A Critical Companion to
Beowulf

A Critical Companion to

Beowulf

Andy Orchard

D. S. BREWER

First published 2003
Reprinted in paperback 2004, 2007
D. S. Brewer, Cambridge

Transferred to digital printing

ISBN 978-1-84384-029-9

D. S. Brewer is an imprint of Boydell & Brewer Ltd
PO Box 9, Woodbridge, Suffolk IP12 3DF, UK
and of Boydell & Brewer Inc.
668 Mt Hope Avenue, Rochester, NY 14620, USA
website: www.boydellandbrewer.com

A CiP catalogue record for this book is available
from the British Library

This publication is printed on acid-free paper

Contents

For Michael,
and for Ellen

Illustrations

Acknowledgements

This book has been a long time coming. Since it was first conceived, so too have been two children, Oscar and Ellen, the latter of whom, now five, is proud (for now) to tell her friends that she takes her name from line 3 of *Beowulf*. In the interim, I have changed jobs and cities and continents, and watched the world and the millennium change: but *Beowulf* has been my constant companion.

My debts, intellectual and otherwise, are deep and long-standing, but my academic indebtedness is deepest of all to Michael Lapidge, my some-time supervisor and colleague and now my long-time friend, who I hope will not mind sharing the dedication with a little girl he has known her whole life. I have accumulated many other debts over the years since I first arrived in October 1983 as an awkward undergraduate in the hugely inspiring Department of Anglo-Saxon, Norse, and Celtic in Cambridge, not least to Clare, whom I met that very first day and who has since been my (other) constant companion. The teaching I received there, primarily from Michael, but also from Richard North, Oliver Padel, Ray Page, Patrick Sims-Williams, Sverrir Tómasson, and Neil Wright, has stayed with me ever since, and in different ways I am grateful to them all. During my 'other' undergraduate career, at Oxford, I was lucky enough to be taught by Ursula Dronke, Malcolm Godden, Bruce Mitchell, and Eric Stanley, and it is an honour to add these honoured names to the list of those I owe. Back at Cambridge, by now teaching in my old undergraduate department, I learned what it was to be an academic from the likes of Lesley Abrams, Paul Bibire, David Dumville, Simon Keynes, Rosalind Love, Máire Ní Mhaonaigh, Erich Poppe, and Martin Syrett; and in essence this book derives in no small measure from the team-taught Cambridge *Beowulf*-seminars I shared then with Michael and Paul, which offered some of the most rewarding and exciting teaching-experiences of my career so far. Likewise, one of the great pleasures of those Cambridge years was sharing an office in Emmanuel College with the late Peter Clemoes, with whom I had long daily conversations, occasionally about Old English: he too taught me much.

This side of the Atlantic, I have benefited greatly from the intellectual stimulation of colleagues and friends, among whom Fred Biggs, Bob Bjork, Roberta Frank, Tom Hall, Bob Hasenfratz, Jack Niles, Katherine O'Brien O'Keeffe, and Paul Szarmach deserve special mention. It is a particular pleasure in a book which aims to look forward as well as back to acknowledge the influence of generations of students, some of whose work I am delighted to cite in the Bibliography: the published and unpublished work of Chris Abram, Clare Lynch, Alison Powell, Christine Rauer, Manish Sharma, and Emily Thornbury (for example) has hugely helped their former supervisor in the writing of this book. Other localised debts to students past and present are acknowledged in the footnotes. I am also extremely grateful to the Toronto graduates who formed with me, a new arrival, an impromptu *Beowulf* reading-group and who through their mingled enthusiasm and scepticism brought me to a deeper understanding of the text: thanks for both beer and *Beowulf* go to Aidan Conti, Gabriella Corona, Jonny Grove, Holly Jagger, Robin Norris, Manish Sharma, and Samantha Zacher.

My admiration and gratitude for the map and genealogies so beautifully drawn by Katharine Scarfe Beckett are likewise profound; it is good to see in her map Grendel right at the centre, where he belongs, and to view the world of *Beowulf* as it is: filled with monsters, mighty-sounding tribes, and artful allusions to Germanic song and story. Likewise, the clear and helpful genealogies are a welcome addition, and provide an indispensable aid to unravelling the sometimes complex family-ties between the poem's many characters. I am also grateful to Jens Wollesen for his help in preparing the plates, and to Anthony Adams for his assistance with the Indexes.

Several have had the mischance to read or hear parts of this book, and I am thankful for all their comments over the years. I am particularly grateful to the two who have read the thing through entirely: Clare Orchard and Samantha Zacher. The faults are not theirs: they both saved me from many. A special word of thanks must go to Caroline 'Patience' Palmer at Boydell and Brewer, who was forced to drink and dance with me at several successive conferences in order to extract this book. I am truly sorry to have made her suffer. After such a long and solitary gestation, it seems only appropriate to finish this Janus-faced book today, at the beginning of a new year, on the feast-day of St Simeon Stylites, and the birthday of Helle Falcher Petersen, now and always my favourite Dane.

Andy Orchard
Toronto
5.i.02

Note on the Paperback Edition
For assistance in the preparation of the paperback edition, which corrects a number of typographical errors in the original text, I am grateful to Christine Rauer and Samantha Zacher.

Toronto
14.xii.03

Abbreviations

AB	*Analecta Bollandiana*
ABäG	*Amsterdamer Beiträge zur älteren Germanistik*
ABR	*American Benedictine Review*
AIUON	*Annali, Istituto Universitario Orientale di Napoli: sezione germanica*
AM	*Annuale Mediaevale*
ANF	*Arkiv för Nordisk Filologi*
ANQ	*American Notes and Queries*
Antiquity	*Antiquity: a Quarterly Journal of Archaeology*
ASnSL	*Archiv für das Studium der neueren Sprachen und Literaturen*
ASE	*Anglo-Saxon England*
ASPR	The Anglo-Saxon Poetic Records, ed. G. P. Krapp and E. V. K. Dobbie, 6 vols. (New York, 1931–42)
ATfS	*Antikvarisk Tidskrift för Sverige*
BEASE	*The Blackwell Encyclopaedia of Anglo-Saxon England*, ed. Lapidge et al.
BGdSL	*Beiträge zur Geschichte der deutschen Sprache und Literatur*
BJRL	*Bulletin of the John Rylands Library*
BRASE	Basic Readings in Anglo-Saxon England
CCSL	Corpus Christianorum, Series Latina
CE	*College English*
CL	*Comparative Literature*
CSASE	Cambridge Studies in Anglo-Saxon England
CSEL	Corpus Scriptorum Ecclesiasticorum Latinorum
E&S	*Essays and Studies by Members of the English Association*
EEMF	Early English Manuscripts in Facsimile
EETS	Early English Text Society
EGS	*English and Germanic Studies*
ELH	*ELH, or Journal of English Literary History*
ELN	*English Language Notes*
ES	*English Studies*
ESC	*English Studies in Canada*
EStn	*Englische Studien*
GR	*Germanic Review*
GRM	*Germanisch-romanische Monatsschrift*
ÍF	Íslenzk fornrit
JAF	*Journal of American Folklore*
JEGP	*Journal of English and Germanic Philology*
JFI	*Journal of the Folklore Institute*
LSE	Leeds Studies in English and Kindred Languages
MÆ	Medium Ævum

MESN	*Medieval English Studies Newsletter*
MGH	Monumenta Germaniae Historica
MH	*Medievalia et Humanistica*
MLN	*Modern Language Notes*
MLQ	*Modern Language Quarterly*
MLR	*Modern Language Review*
MP	*Modern Philology*
MRTS	Medieval and Renaissance Texts and Studies
MS	Mediaeval Studies
Neophil	Neophilologus
NM	*Neuphilologische Mitteilungen*
NMS	*Nottingham Mediaeval Studies*
NQ	*Notes and Queries*
OEC	Old English Colloquium
OEN	*Old English Newsletter*
OT	*Oral Tradition*
PBA	*Proceedings of the British Academy*
PL	Patrologia Latina, ed., J. P. Migne, 221 vols. (Paris, 1844–64)
PLL	*Papers on Language and Literature*
PMAM	*Proceedings of the Medieval Association of the Mid-West*
PMLA	*PMLA, or Publications of the Modern Language Association*
PPMRC	*Proceedings of the Patristics, Medieval, and Renaissance Conference*
PQ	*Philological Quarterly*
PRIA	*Proceedings of the Royal Irish Academy*
RES	*Review of English Studies*
RUO	*Revue d'Université d'Ottawa*
SBVS	*Saga-Book of the Viking Society*
SEL	*Studies in English Literature* (Tokyo)
SI	*Studia Islandica*
SF	*Southern Folklore*
SN	*Studia Neophilologica*
SP	*Studies in Philology*
SS	*Scandinavian Studies*
TCAAS	*Transactions of the Connecticut Academy of Arts and Sciences*
TOES	Toronto Old English Studies
TRHS	*Transactions of the Royal Historical Society*
TSL	*Tennessee Studies in Literature*
TSLL	*Texas Studies in Literature and Language*
UCPE	*University of California Papers on English*
UES	*Unisa English Studies*
UTQ	*University of Toronto Quarterly*
YES	*Yearbook of English Studies*
ZAA	*Zeitschrift für Anglistik und Amerikanistik*
ZdA	*Zeitschrift für deutsches Altertum und deutsche Literatur*
ZdP	*Zeitschrift für deutsche Philologie*

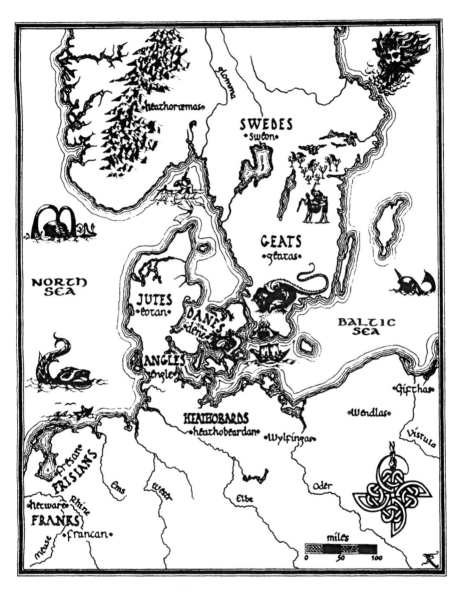

Map of Scandinavia in Beowulf's day

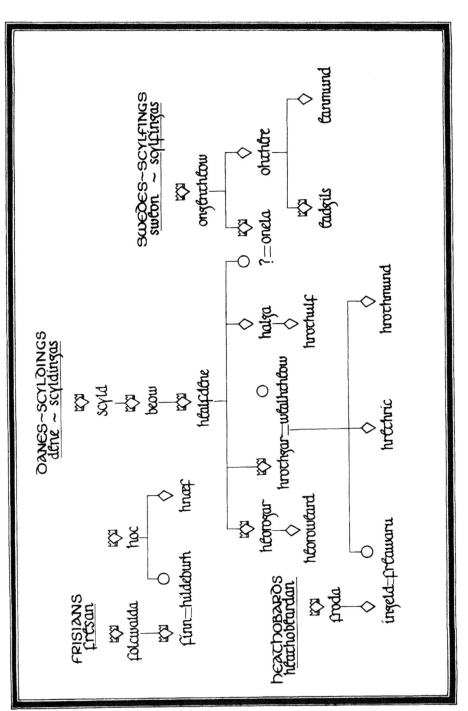

Genealogy I: The Danes, Swedes, Frisians, and Heathobards

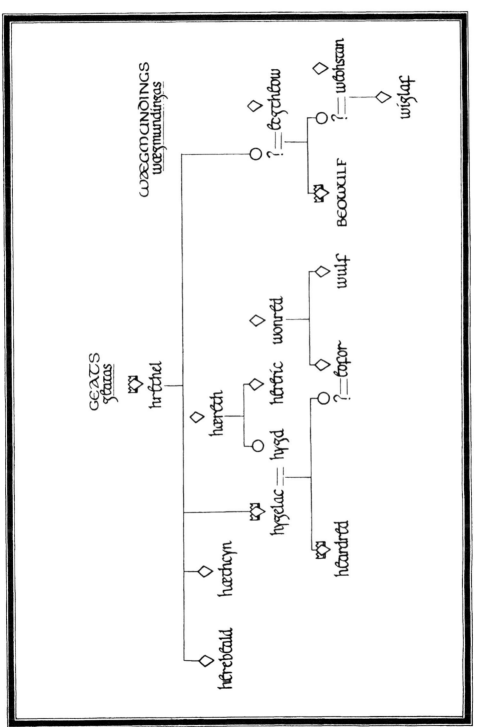

Genealogy II: The Geats and Wægmundings

Beowulf: a brief summary of the plot

Part I: young Beowulf in Denmark (lines **1–2199**)

The history of the Danish royal dynasty is traced back to their eponymous founder, Scyld Scefing, whose mysterious arrival and equally mysterious departure are described in detail (lines **1–52**); the Scyldings thrive, until Scyld's great-grandson Hrothgar, crowning a reign of fifty years, builds his magnificent hall, Heorot, and is immediately attacked by a monstrous fen-dwelling exile called Grendel, who preys on the once proud Danes (lines **53–146a**). After twelve murderous years, a young warrior from the neighbouring land of the Geats, Beowulf, whose own father had been given help and shelter by Hrothgar, hears of Grendel's depredations and comes with a small band of Geatish warriors to offer assistance (lines **146b–498**). After his fitness for such a task is questioned by Unferth, a leading Dane, Beowulf emphasises his monster-slaying past, and undertakes to take on Grendel alone and unarmed (lines **499–661**). Feasting follows, after which both companies of Danes and Geats fall asleep (lines **662–702a**). Grendel enters, devours a sleeping Geat, and grabs at Beowulf (lines **702b–749**). They wrestle, and in the ensuing struggle the hall is smashed inside; Beowulf's men attempt to help, but their swords will not bite on Grendel's hide (lines **750–805a**). Grendel attempts to flee, but Beowulf keeps a grip on his arm, tearing it from the socket; Grendel escapes into the night (lines **805b–836**). The next day, an assembled band of Danes and Geats marvel at Grendel's massive claw, and together they follow Grendel's bloody tracks to the monster-mere, where they see blood on the water, and assume that Grendel is dead (lines **837–63**). In high spirits, they gallop home, celebrating Beowulf in song, and comparing him to the mighty dragon-slaying hero Sigemund (lines **864–924**); back at Heorot, rich rewards are given (lines **925–1062**). The Danes hold a celebration-feast at which the ancient tale of Finn, his wife Hildeburh, and the avenging warrior Hengest is told (lines **1063–1162a**). Afterwards Wealhtheow, Hrothgar's queen, seeks in vain assurances from all parties that recent events will not harm the chances for her own sons to succeed to the Danish throne (lines **1162b–1233a**). The rejoicing Danes and Geats fall asleep (lines **1233b–1255a**).

Out of the darkness, Grendel's monstrous mother comes, seeking revenge for her son (lines **1255b–1282a**). She snatches a sleeping Dane, one of Hrothgar's closest colleagues, and escapes into the night (lines **1282b–1309**). The next morning, Beowulf, who had been sleeping elsewhere, is informed of the attack, and immediately offers to seek revenge (lines **1310–98**). A group of Geats and Danes travel back to the monster-mere, finding the head of the murdered Dane along the way (lines **1399–421**); they sit at the edge of the mere, and there kill one of the monstrous creatures they find (lines **1422–41a**). Beowulf accepts the offer of a borrowed sword from Unferth, strips to his mailcoat, and plunges into the mere (lines **1441b–1495a**). Tusked monsters try to penetrate his armour, but are thwarted; Grendel's mother, sensing an intruder, seizes Beowulf and drags him down to the lair she has ruled for fifty years, and where, miraculously, Beowulf finds himself in a waterless illuminated hall (lines **1495b–1512**). They fight, but Unferth's sword will not bite, and things look bleak for Beowulf until, through divine intervention, he is able to get hold of a giant sword hanging on the wall (lines **1513–62**). With this weapon he dispatches Grendel's mother and, seeing Grendel's body, beheads him too (lines **1563–90**). The waiting Danes and Geats see blood appear in the water and fear the worst: the Danes leave, but the Geats stay behind, hoping that their lord has survived (lines **1591–605a**). The heat and venom in Grendel's blood melt the sword-blade like ice, and Beowulf swims back up through the waters of the monster-mere carrying the sword-hilt and Grendel's head (lines **1605b–1625**). The Geats are delighted to see their lord safe, and assist in carrying the booty back to Hrothgar (lines **1626–50**), who listens rapt to Beowulf's account of his adventures as he hands over the spoils (lines **1651–86**). Hrothgar ponders the mighty hilt, and praises Beowulf, noting his potential as a king, and issuing a long sermon on the dangers of pride (lines **1687–784**); great treasures are given to Beowulf and his men before all retire (lines **1785–1802b**). The Geats make their farewells and leave, with the customary exchange of gifts (lines **1803–1903a**). Back in the land of the Geats, Beowulf gives a full account to his uncle and king, Hygelac, demonstrating considerable political judgement in his assessment of likely feuds ahead between Hrothgar and his future son-in-law, Ingeld (lines **1903b–2151**); once again, gifts are exchanged (lines **2152–99**).

Part II: old Beowulf in Geatland (lines **2200–3182**)

The story flashes forward more than half a century, and now Beowulf is king. Hygelac had been killed in a rash raid in Francia, and although Beowulf had been offered the crown by Hygelac's widow, Hygd, he at first turned it down in favour of Hygelac's young son, Heardred, whom he served loyally until the latter was killed in the latest round of warring between the Geats and their powerful neighbours, the Swedes (lines **2200–8a**). After fifty years on the throne, Beowulf learns that the land of the Geats is threatened by a fire-breathing flying dragon, roused to anger by the theft of a cup from its treasure-hoard (lines **2208b–2231a**). The history of the hoard is described, abandoned by the last of a lost race, and found by the dragon three hundred years before (lines **2231b–2286**). The dragon attacks human dwellings, bent on vengeance (lines **2287–344**). The poet reviews the aged Beowulf's career, as he resolves to face the dragon alone, armed only with his mailcoat, sword, and a specially made iron shield (lines **2345–400**). He goes to battle accompanied by eleven retainers, with the thief the thirteenth man, acting as guide (lines **2401–24**). Beowulf utters a lengthy final speech before the fight, pondering the sad lot of two other aged kings, namely Hrethel of the Geats and Ongentheow of the Swedes (lines **2425–537**). He summons the dragon from its lair with a loud shout, and the fight proceeds in three distinct phases, after the first of which his sword has failed, and by the end of the second of which it has become painfully clear that Beowulf cannot succeed on his own (lines **2538–601**). Beowulf's men are too frightened to help, all except Wiglaf, who, as the last of the Wægmundings, is of his own kin (lines **2602–60**). With Wiglaf's help, Beowulf kills the dragon with his single-bladed knife, but is mortally wounded in the process (lines **2661–715a**). As Beowulf lays dying, Wiglaf plunders the dragon's hoard, and Beowulf, having bequeathed the kingdom to Wiglaf and given detailed instructions about his own funeral, gazes on the treasure as he dies (lines **2715b–2820**). Wiglaf rebukes the cowards and assumes command (lines **2821–91**). A messenger is sent to relay the sorry news to the rest of the Geats, and in the process he foretells a fresh wave of warfare from the Swedes (lines **2892–3027**). The Geats travel to see the dead Beowulf and the dragon side by side, and Wiglaf leads a party of men to plunder the dragon's cursed hoard (lines **3028–57**). His people bury Beowulf on a headland by the sea, along with the dragon's treasure, and (in part at least) according to his own instructions (lines **3058–168**). They sing his praises as the poem ends (lines **3169–82**).

1

Foreword: Looking Back

A hundred years ago, a reader of *Beowulf* had access to an impressive array of tools: scholarship on the poem was both vigorous and wide-ranging. Bibliographical guidance and general background were provided by (amongst others) Richard P. Wülcker, Stopford Brooke, and Alois Brandl.[1] The compendious dictionary now known simply as 'Bosworth–Toller' had just appeared in its original form,[2] and the last few years of the nineteenth century had seen the publication of not one but two dictionaries of Old English specifically designed for students.[3] Within little more than a decade from the beginning of the twentieth century Albert Cook would publish a concordance to *Beowulf*,[4] and scholars would have access to a massively revised version of Christian W. M. Grein's mighty guide to Old English poetic diction, first published half a century earlier.[5] Editions of *Beowulf* were proliferating, in part in reaction to the eccentric text edited by Ludwig Ettmüller in 1875: a twenty-year period either side of 1900 saw a revision by Adolf Socin of Moritz Heyne's edition of a quarter of a century before, as well as a new edition by Alfred J. Wyatt, itself later comprehensively revised,[6] and two further texts by Moritz Trautmann and Ferdinand Holthausen.[7]

All this editorial activity was set against the background of the collective editions of Old English prose and verse by Christian W. M. Grein and Richard P. Wülcker.[8] Among a growing range of renderings, *Beowulf* was translated in

---

1 Wülcker, *Grundriss zur Geschichte der angelsächsischen Literatur*, which appeared in 1885, had an excellent bibliography, while surveys of Old English literature were successively provided by Wülcker, *Geschichte der englischen Literatur* (1896); Brooke, *English Literature from the Beginning to the Norman Conquest* (1898); Brandl, 'Die angelsächsische Literatur' (1901–9).

2 Bosworth and Toller, *An Anglo-Saxon Dictionary*. The *Dictionary* was first published in the years 1881–98, to be followed by a *Supplement* (1908–21) and *Addenda and Corrigenda* (1972).

3 Hall, *A Concise Anglo-Saxon Dictionary for the Use of Students* (published in 1894); Sweet, *The Student's Dictionary of Anglo-Saxon* (published in 1897).

4 Cook, *A Concordance to Beowulf* (published in 1911).

5 Grein, *Sprachschatz der angelsächsischen Dichter* first appeared in the years 1861–4; a revised edition by Köhler, with the help of Holthausen, appeared in 1912.

6 Wyatt's edition, simply called *Beowulf*, first appeared in 1894, and was comprehensively revised (with a much more extensive title) by Chambers in 1914.

7 Trautmann, ed., *Das Beowulflied* (which appeared in 1904); Holthausen, ed., *Beowulf nebst dem Finnsburg-Bruchstück* (produced in the years 1905–6).

8 The Grein–Wülcker *Bibliothek der angelsächsischen Poesie* came out in three volumes from Cassel in the years 1881–98, based on Grein's two-volume publication from Göttingen (1857–8); the thir-

1895 by a famous artist (in collaboration with an Anglo-Saxon scholar) into verse,[9] and in 1892 and again in 1901 by other noted Anglo-Saxon scholars into prose.[10] Study of the metre of *Beowulf* had been put on a new footing by the publication in 1893 of Eduard Sievers' hugely important study of Germanic metre,[11] and if the detailed study of the manuscript-context and scribal transmission of the poem had to wait until after the First World War,[12] Julius Zupitza had already published a widely available manuscript-facsimile of *Beowulf* itself.[13] Likewise, if a (still less than satisfactory) edition of the prose texts of the *Beowulf*-manuscript did not appear until 1924,[14] a number of separate editions and discussions of all four other texts in the *Beowulf*-manuscript (including *Judith*) had already appeared by 1906.[15]

In late nineteenth-century Germany, a cottage-industry busily collected parallels not only between various Old English poems, but across the whole spectrum of Germanic verse; and fierce debate raged about the precise significance of such parallels, which were argued on the one hand to reflect a common Germanic stock of formulas, and on the other conscious borrowing between poets.[16] Source-study of *Beowulf* had become a particular focus for enquiry ever since the Icelander Guðbrandur Vigfússon had drawn attention to perceived parallels between *Beowulf* and *Grettis saga* in 1878;[17] nor were sources sought

teen–volume *Bibliothek der angelsächsischen Prosa* came out from Cassel over the period 1872–1933.

9   Morris and Wyatt, trans., *The Tale of Beowulf*. William Morris undertook an impressive number of artistic and cultural initiatives, and published translations not only of *Beowulf*, but also of a range of Norse texts, as well as the *Odyssey*. See further Tilling, 'William Morris's Translation of *Beowulf*'.

10   Earle, trans., *The Deeds of Beowulf*; Hall, trans., *'Beowulf' and the 'Fight at Finnsburg'*. The latter translation was revised by Wrenn, with a fascinating introduction by Tolkien, in 1940.

11   Sievers, *Altgermanische Metrik*; see too his important 'Miscellen zur Angelsächsischen Grammatik', published in 1884.

12   As early as 1876, Eugen Kölbing, 'Zur Béowulf-handschrift', had published a detailed collation of the manuscript, but most of the detailed discussion of the manuscript took place in successive editions, bar one flare-up in 1890, when a nasty spat developed in a single issue of *MLN* between Charles Davidson and C. F. McClumpha over 'Differences between the Scribes of Beowulf' (the focus was on the use of þ and ð). In this respect, Förster, *Die 'Beowulf'-Handschrift*, published in 1919, represents a great leap forward: previous studies are generally very brief, such as Sisam, 'The *Beowulf* ms'.

13   Zupitza, *Beowulf: Autotypes of the Unique Cotton MS. Vitellius A. XV in the British Museum, with a Transliteration*, first appeared in 1882, and was revised by Norman Davis in 1959.

14   The edition in question is by Rypins, ed., *Three Old English Prose Texts in MS Cotton Vitellius A. xv*. The latest (posthumous) edition of the *Life of St Christopher*, by Phillip Pulsiano, looks set to appear in 2002.

15   Earlier editions of the prose texts include Baskervill, 'The Anglo-Saxon Version of the *Epistola Alexandri ad Aristotelem*' (1881); Einenkel, 'Das altenglische Cristoforus-fragment' (1895); Knappe, *Das angelsächsische Prosastück Die Wunder des Ostens* (1906). Special mention might be made in this context of Cook's 1888 edition of *Judith*, which is a model of its kind.

16   Important stages in the debate in the last two decades of the nineteenth century include Fritzsche, 'Das angelsächsische Gedicht *Andreas* und Cynewulf' (1879); Sarrazin, '*Beowulf* und Kynewulf' (1886); *idem*, *Beowulf-Studien: Ein Beitrag zur Geschichte altgermanischer Sage und Dichtung* (1888); Kail, 'Über die Parallelstellen in der angelsächsischen Poesie' (1889); Meyer, *Die altgermanische Poesie nach ihren formelhaften Elementen beschrieben* (1889); Kistenmacher, *Die wörtlichen Wiederholungen im Béowulf* (1898). As an index of the influence of this activity in the English-speaking world, see, for example, the publication as early as 1904 of Luehrs, 'A Summary of Sarrazin's "Studies in Beowulf"'.

17   See, for example, Vigfusson, 'Prolegomena', p. xlix, n. 1; Vigfusson and Powell, *Corpus Poeticum Boreale*; Gering, 'Der Béowulf und die isländische Grettissaga'; Boer, 'Zur Grettissaga' (all published before 1900).

solely in Norse: other texts in a variety of languages were all being studied for their possible links to *Beowulf*.[18]

Although the whole field of what would now be termed 'literary criticism' was at the turn of the nineteenth century still in its infancy,[19] nonetheless questions were being raised about the roles which (for example) the monsters, Christianity, and women played in the poem.[20] If literary criticism is the one central area that has truly blossomed (indeed, some might say overgrown) over the last hundred years, the debt owed by modern scholarship to that of the late nineteenth and early twentieth century as a whole is profound, if often unacknowledged,[21] and it striking to see the extent and range of academic activity centred on *Beowulf* at that time.

Plus ça change: a hundred years later, the principal areas of scholarly inquiry into *Beowulf* remain substantially the same, although the sheer number of dedicated publications has become somewhat bemusing.[22] Whereas in 1936 J. R. R. Tolkien could humbly call himself an 'unworthy successor and beneficiary of Joseph Bosworth' because on his own admission he had not been 'a man so diligent in [his] special walk as duly to read all that has been printed on, or touching on, this poem',[23] it might fairly be said that none of his successors in this 'special walk' would now dream of doing so. Indeed, such has been the proliferation of books and articles on *Beowulf* in recent years (with a new item a week appearing on average over the last decade),[24] that simply controlling the secondary material has become a near-impossible task.[25] Happily, however, those reading *Beowulf* have for more than three decades had the advantage of extensive bibliographies published annually in academic journals,[26] as well as a range of other bibliographical tools.[27]

---

[18] See, for example, Cook, 'An Irish Parallel to the Beowulf Story'; Klaeber, 'Aeneis und Beowulf'; Suchier, 'Über die Sage von Offa und Þrytho'.

[19] A symptom of the relative newness of the field is the comparative dearth of *Festschriften* in the area; that for F. J. Furnivall (*An English Miscellany: Presented to Dr Furnivall in Honour of his Seventy-fifth Birthday*) was published in Oxford in 1901, and while it contains eight items relating to Old English, none is directly relevant to the study of *Beowulf*.

[20] Important in this context (if now distinctly dated) are Skeat, 'On the Signification of the Monster Grendel' (published in 1886); Burton, 'Woman in Old English Poetry' (which appeared in 1895); Blackburn, 'The Christian Coloring in the *Beowulf*' (published in 1897). Sweringen, 'Women in the Germanic Hero-Sagas', is also of relevance here, although it did not appear until 1909, the year which also saw the appearance of Schück, *Studier i Beowulfsagen*.

[21] Excellent overviews tracing the development of scholarship over the period are offered by Stanley, *In the Foreground*, pp. 1–68, and (especially) by Haarder and Shippey, ed., *Beowulf: the Critical Heritage*, esp. pp. 77–497, which covers a wide range of views across the nineteenth century.

[22] Cf. Robinson, '*Beowulf* in the Twentieth Century'.

[23] Tolkien, '*Beowulf*: the Monsters and the Critics', p. 245; Tolkien is referring to a disparaging comment made about Bosworth himself by Oswald Cockayne.

[24] Cf. Hasenfratz, 'A Decade's Worth of *Beowulf* Scholarship: Observations on Compiling a Bibliography'.

[25] A measure of the sheer volume of scholarship surrounding the poem is perhaps to be gauged by the fact that in 1974 a critical bibliography of translations of the poem (Tinker, *Translations of Beowulf*, now badly in need of updating and revision) could run to some 180 pages.

[26] In general, one follows the annual bibliographies published in *ASE* (1972–) and *OEN* (1967–), although increasingly the on-line MLA-bibliography (also available on CD-ROM) is of use. Plans are afoot to create an electronic bibliography, based on those in *ASE*, which will make available to individual scholars bibliographical resources at present mostly found in research-libraries.

[27] Important in this context are the general bibliography by Greenfield and Robinson (as well as the

Echoing events at the turn of the nineteenth century, the turn of the twentieth saw the production of some fine translations of *Beowulf*, including one by a Nobel Laureate and another by a noted Anglo-Saxon scholar;[28] at least three new editions appeared in the space of three years (two of them designed for students), and the *Beowulf*-manuscript itself was finally made available on CD-ROM.[29] Work proceeded steadily on the mighty *Toronto Dictionary of Old English*, a unique enterprise founded on the whole corpus of surviving texts; the corpus itself was made widely available some time ago.[30] Source-study became an active area of interest during the last decade or so of the twentieth century: two large international projects on the use made of written sources in Anglo-Saxon England came to fruition in parallel,[31] and at the same time attention became increasingly focused on parallels and analogues to *Beowulf* from a variety of new sources.[32] The last few years have brought a complete revolution in our perception of Anglo-Latin literature, largely through the work of Michael

---

select bibliography by Robinson alone), and (specifically for *Beowulf*) the annotated bibliographies by Fry, Hasenfratz, and Short (details of which are to be found in sections A and C of the Bibliography). Also valuable are the annotated bibliographies of North American doctoral dissertations on Old English and Old Norse-Icelandic (both containing numerous items relating to *Beowulf*) by Pulsiano and Wolf (details in section A of the Bibliography), nowadays to be supplemented by the electronic indexes to 'Dissertations Abstracts International'. The extensive single-volume encyclopedias on Anglo-Saxon England by Lapidge *et al.* and by Szarmach *et al.*, as well as that on medieval Scandinavia by Pulsiano (details in section A of the Bibliography) are also extremely useful for general orientation.

28 Heaney, trans., *Beowulf: a New Translation*; Liuzza, trans., *Beowulf: a New Verse Translation*. There is a useful and interesting comparative review of both translations by Frank Kermode, 'Geat of Geats'. A representative range of other translations of the poem is offered as section E of the Bibliography: these include renderings into both prose (Bradley, Donaldson, Gordon, Gummere, Hall, Hieatt, and Swanton) and verse (Alexander, Bone, Crossley-Holland, Hudson, Kennedy, Lehmann, Leonard, Morgan, Raffel, and Rebsamen). Special mention might be made of Porter's word-for-word translation, and the freer renderings by Greenfield and Swearer *et al.* I also include here the translation of *Beowulf* into Modern Icelandic by Halldóra Björnsson, which strikingly demonstrates the links between the Old English and Old Norse-Icelandic literary traditions; likewise I give reference to the versions by Conybeare, Grundtvig, and Kemble which are so central to any perception of the beginnings of *Beowulf*-scholarship. Handy selections from a variety of translations are offered by Liuzza, trans., *Beowulf: a New Verse Translation*, pp. 212–31; McClintock, 'Translation and *Beowulf* in Translation'. See too the 'Alternative *Beowulf*' website, details of which are in section C of the Bibliography.

29 Alexander, ed., *Beowulf*; Jack, ed., *'Beowulf': a Student Edition*; Mitchell and Robinson, ed., *Beowulf*. A complete electronic facsimile appeared in Kiernan, ed., *Electronic 'Beowulf'*; this extraordinarily useful tool contains far more than simply high-quality facsimiles of the manuscript, however: also included are (for example) several early modern transcriptions of the text, and a new edition, glossary, and bibliography of *Beowulf* itself. I include in section D of the Bibliography a range of other editions that I have found useful in writing this book: Klaeber's edition remains in many ways the most useful and authoritative, but I have also consulted (in addition to those already noted) the editions of Chickering, Crépin, Grundtvig, Kemble, Magoun, Nickel, Sedgefield, Thorpe, and Wrenn.

30 Healey, *et al.*, ed., *Dictionary of Old English*; *Dictionary of Old English Corpus in Electronic Form*, ed. Healey *et al.*; Venezky and Healey, ed., *Microfiche Concordance to Old English*; for details of the website, see section C of the Bibliography.

31 The projects in question are *Fontes Anglo-Saxonici* and *SASLC: Sources of Anglo-Saxon Literary Culture*; for websites relating to both, see section C of the Bibliography.

32 The general situation is well summarised by Andersson, 'Sources and Analogues'. Books of particular interest in this context, all published during the years 1992–2000, include Lionarons, *The Medieval Dragon*; Orchard, *Pride and Prodigies*; Rauer, *Beowulf and the Dragon*; Stitt, *'Beowulf' and the Bear's Son*.

Lapidge, and it is clear that Anglo-Saxonists of the future will need to be more conversant with (and appreciative of) the Latin literature of Anglo-Saxon England than they have (generally speaking) proved so far.[33] Another area in which much work has been done in recent years has been that of Old English metre, with *Beowulf* still basically perceived as a principal focus of enquiry: the proliferation of publications in recent years is striking, to say the least.[34] The material culture and the cultural world of the poem have also inspired several studies over the last twenty years or so,[35] and at the same time there has been renewed focus on the manuscript, primarily based around questions of the dating of the manuscript and of *Beowulf* itself.[36]

Indeed, deep and often bitter disagreements about the date of *Beowulf* can be

33 See Lapidge, *Anglo-Latin Literature, 600–899; idem, Anglo-Latin Literature, 900–1066*. Post-Conquest material is dealt with by Rigg, *A History of Anglo-Latin Literature*.

34 The recent trend could perhaps be said to have been sparked off by the publication in 1942 (and revision in 1966) of Pope, *The Rhythm of 'Beowulf'*; important books on the topic published since then include Bliss, *The Metre of Beowulf* (to be used alongside his 'The Scansion of *Beowulf*' and *Introduction to Old English Metre*; see too Vickman, 'A Metrical Concordance to *Beowulf*'); Cable, *The Meter and Melody of 'Beowulf'*; Creed, *Reconstructing the Rhythm of 'Beowulf'*; Fulk, *A History of Old English Meter*; Hoover, *A New Theory of Old English Meter*; Hutcheson, *Old English Poetic Metre*; Kendall, *The Metrical Grammar of 'Beowulf'*; Renoir and Hernández, ed., *Approaches to Beowulfian Scansion*; Russom, *Old English Meter and Linguistic Theory; idem, 'Beowulf' and Old Germanic Metre*; Suzuki, *The Metrical Organization of 'Beowulf'*. A useful overview is offered by Stockwell, 'On Recent Theories of Metrics and Rhythm in *Beowulf*'. Supplementary material is to be found in a number of articles, including Baum, 'The Meter of the *Beowulf*'; Bliss, 'The Appreciation of Old English Metre'; *idem*, 'The Origin and Structure of the Old English Hypermetric Line'; Blockley and Cable, 'Kuhn's Laws, Old English Poetry, and the New Philology'; Frese, 'The Scansion of *Beowulf*: Critical Implications'; Hoover, 'Evidence for the Primacy of Alliteration in Old English Metre'; Russom, 'Purely Metrical Replacements for Kuhn's Laws'; Stockwell and Minkova, 'Old English Metrics and the Phonology of Resolution'; *idem*, 'Prosody'; Suzuki, 'Anacrusis in the Meter of *Beowulf*'. A website containing 'Electronic Scansions for Old Germanic Metre' has been posted by Russom: details are in section C of the Bibliography.

35 Useful contributions (including some that predate 1981) include Bazelmans, *By Weapons Made Worthy*; Christensen, 'Lejre beyond Legend'; Cramp, '*Beowulf* and Archaeology'; *idem*, 'The Hall in *Beowulf* and in Archaeology'; Davidson, 'The Hill of the Dragon'; Hill, 'Beowulf and the Danish Succession'; *idem*, 'Hrothgar's Noble Rule'; *idem, The Cultural World in 'Beowulf'; idem*, 'Social Milieu'; Hills, '*Beowulf* and Archaeology'; Osborn, 'Two-Way Evidence in *Beowulf* Concerning Viking-Age Ships'; Owen-Crocker, *The Four Funerals in 'Beowulf'*; Webster, 'Archaeology and *Beowulf*'; Whitbread, '*Beowulf* and Archaeology'; Whitelock, 'Anglo-Saxon Poetry and the Historian'. The connection of *Beowulf* to the burial at Sutton Hoo has become something of a separate cottage-industry: cf. Carver, ed., *The Age of Sutton Hoo*; Creed, 'Sutton Hoo and the Recording of *Beowulf*'; Girvan, *Beowulf and the Seventh Century*; Newton, *The Origins of 'Beowulf' and the Pre-Viking Kingdom of East Anglia*; Pearson, van de Noort, and Woolf, 'Three Men and a Boat: Sutton Hoo and the East Saxon Kingdom'; Raw, 'Royal Power and Royal Symbols in *Beowulf*'; Scull, 'Before Sutton Hoo: Structures of Power and Society in Early East Anglia'; Wrenn, 'Sutton Hoo and *Beowulf*'. For a refreshingly contrary view, see Frank, '*Beowulf* and Sutton Hoo: the Odd Couple'.

36 Noteworthy contributions (again, including some that predate 1981) include Clement, 'Codicological Consideration in the *Beowulf* Manuscript'; Dumville, 'Beowulf Come Lately'; *idem*, 'The *Beowulf*-Manuscript and How Not to Date It'; Gerritsen, 'British Library MS Cotton Vitellius A.xv – a Supplementary Description'; *idem*, 'Have with You to Lexington! The *Beowulf* Manuscript and *Beowulf*'; *idem*, 'A Reply to Dr Kiernan's "Footnote"'; *idem*, '*Beowulf* Revisited'; Kiernan, '*Beowulf' and the 'Beowulf' Manuscript*; *idem*, 'A Long Footnote for J. Gerritsen's "Supplementary" Description of BL Cotton MS Vitellius A.XV'; *idem*, 'The State of the *Beowulf* Manuscript 1882–1983'; *idem*, 'Old Manuscripts / New Technologies'; *idem*, 'The Eleventh-Century Origin of *Beowulf* and the *Beowulf* Manuscript'; *idem*, 'The Legacy of Wiglaf: Saving a Wounded Beowulf'; Kim, 'Monstrous and Bloody Signs: the *Beowulf* Manuscript'; Lapidge, 'The Archetype of *Beowulf*'; Lucas, 'The Place of *Judith* in the *Beowulf*-Manuscript'; Orchard, *Pride and Prodigies*; Pickles, 'Studies in the Prose Texts of the *Beowulf* Manuscript'; Rose, 'The Kiernan Theory Revisited';

said to be one of the constant themes of *Beowulf*-scholarship from the very beginning, and the twentieth century saw its own share of deep and sometimes acrimonious disputes.[37] There is still no consensus on the date of the poem,[38] with current estimates ranging from the seventh century to the eleventh (and indeed every century in between).[39] Moreover, if the period of composition of the poem remains unresolved, so too have there been recent disagreements about the related question of its provenance: *Beowulf* has been situated all over England, with suggestions of the place of composition now including Northumbria, Mercia, Wessex, East Anglia, and even Kent.[40] If it is no longer fashionable to consider *Beowulf* to be made up of a collection of individual lays inherited from earlier tradition and pieced together by a compiling poet,[41] the profound and continuing effect on *Beowulf*-scholarship from 1953 on of the so-called 'oral-formulaic' theory has ensured that no serious student of the poem

Sisam, 'The Authority of Old English Poetical Manuscripts'; *idem*, 'The Compilation of the Beowulf Manuscript'; Smith, 'The Provenance of the *Beowulf*-Manuscript'.

37 A useful summary is offered by Chase, 'Opinions on the Date of *Beowulf*, 1815–1980'.

38 An entire book of collected essays, edited by Chase (*The Dating of 'Beowulf'*), came out of a conference on the topic held in Toronto in 1980, and is remarkable for the diversity of opinions expressed: the title of the concluding paper by Stanley, 'The Date of Beowulf: Some Doubts and No Conclusions', summarises the outcome. Apart from the articles by Chase and Stanley already noted, the volume contained the following papers: Boyle, 'The Nowell Codex and the Dating of *Beowulf*'; Cable, 'Metrical Style as Evidence for the Date of *Beowulf*'; Cameron, *et al.*, 'A Reconsideration of the Language of *Beowulf*'; Chase, 'Saints' Lives, Royal Lives, and the Date of *Beowulf*'; Clemoes, 'Style as a Criterion for Dating the Composition of *Beowulf*'; Frank, 'Skaldic Verse and the Date of *Beowulf*'; Goffart, '*Hetware* and *Hugas*: Datable Anachronisms in *Beowulf*'; Kiernan, 'The Eleventh-Century Origin of *Beowulf* and the *Beowulf* Manuscript'; McTurk, 'Variation in *Beowulf* and the Poetic *Edda*: a Chronological Experiment'; Murray, 'Beowulf, the Danish Invasions, and Royal Genealogy', in *Dating of 'Beowulf'*; Page, 'The Audience of *Beowulf* and the Vikings'; Pope, 'On the Date of Composition of *Beowulf*'. Two important papers delivered at the same conference did not appear in the final volume, but are nonetheless of great interest in this context, namely Dumville, '*Beowulf* and the Celtic World: the Uses of the Evidence', and Lapidge, '*Beowulf*, Aldhelm, the *Liber Monstrorum* and Wessex'. Other discussions of the dating of *Beowulf* outside the Chase volume that are noteworthy for one reason or another include: Amos, 'An Eleventh-Century *Beowulf*?'; *idem*, *Linguistic Means of Determining the Dates of Old English Literary Texts*; Andersson, 'The Dating of *Beowulf*'; Bjork and Obermeier, 'Date, Provenance, Author, Audiences'; Bolton, *Alcuin and 'Beowulf'*; Bond, 'Links between *Beowulf* and Mercian History'; Busse and Holtei, 'Beowulf and the Tenth Century'; Collins, 'Blickling Homily XVI and the Dating of *Beowulf*'; Fulk, 'Dating *Beowulf* to the Viking Age'; *idem*, 'Contraction as a Criterion for Dating Old English Verse'; Girvan, *Beowulf and the Seventh Century*; Jacobs, 'Anglo-Danish Relations, Poetic Archaism, and the Date of *Beowulf*'; Meaney, 'Scyld Scefing and the Dating of *Beowulf* – Again'; Poussa, 'The Date of *Beowulf* Reconsidered: the Tenth Century'; Pulsiano and McGowan, '*Fyrd*, *here* and the Dating of *Beowulf*'; Smith, 'Ships and the Dating of *Beowulf*'; Thundy, '*Beowulf*: Date and Authorship'; Wetzel, 'Die Datierung des *Beowulf*: Bemerkungen zur jüngsten Forschungsentwicklung'; Whitelock, *The Audience of 'Beowulf'*; Wright, '*Merewioingas* and the Dating of *Beowulf*'.

39 For useful overviews of the dating controversy, see, for example, Liuzza, 'On the Dating of *Beowulf*'; Müller-Zimmermann, 'Beowulf: zur Datierungs- und Interpretationsproblematik'; Tristram, 'What's the Point of Dating "Beowulf"?'.

40 See, for example, the arguments of Girvan, *Beowulf and the Seventh Century* (Northumbria); Whitelock, *The Audience of 'Beowulf'* (Mercia); Lapidge, '*Beowulf*, Aldhelm, the *Liber Monstrorum* and Wessex'; Newton, *The Origins of 'Beowulf' and the Pre-Viking Kingdom of East Anglia*; Mussett and Wilkinson, *Beowulf in Kent*.

41 Among the leading exponents of so-called *Liedertheorie* were Müllenhof, 'Die innere Geschichte des *Beovulfs*'; Ettmüller, *Engla and Seaxna Scôpas and Bôceras*; *idem*, *Carmen de Beovvlfi Gavtarvm regis rebvs*; but the desire to break the poem down into constituent parts is also seen in such later works as Magoun, '"*Beowulf A*": a Folk-Variant'; *idem*, '*Beowulf B*: a Folk-Poem on Beowulf's Death'. But see Brodeur, '*Beowulf*: One Poem or Three?'.

can be unaware of the extent to which much of the imagery and phrasing of *Beowulf* recurs,[42] not only within the poem itself, but in the manuscript, other extant Old English texts,[43] and even surviving works from other Germanic traditions.[44] If for some at least the traditional nature of the *Beowulf*-poet's technique has seemed to undermine the extent of his individual artistry,[45] the debate in recent years has at least focused attention on reading the poem primarily as a poem.

At the root of all these wrangles lies the continuing attempt to assess *Beowulf* as a work of literature, a move inspired in large part by Tolkien's groundbreaking British Academy lecture on '*Beowulf*: the Monsters and the Critics'. Perhaps no single paper on *Beowulf* has spawned so many imitators, although Tolkien himself was not without his critics:[46] the period after the Second World War saw *Beowulf* increasingly appreciated as a literary masterpiece, with a proliferation of books and articles devoted to its study. Within the last decade or so alone there have been a large number of monographs and volumes of collected essays devoted to the poem,[47] not to mention those collected works of individual scholars or the growing number of *Festschriften* which contain significant discussion of the work.[48] In the evolving debate, *Beowulf* has been

---

42 For a partial index, see, for example, Appendixes II and III below.

43 See further below, pp. 163–8.

44 Magoun, 'The Oral-Formulaic Character of Anglo-Saxon Narrative Poetry', is the first to apply to Old English in general (and *Beowulf* in particular) the theories of Parry and Lord about the primary importance of repeated formulaic expressions in oral poetry. For the main expressions of the original theory (developed over many years), see, for example, Parry, *The Making of Homeric Verse*; Lord, *The Singer of Tales*; idem, 'Beowulf and Odysseus'; idem, *The Singer Resumes the Tale*. The secondary literature on oral-formulaic theory is vast, and to some extent is best traced through the sensitive and thought-provoking writings of John Miles Foley, whose *Oral-Formulaic Theory and Research: an Introduction and Annotated Bibliography* (updated through 1992 on its website: see section C of the Bibliography) remains a most useful tool. Some of Foley's works of particular relevance to *Beowulf* include 'Formula and Theme in Old English Poetry'; *The Theory of Oral Composition*; *Traditional Oral Epic*; *Immanent Art*; *The Singer of Tales in Performance*; *Homer's Traditional Art*. Overviews of the theory as applied to Old English are found in Olsen, 'Oral-Formulaic Research in Old English Studies: I'; idem, 'Oral-Formulaic Research in Old English Studies: II'; Orchard, 'Oral Tradition'.

45 Perhaps the most compelling defence of the originality and artistry of the *Beowulf*-poet remains Brodeur, *The Art of 'Beowulf'*. See too his excellent analysis of individual style in 'A Study of Diction and Style in Three Anglo-Saxon Narrative Poems'. For other views see, for example, Benson, 'The Originality of *Beowulf*'; Griffith, 'Convention and Originality in the Old English "Beasts of Battle" Typescene'. An interesting example of how a response to oral-formulaic theory can affect the ways in which an extremely sensitive and thoughtful literary critic approaches the text can be sensed by comparing Irving, *A Reading of 'Beowulf'*, with his later *Rereading 'Beowulf'*, where many of the notions of oral-formulaic theory have been assimilated.

46 Notably Gang, 'Approaches to *Beowulf*'; Sisam, *The Structure of 'Beowulf'*.

47 Good selections of critical essays published within the last ten years or so include Baker, ed., *'Beowulf': Basic Readings*; Bjork and Niles, ed., *'Beowulf' Handbook*; Fulk, ed., *Interpretations of 'Beowulf'*. Earlier selections that are still useful include Fry, ed., *The 'Beowulf'-Poet*; Nicholson, ed., *An Anthology of 'Beowulf' Criticism*.

48 Among those *Festschriften* written in the past four decades that contain a good deal of material relating to *Beowulf* are *Words and Works*, ed. Baker and Howe; *The Wisdom of Poetry*, ed. Benson and Wenzel; *Franciplegius*, ed. Bessinger and Creed; *Modes of Interpretation*, ed. Brown, et al.; *Old English Studies*, ed. Burlin and Irving; *Heroic Poetry in the Anglo-Saxon Period*, ed. Damico and Leyerle; *English and Medieval Studies*, ed. Davis and Wrenn; *Studies in Old English Literature*, ed. Greenfield; *Magister Regis*, ed. Groos, et al.; *Old English and New*, ed. Hall, et al., *Words and Works*, ed. Korhammer; *Learning and Literature in Anglo-Saxon England*, ed. Lapidge and Gneuss; *Prosody and Poetics in the Early Middle Ages*, ed. Toswell; *Studies in English Language and Literature*, ed.

on the receiving end of many of the newest developments in critical theory,[49] as the poem reaches new audiences and benefits from fresh perceptions unimagined by previous generations; a case in point is the growing focus in recent decades of the roles of women and gender in the poem.[50]

But perhaps the real revolution of the twentieth century was that which moved the study and appreciation of *Beowulf* irreversibly away from being bound by the printed word on the page. Now, one can hear part or all of the poem read in a great variety of voices,[51] and analyse the poem through a range of electronic and other media: the challenge for the modern student of *Beowulf* is to negotiate the bewildering array not only of books and articles and images (the traditional paraphernalia of academic criticism), but now of sounds and bytes and pixels and sound-bites, all competing for the attention of the diligent student of the text.[52] This book is intended partly as a guide to previous scholarship, and partly (with apologies to future generations) as an incitement to more; although not all the views expressed here are mainstream ones, it is hoped that the Bibliography reflects a representative range of opinions, in so far as the selections of any single scholar are able to conceal an individual's idiosyncratic prejudices.

Chapter 2 ('Manuscript and Text') considers the sole manuscript containing *Beowulf,* and its fate at the hands of successive generations of critics, readers, and scholars over the past thousand years. After a brief description of the manuscript's history since it was first written, attention is drawn to the continuing controversy surrounding the precise dating of the two scribal hands, as well as to such debates as to whether, which, and when those other texts now found alongside *Beowulf* in the manuscript were ever part of an original compiler's plan. The old notion that the manuscript was intended as an English 'Book of Monsters' is discussed, and particular attention is focused on apparent links between *Beowulf* and *The Letter of Alexander to Aristotle,* the text which (at

Toswell and Tyler. Useful collections of critical essays by a single scholar include Greenfield, *Hero and Exile*; Mitchell, *On Old English*; Robinson, *The Tomb of Beowulf*; Stanley, *A Collection of Papers.*

49 For an overview, see Lerer, '*Beowulf* and Contemporary Critical Theory'. See too Frantzen, *Desire for Origins*, and a number of the papers collected in Frantzen, ed., *Speaking Two Languages.*

50 Examples with particular relevance or interest for a reading of *Beowulf* include Albano, 'The Role of Women in Anglo-Saxon Culture'; Alfano, 'The Issue of Feminine Monstrosity'; Chance, *Woman as Hero in Old English Literature*; Damico and Olsen, ed., *New Readings on Women in Old English Literature*; Fee, '*Beag & beaghroden*'; Fell, *Women in Anglo-Saxon England*; Hansen, 'From *freolicu folccwen* to *geomuru ides*'; Haruta, 'The Women in *Beowulf*'; Judd, 'Women before the Conquest'; Olsen, 'Women in *Beowulf*'; *idem*, 'Gender Roles'; Overing, *Language, Sign, and Gender in Beowulf*; *idem*, 'The Women of *Beowulf*: a Context for Interpretation'; Strauss, 'Women's Words as Weapons: Speech as Action in *The Wife's Lament*'.

51 A range of recordings is listed in section F of the bibliography. Complete recordings of *Beowulf* in Old English (very different in style and speed of delivery) have been made by Kemp Malone and Trevor Eaton; selections by noted Anglo-Saxon scholars include recordings by Jess Bessinger, Arthur Brodeur, Neville Coghill, Robert Creed, Norman Davis, Ted Irving, and John Pope. Cf. the review of Eaton's recording by Orchard, 'Unrecoverable Magic'. I also include here the readings in Modern English by Seamus Heaney and Julian Glover, since both do much to emphasise the dramatic potential of the piece. Other recordings in Old English are also available on the Web, via the 'Old English Pages' noted in section C of the Bibliography.

52 For a variety of web-based media relating to the poem, see section C of the Bibliography; see too Osborn, 'Translations, Versions, Illustrations'.

present) immediately precedes it. From consideration of the manuscript-context of the poem, the discussion turns to the ways in which the manuscript-text of the poem has been altered by its editors, and also to evidence that the *Beowulf*-manuscript is but the last of an unknowable number of written texts of the poem; it is argued that the scribes themselves often seem to be performing similar functions to those of modern editors, and that close analysis of the errors to which they seem prone (some of which they evidently caught and corrected themselves) can provide a useful index against which conjectural emendations of the past may be measured, and new emendations proposed.

Chapter 3 ('Style and Structure') focuses on different patterns of repetition and variation within the poem, and considers the extent to which the *Beowulf*-poet can be regarded as an original artist working within an older and far broader poetic tradition. Repetition within the text at a number of levels of diction is considered: repeated sounds, words, compounds, phrases, and themes are all analysed, and particular attention is paid to the patterns of formulaic repetition that pervade the text. Alongside repetition, the contrasting principle of variation is considered, and the ways in which the poet is able to use changes of pace, metre, and diction, as well as a range of unusual or unexpected juxtapositions to lend texture to his text. A number of examples of punning and *double entendre* are highlighted, and it is argued that the numerous examples of sound- and word-play so freely employed by the *Beowulf*-poet are not simply ornamental, but instead offer strong clues to the ways in which the poet intended the text to be read (or rather heard).

Chapter 4 ('Myth and Legend') explores the ways in which the *Beowulf*-poet made use of a number of aspects of the inherited Germanic past, and often seems to have viewed that pre-Christian heritage with deep sympathy, if not favour. Particular focus is given on the one hand to the legendary figures of Scyld Scefing, Sigemund, and Ermanaric, parts of whose tales are embedded in the text, and on the other to a number of episodes from pagan myth to which (perhaps more suprisingly) the *Beowulf*-poet seems consciously to allude. Parallels and analogues from the Germanic tradition (notably from later Old Norse-Icelandic texts) to a range of themes and scenes from *Beowulf* are suggested, and it is argued that if the *Beowulf*-poet often seems to present a different perspective on shared material, he often likewise seems to do so for specific literary purposes of his own. The analysis strongly suggests that the *Beowulf*-poet consciously and creatively shaped and adapted the existing tales and traditions he adopted into his own.

Chapter 5 ('Religion and Learning') discusses the ways in which the literate and Latinate world of Christian learning may have influenced the poet, both directly and indirectly. The *Beowulf*-poet's use of biblical language and imagery is considered, as well as the extent to which some of the themes and ideas in the poem may derive from patristic and hagiographical sources. It is suggested that the *Beowulf*-poet may have drawn on details of the biblical narratives surrounding Old Testament heroes such as David, Samson, Moses, or Judas Maccabaeus in much the same way as he did with regard to figures from Germanic myth and legend, and with much the same literary intent: the better to highlight the virtues of his own hero, Beowulf. Parallels and analogues from the

Classical tradition are briefly described, as well as the poet's possible debt to the vernacular homiletic tradition; likewise the considerable overlap between the language of *Beowulf* and that of other extant Old English poems with a distinctly Christian or biblical theme (notably *Andreas*, *Genesis A*, and *Exodus*) is analysed; the possibility of direct literary links with such texts is suggested. Other Christian-Latin texts that make use of aspects of the Germanic heroic tradition (such as the *Liber monstrorum* or the *Waltharius*) are also considered for the considerable light they shed on the originality of the *Beowulf*-poet himself.

Chapter 6 ('Heroes and Villains') concentrates on the significant *dramatis personae* of the text, and shows the careful sympathy with which many of the minor figures are depicted. The so-called 'Finn-episode' is analysed in detail, and its brooding quality is emphasised by comparison with the surviving *Finnsburh fragment*, which describes some of the same events. The *Beowulf*-poet's focus on the aftermath of heroic violence, rather than on the violence itself, is highlighted, and it is suggested that in this episode, as elsewhere in the text, *Beowulf* is a poem not so much about action as reaction. Certainly, the particular attention in the episode paid to the reactions of Hildeburh and Hengest to the dilemmas they face as a result of the culture of heroic violence is noteworthy, but the focus throughout the episode (as elsewhere in *Beowulf*) is often more on the victims than the victors, a curious circumstance given the ostensibly celebratory backdrop to the telling of the tale itself. Likewise discussed are the depictions of Grendel and his mother, especially in their battles with Beowulf, where again the *Beowulf*-poet is often at pains to present the monsters' perspectives with the same scrupulous concern as that of the poem's eponymous hero. It is suggested that just as there is significant blurring of the distinctions between monsters and men and past and present in the poem, so too there are few figures who are painted in purely black-and-white terms.

Chapter 7 ('Words and Deeds') directs attention to the major role that speeches, which comprise nearly 40 per cent of *Beowulf*, play within the text. The sheer variety of speech-acts within the poem is explored in detail, as is the highly formalised nature of their phrasing. The extent to which the poet uses speech to define character is assessed, as well as the important structural role that speech-acts play within the narrative: the radically different patterning of speeches in different parts of the poem is underlined. The complex sequence of speeches that punctuate the narration of Beowulf's arrival in Denmark is likewise considered in detail, as are the speeches of Beowulf himself, who, it is argued, is a witty as well as wordy speaker. The continual emphasis throughout the text on the difference between words and deeds is underlined, and it is suggested that such a distinction is used to polarise both characters and events in *Beowulf*.

Chapter 8 ('*Beowulf*: Beyond Criticism?') considers the way in which the poet often seems to undermine his characters as soon as they are introduced: even Beowulf is seen as strictly circumscribed in this way. Mankind, the poet continually reminds us, has no ultimate knowledge of how things will turn out: and different people see the same things in deeply different ways. The explicit criticisms found in Beowulf's opening exchange with Unferth are used as examples to explore other more implicit criticisms of individuals and their viewpoints within the text, and it is suggested that the *Beowulf*-poet, a Christian attempting to assess pre-Christian deeds and times, deliberately and repeatedly offers multiple and varied perspectives on the same event or character in order to highlight the extent to which no final judgments on the glory-days of yore can be offered by even the most disinterested human observer: in the poet's view, apparently, only God, the final arbiter, can truly deem the truth.

The main chapters, then, though discrete units in themselves, can be seen to be roughly arranged to reflect a range of perspectives on *Beowulf*. Chapters 2 and 3 focus on the visual and verbal aspects of the poem; Chapters 4 and 5 on its cultural and literary background; Chapters 6 and 7 on narrative themes and technique; and Chapter 8 argues that the multiplicity of views held by recent readers of the poem is encouraged, indeed demanded, by the text itself. A brief 'Afterword' looks forward to future trends in scholarly criticism of *Beowulf*, in so far as they can be determined with any confidence at this distance. An Appendix aimed at helping to locate any line of the poem within the manuscript gives a key to the foliation of *Beowulf*, and is followed by two further Appendixes attempting to chart repeated formulas within *Beowulf*; all three Appendixes are intended to enable readers to orient themselves within the text. The 'List of passages cited and discussed', 'Index of scholars cited', and 'General index' should likewise assist readers in finding their way around this book.

Like Kenneth Sisam, 'in a place far from libraries I have often read the text of *Beowulf* for pleasure';[53] and assuredly there is no better reason, and perhaps no better place. At such times, however, I have often felt the need for a *Companion* to steer me towards subsequent research when time allowed, perhaps to provoke me with its blinkered views, and to assure me that for all of us who read *Beowulf* primarily for pleasure, there remains much work to be done. And that is the book I have tried to write.

---

[53] Sisam, *The Structure of 'Beowulf'*, p. 1.

2

Manuscript and Text

The 'Beowulf'-manuscript: history, script, and contents

The manuscript that survives today in London as British Library, Cotton, Vitellius A. XV is itself in appearance the 'ruin' that the mighty poem to which it is sole witness has sometimes been held to be;[1] certainly, both *Beowulf* and the manuscript which contains it bear the scars of successive generations.[2] The extant manuscript is composite, probably assembled by the celebrated Elizabethan antiquary Sir Robert Bruce Cotton (1571–1631), from at least two quite separate codices.[3] The manuscript now opens with material in a mid-twelfth-century hand (the so-called Southwick codex, fols. 1–90),[4] including the sole witness to King Alfred's version of Augustine's *Soliloquies*, and concludes with material in two earlier hands (the so-called Nowell codex, fols. 91[94]–206[209]);[5] it is this second codex (named from an inscription on its title-page at the head of its first leaf which identifies Laurence Nowell (*c.* 1510/20–*c.* 1571) as its owner) which is usually called the *Beowulf*-manuscript.[6]

Although the combined manuscript apparently passed into the possession of the British Museum soon after its foundation in 1753, it had by then already suffered greatly, most seriously in the calamitous fire that swept through the Cotton collection on Saturday, October 23, 1731, damaging or destroying around 200 items when they were stored in the ominously named Ashburnham House. A contemporary account describes how some of the manuscripts were

1 Compare the words of the Danish translator Adolf Hansen: 'som vi nu have Digtet, er det som en Ruin' ('as we now have the poem, it is like a ruin'), writing a century ago in Clausen, ed., *Illustreret Verdens-Litteraturhistorie*, III, p. 11, quoted by Haarder, *Beowulf: the Appeal of a Poem*, p. 89.

2 For a brief account of the *Beowulf*-manuscript, see Donald Scragg, *BEASE*, pp. 62–3. A number of facsimiles have been produced by Zupitza, Malone, and Kiernan (see section C of the Bibliography).

3 For a brief account of Cotton, see James P. Carley, *BEASE*, p. 124.

4 For speculation about the interval, see, for example Smith, 'The Provenance of the *Beowulf*-Manuscript'.

5 Apart from the careful description in Malone's facsimile, see in particular the detailed accounts by Boyle, 'The Nowell Codex and the Poem of *Beowulf*'; Gerritsen, 'British Library MS Cotton Vitellius A.xv – a Supplementary Description'. See too Malone, 'Readings from Folios 94 to 131, Cotton Vitellius A xv'. Following Kiernan, *'Beowulf' and the 'Beowulf'-Manuscript*, pp. 71–2 and 81–5, I use the older system of numbering the folios of the *Beowulf*-manuscript, rather than the so-called 'new' foliation, introduced in 1884, which at some points in the discussion I have inserted in square brackets. For the foliation of *Beowulf*, see Appendix I below, pp. 267–73.

6 For a brief account of Nowell, until recently confused with his namesake cousin the Dean of Lichfield, see James P. Carley, *BEASE*, p. 336.

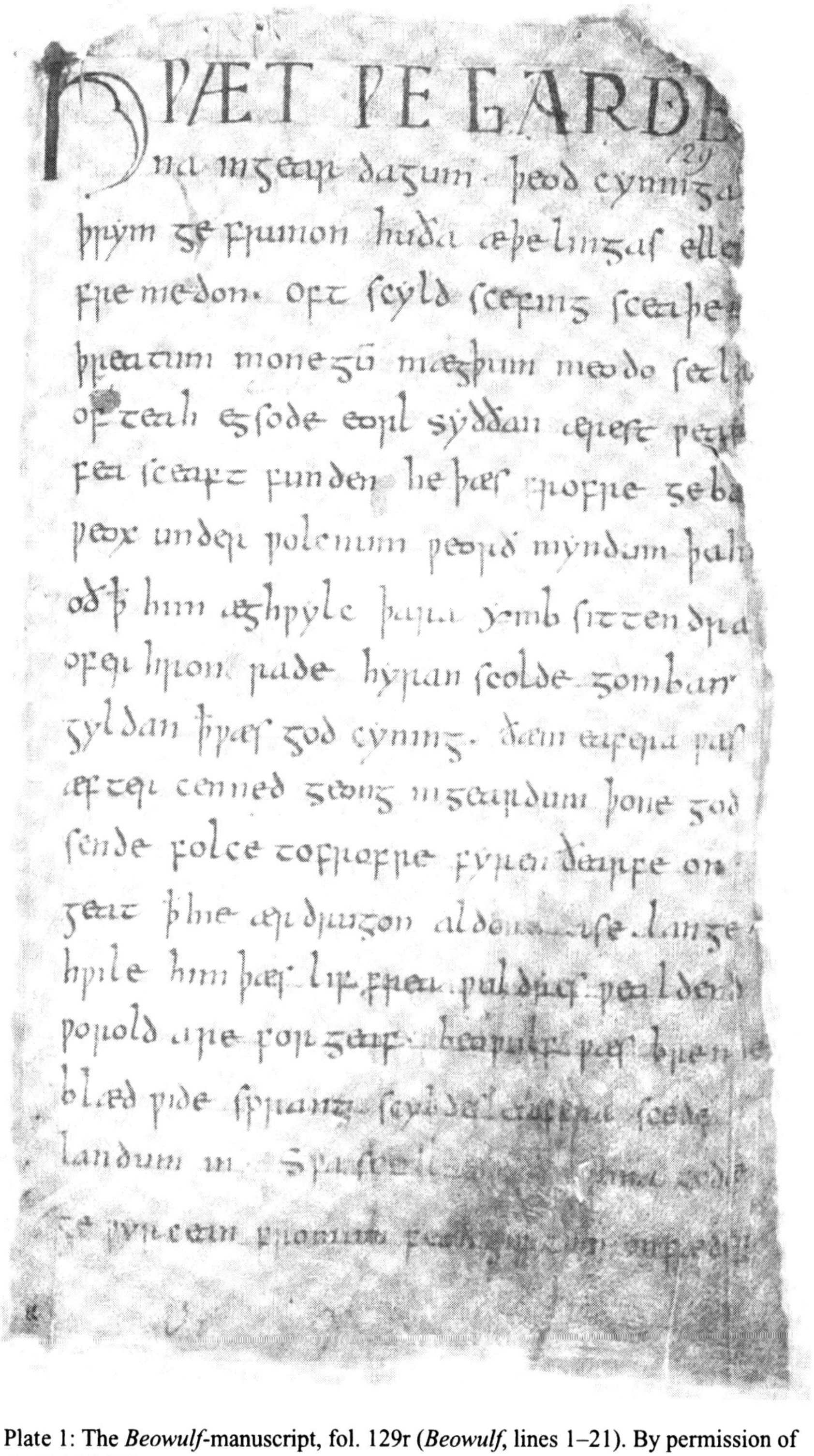

Plate 1: The *Beowulf*-manuscript, fol. 129r (*Beowulf*, lines 1–21). By permission of the British Library

Plate 2: The *Beowulf*-manuscript, fol. 95r (*Wonders*, sections 13–15). By permission of the British Library

Plate 3: The *Beowulf*-manuscript, fol. 95v (*Wonders*, sections 15–16). By permission of the British Library

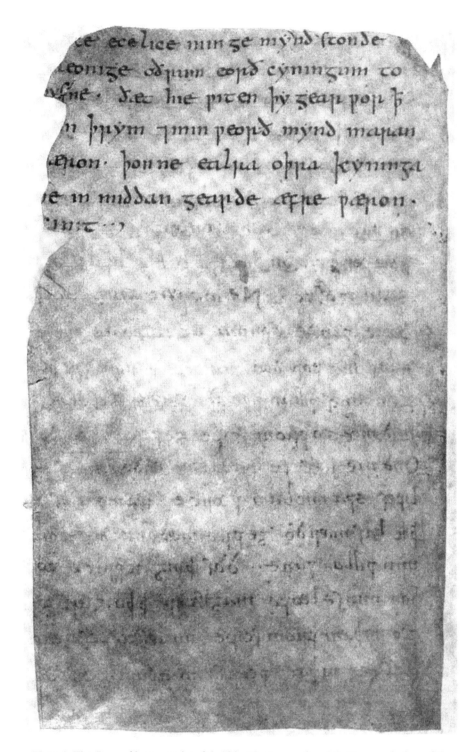

Plate 4: The *Beowulf*-manuscript, fol. 128v (*Letter*, section 41). By permission of the British Library

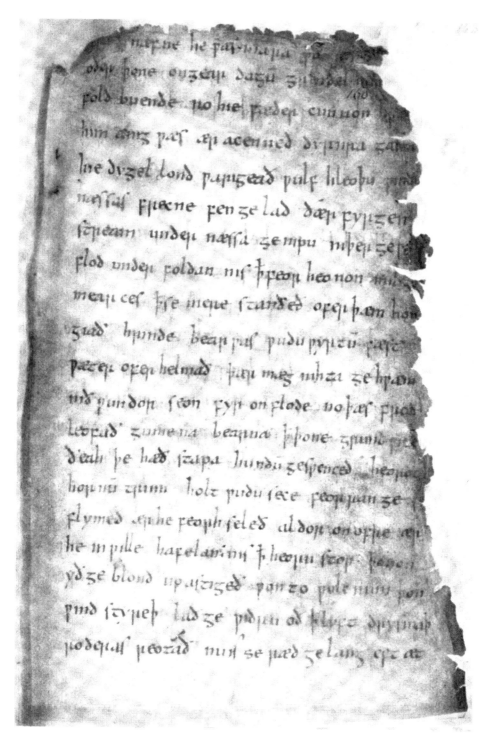

Plate 5: The *Beowulf*-manuscript, fol. 160r (*Beowulf*, lines 1352b–1377a).
By permission of the British Library

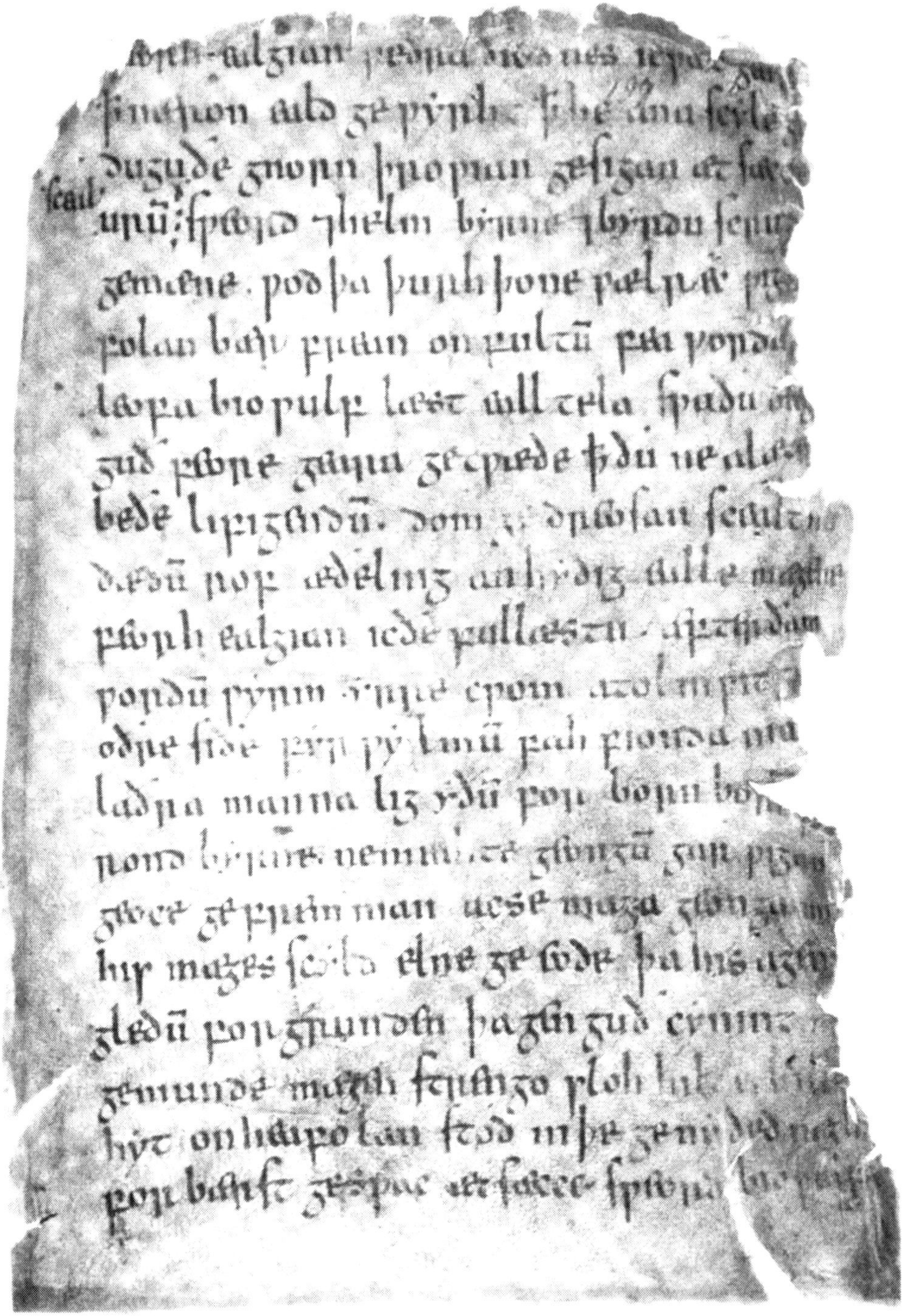

Plate 6: The *Beowulf*-manuscript, fol. 189A(197)r (*Beowulf*, lines 2655b–2682a).
By permission of the British Library

only saved by breaking open the backs of the flaming presses and throwing the books out of the window.[7] The fire destroyed the threads and folds of the gatherings of both the Southwick and Nowell codices, so obscuring their original construction; the leaves are now mounted separately in nineteenth-century paper frames. Although the *Beowulf*-manuscript escaped the worst ravages of the fire, which left some of the Cotton manuscripts 'burnt to a crust',[8] its margins were singed, and many individual letters were lost, later crumbled, or became obscured by the paper frames. In these circumstances, the testimonies of witnesses who saw the manuscript (and indeed the collection) both before and soon after the fire of 1731 take on the highest importance.[9]

Of these, an early and useful account is given by the pioneering palaeographer, Humfrey Wanley (1672–1726),[10] who in 1705 printed transcriptions of lines 1–19 and 53–73 of *Beowulf*.[11] As well as supplying useful testimony that by this date the Southwick and Nowell codices were bound together (but of clearly different origins), Wanley offers a poignant description of *Beowulf* as 'a most noble text written in poetry' (*Tractatus nobilissimus Poetice scriptus*).[12] Important evidence for establishing the text of *Beowulf* is provided by the two complete transcripts of the poem made at the instigation of the Icelander Grímur Jónsson Thorkelin (1752–1829),[13] since although he did not see the *Beowulf*-manuscript until it had already been damaged by fire and moved to the British Museum, it is clear that there has been palpable damage since then. In 1787 Thorkelin commissioned a copyist to transcribe the poem, and in 1789 made a second copy himself; he used the two resulting transcriptions, now known as 'Thorkelin A' and 'Thorkelin B' respectively, to produce his own rather crude first edition of the poem in 1815.[14] The value of these (admittedly often inaccurate) transcripts cannot be overstated: Kevin Kiernan has estimated that between them they restore or help to restore around 2,000 letters of the text lost before the manuscript was rebound in 1845.[15]

The *Beowulf*-manuscript itself is the work of two scribes, writing quite

---

7 'A NARRATIVE of the Fire which happened at *Ashburnham-House, Oct.* 23, 1731. and of the Methods used for preserving and recovering the Manuscripts of the Royal and *Cottonian* Libraries', British Library, MS 24,932, p. 11; see further Kiernan, *'Beowulf' and the 'Beowulf'-Manuscript*, p. 68.

8 See Planta, *Catalogue*, pp. xiii–xiv; Prescott, ' "Their Present Miserable State of Cremation" '.

9 For a full account of the earliest descriptions of the *Beowulf*-manuscript, including a painstaking description of how the various foliations developed, see Kiernan, *'Beowulf' and the 'Beowulf'-Manuscript*, pp. 85–119.

10 For a brief account of Wanley, see Simon Keynes, *BEASE*, pp. 466–7; see too Wright, 'Humfrey Wanley: Saxonist and Library-Keeper'; Milton McC. Gatch, 'Humfrey Wanley (1672–1726)', in *Medieval Scholarship*, ed. Damico, pp. 45–57.

11 Wanley, *Librorum Veterum Septentrionalium . . . Catalogus*, p. 218.

12 *Ibid.*, p. 218.

13 For a brief account of Thorkelin, see Donald Scragg, *BEASE*, pp. 446–7.

14 Thorkelin, ed., *De Danorum Rebus Gestis*. See too Malone, ed., *The Thorkelin Transcripts of Beowulf*; Kiernan, *The Thorkelin Transcripts of Beowulf*; Hall, 'The First Two Editions of *Beowulf*'; Gerritsen, 'The Thorkelin Transcripts'; *idem*, 'What Use are the Thorkelin Transcripts of *Beowulf*?'. See too Bjork, 'Grímur Jónsson Thorkelin's Preface to the First Edition of *Beowulf*, 1815'.

15 Kiernan, *The Thorkelin Transcripts*, p. 144.

distinct styles of Insular minuscule script. David Dumville provides a conveniently succinct summary of their separate styles and stints:[16]

> Scribe A, writing a minuscule characterised especially by extended descenders and ascenders, was responsible for lines 1–1939 (*scyran*) of *Beowulf* (fols. 129[132]r–172[175]v3). Scribe B, writing a rather crude, late Square minuscule script, completed the poetic half-line and the poem, lines 1939 (*moste*)–3182 (fols. 172[175]v4–198[201]v). Both scribes were also responsible for writing other texts now contained within the 'Nowell Codex' (viz. fols. 91[94]–206[209] of the Cotton volume): scribe A wrote the prose texts; scribe B copied the surviving leaves of the poem *Judith*. No other specimen of either scribe's work has ever been discovered; nor have any closely related scribal performances been identified.

Moreover, scribe A, although apparently completing his stint first, writes with a more modern hand than scribe B; Dumville estimates that if the hands were assessed in isolation, hand A would be dated around the beginning of the eleventh century, while that of hand B would be dated to the end of the tenth: the often-quoted dating by Neil Ker to sometime around the turn of the tenth century ('s. X/XI') therefore represents something of a compromise.[17] Dumville goes on to provide a still more narrow dating-band, stating that: 'It is in the highest degree unlikely that the *Beowulf*-manuscript was written later than the death of Æthelred the Unready (1016), or earlier than the mid-point of his reign (which fell in A.D. 997).'[18] This suggestion was made in direct response to an argument put forward by Kevin Kiernan that Ker's dating range permitted an attribution of the writing of the *Beowulf*-manuscript to the English reign of Cnut (1016–35),[19] a late dating which others (notably Johan Gerritsen) had attacked for a variety of reasons.[20] More recent attempts by Kiernan to bolster his own arguments have led to spirited rejoinders by both Gerritsen and Dumville: after much heat (and some light), the battle-lines remain essentially where they were before.[21]

The 3,182 lines of *Beowulf* are written on both sides of seventy leaves: scribe A wrote the first eighty-seven sides (roughly lines 1–1935a), plus the first three lines of fol. 172v; scribe B completed the last seventeen lines of fol. 172v and wrote the last fifty-two sides (comprising roughly lines 1958–3182).[22] During his stint, therefore, scribe A averaged 22.24 lines of verse per page (or about 356

---

[16] Dumville, 'Beowulf Come Lately', p. 50. For examples of scribe A's hand, see Plates 1–5 above; for scribe B, Plate 6.

[17] *Ibid.*, p. 55; Ker, *Catalogue*, p. 281 (no. 216).

[18] Dumville, 'Beowulf Come Lately', p. 63.

[19] See in particular Kiernan, *'Beowulf' and the 'Beowulf'-Manuscript*, esp. pp. 13–63; Kiernan, 'The Eleventh-Century Origin of *Beowulf*'.

[20] Gerritsen, 'British Library MS Cotton Vitellius A.xv – a Supplementary Description'; Gerritsen, 'Have with You to Lexington! The *Beowulf* Manuscript and *Beowulf*'; Clement, 'Codicological Consideration in the *Beowulf* Manuscript'; Fulk, 'Dating *Beowulf* to the Viking Age'; Fulk, *History of Old English Meter*, pp. 249 and 273–4.

[21] Kiernan, 'A Long Footnote'; Kiernan, 'The Legacy of Wiglaf'; Kiernan, 'Re-Visions', in his *'Beowulf' and the 'Beowulf'-Manuscript*, pp. xv–xxviii; Gerritsen, 'A Reply to Dr Kiernan's Footnote'; Gerritsen, *'Beowulf* Revisited'; Dumville, 'The *Beowulf*-Manuscript and How Not to Date It'.

[22] See Appendix I below, from which all the data from the following paragraph derive, for details.

lines per quire of sixteen sides), and scribe B 23.58 (or about 377 lines per quire of sixteen sides). The slight difference would seem negligible, were it not for the fact that both scribes dramatically increase the number of verse-lines per side towards the end of their stint, so skewing the average in both cases. For the first sixty-eight sides (fols. 129r–162v, comprising lines 1–1491a), scribe A regularly rules twenty lines per page,[23] and manages an average of only 21.93 lines of verse, but then suddenly rules sixteen sides for twenty-two lines (fols. 163r–170v, comprising lines 1491b–1874a). At his previous rate of progress, one would expect around 350 lines of verse to fit on the next sixteen sides, but in fact the scribe manages 383. By contrast, scribe B, who mostly fits in twenty-one lines per page,[24] and in general uses far more abbreviations than scribe A,[25] nonetheless writes only 340 lines of verse on his first sixteen sides (fols. 173r–180v; lines 1958–2296a).[26] Yet on the last sixteen sides written (fols. 190r–198v), scribe B manages to squeeze in an astonishing 427 (lines 2756–3182). It is hard to avoid the conclusion that both scribes were anxious to complete their stints within a set space, that both altered the density of their writing to include more verses per page in accordance with calculations of how much extra space would be required, and that both were therefore copying from exemplars.

The combination of two scribal hands of apparently differing dates in the same manuscript, although a defining characteristic of the *Beowulf*-manuscript, is not unique; Ker also assigns to the manuscript of the so-called Blickling Homilies (Princeton, Scheide Library 71) the same compromise date as the *Beowulf*-manuscript ('s. X/XI') since it too exhibits two scribal hands which, if considered separately, would have been assigned different dates.[27] Such an apparent connection between the two manuscripts, combined with the much-discussed textual parallel between St Paul's description of Hell in Blickling Homily XVI and that of the monster-mere in *Beowulf*,[28] has encouraged Kiernan to argue that the manuscripts containing *Beowulf* and the Blickling Homilies came from the same scriptorium, an intriguing suggestion which

---

[23] It is important to note that all the other texts in the *Beowulf*-manuscript written by scribe A (*Life of Christopher*, *Wonders*, and *Letter of Alexander*) are likewise written with twenty lines per page; the opening page of *Beowulf*, however, although ruled for twenty lines, in fact contains only nineteen: two lines are occupied by the opening line of capital letters. Boyle, 'The Nowell Codex', p. 24, provides a useful summary table.

[24] The exceptions are fols. 173r–174r and 176v–178v which contain twenty lines, and the last page of the poem, onto which twenty-two lines are crammed. That twenty lines per page was the norm for scribe B seems confirmed by the fact that the whole of *Judith* is so written.

[25] Cf. Dobbie, ed., *Beowulf and Judith*, pp. xxvii–xxix.

[26] Again, *Judith* provides a useful point of comparison for the normal practice of scribe B: the eight extant folios (199r–206v) contain 343 lines of verse on sixteen sides, with the last few lines of the poem added in an early modern hand at the foot of the final folio. Dobbie, ed., *Beowulf and Judith*, p. xvii, comparing the hands of scribes A and B, notes that 'the hand of the second scribe is much larger and more regular, with heavy shading of the vertical strokes'.

[27] Ker, *Catalogue*, p. 451 (no. 382); see too the facsimile by Willard, ed., *The Blickling Homilies*.

[28] On this textual connection, see, for example, Orchard, *Pride and Prodigies*, pp. 39–42; Brown, '*Beowulf* and the *Blickling Homilies*'; Collins, 'Blickling Homily XVI and the Dating of *Beowulf*'; Wright, *The Irish Tradition in Old English Literature*, pp. 116–38. See too below, pp. 30, 33, and 157–8.

Kiernan supports by a detailed comparison of the writing-areas, rulings, and codicological arrangements of the two manuscripts.[29]

Kiernan's argument would carry more force were it not for the fact that the *Beowulf*-manuscript and that containing the Blickling Homilies are not alone in exhibiting more than one scribal hand: at least three further manuscripts not only witness multiple scribal hands, but are dated by Ker to precisely the same period as those containing the Blickling Homilies and *Beowulf* ('s. X/XI'): Cambridge, Trinity College R. 5. 22 (717), fols. 72–158; London, British Library, Cotton Julius A. X, fols. 44–175; London, British Library, Cotton Otho B. II + Otho B. X, fols. 61, 63, and 64.[30] This kind of combination of scribal hands seems therefore not unusual for the period;[31] much more striking is the fact that scribe B of the *Beowulf*-manuscript appears to take over in mid-line and perhaps even in mid-word, leading Leonard Boyle to the arresting (if unlikely) suggestion concerning scribe A that: '[p]erhaps the plain truth is that he had taken ill, and died'.[32]

But if much ink has been spilt over the combination of scribal hands in the *Beowulf*-manuscript, and the subsequent implications for dating, so too opinions are divided over the reasons for the inclusion of *Beowulf* in the manuscript at all. The present contents of the *Beowulf*-manuscript can be summarised as follows:[33]

1. *The Passion of Saint Christopher*, incomplete at the beginning (fols. 93[94]r–97[98]r);[34]
2. *The Wonders of the East*, illustrated in colour (fols. 97[98]v–103[106]v);[35]
3. *The Letter of Alexander to Aristotle* (fols. 104[107]r–128[131]v);[36]
4. *Beowulf* (fols. 129[132]r–198[201]v);
5. *Judith*, incomplete at the beginning and end (fols. 199[202]r–206[209]v).[37]

---

29 Kiernan, *'Beowulf' and the 'Beowulf'-Manuscript*, pp. xix–xxii.
30 Ker, *Catalogue*, pp. 132–3, 205–6, and 222–3 (nos. 87, 161, and 175); Gneuss, *Handlist*, nos. 180, 338, and 353. I am grateful to David Dumville for pointing me towards these manuscripts.
31 This observation becomes particularly pointed when one realises that Ker only dates a dozen manuscripts (including the three listed here, the *Beowulf*-manuscript, and that containing the Blickling Homilies) with the notation 's. X/XI': Ker, *Catalogue*, nos. 15, 87, 161, 175, 184, 216, 220, 231, 240, 334, 364, and 382; Gneuss, *Handlist*, nos. 11, 180, 338, 353, 360, 399, 403, 421, 436, 640, 879, and 905. See further Cameron, *et al.*, 'A Reconsideration of the Language of *Beowulf*', p. 37.
32 Boyle, 'The Nowell Codex', p. 32. Boyle's rather dramatic view is challenged by Gerritsen, 'Have with you to Lexington', p. 16, who notes other examples of the same sudden changes of hands in, for example, London, British Library, Cotton Vitellius D. XI (Ker, *Catalogue*, pp. 292–8 [no. 222]), a mid-eleventh-century manuscript containing homilies for various saints' days (the change occurs at 54r21), and London, British Library, Harley 107 (Ker, *Catalogue*, p. 303 [no. 227]), a mid-eleventh-century manuscript containing, amongst other items, Ælfric's *Grammar* (the change occurs at 49r2).
33 The foliation given here is that of 1884, which is followed in the facsimile edition by Malone. See further Malone, ed., *The Nowell Codex*, pp. 12–14; Newton, *The Origins of 'Beowulf'*, p. 2; Sisam, *Studies*, p. 65; Boyle, 'The Nowell Codex and the Poem *Beowulf*', p. 24.
34 Rypins, ed., *Three Old English Prose Texts*, pp. 68–76. See too Orchard, *Pride and Prodigies*, pp. 12–14; Pickles, 'Studies in the Prose Texts of the *Beowulf* Manuscript', pp. 15–33.
35 Rypins, ed., *Three Old English Prose Texts*, pp. 51–67; James, ed., *Marvels of the East*; McGurk, *et al.*, ed., *An Eleventh-Century Anglo-Saxon Illustrated Miscellany*; Orchard, *Pride and Prodigies*, pp. 175–203. See too Andy Orchard, 'Marvels of the East', *BEASE*, p. 304.
36 Rypins, ed. *Three Old English Prose Texts*, pp. 1–50; Orchard, *Pride and Prodigies*, pp. 116–39 and 204–53; See too Kathryn Powell, 'Alexander the Great, Letter to Aristotle', *BEASE*, p. 27.
37 Griffith, ed., *Judith*; Orchard, *Pride and Prodigies*, pp. 4–9.

As it survives, then, the manuscript therefore contains three prose texts (items 1–3), all written by scribe A, followed by two poems (items 4–5), the writing of which part of *Beowulf* (from line 1939a on) and all of *Judith* are the work of scribe B. This is the order of the texts as reported by Wanley in 1705, who also confirms that by that date both *Christopher* and *Judith* were in their present incomplete state.[38]

The original position of *Judith* within the manuscript has, however, been called into question by Peter Lucas, who argues on the basis of both codicology and language that *Judith* most likely originally preceded *Christopher*, with which it shares a number of linguistic features not found in the other texts.[39] Although all the texts in the *Beowulf*-manuscript can be said in some sense to consider pagan (or at least pre-conversion) days of yore, such an arrangement would distinguish those texts which deal with an Old Testament or conversion-period past (*Judith* and *Christopher*) from those which describe pre-Christian antiquity (*Wonders* and the *Letter*) or pre-Christian Scandinavia (*Beowulf*). Lucas bolsters his argument that *Judith* and *Christopher* belong together by focusing on a linguistic feature of the manuscript as a whole, namely that both scribes occasionally produce *io*-spellings where one would expect *eo*.[40] As Kenneth Sisam had observed, there are no such *io*-spellings whatsoever either in the nine manuscript pages of *Christopher* (written by scribe A) or in the sixteen manuscript pages of *Judith* (written by scribe B), whereas all the other texts have them;[41] indeed, in *Beowulf* itself scribe B shows a particular fondness for *io*-spellings: in his stint there are 115 such spellings in fifty-three manuscript pages (2.2 per page), as against only eleven in the eighty-seven manuscript pages of scribe A's stint (roughly 1 every 7.9 pages).[42] Such figures seem to indicate that scribe B tended to retain *io*-spellings, while scribe A tried to eliminate them;[43] and this is but one of several differences in the spellings employed by the two scribes of the *Beowulf*-manuscript.[44] As Kenneth Sisam concludes, moreover, such a distribution of *io*-spellings 'suggests that both *Christopher* and *Judith* were added to a collection characterised by *io*-spellings'.[45] Certainly, other spelling-variants also connect the other three texts: all three have occasional *u* for medial *f*, and the *Letter* and *Beowulf* share genitive plural endings in -*o*, all in scribe A's stint.[46]

---

[38] Wanley, *Antiquæ Literaturæ Septentrionalis Liber Alter*, pp. 218–19.

[39] Lucas, 'The Place of *Judith*'; see too Griffith, ed., *Judith*, 1–8.

[40] Lucas, 'The Place of *Judith*', pp. 473–4.

[41] According to Sisam, *Studies*, p. 92, *Wonders* has two *io*-spellings in seventeen manuscript pages, and the *Letter* has sixty-six such spellings in fifty pages.

[42] Sisam, *Studies*, pp. 92–3; see too Lucas, 'The Place of *Judith*', p. 474. The figures derive ultimately from Rypins, *Three Old English Texts*, p. xix.

[43] For some interesting illustrations of how scribe B occasionally corrected his original *io*-spellings, see Kiernan, *Beowulf and the Beowulf-Manuscript*, pp. xxvi–xxvii.

[44] For a useful list of some such variants, see Griffith, ed., *Judith*, pp. 11–18. There are many examples in *Beowulf*: see below, n. 61.

[45] Sisam, *Studies*, p. 68.

[46] Sisam, *Studies*, pp. 64, 85–6, and 94. In the case of both *Wonders* and the *Letter*, the putative medial -*u*- has been copied as -*n*-: the *Letter* has *hleonige* for *hleouige* (128v2) and *Wonders* has *leone* for *leoue* six times (97v10 and 20, 99r7, 96r2 and 19, and 101v7 [there were probably another two examples at 98r4 and 96v8 that have now disappeared as a result of physical damage to the manuscript]);

The 'Beowulf'-manuscript as a 'Book of monsters'

There are further indications that the texts in the *Beowulf*-manuscript were originally composed in different dialects,[47] and at different dates, leading Sisam to conclude that the core-collection of *Wonders*, the *Letter*, and *Beowulf* was put together because of a compiler's interest in texts about monsters.[48] It is certainly true that while both *Wonders* and the *Letter* depict lands far removed in both geography and chronology from those described in *Beowulf*, there are a number of thematic similarities which link all three texts. Like *Beowulf* (but more in the manner of a travelogue), *Wonders* depicts a natural world essentially inimical to men,[49] inhabited by dragons and other man-eating creatures; the land beyond the so-called River Brixontes, for example, is described as follows (sections 13–16):[50]

> Begeondan Brixonte þære ea, east þonon, beoð men acende lange ˥ micle, þa habbað fet ˥ sconcan .XII. fota lange, sidan mid breostum seofon fota lange. Hostes hy synd nemned. Cuðlice swa hwylcne man swa hy gelæccað, þonne fretað hi hyne. Ðonne seondon wildeor þa hatton Lertices. Hy habbað eoseles earan ˥ sceapes wulle ˥ fugeles fet. Þonne syndon oþere ealond suð from Brixonte on þon beoð [men] buton heafdum, þa habbað on hyra breostum heora eagan ˥ muð. Hy seondan eahta fota lange ˥ eahta fota brade. Ðar beoð cende [dracan] þa beoð on lenge hundteontige fotmæla lange ˥ fiftiges, hy beoð greate swa stænene sweras micle. For þara dracena micelnesse ne mæg nan man nayþelice on þæt land gefaran.

> [Beyond the River Brixontes, east from there, there are people born big and tall, who have feet and shanks twelve feet long, flanks with chests seven feet long. They are of a black colour, and are called Hostes ['enemies']. As certainly as they catch a person they devour him. Then there are on the Brixontes wild animals which are called Lertices. They have donkey's ears and sheep's wool and bird's feet. Then there is another island, south of the Brixontes, on which there are born men without heads who have their eyes and mouth in their chest. They are eight feet tall and eight feet wide. Dragons are born there, who are one hundred and fifty feet long, and are as thick as great stone pillars. Because of the abundance of the dragons, no one can travel easily into that land.]

Beowulf has *hliuade* in line 1799b. The genitive plurals in -*o* in *Beowulf* are *yldo* (line 70a) and *hynðo* (line 475a); the five such spellings in the *Letter* are *siðfato* (115v11), *leohtfato* (121r8), *earfeðo* (122r15), *Medo* (108v3), and *ondswaro* (109r13); for other such spelings elsewhere in the extant corpus, see Klaeber, 'A Few *Beowulf* Notes', p. 17, based on Sievers, 'Miscellen', p. 230.

47 For *Judith*, see Griffith, ed., *Judith*, pp. 11–25 and 44–7; for the other texts, see Orchard, *Pride and Prodigies*, p. 3. The phonology of the *Letter* has been minutely documented by Braun, *Lautlehre der angelsächsischen Version der 'Epistola Alexandri ad Aristotelem'*.

48 Sisam, *Studies*, pp. 64–7 and 96, where, however, *Christopher* is also included, since the eponymous saint is depicted with the head of a dog. For further arguments which would also include *Judith* in such a scheme, see Taylor and Salus, 'The Compilation of Cotton Vitellius A XV'; Orchard, *Pride and Prodigies*, pp. 1–27.

49 For the notion that the natural world is depicted as essentially hostile in *Beowulf*, see Neville, *Representations of the Natural World*, esp. pp. 70–84 and 129–38.

50 For the text, see Rypins, ed., *Three Prose Texts*, pp. 58–9; for the section-numbers and translation, see Orchard, *Pride and Prodigies*, pp. 184–203, which is based on the variant version of the text found in London, British Library, Cotton Tiberius B. V, fols. 78v–87v. See too Plates 2–3 for the text and accompanying pictures in the *Beowulf*-manuscript.

Such a description of the utter hostility of such monstrous creatures to men essentially accords with what one finds in *Beowulf*; monster-slaying in response to man-killing is man's natural reaction in both.[51] *Wonders* also supplies an analogue for the *Beowulf*-poet's description that from Grendel's eyes there shone 'an unlovely light, most like a flame' (line 727: *ligge gelicost leoht unfæger*), both in its account of an unnamed island, the eyes of whose inhabitants 'shine as brightly as if one had lit a great lantern on a dark night' (section 3: *scinaþ swa leohte swa man micel blacern onæle þeostre nihte*) and in its description of a two-headed serpent the eyes of which 'shine at night as brightly as lanterns' (section 5: *scinað nihtes swa leohte swa blæcern*). The figure of Alexander the Great, interestingly in his role of monster-slayer, links both *Wonders* (sections 2, 27, and 30) and the *Letter*,[52] as does their shared interest in the monstrous *healfhundingas* (*Wonders*, section 7; *Letter*, section 29), the dog-headed race of men to which Saint Christopher is also said to belong.[53] Indeed, the juxtaposition of the *Letter* and *Beowulf* in the manuscript has seemed significant to some,[54] and Sisam's arguments concerning the putative original association of the two texts in an earlier manuscript-collection, to which in stages were added *Wonders*, *Christopher*, and *Judith*, surely invite further study of their close thematic links.[55]

'Beowulf' and 'The Letter of Alexander to Aristotle': connected texts?

The more explicitly martial and heroic flavour of the *Letter*, when compared to the other prose texts in the *Beowulf*-manuscript, provides an obvious parallel to *Beowulf*, and the Anglo-Saxon author of the *Letter* clearly warms to his theme, often expanding his Latin source in a manner which tends to shift the focus onto the character of Alexander himself. An example is provided by the way in which the Anglo-Saxon author treats Alexander's pride in the appearance of his men, which in the Latin is rather simply expressed (section 11):[56]

Et sane miles ita locupletatus erat, ut vix ferre pondus auri posset. Accedebat quoque armorum non parva gravitas, quia omnia ego incluseram laminis. Ita totum agmen me veluti sidere aut fulgore clarum radiantibus auro insignibusque sequebatur cum signis et vexillis. Eratque inter varietates spectaculum in conspiciendo talem exercitum, quia ornatu pariter et inter gentes ceteras eminebat. Ego certe respiciens felicitatem meam insigni numero iuventutis immenso afficiebar gaudio.

[And indeed each soldier was so wealthy that he could scarcely carry the mass of gold. In addition there was no small weight of armour, because I had encased everything in metal plates. So the whole army was following me,

---

51 For an excellent overview of the theme, see the lavishly illustrated article by Ruggerini, 'L'eroe germanico contro avversari mostruosi'.
52 Cf. Tristram, 'Der Insulare Alexander'; *idem*, 'More Talk of Alexander'.
53 See Orchard, *Pride and Prodigies*, pp. 12–18.
54 See, for example, Orchard, *Pride and Prodigies*, pp. 116–39.
55 See above, n. 48.
56 For variant texts in the Latin, see, for example, Boer, ed., *Epistola Alexandri*.

bright like a star or a bolt of lightning, shining with gold and resplendent, with banners and pennants. And it was a sight to see such an army in its different array, since in ornament it was outstanding equally even among other nations. And I, indeed, gazing on my good fortune in the splendid number of young men was touched by great joy.]

The Old English is version is rather longer, and palpably different in tone:

Ond efne swiðe þa mine þegnas ꝺ eal min weorod wæs gewelgod þæt hie uneðe ealle þa byrðene þæs goldes mid him aberan ꝺ alædan meahton. Swelce eac heora wæpena noht lytel byrðen wæs for þon eal heora wæpenu þæra minra þegna ꝺ ealles mines weoredes ꝺ heriges ic [het] hie mid gyldenum þelum bewyrcean. Ond eall min weorod wæs on þa gelicnesse tungles oððe ligite for þære micelnisse þæs goldes. Hit scan ꝺ berhte foran swa ymb me uton mid þrymme ꝺ herebeacen ꝺ segnas beforan me læddon. Ond swa micel wundor ꝺ wæfersien wæs þæs mines weoredes on fægernisse ofer ealle oþre þeodkyningas þe in middangearde wæron. Ða sceawede ic seolfa ꝺ geseah mine gesælinesse ꝺ min wuldor ꝺ þa fromnisse minre iuguðe ꝺ gesælignisse mines lifes, þa wæs ic hwæthwugo in gefean in minum mode ahafen.

[And indeed my thegns and all my troop had gained so much wealth that they could only with difficulty bring and carry with them the burden of all that gold. Also their weapons were no little burden because I had commanded that all the weapons of my thegns and all my troop and army be covered with gold plate. And all my troop looked like stars or lightning because of the amount of the gold. It shone and glittered before me and around me in glory, and they led before me war-banners and standards. And so great was the sight and spectacle of that troop of mine in splendour beyond all the other mighty kings there have been in the world. When I myself gazed and saw my prosperity and my glory and the success of my youth and the prosperity of my life, I was somewhat uplifted with joy in my heart.]

The richness of the diction is best exemplified by the extensive use of (often alliterating) doublets (*mine þegnas ꝺ eal min weorod*; *scan ꝺ berhte*; *wundor ꝺ wæfersien*; *sceawede ic seolfa ꝺ geseah*; *mine gesælinesse ꝺ min wuldor, þa fromnisse minre iuguðe ꝺ gesælignisse mines lifes*);[57] the emphasis on Alexander himself is highlighted by a fourfold increase in the use of first-person references, as well as by an alteration of an anonymous reference to other 'nations' (*gentes*), to one to 'mighty kings' (*þeodcyninga*). The use of the latter compound is particularly intriguing, not only since the word occurs no fewer than eight times in *Beowulf* alone, but also because it is only one of a number of compounds with an evidently heroic and poetic flavour, some shared with *Beowulf*, that are found in the text of the *Letter*.[58]

---

[57] On the style of the *Letter* in general, see further Orchard, *Pride and Prodigies*, pp. 132–7.

[58] The compound *þeodcyning* and its variants is found fifteen times in surviving Old English poetry (*Beowulf*, lines 2a, 2144a, 2579a, 2694b, 2963a, 2970a, 3008a, and 3086; *Death of Edward*, line 34b; *Fates of the Apostles*, line 18b; *Genesis*, lines 1865a and 1869a; *Judgement Day II*, line162b; *Riddle 67*, line 1a; *Soul and Body I*, line 12b), but, apart from its appearance in the *Letter* here, only one other time in prose (Napier Homily XXIX: Napier, ed., *Wulfstan*, p. 138, line 14). Bately, 'Old English Prose before and during the Reign of Alfred', p. 113, notes of the *Letter* 'a fondness for compounding of a type typical of poetry'. Bately's list contains five compounds otherwise attested only

Other similarities between the vocabulary of *Beowulf* and the *Letter* are likewise suggestive. So, for example, the verb *sceawian* ('to gaze upon', 'to examine') is found frequently in both *Beowulf* and the *Letter*, but occurs in none of the other three texts in the *Beowulf*-manuscript. Moreover, the usage of this verb is markedly similar in both cases. The verb *sceawian* occurs no fewer than nineteen times in *Beowulf*,[59] with a strikingly limited set of objects: the things 'gazed upon' or 'examined' in the poem include Grendel's trail (lines 132b, 840b, and 843b); the omens consulted by the Geats before Beowulf's departure (line 204b); Grendel's hand (line 983b); Grendel's mother's trail (line 1391b); the monster-mere (line 1413b); the dead creature from the monster-mere (line 1440b); the hilt from the monster-mere (line 1687b); the plundered cup from the dragon's hoard (line 2285b); the dragon (line 2402b); the dragon's hoard (lines 2744a, 2748b, 3075b, 3084b, and 3104b); the treasure from the dragon's hoard brought to the dying Beowulf (line 2793b); and, indeed, perhaps most strikingly in this context, the dead Beowulf himself (line 3008b and 3032b).[60] As if to underline the monstrous, uncanny, or otherworldly associations of all the objects 'gazed upon' or 'examined' in the poem, the verb *sceawian* is often found in close proximity to the word *wundor* ('wonder', 'marvel') and its cognates, which together occur some twenty-three times in the poem:[61] so, for example, after Grendel's escape from Heorot, many nobles travel great distances 'to gaze upon the wonder' of Grendel's tracks (*wundor sceawian*, line 840b).[62] More startling, perhaps, is the use of the same half-line (*wundur sceawian*, line 3032b) to describe how the tearful Geatish troops 'gaze upon the wonder' of their dead king; but the poet has carefully set the scene by having the messenger earlier invite the people to 'gaze upon' Beowulf's corpse (*sceawian*, line 3008b),[63] and, after all, we are told that Beowulf 'died a wondrous death' (*wundordeaðe*

in poetry, including two compounds shared with *Beowulf*: *byrnwiga* (*Letter*, section 8; *Beowulf*, line 2918a; *Judith*, line 39a; *Wanderer*, line 94b); *hronfisc* (*Letter*, section 29; *Beowulf*, line 540b). Bately also lists three unique compounds from the *Letter*, namely *stanhol* (*Letter*, section 9), *longscaft* (*Letter*, section 17), and *godmægen* (*Letter*, section 31). In general, throughout this book quotations from Old English poems will be taken from ASPR, unless otherwise indicated.

59   I discount here the compound noun *leassceawere*, unique to *Beowulf*, which is found at line 253a, and apparently means 'spy'.

60   The occurrence of the word *gesceawod* in line 3075b forms part of a notorious crux, but could certainly refer to the dragon's hoard; the phrase *wundur sceawian* (line 3032b) could equally refer to the dead dragon and/or the dead Beowulf. See further below, pp. 86–7.

61   At lines 771a (*wundor*), 840b (*wundor*), 920a (*searowundor*), 931a (twice: '*wunder æfter wundre*'), 995b (*wundorsiona*), 1162a (*wunderfatum*), 1365b (*niðwundor*), 1440a (*wundorlic*), 1452b (*wundrum*), 1509b (*wundra*), 1607b (*wundra*), 1681a (*wundorsmiþa*), 1724b (*wundrum*], 1747a (*wunderbebodum*), 2173a (*wundurmaððum*), 2687a (*wundrum* [manuscript *wundum*]), 2759a (*wundur*), 2768b (*hondwundra*), 3032b (*wundur*), 3062b (*wundur*), and 3103a (*wundur*). One notes in passing the consistent spelling in -*wund[u]r*- of the B-scribe (after line 1939b), by contrast with the A-scribe.

62   Likewise in the space of a single line the poet describes how the creature from the monster-mere killed by Beowulf before his descent to fight Grendel's mother is a 'wondrous wave-crosser' (*wundorlic wægbora*, line 1440a), and notes that 'men gazed upon [it]' (*weras sceawedon*, line 1440b). Similarly one might note that in two consecutive lines Wiglaf invites the Geatish warriors to 'gaze upon' the 'wonder' of the dragon's hoard (lines 3103–4).

63   A further connection between lines 3008b and 3032b is that in each case stress is laid in almost identical terms on the fact that the dead Beowulf had been a great ring-giver (*þe us beagas geaf*, line 3009b; *þone þe him hringas geaf*, line 3034b).

swealt, line 3037b). It is as if in death Beowulf becomes something of a marvel himself.[64] The same verb occurs no fewer than ten times in the *Letter* too, each time describing one of the many wonders Alexander encounters on his travels.[65] In this case, the collocation with the element *-wund(o)r-/wunder-* is still more striking than in *Beowulf*: all thirteen of the occurrences of the element *-wund(o)r- /wunder-* are found in close proximity to those of the verb *sceawian*, as is illustrated in Table I below, which also plots the relevant words in the Latin source-text, in so far as they can be determined.[66]

The particular clustering of such collocated terms at the beginning of the *Letter* underlines the fact that wonders are clearly a major theme of the text, and indeed such collocations occur throughout, right up until the final scenes. What is immediately apparent from the following Table is the fact that, of no fewer than ten sections of the *Letter* which contain either part of the verb *sceawian* or the element *wund(o)r-/wunder-*, only two (sections 14 and 25) fail to contain both. That this close collocation of forms is a deliberate strategy on the part of the translator seems confirmed by the wide diversity in the Latin words used in the source-text: of its ten occurrences in the text, the Old English *Letter* exhibits some form of the verb *sceawian* some six times where either the word translated has no visual connotations or there is no equivalent term in the Latin at all;[67] likewise, of the thirteen occurrences of the element *-wund(o)r-/wunder-*, less than half translate the equivalent Latin element *(-)mir-*.[68] Such a shared association of such frequently occurring terms in both *Beowulf* and the *Letter* is the more striking in that not only do *Christopher*, *Wonders*, and *Judith* contain no examples of the verb *sceawian* at all, but (perhaps more surprisingly) only one each of the form *-wund(o)r-*;[69] moreover, few other texts in the extant corpus of Old English collocate the same terms with any frequency at all.[70]

There are still other parallels to be perceived between the *Letter* and *Beowulf*, particularly with regard to the monstrous creatures that both Beowulf and Alexander encounter. In the poem, Beowulf is accompanied by Geatish and Danish warriors to the monster-mere, which is set in wilderness not far from the human habitation at Heorot and surrounded by towering trees and cliffs (lines

---

64 See further, for example, Robinson, *Tomb of Beowulf*, pp. 3–19.

65 In the following references, section-numbers refer to Orchard, *Pride and Prodigies*. Two gatherings of eight leaves (fols. 107–14 and 115–22) have been bound out of sequence, hence the disjunction between the order of folios and section-numbers at this point. I am grateful to Charles Stone for pointing out to me the relative frequency of this verb in the *Letter*.

66 It might be pointed out that in his glossary Rypins only indicates eleven of the thirteen relevant occurrences of the element *-wund(o)r-*: he omits the two references in 106v19 and 123v8.

67 In sections 9, 25, and 34 there is no direct Latin equivalent for the form of *sceawian* employed in the *Letter*, while in three other cases the only Latin equivalent involves a verb of motion (section 8, *inuasimus* ['we invaded']; section 29, *adire* ['to approach']; section 36, *perambulare* ['to wander through']).

68 The exceptions are found in sections 1, 11, 25, 26, 29, 34, and 36.

69 *Judith* has *wundrum* in line 8b, *Christopher* has *wundor* at 92r10, and *Wonders* has *wundrende* at 103v10 (section 30); neither of the last two references is noted by Rypins.

70 Many of the examples derive from the gloss *[be]sceawige wundra* ['I shall gaze on wonders'] for the Vulgate *considerabo mirabilia* of Psalms 118.18; apart from the translator of the *Letter* and the Beowulf-poet, Wærferth is the only Old English author to use the collocation with any frequency, in his translation of Gregory's *Dialogues*.

Table I: The distribution of (-)*sceaw-* and *wund(o)r / wunder*-forms in
The Letter of Alexander to Aristotle

section 3: the earth as a source of wonder

104v10	*wundorlicra*	*prodigia*
104v12	*wundrienne*	*mirandum est*
104v14	*sceawigendum*	*contemplaris* (?)
104v16	*wundorlice*	–
104v16	*sceawigað*	*intueri*

section 8: the marvellous palace of Porus

106r5	*wundorlice*	*mira*
106v1	*sceawedon*	*inuasimus* (?)
106v11	*wundrode*	*miratus sum*
106v19	*wunderlice*	*miri*

section 9: the marvellous fertility of Caspia

115r14	*wundrade*	*ammirarer*
115r18	*sceawigean*	–

section 11: the wondrous spectacle of Alexander's army

116v12	*wundor*	*spectaculum*
116v15	*sceawede*	*respiciens*

section 14: the army gets restless

118v7	*wundredon*	*mirabantur*

section 25: the camp of King Porus

109v18	*gesceawod*	–

section 26: wonderful and noteworthy things

110v3	*wunderlicra*	*memorabile*
110v3	*sceawian*	*cerneremus*

section 29: the wondrous Ictifafonas

112r10	*sceawigon*	*adire*
112r19	*wunderlices*	*dignum spectaculum*

section 34: the marvellous grove of India

123v6	*sceawodon*	–
123v8	*wundrade*	–

section 36: the wondrous trees of the Sun and the Moon

124r14	*sceawigan*	*perambulare*
124v3	*wunderlicre*	–

1408–17a);[71] in the *Letter*, Alexander and his men come across a river in the wilderness when they are beset by thirst (section 12):

> Ond þa mid þy þe þæt min werod gehyrted ⁊ gestilled wæs, þa ferdon we forð þy wege þe we ær ongunnon ða næs long to þon in þæm westenne þæt we to sumre ea cwoman. On þære ea ofre stod hreod ⁊ pintreow ⁊ abies þæt treowcyn ungemetlicre gryto ⁊ micelnysse þy clyfe weox ⁊ wridode.

> [And when my troop was heartened and calmed by this, we went ahead on the route we had taken before, and it was not long until we came to a certain river in the wilderness. On the river-bank there stood reeds and pines, and silver-fir trees of huge size and stature grew and flourished on the cliff-edge.]

It is useful to compare the Latin source at this point (section 12):

> Quae res cum animaequiorem fecisset exercitum, ceptum iter institui. Nec longe mihi in desertis locis flumen apparuit cuius ripas pedum sexagenum arundo uestiebat, pinorum abietumque robora uincens grossitudine, qua Indi materia ad constituenda aedificia utebantur.

> [After that event had made the army more settled, I continued on the journey we had begun. Not far away in the desert there appeared to me a river, the banks of which were covered by reeds sixty feet high, surpassing in their girth the trunks of pines or silver-firs, and the Indians used that material to construct buildings.]

Apart from the confusion and conflation of tree-types, the Anglo-Saxon author has omitted the anthropological observation on native building-practices, and instead inserted without warrant a reference to a cliff-edge, and an alliterative doublet (*weox ⁊ wridode*). It is interesting to note that both elements can be paralleled in *Beowulf*: the cliffs around the monster-mere are mentioned in both descriptions in the poem (lines 1357b–1379 and 1408–17a), while the doublet *weox ⁊ wridode* occurs only three other times in extant Old English, in *Beowulf* (line 1741a: *weaxeð ond wrideð*), *Genesis A* (line 1532a: *weaxað and wridað*),[72] and Blickling Homily XVI (*geweox ond gewridode*);[73] this last instance is the more intriguing in that the homily in question is precisely that which contains a further parallel for the description of the monster-mere, so suggesting a rather more complex interrerlationship between *Beowulf*, the *Letter*, and Blickling Homily XVI than has been considered so far.[74]

In the *Letter*, Alexander and his men do not have to travel far along this river before they come to human habitation. What happens next again offers suggestive parallels with *Beowulf* (section 15):

> Ferdon we þa forð be þære ea ofre, ða wæs seo eatoðe tid dæges. Þa cwoman we to sumre byrig, seo burh wæs on midre þære ea in anum eglonde

---

71 Hrothgar tells Beowulf that the monster-mere is close at hand (lines 1361–2: *nis þæt feor heonon/ milgemearces þæt se mere standeð*).

72 On the relationship between *Genesis A* and *Beowulf*, see further below, pp. 167–8.

73 Morris, ed., *Blickling Homilies*, p. 199, line 2; see further Clemoes, 'Style as a Criterion for Dating the Composition of *Beowulf*', pp. 180–1.

74 See above, p. 21, n. 28, and below, pp. 33 and 157–8.

getimbred. Wæs seo burh mid þy hreode ⁊ treowcynne þe on þære ea ofre
weox ⁊ we ær biwriton ⁊ sægdon asett ⁊ geworht. Ða gesawon we in þære
byrig ⁊ ongeaton Indisce men fea healf nacode eardigende. Ða hie þa us
gesawon hie selfe sona in heora husum deagollice hie miþan ða wilnade ic
þara monna onsyne to geseonne, þæt hie us fersc wæter ⁊ swete getæhton.
Mid þy we ða longe bidon ⁊ us nænig mon to wolde þa het ic fea stræla sendan
in þa burh innan, to þon gif hie hiera willum us to noldon þæt hie for þæm ege
þæs gefeohtes nede scoldon. Ða wæron hie þy swyðor afyrhte ⁊ hie fæstor
hyddan. Þa het ic .CC. minra þegna of greca herige leohtum wæpnum hie
gegyrwan, ⁊ hie on sunde to þære byrig foron ⁊ swumman ofer æfter þære ea
to þæm eglande. Þa hie ða hæfdon feorðan dæl þære ea geswummen, ða
becwom sum ongrislic wise on hie. Þæt wæs þonne nicra mengeo on onsione
maran ⁊ unhyrlicran þonne ða elpendas in ðone grund þære ea ⁊ betweoh ða
yða þæs wæteres þa men besencte ⁊ mid heora muðe hie sliton ⁊ blodgodon ⁊
hie ealle swa fornamon, þæt ure nænig wiste hwær hiora æni cwom. Ða wæs
ic swiðe yrre þæm minum ladþeowum, þa us on swylce frecennissa gelæddon.
Het hiera ða bescufan in þa ea .L. ⁊ .C. ⁊ sona þæs ðe hie inne wæron, swa
wæron þa nicoras gearwe tobrudon hie swa hie þa oðre ær dydon, ⁊ swa þicce
hie in þære ea aweollon swa æmettan ða nicras, ⁊ swilc unrim heora wæs. Þa
het ic blawan mine byman ⁊ þa fyrd faran.

[Then we went forth along the bank of the river, at the eighth hour of the day.
Then we came to a village, built in the middle of the river on an island. The
village was built and constructed from the reeds and trees that grew on the
river-bank, and which we have written about and described already. When we
looked into the village we saw dwelling in it a few half-naked people. But as
soon as they themselves saw us they hid themselves furtively in their houses. I
wanted to catch sight of these men, to find out about clean fresh water. After
we had waited a long time and none of them would emerge, I ordered a few
arrows to be shot into the village, so that if they would not come out to us
voluntarily, they should of necessity, through fear of battle. Then they were
still more greatly afraid, and hid themselves more securely. Then I ordered
two hundred of my thegns from the Greek army to arm themselves with light
weapons and go over to the village by swimming, and they swam over across
the river to that island. And when they had swum about a quarter of the river,
something terrible happened to them. There appeared a multitude of
water-monsters, larger and more terrible in appearance than the elephants,
who dragged the men through the watery waves down to the river bottom, and
tore them to bloody pieces with their mouths, and snatched them all away so
that none of us knew where any of them had gone. Then I was very angry with
my guides, who had led us into such danger. I ordered that one hundred and
fifty of them be shoved into the river, and as soon as they were in [the water],
the water-monsters were ready, and dragged them away just as they had done
with the others, and the water-monsters seethed up in the river as thick as ants,
they were so innumerable. Then I ordered the trumpets to be sounded, and the
army to head off.]

The Latin source makes it clear that this 'multitude of water-monsters' (*nicra
mengeo*) is in fact a herd of hippopotami, whose actions, moreover, are
described in rather less dramatic terms (section 15):

hippotami inter profundos aquarum emersi apparuerunt gurgites raptosque in uertice crudeli poena uiros flentibus nobis adsumpserunt.

[hippopotami, that had been emersed in the deep currents of the waters, appeared, snatched the men in their mouths and took them off in a cruel punishment while we wept.]

Some manuscripts have the variant *in uorticem* ('into the surging water') for the problematic phrase *in uertice* (literally 'in the top', and so perhaps 'in their mouths'), and such a reading may well lie behind the Old English version,[75] although the sentence as a whole hardly warrants the expansive and gory treatment it receives: there is little but the Anglo-Saxon author's imagination behind the notion that the 'multitude of water-monsters . . . dragged the men through the watery waves down to the river bottom, and tore them to bloody pieces with their mouths, and snatched them all away so that none of us knew where any of them had gone' (*nicra mengeo . . . in ðone grund þære ea ꝼ betweoh ða yða þæs wæteres þa men besencte ꝼ mid heora muðe hie sliton ꝼ blodgodon ꝼ hie ealle swa fornamon, þæt ure nænig wiste hwær hiora æni cwom*). It is worth noting that in describing the cruel fate of the hapless guides forced into the river the Anglo-Saxon author again makes explicit the fact that the water-monsters 'dragged them away just as they had the others' (*gearwe tobrudon hie swa hie þa oðre ær dydon*), while the Latin simply notes that the hippopotami 'dealt out to them their just deserts' (*dignos iusta poena affecere*).

But the notion of being dragged down to the depths by water-monsters occurs twice in two parallel incidents in *Beowulf*. The first is described by Beowulf himself in his account of his swimming-match with Breca (lines 549–58):

> 'Wæs merefixa   mod onhrered;
> þær me wið laðum   licsyrce min,   550
> heard, hondlocen,   helpe gefremede,
> beadohrægl broden   on breostum læg
> golde gegyrwed.   Me to grunde teah
> fah feondscaða,   fæste hæfde
> grim on grape;   hwæþre me gyfeþe wearð   555
> þæt ic aglæcan   orde geræhte,
> hildebille;   heaþoræs fornam
> mihtig meredeor   þurh mine hand.'

[‘The spirit of the sea-fishes was stirred up; there my mail-shirt, hard, hand-woven, gave me help against enemies, the braided battle-garment lay on my breast, decorated with gold. A hostile and fiendish attacker dragged me to the bottom, held me firm, grim in its grip; yet it was granted to me that I should pierce the awesome assailant with my point, my battle-blade; the rush of war took off the mighty sea-beast through my hand.’]

The conclusion of this episode is echoed a few lines later (lines 574–5a), when Beowulf describes how he despatched some other 'water-monsters': 'yet it was

---

[75] On the relationship between the Latin and the Old English texts, see Orchard, *Pride and Prodigies*, pp. 132–9.

granted to me that I slew with my sword nine water-monsters' (*Hwæþere me gesælde þæt ic mid sweorde ofsloh / niceras nigene*). The second incident in which a mail-clad warrior is dragged down to the depths by a water-monster occurs almost a thousand lines later, but is clearly intended to echo the first; once again Beowulf's mailshirt saves him, as he is dragged down by Grendel's mother to her lair at the bottom of the monster-mere (lines 1501–12a):[76]

> Grap þa togeanes, guðrinc gefeng
> atolan clommum.   No þy ær in gescod
> halan lice;   hring utan ymbbearh,
> þæt heo þone fyrdhom   ðurhfon ne mihte,
> locene leoðosyrcan laþan fingrum.　　　　　　　　　1505
> Bær þa seo brimwylf,   þa heo to botme com,
> hringa þengel   to hofe sinum,
> swa he ne mihte,   no he þæs modig wæs,
> wæpna gewealdan,   ac hine wundra þæs fela
> swencte on sunde,   sædeor monig　　　　　　　　　　1510
> hildetuxum   heresyrcan bræc,
> ehton aglæcan.

[Then she made a grasp towards him, seized the warrior with her dread claws; yet she did not injure his unharmed body; the rings protected him without, so that she could not penetrate the battle-coat, the linked mail-shirt, with hostile fingers, When she came to the bottom the sea-wolf carried the prince of rings to her home, so that he could not, however brave he was, wield weapons, but a host of strange creatures oppressed him in the swell, many a sea-beast struck his war-shirt with their battle-tusks, pursued the awesome assailant (or 'awesome assailants pursued [him]').]

That the author of the *Letter* should have elaborated two parallel scenes of warriors dragged down to watery depths by monstrous creatures is striking enough, but it may be equally significant that the author should choose the distinctly uncommon word *nicor* ('water-monster') to describe the hippopotami of his source. The word *nicor* and its variant forms occurs only twelve times in extant Old English, and apart from its four occurrences in the *Letter*,[77] is found five times in *Beowulf* (lines 422a, 575a, 845b, 1411b, and 1427b) and three times in Blickling Homily XVI,[78] once more in precisely the passage which offers a parallel for the description of the monster-mere in *Beowulf*.[79] In none of these other cases is the word used to render a Latin term for 'hippopotamus', although the beast was known to at least some Anglo-Saxons:[80] in the so-called Cleopatra glossary, the word *ipotamus* has been rendered by some etymologically-minded Anglo-Saxon as *sæhengest* ('sea-horse').[81] It is tempting

---

76 The manuscript reads *brim wyl* (line 1506a); *þæm* (line 1508b: dittography with following *modig?*); *swecte* (line 1510a: failure of nasal suspension?).

77 At 119r20 (*nicra*, misread by Rypins as *mera*), 119v10 (*nicoras*) and 12 (*nicras*), and 111r5 (*niccres*).

78 Morris, ed., *The Blickling Homilies*, p. 209, lines 34 and 36, and p. 211, line 5.

79 See above, p. 30.

80 Davis, ' "Hippopotamus" in Old English'.

81 Stryker, ed., 'The Latin-Old English Glossary in MS. Cotton Cleopatra A. III', gloss 3386; the word *sæhengest* is also found in *Andreas*, line 488a, as an unremarkable kenning for 'ship'.

to ascribe both the use of the term *nicor* and the notion that Alexander's men were dragged down to their deaths to the direct influence of *Beowulf* on the *Letter.*

Such a notion becomes still more attractive when other parallels are considered. After the incident with the hippopotami, Alexander's men are directed by the (now subdued) locals to 'a certain very large lake' (*sumne swiðe micelne mere*), again near human habitation, which is 'entirely overgrown with trees a mile deep' (*eall mid wudu beweaxen mile brædo*), and infested with serpents and reptiles of all kinds (sections 16–18); here again the general resemblance to the monster-mere seems striking enough, although in this case all three of the features highlighted here are found in the Latin original, although once more in a less well-developed form.[82] Moreover, later on the *Letter,* Alexander and his men encounter a terrifying and murderous beast the skin of which seems impervious to their blades (section 27):

> Ða wæs þæt lond eall swa we geferdon adrugad ꝺ fen ꝺ cannon ꝺ hreod weoxan. Ða cwom þær semninga sum deor of þæm fenne ꝺ of ðæm fæstene, wæs þæm deore eall se hrycg acæglod swelce snoda hæfde þæt deor seonowealt heafod swelce mona ꝺ þæt deor hatte *quasi caput luna* ꝺ him wæron þa breost gelice niccres breastum ꝺ heardum toðum ꝺ miclum hit wæs gegyred ꝺ geteþed. Ond hit þa þæt deor ofsloh mine þegnas twegen. Ond we þa þæt deor nowþer ne mid spere gewundigan ne meahte ne mid nænige wæpne, ac we hit uneaþe mid isernum hamerum ꝺ slecgum gefyldon ꝺ hit ofbeoton.

> [Then all the land through which we passed was dried up and marshy, and canes and reeds grew there. Then there came suddenly out of the fen and fastness a beast, and the beast's back was all studded with pegs like a snood, and the beast had a round head like the moon, and the beast was called *Quasi caput luna* ['moon-head'], and it had a chest like a water-monster's chest and it was armed and toothed with hard and large teeth. And that beast slew two of my thegns. And we were unable to wound that beast with spears in any way, nor with any kind of weapon, but with difficulty we beat it and subdued it with iron mallets and sledge-hammers.]

Again, comparison with the Latin original is instructive:

> Palus erat sicca et coeno habundans. Per quam cum transire temptaremus, belua noui generis prosiliuit serrato tergo hippotami pectore, duo capita habens, unum leaenae simile, corcodrillo gerens alterum simillimum duris munitum dentibus, quod caput duos milites repentino occidit ictu. Quam ferreis uix umquam comminuimus malleis, quam hastis non ualuimus transfigere. Admirati autem sumus diu nouitatem eius.

> [There was a dry marsh, thick with mud, and when we tried to cross it, a beast of a new kind burst forth, with a jagged back, a chest like that of a hippopotamus, with two heads, one like that of a lioness, the second most like a croco-

---

82 The mere is described simply as a 'big lake . . . surrounded by a thick and very ancient wood, and a mile across' (*ingens . . . stagnum . . . coronatum uetustissima abundantique silua, mille passus tamen patens*); the Anglo-Saxon author has evidently transferred the breadth of the mere to its surrounding forest.

dile, furnished with hard teeth, and that head killed two soldiers with a sudden blow. We scarcely ever weakened it with iron hammers, and we could not pierce it with spears. But we were long amazed at its novelty.]

Here too, notwithstanding the fact that the Anglo-Saxon author appears to have been using a variant text, there are signs of considerable and significant elaboration here.[83] Apart from the usual rash of doublets (*adrugad 7 fen; cannon 7 hreod; of þæm fenne 7 of ðæm fæstene; heardum toðum 7 miclum; gegyred 7 geteþed; mid isernum hamerum 7 slecgum; gefyldon 7 hit ofbeoton*), none of which has any warrant in the original, the author has added more information that emphasises through alliteration both the fact that the creature came 'out of the fen and fastness' (*of þæm fenne 7 of ðæm fæstene*), and that the creature was impervious not only to spears, but to 'any kind of weapon' (*ne mid nænige wæpne*). Grendel, of course, is said in *Beowulf* to inhabit the 'fen and fastness' (line 104a: *fen ond fæsten*) in the only other extant example of the phrase; and Grendel too is impervious to ordinary blades, as Beowulf's men discover when they attempt to help their lord (lines 798–805a):[84]

> Hie þæt ne wiston,   þa hie gewin drugon,
> heardhicgende   hildemecgas,
> ond on healfa gehwone   heawan þohton,   800
> sawle secan,   þone synscaðan
> ænig ofer eorþan   irenna cyst,
> guðbilla nan,   gretan nolde,
> ac he sigewæpnum   forsworen hæfde,
> ecga gehwylcre.   805

[They did not know, when they entered the fray, stout-hearted sword-warriors, and thought to hew on every side, to reach the soul, the sinful destroyer, that no war-sword on earth, best of blades, would touch him, but he had bewitched victorious weapons, every blade.]

The tissue of echoes and parallels, both verbal and thematic, that links the *Letter* and *Beowulf* is perhaps best explained by the notion that the author of the *Letter* knew the poem at first hand, and consciously developed hints in his original text in a way which deliberately drew on aspects of *Beowulf*. Such a possibility is the more intriguing in the light of suggestions by Janet Bately that the *Letter* was composed in the ninth or early tenth century,[85] and by Kenneth Sisam that if there is evidence that the *Letter* and *Beowulf* were associated in the manuscript before *Wonders* was added to the collection, then other evidence in the *Letter* itself is 'against a manuscript association with *Beowulf* going as far back as the early tenth century'.[86] At what stage any putative influence between the texts might have occurred (not to mention between one or both and Blickling Homily

---

[83] Some variant versions of the Latin text have *canna* ('cane') for *coeno* ('mud') and *lunae* ('moon') for *leaenae* ('lioness'); evidently these were the readings seen by the Anglo-Saxon author.

[84] For comment on the apparent bewitching of the blades, see Rogers, '*Beowulf*, line 804'.

[85] Bately, 'Old English Prose', p. 113.

[86] Sisam, *Studies*, p. 94.

XVI) remains unclear, but undoubtedly the *Letter* makes a fine companion-piece to *Beowulf*, and perhaps deserves to be read more widely as such.

One final parallel between *Beowulf* and the text that immediately precedes it in the *Beowulf*-manuscript may be relevant here. *Beowulf* ends with the funeral of its hero, and the establishment of a mighty monument to his courage in the form of a burial-mound on a promontory by the sea, according to the wishes of Beowulf himself (lines 2802–8):[87]

> 'Hataŏ heaŏomære   hlæw gewyrcean
> beorhtne æfter bæle   æt brimes nosan;
> se scel to gemyndum   minum leodum
> heah hlifian   on Hronesnæsse,   2805
> þæt hit sæliŏend   syŏŏan hatan
> Biowulfes biorh,   ŏa ŏe brentingas
> ofer floda genipu   feorran drifaŏ.'

['Have those famed in battle construct a burial-mound, bright after the pyre, at the promontory of the flood, which shall tower high on Whale's Ness as a memorial to my people, so that afterwards seafarers will call it Beowulf's Barrow, as they drive from afar their tall ships over the mists of the seas.']

The description of the proposed monument as 'bright' (*beorhtne*) is particularly noteworthy, and has led some to consider what is planned almost as a kind of lighthouse.[88] Certainly, the poet's later description of the building of this barrow again seems to stress its unique quality; at all events, Beowulf's instructions are seen to have been carried out, and even exceeded (lines 3156–62):[89]

> Geworhton ŏa   Wedra leode
> hlæw on hliŏe   se wæs heah ond brad
> wegliŏendum   wide gesyne
> ond betimbredon   on tyn dagum
> beadurofes becn,   bronda lafe   3160
> wealle beworhton   swa hyt weorŏlicost
> foresnotre men   findan mihton.

[Then the people of the Geats made a burial-mound on the cliff, and it was high and broad and visible from afar to sea-travellers; and in ten days they constructed the beacon of the man brave in battle, surrounded the remnants of the flames with the most splendid wall that the wisest men could devise.]

---

[87] For a thought-provoking analysis of the circumstances surrounding Beowulf's funeral and burial, see Robinson, 'The Tomb of Beowulf', pp. 3–19.

[88] See, for example, Neville, *Representations of the Natural World*, p. 138.

[89] The manuscript is damaged at this point, and the text is problematic; here I follow Mitchell and Robinson, ed., *Beowulf*, pp. 160–1.

The Geats conclude this solemn construction with a still more solemn ceremony:[90] twelve warriors ride around the mound reciting songs of mournful praise, as the poem ends (lines 3169–82).[91] As Fred Robinson observes:[92]

> the monuments and ceremony that Beowulf's survivors provide go far beyond anything he requests in his dying speech. He says nothing about having a splendid wall built around his *becn* and enshrining his ashes within it; he says nothing about filling the structure with treasure and certainly nothing about ritual chants and processions.

The use of the term *becn* ('beacon') in this passage is the more striking in that it echoes precisely Beowulf's own use of the word 'bright' (*beorhtne*, line 2803) in his earlier description of the burial-mound; certainly, the two terms are associated elsewhere in the poem in the only other instances of the word *be(a)c(e)n*: the sun is described as 'the bright beacon of god' (*beorht beacen godes*, line 570a), and a sign from the dragon's hoard is called 'brightest of beacons' (*beacna beorhtost*, line 2777a). But the notion of a burial-mound full of treasure giving off light is a commonplace of Norse literature,[93] and is often a prelude to precisely the kind of gravemound-battle with a dead pagan warrior which in its narrative detail offers so many parallels to the monster-fights in *Beowulf* itself.[94]

The heroic concern for a bright and lasting monument that is exhibited by its hero at the end of *Beowulf* closely echoes that found at the very end of the Latin source for the *Letter* (section 41), which has Alexander, after hearing a prophecy that he will soon die, giving orders for a similar structure:

> Atque in ultima India ultra Liberi et Herculis trophea, quae centum erant, ego quinque mea aurea altiora denis pedibus statui imperaui, quae miraculo futura sunt, carissime praeceptor, posteris saeculis non paruo. Nouum perpetuumque statuimus uirtutibus monimentum inuidendum, ut immortalitas esset perpetua et nobis opinio et animi industriae, optime Aristoteles, indicium.

> [And in the farthest reaches of India, beyond the monuments of Bacchus and Hercules, which were a hundred [feet tall], I ordered my five golden trophies to be set up, ten feet taller, to be no small wonder, dearest teacher, to coming generations. We have set up to be gazed upon [or 'envied'] a new and permanent monument to courage, so that there might be for us immortality and esteem forever, and a sign, finest Aristotle, of the exertion of the spirit.]

---

90 Cf. Rosier, 'The Two Closings of *Beowulf*'.

91 Cf. Puhvel, 'The Ride around Beowulf's Barrow'.

92 Robinson, 'The Tomb of Beowulf', p. 17.

93 See, for examples, Stitt, *'Beowulf' and the Bear's Son*, pp. 129–69. Many of these light-giving barrows containing monstrous dead pagans are, like Beowulf's, specifically described as being situated by the sea; one can therefore make a case that (from a Christian perspective, at least) Beowulf the monster-slayer becomes a monster himself. See further Orchard, *Pride and Prodigies*, esp. pp. 167–8.

94 See, for example, Stitt, *'Beowulf' and the Bear's Son*; Orchard, *Pride and Prodigies*, pp. 140–68; Fjalldal, *Long Arm of Coincidence*. For further discussion of such parallels, see below, pp. 124–5.

A still closer parallel for the construction of sea-side monuments to the courage of a celebrated monster-slayer, moreover, is to be found in the so-called *Liber monstrorum* ('Book of monsters'), a text whose apparently close associations with *Beowulf* have been well-documented.[95] In this case, one of the rare unsourced passages in the text,[96] the hero somewhat ambiguously celebrated is Hercules, the model for Alexander's own exploits (*Liber monstrorum* I.12):[97]

> Quis Herculis fortitudinem et arma non miretur, qui in occiduis Tyrrheni maris faucibus columnas mirae magnitudinis ad humani generis spectaculum erexit, quique bellorum suorum tropaea in Oriente iuxta Oceanum Indicum ad posteritatis memoriam construxit, et postquam paene totum orbem cum bellis peragrasset et terram tanto sanguine maculauisset, sese moriturum flammis ad deuorandum inuoluit?

> [Who does not admire [or 'wonder at'] the courage and weaponry of Hercules, who, at the western entrance to the Tyrrhenian sea, erected pillars of an amazing size as a spectacle for the human race, and who constructed trophies of his wars in the East by the Indian Ocean, as a memorial for posterity, and afterwards travelled in battles through almost the entire world, and spattered the earth with so much blood, and at the point of death wrapped himself in flames to be consumed?]

Such Classical parallels should not, however, obscure the fact that in Anglo-Saxon England, at least during the earlier period, both kings and saints were customarily laid to rest in prominent mounds by the water's edge.[98] Still more significant in this context is the way in which the author of the *Letter* changes utterly the emphasis of the Latin source (section 41, cited above), omitting all classicising references to India, Hercules, or Bacchus, and instead again placing the focus squarely on Alexander, and his own preoccupation with the splendour of his achievements:

> Ond me næs se hrædlica ende mines lifes swa miclum weorce swa me wæs þæt ic læs mærðo gefremed hæfde þonne min willa wære. Ðas þing ic write to þon, min se leofa magister, þæt þu ærest gefeo in þæm fromscipe mines lifes ⁊ eac blissige in þæm weorðmyndum. Ond eac swelce ecelice min gemynd stonde ⁊ hleouige oðrum eorðcyningum to bysne, ðæt hie witen þy gearwor þæt min þrym ⁊ min weorðmynd maran wæron, þonne ealra oþra kyninga þe in middangearde æfre wæron. *Finit.*

> [And to me the swift ending of my life was not so much pain as the fact that I had achieved less glory than I would have wished. I write these things to you, my beloved teacher, that you first can rejoice in the success of my life, and exult in the honours. And also my memory [or 'memorial'] shall forever stand

---

95 For details, see, for example, Lapidge, '*Beowulf*, Aldhelm, the *Liber Monstrorum* and Wessex'; Whitbread, 'The *Liber Monstrorum* and *Beowulf*'; Orchard; *Pride and Prodigies*, pp. 86–115; *idem*, 'The Sources and Meaning of the *Liber monstrorum*'. See too below, pp. 133–7. The *Liber Monstrorum* has been edited by, amongst others, Porsia, ed., *Liber Monstrorum*; Butturff, 'The Monsters and the Scholar'; Orchard, *Pride and Prodigies*, pp. 254–320.
96 See further Orchard, 'The Sources and Meaning of the *Liber monstrorum*'.
97 Orchard, *Pride and Prodigies*, pp. 264–7.
98 See further Clemoes, 'Style as Criterion', pp. 183–4; Clemoes, *Interactions*, pp. 55–6. In both cases, Clemoes cites evidence from Rollason, 'List of Saints' Resting-Places'.

and tower as an example for other earthly kings, so that they know the more readily that my power and my honour were greater than those of all the other kings who have ever lived in the world. *Finit.*]

The *Letter* finishes part-way down folio 128v, followed by a large blank space;[99] facing it, beginning squarely at the head of folio 129r are the opening lines of *Beowulf*, itself a glorious monument to secular heroic endeavour. It is surely incumbent on modern scholars to attempt to assess the precise relationship between the two texts, or at least to read them together, as the compiler of the *Beowulf*-manuscript seems to have intended.[100]

Editing 'Beowulf': from parchment to paper

But if the immediate manuscript-context of *Beowulf* may perhaps provide valuable clues for how the poem was read and understood around the beginning of the eleventh century, when the *Beowulf*-manuscript was written, the fact that the poem does not survive outside that manuscript has inevitably led to careful sifting of every possible clue to the establishment of a reliable text.[101] The chief difficulty lies in ascertaining the extent to which the poem may have been altered in transmission, an essentially insoluble problem which itself hangs on the vexed question of the poem's date:[102] recent voices have argued on the one hand for the existence of some version of *Beowulf* in written form before around 750,[103] and on the other for the *Beowulf*-manuscript itself being (in part at least) an autograph manuscript of the reign of King Cnut.[104] In producing editions of a problematic text using a high proportion of words not found elsewhere in the extant corpus and witnessed in but a single manuscript,[105] *Beowulf*-scholars have been perhaps understandably cautious, and the predominant conservatism of successive editors of the poem has led to the continued acceptance of a whole slew of emendations first proposed by such mighty scholars as John Kemble, Benjamin Thorpe, and N. F. S. Grundtvig during the first half of the nineteenth century.[106] But the last decade or so has seen a welcome (if sometimes highly charged) debate on the methodologies to be employed in the textual criticism

---

99 See Plates 1 and 4 above, pp. 13 and 16.
100 In general, see, for example, Robinson, 'Old English Literature in its Most Immediate Context'.
101 See, for example, Stevick, 'Representing the Form of *Beowulf*', together with his 'Graphotactics' website (details of which are given in section C of the Bibliography).
102 On which vexed question, see above, pp. 5–6.
103 As Lapidge, 'The Archetype of *Beowulf*', p. 41, states: 'many of the literal errors in the transmitted text of *Beowulf* can be economically explained by the hypothesis of an early-eighth-century archetype in Anglo-Saxon set minuscule'. Cf. Fulk, *A History of Old English Meter*, p. 490, who concludes on the basis of a metrical analysis that: '*Beowulf* almost certainly was not composed after ca. 725 if Mercian in origin, or after ca. 825 if Northumbian.'
104 As Kiernan, *'Beowulf' and the 'Beowulf'-Manuscript*, p. 278, puts it, the *Beowulf*-manuscript 'is the archetype of the epic as we now have it'. Kiernan dates the manuscript itself rather later than most other scholars. see pp. 20–2 above.
105 On these words unique to *Beowulf*, see further below, pp. 70–1.
106 Kelly, 'Formative Stages: Part I' and 'Formative Stages: Part II' together offer an indispensable tool for tracing proposed emendations up to 1900. For the editions of Thorpe, Kemble, and Grundtvig, see section D of the Bibliography.

and text-editing of Anglo-Saxon literature in general,[107] with fierce battle-lines drawn between those who, like Eric Stanley, urge caution in abandoning readings preserved by Anglo-Saxon scribes the most incompetent of whose knowledge of Old English surpasses that of any modern critic,[108] and those who, like Michael Lapidge, would encourage sensitive and thoughtful emendation along the lines employed so successfully in the recovery of Classical texts.[109] It is hardly surprising in the context of this ongoing debate that *Beowulf* has provided a number of juicy bones of contention, with some critics (notably Alfred Bammesberger) suggesting emendations to *Beowulf* on an almost annual basis,[110] while others (such as Jack Niles and Kevin Kiernan) seek to defend existing manuscript-readings even at the expense of time-honoured editorial interventions that have long been accepted by most readers and translators of the text.[111] Although an evident *desideratum* of Anglo-Saxon studies is a *variorum* text of *Beowulf* which would seek to catalogue and compare all existing editions and conjectural emendations of *Beowulf*,[112] it is worth noting that despite literally hundreds of proposed emendations scattered through the critical literature, the basic text of the poem has changed little (comparatively speaking) since Kemble's day.

However, it is also important to note that even the most conservative editions of *Beowulf* have tacitly altered the text in a number of significant ways from what is found in the manuscript: modern lineation, capitalisation, word-division, and punctuation have been introduced, and abbreviations have been expanded, sometimes with unfortunate or downright misleading effect.[113] So, for example,

---

107 See, for example, a number of books of collected papers dealing with the theme, such as Scragg and Szarmach, ed., *The Editing of Old English*; Robinson, ed., *The Editing of Old English*; Keefer and O'Keeffe, ed., *New Approaches to Editing Old English Verse*. A useful historical overview is provided by Hall, 'Old English Literature'. See too the thoughtful and thought-provoking comments of Busse, 'Assumptions in the Establishment of Old English Poetic Texts'; *idem, Altenglische Literatur und ihre Geschichte*; Page, 'Back to the Manuscripts: Some Thoughts on Editing Old English Texts'.

108 See, for example, Stanley, 'Unideal Principles of Editing Old English Verse'.

109 See in particular Lapidge, 'Textual Criticism and the Literature of Anglo-Saxon England'; *idem,* 'The Edition, Emendation, and Reconstruction of Anglo-Saxon Texts'.

110 For a representative sample of his work, see, for example, Bammesberger, 'Three Beowulf Notes'; *idem,* 'A Note on *Beowulf* 83b'; *idem,* 'Hidden Glosses in Old English Poetic Texts'; *idem, Linguistic Notes on Old English Poetic Texts*; *idem,* 'Die Lesart in *Beowulf* 1382a'; *idem,* 'The Conclusion of Wealhtheow's Speech (*Beowulf* 1231)'; *idem,* 'Five *Beowulf* Notes'; *idem,* 'A Note on Old English *gedræg/gedreag*'; *idem,* 'Zu *Beowulf* 386–394'; *idem,* 'A Textual Note on *Beowulf* 431–432'; *idem,* 'Beowulf's Descent into Grendel's Mere'; *idem,* 'Beowulf's Last Will'; *idem,* 'The Emendation of *Beowulf,* l. 586'; *idem,* 'The Half-Line *freond on frætewum* (*Beowulf* 962a)'; *idem,* 'The Half-Line *Grendeles mægum* (*Beowulf* 2353b)'; *idem,* 'The Reading of *Beowulf,* l. 31b'; *idem,* 'In What Sense was Grendel an *angeng(e)a*?'; *idem,* 'Old English *reote* in *Beowulf,* line 2457a'; *idem,* 'The Superlative of OE *god* in *Beowulf*'; *idem,* 'What does *he* in lines 1392b and 1394b Refer to?'; *idem,* 'Beowulf's Landing in Denmark'; *idem,* 'Further Thoughts on *Beowulf,* line 1537a: *Gefeng þa be [f]eaxe*'; *idem,* 'The Syntactic Analysis of *Beowulf,* lines 4–5'.

111 See Kiernan, *'Beowulf' and the 'Beowulf' Manuscript,* esp. pp. 171–278; Niles, 'Editing *Beowulf*'.

112 I have in preparation an electronic *variorum* text of *Beowulf*, using hypertext, based mainly on the editions listed in the Bibliography below, pp. 328–9.

113 For details, see Malone, ed., *The Nowell Codex,* pp. 25–6. A case in point is the expansion of the runic symbol .ᛟ. (generally expanded as *eþel*), which appears in *Beowulf* in lines 520b, 913a, and 1702a (as part of the compound .ᛟ. *weard*). I am grateful to Damian Fleming for pointing out to me the possible significance of the preservation of the runic letter in particularly Germanic contexts in the poem; cf. his '*Eþel-weard*: the First Scribe of the *Beowulf*-Manuscript'. See too Senra Silva, 'The Rune "Eþel" and Scribal Writing Habits in the *Beowulf* MS'.

the basic mark of punctuation used in the manuscript itself is the simple point, of which (according to Klaeber and Dobbie) something approaching 700 examples survive in the text of *Beowulf*, occurring about once every four-and-a-half lines;[114] by comparison, only sixteen examples (or about one every twenty lines) are visible in the text of *Judith*, preserved in the same manuscript.[115] In contrast, the recent edition by Mitchell and Robinson (which includes a careful description of their policy in this regard) employs the full panoply of modern punctuation:[116] I count twenty examples in the first twenty-five lines of *Beowulf* alone.[117] Such modern editorial intervention can be misleading, as Bruce Mitchell himself has argued with regard to a range of Old English texts,[118] and it is at all events clear that while modern puctuation is based on syntax,[119] that in the *Beowulf*-manuscript is based on metre: about ninety per cent of the points in the manuscript-text of *Beowulf* occur at the end of a full line, and all but twenty-three of the remainder occur at the end of a half-line.[120] There are therefore a number of cases in which a point appears in the manuscript marking the

114 For the figures, see Klaeber, ed., *Beowulf*, p. c; Dobbie, ed., *Beowulf and Judith*, p. xxx. Rather higher figures are given by Nist, *The Structure and Texture of 'Beowulf'*, pp. 111–12, who counts 838 points at the end of verse-lines, together with forty-seven more at the end of half-lines. By contrast, in the transcript given by Kiernan, ed., *Electronic Beowulf*, I count some 574 single points at the end of complete lines, fifty-seven at the end of a-lines, and twenty-three within individual half-lines. For the last of these categories, see n. 120 below.

115 Dobbie, ed., *Beowulf and Judith*, p. xxx, notes seventeen such points in *Judith*; but see Griffith, ed., *Judith*, pp. 6–7.

116 For details of the policy, see Mitchell and Robinson, ed., *Beowulf*, pp. 172–5. According to the transcript by Kiernan, ed., *Electronic Beowulf*, within the first twenty-five lines of *Beowulf* there are marks of punctuation after lines 1, 3, 8, 11, 15, 17, 19, 23, and 25, and none at all following the a-lines. Modern editions generally include punctuation at the ends of all these lines, except after line 15, which no modern edition punctuates.

117 It should be pointed out, moreover, that Mitchell and Robinson are notably sparing in their imposition of modern punctuation when compared to other editors: comparable figures for punctuation in the first twenty-five lines of *Beowulf* in the editions of (for example) Kiernan, Klaeber, Wrenn, and Dobbie are twenty-eight, twenty-seven, twenty-eight, and thirty-three respectively. Mitchell has for many years been a vigorous proponent of a new system of puctuation for Old English verse (see in particular his 'Dangers of Disguise'), and an example of *Beowulf* punctuated in this fashion appears as an Appendix to Mitchell and Robinson, ed., *Beowulf*, pp. 313–18. Even under the new system, however, I count twenty punctuation-marks in the first twenty-five lines of *Beowulf*. See too Mitchell and Irvine, *'Beowulf' Repunctuated*, where a slightly different set of punctuation marks is employed: I count nineteen in the first twenty-five lines of *Beowulf*.

118 Mitchell, 'The Dangers of Disguise'; see too Mitchell and Irvine, *'Beowulf' Repunctuated*, pp. 1–30.

119 For difficulties regarding especially the paratactic syntax of *Beowulf*, see, for example, Andrew, *Syntax and Style in Old English*, pp. 94–100. For all questions relating to Old English style, the indispensable tool is Mitchell, *Old English Syntax*.

120 The exceptions are in lines 61a (*heorogar.*), 273a (*we.*), 320b (*stig.*), 338a (*þæt.*), 367b (*glædman.*), 423a (*wræc.*), 553b (*grunde.*), 807b (*ellor.*), 1039a (*hilde.*), 1146b (*fin.*), 1159a (*læddon.*), 1585b (*dæs.*), 1974a (*laces.*), 2252a (*ofgeafgesawon.*), 2377a (*hwæðre.*), 2494b (*oððe.*), 2542a (*geseah.*), 2655b (*feorh.*), 2673b (*byrne.*), 2698b (*mægenes.*), 2832b (*lacende.*), 2897a (*leofes.*), and 2902a (*wæl.*). In two of these cases (at 423a and 1159a), the word in question is the last on the page. In the context of scribal corrections to the text (on which see below), it is interesting to note that at 158v14 (= line 1301a) a point has been erased after *mapðum*, and another appears immediately after the following word (*gife.*). The scribe seems to have recognised that the original point was misplaced: it would have come after the first element of the compound *mapðumgife* (as in the examples from lines 807b, 1039a, and 2902a above); the point after *gife* simply marks the caesura. That the scribes could catch one such 'error' but miss twenty-three others might raise a sceptical eyebrow at the claims of those who doggedly defend the integrity of the scribes.

end of a full or half-line where the syntactical sense is clearly incomplete, and (for example) subjects and verbs, or nouns and adjectives in agreement, or auxiliary verbs and dependent infinitives which appear in different half-lines are separated by an intervening point.[121] Naturally, no punctuation is found in any modern edition for any of these occurrences, just as most of the punctuation found in all modern editions has no warrant in the manuscript whatsoever.

Editing 'Beowulf': saving the text

But if modern lineation, capitalisation, word-division, and punctuation have been freely imposed on *Beowulf,* the same cannot be said of most of the words that make up the text, which have remained largely unchanged since the earliest editions first appeared. In recent years, moreover, there has been a definite trend against the over-ready acceptance of even these time-honoured conjectural changes to the manuscript-text.[122] Against such a background, combined with a growing realisation of the importance of considering the immediate manuscript context of the poem, it is perhaps unsurprising that both of the most recent and widely circulating editions should unashamedly make a virtue of their basically conservative texts.[123] Although Bruce Mitchell and Fred Robinson seek to reject what are deemed 'unnecessary emendations', however, I still count over three hundred such deviations from or additions to the manuscript-text, affecting more than one line in ten. The conjectural emendations proposed in this edition appear to assume that the scribes of *Beowulf* could and did commit a whole range of mechanical copying-errors, such as the confusion of individual letter-forms (so-called *translitteratio* or *metacharakterismos*),[124] the omission of

---

121 Several examples are given by Nist, *The Structure and Texture of 'Beowulf'*, pp. 112–13.

122 Useful surveys of the history of text-editing with regard to Old English literature in general and *Beowulf* in particular are found in Stanley, 'Unideal Principles'; Hall, 'Old English Literature'; Fulk, 'Inductive Methods'; *idem*, 'Textual Criticism'.

123 Mitchell and Robinson, ed., *'Beowulf': an Edition*; Kiernan, ed., *Electronic Beowulf*. Mitchell and Robinson, ed., *'Beowulf': an Edition*, pp. 165–75, offer a brief description of how they arrived at their text.

124 So, for example, Mitchell and Robinson implicitly conjecture the confusion of *a* and *æ* (emending *hwaþere* to *hwæþere* in line 578a; *bræde* to *brade* in line 2207b; *wat* to *þæt* in line 2534a), *a* and *e* (emending *steda nægla* to *stedenægla* in line 985a; *ge sacan* to *gesecan* in line 1004a; *frecnen* to *frecnan* in line 1104b; *ed wendan* to *edwenden* in line 1774b; *maþme þy weorþre* to *maþma þy weorþre* in line 1902b; *gelæsta* to *gelæste* in line 2990b; *twelfa* to *twelfe* in line 3170b), *a* and *ea* (emending *brimleade* to *brimlade* in line 1051b; *heand gesteallan* for *handgesteallan* in line 2596b), *a* and *o* (emending *onsole* to *on sale* in line 302a; *hard wyrône* to *hordwyrône* in line 2245b; *hlodon* to *hladan* in line 2775a), *a* and *u* (emending *strade* to *strude* in line 3073b; *un har* to *anhar* in line 357a), *æ* and *o* (emending *mæstan* to *mostan* in line 2247b), *æ* and *e* (emending *sendeþ* for *snædeþ* in line 600a; *secan* to *sætan* in line 1602b), *b* and *h* (emending *hetlic* to *betlic* in line 780a), *c* and *cg* (emending *ec þeo wes* to *Ecgþeowes* in line 957b; *eclafes* to *Ecglafes* in line 980; *sec* to *secg* in line 2863a), *c* and *t* (emending *secan* to *sætan* in line 1602b; *wræce* to *wræte* in lines 2771a and 3060a), *d* and *t* (emending *fædde* for *fætte* in line 1750a), *d* and *þ* or *ô* (emending *hador* to *haôor* in line 414a; *aô* to *ad* in line 1107a; *hord mad mum* for *hordmaômum* in line 1198a; *þeod* to *deod* in line 1278b; *geþinged* to *geþingeô* in line 1837a; *wiôcuône* for *widcuône* in line 1991a; *aô* to *sweorô* to *aôsweord* in line 2064a; *ford* to *forô* in line 2959b; *fædergearwü* for *fæôergearwum* in line 3119a), *e* and *ea* (emending *oncear* to *oncer* in line 1918a), *e* and *ie* (emending *siexbennum* to *sexbennum* in line 2904a), *eo* and *o* (emending *scotenum* to *sceotendum* in line 1026a; *abreotan* for *abroten* in line 1599b; *weordum ond worcum* to *wordum ond weorcum* in line 1833a; *geareofolm* to *gearofolm* in

individual words, perhaps through eye-skip or haplography (the copying of one letter or form for two),[125] dittography (the copying of two letters or forms for one),[126] and metathesis (the transposition of letters or forms).[127] It should be noted that these mechanical copying-errors are conjectured to have occured in the work of both scribes, and amply support the view that each was copying from an exemplar.[128]

An even greater order of conservatism is found in the edition produced by Kevin Kiernan alongside his electronic facsimile of the manuscript and an excellent range of early transcripts.[129] Kiernan is careful to distinguish separate categories of editorial intervention, namely 'restorations' (defined as 'conjectural attempts to recover something lost to the manuscript by some kind of damage') and 'emendations' (defined as 'changes [to] or rejection of something that can be clearly seen in the manuscript'); he accepts some 124 'editorial restorations' (listing some 944 further 'early restorations'), but only ninety-one emendations (about one every thirty-five lines). Kiernan therefore implicitly rejects a large number of emendations suggested by generations of previous scholars in order to correct perceived lapses of alliteration or metre in the transmitted text,[130] arguing that such irregularity should be accepted if the sense is (or can be made) clear.[131] Whereas Kenneth Sisam (amongst others) had high-

line 2085a; *brost* to *breost* in line 2176b; *swona* to *Sweona* in line 2946b), *f* and *p* (emending *for speof* to *forsweop* in line 2814b), *f* and *s* (emending *fela ða* to *se laða* in line 2305a), *f* and *p* (emending *fere fyhtum* for *werefyhtum* in line 457a; *weall* to *fealh* in line 2225b; *fergendra* to *wergendra* in line 2882b), *n* and *d* (emending *be weotene* to *beweotede* in line 1796b), *n* and *nd* (or *dn*) (emending *sele rædenne* to *selerædende* in line 51b; *scotenum* to *sceotendum* in line 1026a; *headabearna* to *Heaða-Beardna* in line 2037b; *headobearna* to *Heaðo-Beardna* in line 2067a), *n* and *r* (emending *hord* to *hond* in line 1520b; *þana* to *þara* in line 2251b; *urder* to *under* in line 2755b; *wonn* to *worn* in line 3154a), *p* and *p* (emending *for speof* to *forsweop* in line 2814b; *speop* to *speow* in line 2854b), *r* and *s* (emending *fæs* to *fær* in line 2230b), *s* and *sc* (emending *scynscapa* to *synscapa* in line 707a), *t* and *d* (emending *hilte cumbor* to *hildecumbor* in line 1022a), *r* and *p* (emending *hwæðre* to *hræðre* in line 2819a), and *þ* and *p* (emending *sona mwatide* to *sona him þa tide* in line 2226b; *wat* to *þæt* in line 2534a). For the use of the term *translitteratio*, see Lapidge, 'The Archetype of *Beowulf*', p. 5.

125 So, for example, Mitchell and Robinson read *minne* for manuscript *mine* in lines 255b and 418b; *Sigemundes secgan* for manuscript *sige munde secgan* in line 875; *eglu unheoru* for manuscript *egl unheoru* in line 987a. For cases in which eye-skip has apparently occured between words with like endings (so-called *homoeoteleuton*), see below, pp. 45–51.

126 So, for example, Mitchell and Robinson read manuscript *se ecghete* for manuscript *se secg hete* in line 84a; *eafora nu* for manuscript *eaforan nu* in line 1738a; *sceata* for manuscript *sceatta* in line 752a; *hæle* for manuscript *helle* at line 1816a; *gefremedon* for manuscript *ge gefremedon* at line 2478b.

127 So, for example, Mitchell and Robinson read *gebruen* for manuscript *gebuen* in line 1285b; *æþelum* for manuscript *hælebum* in line 332b; *hwæper* for manuscript *hwæpre* in line 1314a; *ægwæðer* for manuscript *ægwæðre* in line 2844a. See too Robinson, 'Metathesis in the Dictionaries'.

128 As Kiernan, *'Beowulf' and the 'Beowulf'-Manuscript*, p. 193, acknowledges, although he believes that scribe B was working from a different exemplar to scribe A.

129 Kiernan, ed., *Electronic Beowulf*. Kiernan's edition of *Beowulf* has 3,184 lines, compared to the 3,182 of most modern editions, since (for example) he rejects a number of emendations which fill out apparently defective lines (for example at lines 389b–90a), and rearranges what most editors perceive as a hypermetric passage in lines 1162–8 (his lines 1161–70). I retain the traditional line-numbering, for ease of comparison, but cite Kiernan's line-numbers in square brackets where appropriate.

130 See further Prokosch, 'Two Types of Scribal Error in the *Beowulf* MS'; Andrew, 'Scribal Error and its Sources', in his *Postscript on 'Beowulf'*, pp. 133–52; Lehmann, 'On Posited Omissions in the *Beowulf*'; Taylor and Davis, 'Some Alliterative Misfits in the *Beowulf* MS'.

131 Kiernan, *'Beowulf' and the 'Beowulf'-Manuscript*, pp. 172–91.

lighted the possibility of widespread scribal error,[132] Kiernan (following the exhaustive work of Tilman Westphalen) stresses instead the extent to which the scribes of *Beowulf* appear to have checked and corrected their work.[133] Noting in the manuscript-text of *Beowulf* 'about 180 positive examples of intelligent scrutiny on the part of the scribes', Kiernan argues that 'the sheer bulk of the erasures and written corrections is testimony to the integrity of the scribes and the reliability of their final copy'.[134] Such an argument would carry more weight were it not for the fact that notwithstanding this 'intelligent scrutiny on the part of the scribes', the extant text is far from clean, and Kiernan's own suggested emendations do not differ significantly in type and quality from those of other editors. So, for example, even in this ultra-conservative edition there is tacit acknowledgment that the scribes of *Beowulf* could and did indeed commit each of the four kinds of mechanical copying-error identified above, namely *translitteratio*,[135] omission through eye-skip or haplography,[136] dittography,[137] and metathesis.[138]

Editing 'Beowulf': the scribes as editors

In fact, one could argue that the two scribes of the *Beowulf*-manuscript were in a sense acting as the poem's first identifiable 'editors',[139] since a number of their corrections to their own work, as highlighted by Kiernan and Westphalen, likewise fall into the same four categories of mechanical copying-errors already

132 Sisam, 'The Authority of Old English Poetical Manuscripts'.
133 Kiernan, *'Beowulf' and the 'Beowulf'-Manuscript*, pp. 191–218; Westphalen, *Beowulf 3150–55*, esp. 107–8. Cf. the review of Westphalen's work by Kemp Malone.
134 Kiernan, *'Beowulf' and the 'Beowulf'-Manuscript*, p. 195.
135 So, for example, Kiernan conjectures the confusion of *a* and *u* (emending manuscript *wudu* to *wado* in line 581[580]a), *b* and *h* (emending manuscript *hetlic* to *betlic* in line 780[779]a), *c* and *o* (emending manuscript *swicðole* to *swioðole* in line 3145[3147]a), *d* and *ð* or *þ* (emending manuscript *mid gripe* to *niðgripe* in line 976[975]a, *standeð* to *standeð* in line 1362[1364]b, *gepinged* to *gepinged* in line 1837[1840]a, *wið cuðne* to *widcuðne* in line 1991[1994]a, and *fædergearwū* to *fædergearwum* in line 3119[3121]a), *f* and *s* (emending *fela ða* to *se laða* in line 2305[2306]a), *n* and *m* (emending manuscript *mid gripe* to *niðgripe* in line 976[975]a and *hrusam* to *hrusan* in line 2279[2280]a), *n* and *r* (emending manuscript *hord swenge* to *hondswenge* in line 1520[1522]b, *hard wyrðne* to *handwyrðne* in line 2245[2246]b, *urder* to *under* in line 2755[2756]b, and *wonn* to *worn* in line 3154[3156]a), *p* and *ρ* (emending *speop* to *speow* [= *speoρ*] in line 2854[2855]b), and *u* and *ū* (emending *galg treowu* to *galgtreowum* [= *galgtreowū*] in line 2940[2941]b).
136 So, for example, Kiernan conjectures the omission of *wolde* in line 139b, *sona* in line 149b, *guman* in line 652[651]b (after *guma* in line 652[651]a), *dæd* in line 954[953]b (after *dædum* in line 954[953]a), *hafenian* in line 1372[1374]a (after *hafelan*), *grund* in line 2139[2142]a (part of *grundsele*, preceding *grendeles*), *heaþo* in line 2488[2489]a, *gefrægn* in line 2694[2695]b, *feðan* in line 2941[2942]a, *wean* in line 3000[3002]b, *siðe* in line 3101[3103]b, and *on* in line 3102[3104]b (after *seon ⁊ secean* in line 3102[3104]a).
137 So, for example, Kiernan conjectures *gefremedon* for manuscript *ge gefremedon* in line 2478[2479]b.
138 So, for example, Kiernan conjectures *hleo* for manuscript *heol* (altered to *hol*) in line 1229[1231]b, *eorl scolde* for manuscript *scolde eorl* in line 1328[1330]b, *herode* for manuscript *heorde* in line 2930[2931]b, and *þæt gifeðe wæs* for manuscript *wæs þæt gifeðe* in line 3085[3087]b.
139 Cf. Duggan, 'Scribal Self-Correction and Editorial Theory'; Moffat, 'Anglo-Saxon Scribes and Old English Verse'.

described.[140] Of these, metathesis is least well-attested: I count only a single case where *wlocn* has been corrected by the scribe to *wolcn*.[141] Likewise, scribal correction of haplography of individual letters is relatively rare, and largely restricted to the stint of scribe B;[142] both scribes, however, are prone to the kind of eye-skip induced by repetition of the same elements within (and especially at the end of) words (also known as *homoeoteleuton*), and both scribes correct such errors where they find them.[143] More frequent are the several instances of dittography, both of individual letters and of whole words, that have been caught and corrected by the scribes themselves;[144] in at least one clear instance, the word *hilde* appears both as the last word on fol. 151r and the first on fol. 151v, and the dittography across a page-break has remained undetected by the scribes' alleged 'intelligent scrutiny'. Most frequent of the scribal corections are numerous cases of *translitteratio*,[145] with an intriguing overlap with precisely

---

140 See nn. 135–8 above.

141 At 137r14 (= line 331b).

142 So, for example, we find correction of *sine* to *sinne* at 180v8 (= line 2283[2284]a); *bil* to *bill* at 190r18 (= line 2777[2778]b); *gemete* to *gemette* at 190v14 (= line 2785[2786]b). Cf. Hulbert, 'The Accuracy of the B-Scribe of *Beowulf*'.

143 So, for example, we find *gellum* corrected to *gesellum* at 162v11 (= line 1481[1483]a); *gweox* corrected to *geweox* at 167v3 (= line 1711[1714]a); *ungefelice* corrected to *ungedefelice* at 184r8 (= line 2435[2436]b); *ac* corrected to *ac ic* at 186r3 (= line 2522[2523]a).

144 So, for example, we find correction of dittography of individual letters in the following cases: *steappa* corrected to *steapa* in 157v3 (= line 1245[1247]a); *gryrre* corrected to *gryre* in 158r16–17 (= line 1282[1284]b); *findaan* corrected to *findan* in 160v2 (= line 1378[1380]b); *sceall* corrected to *sceal* in 170v11 (= line 1862[1865]a). Recognition of a similar kind of copying-error has presumably led to the correction of *weorðpan* to *weorþan* at 167r22 (= line 1707[1710]b). It will be noted that all of these examples are in the stint of scribe A; scribe B seems rather less prone to this particular kind of copying-error. In the case of dittography of entire words, however, both scribes are culpable: we find, for example, *hlaford hlaford* corrected to *hlaford* at 135v15 (= line 267b); *man man* corrected to *man* at 141r20 (= line 503[502]b); *moste moste* corrected to *moste* at 149r20 (= line 894[893]b); *ende ende* corrected to *ende* at 168v2 (= line 1753[1756]a); *to to* corrected to *to* at 169v11 (= line 1815[1818]a); *manigra manigra* corrected to *manigra* at 176r6 (= line 2091[2094]a); *bronde bronde* corrected to *bronde* at 176v19 (=line 2126[2129]a); *leodû leodû* corrected to *leodû* at 181r14 (= line 2310[2311]a); *he he* corrected to *he* at 182v16 (= line 2378[2379]b); *his his* corrected to *his* at 189A(197)v19 (= line 2676[2677]b; *hyrde hyrde* corrected to *hyrde* at 198r9 (= line 3133[3135]b); *to to* corrected to *to* at 198r11 (line 3136[3138]b).

145 So, for example, *translitteratio* of *a* and *æ* is implied by the correction of *sacce* to *sæcce* at 173v11 (= line 1989[1992]a), *blædan* to *hladan* at 176v20 (= line 2126[2129]b), *faðmie* to *fæðmie* at 188v19 (= line 2652[2653]b), and *het wære* to *hetware* at 193r6 (= line 2916[2917]a). Likewise, the *translitteratio* of other letter-forms is implied by the following corrections: *translitteratio* of *æ* and *o* in the correction of *moste* to *mæste* at 153v5 (= line 1079[1078]b); of *a* and *u* in the correction of *maðmam* to *maðmum* at 194v3 (= line 2993[2994]b); of *b* and *h* in the correction of *blædan* to *hladan* at 176v20 (= line 2126[2129]b); of *b* and *þ* in the correction of *þurh* to *burh* at 196v6 (= line 3100[3102]a); of *c* and *cg* in the correction of *ecþeow* to *ecgþeow* at 135v11 (= line 263b); of *c* and *g* in the correction of *aglægean* to *aglæcean* at 192v18 (= line 2905[2906]a); of *c* and *t* in the correction of *wac* to *wat* at 170r5 (= line 1830[1833]b); of *d* and *ð* in the correction of *sceaðen* to *sceaden* at 172v3 (= line 1939[1942]a), *sweorð* to *sweord* at 175v2 (= line 2064[2067]a), and *wearð* to *weard* at 187r14 (= line 2580[2581]b); of *e* and *i* in the correction of *wælric* to *wælrec* at 189A(197)r5 (= line 2661[2662]a); of *f* and *s* in the correction of *fæft* to *fæst* in 136v6 (= line 303a); of *h* and *þ* in the correction of *þis* to *his* at 138r17 (= line 375b); of *i* and *u* in the correction of *dungum* to *dingum* at 174r5 (= line 2004[2007]a); of *l* and *r* in the correction of *wyrmū* to *wylmū* at 189A(197)r13; of *m* and *n* in the correction of *hram* to *hran* at 146v5 (= line 722[721]b) and *bumden* to *bunden* at 158r19 (= line 1285[1287]a); of *n* and *nd* in the correction of *scyppen* to *scyppend* at 132r13 (= line 106a); of *n* and *r* in the correction of *holdre* to *holdne* at 138r15 (= line 376b) and *werede* to *wenede* at 169v18 (= line 1821[1824]a); and of *r* and *s* in the correction of *wære* to *wæs* at 139r5 (= line 407[406]a).

the kinds of *translitteratio* conjectured by generations of modern editors not only of *Beowulf* but a range of other surviving poems.[146]

Several of the corrections to the work of scribe A are apparently the work of scribe B, so arguing for latter's supervisory capacity and seniority as copyist, a fact perhaps underlined by his use of a slightly more archaic script.[147] For this and other reasons, Kiernan argues that scribe B's role is quasi-authorial, and that the *Beowulf*-manuscript 'is the archetype of the epic as we now have it'.[148] In this context, the 'non-correction' of what scribe B (in common with all modern editors) obviously felt to be a gap in scribe A's text at 160r17 (= line 1372[1374]a) is surely significant: he uses his normal insertion-mark (a comma,

[146] An incomplete survey of the critical apparatus to the first four volumes of the ASPR reveals the following cases of common types of supposed *translitteratio*, either emended by the editors or corrected by the scribes: *translitteratio* of *a* and *u* in *Genesis A* 2662b *ærendu* for *ærenda*; *Exodus* 326b *þracu* for *þraca*, 442a *sand* for *sund*; *Andreas* 424b *sund* for *sand*, 1545b *wadu* for *wudu*; *Dream of the Rood* 117b *anforht* for *unforht*; *Elene* 119a *heorugrimme* for *heora grimme*; *Christ I* 18a *þu* for *þa*; *Christ III* 978b *þa* for *þu*; *Guthlac A* 299b *abanne* for *abunne*; *Phoenix* 72b *waniað* for *wuniað*, 171b *holtwuda* for *holtwudu*; *translitteratio* of *n* and *r* in *Genesis A* 2252b *Agar* for *agan*, 2645b *þæne* for *þære*, 2751b *arna* for *arra*; *Exodus* 321b *leon* for *leor*; *Elene* 1183b *foran* for *fonan*; *Christ III* 927a *gehwone* for *gehwore*; *Phoenix* 336a *gehwone* for *gehwore*; *translitteratio* of *p* and *þ* in *Genesis A* 2645a *beheopan* for *beheopan*, 2730b *flettpaðas* for *flett þaðas*; *Christ and Satan* 78a *spearcade* for *speartade* (with scribal correction to *spearcade*), 318b *hreopan* for *hreopan*; *Elene* 996b *sponrade* for *sponrade*; *Guthlac B* 875b *stopum* for *stopum*; *Juliana* 294a *bispeop* for *bispeop*; *translitteratio* of *c* and *t* in *Christ and Satan* 78a *spearcade* for *speartade* (with scribal correction to *spearcade*); *Andreas* 332b *sceatas* for *steatas* (scribal correction); *translitteratio* of *d* and *ð* in *Genesis A* 1642b *frod* for *forð* (with metathesis), 1986b *þryðge* for *þrydge*, 2007b *ahyðdan* for *ahudan* (with haplography), 2758b *weard* for *wearð* (but *cf.* 2757b *wearð*); *Exodus* 113b *sceado* for *sceaðo*; *Daniel* 35a *wisde* for *wisðe*, 615a *wod* for *woð*; *Christ and Satan* 188b *sidas* for *sidas*; *Andreas* 219b *wyrðeð* for *wyrðeð*, 309b *bedæled* for *bedæleð*, 394b *duguð* for *dugud*; *Fates of the Apostles* 43b *gelædde* for *gelæððe* (scribal correction); *Soul and Body I* 38b *god* for *goð*; *Elene* 14a *guðweard* for *guð weard*, 531a *gehðum* for *gehðu*, 1294a *ældes* for *eðles* (plus metathesis); *Christ I* 4a *heafod* for *heafoð*, 69a *genedde* for *geneðde*, 364b *genyrwad* for *genyrwað*; *Christ II* 539b *hreðer* for *hreder*, 698b *lixed* for *lixed*, 710b *blæd* for *blæð*, 790b *ðy reþran* for *dyreþran*, 795b *læded* for *lædað*; *Christ III* 961b *gesargad* for *gesargað*, 1337b *mædleð* for *mædleð*, 1597b *bidfæstne* for *bið fæstne* (see too *Christ I* 118a *sceadu*, 137b *toweard*, 257b *eowde*; *Christ II* 482a *widwegas*; *Christ III* 970b *gesargad*, 1311a *unbeted*, 1490b *gefæstnad*: in each case, manuscript *ð* has been altered to *d*); *Guthlac A* 71b *bimutad* for *bimutað*, 105b *weard* for *wearð*, 153b *gecostad* for *gecostaº*, 245b *geðringan* for *gedrin gan*, 296a *wid* for *wið*, 391a *onwylled* for *onwyl leð*, 867b *gynnwised* for *gynn wiðeð*; *Guthlac B* 1040a *geswedrad* for *ge swedrad*; *Phoenix* 103a *sidne* for *siðne*, 156b *side* for *siðe* (scribal correction), 294a *wrixled* for *wrixleð*, 393a *geascad* for *geascað siðe* (scribal correction), 491b *læded* for *lædaþ*, 635a *singað* for *singad*; *Phoenix* 648b *onwæcned* for *on wæcned*; *Juliana* 338b *ne oðcyrreð* for *neod cyrreð*; *Seafarer* 79b *blæd* for *blæð*; *Widsith* 103a *Đonne* for *dón*; *Maxims I* 56b *geþingad* for *geþingað* (scribal correction), 109b *alyfed* for *alyfeð*; *Panther* 38a *þeodwiga* for *þeoð wiga*, 39b *gewbiesgad* for *ge biesgað*, 41a *gewelgad* for *gewelgað*, 59a *grund* for *grunð* (scribal correction), 71a *ungnyðe* for *ungnyde*; *Deor* 30b *earfoða* for *earfoda*; *Riddle 5.6 forwurðe* for *for wurde*; *Riddle 13.6 siðe* for *side*; *Riddle 20.3 seomað* for *seomad*; *Judith* 165a *þeodnes* for *þeoðnes*. I have in preparation an electronic database of scribal corrections and editorial emendations of the extant poetic corpus.

[147] Dumville, 'Beowulf Come Lately', p. 55. The corrections in question are of *scyppen* to *scyppend* at 132r13 (= line 106a), of *beortre* to *beorhtre* at 133r20 (= line 158a), of *dolscaðan* to *dolsceaðan* at 140v14 (= line 479[478]a), *o* to *on* at 142r13 (= line 537[536]a), *wealhþeo* to *wealhþeow* at 144r5 (= line 612[611]b), of *ængum* to *ænigum* at 147r11 (= line 793[792]b), of *on* to *in* at 158v15 (= line 1302[1303]b), of *gan* to *gang* at 160v14 (= line 1391[1393]b), of *feh* to *fehð* at 168v3 (= line 1755[1758]b), of *dogor* to *dogore* at 169r19 (= line 1797[1800]b), and of *hrepe* to *hraþe* at 171v20 (= line 1914[1917]a). See further Kiernan, *'Beowulf' and the 'Beowulf'-Manuscript*, pp. 272–7, who argues that 'most of the second scribe's alterations in the first scribe's copy are emendations rather than corrections'.

[148] Kiernan, *'Beowulf' and the 'Beowulf'-Manuscript*, p. 278.

so distinguishing his insertions from those of scribe A), but refrains from actually inserting anything at all. Kiernan argues that this non-correction 'strongly implies that the second did not have an exemplar to refer to when he read and altered the first scribe's work',[149] an argument which ignores the possibility that scribe A's exemplar was itself defective, and scarcely squares with Kiernan's own case for scribe B's creative role. The passage in question is a justly celebrated description of how a hunted hart would rather die on the edge of the monster-mere than plunge in, and reads as follows (lines 1368–72):[150]

> Ðeah þe hæðstapa   hundum geswenced,
> heorot hornum trum,   holtwudu sece,
> feorran geflymed,   ær he feorh seleð,   1370
> aldor on ofre,   ær he in wille
> hafelan [. . .]   Nis þæt heoru stow.

> [Even though the heath-stepper, driven by the hounds, a hart strong in its horns, may seek the wooded forest, chased from afar, he will give up his life, his spirit on the brink, rather than [. . .] his head within; that is no pleasant place.]

There is an evident break in sense and metre in line 1372a, although the manuscript moves smoothly from *hafelan* to *nis* with only scribe B's comma to indicate an omission.[151] The two most favoured modern emendations are both based partly on literary considerations: Holthausen and Klaeber supply *beorgan* ('to save'), citing as parallel line 1293a (*feore beorgan*; 'to save [her] life');[152] but most other editors (following Kemble) have favoured supplying *hydan* ('to hide'), presumably influenced at least in part by the fact that the three preceding lines all contain double alliteration (as would 1372, if the addition of *hydan* were accepted), and that such sequences of double alliteration in 'set-piece' passages are relatively common in *Beowulf*, where sound-play is often used to highlight particular portions of the narrative.[153] Paying greater attention to the palaeographical possibilities, however, Johan Gerritsen and Alfred Bammesberger have both independently suggested that the missing word is neither *beorgan* nor *hydan*, but *helan* ('to hide', 'to conceal');[154] as both point out, eye-skip through *homoeoteleuton* from one word to another is particularly possible if we suppose that the phrase in question originally comprised two words (*hafelan helan*) which both shared the same last four letters. Such a suggestion has a number of attractions, not least because it makes perfect sense,

---

149 *Ibid.*, p. 277.

150 For the manuscript at this point, see Plate 5 above, p. 17, esp. lines 14–17. For literary discussion of the passage, see, for example, Faraci, 'La caccia al cervo nel *Beowulf*'; Higley, '*Aldor on ofre*, or The Reluctant Hart '. For a parallel to the scene from a much later Latin text, see Rigg, '*Beowulf* 1368–72: an Analogue'.

151 See in general Lowe, 'The Oldest Omission Signs in Latin Manuscripts'.

152 One might also cite *Andreas*, line 1538b, which also reads *feore beorgan*: the half-line is one of a number uniquely shared by *Beowulf* and *Andreas*, on the relationship between which see below, pp. 163–6.

153 See further below, pp. 61–9.

154 Gerritsen, 'Emending *Beowulf* 2253 – Some Matters of Principle', pp. 451–2; Bammesberger, 'Five *Beowulf* Notes', pp. 250–2.

and manages to maintain both the double alliteration (as the addition of *hydan* would also do) and the assonance (as, ironically enough, is witnessed in the supposed parallel *feore beorgan* in line 1293a) that is characteristic of the aural embellishment of the text at key moments.[155] Moreover, precisely such ornamentation is evident in this very passage, which as it stands provides examples of sustained alliteration (three out of five lines alliterate on *h*, which indeed appears in every line; four of the five lines end in words which alliterate on *s-*),[156] end-rhyme (*geswenced . . . geflymed; hornum trum*), and assonance (four out of five lines feature words in *-l-*); all three of these features would only be enhanced by the acceptance of *helan*.[157] Here, as elsewhere, one need not overstate the 'intelligent scrutiny' of scribe B; assumption of a well-attested mechanical copying error at some stage in the text's transmission is all that is required.

In much the same way, Kiernan seeks to defend scribe B's initial inadvertent use of the word *fyrwyrmum* ('fire-dragons'), subsequently corrected to *fyrwylmum* ('fire-surges'), claiming it as an example of where scribe B 'was clearly following the sense of the text'.[158] True enough, the word occurs in the general context of the dragon-fight, and in the extant corpus the term *fyrwylm* only appears here (*fyrwyr* does not occur at all). But again, the wider context makes the explanation of a mechanical copying-error far the most likely (lines 2669–72a):[159]

> Æfter ðam wordum   wyrm yrre cwom,
> atol inwitgæst,   oðre siðe   2670
> fyrwylmum fah   fionda niosian,
> laðra manna.
>
> ['After those words, the dragon advanced angily, the dread hostile spirit, a second time, stained with fire-surges, to seek out the foes, the hateful men.']

It is hard to see how anyone 'following the sense of the text' would suppose that the dragon was 'stained with fire-dragons', but quite likely that a scribe copying the sequence *wyrm yrre . . . fyr* would initially write *wyrmum* through dittography; the form *fyr* immediately precedes, and the two words *wyrm yrre* in fact appear in the manuscript-line directly above. The textual context may have had some influence on the scribe's initial choice, but the manuscript context alone is surely sufficient to account for his action.

---

155 See below, pp. 61–6.
156 Indeed, if we extend consideration of the passage further, to line 1374, it is clear that six out of seven lines end in words alliterating on *s-*, with words alliterating on *s-* and *st-* evidently distinguished; the sequence runs as follows: *geswenced . . . sece . . . seleð . . . [wille] . . . stow . . . astigeð . . . styreþ*.
157 Likewise, the last half-line of the sequence echoes the alliterative elements of the first (*heoru stow* echoes *hæðstapa*), although this would of course be the case whatever emendation were accepted.
158 Kiernan, *'Beowulf' and the 'Beowulf'-Manuscript*, p. 216.
159 For the manuscript at this point, see Plate 6 above, p. 18, esp. lines 11–14.

Editing 'Beowulf': explaining scribal errors

Similar arguments can be brought to bear to explain apparent errors that remain unemended by either scribe, but which have been faulted (and corrected) by modern editors. It is easy to imagine how a native speaker of Old English might copy the phrase *gewat him on nacan* ('he went on [board] ship', line 1903a): the phrase makes sense in isolation, the prepositional use of *on* is well-attested in the poem, and some influence of the forms immediately preceding and following *nacan* (namely *on* and *drefan*) is possible; nonetheless, most editors emend to *naca*, since the wider context seems to demand the alternative adverbial sense of *on* ('the ship went on').[160] Likewise, simple dittography seems to account for the copying of the perfectly normal form *eaforan* in Hrothgar's explanation of his knowledge of Beowulf through the latter's father, Ecgtheow; as it stands, the phrase is, however, hard to construe (*is his eaforan nu heard her cumen, sohte holdne wine*, lines 375b–376),[161] but the widely-accepted emendation to *eafora* makes better sense ('his son has now come here bravely, sought out a trusted friend'). It has recently been argued that Thorkelin's own transcript of *Beowulf* (the so-called Thorkelin B transcript) is less reliable that that commissioned by him from a third party (Thorkelin A), precisely because Thorkelin's own (rather less than perfect) knowledge of Old English influenced him in his copying.[162] The same of course, might be said in spades for both scribes of the *Beowulf*-manuscript, and should perhaps deter us from placing too much blind faith in their transmitted text.

So much is further clear from a number of cases where eye-skip has been suggested where the metre or meaning seems defective, as in the following passage, describing the reaction of the Danes to Grendel's initial attacks (lines 138–40a):

> Þa wæs eaðfynde þe him elles hwær
> gerumlicor ræste [. . .]
> bed æfter burum   140

['Then it was easy to find [a man] who elsewhere [. . .] a roomier resting-place for himself, a bed among the out-buildings.']

The problem evidently lies in line 139b, where the scribe has perhaps mistaken the noun-form *ræste* for a version of the preterite of the verb *restan* ('rest'; the

---

160 For a similar kind of error, cf. line 2448b, where the manuscript clearly reads *ond he him helpan ne mæg* ('and he cannot help him'), so anticipating the infinitive required by the auxiliary verb *mæg* that in fact occurs at line 2449b (*ænige gefremman*). The presence of the otherwise unexplained adjective *ænige* provides reason enough to emend the verb *helpan* to the noun *helpe* ('help') so providing an object for the infinitive *gefremman* and a referent for the adjective *ænige*.

161 Kiernan, ed., *Electronic 'Beowulf'*, wants to defend the manuscript-reading as a dative plural; but apart from exciting wild speculation about what Ecgtheow was up to while in exile in Denmark (if the sense is that Beowulf has come visiting others of Ecgtheow's sons), it is far from clear that such an explanation will serve.

162 Ironically enough, the case is most cogently made by Kiernan, *The Thorkelin Transcripts*, esp. pp. 97–99. See too the rigorously critical examination of Kiernan's assertions about the transcripts by Gerritsen, 'What Use are the Thorkelin Transcripts of *Beowulf*?'.

preterite would be *reste*, as at line 1799a);[163] clearly some verb is required, and most editors have accepted Grein's proposed addition of *sohte* ('sought'), especially because eye-skip from *ræste* to *sohte (or any other preterite verb-form in -*te*) seems easy to assume. Similar sensitivity to the surrounding context may help in assessing both the manuscript evidence (and the proposed emendations) for the introduction to Beowulf's penultimate speech before dying (lines 2794–808). The general situation is clear: Wiglaf emerges from the dragon's barrow, bearing treasure, to find Beowulf close to death; he sprinkles him with water, and Beowulf is rallied enough to begin what will be his final speech (lines 2788–93):[164]

> He ða mid þam maðmum   mærne þioden,
> dryhten sinne,   driorigne fand
> ealdres æt ende;   he hine eft ongon   2790
> wæteres weorpan,   oðþæt wordes ord
> breosthord þurhbræc;
> gomel on giohðe   gold sceawode.

> [He [= Wiglaf] then with those treasures found the glorious prince, his own lord covered in blood, at the end of his life; he began again to sprinkle him with water, until the beginning of a speech burst forth from the breast-hoard; old, in pain, he gazed on the gold.]

Although most editors have proposed a variety of half-lines to fill out the apparently missing line 2792b, others have urged caution, arguing that the demands of sense are fully met by the text as it stands, and that the isolated half-line constitutes 'the strategic use of a dramatic pause'.[165] Such a pause would surely be most effective immediately before the speech, however, notwithstanding the fact that the following verse (line 2793) provides a parallel with two further episodes in the poem: first, that in which Hrothgar gazes in uncomprehending awe at the giant sword-hilt from the monster mere (*Hroðgar maðelode, hylt sceawode*, line 1687), and, second, that in which the thief's lord (who may be Beowulf himself) first gazes on the cup ransacked from the dragon's hoard (*frea sceawode*, line 2285b). Stylistic considerations may better account for the apparent gap here: the assonance of *wordes ord breosthord* is clear, and most editors wishing to fill the perceived lacuna supply a half-line concluding with (*ge*)*spræc* ('spoke'), a form that could easily be lost through eye-skip from *þurhbræc*;[166] a broad parallel is provided by the extent to which, for example, eye-skip through

---

163   For possible scribal confusion of *æ* and *e*, see n. 124 above.

164   In fact, the final speech is interrupted by the narrator describing Beowulf bestowing gifts on Wiglaf; see further below, pp. 52–3.

165   Thus Niles, 'Editing *Beowulf*', pp. 455–6, citing the stray half-line (and the general situation of a warrior's dying speech) in *The Battle of Maldon*, line 172 as a parallel. There are other verbal parallels linking *The Battle of Maldon* to *Beowulf*; the possibility of direct influence is perhaps worth exploring. For other such apparent borrowings, linking *Beowulf* to a range of extant Old English poems, see below, pp. 163–8.

166   In their edition, Mitchell and Robinson suggest supplying *Bregorof gespræc* ('the powerful one spoke'), on the grounds that 'it resembles the preceding half-line at both beginning and end and so could have been skipped easily in copying' (p. 146); they cite as parallel to their hypothesized 2792b–2793a the phrase *worn eall gespræc, gomel on gehðo* (lines 3094b–5a).

homoeoteleuton in the Vercelli homilies is most common where the rhetorical style of the author favours the repetition of aural effects.[167]

Rather different considerations come into play in the possible emendation of what has been perceived as a similar gap between lines 389a and 390b, where most editors supply two half-lines (at 389b and 390a) to fill out evident failures in the alliteration of those lines. The lines in question represent a transition between two speeches, the first of which is by Hrothgar, speaking to Wulfgar, and welcoming the arrival of the Geats; his speech apparently concludes: 'Tell them further in words, that they are welcome to the people of the Danes' (*Gesaga him eac wordum, þæt hie sint wilcuman / Deniga leodum*, lines 388–389a). The second speech at issue is by Wulfgar, speaking to the Geats, which apparently begins: 'my victorious lord, prince of the East-Danes, has commanded that you be told that he knows your lineage' (*Eow het secgan sigedryhten min / aldor East Dena, þæt he eower æþelu can*, lines 391–2). The perceived difficulty stems from the fact that in the manuscript the transition between these two speeches is accomplished by the single half-line 'he spoke a word within' (*word inne abead*, line 390b), which not only omits both to introduce Wulfgar, the speaker of the lines following, and to explain how he physically gets from Hrothgar to the Geats, but also fails to alliterate with line 389a, which immediately precedes it in the manuscript. Despite recent spirited attempts to defend the manuscript reading as it stands by such senior scholars as (for example) Jack Niles, Allen Frantzen, and Kevin Kiernan,[168] the abruptness of the transition cannot be denied.[169] A wider consideration both of scribal practice in the *Beowulf*-manuscript and of the poet's practice with regard to transitions between speeches, however, only serves to heighten concern at the wisdom of accepting either the manuscript reading as it stands or the majority of the proposed suppletions of the text (which generally add two half-lines, the smallest number which will logically serve to produce two alliterating lines at 389–90).

First, it has been argued that the *Beowulf*-poet is exceedingly careful about the disposition of his (many) speeches,[170] and that in over forty separate

---

167 So, for example, it is striking to note from the critical apparatus of Scragg, ed., *The Vercelli Homilies*, that he identifies no fewer than ten examples of *homoeoteleuton* in Vercelli X alone (at X.24–5, 25, 26, 29–30, 58, 71–2, 104, 137–8, 160–1, and 203), as against only twenty-three examples in the other twenty-two homilies combined (at II.3; III.159–60; IV.296–7; V.121–2 and 149; VII.75 and 117; IX.58 and 111–12; XVI.155–6; XVIII.161–2; XIX.24, 33–4, 48, 108, and 170; XXII.37, 144, and 189; XXIII.10–13 and 38–9). Vercelli X is noted for its highly crafted rhetorical style, on which see Zacher, 'Sin, Syntax, and Synonyms'; I am grateful to the author for allowing me pre-publication access to her paper.

168 Niles, '*Beowulf* and the Ballads', p. 456; Frantzen, 'Writing the Unreadable *Beowulf*', pp. 338–9; Kiernan, *Beowulf and the Beowulf Manuscript*, p. 187.

169 A rather different strategy is employed by Robinson, 'Textual Notes on *Beowulf*', pp. 109–10, who notes that in lines 965a and 1073b the scribe apparently copied a synonym for the intended word (manuscript *handgripe* at line 865a will not alliterate, synonymous *mundgripe* will; manuscript *hildplegan* at line 1073b will not alliterate, synonymous *lindplegan* will), and suggests replacing *leodum* in line 389a with the nearly synonymous *weorode* ('troop', 'band'). The solution is ingenious, but subject to the same general objections as the others which retain the manuscript-reading. See below.

170 See further below, pp. 203–27. For an outline of the speech-acts in *Beowulf*, see Table IV below, pp. 206–7.

speech-acts only elsewhere fails to indicate the speaker (whether by name, description, or epithet) on four occasions.[171] Even these four examples, however, do not offer really convincing parallels for accepting the half-line *word inne abead* (line 390b) as the sole link between Hrothgar's speech and Wulfgar's, since in every other case the transition occurs between speeches by the same character. Among the briefest of such transitions between speeches is found in Beowulf's last address to his men before the dragon-fight, when he breaks off before speaking to them for the final time (lines 2516–18a). Although the transition here is briefer than that found elsewhere, there is still no real parallel with what the manuscript provides between Hrothgar's speech and Wulfgar's: Beowulf's last speech to his men is in fact interrupted twice in quick succession (at lines 2510–11a and 2516–18a), as the poet twice stresses that Beowulf is talking for the last time (*niehstan siðe*, line 2510a; *hindeman siðe*, line 2517b), and the wider context gives no room for doubt that in the final transition it is Beowulf who is speaking.[172]

A quite different kind of linking device is used in all three of the remaining cases where a speaker, continuing his own speech is not explicitly identified. So, for example, on his return to Heorot, Beowulf breaks off from his lengthy description of his adventures in Denmark (lines 2000–151) to have Hrothgar's treasures brought in for presentation to Hygelac, before resuming speech to commend the gifts to his lord (lines 2155–62). In this case, however, the transition between speeches is accomplished in three full lines (lines 2152–4), and carefully choreographed by the poet, who marks the beginning and end of the transition by a pair of chiastically arranged verbal phrases describing how Beowulf had the treasure brought in, and how he resumed his speech (*Het þa in beran . . . gyd æfter wræc*, lines 2152a and 2154b). Similar patterns of verbal phrasing signal the transitions between other speeches by the same character where the pronoun is understood, as when Beowulf (in what is probably intended as a parallel scene to Beowulf's gift-giving to Hygelac) interrupts his last speech in order to commend his neck-ring, arm-ring, helmet, and mail-coat to Wiglaf:[173] the transition takes four full lines (lines 2809–12), beginning with a description of action (*Dyde him of healse*, line 2809a), and ending with an introduction to speech (*het hyne brucan well*, line 2812b). Even though the context is rather different (since he is addressing two different audiences), a very

---

171 For an excellent brief analysis of the difficulties of accepting the manuscript-reading as it stands, see Handelman, 'Wulfgar at the Door', to which I am indebted for part of the following discussion; see too Tripp, 'Wulfgar at the Door?'. The transitions in question occur at lines 2152–4, 2516–2518a, and 2809–12 (where Beowulf is speaking); and at lines 2661–2 (where Wiglaf is speaking). A further such example where the speaker is not explicitly identified is that at 2792b, where, however, there are textual difficulties: see above, p. 50.

172 Quite apart from anything else, he is the only one present who has 'dear companions' whom he might 'address' at this point (*Gegrette ða . . . swæse gesiðas*, lines 2516a and 2518a).

173 One might, for example, compare the closing words of Beowulf's speech to Hygelac ('Enjoy it all well' [*Bruc ealles well*, line 2162b]) with the last words of the transition of the speech to Wiglaf ('He told him to enjoy [it all] well' [*het hyne brucan well*, line 2812b]); it is certainly striking that when Hrothgar gives Beowulf the treasures he eventually passes on to Hygelac, he too tells him to enjoy them well (*het hyne wel brucan*, line 1045b). If one takes (as I do) the *beah* ('[arm]-ring') of line 2812a to be different from the *hring* ('[neck]-ring') of line 2809b, then both Hygelac and Wiglaf receive four treasures.

similar transition takes place (lines 2661–2) between Wiglaf's speeches, first to the faithless retainers before he enters the dragon-fight (lines 2633–60), and then to Beowulf, as he joins him in the fray (lines 2663–8): here again the transition is bounded by half-lines describing first action, then speech (*Wod þa þurh þone wælrec*, line 2661a; *fea worda cwæð*, line 2662b).[174]

Such evidence emphatically throws into doubt the manuscript-reading at 389b–90a, since as it stands the transition between the two different speakers, Hrothgar and Wulfgar, is not simply abrupt, but quite contrary to the highly choreographed introductions to speeches found elsewhere in the poem. A further problem is raised by the fact that acceptance of the transmitted text would entail that Hrothgar's speech terminates at line 389a, making it the only one of over forty separate speech-acts in *Beowulf* not to conclude with a b-line. That the *Beowulf*-poet was careful in the layout of his speeches is apparent from the discussion above, and moreover it is surely striking that (ignoring the apparent exception here) if none of the speeches in Beowulf end with an a-line, they likewise only begin with a b-line in a highly restricted set of circumstances, namely when the speech in question is the second or third speech in a series or exchange spoken together.[175] Otherwise, speeches tend to begin with an a-line and end with a b-line: such is surely the model to be followed in suggesting emendations for the otherwise unremarkable transition between Hrothgar's speech and Wulfgar's in this highly patterned series of exchanges that preface Beowulf's arrival into Heorot.[176]

Examination of the manuscript is instructive at this point, since, as Johan Gerritsen has noted: '[t]here is a clear step in the writing between *deniga* and *leodum* [line 389a], such as one may find when the pen has temporarily left the writing surface, whether because the writer had to take ink or because he had to look at his exemplar for more text'.[177] One might well invoke the principle of scribal eye-skip here again, and note that if the phrase *Deniga leodum* is found as a formula in *Beowulf* (lines 389a, 1323a, and 1712b) so too is the phrase *Wedera leodum* ('people of the Geats', lines 697b and 1894b), which would provide a perfect alliterative foil for the half-line *word inne abead* (line 390b), so naming the folk to whom Wulfgar addressed his speech.[178] If such a suggestion for line 390a is accepted, then there is simply no way of knowing how much has been lost between line 389a (*Deniga leodum*) and a suggested new line 390a (*Wedera leodum*); it seems unlikely that the poet would have two consecutive

---

174 It might be noted that the majority of these transitions between speeches by the same speaker take place in the latter part of the poem, where the speech-patterning in general is quite distinctive; see further below, pp. 227–37.

175 The speeches in question are at 287b–300 (the third in the exchange between Beowulf and the coast-guard); 342b–347 and 350b–355 (the second and third in the exchange between Beowulf and Wulfgar); 2511b–2515 and 2518b–2537 (the second and third in the series spoken by Beowulf to his men before the dragon-fight); and 3114b–3119 (the second in the series spoken by Wiglaf to the Geatish people outside the dragon's barrow). See further Table IV below, pp. 206–7.

176 On which see further below, pp. 208–18.

177 Gerritsen, 'Emending *Beowulf* 2253', p. 451. It is curious to note that although it appeared in the same journal a year earlier, Gerritsen makes no mention of Handelman, 'Wulfgar at the Door', which offers much support for his analysis from a more literary perspective.

178 Gerritsen, 'Emending *Beowulf* 2253', p. 451, notes that 'it is . . . hard to imagine that the on-verse of 390 . . . could have begun with anything else than *Wedera*'.

a-lines with *leodum*,[179] and the patterning of the other speeches would indicate that whatever has been lost, there had to have been enough space to terminate Hrothgar's speech with a b-line, identify Wulfgar as the speaker of the following speech, and describe his movement from Hrothgar to the Geats. Despite the outrage expressed by such stalwart defenders of the manuscript as Kevin Kiernan that '[b]ecause there is no alliteration [between lines 389a and 390b], editors invent a great lacuna of two half-lines between *leodum* and *word*',[180] it seems likely that the 'great lacuna' supposed in this passage should in fact be greater still.[181]

Editing 'Beowulf': the case for continuing emendation

Taken together, such examples might well offer encouragement to further emendation, even of passages which have so far largely escaped editorial attention. So, for example, the burial-ship that bears Scyld Scefing away on his last voyage is described as *isig ond utfus* ('icy and eager to be away', line 33b). Despite the efforts of several scholars to explain the term *isig*, the word has continued to puzzle: most of the doublets in *Beowulf* combine homonyms or antonyms, and there seems no necessary context for the combination used here.[182] The most elegant solution may be that offered in an unpublished lecture by Alistair Campbell, who suggested that scribal confusion of *s* for *l* caused the form *isig* to be written for a putative earlier form **ilig*, 'speedy', cognate with Old High German *ilig* (Modern German *eilig*, 'quick', 'urgent'), and so providing an excellent match for *utfus* ('eager to be away').[183] While Campbell's suggested

---

179 Some rough indication of the possible gap between lines 389a and 390b is offered by the juxtaposition in Hrothgar's so-called sermon of the phrases *leodum þinum* (line 1708b; referring to the Geats) and *Deniga leodum* (line 1712b). One should, however, also bear in mind the immediate juxtaposition in consecutive lines of *Denigea leode* and *Wedera leodum* in lines 696a snd 697b respectively. It might be pointed out that those who defend the manuscript-reading as it stands are prepared to accept the juxtaposition *wordum . . . word* in consecutive lines; see too Handelman, 'Wulfgar at the Door', p. 477, n. 10. Further indication that a gap greater than supposed by most editors is offered by the swift repetition of the term *wilcuman* ('welcome') in lines 388b and 394b; the whole passage is evidently deliberately echoed when the Geats return to the Danish coast and the coastguard bids them welcome (*cwæð þæt wilcuman Wedera leodum*, line 1894). On the use by the *Beowulf*-poet of repeated elements in close proximity as a stylistic and structuring device, see below, pp. 78–85.

180 Kiernan, *Beowulf and the Beowulf Manuscript*, p. 187.

181 One might also point to the evident lacuna in both metre and sense at 1803a, apparently caused by a form of eyeskip from *ða com beorht scacan* (line 1802b: 'then there came brightly hastening') to *scaþan onetton* (line 1803b: 'Warriors hastened'): the two forms *scacan* and *scaþan* appear consecutively in the manuscript, and are similar enough to cause such eye-skip; the parallel meanings of *scacan* and *onettan* may well have assisted the confusion. The minimal required addition of a single half-line at 1803a has been variously supplied as *scima æfter sceadwe* ('brightness after shadows'; Sievers' suggestion) or *scima ofer sceadwa* ('brightness over the shadows'; Klaeber's suggestion); both would provide the alliterative link between lines 1802–3, as well as between the human and natural worlds (for a similar construction earlier in the poem, see below, pp. 65–6); but we cannot be sure that only a single half-line has been lost.

182 See, for example, the explanations of Porru, '*Beowulf*, v. 33: *isig ond utfus*'; Liberman, 'The "Icy" Ship of Scyld Scefing'.

183 For the attribution of this emendation to Campbell, see Howlett, *British Books*, p. 509.

emendation is made on purely philological grounds, it may find some palaeographical support in the fact that both scribes occasionally employ 'a form like the modern long *s*',[184] a form perhaps more easily confusable with *l* than the alternatives, which are also found in the manuscript. A further interesting example of a hitherto unemended form that may repay closer attention is provided by the introductory description of Beowulf as one 'who was the strongest in might of mankind on that day of this life' (*se wæs moncynnes mægenes strengest on þæm dæge þysses lifes*; lines 196–7), since the phrase is repeated almost verbatim at the opening of the fight with Grendel (*se þe monna wæs mægene strengest on þæm dæge þysses lifes*; lines 789–90). The difference between lines 196b (*mægenes strengest*) and 789b (*mægene strengest*) is one that could certainly be explained mechanically either by haplography (*s* for *ss*) or dittography (*ss* for *s*); and it is interesting to note that in both cases the relevant ending has been attracted to that of surrounding words: in 196b we find *mægenes* alongside *moncynnes*, *þysses*, and *lifes*; and in 789b we find *mægene* alongside *helle*, *hine*, *fæste* (all in line 788), and *dæge*. That a related description of Beowulf by Hrothgar later in the poem calls him 'strong in might and intelligent in mind, a wise word-speaker' (*mægenes strang ond on mode frod, wis wordcwida*, lines 1844–5a)[185] might appear to strengthen the case that in *Beowulf* the adjective *strang* ('strong') governs the genitive, and that haplography has occured in line 789b, were it not apparent that a number of other adjectives in the poem seem to govern both genitive and dative cases.[186]

It will be clear from the above analysis, however, that even after the assiduous attention of successive generations of modern readers, the *Beowulf*-manuscript still rewards careful study. The widespread availability of high-quality facsimiles and the continued comparison of earlier transcripts and editions can (and surely should) only stimulate further research and the proposal of still more conjectural emendations to the text. The bare fact of the uniqueness of the text surviving in the *Beowulf*-manuscript, once one accepts that the scribes were copying from a pre-existing source, makes the full extent of scribal error and interference essentially unknowable, but by following the clues the scribes themselves offer about the errors to which they were prone, and by evaluating conjectural emendations against those supposed with regard to other Old English poems (a few of which do indeed survive in multiple copies),[187] it

---

184 Malone, *Nowell Codex*, p. 18, who notes (writing in 1963) that the form was 'still used within living memory though no longer current'.

185 On this 'thought, word, and deed' triad, see below, pp. 73, 146, 218, and 255.

186 See Rudanko, *Towards Classifying Verbs and Adjectives Governing the Genitive in 'Beowulf'*. It is worth noting, however, that *strang* is one of eight adjectives governing the genitive comprising Rudanko's Class II.a, and referring to 'health . . . physical strength, or mental presence' (pp. 80–6: the others are *cræftig*, *gemyndig*, *gesund*, *hal*, *heard*, *seoc*, and *wis*), and that he quotes eighteen examples where these adjectives clearly govern a genitive, two where the adjective *seoc* ('sick') governs a dative with a clear difference in meaning ('cause', rather than 'the respect in which [the noun agreeing with the adjective is sick', pp. 83–4); the only other case where an adjective from this group apparently governs the dative is precisely the example from line 789b under discussion.

187 See now Orton, *The Transmission of Old English Poetry*, for a full analysis of all Old English poetry surviving in multiple copies, comprising roughly 2.2 per cent of the extant corpus.

should be possible to exercise some control over the level and type of emendation proposed. But, as we have seen, conjectural emendation (however brilliant) should never be so myopic as to exclude the wider context: all such conjectures surely need to be evaluated carefully against the style of the language and the structure of the text, the topic to which we now turn.

3

Style and Structure

The style of 'Beowulf': beginning at the beginning

The richness of diction in *Beowulf* has long been the subject of intensive study; indeed, the language and style of the poem are often seen as the yardstick against which other texts, particularly in vernacular verse, have come to be measured.[1] Likewise, there has been a growing realisation that the very structure of *Beowulf* can best be perceived through a closer understanding of the techniques of composition employed.[2] For almost half a century, *Beowulf* has been the primary battlefield upon which the sometimes heated skirmishes of the so-called oral-formulaic debate have taken place, and it would be no exaggeration to say that the whole issue of the precise implications of *Beowulf*'s clearly formulaic style of composition has (rightly or wrongly) dominated recent literary appreciation of the text.[3] The result has been to place *Beowulf* squarely at the centre of critical discussion concerning the creative tension between a series of conflicting influences (native and imported; traditional and innovative; Germanic and Latinate; secular and Christian; oral and literate; popular and elite) that is perhaps the hallmark of Anglo-Saxon literature as a whole.[4]

The language of *Beowulf* can largely be said to be based on two opposing principles, namely repetition and variation, which essentially both perform the same function: setting separate elements side by side for the purpose of compar-

---

[1] Discussions of the style of *Beowulf* include: Andrew, *Syntax and Style in Old English; idem, Postscript on 'Beowulf'*; Batchelor, 'The Style of the *Beowulf*'; Blomfield, 'The Style and Structure of *Beowulf*'; Brodeur, 'A Study of Diction and Style in Three Anglo-Saxon Narrative Poems'; *idem, The Art of 'Beowulf'*; Campbell, 'The Old English Epic Style'; Clemoes, 'Style as a Criterion for Dating the Composition of *Beowulf*'; Donoghue, *Style in Old English Poetry*; Gradon, *Form and Style in Early English Literature*; Niles, 'Compound Diction and the Style of *Beowulf*'; Robinson, *'Beowulf' and the Appositive Style*; Schaefer, 'Rhetoric and Style'; Storms, 'The Subjectivity of the Style of *Beowulf*'; Taylor, 'The Epithetical Style in *Beowulf*'. Cf. too Godden, 'Literary Language'; Huppé, *The Web of Words*; Wyld, 'Diction and Imagery in Anglo-Saxon Poetry'. For a useful summary of the critical history of the topic for Old English verse in general, see Calder, 'The Study of Style in Old English Poetry'.

[2] See further below, pp. 78–85.

[3] For overviews of the whole debate, see Olsen, 'Oral-Formulaic Research in Old English Studies: I'; *eadem*, 'Oral-Formulaic Research in Old English Studies: II'; Orchard, 'Oral Tradition'. Many of the more important studies are listed below, pp. 85–6.

[4] Cf. the subtitles used by Liuzza, trans., *Beowulf: a New Verse Translation*: '*Beowulf* Between Myth and History' (p. 13); '*Beowulf* Between Song and Text' (p. 20); '*Beowulf* Between Court and Cloister' (p. 31).

ison or contrast. Fred Robinson has most fully articulated this aspect of what he has termed 'the appositive style',[5] building on the work of others who have focused on one or other of the principles of repetition and variation.[6] Such principles operate at a number of levels of diction, and can be perceived at the sub-verbal level (in the form of alliteration, assonance, dissonance, and rhyme), as well as at the levels of words, compounds, phrases, paragraphs, and themes. Often, the same principles of repetition and variation can be seen to lend structure to the poem as a whole, and work alongside (and occasionally against) existing scribally imposed divisions of the text, whether by capitalisation, pointing, spacing, or the use of roman numerals to break the text down into separate sections or fitts.[7] Other more clearly aurally-derived techniques of repetition are used to divide the poem into verse-paragraphs,[8] whether through repetition of sounds, words, or phrases at the beginning and end of such paragraphs (the so-called 'envelope-pattern'),[9] or the repetition of sounds, words, or phrases at the beginning of successive verse-paragraphs (a technique sometimes described as 'incremental repetition', and parallel to that of anaphora in Classical rhetoric).[10] Like many other composers of Old English verse, the *Beowulf*-poet also uses a range of pithy, self-contained and understated phrases,[11] often couched in the form of a proverb or other gnomic expression, more or less as marks of aural punctuation:[12] on a number of occasions such gnomic phrases start or end speeches or fitts, or break down the narrative into more manageable sections.

Several of these characteristic stylistic traits can be seen in the very opening lines of the poem (lines 1–11), which celebrate the heroic endeavours of bygone days that will prove the poet's main stated theme, as follows (with structural alliteration within the line highlighted in bold, and ornamental interlinear alliterative effects underlined):[13]

---

5   Robinson, *'Beowulf' and the Appositive Style*.
6   Cf. esp. Brodeur, *The Art of 'Beowulf'*, pp. 1–70.
7   See further Table II and the discussion below, pp. 91–7.
8   On the use of such techniques in Old English poetry in general, see, for example, Orchard, 'Oral Tradition'; *idem*, 'Re-reading *The Wanderer*'. See too Stévanovitch, *Beowulf': de la forme au sens*.
9   On the envelope-patttern (sometimes called ring-composition), see Bartlett, *The Larger Rhetorical Patterns in Anglo-Saxon Poetry*, pp. 9–29; Battles, 'The Art of the Scop', pp. 241–305; Dane, 'The Notion of Ring Composition in Classical and Medieval Studies'; Niles, 'Ring-Composition and the Structure of *Beowulf*'; *idem*, *Beowulf: the Poem and its Tradition*, pp. 152–62; Parks, 'Ring Structure and Narrative Embedding in Homer and *Beowulf*'; Pasternack, *The Textuality of Old English Poetry*, pp. 120–46; Tonsfeldt, 'Ring Structure in *Beowulf*'. See too Stévanovitch, 'Envelope Patterns and the Unity of the Old English *Christ and Satan*'; *idem*, 'Envelope Patterns in *Genesis A* and *B*'.
10 The standard study remains that of Jackson, 'Incremental Repetition in the Early Welsh *Englyn*'; see too Bartlett, *The Larger Rhetorical Patterns in Anglo-Saxon Poetry*, pp. 4–61; Orchard 'The *Hisperica famina* as Literature'.
11 Cf. Bracher, 'Understatement in Old English Poetry'.
12 See in general, for example, Burlin, 'Gnomic Indirection in *Beowulf*'; Cavill, '*Beowulf* and *Andreas*: Two Maxims'; *idem*, *Maxims in Old English Poetry*; Greenfield, 'Of Words and Deeds: the Coastguard's Maxim Once More'; Karkov and Farrell, 'The Gnomic Passages of *Beowulf*'; Kaske, 'The Coastwarden's Maxim in *Beowulf*: a Clarification'.
13 The manuscript reads *eorl* at line 6a and *þara* for *þær* in line 9; for *þær* (line 9), see Jack, ed., *Beowulf*, p. 28; Pope, 'Irregular Anacrusis', pp. 105–10.

Hwæt! We Gardena   in geardagum,
þeodcyninga,   þrym gefrunon,
hu ða æþelingas   ellen fremedon.
Oft Scyld Scefing   sceaþena þreatum,
monegum mægþum,   meodosetla ofteah,   5
egsode eorlas.   Syððan ærest wearð
feasceaft funden,   he þæs frofre gebad,
weox under wolcnum,   weorðmyndum þah,
oðþæt him æghwylc þær   ymbsittendra
ofer hronrade   hyran scolde,   10
gomban gyldan.   Þæt wæs god cyning.

[Listen! We have heard of the power of the mighty kings of the
Spear-Danes in bygone days, how those [or 'then'] princes did bold
deeds. Often Scyld Scefing snatched off mead-benches from bands of
foes, from many nations, spread awe amongst warriors since first he was
discovered destitute; he had comfort for that: he grew under the skies,
flourished in glorious deeds, until each of the neighbouring peoples
there over the whale's riding had to obey, pay tribute. That was a good
king.]

These opening lines of the poem, which in a wholly self-contained fashion
describe the mysterious arrival and equally mysterious departure of the intrigu-
ingly named Scyld Scefing ('Shield, son of Sheaf'), from whom the Danish
royal house is descended, establish many of the themes of the poem as a whole,
and set up resonances which can still be perceived in the closing lines of the
poem. It has often been observed that *Beowulf* begins and ends with a funeral,[14]
but the tone of the opening and closing sections (let alone the rest of the poem)
is far from consistently elegiac.[15] The martial valour celebrated in these first
eleven lines of the poem is precisely what is picked up time and again in the
course of the poem: 'bold deeds' (*ellen*) lie at the heart of *Beowulf*, which richly
depicts the doings and foreign forays of successive generations of 'mighty
kings' (*þeodcyninga*).[16] The venerable antiquity of the action 'in days of yore' is
stressed in the opening line (*geardagum*), and perhaps again in the third line, if
ða is taken (as it well might be) not as the definite article, but as the adverb
'then'.[17] Such possibilities of multiple and layered meanings are the hallmark of
the *Beowulf*-poet, as we shall see.[18]

But aside from setting a stirring scene, these opening lines are a typical

---

14 See, for example, Bonjour, *Digressions*, pp. 1–11.

15 Cf. Tolkien, '*Beowulf*: the Monsters and the Critics', p. 275: '*Beowulf* is not an "epic", nor even a
magnified "lay". No term borrowed from Greek or other literatures exactly fit: there is no reason why
they should. Though if we must have a term, we should choose rather "elegy". It is an heroic-elegiac
poem.'

16 It is instructive to note that the term *ellen* or its compounds occur no fewer than twenty-five times in
the course of the poem (lines 3b, 86a, 340a, 358a, 573b, 602a, 637a, 661a, 828a, 876a, 900a, 902a,
958a, 1464a, 1471a, 1787b, 2122a, 2349a, 2399a, 2643a, 2695b, 2706b, 2787a, 3063a, and 3173b), if
we assume that the reference to Grendel as an *ellengæst* (line 86a) is not a scribal error for *ellorgæst*
or *ellorgast* (as in lines 807b, 1349a, and 1617a); *þeodcyning* is found (with various spellings)
perhaps eight times (lines 2a, 2144a, 2579a, 2694b, 2963a, 2970a, 3008a, and [perhaps] 3086a).

17 Cf. Howlett, *British Books in Biblical Style*, p. 506 (arguing from parallelism with *in geardagum*).

18 See below, pp. 238–64.

example of this poet's art. The initial call to attention (*Hwæt*) is echoed in a number of other Old English poems,[19] as is the use of the 'we have heard' formula,[20] appealing to a supposed common knowledge of famed past events; a related device ('I have heard') is found elsewhere in *Beowulf* (lines 74, 776, 1011, 1197, and 2163), but this is the only time in the poem when the poet uses the inclusive first-person plural form.[21] The passage ends with a pithy self-contained half-line (*þæt wæs god cyning*), that is likewise echoed elsewhere in the poem (at lines 863b and 2390b). The diction of this passage, as in Old English poetry in general and *Beowulf* in particular, is richly noun-based: in these eleven lines we find nineteen nouns but only ten finite verbs and (unusually for a passage of this length in *Beowulf*) only three adjectives.[22] Several of the finite verbs, moreover are rather bland and colourless (such as *fremedon* ['did'], *wearð* ['was'], *scolde* ['had to'], and *wæs* ['was']), and again underline the relative importance of the nouns, and more specifically of the compound nouns. The proportion of compound nouns here (seven out of nineteen, of which one, *meodosetla*, is unique to the poem) signals their weight; in the 3182 lines of *Beowulf*, Arthur Brodeur, in the course of a masterful analysis, counted 903 distinctive noun-compounds (as opposed to 675 distinctive simplexes), 518 of which are unique to *Beowulf*, and 578 of which occur only once in the poem.[23]

The poet emphasises two such compounds in the opening line of the poem, highlighting their importance through the extra ornament of cross-alliteration.[24] That the structural alliteration of this line (*Gar-Dena . . . geardagum*) should rely on recognition of an identity between two pronunciations of *g* (guttural and palatal respectively), a distinction that apparently arose in the eighth century, has been used by some to argue that the poem must predate such a linguistic innovation; it seems at least as likely that the poet is emphasising the archaic nature of his theme by recourse to an archaic and (by the time of the poet) utterly traditional alliterative pattern.[25] In other respects, moreover, in this passage the poet clearly emphasises his material through alliterative ornament.

---

19 See, for example, line 1 of *Exodus, Andreas, Fates of the Apostles, The Dream of the Rood, Juliana, Vainglory, Solomon and Saturn, Judgment Day II*, and *Metrical Charm 2*, not to mention several sections of the *Metres of Boethius* and the *Paris Psalter*.

20 For a study of the use of this and related formulas ('I have heard'; 'as I have heard tell') see Parks, ' "I Heard" Formulas in Old English Poetry'.

21 See further below, pp. 99–100.

22 Nouns (compound nouns are marked with an asterisk): *Gar-Dena*, geardagum*, þeodcyninga*, þrym, æþelingas, ellen, Scyld Scefing, sceaþena, þreatum, mægþum, meodosetla*, eorl[as], frofre, wolcnum, weorðmyndum*, ymbsittendra*, hronrade*, gomban*, and *cyning*; verbs: *gefrunon, fremedon, ofteah, egsode, wearð, gebad, weox, þah, scolde*, and *wæs*; adjectives: *monegum, feasceaft* and *god*.

23 Brodeur, *Art of Beowulf*, pp. 1–38. For a further analysis of the poet's use of such compounds, see below, pp. 69–72.

24 I count perhaps 111 examples of cross-alliteration in the poem as a whole: lines 1, 19, 32, 34, 39, 64, 88, 98, 201, 209, 282, 355, 374, 418, 525, 535, 566, 589, 591, 653, 699, 730, 779, 803, 829, 893, 907, 919, 971, 1016, 1131, 1140, 1143, 1182, 1184, 1201, 1203, 1222, 1262, 1301, 1314, 1341, 1342, 1403, 1406, 1443, 1445, 1472, 1475, 1482, 1488, 1535, 1573, 1599, 1611, 1644, 1721, 1728, 1732, 1824, 1826, 1849, 1892, 1910, 1933, 1939, 1968, 2020, 2030, 2053, 2066, 2091, 2158, 2181, 2186, 2187, 2204, 2223, 2235, 2261, 2267, 2337, 2377, 2385, 2397, 2465, 2479, 2515, 2567, 2615, 2637, 2651, 2669, 2726, 2745, 2794, 2875, 2907, 2954, 2970, 2973, 2998, 3058, 3066, 3074, 3081, 3089, 3107, 3162, 3164, and 3180.

25 Cf. Amos, *Linguistic Means of Determining the Dates of Old English Literary Texts*, pp. 100–2. On

Beowulf is relatively unexceptional in its use of double alliteration (in which both stressed syllables of the a-line alliterate with the first stressed syllable of the b-line), by comparison with other Old English poems.[26] It is therefore striking that the six lines which exhibit this pattern (lines 4–8 and line 11) should all cluster in the verses which introduce Scyld Scefing. That the final line of the passage (line 11) should contain double alliteration is perhaps also significant (line 12 does not): the same pattern of continued double alliteration is found at the end of the fitt (lines 48–52) and, indeed, the poem (lines 3181–2). At the very beginning of his poem, then, the *Beowulf*-poet effectively lays out his stall, using a range of devices to underscore his story at all levels of diction.

The wall of sound: alliteration, assonance, rhyme, and other sub-verbal effects

The most obvious form of aural repetition at the sub-verbal level of diction in *Beowulf* is alliteration, which the poet uses artfully in a number of ways.[27] The importance of alliteration as the underlying principle of Old English verse has been underlined several times in recent years, as has the propensity of many poets to employ specific alliterative patterning both within and between lines not only to highlight particular passages but for structural effect.[28] The *Beowulf*-poet's favoured form of artful alliteration appears to lie in the clustering of double alliteration, a pattern he repeats throughout the text to highlight a large number of key passages in the poem. *Beowulf* is proportionately rich in double alliteration: almost half of the lines in the poem contain the feature.[29] But such a raw statistic masks the way in which the *Beowulf*-poet employs double alliteration in irregular clusters: there are large tracts of the piece which contain little or no examples of double alliteration at all. That clusters of double alliteration can form a bridge linking adjacent passages is in fact perfectly illustrated at the junction between the first (unnumbered) fitt, or manuscript-section of the poem,[30] and what in the manuscript is fitt I: the linked passages describe first the funeral of Scyld Scefing, and then the rise of his son, Beow (lines 47–58):[31]

the difficulty of using such linguistic criteria, see too Cameron, *et al.*, 'A Reconsideration of the Language of *Beowulf*'; Bately, 'Linguistic Evidence as a Guide to the Authorship of Old English Verse'.

26 For a useful table giving the percentages of double alliteration found in a number of Old English poems, see Hutcheson, *Old English Poetic Metre*, p. 271.

27 On the *Beowulf*-poet's use of sound-effects in general, see, for example, Barquist, 'Phonological Patterning in *Beowulf*'; Borroff, 'Systematic Sound Symbolism in the Long Alliterative Line in *Beowulf* and *Sir Gawain*'; Creed, 'The *Beowulf*-Poet: Master of Sound-Patterning'; *idem*, 'Between the Lines: Subdominant-to-Dominant Patterning in *Beowulf*'.

28 See, for example, Bennett, 'Extra Alliteration as a Stylistic Device in *Beowulf*'; Cronan, 'Alliterative Rank in Old English Poetry'; Lehmann and Tabusa, *The Alliterations of the 'Beowulf'*; Orchard, 'Artful Alliteration in Anglo-Saxon Song and Story'; Reinhard, *On the Semantic Relevance of the Alliterative Collocations in 'Beowulf'*; Standop, 'Alliteration und Akzent: "schwere" und "leichte" Verse im *Beowulf*'; Taylor and Davis, 'Some Alliterative Misfits in the *Beowulf* MS'.

29 See the table referred to in n. 26 above.

30 On the fitt-divisions in *Beowulf*, see Table II below, pp. 94–5. The fitt-division here comes after line 52.

31 The manuscript reads *sele rædenne* at line 51b, and *beowulf* at line 53b. For the name of Scyld's son as Beow (rather than manuscript 'Beowulf'), see below, pp. 103–4.

> Þa gyt hie him asetton   segen gyldenne
> heah ofer heafod,   leton holm beran,
> geafon on garsecg;   him wæs geomor sefa,
> murnende mod.   Men ne cunnon   50
> secgan to soðe,   selerædende,
> hæleð under heofenum,   hwa þæm hlæste onfeng.
>   Ða wæs on burgum   Beow Scyldinga,
> leof leodcyning,   longe þrage
> folcum gefræge   (fæder ellor hwearf,   55
> aldor of earde),   oþþæt him eft onwoc
> heah Healfdene;   heold þenden lifde,
> gamol ond guðreouw,   glæde Scyldingas.

[Then they set above him a golden standard, high over his head, let the sea carry him, gave him to the ocean; their spirits were sad, hearts grieving. Folk cannot say for sure, hall-counsellors, heroes under the heavens, who received that load. Then there was in the strongholds Beow of the Scyldings, a beloved king of the people; for a long time famed among folk – his father had passed away, the prince from the land – until after him arose high Healfdene, who governed while he lived, ancient and battle-fierce, the happy Scyldings.]

The clustering of double alliteration here seems self-conscious, effectively dividing the passage equally into two sections of six lines each (lines 47–52 and 53–8), with five lines of double alliteration preceded by a line of single alliteration in each. Certainly the strike-rate of double alliteration in these dozen lines (at over 80 per cent) seems unusually high: less than half of the next forty lines exhibit the feature.[32]

In introducing Grendel, the poet likewise uses a condensed variety of alliterative effects in a single passage (lines 86–98):[33]

> Ða se ellengæst   earfoðlice
> þrage geþolode,   se þe in þystrum bad,
> þæt he dogora gehwam   dream gehyrde
> hludne in healle;   þær wæs hearpan sweg,
> swutol sang scopes.   Sægde se þe cuþe   90
> frumsceaft fira   feorran reccan,
> cwæð þæt se ælmihtiga   eorðan worhte,
> wlitebeorhtne wang,   swa wæter bebugeð,
> gesette sigehreþig   sunnan ond monan
> leoman to leohte   landbuendum   95
> ond gefrætwade   foldan sceatas
> leomum ond leafum,   lif eac gesceop
> cynna gehwylcum   þara ðe cwice hwyrfaþ.

[Then the mighty spirit, who waited in the darkness, endured grievously for a time that he heard each day joy, loud in the hall; there was the

---

32 I count double alliteration in lines 60–1, 65, 67, 69, 75–7, 79, 81–3, 87, 89, 91, 93–5, and 97.

33 I end the passage at this point out of simple convenience; it has been argued that the following lines, usually taken to refer to Grendel (lines 99–101, cited below), can also be read as part of the pre-lapsarian fall. See further Ball, '*Beowulf* 99–101', and below, pp. 137–8.

sound of the harp, the clear voice of the poet. The one who could recount from past ages the first-making of men spoke, said that the Almighty created the earth, the fair bright plain which water encircles; triumphing in might he set the sun and the moon as lamps to give light to the dwellers on earth, and he adorned the earth's corners with branches and leaves; he also fashioned life for each of the kinds that move around alive.]

Of the thirteen lines which comprise this passage, no fewer than eight exhibit double alliteration (lines 87, 88–91, 93–5, and 97), three cross-alliteration (lines 88, 93, and 98), and seven interlinear alliteration (lines 88–90, 92–3, and 96–7). A handful of examples of paronomasia or wordplay (*leoman . . . leomum*, lines 85a and 97a; *leafum . . . lif*, line 97) complete the picture. The effect is almost unparalleled within *Beowulf*, and serves to demonstrate part of the range of effects this skilful poet had at his disposal to highlight individual passages.

It seems likewise significant that the next important cluster of double alliteration comes in the celebrated passage that first links Grendel with the kin of Cain, and concludes the first numbered fitt (lines 99–110):[34]

> Swa ða drihtguman   dreamum lifdon
> eadiglice,   oððæt an ongan   100
> fyrene fremman   feond on helle.
> Wæs se grimma gæst   Grendel haten,
> mære mearcstapa,   se þe moras heold,
> fen ond fæsten;   fifelcynnes eard
> wonsæli wer   weardode hwile,   105
> siþðan him scyppend   forscrifen hæfde
> in Caines cynne.   Þone cwealm gewræc
> ece drihten,   þæs þe he Abel slog;
> ne gefeah he þære fæhðe,   ac he hine feor forwræc,
> metod for þy mane,   mancynne fram.   110

[So those noble warriors lived in joy, happily, until one began to perform wickedness, a fiend in hell. That grim spirit (or 'guest', 'stranger') was called Grendel, a well-known march-stepper, who ruled the wetlands, the fens and fastnesses; the unhappy man occupied for a time the dwelling-place of the monster-kin, once the Creator had proscribed him (or 'them') among the kin of Cain: the eternal Lord wrought vengenance for that killing, when he slew Abel. He did not rejoice in that feud, but God drove him far away from mankind for that crime.]

A number of points are worth making about this passage, which is otherwise notable for a number of instances of paronomasia or wordplay (*mær-/mearc-/mor-*, line 103; *wer/weard-*, line 105; *-feah/fæhð-*, line 109; *man-/man-*, line 110).[35] At first glance, a clear contrast is made between the joys of the happy

34 In line 107a, *caines* has apparently been altered from manuscript *cames*, whereas at line 1261b Cain is written *camp*. See further Pulsiano, ' "Cames cynne": Confusion or Craft?'.

35 On the significance of the pun *mær-/ mearc-/ mor-*, which occurs elsewhere in the poem, see Sharma, 'Movement and Space as Metaphor in Old English Poetry', pp. 207–39.

Danes (*dreamum lifdon eadiglice*, lines 99–100) and the sorrows of Grendel and Cain (*grimma*, line 102b; *wonsæli*, line 105a; *Ne gefeah*, line 109a). But although both the latter are exiled far from men (*feor . . . mancynne fram*, lines 109–10), we know than Cain was a man, as too is Grendel (*wer*, line 105a). Both act like kings already mentioned in the poem: like Healfdene, Grendel 'ruled' his domain (*heold*, lines 57b and 103b), whilst the descent of monsters from Cain is described in similar terms to that of the Danish royal house from Beow, Scyld's son (*onwoc*, line 56b; *wocun*, line 60a; *onwocon*, line 111b). Other resonances which run through the rest of the poem are established here. The reversal the Danes experience at Grendel's hands occurs, we later learn, after Hrothgar has ruled the kingdom for fifty years (*ic Hring-Dena hund missera weold under wolcnum*, lines 1769–70), until the singular creature, already present close at hand, turns against them (*oððæt an ongan*, line 100); in precisely parallel terms we learn that Beowulf ruled the Geats for fifty years until another singular creature, the dragon, already present close at hand, wreaks its vengeance (*He geheold tela fiftig wintra . . . oððæt an ongan*, lines 2208–10;[36] *Ic ðæs leode heold fiftig wintra*, lines 2732b–3a). It is further striking to note that the poet uses very similar language to describe how Grendel's mother ruled the monster mere for fifty years until another singular creature, this time Beowulf himself, invades her realm (*floda begong . . . beheold hund missera*, lines 1498b–9).[37] In this way, the poet appears through verbal repetition to cause thematic links to be made across stretches of narrative, and in this case the effect of the repetition is for the distinctions between the worlds of monsters and men to become blurred.[38]

Likewise, the extensive use of double alliteration (and other sub-verbal effects) highlights the description of Beowulf's first entrance into Heorot and his introductory speech to Hrothgar (lines 399–414):[39]

> Aras þa se rica, ymb hine rinc manig,
> þryðlic þegna heap; sume þær bidon,   400
> heaðoreaf heoldon, swa him se hearda bebead.
> Snyredon ætsomne, þa secg wisode,

---

36 However, Shippey, *Old English Verse*, p. 38, says of the apparent echoes between the advents of Grendel and the dragon that: 'Probably the parallelism is not deliberate. For poets of this type it is natural to see joy growing into sorrow, and to pull the two opposites together, carefully linked within a sentence.' But, as we shall see, such verbal repetition is by no means isolated, and seems part of this poet's stock-in-trade as a structuring device.

37 One might also note what is said of the dragon, which 'ruled for three hundred years, until one man enraged him in his heart' (*þreo hund wintra heold . . . oððæt hyne an abealch mon on mode*, lines 2278b–81a).

38 See further below, pp. 162, 196, and 256.

39 There is no gap in the manuscript to indicate an apparently missing half-line (or, as I suspect, more) at line 403b; likewise, the manuscript reads *hador* at line 414a (for *ð/d*-confusion, see above, pp. 42–6). I take the otherwise unattested reading *hador* from Mitchell and Robinson, ed., *Beowulf*, p. 62, and agree that the word probably means something like 'vault'; the poet has produced a fine series of nesting images, with Beowulf and his men passing under the protecting vault of Heorot's roof (*under Heorotes hrof*, line 403a), as Beowulf himself walks under the protecting vault of his helmet (*heard under helme*, line 404a), and talks about the evening sun passing under the protective vault of the sky (*under heofenes hador*, line 414a). Cf. Grein, *Sprachschatz der angelsächsischen Dichter*, p. 306, where the word *heador* is glossed as *receptaculum* ('shelter').

under Heorotes hrof
heard under helme,   þæt he on heoðe gestod.
Beowulf maðelode   (on him byrne scan,   405
searonet seowed   smiþes orþancum):
'Wæs þu, Hroðgar, hal!   Ic eom Higelaces
mæg ond magoðegn;   hæbbe ic mærða fela
ongunnen on geogoþe.   Me wearð Grendles þing
on minre eþeltyrf   undyrne cuð;   410
secgað sæliðend   þæt þæs sele stande,
reced selesta,   rinca gehwylcum
idel ond unnyt,   siððan æfenleoht
under heofenes haðor   beholen weorþeð.'

[The mighty man arose, and many a man with him, a powerful throng of thegns; some remained there, guarded the battle-equipment as the brave man bid. They hastened together as the man led them, under Heorot's roof; [he went?] brave under his helmet, so that he stood inside. Beowulf spoke (on him his corselet shone, the cunning weaving sewn through a smith's great skill): 'May you, Hrothgar, be well! I am Hygelac's kinsman and close thegn; I have acomplished many great deeds in my youth. The matter of Grendel was made no secret to me in my native land; seafarers say that this building, best of halls, stands empty and useless to every man, once the evening's light becomes hidden under the vault (?) of heaven'.]

There are a number of effects employed in this passage, which clearly describes an important point in the narrative of the poem as a whole.[40] Apart from the insistent use of double alliteration, one might note some interesting examples of interlinear alliteration: lines 403–4, whatever one makes of the apparently defective line 403, clearly contain continued (double?) alliteration on *h*;[41] and lines 400–1 and 411–12 are linked both by alliteration and paronomasia through the pairs *bibead . . . bidon* and *sele . . . selesta*). Still more intriguing are the verbal and thematic repetitions found in the passage. The identical half-line *heard under helme* (line 404a: 'brave under the helmet') is found earlier in the poem (line 342a) in precisely the same context, introducing Beowulf's first speech to the coastguard. Likewise, the only other time the phrase is used in the entire poem, it again refers to Beowulf, as he sets off to fight the dragon after making his final boast (lines 2538–41):

Aras ða bi ronde   rof oretta,
heard under helme,   hiorosercean bær
under stancleofu,   strengo getruwode   2540
anes mannes.   Ne bið swylc earges sið.

[Then the bold warrior arose by his shield, hard under his helmet, he bore his battle-shirt under the stone cliffs, put his faith in the strength of a single man: such is not the coward's way.]

In this case, the poet cleverly repeats an emphasis on the defensive armour (*ronde . . . helme . . . hiorosercean*) and sole strength (*strengo . . . anes mannes*) in which he puts his faith as Beowulf dashes off to die: none of these things can save him.[42] But it is striking to note that the repeated half-lines 2539a and 404a are not the only parallels to link these passages: lines 399a and 2538a are the only examples of the *Aras þa*-formula in the entire poem, and the series of half-lines *under Heorotes hrof . . . heard under helme* and *heard under helme . . . under stancleofu* (lines 403a/404a and 2539a/2540a) represent the the only pairs in which the preposition *under* is used in consecutive lines. As we shall see, such complex patterns of verbal repetition are widely used in *Beowulf* for a variety of effects.[43]

Rhyme is another feature of the sound-patterning of *Beowulf* which perhaps warrants more attention than it has received so far;[44] certainly, this particular brand of aural ornamentation is a key feature of such self-contained phrases as *frod ond god* (line 279a), *hond ond rond* (line 656a; cf. *hond rond gefeng*, line 2609b), *sæl ond mæl* (line 1008b; cf. *sæla ond mæla* in line 1611a), *ge wið feond ge wið freond* (line 1864a), and (perhaps) *swelan ond swellan* (line 2713a).[45] Even individual compounds, such as the evidently tautologous *þryðswyð* ('powerful in might', lines 131a and 736b) or the equally perplexing *foldbold* ('ground-building'), both of which are unique to the poem, have apparently been coined for their sheer playfulness; and a poet who can delight in such sonorous phrases as *swiðferhþes sið* (line 908a), *fylle gefægon, fægere geþægon* (line 1014), *suhtergefæderan . . . ætgædere* (line 1164), *flod blode weoll* (line 1422a),[46] *snyttru bryttað* (line 1726b), *guðum cuð* (line 2178a), *broðor oðerne* (line 2440a), *wordes ord breosthord* (lines 2791b–2792a), and *wordgyd wrecan ond ymb wer sprecan* (line 3173) is surely composing for the ear rather than the eye. The last three lines of the poem combine a number of these sub-verbal effects beautifully, and draw the poem to a fitting close (lines 3180–2):[47]

> cwædon þæt he wære   wyruldcyninga
> mannum mildust   ond monðwærust,
> leodum liðost   ond lofgeornost.

---

42 For a comparable passage, see below, p. 234.

43 See below, pp. 78–85.

44 See in general Stanley, 'Rhymes in English Medieval Verse: from Old English to Middle English'.

45 See further Berendsohn, *Zur Vorgeschichte des 'Beowulf'*, pp. 187–8, who, however, also includes a number of phrases where a single word is repeated. On the latter collocations, see below, pp. 78–9.

46 Cf. Cook, '*Beowulf* 1422'.

47 There are a number of textual difficulties with these lines: the manuscript clearly reads *wyruldcyning* at 3180b and only the first three and last three letters of *monðwærust* (line 3181b) are visible. A different kind of problem is presented by the final letter of *mannū* (= *mannum*) in line 3181a, long read (and translated) as an -*a*. Aesthetic reasons surely support reading *mannum* here, to provide a closer parallel to the following line; and surely the *Beowulf*-poet would not wish to vary the mighty *wyruldcyning* with the mundane *manna. On the difficulties of these lines, see further, for example, Clark, '*Beowulf*: the Last Word'; Cronan, '*Lofgeorn*: Generosity and Praise'; Deskis, 'An Addendum to Beowulf's Last Words'; Frank, 'Old Norse Memorial Eulogies and the Ending of *Beowulf*'; Harris, 'Beowulf's Last Words'; Malone, 'A Reading of *Beowulf* 3169–3182'; Mitchell, 'Linguistic Facts and the Interpretation of Old English Poetry', p. 12; Owen-Crocker, *The Four Funerals in 'Beowulf'*, pp. 103–5; Richards, 'A Reexamination of *Beowulf* ll. 3180–3182'; Riley, '*Beowulf*, Lines 3180-82'; Wieland, '*Manna mildost*: Moses and Beowulf'; Wright, 'Moses, *manna mildost* (*Exodus*, 550a)'.

[They said that he was of worldly kings the mildest to men and the most gracious, the kindest to nations, and the keenest for fame.]

The sound-play of *wær-*/*wyr-* and *man-*/*mon-* in the opening two lines of this passage gives way to double alliteration, end-rhyme, and precisely repeated rhythms in the last two. With such a range of sound-effects this essentially aural poem draws to a close.

The rhythmical effect found in the closing lines of the poem is all the more striking since such a use of repeated rhythms is in fact not very common in *Beowulf*, where the repetition of the same rhythm over successive lines seems rather to be used to delimit or highlight particular passages. The long lines that introduce the entrance of the stately Wealhtheow into Heorot after the trauma of the telling of the Finn-episode, for example, beautifully set off a self-contained vignette of the Danish court (lines 1162b–1168a):[48]

> þa cwom Wealhþeo forð
> gan under gyldnum beage,   þær þa godan twegen
> sæton suhtergefæderan;   þa gyt wæs hiera sib ætgædere,
> æghwylc oðrum trywe.   Swylce þær Unferþ þyle   1165
> æt fotum sæt frean Scyldinga;   gehwylc hiora his ferhþe treowde,
> þæt he hæfde mod micel,   þeah þe he his magum nære
> arfæst æt ecga gelacum.

[Then Wealhtheow came forth, striding under a golden diadem, where the goodly pair sat together, uncle and nephew; at that time their kinship was still intact, each true to the other. Likewise, Unferth the *þyle* sat there at the foot of the lord of the Scyldings; each of them trusted his spirit, that he had great courage, even though he was not merciful to his kinsmen at the play of swords.]

The significance of other clusters of long lines (at lines 1705–7 and 2995–6) is more difficult to assess;[49] the first comes in the middle of Hrothgar's so-called 'sermon',[50] while the second has recently been dismissed as a possible interpolation.[51] It is interesting to note that another passage in Hrothgar's sermon that relies on repeated rhythms and on anaphora has also been signalled as a possible interpolation (lines 1762b–1768):[52]

---

48 The manuscript reads *hun ferþ* at 1164b; the half-line 1166a recurs almost verbatim, following the whole line at line 500 (*þe æt fotum sæt frean Scyldinga*). For a fuller discussion of the narrative significance of these lines, see below, pp. 180–1 and 246–7. On the use of rhythm to set off sections of Old English verse, see, for example, Bartlett, *The Larger Rhetorical Patterns in Anglo-Saxon Poetry*, pp. 62–71.

49 According to Vickman, *A Metrical Concordance to 'Beowulf'*, p. 46, there are also isolated hypermetric half-lines at line 2173a (again referring to the necklace that Wealhtheow gives to Beowulf after the Finn-episode) and 2297a.

50 On which see more below, pp. 158–62.

51 Lapidge, 'The Archetype of *Beowulf*', pp. 37–8. A close parallel to line 2995a (*londes ond locenra beaga*) is found in *Andreas*, line 303a (*landes ne locenra beaga*), and is one of a number of verbal parallels which, it has been suggested, demonstrate direct borrowing from *Beowulf* by the *Andreas*-poet (on which see more below, pp. 163–6); if so (and if these lines are indeed an interpolation into *Beowulf*), such interpolation must have taken place *before* any putative borrowing could occur.

52 On the passage as a possible interpolation, see Lapidge, 'The Archetype of *Beowulf*', pp. 38–40.

Eft sona bið
þæt þec adl oððe ecg   eafoþes getwæfeð,
oððe fyres feng,   oððe flodes wylm,
oððe gripe meces,   oððe gares fliht,   1765
oððe atol yldo;   oððe eagena bearhtm
forsiteð ond forsworceð;   semninga bið
þæt ðec, dryhtguma,   dead oferswyðeð.

[Soon it will turn out that sickness or sword will separate you from your
strength, or the fire's embrace or the flood's surge, or the bite of a blade,
or the flight of a spear, or dreaded old age, or the brightness of your eyes
shall fail and grow dim; finally it shall be that death, noble warrior, shall
overpower you.]

Certainly, these lines have much in common with a number of Old English
homilies and sermons, which often use similar runs of repeated rhythmical
phrasing to highlight key passages,[53] and the effect seems deliberately chosen
here to underscore the different tone of what is being said at this point.
Beowulf's oath to Hrothgar to pursue Grendel's mother remorselessly may also
be of relevance here, since it relies on an apparently similar technique (lines
1392–4):

Ic hit þe gehate,   no he on helm losaþ,
ne on foldan fæþm,   ne on fyrgenholt,
ne on gyfenes grund,   ga þær he wille.

[I promise you: he shall not disappear under cover, neither in the bosom
of the earth, nor in the mountain wood, nor in the bottom of the sea,
wherever he goes.]

In this case, however, while biblical and Vergilian parallels have been
suggested,[54] the phrasing of this promise looks most similar to Norse formulas
dealing with the prosecution of outlaws, of which an excellent example is found
in the much later Icelandic *Grettis saga*,[55] a text which has been seen to contain
a number of parallels and analogues to *Beowulf*.[56] Such a parallel is the more
interesting since Grendel himself is not only of the kin of Cain,[57] but is depicted
(rather sympathetically) as something of an exile or outlaw:[58] once again, the

53 See further below, pp. 159–61.
54 Klaeber, *Beowulf*, p. 184.
55 Jónsson, ed., *Grettis saga*, pp. 232–3 (ch. 72); Fox and Pálsson, trans., *Grettir's saga*, p. 150.
56 See further below, pp. 124 and 142.
57 On Grendel as part of the kin of Cain see, for example, Bandy, 'Cain, Grendel, and the Giants of
    Beowulf'; Crawford, 'Grendel's Descent from Cain'; Donahue, 'Grendel and the *Clanna Cain*';
    Emerson, 'Legends of Cain, Especially in Old and Middle English'; Feldman, 'Grendel and Cain's
    Descendants'; Mellinkoff, 'Cain's Monstrous Progeny in *Beowulf*: Part I, Noachic Tradition'; *idem*,
    'Cain's Monstrous Progeny in *Beowulf*: Part II, Post-Diluvian Survival'; Orchard, *Pride and Prod-
    igies*, pp. 58–85; Peltola, 'Grendel's Descent from Cain Reconsidered'; Williams, *Cain and Beowulf:
    a Study in Secular Allegory*.
58 For a range of attitudes towards Grendel, see, for example, Andrew, 'Grendel in Hell'; Baird,
    'Grendel the Exile'; Bammesberger, 'In What Sense was Grendel an *angeng(e)a*?'; Britton, 'Unferth,
    Grendel and the Christian Meaning of *Beowulf*'; Chapman, 'Alas, Poor Grendel'; Florey, 'Grendel,
    Evil, "Allegory", and Dramatic Development in *Beowulf*'; Greenfield, 'The Formulaic Expression of
    the Theme of "Exile" in Anglo-Saxon Poetry'; Johansen, 'Grendel the Brave?'; Malmberg, 'Grendel

style of discourse seems specially tailored to fit the needs of the text. At all events, immediately following this vow, which might be seen as a purely rhetorical outburst, Beowulf is soon to take his pursuit literally underground, beneath mountain-forests, and on the sea-bed in his relentless search for Grendel's mother into her lair, which this promise neatly (if perhaps from Beowulf's own view, unintentionally) describes.[59]

Varying words: synonyms, compounds, and unique forms

The greatly varied manner in which Beowulf describes the monster-mere highlights another important aspect of the *Beowulf*-poet's technique, namely the sheer number of words, compounds, and coinages at his disposal. Several studies (especially by Caroline Brady) have demonstrated the ingenuity of the *Beowulf*-poet in this respect.[60] To discuss even such a commonplace concept (in this context) as 'sword', the poet could use a number of simple terms (such as *bil, brond, ecg, heoru, mece*, or *sweord*) offering a range of alliterative possibilities.[61] By the use of metonymy (for example, by using the word *iren* ['iron']) or by specifying a type of sword (such as a short-sword or *seax*), or by naming a specific weapon (such as Hrunting, Unferth's sword, or Nægling, used by Beowulf against the dragon), the poet could slightly increase his range of reference. But by compounding these simple words, he could add to the list the terms *beadomece, guðbil, guðsweord, hildebil, hildemece, wigbil*, all of which essentially mean 'battle-sword'; he could form other compounds based on these words to describe other attributes of the weapon, such as *ealdsweord* ('old sword'), *gomelswyrd* ('old sword'), *hæftmece* ('hilted sword'), *maðþumsweord* ('treasure-sword'), *wægsweord* ('wave-patterned sword'); he could describe a type of sword (such as *brogdenmæl, hringmæl, sceadenmæl*, or *wundenmæl*, all of which are varieties of damascened or otherwise adorned weapons); or he could introduce metaphor, and refer to a sword as a 'battle-light' (*beadoleoma* or *hildeleoma*) or a 'war-friend' (*guðwine*).[62] These last two examples are impor-

and the Devil'; Orchard, *Pride and Prodigies*, pp. 28–57; Storms, 'Grendel the Terrible'; Williams, 'The Exile as Uncreator'; Zachrisson, 'Grendel in *Beowulf*'. Particular mention should be made of John Gardner's novel, *Grendel*, which seeks to tell the story of *Beowulf* from the monster's point of view.

59 See, for example, Cornelius, 'Palus inamabilis'; Lawrence, 'The Haunted Mere in *Beowulf*'; *idem*, 'Grendel's Lair'; Malone, 'Grendel and his Abode'; Schrader, 'Sacred Groves, Marvellous Waters, and Grendel's Abode'.

60 See, for example, Brady, 'The Synonyms for "Sea" in *Beowulf*'; *idem*, ' "Weapons" in *Beowulf*'; *idem*, ' "Warriors" in *Beowulf*'. Useful general studies include Carr, *Nominal Compounds in Germanic*; Gardner, *Semantic Patterns in Old English Substantival Compounds*; Niles, 'Compound Diction and the Style of *Beowulf*'. More specific analyses are those by, for example, Bryan, '*Ærgod* in *Beowulf*, and other Old English Compounds of *ær*'; Hulbert, 'A Note on Compounds in *Beowulf*'; Magoun, 'Recurring First Elements in Different Nominal Compounds in *Beowulf* and the *Elder Edda*'; Mazo, 'Compound Diction and Traditional Style in *Beowulf* and *Genesis A*'; Menzer, '*Aglæcwif* (*Beowulf* 1259a): Implications for -*wif* Compounds, Grendel's Mother, and Other *aglæcan*'; Vickrey, 'On the *eorð*-Compounds in the Old English Finn-Stories'.

61 On the significance of swords in *Beowulf*, see below, pp. 76, 81–2, 135–6, and 198–9.

62 Such metaphorical compounds are customarily called 'kennings' after the Old Norse-Icelandic formulation. See further, for example, Gardner, 'The Application of the term "Kenning" '.

tant in underlining the flexibility of the *Beowulf*-poet's diction, since both *hildeleoma* and *guðwine* occur elsewhere in the poem in senses other than 'sword': if the poet apparently refers to the sword Hrunting as a 'war-friend' (*guðwine*) at line 1810a,[63] he certainly later refers to human warriors as 'war-friends' (*guðwinum*, line 2735a), and if a warrior can place a 'battle-light' (*hildeleoman*, line 1143b) that is also referred to as the 'best of swords' (*billa selest*, line 1144a) on Hengest's lap to stir him to vengeance, so too the dragon can attack Beowulf with a 'battle-light' (*hildeleoman*, line 2583a) that is also described as a 'murderous fire' (*wælfyre*, line 2582a). In the latter case, the poet is playing on a poetic commonplace: if a human warrior can wield a sword like a flame, then a dragon can surely wield a flame like a sword.[64]

To some extent, the creativity of the *Beowulf*-poet in forming compounds can likewise be seen simply with respect to those words based on words for 'war' or 'battle'; such forms are certainly frequent within the poem, and the degree to which the poet seems at pains to vary his precise choice of words is simply staggering. In creating such compounds, the poet makes use of a number of elements, including the common simplexes *wig* ('war', 'warfare'), *hild* ('war', 'battle'), *guð* ('war', 'battle'), and *beadu* ('battle', 'fighting'), of which the last three words are only attested in verse, as well as the compounding element *heaðo*- ('battle', 'war'), which is never found as a simplex, and is (apart from a handful of names) entirely restricted to verse. Yet from these five simple mainly poetic elements, the *Beowulf*-poet creates a huge variety of noun- and adjective-compounds, the great majority of which are not witnessed outside the poem in any surviving Old English texts. Such words, often termed *hapax legomena* (from the Greek; literally 'those [words] which are said once'), were evidently an important part of the *Beowulf*-poet's creative technique.[65] A complete list of noun- and adjective compounds in *Beowulf* generated from these five compounding elements alone would run as follows (an asterisk indicates *hapax legomena*):

> *beadogrima* ('battle-mask', line 2257a), *beadohrægl* ('battle-garment', line 552a), *beadoleoma* ('battle-light', line 1523a), *beadomece* ('battle-sword', line 1454a), *beadufolm* ('battle-hand', line 990a), *beadulac* ('battle-play', line 1561a), *beadorinc* ('battle-warrior', line 1109a), *beadurof* ('battle-bold', line 3160a), *beadurun* ('battle-rune', line 501a), *beaduscearp* ('battle-sharp', line 2704a), *beaduscrud* ('battle-clothing', lines 453a and 2660a), *beaduserce* ('battle-coat', line 2755a); *guðbeorn*

---

63 For a discussion of the word in context, see below, pp. 75–6; it is possible that the poet deliberately chooses the word to refer ambiguously to either Unferth or his sword.

64 That the kenning 'battle-flame' for sword is part of the inherited Germanic poetic tradition seems attested by the existence of parallel compounds such as *gunnlogi* in Norse. Cf. Egilssson, *Lexicon Poeticum*, p. 209.

65 Some critics interpret the term *hapax legomena* (the singular form is *hapax legomenon*) strictly, and only employ it to refer to words attested only once in the extant corpus. Such a usage, while undoubtedly correct, would of course obscure a poet's repeated use of his own unique coinage for literary effect. So, for example, Lucas, ed., *Exodus*, marks only those words unique in the corpus, while Irving, ed., *Exodus*, marks for particular interest those words which only appear in *Exodus*. Thus Irving highlights (for example) *meredeað* ('sea-death': *Exodus*, lines 465a and 513b) and *sigerice* ('victory-realm': *Exodus*, lines 27a and 563a), while Lucas does not.

('war-warrior', line 314b), *guðbill* ('war-blade', lines 803a and 2584b), **guðbyrne* ('war-corselet', line 321b), **guðcearu* ('war-care', line 1258a), **guðcræft* ('war-skill', line 127a), *guðcyning* ('war-king', lines 199b, 1969a, 2563a, and 2677b), **guðdeað* ('war-death', line 2249b), **guðfloga* ('war-flier', line 2528a), *guðfreca* ('war-combatant', line 2414a), *guðfremmende* ('war-protagonist', line 246a), **guðgeatwa* ('war-gear', lines 395b and 2636a), **guðgewæde* ('war-dress', lines 227a, 2617b, 2623b, 2730a, 2851a, and 2871b), **guðgeweorc* ('war-deed', lines 678a, 981b, and 1825a), **guðhelm* ('war-helmet', line 2487a), **guðhorn* ('war-horn', line 1432a), **guðhreð* ('war-glory', line 819a), **guðleoð* ('war-song', line 1522a), **guþmod* ('war-minded', line 306a), **guðreow* ('war-fierce', line 58a), *guðræs* ('war-rush', lines 1577b, 2426b, and 2991a), *guðrinc* ('war-warrior', lines 838b, 1118b, 1501b, 1881a, and 2648a), *guðrof* ('war-bold', line 608a), **guðsceaða* ('war-ravager', line 2318a), **guðscear* ('war-carnage', line 1213a), *guðsearo* ('war-accoutrements', line 328a), **guðsweord* ('war-sword', line 2154a), **guðwerig* ('war-weary', line 1586a), **guðwiga* ('war-fighter', line 2112a), **guðwine* ('war-friend', line 1810a and 2735a); *heaðobyrne* ('battle-byrnie', line 1552a), **heaþodeor* ('battle-brave', line 772a), **heaðofyr* ('battle-fire', lines 2522a and 2547a), *heaðogrim* ('battle-grim', lines 548a and 2691a), *heaþoliþende* ('battle-sailor', lines 1798a and 2955a), **heaðolac* ('battle-play', lines 584a and 1974a), **heaðomære* ('battle-famed', line 2802a), **heaðoræs* ('battle-rush', lines 526a, 557b, and 1047b), **heaðoreaf* ('battle-plunder', line 401a), *heaðorinc* ('battle-warrior', lines 370a and 2466a), *heaþorof* ('battle-bold', lines 391a, 864a, and 2191a), **heaðoscearp* ('battle-sharp', line 2829a), **heaðosioc* ('battle-wounded', line 2754a), **heaðosteap* ('battle-towering', lines 1245a and 2153a), **heaðoswat* ('battle-blood', lines 1460a, 1606a, and 1668a), **heaðusweng* ('battle-stroke', line 2581a), **heaðotorht* ('battle-clear', line 2553a), **heaðowæd* ('battle-dress', line 39b), **heaðoweorc* ('battle-work', line 2892a), *heaðowylm* ('battle-surge', line 82b and 2819a); **hildebill* ('battle-blade', lines 557a, 1520a, 1666b, and 2679a), **hildebord* ('battle-shield', lines 397a and 3139b), **hildecumbor* ('battle-banner', line 1022a), **hildecyst* ('battle-virtue', line 2598a), *hildedeor* ('battle-brave', lines 312a, 834a, 1646a, 1816a, 2107a, 2183a, 3111a, and 3169b), *hild(e)freca* ('battle-combatant', lines 2366a and 2205b), *hildfruma* ('battle-chief', lines 1678a, 2649a, and 2835a), *hildlata* ('battle-sluggish', line 2846a), **hildegeatwe* ('battle-equipment', lines 674b and 2362a), **hildegicel* ('battle-icicle', line 1606b), **hildegrap* ('battle-grasp', line 1446a and 2507a), **hildehlæmm* ('battle-crash', lines 2201a, 2351a, and 2544a), **hildeleoma* ('battle-light', lines 1143b and 2583a), **hildemece* ('battle-sword', line 2202b), **hildemecg* ('battle-fighter', line 799b), **hilderæs* ('battle-rush', line 300a), **hilderand* ('battle-shield', line 1242b), *hilderinc* ('battle-warrior', lines 39a, 57a, 169a, 986a, 1307a, 1495a, 1576a, 3124a, and 3136a), **hildesceorp* ('battle-armour', line 2155a), **hildesetl* ('battle-seat', line 1039a), **hildestrengo* ('battle-strength', line 2113a), **hildeswat* ('battle-blood', line 2558a), **hildetux* ('battle-tusk', line 1511a), **hildewæpen* ('battle-weapon', line 39a), **hildewisa* ('battle-leader', line

1064b); *wigbealu ('war-harm', line 2046a), *wigbill ('war-blade', line 1607a), wigbord ('war-shield', line 2339a), wigcræft ('war-skill', line 2953a), *wigcræftig ('war-strong', line 1811a), *wigfreca ('war-combatant', lines 1212a and 2496a), *wigfruma ('war-chief', lines 664a and 2261a), *wiggetawa ('war-gear', line 368a), wiggeweorþad ('war-distinguished', line 1783a), *wiggryre ('war-terror', line 1284a), *wigheafola ('war-peak', line 2661b), *wigheap ('war-band', line 477a), *wighete ('war-hatred', line 2120a), *wighryre ('war-fall', line 1619a), wigsigor ('war-victory', line 1554a), wigsped ('war-success', line 697a).

That these five compounding elements should between them generate 103 distinct compounds in *Beowulf* is striking enough; that no fewer than seventy-five of those 103 compounds should be unattested outside the poem is surely some index of the *Beowulf*-poet's creativity. Moreover, in producing these 103 compounds, the five initial elements combine with as many as seventy-eight different final elements, with relatively little overlap;[66] by such raw measurements is the originality and ingenuity of the *Beowulf*-poet made plain.

Yet even as we celebrate and appreciate the sheer extent of the *Beowulf*-poet's 'word-hoard', we should acknowledge that not all of the diction can be described as brilliant: the hard practicalities of alliterative composition also give rise to a significant number of tautologous compounds and phrases: while we may applaud the *Beowulf*-poet's ingenuity, it is perhaps only the blinkered eye of faith that can see clear poetic merit in such compounds as *healærn* (line 78a) or *healreced* (lines 68a and [by emendation] 1981a),[67] which although unique to *Beowulf* in the surviving corpus appear to mean merely 'hall-hall'. One might perhaps find more to admire in the sheer creative range of 'treasure-treasure' compounds in *Beowulf*, including *hordmaðum* (line 1198a), *maþmgestreon* (line 1931a), *sincmaþum* (line 2193a), and *sincgestreon* (lines 1092b and 1226a).[68] It would be dangerous, moreover, to dismiss entirely the creative possibilities of such apparently tautologous compounds: the term 'wood-wood' (*holtwudu*) is found at line 1369b to mean 'forest', but at line 2340a to mean '(wooden) shield'. At the very least, we can surely claim that even in his deployment of the basic principle of repetition, the usage of the *Beowulf*-poet is truly varied.

---

66 Overlap occurs in the following cases: *guðbill*, *hildebill*, and *wigbill*; *hildebord* and *wigbord*; *heaþobyrne* and *guðbyrne*; *guðcræft* and *wigcræft*; *heaðodeor* and *hildedeor*; *guðfreca*, *hild(e)freca*, and *wigfreca*; *hildfruma* and *wigfruma*; *guðgeatwa*, *hildegeatwe*, and *wiggetawa* (taking the second elements as identical); *beadolac* and *heaðolac*; *beadoleoma* and *hildeleoma*; *beadumece* and *hildemece*; *guðræs*, *heaðoræs*, and *hilderæs*; *beadurinc*, *guðrinc*, *heaþorinc*, and *hilderinc*; *beadurof*, *guðrof*, and *heaðorof*; *beaduscearp* and *heaðoscearp* (taking the second elements as identical; in fact the manuscript reads *heaðoscearde*); *hildeswat* and *heaðuswat*; *guðgeweorc* and *heaðoweorc* (taking the second elements as identical).

67 The manuscript originally read *reced* at line 1981a, with *side* added above the line by the B-scribe. But the line is short without *side*, and alliteratively defective with it, hence the emendation. For a spirited defence of the corrected manuscript-reading, both here and elsewhere in the text, see Kiernan, *'Beowulf' and the Beowulf Manuscript*, pp. 206–11.

68 A similarly tautologous phrase is 'day-tally of days' (*dogera dægrim*, line 823a); for a useful list of what he describes as *Doppelformen* ('double forms'), see Berendsohn, *Zur Vorgeschichte des 'Beowulf'*, pp. 186–7.

Trading words: variation, wordplay, and other verbal effects

In producing such compounds, whether tautologous or not, the *Beowulf*-poet is effectively offering a number of snap-shots or perspectives both simultaneously and in sequence, and allowing the audience the chance to savour (or not) the multiplicity of meanings offered.[69] This technique, commonly described as 'variation', is attested widely in surviving Old English verse, but its use has been noted (and studied) most fully in *Beowulf*.[70] An extensive example of such variation occurs the first time that Wiglaf is introduced, when he is effectively characterised no fewer than five times in swift succession (lines 2602–5):

> Wiglaf wæs haten   Weoxstanes sunu,
> leoflic lindwiga,   leod Scylfinga,
> mæg Ælfheres;   geseah his mondryhten
> under heregriman   hat þrowian.   2605

> [He was called Wiglaf, Weohstan's son, a dear shield-warrior, a prince of the Scylfings, Ælfhere's kinsman; he saw his lord suffering heat under the battle-helmet.]

Such a portentous introduction undoubtedly fits Wiglaf's importance as a central figure in the last six hundred lines of the poem, but it is perhaps worth pausing to consider how much information is actually imparted here: this is the first time that Wiglaf, Weohstan, or Ælfhere have been mentioned at all, and the last-named is never mentioned again. A similarly impressive tally of epithets is used by Hrothgar, lamenting the death of his trusted companion Æschere at the hands of Grendel's mother (lines 1323b–8a):

> 'Dead is Æschere,
> Yrmenlafes   yldra broþor,
> min runwita   ond min rædbora,   1325
> eaxlgestealla,   ðonne we on orlege
> hafelan weredon,   þonne hniton feþan,
> eoferas cnysedan.'

> ['Æschere is dead, Yrmenlaf's elder brother, my close confidant and my counsel-giver, my shoulder-companion when in battle we protected our heads as footsoldiers clashed, struck boar-helmets.']

Again, we note that Æschere is characterised with respect to a figure who never appears in the poem again,[71] before being described in three parallel terms (*runwita*, *rædbora*, and *eaxlgestealla*) that apparently link him with the 'thought, word, and deed' theme that is found elsewhere in the poem.[72] As with

---

[69] See further below, pp. 240–56.
[70] The classic studies remain those of Brodeur, *The Art of 'Beowulf'*, pp. 39–70, and Robinson, *'Beowulf' and the Appositive Style*. See too Berendsohn, *Zur Vorgeschichte des 'Beowulf'*, pp. 181–6; McTurk, 'Variation in *Beowulf* and the Poetic *Edda*: a Chronological Experiment'; O'Brien O'Keeffe, 'Diction, Variation, and the Formula'; Robinson, 'Variation: a Study in the Diction of *Beowulf*'; *idem*, 'Two Aspects of Variation in Old English Poetry'.
[71] On the mysterious Yrmenlaf, see further below, p. 169.
[72] See below, pp. 146, 218, and 255.

the introduction to Wiglaf, the sense is very much one of variation being used for purely rhetorical effect, to focus attention on a particular figure or scene.

In this context, one might consider what is evidently a set-piece description in the poem, as Beowulf's sea-voyage to Denmark is carefully depicted (lines 210–28):[73]

Fyrst forð gewat. Flota wæs on yðum,		210
bat under beorge. Beornas gearwe		
on stefn stigon; streamas wundon,		
sund wið sande; secgas bæron		
on bearm nacan beorhte frætwe,		
guðsearo geatolic; guman ut scufon,		215
weras on wilsið, wudu bundenne.		
Gewat þa ofer wægholm, winde gefysed,		
flota famiheals fugle gelicost,		
oðþæt ymb antid oþres dogores		
wundenstefna gewaden hæfde		220
þæt ða liðende land gesawon,		
brimclifu blican, beorgas steape,		
side sænæssas; þa wæs sund liden,		
eoletes æt ende. Þanon up hraðe		
Wedera leode on wang stigon,		225
sæwudu sældon (syrcan hyrsedon,		
guðgewædo), gode þancedon		
þæs þe him yþlade eaðe wurdon.		

[Time passed on; the vessel was on the waves, the boat beneath the headland. Warriors eagerly embarked by the prow – the tides eddied, the stream against the sand; the men bore into the bosom of the craft bright ornaments, splendid war-gear; the lads shoved out the braced timbers, men on a longed-for trip. Then there passed over the wavy sea, driven by the wind, the foamy-necked vessel, most like a bird, until in due time on the next day the braced prow had travelled so that the sailors saw land, sea cliffs glistening, steep headlands, broad promontories; then the passage was crossed, at the end of the watery way. From there swiftly the people of the Weder-Geats disembarked on land, made fast the sea-timbers – mail-coats rang, battle-dress; they gave thanks to God that their sea-voyage had been easy.]

The sheer variation in language here is striking. The passage contains a rich array of between six and eight synonyms for each of the four key concepts (poetic usages are indicated with an asterisk): men (*beornas* * . . . *secgas* * . . . *guman* * . . . *weras* . . . *liðende* . . . . *Wedera leode* *), ship (*flota* . . . *bat* . . . *stefn* . . . *nacan* * . . . *wudu bundenne* * . . . *flota* . . . *wundenstefna* * . . . *sæwudu* *), sea (*yðum* . . . *streamas* * . . . *sund* * . . . *wægholm* * . . . *sund* * . . . *eoletes* *), and land (*under beorge* . . . *sande* . . . *land* . . . *brimclifu* * . . . *beorgas* . . . *sænessas* * . . .

[73] On this and a related passage later in the poem, see, for example, Ramsey, 'The Sea Voyages in *Beowulf*'. Cf. Cook, 'Beowulfian and Odyssean Voyages'; Fry, 'Launching Ships in *Beowulf* 210–216 and *Brunanburh* 32b–36'; Greenfield, '*Beowulf* 207b–228: Narrative and Descriptive Art'.

wang).[74] All but one of the compounds in the preceding list are unique to *Beowulf*.[75] The sound of sea against sand is surely imitated in the assonance of *wundon sund wið sande* (lines 212b–13a), and the same combination of sounds echo throughout the rest of the passage until the sea-voyage is over (*bundenne . . . winde . . . wundenstefna . . . liðende . . . . land . . . sund . . . ende*). Another example of assonance (*beorge . . . beornas . . . bæron . . . bearm . . . beorhte*) effectively delimits and characterises precisely those lines which deal with the preparations for the voyage (lines 211–14), and the poet underlines the integrity of these verses by providing four consecutive b-lines with exactly the same metre (*Beornas gearwe, streamas wundon, secgas bæron,* and *beorhte frætwe*).[76] The voyage proper begins at line 216, indicated by the repetition of *gewat* (lines 210 and 216) and *flota* (lines 210 and 217) from the beginning of the passage, and the whole section ends at the disembarkation with a series of four consecutive b-lines ending with a third-person plural preterite verb (lines 225–8: *stigon . . . hrysedon . . . þancedon . . . wurdon*), and an example of paronomasia or wordplay (*yþ-/ eað-*, line 228). In such passages the poet's careful craft is manifest.

Similarly close attention to phrasing at even the most apparently mundane parts of the poem demonstrate the high artistry that the *Beowulf*-poet is able to bring to bear. So, for example, before departing from Denmark after killing Grendel's mother, Beowulf apparently hands back Hrunting (the sword which had failed him) to its owner, Unferth, in a manner described with great ceremony (lines 1807–12):[77]

Heht þa se hearda   Hrunting beran
sunu Ecglafes,   heht his sweord niman,
leoflic iren;   sægde him þæs leanes þanc,
cwæð, he þone guðwine   godne tealde,   1810
wigcræftigne,   nales wordum log
meces ecge;   þæt wæs modig secg.

[Then the hardened warrior ordered Hrunting to be carried to the son of Ecglaf, bid him take his sword, the precious blade; he said thanks to him for the loan, said that he reckoned it [or 'him'] a good friend in conflict, strong in battle. In no way did he decry in words the weapon's edge: that was a brave man.]

---

74   See further the comments of Tolkien in Clark Hall, trans., *Beowulf*, pp. xxxviii–xlii. See too Evans, 'The Sequence of Events in *Beowulf*, ll. 207–16'.

75   The exception is *sæness*, found twice in two separate Aldhelm-glossaries (Goossens, ed., *The Old English Glosses of MS. Brussels, Royal Library 1650*, no. 654; Napier, ed., *Old English Glosses*, 1.577), glossing Latin *promontorio* (alternatively spelt *promunctorio*).

76   On the artful use of repeated metre, see, for example, Scragg, 'The Nature of Old English Verse'; cf. above, pp. 66–9.

77   Assuming that *leanes* (line 1809b) is a variant spelling of *lænes*. The alternative, favoured by (for example) Jack, *Beowulf*, p. 134, that here Unferth is presenting Hrunting (which has been quietly returned to him in the interim) to Beowulf seems somewhat strained, and requires *se hearda . . . sunu Ecglafes* to be read together; by contrast, *se hearda* is certainly used alone of Beowulf, at lines 401b and 1963a.

The formalism of this passage, with its anaphora (*Heht . . . heht*), near-rhyme (*ecge . . . secg*), and final closing formula (*þæt wæs modig secg*),[78] certainly highlights the remarkable reconciliation that has taken place between Beowulf and his sometime detractor:[79] the delicious ambiguity of whether it is Unferth or his sword that is reckoned by Beowulf a 'good friend in conflict, strong in battle' (*guðwine godne . . . wigcræftigne*, lines 1810–11) underlines Beowulf's own generosity, since whilst he knows that both Unferth and Hrunting ultimately failed against Grendel and his mother, nonetheless they are not utterly disgraced. The blurring of the images of swords and men is beautifully encapsulated by the choice of the word *secg* (which the poet uses both to mean 'man', as here, and 'sword' [line 864a]), the pairing of swords and men across the caesura in line 1812, and (especially) the reinforcing soundplay in the same line (*meces ecge . . . secg*).[80]

Wordplay and localised sound-effects are the *Beowulf*-poet's stock-in-trade, and again emphasise the extent to which the poem is essentially aural in nature, and deserves to be heard.[81] Again, even a relatively short transitional section of the poem, such as when he describes the end of the anonymous messenger's speech to the Geats, predicting their dire fate, before they all travel to the headland to view their dead king and the dragon together (lines 3028–30a):

> Swa se secg hwata   secggende wæs
> laðra spella;   he ne leag fela
> wyrda ne worda.   Weorod eall aras.
>
> [Thus the brave man was speaking of hateful tidings; nor did he overstate the deeds or words. The whole troop rose.]

Beginning with wordplay (*secg . . . secggende*),[82] continuing with a series of words apparently picked in part for their shared ending (*hwata . . . laðra spella . . . fela wyrda ne worda*), the poet focuses on one of his main themes, namely the difference between words and deeds,[83] again through the mechanism of wordplay or paronomasia (*wyrda ne worda weorod*), as well as through the structure of the whole passage, which moves from one to the other. The final self-contained half-line of the passage is perhaps intended to recall other earlier such formulations, notably *Werod eall aras* (line 651b) and *Duguð eal aras* (line 1790b); in both cases, the phrase occurs (as here) immediately after a description of feasting. In this case, however, the feasting is not *of* humans, but *on* humans: the messenger has been describing the carnage that will be the lot of the hapless Geats. The second of these occurrences of the phrase occurs after

---

78 The most common related closing formula is of course 'that was a good king' (*þæt wæs god cyning*, lines 11b, 863b, and 2390b).
79 On the verbal conflict between Unferth and Beowulf, see below, pp. 246–55.
80 For the phrase *meces ecge* as a possible pun on *mece secge*, see below, pp. 185–6 and 240–1.
81 A sometimes fanciful set of perceived aural puns is given by Tripp, 'Humor, Wordplay, and Semantic Resonance in *Beowulf*'. Cf. *idem*, *Literary Essays on Language and Meaning in the Poem Called 'Beowulf'*.
82 For a similar kind of wordplay in consecutive half-lines, compare (for example) *gehyrde . . . hyrde* (lines 609b–10a).
83 On the poet's repeated interest on the difference between words and deeds, see below, pp. 204–37.

the end of Hrothgar's sermon, when the poet simply offers a thumbnail sketch of a feast, apparently expecting his audience to fill in the blanks (as it were) based on his own previous descriptions (lines 1787–92a):

> Þa wæs eft swa ær   ellenrofum
> fletsittendum   fægere gereorded
> niowan stefne.   Nihthelm geswearc
> deorc ofer dryhtgumum.   Duguð eal aras.   1790
> Wolde blondenfeax   beddes neosan,
> gamela Scylding.

> [Then again as before a feast was finely prepared for the courageous ones sitting in hall, on a new occasion. The shadow of night grew dark over the noble warriors; the whole troop rose. The grey-haired one, the aged Scylding, wanted to go to bed.]

It seems possible that the poet is punning here on two semantically related sets of homonyms: *gereordian*, 'to prepare a feast' (as in *fægere gereorded*, line 1788b), and *reord*, 'speech', 'voice' (as in line 2555a), *reordian*, 'speak', 'talk' (as in line 3025); *stefn*, 'period', 'time' (as in *niowan stefne*, line 1789a), and *stefn*, 'voice' (as in 2552b). If such a pun is accepted, the poet seems to be supporting the notion that after Hrothgar's sombre speech there is a complete change of tone. The poet states that the feasting until Hrothgar goes to bed occured 'again as before' (*Þa wæs eft swa ær*, line 1787a), and indeed the phrase itself occurs in a precisely similar situation, in the context of the initial feast of welcome that greets Beowulf's arrival (*Þa wæs eft swa ær*, line 642a). Other similarities of diction and image between the latter two passages only confirm the parallel: in both cases there is gleeful celebration (*ðeod on sælum, sigefolca sweg*, lines 643b–44a; *fægere gereorded, niowan stefne*, lines 1788b–89a), before night falls (*nipende niht ofer ealle, / scaduhelma gesceapu scriðan cwoman*, lines 649–50; *Nihthelm geswearc, / deorc ofer dryhtguman*, lines 1789b–90a), when the assembled company arise (*Werod eall aras*, line 651b; *Duguð eal aras*, line 1790b), and Hrothgar goes to bed (*sunu Healfdenes secean wolde æfenreste*, line 646b; *Wolde blondenfeax beddes neosan, / gamela Scylding*, lines 1791–2a).

The poet apparently draws attention to the parallels between these two scenes of feasting only to emphasise the differences: in the first case the onset of night introduces the approach of Grendel; whilst here an evil outcome, though signalled, is averted. We are told that Beowulf slept 'until a dark raven, glad-hearted, announced heaven's joy' (*oþþæt hrefn blaca heofones wynne bliðheort bodode*, lines 1801–2a). The chiastic alliteration that links the 'dark raven' with its description as 'glad-hearted' is striking (*hrefn blaca . . . bliðheort*, lines 1801a and 1802a), and surely hints at artifice.[84] The poet seems to be toying with the audience's expectations of still more grief to come, as previ-

---

[84] On the unusual appearance of the raven here, see, for example, Damon, 'The Raven in *Beowulf* 1801'; Horowitz, 'The Ravens in *Beowulf*'; Hume, 'The Function of the *hrefn blaca*: *Beowulf* 1801'; Lapidge, '*Beowulf* and Perception', pp. 64–7; Puhvel, 'The Blithe-Hearted Morning Raven in *Beowulf*'.

ously: after all, as the poet has already said himself: 'Then there was after the feasting the commencement of weeping, a great sound in the morning' (*Þa wæs æfter wiste wop up ahafen, micel morgensweg*, lines 129–30a). Later in the poem the messenger of the Geats predicts a similarly ominous outcome (lines 3021b–7):

> Forðon sceall gar wesan
> monig morgenceald   mundum bewunden,
> hæfen on handa,   nalles hearpan sweg
> wigend weccean,   ac se wonna hrefn
> fus ofer fægum   fela reordian,   3025
> earne secgan   hu him æt æte speow,
> þenden he wið wulf   wæl reafode.

[For there shall be many a spear, cold with chill of morning, grasped in the fist, held in the hand: no sound of harp shall rouse the warrior, but the dark raven eager above the doomed shall say much, tell the eagle how things went at the feasting, when he plundered the slain with the wolf.]

Here again, just as before, ravens unequivocally betoken grief. Such a grim prospect does not, however, face the departing Beowulf, as he takes his leave of the Danes twelve hundred lines earlier: instead we see how the poet has subverted expectations through the clever use of verbal repetition as a device to associate quite disparate parts of his poem.

Parallels and echoes: incremental repetition and the envelope pattern

It will be clear from the above discussion that, as with alliteration, assonance, rhyme, and other sound-patterning, the *Beowulf*-poet uses the technique of repeating particular words and phrases both as a structural and as an ornamental device. Successive studies of the repetition of individual words within passages have underlined the extent to which the use of such 'echo-words' can help to 'generate composition', effectively aiding the poet in the making of his poem.[85] But repeated words and phrases are also used to 'bracket off' discrete sections of the narrative into self-contained units. So, for example, Grendel's advance on Heorot is delimited by a threefold repetition of the the word *com* ('he came'), as the monster approaches closer and closer, from out of the dark night, from off the moor, and right up to the building itself (*Com on wanre niht . . . Ða com of more . . . Com þa to recede*);[86] the term 'incremental repetition' has been coined to describe such an effect, which is widespread in medieval texts.[87] Likewise,

---

[85] I use these terms following the important articles by Beaty, 'The Echo-Word in *Beowulf*', and Rosier, 'Generative Composition in *Beowulf*'. See too Battles, 'The Art of the Scop', pp. 168–240; Gardner, 'How Free Was the *Beowulf* Poet?'; *idem*, 'Compositional Techniques of the Beowulf Poet'. The technique is also employed by Anglo-Saxon poets composing in Latin: see, for example, Orchard, 'Wish you were here: Alcuin's Courtly Verse and the Boys Back Home', pp. 39–41.

[86] For further discussion of this central scene, see further below, pp. 189–91.

[87] See further n. 10 above.

the whole episode of Sigemund and Heremod (lines 867b–915) is bracketed off by incremental repetition describing the warriors joyfully racing their horses back from the monster-mere, happy in the belief that Grendel is dead (lines 864–7a and 916–17a):

> Hwilum heaþorofe   hleapan leton,
> on geflit faran   fealwe mearas
> ðær him foldwegas   fægere þuhton,
> cystum cuðe.
> . . .
> Hwilum flitende   fealwe stræte
> mearum mæton.
>
> [At times the battle-brave ones let their pale horses gallop, contend in races where the tracks seemed good to them, noted for fine qualities . . . At times contending they raced with their horses along the pale paths.]

By contrast, the return of this triumphant party back to Heorot from the monster-mere is marked by an ebullient speech from Hrothgar that immediately follows, beginning and ending with parallel invocations to God in a clear envelope pattern (lines 928–9b and 955b–6):

> Ðisse ansyne   Alwealdan þanc
> lungre gelimpe!
> . . .
>   Alwalda þec
> gode forgylde,   swa he nu gyt dyde!
>
> [For this sight may thanks go immediately to the all-powerful . . . may the all-powerful repay you with good, as he has done up till now.]

The beginning of the rest of Hrothgar's speech is, moreover, chiefly notable for ornamental alliteration on *w-*, which appears in six of the following nine lines (lines 930b–939a):[88]

> | a mæg god wyrcan | 930 |
> | --- | --- |
> | wunder æfter wundre,   wuldres hyrde. | |
> | Þæt wæs ungeara   þæt ic ænigra me | |
> | weana ne wende   to widan feore | |
> | bote gebidan,   þonne blode fah | |
> | husa selest   heorodreorig stod, | 935 |
> | wea widscofen   witena gehwylcum | |
> | ðara þe ne wendon   þæt hie wideferhð | |
> | leoda landgeweorc   laþum beweredon | |
> | scuccum ond scinnum. | |

---

[88] The manuscript reads *gehwylcne* at 936b, but cannot be so construed. Note how the alliteration in this passage is supported by the repeated phrasing (*ne wende . . . to widan feore*, line 933; *ne wendon . . . þæt hie wideferhð*, line 937), so aligning Hrothgar with his own wise counsellors. It is worth pointing out that Beowulf's reply is equally decorous: four out of six lines in his answer contain alliteration on *f-* (lines 968–73).

[Ever may God work wonder after wonder, master of glory. It was only recently that I did not ever expect to experience any end to my woes, when the best of houses stood stained with blood, dripping with gore, an all-embracing woe for each of the wise men who never expected that they should defend the stronghold of the people from hostile demons and wicked spirits.]

Such a combination of aural effects, both structural and ornamental, within a relatively short space of text is testimony to the range of techniques available to the *Beowulf*-poet at any one time.

A further example of how the envelope-pattern can be used to mark off a set-piece scene comes in the poet's account of Beowulf's preparations to fight Grendel's mother. Of all the elaborate descriptions in the poem, this arming-scene (which brings fitt XXI to an end) is perhaps closest in scale to what one finds in Classical epic (lines 1441b–1472):[89]

Gyrede hine Beowulf		
eorlgewædum,	nalles for ealdre mearn.	
Scolde herebyrne	hondum gebroden,	
sid ond searofah,	sund cunnian,	
seo ðe bancofan	beorgan cuþe,	1445
þæt him hildegrap	hreþre ne mihte,	
eorres inwitfeng,	aldre gesceþðan;	
ac se hwita helm	hafelan werede,	
se þe meregrundas	mengan scolde,	
secan sundgebland	since geweorðad,	1450
befongen freawrasnum,	swa hine fyrndagum	
worhte wæpna smið,	wundrum teode,	
besette swinlicum,	þæt hine syðþan no	
brond ne beadomecas	bitan ne meahton.	
Næs þæt þonne mætost	mægenfultuma	1455
þæt him on ðearfe lah	ðyle Hroðgares;	
wæs þæm hæftmece	Hrunting nama.	
þæt wæs an foran	ealdgestreona;	
ecg wæs iren,	atertanum fah,	
ahyrded heaþoswate;	næfre hit æt hilde ne swac	1460
manna ængum	þara þe hit mid mundum bewand,	
se ðe gryresiðas	gegan dorste,	
folcstede fara;	næs þæt forma sið	
þæt hit ellenweorc	æfnan scolde.	
Huru ne gemunde	mago Ecglafes,	1465
eafoþes cræftig,	þæt he ær gespræc	
wine druncen,	þa he þæs wæpnes onlah	
selran sweordfrecan.	Selfa ne dorste	
under yða gewin	aldre geneþan,	
drihtscype dreogan;	þær he dome forleas,	1470

---

[89] On the relationship of such self-contained sequences to the fitt-structure of the poem, see below, pp. 91–7.

ellenmærðum.   Ne wæs þæm oðrum swa,
syðþan he hine to guðe   gegyred hæfde.

[Beowulf dressed himself in warrior's garb; he did not care for his life.
The war-corselet, woven by hand, broad and cunningly decorated, had
to test the water, the one that was able to protect his body so that hostile
grasp, the wicked grip of an angry foe should not harm his heart, his
life; but the bright helmet, which had to mingle with the bottom of the
mere, seek the surging water, guarded his head, adorned with gold,
encircled with lordly bands, just as in ancient days a weapon-smith had
made it, formed it marvellously, set it round with boar-images, so that
afterwards no sword or battle-blade could bite it. That was not the least
of powerful aids that Hrothgar's *þyle* lent him in his need: the name of
that hilted sword was Hrunting; that was one of the foremost of ancient
treasures: its edge was iron, gleaming with venom-twigs, hardened by
battle-blood; it had never failed in battle any man who grasped it in his
hand, who dared enter on dangerous deeds, the meeting-place of foes;
that was not the first time that it had to perform a courageous act.
Indeed, the son of Ecglaf, mighty in strength, did not recall what he had
previously said, drunk with wine, when he lent that weapon to a better
swordsman. He himself did not dare to risk his life under the turmoil of
the waves, perform a heroic deed; for that he lost his glory, his fame for
courage. It was not so for the other man, once he had dressed himself for
battle.]

The whole description is enclosed in an envelope-pattern (*Gyrede . . . gegyred*),
and begins with an approving glance at Beowulf's insouciance – 'he did not care
for his life' (*nalles for ealdre mearn*, line 1442b) – that the poet is shortly to
connect with great deeds of derring-do (lines 1534b–1536, emphasis added):

> Swa sceal man don,
> þonne he æt guðe   gegan þenceð   1535
> longsumne lof,   *na ymb his lif cearað.*

[So must a man do when he thinks to gain in battle long-lasting fame: he
will have no care for his life.]

In his description of Beowulf's preparations for the fight, the poet focuses carefully in turn on his mail-coat (lines 1443–7), his helmet (lines 1448–54), and his
(borrowed) sword (lines 1455–64).[90] As commonly in such epic lists of three,
attention is focused on the first and last items, namely the mailcoat, which plays
a crucial role in getting Beowulf to the bottom of the mere, and on the sword,
which becomes a focal point in the actual conflict. The increasing length of the
descriptions of the three items again underlines the importance of the sword,
and highlights the role played by its lender, Unferth;[91] in a characteristically
loaded echo, the poet stresses that he himself did not dare 'to risk his life under
the turmoil of the waves' (*under yða gewin aldre geneþan*, line 1469), so
evidently recalling Unferth's earlier taunt to Beowulf about the time when he

---

[90] Cf. the discussion of Clark, 'Beowulf's Armor'; McGuinness, 'Beowulf's Byrnies'.
[91] On Unferth's wider role in the poem, see below, pp. 246–56.

and Breca 'risked their lives' on the waves (*on deop wæter aldrum nehdon*, lines 509b–510a; *on garsecg . . . aldrum neðdon*, lines 537b–538a). Here, as before, the poet is at pains to establish associations between widely separated scenes in the poem through verbal repetition, so providing a complex series of cross-references within the text.

It should be stressed, however, that although verbal parallels and verbatim repetition play a key role in the structuring of the text, parallels of meaning or theme could be employed in the same way. So, for example, during Beowulf's fight with Grendel, the perception of the terrified Danes in the hall, onlookers in a battle in which they cannot play a useful part, is depicted in another brief passage marked off by a clear envelope pattern in which, however, none of the key words actually recurs (lines 767–70):[92]

> Dryhtsele dynede;   Denum eallum wearð,
> ceasterbuendum,   cenra gehwylcum,
> eorlum ealuscerwen.   Yrre wæron begen,
> reþe renweardas.   Reced hlynsode.   770

> [The noble hall resounded; there was for all the Danes, for the fortress-dwellers, for each of the bold ones, for the warriors, great terror. Both were enraged, the angry hall-guardians: the building crashed.]

The ferocity of the combatants is emphasised, as is their essential identity: to the onlooking Danes both Beowulf and and Grendel are 'hall-guardians', and both the cause of the 'great terror' they feel. The problematic nature of the term *ealuscerwen* has long puzzled scholars, and the closely-varied fourfold dative description of the onlookers (*Denum eallum . . . ceasterbuendum . . . cenra gehwylcum . . . eorlum*) presents such a delayed build-up to its deployment as to suggest that it was something of a trump-card that the poet was playing.[93] A broad parallel to the construction (and, surely, to the general scene) is offered by the later discovery by the Danes of the head of Æschere by the monster-mere (lines 1417b–1421):[94]

> Denum eallum wæs,
> winum Scyldinga,   weorce on mode
> to geþolianne,   ðegne monegum,

---

92 Cf. Berkhout and Medine, '*Beowulf* 770a: *reþe renweardas*'.

93 Discussion of the term usually centres around the appearance of a similar term in *Andreas*; see further below, pp. 163–6. A characteristically clear-sighted analysis of the difficulties of interpretation is offered by Mitchell, 'Literary Lapses: Six Notes on *Beowulf* and Its Critics', pp. 4–7. For attempts to explain the term by reference to sources in Latin, Welsh, and Norse, see, for example, Heinemann, '*Ealuscerwen-Meoduscerwen*, the Cup of Death and *Baldrs Draumar*'; Rowland, 'OE *ealuscerwen/ meoduscerwen* and the Concept of "Paying for Mead" '.

94 One might also note that the description of the finding of Æschere's head occurs almost parenthetically between two accounts of the bloody and turbid water of the mere: we are told that 'the water stood beneath, gory and disturbed' (*wæter under stod, dreorig ond gedrefed*, lines 1416b–17a), and (with rhyme and assonance) that 'the swell seethed with blood . . . with hot gore' (*flod blode weol . . . hatan heolfre*, lines 1422a–1423a); by providing such a background to the grim discovery, the poet has brilliantly contextualised this gory scene.

oncyð eorla gehwæm,   syðþan Æscheres   1420
on þam holmclife   hafelan metton.

[For all the Danes, the friends of the Scyldings, there was grief to suffer
in the heart, for many a thegn, sorrow for each of the warriors, once they
came across Æschere's head on the sea-cliff.]

Here again a fourfold dative construction (*Denum eallum . . . winum Scyldinga
. . . ðegne monegum . . . eorla gehwæm*) is used to delay the revelation of the
dread discovery of Æschere's head. At all events, the base-meaning 'terror' for
ealuscerwen seems sanctioned by a further parallel dative construction, again in
a passage describing the reaction of the Danes to the unearthly din made by
Grendel (lines 782b–790):

> Sweg up astag
> niwe geneahhe;   Norðdenum stod
> atelic egesa,   anra gehwylcum
> þara þe of wealle   wop gehyrdon,   785
> gryreleoð galan   godes ondsacan,
> sigeleasne sang,   sar wanigean
> helle hæfton.   Heold hine fæste
> se þe manna wæs   mægene strengest
> on þæm dæge   þysses lifes.   790

[A sound rose up, wholly without parallel; for the North-Danes there
arose a dread terror, for every single one of those who heard the cry
from the outer wall, God's adversary chanting a terrible lay, a song
without victory, hell's captive bemoaning his wound. There held him
fast the one who was the strongest in might of men on that day of this
life.]

In this case, the phrase *atelic egesa* ('dread terror', line 784a) does duty for the
puzzling term *ealuscerwen* in a parallel syntactical structure just a few lines
before; the association seems inescapable, just as the wholesale repetition here
of the characterisation of Beowulf as 'the one who was the strongest in might of
men on that day of this life' (*se þe manna wæs mægene strengest / on þæm dæge
þysses lifes*, lines 789–90) seems consciously to recall the earlier description of
him on strikingly similar terms (*se wæs moncynnes mægenes strengest / on þæm
dæge þysses lifes*, lines 196–7).[95]

Other parallels of diction and scene are used to associate characters and
create links between apparently disparate scenes, so lending structure to the
whole. So, for example, the second time that Hygd is mentioned in the poem,
bustling around the hall serving drinks (lines 1980b–1983a), she is described as
'Hæreth's daughter' (*Hæreðes dohtor*, line 1981b), just as she had been when
first described (line 1929a). After a brief enquiry from Hygelac, Beowulf
launches into one of the longest speeches in the poem (lines 2000–151),
mentioning first his victory over Grendel, before describing his reception at
Heorot (lines 2014–31):

---

[95] See further above, p. 55.

'Weorod wæs on wynne;   ne seah ic widan feorh
under heofones hwealf   healsittendra   2015
medudream maran.   Hwilum mæru cwen,
friðusibb folca,   flet eall geondhwearf,
bædde byre geonge;   oft hio beahwriðan
secge sealde,   ær hie to setle geong.
Hwilum for duguðe   dohtor Hroðgares   2020
eorlum on ende   ealuwæge bær;
þa ic Freaware   fletsittende
nemnan hyrde,   þær hio nægled sinc
hæleðum sealde.   Sio gehaten is,
geong, goldhroden,   gladum suna Frodan;   2025
hafað þæs geworden   wine Scyldinga,
rices hyrde   ond þæt ræd talað,
þæt he mid ðy wife   wælfæhða dæl,
sæcca gesette.   Oft seldan hwær
æfter leodhryre   lytle hwile   2030
bongar bugeð,   þeah seo bryd duge.'

[‘The company was joyful: I never saw under the vault of the sky greater
mead-pleasure for those sitting in a hall. At times the renowned queen,
the peace-pledge of nations, passed right around the hall, urged on the
young men, often she gave a man a twisted circlet, before she went to
her seat; at times before the experienced warriors Hrothgar's daughter
carried the ale-cup to the warriors in turn, and I heard those sitting in the
hall name her Freawaru, as she gave the precious vessel to the warriors.
Young and gold-adorned, she is promised to Froda's gracious son; the
lord of the Scyldings, the guardian of his people, has brought it about
(and reckons it a wise policy) that he should settle a great number of
conflicts, murderous feuds, with that woman. The killing-spear seldom
stays idle anywhere for a brief time after a man dies, although the bride
is fine.']

Once again, ominous words, here in the form of a gnomic utterance, bring a
passage of praise to a close. There has been no previous mention of Freawaru,
nor of the joint role she plays in Heorot serving the men:[96] here it would appear
that while Wealhtheow serves the younger warriors, Freawaru does parallel
service (*Hwilum . . . Hwilum*, lines 2016b and 2020a) for the tried and tested
men. Like her mother, a celebrated 'peace-pledge of nations' (*friðusibb folca*,
lne 2017a), Freawaru is to be sent abroad to cement an uneasy accord after a
period of strife. This episode, coming hard on the heels of the accounts of Hygd
(who serves drink in the same way, lines 1980b–1983a) and Thryth, suggests
careful patterning on the part of the poet, who has thereby effected a contrast
between accounts in Denmark of three mature matrons mindful of their sons
(Wealhtheow, Hildeburh, and Grendel's mother), and those in the land of the
Geats of three young princesses married off abroad (Hygd, Freawaru, and
Thryth).[97]

The extent to which the poet of *Beowulf* uses repetition at the sub-verbal,

---

96 For other differences, see below, pp. 184 and 242–4.
97 On the structural role of women in the poem, see further below, p. 148.

verbal, and phrasal levels of diction is abundantly clear from the passages already cited; little wonder, then, that such a formulaic technique should have come under close scrutiny by generations of scholars attempting to characterise the art and craft of the *Beowulf*-poet, who seems especially adept among composers of extant Old English verse at bringing what appear to be aspects of an original and individual style to a common inherited tradition.

Repeated words and formulaic phrasing

Beowulf has long been characterised as a poem largely composed of repeated phrases: as early as 1898 Richard Kistenmacher attempted the systematic collection of such formulaic phrases,[98] and it is interesting to see the extent to which his work anticipates that of Robert Creed,[99] working nearly sixty years later and filled with the zeal of oral-formulaic theory, which had only first been applied to *Beowulf* a few years before.[100] Since then there has been a veritable frenzy of activity initially designed to demonstrate that *Beowulf* was not simply formulaic, but oral,[101] with a welter of counter-arguments seeking to show that not only were literate Anglo-Saxons perfectly capable of formulaic composition in Old English verse, but that in some instances they were equally prone to formulaic composition in Old English prose, in Anglo-Latin verse, and even in

---

[98]   Kistenmacher, *Die wörtlichen Wiederholungen im Bêowulf.* For other attempts to catalogue so-called *Parallelstellen* in *Beowulf*, see above, p. 2.

[99]   Creed, 'Studies in the Techniques of Composition', remains the most comprehensive attempt to date to record formulaic repetition in *Beowulf.*

[100] The seminal article is that by Magoun, 'The Oral-Formulaic Character of Anglo-Saxon Narrative Poetry'.

[101] The secondary literature is extensive, see above, p. 7 for overviews. Among the more notable contributions to the debate have been, for example, Amodio, 'Affective Criticism, Oral Poetics, and Beowulf's Fight with the Dragon'; Anderson, 'Formulaic Typescene Survival'; Cassidy, 'How Free Was the Anglo-Saxon Scop?'; Clark, *Theme in Oral Epic and in 'Beowulf'*; Creed, 'Studies in the Techniques of Composition of the "Beowulf" Poetry'; *idem*, 'The *Andswarode*-System in Old English Poetry'; *idem*, 'The Making of an Anglo-Saxon Poem'; *idem*, 'On the Possibility of Criticizing Old English Poetry'; *idem*, 'The Singer Looks at His Sources'; *idem*, ' ". . . Wel-hwelc Gecwaeþ . . .": the Singer as Architect'; *idem*, 'The *Beowulf*-Poet: Master of Sound-Patterning'; *idem*, 'The Remaking of *Beowulf*'; Diamond, 'Theme as Ornament in Anglo-Saxon Poetry'; Doane, 'Oral Texts, Intertexts, and Intratexts: Editing Old English'; Foley, 'Formula and Theme in Old English Poetry'; Fry, 'Old English Fomulas and Systems'; *idem*, 'Old English Formulaic Themes and Type-Scenes'; Greenfield, 'The Formulaic Expression of the Theme of "Exile" in Anglo-Saxon Poetry'; Hart, 'Tectonic Design, Formulaic Craft, and Literary Execution'; Jager, 'Speech and Chest in Old English Poetry: Orality or Pectorality?'; Lewis, '*Beowulf* 992A: Ironic Use of the Formulaic'; Moisl, 'Anglo-Saxon Royal Genealogies and Germanic Oral Tradition'; Niles, 'Formula and Formulaic System in *Beowulf*'; *idem*, 'Toward an Anglo-Saxon Oral Poetics'; *idem*, 'Understanding *Beowulf*: Oral Poetry Acts'; O'Brien O'Keeffe, 'Diction, Variation, and the Formula'; Olsen, '*Beowulf*'; Opland, *Anglo-Saxon Oral Poetry*; Parks, ' "I Heard" Formulas in Old English Poetry'; Renoir, 'Old English Formulas and Themes as Tools for Contextual Interpretation'; Riedinger, 'The Old English Formula in Context'; *idem*, 'The Formulaic Relationship between *Beowulf* and *Andreas*'; Rogers, 'The Crypto-Psychological Character of the Oral Formula'; Schaefer, *Vokalität*; Sorrell, 'Oral Poetry and the World of *Beowulf*'; Stevick, 'The Oral-Formulaic Analysis of Old English Verse'; Whallon, 'Formulas for Heroes in the *Iliad* and in *Beowulf*'; *idem*, *Formula, Character, and Context*; *idem*, *Inconsistencies*; Whitman, 'The Meaning of "Formulaic" in Old English Verse Composition'.

Anglo-Latin prose.[102] The focus of enquiry has now shifted somewhat away from an insistence on the orality of formulaic composition, and instead onto the originality and artistry of the individual authors who chose to produce using traditional techniques of composition, transmission, and performance.[103]

The extent to which the diction of *Beowulf* can be described as formulaic can to some degree be traced through Appendixes II and III below, which together chart formulaic repetition in around 40 per cent of the lines in the poem.[104] In fact, however, relatively few self-contained lines in the poem are recycled verbatim: such repetition accounts for less than 1 per cent of the lines in *Beowulf*.[105] Such a figure is substantially smaller than that found in other formulaic texts routinely compared with *Beowulf*: after an analysis of the first 3,182 lines of the *Iliad*, for example, William Whallon concludes that *Beowulf* is 'less than a third as formulaic'.[106] Moreover, nearly half of these whole-verse repetitions comprise three simple parallel statements: 'Beowulf spoke, son of Ecgtheow' (*Beowulf maþelode, bearn Ecgþeowes*, first appearing at line 529); 'Hrothgar spoke, protector of the Scyldings' (*Hroðgar maþelode, helm Scyldinga*, first appearing at line 371); 'Wiglaf spoke, son of Weohstan' (*Wiglaf maðelode Weohstanes sunu*, first appearing at line 2862).[107]

Much more common are those lines in *Beowulf* where a whole line is confected from two half-lines found verbatim elsewhere in the poem; so, for example, the notion that folk travelled 'throughout far distances to view the wonder' of Grendel's tracks (*geond widwegas wundor sceawian*, line 840) is not repeated precisely elsewhere in the poem, though both its constituent half-lines are: line 840a appears verbatim as line 1704a, when Hrothgar extols the fame of Beowulf 'throughout far distances', and line 840b is repeated as line 3032b, when the sorry Geats go 'to view the wonder' of the dead Beowulf and the

---

102 For a sustained argument against applying the original assumptions of oral-formulaic theory to Old English poetry, see Watts, *The Lyre and the Harp*; the notion that literate Anglo-Saxons could likewise compose formulaic Old English verse was first demonstrated by Benson, 'The Literary Character of Anglo-Saxon Formulaic Poetry'. Studies which seek to extend the parameters of the debate into other areas of Anglo-Saxon composition include Lapidge, 'Aldhelm's Latin Poetry and Old English Verse'; Orchard, 'Crying Wolf: Oral Style and the *Sermones Lupi*'; *idem*, *The Poetic Art of Aldhelm*, pp. 73–125; *idem*, 'Old Sources, New Resources: Finding the Right Formula for Boniface'; *idem*, 'Both Style and Substance: the Case for Cynewulf'.

103 See, for example, the comments of the most prolific and influential writer of oral-traditional literature, John Miles Foley, writing at the beginning of the first chapter of his latest book, significantly entitled *Homer's Traditional Art* (p. 13): 'This volume focusses on the roots of Homeric epic in an ancient Greek oral tradition, exploring Homeric art not as a literary triumph over that heritage but as the direct product of its unique, empowering agency. That is, it considers how the bard and his tradition employed a dedicated medium for expression to achieve a more than literary art.' One might well argue that, *mutatis mutandis*, the time is ripe for an analysis of the traditional art of *Beowulf*.

104 In the analysis that follows, I have made extensive use of both Appendixes, to which reference should be made for verification and full texts of the lines cited.

105 Whole-verse repetition occurs at lines 75 and 1771; 197, 790, and 806; 371, 456, and 1321; 500 and 1166a; 529, 631, 957, 1383, 1473, 1651, 1817, 1999, and 2425; 1271 and 2182; 1685 and 1956; 2052 and 3005; 1646 and 1816; 2862 and 3076. Repetition that carries over a single line occurs at lines 133–4 and 191–2; 196–7 and 789–90; 200–1 and 1597–8; 302–3 and 1917–18; 416–17 and 1591–2; 672–3 and 1696–7; 796–7 and 2655–6; 946–7 and 1758–9; 949–50 and 660; 1046–7 and 3141–2; 1052–3 and 1902–3; 1386–7 and 2342–3; 1484–5; 1684–6 and 2382–3; 2335–6 and 3036–7; 2350–1 and 2543–4; 2918–19 and 2974–5.

106 Whallon, *Formula, Character, and Context*, p. 82.

107 Compare Table IV below, pp. 206–7.

dragon together.[108] Outside *Beowulf*, the phrase *wundor sceawian* is not found in extant poetry, but by contrast *geond widwegas* occurs twice.[109] Likewise, both elements of a line describing how at the death of Hygelac 'worse war-fighers plundered the slain' (*wyrsan wigfrecan wæl reafodon*, line 1212) recur elsewhere: Beowulf boasts how Hygelac had no need to seek out 'worse warfighters' while he was alive (line 2496a), while the messenger of the Geats gloomily predicts how in times to come, the beasts of battle will talk among themselves, and the raven will tell the eagle what good feasting he had when he 'plundered' the slain with the wolf (*wæl reafode*, line 3027b).[110] Several other lines in *Beowulf* are repeated piecemeal in this way.[111]

At the level of the half-line, of course, verbatim repetition is commensurately still more common,[112] and the real flexibility of the formulaic technique of composition employed by the *Beowulf*-poet becomes clear. In several cases, the poet is able to repeat formulas (and double their alliterative potential) by simply reversing the constituent elements: if he can say of the retainers of Scyld Scefing, sending their lord back into the unknown that 'their spirit was sad' (*him wæs geomor sefa*, line 49b), he can say the same of the brooding Beowulf, waiting to fight the dragon (*him wæs geomor sefa*, line 2419b), but vary the elements when describing Wiglaf, pondering his lord's solitary lot (*him wæs sefa geomor*, line 2632). A 'famous prince' can be called either a *mære þeoden* (lines 129b, 201a, 345a, 797a, 1046b, 1598a, 1715a, 1992a, 2384a, 2572a, 2788b, and 3141b) or (should alliteration demand it) a *þeoden mære* (lines 353a and 2721a); Hrothgar, 'son of Healfdene', can be described as both *sunu Healfdenes* (lines 268a, 344b, 645a, and 1040b) and *Healfdenes sunu* (line 1009b); Wiglaf, 'son of Weohstan', can be both *sunu Wihtstanes* (lines 2752b and 3120b) and *Wihtstanes sunu* (lines 2862b and 3076b); and even 'dear Beowulf' himself can be both *Beowulf leofa* (lines 1216b and 1758b) and *leofa Beowulf* (1854b, 1987b, and 2663a).[113]

The flexibility of the formulaic system becomes still more apparent when it is realised that synonyms and even metrical equivalents can be freely substi-

---

108 In fact, line 3032b is written as *wundur sceawian*, so displaying scribe B's characteristic spelling of the form; on the customary collocation of the words *wund[o]r* and *sc[e]aw-* in the *Beowulf*-manuscript, see above, pp. 27–9.

109 At *Christ II*, line 482, and in the *Paris Psalter*, 144.20, line 4.

110 On the so-called 'beasts of battle motif', especially as it appears in *Beowulf*, see, for example, Bonjour, '*Beowulf* and the Beasts of Battle'; Griffith, 'Convention and Originality in the Old English "Beasts of Battle" Typescene'; Magoun, 'The Theme of the Beasts of Battle in Anglo-Saxon Poetry'.

111 See, for example, the entries in Appendix II below under lines 35, 150, 227, 232, 268, 289, 383, 427, 512, 561, 1245, 1307, 1311, 1327, 1381, and 1646; other examples can, of course, be easily found.

112 For instances of repetition restricted to individual half-lines within the first fifty lines of *Beowulf* alone, see, for example, the entries in Appendix II below under lines 6, 9, 11, 16, 17, 29, 30, 32, 34, 40, 41, 44, 45, 46, 47, and 50.

113 There are a host of similar examples: cf. *sweotolan tacne* (line 141b) and *tacen sweotol* (line 833b); *feond mancynnes* (line 164b) and *mancynnes feond* (line 1276a); *Deniga leodum* (lines 389a, 696a, 1323a, 1712b, and 2125b) and *leode Deniga* (line 599a); *leode mine* (lines 415b, 1336b, and 1345b) and *minum leodum* (lines 2797b and 2804b); *feorran ond nean* (line 839b) and *nean ond feorran* (lines 1174a and 2317b); *het hine wel brucan* (line 1045b) and *het hyne brucan well* (line 2812b); *þa wæs frod cyning* (line 1306b) and *wæs ða frod cyning* (line 2209b); *Geata dryhten* (lines 1484b, 1831a, 2483a, 2560b, 2576a, and 2991b) and *dryhten Geata* (lines 2402a and 2901a).

tuted. So, for example, a 'band of men' can be described as *æþelinga gedriht* (line 118b), *eorla gedriht* (lines 357b and 431b), *secga gedriht* (lines 633b and 1672b), or *hæleþa gedryht* (line 662a); one can 'risk [one's] life' in various ways (*feore gedigde*, line 578b; *aldre gedigest*, line 661b; *ealdre gedigde*, line 1655b); when a 'whole troop arose' on different occasions, it could be described in different ways (*werord eall aras*, line 651b; *duguð eal aras*, line 1790b; *weorod eall aras*, line 3030b);[114] the notions that 'soonest is best', 'battle is impending', or 'flame must consume' can each be depicted by two distinct but clearly related phrases (*ofost is selest*, line 256b, and *nu is ofost betost*, line 3007b; *hild onsæge*, line 2076b, and *guð onsæge*, line 2483b; *þa sceall brond fretan*, line 3014b, and *nu sceal gled fretan*, line 3114b); and 'grief' or 'strife' can be 'renewed' in three quite different ways (*cearu wæs geniwod*, line 1303b; *sorh is geniwod*, line 1322b; *wroht wæs geniwod*, line 2287b). Nor was the simple substitution of synonyms the only option: metrically equivalent words and phrases would work just as well. If something could be said to be 'most like a bird' (*fugle gelicost*, line 218b), something else could be 'most like flame' or 'steel' or 'ice' (*ligge gelicost*, line 727a; *style gelicost*, line 985b; *ise gelicost*, line 1608b); if something could be 'urged on by wind' (*winde gefysed*, line 217b), something else might be 'urged on by war' or 'fire' or even 'its own heart' (*guþe gefysed*, line 630b; *fyre gefysed*, line 2309a; *heorte gefysed*, line 2561b). The formulaic world of *Beowulf* is a world of delicious linguistic possibilities: one can be drunk on 'wine' or 'beer',[115] be mindful of 'noble things', 'songs', 'gifts', 'glories', 'miseries', 'pleasures', or 'feuds',[116] die of 'mortal wounds' or 'wounds inflicted by a *sax*',[117] and still 'not shrink back at all' from either 'life' or 'the feud'.[118]

The substitution of metrically equivalent words or phrases, moreover, further permits the use of quite different parts of speech within the same formulaic system.[119] So, for example, there are no fewer than five half-lines of precisely the same form 'X under clouds' scattered throughout the poem, and employing verbs, nouns, and adjectives, as necessary: Scyld Scefing 'grew under clouds' (*weox under wolcnum*, line 8a), Grendel 'strode under clouds' (*wod under wolcnum*, line 714a), and Hrothgar 'ruled under clouds' (*weold under wolcnum*, line 1770a); the shadows of night passed 'dark under clouds' (*wan under wolcnum*, line 651a); and likewise there darkened in Grendel's mere the 'water under the clouds' (*wæter under wolcnum*, line 1770a).[120] Such freedom allows the possibility of what Rand Hutcheson, who has produced the fullest list of such formulaic metrical verse-types to date, calls 'interlocking formula[s]:

---

114 Cf. above, pp. 76–7.
115 Cf. *beore druncne*, line 480; *beore druncen*, line 531a; *wine druncen*, line 1467a.
116 cf. *cynna gemyndig*, line 613b; *gidda gemyndig*, line 868b; *geofena gemyndig*, line 1173b; *mærða gemyndig*, line 1530a; *bealewa gemyndig*, line 2082b; *hroþra gemyndig*, line 2171b; *fæhða gemyndig*, line 2689b.
117 Cf. *feorhbennum seoc*, line 2740a and *sexbennum seoc*, line 2904a.
118 Cf. *nalles for ealdre mearn*, line 1442b and *nalles for fæhðe mearn*, line 1537b.
119 The notion of formulaic systems, especially within *Beowulf*, is explored most fully by Fry, 'Old English Fomulas and Systems'; Niles, 'Formula and Formulaic System in *Beowulf*'; Riedinger, 'The Old English Formula in Context'.
120 Cf. the discussion by Liuzza, trans., *Beowulf: a New Verse Translation*, p. 22.

verses representing formula[s] that share a common element with a third verse'.[121] While on the surface, only identity of metre would seem to associate the two half-lines *weorðmyndum þah* ('he throve with honours', line 8b) and *beotwordum spræc* ('he spoke with boasting words', line 2510b), outside *Beowulf* the existence of an apparently connected set *beotwordum spræc* (*Juliana*, line 185a) / *hospwordum spræc* (*Juliana*, line 189b) / *gylpwordum spæc* (*Battle of Maldon*, line 274b) / *wurðmyndum spræc* (*Exodus*, line 258b) seems to bridge that gap.[122]

Such extraordinary flexibility within the interconnected systems of formulas available to a creative poet such as that of *Beowulf* makes the appeal to identical formulaic phrasing in the conjectural emendation of apparent gaps or flaws in the transmitted text a more problematic procedure than perhaps has been acknowledged to date.[123] Although formulaic phrasing certainly seems useful in restoring a number of readings now lost either through physical damage to the manuscript,[124] or through obvious scribal errors of one sort or another,[125] there are other cases where it seems at least possible that the poet was deliberately varying his use of formulas for local effect. It seems relatively safe, for example, to add the word *æþeling* to existing *ærgod* in line 1329a, on the grounds that the phrase *æþeling ærgod* ('prince good of old') is witnessed in the manuscript at lines 130a and 2342a, and both sense and metre seem to require something; likewise, it seems appropriate to add the word *wen* on the grounds of alliteration, sense, and metre to the otherwise defective phrase *ðæs ðe ic hafo* in line 3000b, on the model of the parallel phrase *þæs ic wen hæbbe* ('as I expect') in line 383b. But it seems easier to account for the omission of the element *grund*- ('ground') through eyeskip in line 2139, which in the manuscript has a light and non-alliterating a-line (*in ðam sele Grendeles modor* ['in the hall of Grendel's mother']), than to restore the (otherwise perfectly acceptable) phrase *in ðam guðsele* ('in the war-hall') on the basis of line 443a (*in þæm guðsele*). Similarly, the omission through eyeskip of an infinitive after *hafelan* in line 1372b makes more sense if the word *helan* is restored, rather than the synonymous *hydan* that

---

121 Hutcheson, *Old English Poetic Metre*, pp. 303–16; the definition is given at p. 303.
122 For the possibility of a more direct connection between these texts, see below, pp. 163–8.
123 See above, pp. 44–56.
124 A number of cases are highlighted in Appendix II below; see particularly, for example, the restoration of *segen gyldenne* (for manuscript *segen g . . . denne*) at line 47b, on the model of *segen gyldenne* in line 1021a; the restoration of *swa hit gedefe bið* (for manuscript *swa hit ğd . . .*) at line 3174b on the model of *swa hit gedefe wæs* in lines 561b and 1670b; the restoration of *mærða gemunde* (for manuscript *m . . . gemunde*) at line 2678a on the model of *gemyne mærþo* in line 659a and *mærða gemyndig* in 1530a. Other examples are found in lines 723b, 762b, 2146b, 2220b, and 2727a.
125 So, for example, it seems clear that line 148a should read *wine Scyldinga* (whereas the manuscript reads *wine scyldenda*) on the model of lines 30b, 170b, 1183a, 1418a, 2026b, and 2101b; likewise, the manuscript-reading *sele ædenne* at line 51b represents a common scribal error: most editors restore *selerædende* on the model of line 1346a; the apparent dittography *oft ge gefremedon* at line 2478b can be restored to *oft gefremedon* on the model of *oft gefremede* in line 165b; at line 465b the manuscript reads *folce deninga* for *folce Deniga*, presumably because the scribe has been influenced by the preceding *Arscyldinga*; cf. *folces Denigea* at line 1582a. Other examples of unusual or impossible scribal spellings that can apparently be restored on the basis of formulaic phrasing are found at lines 302a, 581a, 652a, 1278b, 1333a, 1599b, 1833a, 1918a, 2225b, 2325b, 2596b, 2793a, 2814b, 2946b, and 3060a.

the appearance of the phrase *hafelan hydan* ('to hide [the] head') in line 446a might suggest.[126] It is tempting to emend one or other of the phrases *ecgum dyhtig* (line 1287a) and *ecgum þyhtig* (line 1558b), to make them match, but although such an emendation is easily defensible on the grounds that the scribes commonly confuse *d* and *þ*,[127] both forms seem possible, and the meaning ('strong in edge') in both cases is essentially the same; ditto with the phrases *hringa þengel* (line 1507a) and *hringa fengel* (line 2345b): both mean 'prince of rings'.[128] Still other common editorial choices simply seem baffling when viewed in a formulaic context: the first two words of the phrase *ac se æglæca* in line 159a have long been lost due to a gap at the edge of the manuscript, but have nonetheless somehow become fixed in the editorial tradition of the poem despite the existence of the formulaic phrase *atol æglæca* ('awesome dread assailant') at lines 592a, 732a, and 816a.[129] And just as Unferth long ago in the editorial tradition of *Beowulf* lost the initial *H* that begins his name on all four occasions that it appears (at lines 499a, 530b, 1165b, and 1488a), so too editors commonly emend to *ondslyht* ('onslaught', 'counterblow') the manuscript reading *hond slyht* ('hand-slaughter', 'hand-blow') on both occasions that the word occurs in a clearly formulaic context (at lines 2929b and 2972b).[130] More-over, editors of *Beowulf* may not be the only ones to have been affected by the formulaic language of the text; Katherine O'Brien O'Keeffe has shown how scribes commonly substituted one formula for another in copying,[131] and such a process may help to explain how the entire line *æfter hæleða hryre hwate Scyldingas* ('after the fall of heroes, the brave Scyldings') can appear in context as line 2052 and again, bizarrely, as line 3005; as Klaeber puts it: 'the line as it stands in the [manuscript] has the air of an intruder',[132] and various imaginative attempts to defend the manuscript-reading seem unconvincing.[133]

But if the fact of formulaic verbal repetition in *Beowulf* is undeniable, there is still discussion as to its precise significance, and whether what at one level can simply be seen as a useful inherited compositional technique has any wider purpose in associating scenes, characters, and themes. We have already seen how the *Beowulf*-poet uses the repetition and variation of sounds, words, and phrases frequently to lend both structure and texture to his text; but it can be seen time and again how repetition at other levels of discourse strongly supports

---

126 See further above, pp. 46–8.
127 See further above, pp. 42–6.
128 More understandable is the emendation of both occurrences of the personal name in the phrase *Hemminges mæg* ('Hemming's kinsman'), used twice in quick succession at lines 1944b and 1961b: the manuscript reads *hem ninges* and *hem inges* respectively.
129 On the meaning of *æglæca*, see, for example, Gillam, 'The Use of the Term *æglæca* in *Beowulf* at Lines 813 and 2592'; Kuhn, 'Old English *aglæca* – Middle Irish *ochlach*'; Nicholls, 'Bede "Awe-Inspiring" not "Monstrous": Some Problems with Old English *aglæca*'.
130 One might compare the customary editorial emendation of manuscript *handlean* to *andlean* in line 1541b, again in a common formulaic context.
131 O'Keeffe, *Visible Song*.
132 Klaeber, ed., *Beowulf*, p. 224.
133 For a useful summary, see Jack, ed., *Beowulf*, p. 200. As Klaeber, ed., *Beowulf*, pp. 224–5, commenting on the complexity of allusion assumed by those who would seek to defend the manuscript-reading, puts it: 'it is doubtful whether such a procedure on the part of the poet would have been fair to the readers'.

the notion that the *Beowulf*-poet also uses patterns of repeated and deliberately varied themes and scenes to provide the opportunity for his audience to make other, broader connections between disparate elements in the text. In short, it is the basic elements of *Beowulf*'s style (namely repetition and variation, together the products of apposition) that give the poem its basic structure.

Repetitions of theme and scene: the fitt-divisions and the wider structure

Scholarly debate on the structure of *Beowulf* has been extensive (and occasionally acrimonious) for years.[134] Even granted the grudging critical acceptance of the essential unity of the poem that survives,[135] the older notions of the text as simply focusing on the one hand on the three monster-fights, or on the other on the periods of Beowulf's youth and age, have slowly given way to suggestions that the patterning within the poem is much more complex and interwoven than even that stark bipartite or tripartite choice might imply.[136] The year 1967 saw two important contributions to the debate, with John Leyerle developing his earlier notion of the poem as based on the same interlace-pattern as found widely in Insular art, and Eamonn Carrigan proposing a highly involved mathematical structure based on the numbered sections in the manuscript;[137] more recent contributions, by Thomas Elwood Hart and David Howlett, have been still more ingenious and complex.[138] As with so many aspects of the poem, both visual and aural patterns have been invoked in the search for the structure and meaning of *Beowulf*.

With regard to its larger structure, the very fact that *Beowulf* begins and ends

---

134　There have been a number of studies which attempt to deal with the whole question of the structure of *Beowulf*, including Abraham, 'The Decorum of *Beowulf*'; Andersson, 'Tradition and Design in *Beowulf*'; Blomfield, 'The Style and Structure of *Beowulf*'; Bloomfield, ' "Interlace" as a Medieval Narrative Technique, with Special Reference to *Beowulf*'; Brodeur, 'The Structure and the Unity of *Beowulf*'; Burlin, 'Inner Weather and Interlace'; Carrigan, 'Structure and Thematic Development in *Beowulf*'; Chance, 'The Structural Unity in *Beowulf*'; Crépin, 'Wealhtheow's Offering of the Cup to Beowulf'; Eller, 'Semantic Ambiguity as a Structural Element in *Beowulf*'; Gardner, 'Fulgentius's *Expositio Vergiliana Continentia* and the Plan of *Beowulf*'; Hieatt, 'Envelope Patterns and the Structure of *Beowulf*'; Hume, 'The Theme and Structure of *Beowulf*'; Köberl, 'Referential Ambiguity as a Structuring Principle in *Beowulf*'; Kuhn, '*Beowulf* and the Life of Beowulf'; Leyerle, 'The Interlace Structure of *Beowulf*'; Locherbie-Cameron, 'Structure, Mood and Meaning in *Beowulf*'; Nicholson, 'The Literal Meaning and Symbolic Structure of *Beowulf*'; idem, 'The Art of Interlace in *Beowulf*'; Niles, 'Ring-Composition and the Structure of *Beowulf*'; Nist, *The Structure and Texture of Beowulf*; Owen-Crocker, *The Four Funerals in 'Beowulf*'; Parks, 'Ring Structure and Narrative Embedding in Homer and *Beowulf*'; Richardson, 'Imperfective Aspect and Episode Structure in *Beowulf*'; Shaw, 'The Speeches in *Beowulf*'; Shippey, 'The Fairy-Tale Structure of *Beowulf*'; idem, 'Structure and Unity'; Sisam, *The Structure of 'Beowulf'*; Stevens, 'The Structure of *Beowulf*; Tonsfeldt, 'Ring Structure in *Beowulf*'.

135　On the notion that the poem was originally composed of a number of self-contained lays, amalgamated by a later poet or poets (so-called *Liedertheorie*), see above, pp. 6–7.

136　An excellent general account of the history of the debate is given by Shippey, 'Structure and Unity'.

137　Carrigan, 'Structure and Thematic Development in *Beowulf*'; Leyerle, 'The Interlace Structure of *Beowulf*'.

138　Hart, 'Tectonic Design, Formulaic Craft, and Literary Execution'; idem, 'Tectonic Methodology and an Application to *Beowulf*'; idem, 'Calculated Casualties in *Beowulf*'; Howlett, 'Form and Genre in *Beowulf*'; idem, 'New Criteria for Editing *Beowulf*'; idem, *British Books in Biblical Style*, pp. 504–40.

with a funeral certainly lends to the poem as a whole the same enve-
lope-patterning that can be seen to operate at lower levels of the text; nor are
these the only funerals in the poem.[139] Other connections and associations seem
self-evident. The anonymous grieving woman at Beowulf's own funeral (lines
3150–5)[140] surely calls to mind Hildeburh grieving for her own dead in the
Finn-episode (lines 1114–18a),[141] just as Sigemund's dragon-slaying (lines
874b–97) surely calls to mind Beowulf's own (lines 2543–820).[142] Still other
similar scenes in the poem, whether of feasting, fighting, sailing, or sleeping, all
seem interconnected by verbal or thematic parallels: it is as if the poet has
extended the patterns of repetition and variation that are his stock-in-trade at the
sub-verbal, verbal, and phrasal levels to the wider levels of theme and scene, and
is inviting his audience continually to compare and contrast different aspects of
his text.[143] Whereas it used to be argued that the many apparent 'digressions' in
the poem, and what Klaeber famously characterised as the poem's 'lack of
steady advance',[144] represented some kind of major structural flaw, it is now
accepted that all of the so-called digressions lend considerable depth and
contrast to the events of the main narrative.[145]

Further analysis has pointed up the existence in *Beowulf* (as in a number of
other works composed using the formulaic techniques of an ultimately orally
derived tradition) of several stock scenes and themes found elsewhere in extant
Old English poetry. The best-attested of such formulaic type-scenes is undoubtedly that of the 'beasts of battle', which occurs more than a dozen times in
surviving Old English verse,[146] but other themes have also been identified in
Beowulf, so linking it not only to other texts within the extant corpus of Old
English poetry, but more widely with texts composed in other languages, and at
other times.[147] It is clear that this kind of set-piece scene provides an essential
building-block in the composition of traditional epics. The occurrence of such
themes, like the clear patterning of repeated sounds, words, phrases and scenes
within *Beowulf*, only underlines the extent to which aspects of an inherited
tradition have been adopted and adapted by the *Beowulf*-poet. The further fact
that, as we shall see, elements of the narrative of *Beowulf* itself seem to resur-
face widely in other literatures composed in a variety of languages and places

---

139 See, for example, the detailed discussion by Owen-Crocker, *The Four Funerals in 'Beowulf'*, esp.
   pp. 9–113. On envelope-patterns, see above, pp. 78–85.
140 Cf. Bennett, 'The Female Mourner at Beowulf's Funeral'; Mustanoja, 'The Unnamed Woman's
   Song of Mourning over Beowulf and the Tradition of Ritual Lamentation'.
141 See further below, pp. 177 and 181.
142 See further below, pp. 234–7.
143 See further below, pp. 238–64.
144 Klaeber, ed., *Beowulf*, p. lvii.
145 Central to this debate was the work of Bonjour, *The Digressions in 'Beowulf'*; see too Bjork,
   'Digressions and Episodes', for a characteristically clear and fair-minded overview. Among more
   recent noteworthy attempts to reassess the whole concept of the digression in *Beowulf* is that by
   Diller, 'Contiguity and Similarity in the *Beowulf* Digressions'.
146 See n. 110 above.
147 See, for example, Clark, *Theme in Oral Epic and in 'Beowulf'*; Crowne, 'The Hero on the Beach';
   Diamond, 'Theme as Ornament in Anglo-Saxon Poetry'; Fry, 'Old English Formulaic Themes and
   Type-Scenes'; *idem*, 'Launching Ships in *Beowulf* 210–216 and *Brunanburh* 32b–36'. On particular
   links perceived between *Beowulf* and Classical epic, see below, pp. 132–3.

seems to show the benefits of considering *Beowulf* not simply as an isolated poem preserved by chance in a single damaged manuscript.[148]

But, as we have seen, that manuscript can still offer useful primary evidence,[149] even about the structure of *Beowulf* itself. Most modern editions of *Beowulf* follow the marked fitt-divisions in the manuscript to a greater or lesser extent; but in the case of these divisions (like the poem itself) the scribes have not left an unproblematic text.[150] Table II, below, shows the distribution of fitt-numbers throughout the poem.[151] Several have evidently been corrected,[152] and three are missing entirely and need to be supplied (XXVIII, XXX, and XXXVIIII). As with a number of other features in the manuscript,[153] the way each scribe indicates a change of fitt is somewhat different: though both use closing punctuation and capitalisation to signal their intent, only scribe A tends to leave a blank line.[154] Notwithstanding such differences, some clear patterns seem to emerge from a consideration of the surviving fitt-divisions. First, the notion of incremental repetition is markedly in evidence: many of the fitts begin in very similar ways. No fewer than ten begin with a variant of the formula 'X *maþelode*' (nos. VI, VII, VIII, XIIII, XX, XXI, XXII, XXIIII, XXVI, and [XXVIIII]), and eleven commence with a simple connective ÐA (nos. I, X, XI, XIII, XVI, XXXIII, XXXVII, XXXVIII, [XXXVIIII], and XLII), mostly capitalised thus (the exceptions are XI, [XXXVIIII], and XLII); other patterns are also discernible, such as *(GE)wat ða . . . (G)Ewiton him ða . . . GEwat him ða . . . GEwiteð þonne* (nos. II, XVII, XXVIII, and XXXV). Such patterning may allow us to feel some confidence in the editorial restoration of *gefrægn* in XXXVII (to match the *Ða ic . . . gefrægn* of XXXVIII),[155] and the notion that the start of [XXX] should indeed be placed at line 2039a, beginning *Oððæt* (compare XXV *Oðþæt*).[156]

Closer examination, however, reveals a number of oddities. It is striking that none of the ten fitts beginning with a variant of the formula 'X *maþelode*'

---

148 For parallels and analogues to parts of the narrative of *Beowulf*, see below, pp. 100–29 and 142–62.
149 See above, pp. 12–56.
150 See further Bradley, 'The Numbered Sections in Old English Poetical MSS'; Conner, 'The Section Numbers in the *Beowulf* Manuscript'; Wells, 'The Sections in Old English Poetry'. A useful discussion of the problems of the fitt-numbering is offered by Kiernan, *'Beowulf' and the 'Beowulf'-Manuscript*, pp. 264–70.
151 In the discussion below, I retain the numbering of the fitts familiar to most readers of the text through the editions of (for example) Klaeber or Mitchell and Robinson, using (as do most editors) upper-case Roman numerals for clarity; the numbers in the manuscript itself are uniformly lower-case Roman. Conner, 'The Section Numbers in the *Beowulf* Manuscript', and Owen-Crocker, *The Four Funerals in 'Beowulf'*, pp. 138–45 both argue on the basis of the corrected numbers and other evidence that the first twenty-four fitts are numbered retrospectively, and that from then on the numbering precedes the fitt. I include Conner's numbering in a second column. For arguments that the fitt-numbering has been misinterpreted, see below, n. 159.
152 Numbers XXIIII–XXVIII represent later corrections, apparently in a later hand, from XXV–XXVIIII; see further Kiernan, *'Beowulf' and the 'Beowulf'-Manuscript*, pp. 265–6.
153 On differences between the scribes, see above, pp. 20–2.
154 Such a practice is in keeping with scribe B's tendency to conserve space, for example, through the more frequent use of abbreviations. See further above, p. 21.
155 Note that fitt XIII also begins with the related formula *mine gefræge*. On such formulas in general, see below, pp. 99–100.
156 On the importance of the word *oþþæt* in the structure of *Beowulf* as a whole, see Irving, *A Reading of 'Beowulf'*, pp. 31–42; Gruber, 'Motion, Perception, and *oþþæt* in *Beowulf*'.

Table II: Fitt-divisions in *Beowulf*

Fitt-number (Klaeber)	Fitt-number (Conner)	Folio	Opening line of fitt (with manuscript capitalisation)	Line-number	No. of lines in fitt
I	1	129r1	HWÆT WE GARDEna in geardagum	1	52
II	2	130r8	ÐA wæs on burgum beowulf scyldinga	53	62
III	3	132v4	(GE)wat ða neosian syþðan niht becom	115	74
IIII	4	134r9	Swa ða mælceare maga healfdenes	189	69
V	5	135v7	Him se yldesta ondswarode	258	62
VI	6	137r3	Stræt wæs stanfah stig wisode	320	51
VII	7	138r13	Hroðgar maþelode helm scyldinga	371	85
VIII	8	140r13	Hroðgar maþelode helm scyldinga	456	43
VIIII	9	141r15	HVNferð maþelode ecglafes bearn	499	60
X	10	142v15	Swa mec gelome laðgeteonan	559	103
XI	11	145r8	ÐA him hroþgar gewat mid his hæleþa gedryht	662	48
XII	12	146r13	Ða com of more under misthleoþum	710	81
XIII	13	147r9	Nolde eorla hleo ænige þinga	791	46
XIIII	14	148r10	ÐA wæs on morgen mine gefræge	837	88
XV	15	150r8	Hroðgar maþelode he to healle geon(g)	925	66
XVI	16	151v5	ÐA wæs haten hreþe Heort innanweard	991	59
XVII	17	152v18	ÐA gyt æghwylcum eorla drihten	1050	75
XVIII	18	154v8	(G)Ewiton him ða wigend wica neosian	1125	67
XVIIII	19	156r18	HIm wæs ful boren ond freondlaþu	1192	59
XX	20	157v10	SIgon þa to slæpe sum sare angeald	1251	70
XXI	21	159r14	Hroðgar maþelode helm scyldinga	1321	62
XXII	22	160v7	(B)EOWVLF maþelode bearn ecgþeo(w)es	1383	90
	23	162v4	BEOWVLF maðelode bearn ecgþeowes	1473	84

XXIII	24	164r15	GEseah ða on searwum sigeeadig bil	1557	94
XXIIII*	25	166r12	BEOwulf maþelode bearn ecgþeowe(s)	1651	89
XXV*	26	168r10	Oðþæt him on innan oferhygda dæl	1740	77
XXVI*	27	169v15	(Be)owulf maþelode bearn ecgþeowes	1817	71
XXVII*	28	171r16	CWOM þa to flode felamodigra	1888	75
XXVIII*	29	173r6	GEwat him ða se hearda mid his hondscole	1963	36
[XXVIIII]		173v20	Biowulf maðelode bearn ecgðioes	1999	40
[XXX]	30	174v19	Oððæt hie forlæddan to ðam lindplegan	2039	105
XXXI	31	177r18	Swa se ðeodkyning beawum lyfde	2144	77
XXXII	32	179r14	Nealles [mid] gewealdum wyrmhord abræc	2221	91
XXXIII	33	181r18	ÐA se gæst ongan gledum spiwan	2312	79
XXXIIII	34	183r9	SE ðæs leodhryres lean gemunde	2391	69
XXXV	35	184v10	GEwiteð þonne on sealman sorhleoð gæleð	2460	142
XXXVI	36	187v12	(W)lGlaf wæs haten weoxstanes sunu	2602	92
XXXVII	37	189A(197)v12	ÐA ic æt þearfe [gefrægn] þeodcyninges	2694	58
XXXVIII	38	189v17	ÐA ic snude gefrægn sunu wihstanes	2752	69
[XXXVIII:]	39	191r13	Ða wæs gegongen gumum unfrodum	2821	71
XL	40	192v8	Heht ða þæt heaðoweorc to hagan biodan	2892	54
XLI	41	193v8	Wæs sio swatswaðu sw[e]ona ond geata	2946	112
XLII	42	195v15	Þa wæs gesyne þæt se sið ne ðah	3058	79
XLIII	43	198r12	Him ða gegiredan geata leode	3137	46

* XXIIII–XXVIII have been altered from XXV–XXVIIII by a later hand

should be in the second part of the poem, that tells of Beowulf's fight with the dragon, even though six of the thirteen designated speech-acts in that section of the poem begin that way (as against twenty of the thirty-two in the first part of the poem).[157] Likewise, it seems curious that four of the first five examples of the '*X maþelode*' formula should refer to Hrothgar, and that all five of the last five examples should refer to Beowulf: up to line 1382 (when Hrothgar predominantly opens the fitt) Beowulf speaks seven times (four times using the formula *Beowulf maþelode*), and after line 1383 (when Beowulf exclusively opens the fitt) Hrothgar speaks twice (both times with the formula *Hroðgar maþelode*). Perhaps most striking of all is the full capitalisation of Beowulf's name at the openings of fitts XXI and XXII (the medial numbers of the sequence), since he has already been named almost a dozen times previously in the nominative case alone.[158]

Such patterning might tempt one to suggest that the fitt-division was authorial,[159] or at least earlier than the manuscript-version that survives (and indeed altered in transmission by the scribes of the *Beowulf*-manuscript in much the same way as the rest of the text).[160] But such a conclusion is not without difficulties of its own, given the wild disparity in length of the surviving fitts, which vary from around forty lines to over 140.[161] Moreover, although many of the fitt-divisions come at logical pauses in the narrative sequence,[162] several seem to cut across natural breaks, and it is easy to suggest alternative placements. As it stands, for example, fitt XXXI begins in the middle of a speech by Beowulf, whereas it might just as well begin only eight lines further on, at the end of same speech, with line 2152a (*Het ða in beran*), which would indeed echo the beginning of the existing fitt XL (*Heht ða þæt heaðoweorc*). Likewise, fitt VIIII begins in the middle of Beowulf's reply to Unferth, the opening of fitt XI interrupts the celebrated *com . . . com . . . com* sequence that describes Grendel's approach to Heorot, the battles with both Grendel and his mother are interrupted by the openings of fitts XII and XXIII,[163] as are the Finn- and

---

157 See Table IV and the discussion below, pp. 205–8, for details.

158 At lines 343a*, 405a*, 506a, 529a*, 631a*, 676a, 957a*, 1024b, 1191a, 1299b, and 1310b (the asterisk denotes the appearance of the word in the formula *Beowulf maþelode*).

159 Among those who use the fitt-divisions to argue for a complex structure to the text are Carrigan, 'Structure and Thematic Development in *Beowulf*'; Howlett, 'Form and Genre in *Beowulf*'; *idem*, 'New Criteria for Editing *Beowulf*'; Nist, *The Structure and Texture of Beowulf*; Owen-Crocker, *The Four Funerals in 'Beowulf'*, pp. 133–57.

160 Compare the conclusion of Mitchell and Robinson, ed., *Beowulf*, p. 7, who point out that in the Junius manuscript the fitt-numbering continues through all four poems *seriatim*, and suggest that 'when scribes A and B were copying *Beowulf*, their exemplar could have been in a manuscript where the fitt numbers started not at I but rather at some advanced number . . . and that in that case the scribes would naturally renumber the fitts, and in the course of doing so, they might well blunder occasionally.'

161 If we accept the modern placement of the missing fitt-numbers [XXVIIII] and [XXX], then fitts XXVIII and [XXVIIII] are only thirty-six and forty lines long respectively; the shortest fitt, the extent of which is clearly indicated in the manuscript, is VII (forty-three lines); the longest fitt is XXXV (142 lines).

162 So, for example, the end of a fitt coincides with the end of a speech in the following cases: III, IIII, V, VI, VIIII, XX, XXVIII, XXXVII, and [XXXVIIII].

163 Cf. Horowitz, 'The Interrupted Battles in *Beowulf*', who argues that in these and other cases the placement of the fitt-division is artful.

Ingeld-episodes by fitts XVII and [XXX], and Hrothgar's sermon, Beowulf's lengthy musings on the sadness of King Hrethel, and the Geatish messenger's woeful prophecy about the fate of his people are all (perhaps mercifully) broken up by the commencements of fitts XXV, XXXV, and XLI respectively. Despite a number (and that is the right word) of sometimes overly ingenious suggestions about the significance of the fitt-numbers,[164] several of which solve certain local difficulties, it remains hard to see a clear pattern to their overall placement.

In the end, it is perhaps fitting that arguments about the structure of *Beowulf* should have recourse to visual as well as aural cues. For a poem which is steeped in the traditional techniques of the ultimately oral Germanic tradition, yet which fairly flaunts its indebtedness to a Christian culture ultimately based on Latin letters, so much seems simply apposite. In the past, critics have been torn as to whether to regard *Beowulf* as primarily a tripartite structure, focusing on the three main monster-fights, or a bipartite structure split between accounts of the hero's youth in Denmark or his old age in Geatland; recently it has even been suggested that in fact the poem has a four-part structure, based on funerals.[165] In truth, however, it seems simplistic to regard *Beowulf* as primarily based on a two-part, three-part, four-part, or even, considering the divisions in the manuscript, a forty-three- (or even forty-four-) part structure. By means of a series of aural (and perhaps visual) cues, the *Beowulf*-poet surely invites his audience to make an intricate network of comparisons and contrasts at every level of diction through the related mechanisms of repetition and variation that lie at the heart of the style and structure of this complex text. Moreover, the same appositional principles of repetition and variation apply not only to the form of the poem but to its content, which (as we shall see) seems drawn from a range of quite disparate sources. It is the variety of such influences, whether oral or written, native or imported, Germanic or Latin-derived, secular or Christian, that will prove the focus for the next two chapters, which consider more closely the literary background to *Beowulf*.

---

[164] See n. 159 above.

[165] Owen-Crocker, *The Four Funerals in 'Beowulf'*. The four funerals of the title are those of Scyld Scefing and Beowulf at either end of the poem, and those associated with the Finn-episode on the one hand and on the other (as Owen Crocker argues on pp. 61–84) the so-called 'lay of the last survivor'.

4

Myth and Legend

Looking back in 'Beowulf'

From its opening line, *Beowulf* firmly asserts itself as a retrospective text, and by situating its story in pre-Christian Scandinavia deliberately distances in both time and space its Anglo-Saxon audience (of whatever date) from the events it describes. But, as Roberta Frank has elegantly shown, the *Beowulf*-poet also demonstrates a keen sense of history, layering his text with considerable skill;[1] if the main events of the poem take place over just a few days on either side of a fifty-year hiatus, we are nonetheless kept (relatively) well-informed about five generations of Danish kings, four of the Geatish royal line, and three more of that of the Swedish kings,[2] not to mention a small band of other kings of peripheral dynasties, such as Offa, celebrated king of the Continental Angles, or Finn, king of the Frisians.[3] From the period before the mysterious arrival of Scyld Scefing at the beginning of the poem, we are aware of still earlier figures, like Sigemund, Heremod, Eormenric, Hama, and Weland, and before them of the time of the biblical Flood, and Cain and Abel, right back to Creation itself.[4] The poem ends with a grim sense of future disaster for Beowulf's people that partly bridges the gap between the Anglo-Saxon audience and the events of the poem proper.

But if the *Beowulf*-poet seems unconcerned about precisely dating the events of his poem, modern scholarship has (in part) supplied the answer: if Hygelac's fatal raid against the Franks (mentioned no fewer than five times in the poem)[5]

---

[1] Frank, 'The *Beowulf* Poet's Sense of History'. See too Chickering, 'Lyric Time in *Beowulf*'; Dean, '*Beowulf* and the Passing of Time'; Green, 'Man, Time, and Apocalypse'; Greenfield, 'Geatish History: Poetic Art and Epic Quality in *Beowulf*'; Hanning, '*Beowulf* as Heroic History'; Helterman, '*Beowulf*: the Archetype Enters History'; Jones, *Kings, Beasts, and Heroes*, pp. 27–41; Loganbill, 'Time and Monsters in *Beowulf*'; McNamara, 'Beowulf and Hygelac'; Nagler, '*Beowulf* in the Context of Myth'; Niles, 'Myth and History'; *idem*, '*Beowulf*': the Poem and its Tradition, pp. 179–96; Risden, *Beasts of Time*.

[2] See the genealogies above, pp. xiv–xv.

[3] See, for example, Eliason, 'The "Thryth-Offa" Digression in *Beowulf*'; Gough, 'The Thrytho Saga, and Offa and Cynethryth of Mercia'; Moore, 'The Thryth-Offa Digression in *Beowulf*'; Rickert, 'The Old English Offa Saga'; Stefanovic, 'Zur Offa-Thryðo-Episode im *Beowulf*'; Suchier, 'Über die Sage von Offa und Þrytho'.

[4] Cf. Niles, '*Beowulf*': the Poem and its Tradition, pp. 181–2.

[5] The raid is mentioned at lines 1202–14a, 2201b, 2354b–66, 2493b–2508, and 2910b–21; see too further below, pp. 114–15, 121, and 134.

can be identified with that of one 'Chlochilaicus' first described in the sixth-century *Historia Francorum* of Gregory of Tours,[6] then it seems to have occurred around the year 520, a date consistent with the death of King Onela of Sweden (if he is rightly identified as King Áli) around the year 535.[7] We are therefore left with a gap of at least 150 years before the composition of *Beowulf*, which no modern scholar seems to suppose to have occurred before 685, the putative rough date of composition of *Cædmon's Hymn*.[8] The extent to which such a gap could been filled (at least in part) by oral traditions is a moot point for modern scholarship, but certainly the *Beowulf*-poet himself seems to claim as much in the opening lines of the poem, with its call for aural attention and identification of himself with the audience as recipients of traditional lore (*Hwæt! We . . . gefrunon*, lines 1a and 2b).[9] Although this is the only occasion on which the first-person plural form is used in such a way,[10] the poet goes on several times in the course of *Beowulf* to punctuate his tale with (mostly) first-person singular formulas such as *ne gehyrde ic* ('I never heard', lines 38a and 1842b), *secgan hyrde* ('heard tell', lines 273b, 882b, 875b, and 1346b), *hyrde ic* ('I heard', lines 62a, 2163a, and 2172a), *mine gefræge* ('as I have heard tell', lines 776b, 837b, 1955b, 2685b, and 2837b), *ic gefrægn* ('I learnt', lines 74a, 1196b, 2484a, 2752a, 2773a, and [by emendation] 2694a), and *ne gefrægn ic* ('I never learnt', lines 575b, 1011a, and 1027a). It is not as if references to books and writing are uncommon in extant Old English verse;[11] but they are alien to the world of *Beowulf*.[12] And while given the extensive evidence for the influence of imported, Christian, Latinate, and written sources on Anglo-Saxon literary culture it would be foolish to dismiss entirely the notion that the *Beowulf*-poet, who was assuredly a Christian, was composing pen in hand after

6   *Historia Francorum* III.3 (ed. Krusch and Levison, p. 99). See the discussion by Chambers, *Introduction*, pp. 381–7; Klaeber, ed., *Beowulf*, p. xxxix. See further Magoun, 'The Geography of Hygelac's Raid'; *idem*, 'Béowulf and King Hygelác in the Netherlands'; Storms, 'The Significance of Hygelac's Raid'.

7   See, for example, Klaeber, ed., *Beowulf*, p. xxxviii. On Onela see, for example, Belden, 'Onela the Scylfing and Ali the Bold'.

8   Compare the view of Fulk, *History of Old English Meter*, p. 390, who concludes on linguistic grounds that *Beowulf* was most probably composed before 725 if Mercian in origin or before 825 if Northumbrian, but that a date as early as *circa* 685 'is considerably less probable'.

9   On these formulas in general, see Parks, ' "I Heard" Formulas in Old English Poetry'.

10 It is interesting to note that the only comparable use of the first-person plural in this way is in the opening speech of Beowulf to the coastguard when he first broaches the question of Grendel's persecution of the Danes 'if it is as we have truly heard tell' (*gif hit is / swa we soþlice secgan hyrdon*, lines 272b–3).

11 So, for example, four times in his own works the poet Cynewulf apparently augments an inherited and aurally-derived formula by stating (somewhat paradoxically) 'Listen! We have heard through holy books' (*Hwæt! We þæt gehyrdon þurh halige bec* [*Fates of the Apostles*, line 63; *Elene*, lines 364, 670, and 852]).

12 See in particular Frantzen, 'Writing the Unreadable Beowulf' (and cf. Bennett, 'The Female Mourner at Beowulf's Funeral'; McNelis, 'The Sword Mightier Than the Pen? Hrothgar's Hilt, Theory, and Philology'). Much of the focus has been on the engraving on the giant sword from Grendel's mere, on which see, for example, Schrader, 'The Language on the Giant's Sword Hilt in *Beowulf*'. On the general topic of literacy and *Beowulf*, see, for example, John, '*Beowulf* and the Margins of Literacy'; Lerer, *Literacy and Power in Anglo-Saxon Literature*; Near, 'Anticipating Alienation: *Beowulf* and the Intrusion of Literacy' (with responses from Frantzen and Overing); Waugh, 'Literacy, Royal Power, and King-Poet Relations in Old English and Old Norse Compositions'.

consulting such materials,[13] it would be equally naive to suppose that even the most educated churchman would be entirely immune from an awareness of native tradition: so much did Ingeld have to do with Christ.[14]

But to look beyond written, Latin, Christian sources for the threads from which the *Beowulf*-poet wove his tale is emphatically not simply to label such threads primarily (or even partially) as 'pagan'.[15] The search for pagan elements in *Beowulf* has a rocky history indeed,[16] and it is as well to remember that throughout the entire span suggested for the composition of *Beowulf* pagan and Christian elements co-existed uneasily in Anglo-Saxon England:[17] Wulfstan, writing in Old English at the beginning of the eleventh century, has as much to say in condemnation of heathen customs and practices, as Aldhelm, writing in Latin at the end of the seventh.[18] In looking back in *Beowulf* we would do well to remember that in the carefully crafted layering of history provided by the poet, his primarily Christian audience had to cast an eye over Beowulf's own time, and then beyond, to a time of secular myth and legend, before catching a glimpse of antediluvian biblical narrative stretching back to the dawn of time, with an antiquity and authority that the people of the poem, however hard they gaze upon it, like Hrothgar staring at the giant sword-hilt, simply cannot comprehend.[19]

Beginnings: Scyld Scefing and the Skjǫldungs

Scyld Scefing is the progenitor of the royal line of the Danes, the father of Beow,[20] great-grandfather of Hrothgar, and the heaven-sent saviour who came to the lordless Danes in the 'dire distress' (*fyrenðearf*, line 14b) that presumably

---

13 See further below, pp. 132–62.
14 On the famous passage in which Alcuin (following Jerome), questions the value of secular literature to Christians (*Quid Hinieldus cum Christo*), see, for example, Frank, 'Germanic Legend in Old English Literature', p. 91. The passage in question is to be found in Alcuin's *Epistola* 124, ed. Dümmler, *Alcuini Epistolae*, p. 183; on the intended recipients of this letter, see Bullough, 'What has Ingeld to do with Lindisfarne?'.
15 For a sensitive overview, see, for example, Harris, '*Beowulf* in Literary History'.
16 Several studies attempt to focus on the pagan elements perceived in *Beowulf*, including Andersson, 'Heathen Sacrifice in *Beowulf* and Rimbert's *Life of Ansgar*'; Benson, 'The Pagan Coloring of *Beowulf*'; Crook, 'Pagan Gold in *Beowulf*'; Fell, 'Paganism in *Beowulf*'; Hill, 'Scyld Scefing and the *stirps regia*'; Irving, 'Christian and Pagan Elements'; Moorman, 'The Essential Paganism of *Beowulf*'; Nicholson, '*Beowulf* and the Pagan Cult of the Stag'; Niles, 'Pagan Survivals and Popular Belief'; North, *Pagan Words and Christian Meanings*; idem, *Heathen Gods in Old English Literature*; Robinson, 'The Language of Paganism in *Beowulf*'; idem, 'A Sub-Sense of Old English *fyrn(-)*'; Schneider, *Sophia Lectures on 'Beowulf'*, pp. 96–114; Stanley, *The Search for Anglo-Saxon Paganism*; idem, '*Hæthenra Hyht* in *Beowulf*'; idem, *Imagining the Past*; Taylor, 'Heorot, Earth, and Asgard'; idem, '*searoniðas*: Old Norse Magic and Old English Verse'; idem, 'The Language of Sacral Kingship in *Beowulf*'; idem, 'Vestiges of Old Norse Charms in *Beowulf*'; Wentersdorf, '*Beowulf*: the Paganism of Hrothgar's Danes'; Wilson, *Anglo-Saxon Paganism*. For useful comparative material from the Old Norse-Icelandic tradition, see too Lönnroth, 'The Noble Heathen: a Theme in the Sagas'.
17 On the vexed question of dating, see above, pp. 5–6.
18 For an overview, see, for example, Stanley, '*Hæthenra Hyht* in *Beowulf*'.
19 Cf. Orchard, *Pride and Prodigies*, p. 67.
20 On the form of the name, see below, pp. 103–4.

resulted from the wicked deeds of Heremod.[21] The B- and C-manuscripts of *The Anglo-Saxon Chronicle* (*sub anno* 855) trace the ancestry of the West-Saxon royal house from Æthelwulf back past Woden to an ark-born son of Noah,[22] in a genealogy which contains a number of the same or similar names; the relevant section reads as follows:[23]

> Geatt Tætwaing, Tætwa Beawing, Beaw Scealdwaing, Scealdwa Heremoding, Heremod Itermoning, Itermon Haðraing, Haþra Hwalaing, Hwala Bedwiging, Bedwig Sceafing, id est filius Noe, se wæs geboren on þære earce Noes.

> [Geatt, son of Tætwa, Tætwa son of Beaw, Beaw son of Scealdwa, Scealdwa son of Heremod, Heremod son of Itermon, Itermon son of Haþra, Haþra son of Hwala, Hwala son of Bedwig, Bedwig son of Sceaf. He is Noah's son, and was born on Noah's ark.]

What in *Beowulf* appears as a direct line of descent Scef–Scyld–Beow is here obscured: although Scealdwa is still the father of Beaw, Scealdwa's own father is given as Heremod, Scyld's presumed predecessor as Danish king in *Beowulf*,[24] with Sceaf listed six generations further back. In his Latin translation of the *Anglo-Saxon Chronicle*, written some time between 975 and 983, Æthelweard offers instead a truncated version of Æthelwulf's genealogy that seems closer to *Beowulf*:[25]

> quintus decimus [pater] Geat, sextus decimus Tetuua, septimus decimus Beo, octauus decimus Scyld, nonus decimus Scef. Ipse Scef cum uno dromone aduectus est in insula oceani que dicitur Scani, armis circundatus, eratque ualde recens puer, et ab incolis illilus terræ ignotus. Attamen ab eis suscipitur, et ut familiarem diligenti animo eum custodierunt, et post in regem eligunt; de cuius prosapia ordinem trahit Aðulf rex.

> [His fifteenth [forefather] was Geat, the sixteenth Tetwa, the seventeenth Beo, the eighteenth Scyld, the nineteenth Scef. That Scef arrived with one light vessel on an oceanic island called Skåne, surrounded by weapons, and he was an extremely young lad, unknown to the inhabitants of that land. Yet he was accepted by them, and they kept him lovingly as a member of the clan, and afterwards picked him as their king; and from his line King Æthelwulf derived his descent.]

In this account, not only is the line of direct descent Scef–Scyld–Beo preserved, but so too is the myth of an unknown progenitor from beyond the sea, although in this case (rather as in the notion that Sceaf is the ark-born son of Noah) it is

---

21 On Scyld and the Scyld-episode in general, see Anderson, 'A Submerged Metaphor in the Scyld Episode'; Benediktsson, 'Icelandic Traditions of the Scyldings'; Cameron, 'Saint Gildas and Scyld Scefing'; Fulk, 'An Eddic Analogue to the Scyld Scefing Story'; Guðnason, *Um Skjöldunga sögu*; Hill, 'Scyld Scefing and the *stirps regia*'; Liberman, 'The "Icy" Ship of Scyld Scefing'; Meaney, 'Scyld Scefing and the Dating of *Beowulf* – Again'; Owen-Crocker, *The Four Funerals in 'Beowulf'*, pp. 11–42; Tolley, '*Beowulf*'s Scyld Scefing Episode'.
22 For the ark-born son of Noah, see Anlezark, 'The Old Testament Patriarchs in Anglo-Saxon England', pp. 62–112; Hill, 'The Myth of the Ark-Born Son of Noah'.
23 O'Brien O'Keeffe, ed., *The Anglo-Saxon Chronicle: MS C*, p. 57.
24 On Heremod, see further below, pp. 104–14.
25 Campbell, ed., *Chronicon Æthelweardi*, p. 33.

Scef, rather than his son Scyld, who is the mysterious arrival.[26] Audrey Meaney has demonstrated that Æthelweard is here making use of material earlier than the common archetype of *The Anglo-Saxon Chronicle* (which she calls 'æ'), and argues that the *Beowulf*-poet must himself have had access to the same material.[27] She goes on to argue that: 'Scyld Scefing and his arrival from overseas cannot have been part of the prologue of *Beowulf* before 858, and almost certainly not before Alfred's reign',[28] a conclusion vigorously opposed by Richard North, who also considers the anomaly that according both to Æthelweard and the augmented version of the genealogy found in *The Anglo-Saxon Chronicle*, it is Sce(a)f, rather than Scyld, who arrives as a foundling from over the sea.[29] It is perhaps unsurprising that William of Malmesbury, writing his *Gesta Regum Anglorum c.* 1125, and clearly using both Æthelweard and *The Anglo-Saxon Chronicle* as sources, should also insist that the name of the foundling child was Sceaf.[30] A still later analogue is found in the thirteenth-century account of a ritual dated to the time of King Edmund (941–6), by which the monks of Abingdon Monastery established their rights to a certain piece of land.[31]

Quod dum servi Dei propensius actitarent, inspiratum est eis salubre consilium et (ut pium est credere) divinitus provisum. Die etenim statuto mane surgentes monachi sumpserunt scutum rotundum, cui imponebant manipulum frumenti, et super manipulum cereum circumspectae quantitatis et grossitudinis. Quo accenso, scutum cum manipulo et cereo, fluvio ecclesiam praetercurrenti committunt, paucis in navicula fratribus subsequentibus. Praecedebat itaque eos scutum et quasi digito demonstrans possessiones domui Abbendoniae de jure adjacentes, nunc huc, nunc illuc divertens; nunc in dextra, nunc in sinistra parte fiducaliter eos praeibat, usquedum veniret ad rivum prope pratum quod Beri vocatur, in quo cereus medium cursum Tamisiae miraculose deserens se declinavit et circumdedit pratum inter Tamisiam et Gifteleia, quod hieme et multociens aestate ex redundatione Tamisiae in modum insulae aqua circumdatur.

[While the servants of God were rather fervently pleading this [case], they were inspired by a plan which was both helpful and (as it is pious to believe), divinely provided. For on an appointed day the monks got up in the morning and took up a round shield, on which they placed a sheaf of corn, and above the sheaf a candle of considered size and thickness. After lighting this, they entrusted the shield with sheaf and candle to the river flowing past the church, with a few brothers following in a little boat. The shield went before them and as if with a finger indicated the adjacent lawful possessions of the house of

---

26 See further Hill, 'Scyld Scefing and the *stirps regia*'.
27 Meaney, 'Scyld Scefing and the Dating of *Beowulf*', pp. 13–22; see too Newton, *The Origins of 'Beowulf' and the Pre-Viking Kingdom of East Anglia*, pp. 71–6.
28 Meaney, 'Scyld Scefing and the Dating of *Beowulf*', p. 21.
29 North, *Heathen Gods in Old English Literature*, pp. 182–94.
30 Mynors, *et al.*, ed. and trans., *William of Malmesbury: Gesta Regum Anglorum*, I.176–7 and II.88–90. See too Dumville, 'The West Saxon Genealogical Regnal List'.
31 Stevenson, ed., *Chronicon Monasterii de Abingdon*, I.89. See too the discussion on this and the earlier passages cited by Tolley, '*Beowulf*'s Scyld Scefing Episode', pp. 9–11; North, *Heathen Gods in Old English Literature*, pp. 182–94.

Abingdon, turning now this way, now that; now to the left, now to the right it faithfully went before them until it came to a meadow which is called Beri, at which the candle, miraculously abandoning the middle current of the Thames, turned off and went around the meadow between the Thames and Iffley, which in winter and many times in the summer is surrounded by water in the manner of an island, thanks to the overflow of the Thames.]

The fact that this extraordinary account is only preserved in a thirteenth-century chronicle need not impugn its authority: the so-called *Abingdon Chronicle* certainly drew on much earlier sources, although that too need not make the details of the ritual contemporary with the mid-tenth-century date they claim. But it is hard to escape the general parallel with the Scyld Scefing episode in *Beowulf*, and certain aspects of the account, for example the casual reference to the round shields that were the norm before the Conquest, or the early form of the place-name *Gifteleia*, seem to suggest at least a certain antiquity for the episode.[32]

What all these analogues, together with others from Norse eddic poetry and Finnish material,[33] do seem to suggest is that behind the tale of Scyld Scefing lies a myth about a fertility god, who came across water.[34] The name of Scyld's own son, Beow,[35] which means 'barley', seems to confirm the notion. In tranferring the tale from father to son and having Scyld be the one to make a mysterious sea-bourne arrival, the *Beowulf*-poet looks ahead to the main events of his story: like Scyld Scefing, Beowulf himself will come unannounced across the sea as a 'shield' or protection to aid the Danes in their 'dire distress' (*fyrenðearf*, line 14); like the 'vigorous' Scyld (*felahror*, line 27a) so too the 'vigorous' Beowulf (*hroran*, line 1629a), who, like Scyld, departs from Denmark in a treasure-laden vessel never to be seen there again, eventually dies and passes into the 'keeping' of an unspecified higher authority (*on Frean wære*, line 27b; *on ðæs Waldendes wære*, line 3109a).[36] And of Beowulf too, the poet seems to say: *þæt wæs god cyning* ('that was a good king!', lines 11b and 2390b).[37]

Comparison with Scyld, however, need not necessarily cast Beowulf in the

---

32 Cf. Tolley, '*Beowulf*'s Scyld Scefing Episode', p. 11.

33 Fulk, 'An Eddic Analogue to the Scyld Scefing Story'; Harris, 'The Dossier on Byggvir, God and Hero'; Tolley, '*Beowulf*'s Scyld Scefing Episode'.

34 Mythological interpretations of *Beowulf* as a whole have been somewhat out of favour since Müllenhof, 'Der Mythus von Beovulf', famously interpreted (for example) Grendel as the North Sea.

35 The spelling of the name of Scyld's son is somewhat controversial: the manuscript clearly reads 'Beowulf' on both occasions (lines 18 and 53) where it occurs, and a case can be made on artistic grounds for pointing up the extent to which the poem's eponymous hero might be said to be a 'spiritual son' of Scyld; however, a form such as 'Beow' is found in the appropriate place in a number of genealogies, and, as Fulk, 'An Eddic Analogue', p. 314, n. 4, indicates, is supported metrically in line 53: it is perhaps more likely that a scribe has anticipated the name of the poem's hero. Cf. the extensive use of capitals to highlight Beowulf's name at the beginnings of fitts XXI and XXII; see Table II above, pp. 94–95.

36 The parallels are the stronger in that these are the only occurrences of *hror* and (in this sense) *wær* in the whole poem.

37 This is to assume that line 2390b indeed refers to Beowulf, as most commentators seem to suppose; the syntax of the sentence might just as easily refer to Onela. The same half-line, unambiguously referring to Hrothgar, appears at line 863b.

best light: Scyld carved out through conquest a country for himself, and, crucially, left his people a long line of kings, while Beowulf famously delays seizing the crown, and leaves his people lordless.[38] Moreover, the anarchic chaos that the Danes suffer before Scyld's arrival is precisely the fate predicted for the Geats after Beowulf's demise, a circularity of circumstance that is only heightened if we assume that the Danes' initial difficulties arise as a direct result of the selfish actions of Heremod, Scyld's immediate predecessor in a number of royal genealogies.[39] Certainly the double gnomic injunction (the first in the poem) that follows the introduction of Scyld's son, Beow, contrasts sharply with what is known elsewhere in *Beowulf* of the illiberal niggardliness of the doomed Heremod (lines 20–5):[40]

> Swa sceal geong guma gode gewyrcean,						20
> fromum feohgiftum   on fæder bearme,
> þæt hine on ylde   eft gewunigen
> wilgesiþas,   þonne wig cume,
> leode gelæsten;   lofdædum sceal
> in mægþa gehwære man geþeon.						25

> [So ought a young man bring about through good actions, with generous gifts of property while under his father's protection, that when he grows old willing retainers will remain with him when war comes, repay their prince; by praiseworthy deeds a man ought to prosper among every nation.]

Beowulf should be so lucky. True enough, like Beow, in his youth Beowulf's 'fame spread widely' (*blæd wide sprang*, line 18b),[41] but although as Beowulf faces the dragon alone Wiglaf twice reminds his retainers of their lord's former generosity (lines 2633–60 and 2864–91), he is the only one to 'repay their prince'.[42] That Scyld himself was luckier, and amply fulfilled the heroic ideal of generosity is made explicit in the description of his funeral that follows: the 'willing companions' of the gnomic passage (*wilgesiþas*, line 23a) are actualised in the 'dear companions' (*swæse gesiþas*, line 29a) who participate in the funeral of 'the Scyldings' friend, the beloved leader of the land' (*wine Scyldinga, leof landfruma*, lines 30b–31a); in what is surely a telling collocation in this context, they 'laid their beloved lord, distributor of rings, in the bosom of the ship, famous by the mast' (*aledon þa leofne þeoden, / beaga bryttan on bearm scipes, / mærne be mæste*, lines 34–6a). In the only other use of the phrase in the poem, Beowulf himself is described as a 'beloved lord' (*leofne þeoden*, line 3079b) by Wiglaf, even as he criticises him for spurning the advice to let the dragon well

---

38 Cf. Hollis, '*Beowulf* and the Succession'; Schrader, 'Succession and Glory in *Beowulf*'.
39 See, for example, above, p. 101.
40 On Heremod, see below, pp. 105–14, 159–61, and 171–2.
41 Harris, 'The Dossier on Byggvir, God and Hero', pp. 13–14, is surely right to assume that (as with Scyld) the *Beowulf*-poet is here punning on Beow's name: the noun *blæd* means both 'fame' 'glory' and 'blossom', 'growth', 'blade (as of grass)', while the verb *springan* means both 'to grow (as a plant)' and 'to spread'. For other puns on names in *Beowulf*, see below, pp. 171–2.
42 One might further note that the Geatish messenger, reporting Beowulf's death, calls him first of all a *wilgeofa* ('willing-giver', line 2900a).

alone.[43] Likewise, in what is surely a deliberate echo, Beowulf's own men, having built his pyre 'laid in the midst their famous prince, grieving warriors, their beloved lord' (*alegdon ða tomiddes mærne þeoden / hæleð hiofende hlaford leofne*, lines 3141–2).[44] In such ways do the resonances of the first lines of *Beowulf* still echo at the end.[45]

Men and monsters: Sigemund and Heremod

But if the *Beowulf*-poet seems content to manipulate myth in the service of his story, so too he seems at times to play fast and loose with legend. If the tale of the sea-bourne arrival of Scyld Scefing has been borrowed from his father for the sake of a parallel with Beowulf and a pun on his name ('shield', 'protector'), then in his account of the dragon-slaying Sigemund, the *Beowulf*-poet from much the same motive apparently transfers a famous exploit from Sigemund's son. The onomastic allusion is in this case more groanworthy,[46] since Sigemund means 'victory-hand' and the episode is recounted after Beowulf's victory has rendered Grendel armless, but the direct comparison of Sigemund and Beowulf is all the more direct. A combined company of Geats and Danes ride back from the monster-mere in high spirits, having seen Grendel's blood in the water, and are busy celebrating Beowulf's deeds (lines 853–63). There follow three related passages describing the journey home, carefully connected by the poet through the repetition of the word *hwilum* ('at times', lines 864a, 867b, and 916a).[47] The first and third of these simply describes the light-hearted horse-races that take place on the way, and these descriptions form an envelope around the central description of how a poet compares Beowulf's own deeds with those of the legendary heroes of the past (lines 867b–915):[48]

> Hwilum cyninges þegn,
> guma gilphlæden,   gidda gemyndig,
> se ðe ealfela   ealdgesegena
> worn gemunde,   word oþer fand   870
> soðe gebunden;   secg eft ongan
> sið Beowulfes   snyttrum styrian
> ond on sped wrecan   spel gerade,
> wordum wrixlan.   Welhwylc gecwæð
> þæt he fram Sigemundes   secgan hyrde   875

---

[43] Like Scyld Scefing, Beowulf is often described as 'beloved' (*leof*) even in death: cf., for example, lines 2823a, 2897a, 2910a, 3108a, and 3142b.

[44] Cf. Owen-Crocker, *The Four Funerals in 'Beowulf'*, pp. 23–7.

[45] It is perhaps more alarming to note a parallel between the way in which the Danes deal with Scyld Scefing and the way in which the Geats dispose of the dragon (cf. *leton holm beran*, line 48b; *leton weg niman*, line 3132b).

[46] I am grateful to Chris Abram for first pointing out to me the significance of the name; cf. Lee, *Gold-Hall and Earth-Dragon*, p. 118.

[47] On this kind of incremental repetition, see above, pp. 78–9 and 84.

[48] The manuscript reads *sige munde* at line 875a, presumably through haplography, and *earfoð* at line 902a, apparently through confusion of the noun *eafoð* ('strength', 'might') with the element *earfoð-* ('hardship').

ellendædum,   uncuþes fela,
Wælsinges gewin,   wide siðas,
þara þe gumena bearn   gearwe ne wiston,
fæhðe ond fyrena,   buton Fitela mid hine,
þonne he swulces hwæt   secgan wolde,   880
eam his nefan,   swa hie a wæron
æt niða gehwam   nydgesteallan;
hæfdon ealfela   eotena cynnes
sweordum gesæged.   Sigemunde gesprong
æfter deaðdæge   dom unlytel,   885
syþðan wiges heard   wyrm acwealde,
hordes hyrde.   He under harne stan,
æþelinges bearn,   ana geneðde
frecne dæde,   ne wæs him Fitela mid.
Hwæþre him gesælde   ðæt þæt swurd þurhwod   890
wrætlicne wyrm,   þæt hit on wealle ætstod,
dryhtlic iren;   draca morðre swealt.
Hæfde aglæca   elne gegongen
þæt he beahhordes   brucan moste
selfes dome;   sæbat gehleod,   895
bær on bearm scipes   beorhte frætwa,
Wælses eafera.   Wyrm hat gemealt.
Se wæs wreccena   wide mærost
ofer werþeode,   wigendra hleo,
ellendædum   (he þæs ær onðah),   900
siððan Heremodes   hild sweðrode,
eafoð ond ellen.   He mid Eotenum wearð
on feonda geweald   forð forlacen,
snude forsended.   Hine sorhwylmas
lemede to lange;   he his leodum wearð,   905
eallum æþellingum   to aldorceare;
swylce oft bemearn   ærran mælum
swiðferhþes sið   snotor ceorl monig,
se þe him bealwa to   bote gelyfde,
þæt þæt ðeodnes bearn   geþeon scolde,   910
fæderæþelum onfon,   folc gehealdan,
hord ond hleoburh,   hæleþa rice,
.ᛉ. Scyldinga.   He þær eallum wearð,
mæg Higelaces,   manna cynne,
freondum gefægra;   hine fyren onwod.   915

[Sometimes the king's thegn, a man filled with eloquent speech, mindful of songs, who remembered many great numbers of ancient traditions, devised another word, truly linked. The man began to recount with skill Beowulf's exploit, and successfully tell a skilful tale, varying words. He told everything that he had heard tell about Sigemund, his mighty deeds, many a strange thing, the Wælsing's struggle, his distant travels, feuds and crimes, those which the children of men did not readily recall, except for Fitela (who was) with him, when he wanted to say some such thing as an uncle to his sister's son, since they were ever comrades in need in every attack: they had laid low with their swords a multitude of giants' kin. On Sigemund there fell after his death-day no small judgment (or 'glory'), after the man keen in battle killed a serpent, the guardian of a hoard. Under a grey stone the prince's son attempted the perilous deed alone: Fitela was not with him; yet it befell him that his sword passed through the wondrous serpent, so that it stuck in the wall, the noble blade; the dragon perished in the slaying. The awesome assailant had brought it about by his valour that he might enjoy the ring-hoard at his own choice. He loaded a sea-boat, the son of Wæls, bore into the ship's bosom bright ornaments; the hot serpent melted away. He was the most widely known of exiles among the nations of men, for his mighty deeds, a protector of warriors – he had prospered for that – since the warlike vigour of Heremod diminished, his vigour and valour. He among the Jutes [or 'giants'] was lured forth into the power of enemies, quickly put to death. Surgings of sorrow oppressed him too long; he turned out for his people, for all the nobles, a source of mortal worries; likewise many a wise man in earlier times often bemoaned the passage of the strong-minded one, who had put faith in him for relief from their miseries, that the prince's son should prosper, take on his father's nobility, maintain the people, the treasure and the stronghold, the kingdom of warriors, the land of the Scyldings. He, Hygelac's kinsman, turned out there to all, to the race of men, to his friends the dearer; sin entered him.]

The passage, as befits one put in the mouth of 'a man filled with eloquent speech', is extremely artfully arranged,[49] including a number of examples of assonance, clustered towards the beginning (*gemyndig . . . gemunde . . . fand . . . gebunden . . . Sigemundes*; *worn . . . word*; *heard . . . hordes hyrde*), and the use of rhyming parallel phrases (*ðæt þæt swurd þurhwod . . . þæt hit on wealle ætstod*, lines 890b and 891b; *draca morðre swealt . . . Wyrm hat gemealt*, lines 892b and 897b).[50] It is clear that Beowulf is somehow being compared and contrasted with two figures from the legendary past, Sigemund and Heremod, who in other sources are often themselves linked.[51] The 'king's thegn' who recites the lay is specifically said to be a man well-versed in ancient lore (*guma gilphlæden, gidda gemyndig, se ðe ealfela ealdgesegena worn gemunde*, lines 868–70a),[52] but the assumption that the poet expected his audience to know the whole background of the material he has recited seems unwarranted:[53] the *Beowulf*-poet goes out of his way to stress that this specific story about Sigemund at least was not common currency, saying that the king's thegn included in his account 'many an unfamiliar thing . . . that the sons of men did not readily know' (*uncuþes fela . . . þara þe gumena bearn gearwe ne wiston*, lines 876b–78). Even the apparent exception to this rule, Fitela (*buton Fitela mid hine*, line 879b), is specifically excluded from the dragon-slaying exploit

---

[49] Cf. the comments of Opland, '*Beowulf* on the Poet'.
[50] On this kind of word- and sound-play in the poem as a whole, see above, pp. 61–9.
[51] Cf. the Norse poems *Hyndluljóð* 2 (Neckel, ed., *Edda*, p. 288), *Hákonarmál* 14 (Jónsson, ed., *Den norsk-islandske skjaldedigtning*, IB.59), and *Eiríksmál* 16 (Jónsson, ed., *Den norsk-islandske skjaldedigtning*, IB.165); cf. Chadwick, *The Cult of Othin*, p. 51; Garmonsway, *et al.*, '*Beowulf' and its Analogues*, pp. 116–17.
[52] See further Nolan and Bloomfield, '*Beotword, gilpcwidas*, and the *gilphlædan* Scop of *Beowulf*'.
[53] See further Eliason, 'The "Improvised" Lay', pp. 178–9.

that is the main focus here (*ne wæs him Fitela mid*, line 889b);[54] the question naturally arises: from where did the king's thegn get his information? Evidence outside *Beowulf* for a knowledge of Sigemund or Sigmundr in Anglo-Saxon England is decidedly thin: it is possible that he is represented on a fragmentary eleventh-century sculpture from Winchester, although quite what a depiction of a character from the heroic past apparently biting off a she-wolf's tongue would be doing in a church-setting seems obscure.[55]

Although perhaps it might be considered overly pedantic, the question of knowledge of Sigemund outside *Beowulf* has a serious point, since this is the only source which attributes a dragon-slaying to Sigemund, rather than to his son. Without exception in the Scandinavian traditions it is the hero Sigurðr the Vǫlsung (Old English Wælsing),[56] rather than his father Sigmundr (Old English Sigemund) or his half-brother Sinfjǫtli (Old English Fitela), who kills the terrible dragon Fáfnir and gains his cursed treasure.[57] The description of this fight in the prose introduction to the eddic poem *Fáfnismál*, moreover, makes it clear that quite a different kind of dragon-fight is envisaged in the Scandinavian sources:[58]

> Sigurðr ok Reginn fóru upp á Gnitaheiði ok hittu þar slóð Fáfnis, þá er hann skreið til vatns. Þar gerði Sigurðr grǫf mikla á veginum, ok gekk Sigurðr þar í. En er Fáfnir skreið af gullinu, blés hann eitri, ok hraut þat fyrir ofan hǫfuð Sigurði. En er Fáfnir skreið yfir grǫfina, þá lagði Sigurðr hann með sverði til hjarta. Fáfnir hristi sik ok barði hǫfði ok sporði.
>
> [Sigurd and Regin went up onto Gnitaheath, and came upon the trail by which Fáfnir slithered to the water. Then Sigurd dug a large hole in the path, and Sigurd entered into it. When Fáfnir slithered away from his gold, he spewed poison, which spurted from above onto Sigurd's head. When Fáfnir slithered over the hole, Sigurd pierced him to the heart with his sword. Fáfnir twisted about, flailing with his head and tail.]

Sigurd essentially ambushes Fáfnir on his way across heathland to water, thrusting up through the dragon's middle; in the case of Sigemund, however, the dragon-fight clearly takes place in a cave by the sea, since Sigemund has to pass 'under the grey stone' (*under harne stan*, line 887b), his sword penetrates (presumably *not* from below) not just the dragon but the cave-wall (*þæt hit on wealle ætstod*, line 891b), and he has to load the treasure onto a sea-boat (*sæbat*

---

[54] It seems somewhat odd to introduce Fitela only to dismiss him ten lines later; the poet's point may well be to provide a contrast with Beowulf's own dragon fight, where he certainly (unlike Sigemund) required assistance in the form of Wiglaf. See further below, pp. 256–63.

[55] See Biddle, 'Excavations at Winchester 1965', pp. 329–32, and his (rather unclear) plate LXIIa. For a (rather unconvincing) argument that elements of the Sigurd-story are carved in Spain, see Breeze, '*Beowulf* 875–902 and the Sculptures at Sangüesa, Spain'; see rather Düwel, 'On the Sigurd Representations in Great Britain and Scandinavia'; King, 'Traces of Sigmund the Wælsing in Popular Tradition'; Margeson, 'The Völsung Legend in Medieval Art'.

[56] On Sigurðr in general, see Ploss, *Siegfried-Sigurd, der Drachenkämpfer*.

[57] Many of the tales surrounding Sigmundr and Sinfjǫtli are conveniently collected in Finch, ed., *Vǫlsunga saga: the Saga of the Volsungs*, chapters 2–12 (pp. 3–22). See further Griffith, 'Some Difficulties', pp. 23–4.

[58] Cf. Neckel, ed., *Edda*, p. 180.

gehleod, line 895b). In other words, the setting and manner of Sigemund's other-wise unattested dragon-fight is precisely that of Beowulf's own, fought against a creature from a cave beside the sea.[59] Other verbal parallels (*under harne stan*, line 887b and 2553b; *þæt swurd þurhwod*, line 890b and *bil eal ðurhwod*, line 1567b; *draca morðre swealt*, line 892b and *oðþæt he morðre swealt*, line 2782b; *selfes dome*, line 895a and *sylfes dome*, line 2776a; *gehleod, bær on bearm scipes*, lines 895b–896a and *him on bearm hladon*, line 2775a) only underline the connection between the two episodes.[60]

If Sigemund is described as 'hard in battle' (*wiges heard*, line 886a), so too is Beowulf (*beadwe heard*, 1539a); if Beowulf can boast earlier in the poem that he has slain the 'kin of giants' (*eotena cynn*, line 421a), so too can Sigemund (*eotena cynnes*, line 883b). Moreover, both the apparent heroes share character-istics of their prey: each is described as an *aglæca* ('awesome assailant', line 893a; cf. *aglæcean*, line 2592a, used of Beowulf and the dragon together).[61] The term (spelt in various ways) is altogether problematic, being used of Grendel (lines 159a, 425a, 433b, 592a, 646b, 732a, 816a, 989b, 1000b, and 1269a), his mother (*aglæcwif*, line 1259a), the dragon (2520a, 2534a, 2557a, 2592a, and 2905a), and, perhaps, the creatures of the monster-mere (line 1512a, although the term could equally refer here again to Beowulf); of the 'human' characters, only Sigemund and Beowulf are so described.[62]

Moreover, the parallels between Sigemund and Beowulf which might be drawn are (as we saw with those between Scyld Scefing and Beowulf) not neces-sarily wholly to the latter's credit. As Mark Griffith has recently shown, the depiction of Sigemund in *Beowulf* is far from simply positive: in particular, the attribution to Sigemund of 'feuds and crimes' (*fæhðe ond fyrena*, line 879a) aligns him squarely with Grendel, of whose acts the phrase has already been used twice in the poem (*fæhðe ond fyrene*, line 137a; *fyrene ond fæhðe*, line 153a).[63] Likewise, many critics have seen in the half-line that describes the rela-tionship between Sigemund and Fitela a loaded reference: according to *Vǫlsunga saga* Sigmundr sired Sinfjǫtli incestuously on his own sister, Signý,[64] making himself both the boy's father and (more significantly) maternal uncle, the closest of male family relationships in the Germanic heroic world.[65] It may

---

59 The general situation is commonly attested elsewhere; cf. (for example) Rauer, *Beowulf and the Dragon*, pp. 112–13 and 120–1, and below, pp. 149–51.

60 Griffith, 'Some Difficulties', pp. 33–4, who recognises most of these verbal parallels, objects that several of them would link Sigemund with Wiglaf, not Beowulf, but this is to ignore the extent to which in the second part of the poem Wiglaf is playing the same role as Beowulf in the first. See further below, pp. 256–63.

61 On the use of the term in *Beowulf*, see above, p. 90.

62 See Griffith, 'Some Difficulties', pp. 34–5.

63 The only other usage of the phrase is by Beowulf himself, much later in the poem (*fæhðe ond fyrene*, line 2480a); as Griffith, 'Some Difficulties', p. 20, points out of the simplex *firen*: 'The word appears seven times before this verse, always of the depredations of Grendel (101a, 137a, 153a, 164a, 628a, 750b, and 811a).' For an alternative view, see Robinson, 'Sigemund's *fæhðe ond fyrena*: *Beowulf* 879a'.

64 Finch, ed., *Vǫlsunga saga: the Saga of the Volsungs*, chapter 7 (pp. 9–10).

65 For a full analysis of the uncle-nephew relationship, see Bremmer, 'The Importance of Kinship'; on a range of meanings of the term *nefa*, see Lowe, 'Never say *Nefa* Again'. Cf. Spolsky, 'Old English Kinship Terms and *Beowulf*'.

be that by omitting the expected Sin- element from Fitela's name the poet is here subtly indicating the sin of incest.[66] In the same way, the poet's use of the description 'many a strange thing' (*uncuþes fela*, line 876b) to denote Sigemund's activities carries interesting implications in a poem in which the term 'strange' (*uncuþ*) is used mainly of Grendel and his kin; Grendel himself has demonstrated 'strange aggression' on his trips to Heorot (*uncuðne nið*, line 276b), Beowulf later boasts of tackling the 'power of the strange one' (*eafoð uncuþes*, line 960a), and both the path to the monster-mere and that to the dragon's lair are described as 'strange' (*uncuð gelad*, line 1410b; *stig . . . uncuð*, lines 2213b–2214a). Finally, the description of Sigemund as 'the most famous of exiles' (*wreccena . . . mærost*, line 898) need not be wholly positive; the same term is used of the mercenary Hengest (line 1137b), and the motivation of being an exile is explicitly excluded as that which drove Beowulf to Denmark in the first place (*nalles for wræcsiðum*, line 338b; compare line 2292a, *wean ond wræcsið*). Given the ambiguous presentation of Sigemund here, and his strong identification in this passage with the performance of deeds of valour (*ellendædum*, lines 876a and 900a; *elne*, line 873b), the stated interest of the *Beowulf*-poet from the outset that it is *ellen* ('valour') that is being celebrated seems still more double-edged.[67]

But if the comparisons apparently being drawn between Sigemund and Beowulf are far from clear-cut, those between Beowulf and Heremod, equally famed (at least at first) for deeds of *ellen* (or even between Heremod and Sigemund), are still more troubling and obscure. That the poet regards Heremod as a Danish king is clear not simply from the reference in this passage to the 'homeland of the Scyldings' (.ᛟ. *Scyldinga*, line 913a),[68] but from two later citations, in which his people are described as 'honourable Scyldings', 'the people of the Danes', and just 'the Danes' (*Ar-Scyldingum*, line 1710b; *Deniga leodum*, line 1712b; *Denum*, line 1720a). This later passage, in which Hrothgar explicitly draws a parallel between Beowulf and Heremod, needs also to be considered here (lines 1707b–24a):[69]

> Ðu scealt to frofre weorþan
> eal langtwidig   leodum þinum,
> hæleðum to helpe.   Ne wearð Heremod swa
> eaforum Ecgwelan,   Ar-Scyldingum;   1710
> ne geweox he him to willan,   ac to wælfealle
> ond to deaðcwalum   Deniga leodum;
> breat bolgenmod   beodgeneatas,
> eaxlgesteallan,   oþþæt he ana hwearf,
> mære þeoden,   mondreamum from.   1715
> Ðeah þe hine mihtig god   mægenes wynnum,
> eafeþum stepte,   ofer ealle men
> forð gefremede,   hwæþere him on ferhþe greow

---

[66] On the similar use of significant names in *Beowulf*, see below, pp. 172–3.
[67] On the central role of *ellen* in *Beowulf*, see above, p. 59.
[68] On the use of the rune .ᛟ. (*eþel*, 'homeland') in the manuscript, see further above, p. 40.
[69] On this passage, see further below, pp. 155–62.

breosthord blodreow.   Nallas beagas geaf
Denum æfter dome;   dreamleas gebad   1720
þæt he þæs gewinnes   weorc þrowade,
leodbealo longsum.   Ðu þe lær be þon,
gumcyste ongit;   ic þis gid be þe
awræc wintrum frod.

[You ought to turn out as a comfort to your people, entirely long-lasting,
a help to warriors. Heremod did not turn out like that for the sons of
Ecgwela, the noble Scyldings; he did not develop for the joy, but for the
slaughter and death of the Danish people; enraged he slew his table
companions, his comrades, until, alone, he turned, the famous prince,
away from the joys of men. Although mighty God had exalted him with
the delights of might and with powers, promoted him above all men, yet
in his heart there grew a bloodthirsty breast-hoard. Not at all did he give
rings to the Danes in pursuit of fame; joyless he lived on, so that he
suffered grief for that struggle, a prolonged misery for his people. Teach
yourself from that; perceive manly virtue: I, old in winters, have told
this tale for your sake.]

Since within *Beowulf* itself we are supplied with a complete genealogy of the
Danish royal house from Scyld Scefing to Hrothgar, it seems logical to assume
that Heremod must belong to an earlier period in their history. The fact that in
the West-Saxon genealogy of Æthelwulf (*sub anno* 856) Heremod is given as the
father of Scealdwa (Old English Scyld),[70] and that it is a common trait for kings
to appear in genealogies as the sons of their predecessors, whatever their
connection, would support the supposition.[71]

Moreover, if Heremod were Scyld's immediate predecessor his subsequent
fall from grace, apparent exile, and the condition in which he abandoned his
beleaguered people would all explain the plight of the Danes before Scyld's
mysterious arrival from across the water.[72] The early thirteenth-century Danish
chronicler Saxo Grammaticus obligingly offers a predecessor to Skioldus (Old
English Scyld) of appropriate wickedness, but unfortunately inappropriate
name, whom he calls Lotherus.[73] Nonetheless, as an example of what was
considered poor kingship, the parallel is instructive:

Sed nec Lotherus tolerabiliorem regem quam militem egit, ut prorsus
insolentia ac scelere regnum auspicari videretur; siquidem illustrissimum
quemque vita aut opibus spoliare patriamque bonis civibus vacuefacere
probitatis loco duxit, regni aemulos ratus quos nobilitate pares habuerat. Nec
diu scelerum impunitus patriae consternatione perimitur, eadem spiritum
eripiente, quae regnum largita fuerat.

[70] See further above, p. 101.
[71] Cf. Davis, 'Cultural Assimilation in the Anglo-Saxon Royal Genealogies'; Sisam, 'Anglo-Saxon Royal Genealogies'.
[72] Chambers, *Introduction*, pp. 89–91
[73] Olrik and Raeder, ed., *Saxonis Gesta Danorum*, I.ii.2 (p. 11); cf. Davidson and Fisher, *Saxo Grammaticus*, I.14–15. See too the online text of the *Gesta Danorum* (details in section C of the Bibliography).

[But Lother did not behave as a king any more tolerably than as a soldier, so that he seemed from the start to inaugurate his reign with arrogance and crime; he deemed it a measure of virtue to deprive everyone most honourable of life and wealth, and so to empty the land of good citizens, reckoning that his equals in rank were his rivals to power. Nor did he last unpunished for long, but he fell in a national revolt, with the same homeland snatching away his life as it had once granted the kingdom.]

If they do not share a name, then Lotherus at least shares with Heremod (whose name means 'war-mind') something of the latter's temperament.[74]

Like Sigemund, Heremod is associated not merely with *ellen*, but with *eotenas* (lines 883b and 902b). Since the latter term is used in *Beowulf* to signal both 'giants' and 'Jutes', it is far from clear that the same referent applies in both cases;[75] many translators consider that Sigemund battled against 'giants', whilst Heremod came to a sticky end amongst 'Jutes',[76] and we have already seen cases where the *Beowulf*-poet uses the same term to refer to different things.[77] The fact that Heremod is depicted as falling 'into the power of enemies' (*on feonda geweald*, line 903a) is particularly intriguing, given that precisely the same phrase has already been used in the poem to describe the wretched fate of Grendel (lines 805b–8):

> Scolde his aldorgedal   805
> on ðæm dæge   þysses lifes
> earmlic wurðan,   ond se ellorgast
> on feonda geweald   feor siðian.

[His parting from life on that day of this life had to be wretched, and the alien spirit had to depart far into the power of fiends (or 'enemies').]

Norman Blake, building on this and other evidence, has argued that Heremod is here effectively damned.[78] In proclaiming that Heremod was a cause of great death among the Danes (*to deaðcwalum Deniga leodum*, line 1712), Hrothgar is simply echoing Beowulf's recent observation of the same trait shared by Grendel (*deaðcwealm Denigea*, line 1670a). Moreover, whilst Grendel, swollen with rage (*gebolgen*, line 723b), had destroyed Hrothgar's hearth-companions (*Hroðgares heorðgeneatas*, line 1580b), the enraged Heremod had done no less to his own Danes (*Breat bolgenmod beodgeneatas*, line 1713). Like Grendel (*dreamum bedæled*, line 721a; *dreama leas*, line 850b; *dreame bedæled*, line 1275a), like Cain (*gewat . . . mandream fleon*, line 1264b), Heremod too

---

74 On the poet's use of meaningful names, see further below, pp. 172–3.
75 See further Kaske, 'The *eotenas* in *Beowulf*'; Stuhmiller, 'On the Identity of the *eotenas*'.
76 It is intriguing to note that, according to a seventeenth-century source reported by Chambers, *Introduction*, p. 97, Lotherus (Heremod's equivalent according to Saxo) was supposed to have fled to the land of the Jutes (*Lotherus . . . superatus in Jutiam profugit*); cf. Heremod's exile (lines 1714–15) and his stay *mid eotenum* (line 902b).
77 See above, pp. 69–70.
78 Blake, 'The Heremod Digressions'. See too n. 80 below. One might also note that according to some later versions of the myth of the death of the god Baldr (possibly alluded to in *Beowulf*: see further below, pp. 116–19), Hermóðr (Old English Heremod) was a son of Óðinn sent down to Hel to plead for Baldr's return.

becomes a lonely outcast from the joys of men (*ana . . . mondreamum from*, lines 1714b–1715; *dreamleas*, line 1720b). Like the magnificent giant hilt without a blade that Hrothgar gazes on but cannot comprehend immediately before speaking of his predecessor's fall from grace (lines 1687–99),[79] Heremod is offered up to Beowulf as a dire warning of how even the finest fighters can fail.[80]

That some kind of comparison or contrast is being drawn between Beowulf, now at the height of his powers, and the fallen idol Heremod is made strikingly clear in the second passage from the blunt comment of Hrothgar that 'I . . . have told this tale for your sake' (*ic þis gid be þe awræc*, lines 1723b–24a), words which could equally mean: 'I . . . have told this tale about you.' In the earlier passage about Heremod, the connection between Heremod and Beowulf is achieved through the use of parallel syntax: Heremod 'turned out for his people, for all the nobles, a source of mortal worries' (*he his leodum weard, / eallum æþelingum to aldorceare*, lines 905b–6); Beowulf 'turned out there to all, to the race of men, to his friends the dearer' (*He þær eallum weard, / mæg Higelaces, manna cynne, / freondum gefægra*, lines 913b–915a). The precise referent of the closing half-line of the passage is, however, decidedly ambiguous: we are simply told that 'sin entered him' (*hine fyren onwod*, line 915b). While modern editors and translators go to some lengths to reassure their readers that Heremod is intended here,[81] an Anglo-Saxon audience might have felt less confident that Beowulf and Heremod were being juxtaposed not so much as opposites as equals.

The way in which the *Beowulf*-poet adopts and adapts into his poem the tales of Scyld Scefing and of Sigemund and Heremod is surely instructive of his attitudes towards the inherited tradition as a whole. Each legendary hero is held up as a point of comparison and contrast with Beowulf himself, and it cannot fairly be said that the results are always flattering. In all three cases, however, the didactic purpose is the same: to provide a fresh perspective on the past. The old tales may have been sanitised, the elements of incest and fertility cults excised, and even aspects of the story changed to protect the (not so) innocent. But the names remain, in part perhaps after the fashion and model of biblical exegetical practice, for their signification and for representation of a wider, deeper tradition, and of a legendary past that the poet cannot quite seem to bring himself to disown. The old gods themselves, however, were a different and (to Christian eyes) more dangerous matter, and if they are present in *Beowulf* at all, it is apparently as euhemerised ciphers, with disfigured names and disguised forms.[82] But if we must dig deep to find traces of pagan myth in the text, it is

---

79 On which lines see further below, pp. 159–61.
80 Cf. Hieatt, 'Modþryðo and Heremod'; Vickrey, '*Egesan ne gymeð* and the Crime of Heremod'.
81 So, for example, bland notes simply assert a change of referent in Jack, ed., *Beowulf*, p. 81; Klaeber, ed., *Beowulf*, p. 166; Liuzza, trans., *Beowulf: a New Verse Translation*, p. 81; Mitchell and Robinson, ed., *Beowulf*, p. 78. Greenfield, trans., *A Readable 'Beowulf'*, p. 67, simply says 'sin dragged Heremod down'.
82 For the identification of three separate myths embedded in *Beowulf* (all discussed below), see Dronke, 'Beowulf and Ragnarǫk', pp. 322–5.

surely striking that the *Beowulf*-poet should so reveal his antiquarian interests as to include them at all.

Divine gifts: the Brosinga mene and the Brísingamen

Following the Finnsburh-episode and Wealhtheow's ill-starred speech to Hrothgar about the Danish succession,[83] we are told that the queen too seeks to reward Beowulf for his deeds against Grendel by presenting him with a splendid neck-ring, alongside other treasures. The poet's description is fulsome (lines 1197–1214):[84]

> Nænigne ic under swegle   selran hyrde
> hordmaðum hæleþa,   syþðan Hama ætwæg
> to þære byrhtan byrig   Brosinga mene,
> sigle ond sincfæt;   searoniðas fealh   1200
> Eormenrices,   geceas ecne ræd.
> Þone hring hæfde   Higelac Geata,
> nefa Swertinges,   nyhstan siðe,
> siðþan he under segne   sinc ealgode,
> wælreaf werede;   hyne wyrd fornam,   1205
> syþðan he for wlenco   wean ahsode,
> fæhðe to Frysum.   He þa frætwe wæg,
> eorclanstanas   ofer yða ful,
> rice þeoden;   he under rande gecranc.
> Gehwearf þa in Francna fæþm   feorh cyninges,   1210
> breostgewædu   ond se beah somod;
> wyrsan wigfrecan   wæl reafeden
> æfter guðsceare,   Geata leode,
> hreawic heoldon.   Heal swege onfeng.

[I never heard under the sky of a better warriors' treasure, since Hama carried off the necklace of the Brosings to the bright stronghold, the jewel and precious setting: he endured the cunning aggression of Eormenric, chose eternal gain. Hygelac of the Geats, Swerting's nephew, had that ring on his last expedition, when he defended his treasure under the standard, protected the plunder of the slain; fate took him off when, out of pride, he sought woe, a feud from the Frisians. He carried those adornments, precious stones, over the cup of the waves, the mighty prince; he died beneath his shield. The king's corpse then passed into the hands of the Franks, his mailcoat and the ring too; less worthy warriors plundered the slain after the slaughter; the people of the Geats occupied the place of carnage. The hall filled with sound.]

---

83 On which see below, pp. 173–87.

84 The manuscript reads *hord mad mum* at 1198a and *here* at 1199a; the readings given here are standard emendations. For an argument for retaining the manuscript-reading *fealh* ('penetrated') for the usual emendation to *fleah* ('fled') of line 1200b, see Hintz, 'The "Hama" Reference in *Beowulf* 1197–1201'; here I follow Mitchell and Robinson, ed., *Beowulf*, in translating the word as 'endured'.

Here, not for the first time in *Beowulf*, the poet introduces an object and immediately flashes forward in its history;[85] moreover, there seems a deliberate contrast drawn between the brave way Hama acquires the so-called *Brosinga mene*, and the rash way Hygelac loses his comparable neck-ring.[86] We are later told in *Beowulf* that on his return to Geatland Beowulf gave the ring to Hygd (lines 2172–6), and must assume that (in a curious continuation of the alternate passing of the ring between men and women) she gave it to her reckless husband for his final trip.[87]

The fleeting reference to Hama here is on the face of it obscure,[88] although its very brevity seems to suggest that the *Beowulf*-poet expected his audience to be as familiar with this story as those of Scyld Scefing, Weland, Sigemund, or Heremod.[89] Elsewhere in extant Old English poetry Hama is mentioned twice in *Widsith*, as the companion of one Wudga (who is presumably to be identified with Widia, son of Weland),[90] while Eormenric is attested both widely in *Widsith* (as Eormanric, lines 8a, 18b, 88a, and 111b) and in *Deor* (line 21), where reference is also made explicitly to Weland (lines 1–6) and implicitly to Widia, his son (lines 8–12); Widia's own adventures are likewise alluded to in *Waldere II* (lines 4–10).[91] Such a nexus of interconnecting references in four Old English poems surviving by chance in three separate manuscripts seems to suggest a rich background of tradition to which poets might be expected to allude.[92] Several of these characters are well-attested in Scandinvian tradition

---

85 On the use of this technique in *Beowulf*, see below, pp. 240–2.

86 On this interpretation, see further Kaske, 'The Sigemund-Heremod and Hama-Hygelac Passages'.

87 Cf. Mizuno, 'The Magical Necklace and the Fatal Corselet in *Beowulf*'.

88 Cf. Garmonsway *et al.*, *Beowulf and its Analogues*, pp. 265–300.

89 It is hard to assess the extent to which material concerning any or all of these characters may have circulated in Anglo-Saxon England. Important attempts to consider the wider picture include Wilson, *The Lost Literature of Medieval England*; Wright, *The Cultivation of Saga in Anglo-Saxon England*.

90 One might note in passing that the references to *Wudgan ond Haman* (line 124b) and to *Wudga ond Hama* (line 130b) in *Widsith* form an envelope-pattern, so marking off a separate passage. The half-line immediately preceding the first of these references mentions one *Wiþergield* (line 124a), who may or may not be identical to the *Wiðergyld* named in *Beowulf*, line 2051b, on whom see further below, pp. 240–7.

91 Note that, according to *Waldere II*, Widia 'hastened forth through the power of giants' (line 10: *ðurh fifela ge[wea]ld forð onette*), since a similar fate is apparently alleged in *Beowulf* for Heremod, who 'among the Jutes [or 'giants'] was lured forth into the power of enemies, quickly put to death' (lines 902b–4a: *mid Eotenum wearð / on feonda geweald forð forlacen, / snude forsended*). See further Zettersten, ed., *Waldere*, p. 27, and n. 80 above.

92 This is to assume no direct influence between the poems, although it is striking that a number of the legends common to both *Beowulf* and *Widsith* come in clusters in the latter poem, and (in general) outside the structural sequence of the text. If the concatenation of names shared with *Beowulf* in the sequence 'X ruled (the tribe of) Y' (*Widsith*, lines 18–34) seems impressive (*Eormanric Gotum . . . Þeodric Froncum . . . Breoca Brondingum . . . Finn Folcwalding Fresna cynne . . . Hnæf Hocingum . . . Sweom Ongendþeow*, lines 18b, 24a, 25a, 27, 29a, and 31b), it may simply reflect a traditional role-call. But the fact that there should immediately follow a digression on Offa (lines 35–44), similar in its expansive praise to that found in *Beowulf* (lines 1944–62), and itself followed by a self-contained allusion to the Ingeld-story (*Widsith*, lines 45–9), may suggest that the latter scenes are interpolations, like the rather out-of-place references by the poet that 'I was with the Israelites and the Assyrians, with the Hebrews and the Indians and the Egyptians' (*Mid Israhelum ic wæs ond mid Exsyringum / mid Ebreum ond mid Indeum ond mid Egyptum*, lines 82–3). Cf. the suggestion by Frank, 'Germanic Legend in Old English Literature', p. 99, that 'Whatever its age, [*Widsith*] was probably not composed at any great remove, in time or place, from *Beowulf*'. For the notion that there

too, and intriguing parallels to this allusion to Hama in *Beowulf* are to be found in the thirteenth-century *Þiðreks saga af Bern*,[93] where the figure Heimir flees the wrath of Erminríkr with a quantity of treasure and weapons and ends up in a monastery.[94] Similarly, the reference to the *Brosinga mene* has a further analogue in Norse myth, where the goddess Freyja is the owner of the marvellous necklace known as the *Brísingamen*, which she gained by sleeping with its dwarf-creators, and which was stolen by Loki, but perhaps recovered by the god Heimdallr, the first element of whose name recalls that of Hama.[95] The notion that a euhemerised version of this myth finds a reflex in *Beowulf* is perhaps less surprising than it might first appear: as we shall see, it has been argued that versions of other Norse myths concerning the gods Baldr and Thor, suitably abstracted from their divine pagan setting, likewise underlie other aspects of the Old English poem.

Divine deaths: Herebeald and Baldr

The childhood memory of his adoption by his maternal grandfather, Hrethel, who brought him up alongside his own three sons, Herebeald, Hæthcyn, and Hygelac (lines 2428–34), triggers in Beowulf, brooding before his final fight, a lengthy meditation on the tragedy that brought Hygelac the crown (lines 2435–71):[96]

'Wæs þam yldestan ungedefelice	2435
mæges dædum morþorbed stred,	
syððan hyne Hæðcyn of hornbogan,	
his freawine, flane geswencte,	
miste mercelses ond his mæg ofscet,	
broðor oðerne blodigan gare.	2440
Þæt wæs feohleas gefeoht, fyrenum gesyngad,	
hreðre hygemeðe; sceolde hwæðre swa þeah	
æðeling unwrecen ealdres linnan.	
Swa bið geomorlic gomelum ceorle	
to gebidanne, þæt his byre ride	2445
giong on galgan, þonne he gyd wrece,	
sarigne sang, þonne his sunu hangað	
hrefne to hroðre, ond he him helpe ne mæg,	
eald ond infrod, ænige gefremman.	
Symble bið gemyndgad morna gehwylce	2450
eaforan ellorsið; oðres ne gymeð	

---

may be direct influence between surviving Old English poems, see below, pp. 163–8. See too Campbell, 'The Old English Epic Style'; *idem*, 'The Use in *Beowulf* of Earlier Heroic Verse'.
93 Jónsson, ed., *Þiðreks saga af Bern*, chapters 288 (pp. 388–9) and 429 (pp. 579–81); Haymes, trans., *The Saga of Thidrek of Bern*, pp. 175–6 and 261.
94 Cf. Klaeber, ed., *Beowulf*, pp. 177–9; Frank, 'Germanic Legend in Old English Literature', p. 104.
95 See especially Damico, '*Sörlaþáttr* and the Hama Episode in *Beowulf*'; Orchard, *Cassell Dictionary of Norse Myth and Legend*, p. 25.
96 The manuscript reads *helpan* at line 2448b; on the emendation to *helpe*, see above, p. 49.

to gebidanne   burgum in innan
yrfeweardas,   þonne se an hafað
þurh deaðes nyd   dæda gefondad.
Gesyhð sorhcearig   on his suna bure   2455
winsele westne,   windge reste
reote berofene.   Ridend swefað,
hæleð in hoðman;   nis þær hearpan sweg,
gomen in geardum,   swylce ðær iu wæron.
Gewiteð þonne on sealman,   sorhleoð gæleð   2460
an æfter anum;   þuhte him eall to rum,
wongas ond wicstede.   Swa Wedra helm
æfter Herebealde   heortan sorge
weallende wæg.   Wihte ne meahte
on ðam feorhbonan   fæghðe gebetan;   2465
no ðy ær he þone heaðorinc   hatian ne meahte
laðum dædum,   þeah him leof ne waes.
He ða mid þære sorhge,   þe him swa sar belamp,
gumdream ofgeaf,   godes leoht geceas,
eaferum læfde,   swa deð eadig mon,   2470
lond ond leodbyrig,   þa he of life gewat.'

[For the eldest a violent death-bed was inappropriately spread through the deeds of his kinsman, when Hæthcyn struck down his lord and friend with an arrow from a horn-bow; he missed his mark and shot down his kinsman, one brother another, with a bloody shaft. That was an assault without compensation, a wrongful act of wickedness, wearying to the heart, nonetheless the prince had to lose his life unavenged. Likewise is it sad for an old man to endure, that his son should swing on the gallows young; then he utters a dirge, a mournful song, when his son hangs as a pleasure for the raven, and, old and very wise, he cannot bring about any help. Every morning there is a reminder of the passing forth of his son; he does not care to wait for another heir within the stronghold, now that one, through the necessity of death, has experienced the last of his deeds. Sore at heart he gazes on his son's dwelling, the deserted banquet-hall, a wind-swept resting-place bereft of joy; the horsemen sleep, warriors in the grave; there is no sound of harp, happiness in the enclosures, as there once had been. He goes to his bed, chants a song of sorrow, one after another; everything has seemed too spacious to him, the fields and dwelling-places. Likewise did the protector of the Weder-Geats bear his swelling heart's sorrow after Herebald; in no way could he remedy the wrong against the killer, none the sooner could he show hatred to that warrior through hostile deeds, although he was not dear to him. With that sorrow, which, sadly had befallen him, he gave up human joy; he chose God's light; he left to his sons, as a fortunate man does, his lands and strongholds, when he departed from life.]

The thematic connection made between the impossibility of either Hrethel or the unnamed father of the hanged man gaining either vengeance or recompense for their sons seems clear enough: Hrethel would hardly wish to exact vengeance from Hæthcyn, and it may well be, as Dorothy Whitelock has suggested, that a judicial hanging (and therefore without recompense) is intended in the second case.[97] Whatever the precise parallels invoked,[98] it is clear enough that Beowulf is here pondering the impotent grief and frustrated desire for requital of two old men in a manner which surely suggests something of his own anguish in the case of the dragon.[99]

Many critics have pointed to the resemblances between the account of the killing of Herebald by his brother Hæthcyn and that of the Norse god Baldr by his brother Hǫðr;[100] the similarities between the name-elements (Baldr / -beald; Hǫðr / Hæth-) certainly underline such an identification, which would then align Hrethel with the Norse god Óðinn, who was the father of both Baldr and Hǫðr.[101] As a god, Óðinn is intimately associated with the dead, with ravens, with death by hanging, with ritual marking with a spear, and with the art of poetry;[102] it is surely striking that Beowulf here mentions that Herebald was struck with a *blodigan gare* ('bloody shaft', literally 'bloody spear': the term seems inappropriate for an 'arrow from a horn-bow' [*of hornbogan . . . flane*], as at lines 2437b and 2438b), and that Hrethel's grief for his son is paralleled by that of a father who sees his son hanged, as a sport for ravens, whilst he laments by singing sad songs. The father of the hanged man is specifically described as an 'old man' (*gomelum ceorle*, line 2444b), and it is worth pointing out that Óðinn himself is several times described in similar ways.[103] Other Norse parallels might be mentioned here too: according to the thirteenth-century *Egils saga*, the tenth-century Icelandic poet Egill Skallagrímsson utters a similar dirge (in which he explicitly describes himself as a follower of Óðinn) for his own dead son (*Egils saga*, chapter 78),[104] whilst the thirteenth-century Icelander Snorri Sturluson gives an account of the events leading up to the accession of King Hugleikr (Old English Hygelac), in which there is a hunting accident in which one of two royal brothers kills the other (*Ynglinga saga*, chapters 22–3).[105]

With customary deftness, moreover, the *Beowulf*-poet incorporates into the passage a phrase which would appear to owe more to the Christian Latin tradition, saying of Hrethel that 'he chose God's light' (*Godes leoht geceas*, line 2469b), presumably a euphemism for 'he died': it is notable, however, that one

97 Whitelock, '*Beowulf* 2444–71'.
98 Cf. Schrader, 'The Deserted Chamber: an Unnoticed Topos in the "Father's Lament" of *Beowulf*'; Wehlau, ' "Seeds of Sorrow": Landscapes of Despair in *The Wanderer*, *Beowulf*'s Story of Hrethel and *Sonatorrek*'.
99 For a sensitive literary reading of the episode, see Georgianna, 'King Hrethel's Sorrow and the Limits of Heroic Action in *Beowulf*'. On the episode as a whole, see further below, pp. 227–37.
100 Cf. (for example) Harris, 'A Nativist Approach to *Beowulf*'; Orchard, *Cassell Dictionary of Norse Myth and Legend*, pp. 12–13. See too Faulkes, trans., *Edda*, pp. 48–51.
101 The same kind of onomastic connection, of course, links the god Heimdallr to the apparently human figure of Hama in *Beowulf*, as we have seen.
102 For a useful overview, see Turville-Petre, *Myth and Religion of the North*, pp. 35–74; cf. Orchard, *Cassell Dictionary of Norse Myth and Legend*, pp. 122–5.
103 In Snorri's account of the death of Baldr, a giantess called Þǫkk ('thanks') effectively condemns Baldr to remain in Hel by refusing to weep for him, saying that: 'alive nor dead I got no benefit from the old man's son' (*Kyks né dauðs / naut'ka ek karls sonar* [Faulkes, ed., *Gylfaginning*, p. 48; Jónsson, ed., *Edda*, p. 68; Faulkes, trans., *Edda*, p. 51), while in the eddic *Hárbarðsljóð* 2 Óðinn is derided by Þórr as 'old man of old men' (*karl karla* [Neckel, ed., *Edda*, p. 78]). I am grateful to Paul Bibire for pointing out to me the significance of these references.
104 Nordal, ed., *Egils saga*, pp. 242–57; cf. Harris, 'A Nativist Approach to *Beowulf*', pp. 51–5.
105 Aðalbjarnarson, ed., *Heimskringla*, I.40–3.

of the only parallel instances of such a phrase in the whole poem also comes in a passage which, it has been argued, may also allude to an event from Germanic myth. In that case, we are told that Hama 'chose eternal gain' (*geceas ecne ræd*, line 1201b)[106] when he carried of the *Brosinga mene* from Ermanaric, who, we might note, was celebrated in Germanic legend for having his own son hanged.[107] In incorporating such phrases into passages which seem to hark back to pagan myth, albeit in a euhemerised and sanitised form, it is as if the *Beowulf*-poet is somehow sanctifying his appeal to the figures of pre-Christian myth and legend. But whereas many of the passages which have been identified as containing echoes of an older tradition appear in episodes which are in some sense outside the main narrative of the poem, the same cannot be said for a further striking set of analogues, which would align Beowulf with the famed pagan god and monster-slayer Thor (*Þórr*) himself.[108]

The end of it all: Beowulf and Thor

As Ursula Dronke puts it: 'It has often been pointed out that Beowulf's fight with the dragon and Þórr's fight with the World-Serpent belong to the same type of dragon-fight: a hero in defence of his people kills a marauding dragon and himself dies in the fight.'[109] Paraphrasing a much earlier source (the eddic poem *Vǫluspá*, which dates to around the same period as the *Beowulf*-manuscript), Snorri Sturluson describes how Thor defeats the terrible Midgard-serpent, and dies:[110]

Þórr ber banaorð af Miðgarðsormi ok stígr þaðan braut níu fet. Þá fellr hann dauðr til jarðar fyrir eitri því, er ormrinn blæss á hann.

[Thor will be the death of the Midgard-serpent, and will step nine paces away from it. Then he will fall dead to the ground because of the venom that the serpent spit at him.]

The general situation is certainly similar to that of Beowulf, fatally poisoned by the dragon's venom, and forced to stagger away and sit down to die (lines 2711b–2717a):[111]

---

106 Cf. Hrothgar's advice to Beowulf to 'choose the better part, eternal gains' (*þæt selre geceos, / ece rædas*, lines 1759b–60a) in his so-called 'sermon', on the Christian connotations of which see further below, pp. 155–62. See too, for example, *Exodus*, line 516b (*ece rædas*); *Daniel*, line 30b (*eces rædes*); *Metres of Boethius* 20, line 224 (*ecne ræd*). In surviving prose, the phrase is entirely restricted to homiletic or religious contexts: cf. Ælfric, *Catholic Homilies* I.vii.197 (Clemoes, ed., *Ælfric's Catholic Homilies*, p. 238: *ecum ræde*); Ælfric, *Hexameron*, line 390 (Crawford, ed., *Exameron Anglice*, line 387: *ecum ræde*); Vercelli Homily XI, line 10 (Scragg, ed., *Vercelli Homilies*, p. 221: *ecan ræd*).

107 Cf. Finch, ed., *Vǫlsunga saga: the Saga of the Volsungs*, chapters 42–3 (pp. 75–7); Faulkes, ed., *Skáldskaparmál*, p. 49; Jónsson, ed., *Edda*, p. 132; Faulkes, trans., *Edda*, p. 104.

108 On Thor in Anglo-Saxon literature, see North, *Heathen Gods in Old English Literature*, pp. 232–41. See too Clunies Ross, 'Two of Þórr's Great Fights according to *Hymiskviða*'.

109 Dronke, '*Beowulf* and Ragnarǫk', p. 313.

110 Faulkes, ed., *Gylfaginning*, p. 50/35–6; Jónsson, ed., *Edda*, p. 72; Faulkes, trans., *Edda*, p. 54.

111 The manuscript reads *beal . . . weoll* at line 2714b, through damage to its edge.

> Ða sio wund ongon,
> þe him se eorðdraca   ær geworhte,
> swelan ond swellan;   he þæt sona onfand,
> þæt him on breostum   bealoniðe weoll
> attor on innan.   Ða se æðeling giong   2715
> þæt he bi wealle   wishycgende
> gesæt on sesse.

[Then the wound which the earth-dragon had given him began to burn and swell; he at once perceived that in his heart there welled with deadly harm poison within. Then the prince went, so that, wise-thinking, he sat down still by the wall.]

But this is not the only connection between Beowulf and Thor, the most celebrated monster-slayer in Norse myth and legend.[112] That Thor was associated with the killing of a variety of monstrous creatures is clear from the accounts of his exploits in a variety of sources. So, for example, in the *Prologue* to his *Gylfaginning*, Snorri Sturluson gives a euhemerised account of Thor which attempts to link him back to the Classical literary tradition:[113]

Einn konungr er þar var er nefndr Munon eða Mennon. Hann átti dóttur hǫfuðkonungs Priami. Sú hét Troan. Þau áttu son, hann hét Tror, þann kǫllum vér Þór. Hann var at uppfœzlu í Thracia með hertoga þeim er nefndr er Loricus. En er hann var tíu vetra þá tók hann við vápnum fǫður síns. Svá var hann fagr álitum, er hann kom með ǫðrum mǫnnum sem þá er fílsbein er grafit í eik. Hár hans er fegra en gull. Þá er hann var tólf vetra þá hafði hann fullt afl. Þá lypti hann af jǫrðu tíu bjarnstǫkkum ǫllum senn ok þá drap hann Loricum fóstra sinn, ok konu hans Lora eða Glora ok eignaði sér ríkit Thracia. Þat kǫllum vér Þrúðheim. Þá fór hann víða um lǫnd ok kannaði allar heims hálfur ok sigraði einn saman alla berserki ok risa ok einn inn mesta dreka ok mǫrg dýr.

[There was a king who was there [in Troy] whose name was Munon or Mennon; he was married to the daughter of the high-king, Priam (she was called Troan). They had a son, who was called Tror, but we call him Thor. He was raised up in Thrace by a commander, who was called Loricus, and when he was ten he inherited his father's weapons. He was as fair in appearance, when he came among other men, as when ivory is inlaid in oak. His hair is fairer than gold. When he was twelve, he had reached his full strength. Then he lifted up twelve bear-skins at once from the ground, killed his foster-father Loricus and his wife Lora or Glora, and took possession of the kingdom of Thrace. We call it Thrudheim. Then he travelled widely across the lands and explored all the continents and alone conquered all berserks and giants and the single greatest dragon and many animals.]

The association with bears here is one that recurs in tales about Thor,[114] and

---

112 On Thor in general, see Turville-Petre, *Myth and Religion of the North*, pp. 75–105; Orchard, *Cassell Dictionary of Norse Myth and Legend*, pp. 161–3.
113 Faulkes, ed., *Gylfaginning*, pp. 4/55–5/6; Jónsson, ed., *Edda*, p. 4; Faulkes, trans., *Edda*, p. 3.
114 See, for example, Coffin, '*Beowulf* and its Relationship to Norse and Finno-Uguric Beliefs and Narratives'; Jorgensen, 'The Two-Troll Variant of the Bear's Son Folktale in *Hálfdanar saga*

links the god with the so-called 'bear's son' folk-motif first studied in detail by Friedrich Panzer and detected by him in *Beowulf*.[115] This is emphatically not to revive the notion, put forward at its most extreme by Skeat,[116] that Beowulf himself is a bear, or that his name means 'bee-wulf' and so 'enemy of the bee', likewise a bear.[117] But Beowulf is at his most bear-like in his slaying of the Frankish champion Dæghrefn, apparently crushed to death to avenge the slaying of Hygelac (lines 2501–8a):[118]

'Syððan ic for dugeðum   Dæghrefne wearð
to handbonan,   Huga cempan;
nalles he ða frætwe   Frescyninge,
breostweorðunge,   bringan moste,
ac in compe gecrong   cumbles hyrde,   2505
æþeling on elne;   ne wæs ecg bona,
ac him hildegrap   heortan wylmas,
banhus gebræc.'

['Since before the hosts I became the hand-slayer of Dæghrefn, the champion of the Hugas. Not at all was he permitted to bring back the accoutrements, breast-adornments, to the Frisian king, but he fell on the battle-field, the standard-bearer, the prince in valour; no sword was his slayer, but a battle-grip shattered the surgings of his heart, his bone-house.']

In killing Dæghrefn as he had disposed of Grendel, without recourse to a weapon of any kind,[119] Beowulf aligns himself again with the god Thor, who elsewhere famously wrestles Elli ('old age') and is never seen wielding a sword.[120] Certainly, the notion that Thor engaged in lone combat with a variety of monsters, culminating in 'the single greatest dragon', matches what we find in *Beowulf*; moreover, still other traditions associated with Thor contain parallels for some puzzling details in the Old English poem.

So, for example, when Beowulf recounts his adventures in Denmark to Hygelac,[121] it has often been noted that a number of new elements are introduced,[122] among which is the name of the Geat devoured by Grendel, and (immediately afterwards) a description of the monster's marvellous *glof* (lines 2085b–2088):

Brönufóstra and *Grims saga loðinkinna*'; Stitt, *'Beowulf' and the Bear's Son*; Wachsler, 'Grettir's Fight with a Bear: another Neglected Analogue of *Beowulf* in the *Grettis Sag[a] Ásmundarsonar*'.

115   Panzer, *Studien zur germanischen Sagengeschichte*.

116   Skeat, 'On the Signification of the Monster Grendel in the Poem of *Beowulf*'.

117   Cf. Klaeber, ed., *Beowulf*, pp. xxv–xxvii. More likely, the etymology of Beowulf's name is Beow-wulf, 'the wolf of (the god) Beow', cf. the common Norse name Þórólfr 'the wolf of (the god) Þórr'.

118   The manuscript reads *fres cyning* at line 2503b and *incempan* at line 2505a, but the emendations accepted here are common ones.

119   On Dæghrefn in general, see, for example, Bonjour, 'The Problem of Dæghrefn'.

120   Faulkes, trans., *Edda*, pp. 44–5. See too Hodges, 'Beowulf's Shoulder Pin'; Peters, 'The Wrestling in *Grettis saga*'; idem, 'The Wrestling in *Beowulf*'.

121   See in general Looze, 'Frame Narratives and Fictionalization'.

122   See, for example, Klaeber, ed., *Beowulf*, p. 201.

'Glof hangode   2085
sid ond syllic,   searobendum fæst;
sio wæs orðoncum   eall gegyrwed
deofles cræftum   ond dracan fellum.'

['A *glof* hung, wide and wonderful, secure with skilful bonds; it was
entirely adorned with cunning, with a devil's skill and dragon-skins.']

That the name of the Geat devoured by Grendel should be Hondscio (line
2075a), an apparently transparent term for 'glove' (compare Modern German
Handschuh), is evidently another example of the *Beowulf*-poet's tendency to
etymologise names.[123] It has been noted that there are parallels between this
passage in *Beowulf* and a much later Icelandic tale of a glove, a cunningly
wrought food-sack, and the god Thor who finds himself unfortunately inside the
one and outside the other.[124] The Icelander Snorri Sturluson describes a humiliating encounter that Thor had at the hands of a huge giant, Skrýmir, apparently
basing his tale on older poetic sources.[125] According to Snorri's account, Thor,
travelling towards the land of the giants with two companions, finds himself
without shelter in a forest, and is forced to improvise:[126]

Þá er myrkt var orðit leituðu þeir sér náttstaðar ok fundu fyrir sér skála
nokkvorn mjǫk mikinn. Váru dyrr á enda ok jafnbreiðar skálanum. Þar leituðu
þeir sér náttbóls. En of miðja nótt varð landskjálpti mikill, gekk jǫrðin undir
þeim skykkjum ok skalf húsit. Þá stóð Þórr upp ok hét á lagsmenn sína, ok
leituðust fyrir ok fundu afhús til hœgri handar í miðjum skálanum ok gengu
þannig. Settist Þórr í dyrrin, en ǫnnur þau váru innar frá honum ok váru þau
hrædd, en Þórr hélt hamarskaptinu ok hugði at verja sik. Þá heyrðu þau ym
mikinn ok gný.

[When it got dark, they looked for a place to spend the night, and found for
themselves a very big hall with a door in one end that was as wide as the hall
itself. They looked for night-shelter there. But in the middle of the night there
was a huge earthquake: the ground shook and shuddered under them, and the
building trembled. Then Thor stood up and called to his companions, and they
looked around and found a side-chamber on the right, half-way down the hall,
and went in. Thor sat by the door, and the others were further inside, and they
were terrified, but Thor gripped the shaft of his hammer and prepared to
defend himself. They heard a great groaning and roaring.]

At dawn, Thor finds the snoring giant Skrýmir, and realises that they have spent
the night in his glove (evidently more of a mitten, since there are apparently no
fingers to it, and the 'side-chamber' turns out to be the thumb). Skrýmir offers

---

123 On which see below, pp. 172–3.
124 Cf. Klaeber, ed., *Beowulf*, p. 205; Laborde, 'Grendel's Glove and his Immunity from Weapons';
     Lerer, 'Grendel's Glove'. For a different view, see Anderson, 'Grendel's *glof* (*Beowulf* 2085b–88),
     and Various Latin Analogues'.
125 Thor's taking refuge inside a glove (and being too afraid even to fart) is referred to in the eddic
     Hárbarðsljóð 26 (Neckel, ed., *Edda*, p. 82), while his inability to untie a food-sack is referred to in
     Lokasenna 60 (Neckel, ed., *Edda*, p. 108).
126 Faulkes, ed., *Gylfaginning*, pp. 37/35–38/1; Jónsson, ed., *Edda*, p. 50; Faulkes, trans., *Edda*,
     pp. 38–9.

Thor and his companions his food-sack, and goes back to sleep, but Thor is quite unable to untie it: 'he couldn't loosen a single knot, or move a strap-end so that it was looser than before' (*engi knút fekk hann leyst ok engi álarendann hreyft, svá at þá væri lausari en áðr*). While Skrýmir's glove, like Grendel's, could certainly be described as 'wide and wonderful' (*sid ond syllic*, line 2086a) his food-bag, like Grendel's, is surely 'secure with skilful bonds' (*searobendum fæst*, line 2086b). The putative links between Beowulf and Thor are the more intriguing since it has long been recognised that euhemerised versions of Norse myth can be detected in a range of sagas,[127] much as elements of the death of Baldr or Heimdallr's theft of the Brísingamen can (as we have seen) appear in *Ynglinga saga* or *Þiðreks saga*. For Christian Icelanders, as for Christian Anglo-Saxons, the myths and legends of the pagan past could apparently afford literary opportunities that were not to be missed, and it is to these later sagas that we now turn.

Aftermath: 'Beowulf' and later Icelandic sagas

For more than a hundred years, a wide range of Icelandic sagas have routinely been compared with various aspects of *Beowulf*.[128] Although parallels and analogues have also been sought for *Beowulf* among a number of Celtic sources,[129]

---

127 See, for example, Harris, 'The Masterbuilder Tale in Snorri's Edda and in Two Sagas'.
128 The secondary literature is vast: see, for example, Albano, 'The Role of Women in Anglo-Saxon Culture'; Arent, 'The Heroic Pattern'; Boer, 'Zur Grettissaga'; Byock, *The Saga of King Hrolf Kraki*, pp. vii–xxviii; Chadwick, 'Norse Ghosts: a Study in the *draugr* and the *haugbúi*'; *idem*, 'The Monsters and Beowulf'; Clark, '*Beowulf* and *Njálssaga*'; Fjalldal, *The Long Arm of Coincidence*; Gering, 'Der Béowulf und die isländische Grettissaga'; Hieatt, 'Beowulf's Last Words vs. Bothvar Bjarki's'; Hill, 'The Confession of Beowulf and the Structure of *Vǫlsunga Saga*'; Jorgensen, 'Grendel, Grettir, and Two Skaldic Stanzas'; *idem*, 'The Two-Troll Variant of the Bear's Son Folktale in *Hálfdanar saga Brönufóstra* and *Gríms saga loðinkinna*'; *idem*, 'Beowulf's Swimming Contest with Breca: Old Norse Parallels'; *idem*, 'The Gift of the Useless Weapon in *Beowulf* and the Icelandic Sagas'; *idem*, 'Additional Icelandic Analogues to *Beowulf*'; Kluge, 'Der Beowulf und die Hrolfs saga kraka'; Lawrence, '*Beowulf* and the *Saga of Samson the Fair*'; Liberman, 'Beowulf-Grettir'; McConchie, 'Grettir Ásmundarson's Fight with Kárr the Old'; McTurk, *Studies in 'Ragnars saga loðbrókar' and its Major Scandinavian Analogues*; Olson, *The Relation of the Hrólfs saga kraka and the Bjarkarímur to Beowulf*; Opland, 'A *Beowulf* Analogue in *Njálssaga*'; Orchard, *Pride and Prodigies*, pp. 140–68; Peters, 'The Wrestling in *Grettis saga*'; *idem*, 'The Wrestling in *Beowulf*'; Puhvel, 'The Aquatic Contest in *Hálfdanar saga Brönufóstra*'; Stedman, 'Some Points of Resemblance between *Beowulf* and the Grettla (or *Grettis saga*)'; Stitt, '*Beowulf*' and the Bear's Son; Taylor, 'Two Notes on *Beowulf*'; Turville-Petre, '*Beowulf* and *Grettis saga*: an Excursion'; Wachsler, 'Grettir's Fight with a Bear'.
129 For those wishing to seek a Celtic connection for *Beowulf*, the following are useful: Borsje, *From Chaos to Enemy*; Bray, *A List of Motifs in the Lives of the Early Irish Saints*; Breeze, '*Beowulf* and *The Battle of Maldon*'; *idem*, '*Wered* "sweet drink" at *Beowulf* 496'; Carney, *Studies in Irish Literature and History*, pp. 77–128; Cook, 'An Irish Parallel to the Beowulf Story'; Donahue, 'Grendel and the *Clanna Cain*'; Dumville, '*Beowulf* and the Celtic World'; Evans, *The Heroic Poetry of Dark-Age Britain*; Kuhn, 'Old English *aglæca* – Middle Irish *ochlach*'; McCone, *Pagan Past and Christian Present in Early Irish Literature*; Nagy, 'Beowulf and Fergus'; Olson, '*Beowulf* and *The Feast of Bricriu*'; Puhvel, 'Beowulf and Celtic Under-Water Adventure'; *idem*, 'Beowulf's Slaying of Daghræfn'; *idem*, 'The Swim Prowess of Beowulf'; *idem*, 'The Blithe-Hearted Morning Raven in *Beowulf*'; *idem*, '*Beowulf*' and Celtic Tradition; *idem*, 'A Scottish Analogue to the Grendel Story'; Scowcroft, 'The Irish Analogues to *Beowulf*'; Sims-Williams, ' "Is it Fog or Smoke or Warriors

not to mention those from still wider afield,[130] in general these have seemed less convincing than those detected among Norse texts. If the fourteenth-century *Grettis saga* has been most closely studied in this respect,[131] over the years the search for parallels has become increasingly focused on the so-called 'legendary sagas' (*fornaldarsǫgur*),[132] several of which seem to share a striking number of narrative details with those found in *Beowulf*.[133] In particular, the so-called 'two-troll' motif seems to provide the closest comparisons to the first two monster-fights in *Beowulf*.

In general in these tales, the hero resolves to break into the mound of a *draugr* or walking corpse, which is usually situated by water; although accompanied by locals, the hero goes on alone, often descending by rope and emerging into a lit chamber. The fight with the *draugr* is a hand-to-hand affair, until the hero spies a sword in the gravemound, and uses it to kill and decapitate the *draugr*. The hero's companions have by this point fled, leaving the hero to emerge from the gravemound carrying spoils.[134] A typical account of such a battle is that in the fourteenth-century *Hrómundar saga Gripssonar*, chapter 4:[135]

Þeir kómu vestan at Vallandi ok fundu hauginn ok rufu þegar. Ok at liðnum sex dǫgum kómu þeir glugga á hauginn. Sáu þeir, at þar sat á stóli dólgr mikill, blár ok digr, allr gulli klæddr, svá at leiptraði af. Rumdi hann mjǫk ok blés at eldi . . . Fór svá Hrómundr niðr í festinni. Var þat á nóttu. Ok er hann kom niðr, bar hann saman fé mikit ok batt í festarenda. Þráinn hafði verit á fyrri dǫgum konungr yfir Vallandi ok vann allt með gǫldrum, gerði margt illt af sér, ok þá hann var svá gamall, at hann kunni eigi at stríða lengr, lét hann setja sik lifanda í hauginn ok mikit fé með sér. Nú sér Hrómundr, hvar sverðit hangir uppi á einni súlu. Hann kippir því ofan, gyrðist með ok gengr fram at stólnum ok mælti: 'Mér mun vera mál ór hauginum, fyrst engi hamlar, eða hverninn vegnar þér, þú hérna, inn gamli? Sástu eigi, at ek bar saman fé þitt, en þu hǫktir kyrr, hundr leiðr, eða hvat var þér í augum, er þú horfðir á, at ek tók sverðit ok menit ok fjǫlda þinna annarra gripa?' . . . Draugr mælti: 'Þat er engi fremd at bera sverð á mik vápnlausan. Heldr vil ek reyna afl við þik ok glímu.' Hrómundr kastar þá sverðinu ok treysti afli sínu.

[They came from the west to Valland, and found the grave-mound, and immediately began to break it open; and after six days they came upon a trap-door

---

Fighting?" '; *idem*, 'Thought, Word, and Deed: an Irish Triad'; Welsh, '*Branwen, Beowulf*, and the Tragic Peaceweaver Tale'; Wright, *The Irish Tradition in Old English Literature*.

130   See, for example, Colgrave, 'A Mexican Version of the "Bear's Son" Folk Tale'; Ogura, 'An Ogre's Arm: Japanese Analogues of *Beowulf*'.

131   For contrasting views, see, for example, Orchard, *Pride and Prodigies*, pp. 140–68; Fjalldal, *The Long Arm of Coincidence*.

132   Jónsson, ed., *Fornaldar sögur Norðurlanda*; see too the online versions of Old Norse-Icelandic sagas, details of which are given in section C of the Bibliography. Cf. Pálsson and Edwards, *Legendary Fiction in Medieval Iceland*; Schlauch, *Romance in Iceland*.

133   See in particular Stitt, '*Beowulf*' and the Bear's Son'.

134   For a series of tables offering detailed comparisons between events in *Beowulf* and in five separate episodes in *Grettis saga*, see Orchard, *Pride and Prodigies*, pp. 142–4, 147, 152, 161, and 164.

135   Jónsson, ed., *Fornaldar sögur Norðurlanda*, II.410–12; Kershaw, *Stories and Ballads of the Far Past*, pp. 66–7.

in the mound. There they saw that a big fiend was sitting on a seat, black and fat, all clad in gold, so that it flashed. He was roaring loudly and blowing on a fire . . . Then Hrómundr climbed down by the rope; it was then night. When he came down, he gathered together alot of treasure, and tied it to the end of the rope. Þráinn had been king over Valland in days gone by, and had won all his victories by magic: he had performed much evil, and when he was so old, that he could not fight any longer, he had caused himself to be shut up in the mound alive, along with much treasure. Now Hrómundr saw where a sword was hanging up on a pillar. He took it down, put it on, and marched up to the seat, saying: 'It's time for me to leave the mound now, since there is no one to stop me. But what's your problem, you there, old bloke? Can't you see that I'm carrying off your treasure, while you just sit still, you son of a bitch? What were you thinking of when you ignored me taking your sword and necklace and many other treasures?' . . . The *draugr* replied: 'It's not brave to take a sword from me when I am unarmed; I'd rather test my strength wrestling with you.' Hrómundr threw the sword down and relied on his strength.]

There are a number of very similar episodes scattered throughout the sagas;[136] the broad similarities of narrative detail to what we find in *Beowulf* will be clear.

But it is important to stress that it is not simply in the case of the monster-fights that one can find parallels between much later *fornaldarsǫgur* and *Beowulf*. Any assessment of Beowulf's aquatic prowess will rest principally on the interpretation of three key episodes, namely the encounter with Breca (lines 506–81a), the descent into the monster-mere (lines 1494b–1512a), and the retreat from Frisia (lines 2359–62).[137] In practice, all three episodes have come under extensive scrutiny, and what might be termed the more 'traditional' view, namely that Beowulf's exhibits marvellous or superhuman characteristics in these episodes, has been steadily eroded.[138] In particular, it has been argued that the encounter with Breca is a rowing-match, rather then the swimming-contest often assumed; that the descent into the monster-mere does not take all day, as sometimes supposed; and that the retreat from Frisia, in which Beowulf carries off thirty coats of mail from his fallen comrades, is accomplished by boat, rather than (as some would say) by swimming across the sea.[139] But it is still striking to

---

[136] See, for example, *Barðar saga Snæfellsáss*, chapter 20; *Egils saga ok Ásmundar*, chapter 7; *Grettis saga*, chapter 18; *Gull-Þóris saga*, chapter 3; *Harðar saga ok hólmverja*, chapter 15; Saxo Grammaticus, *Gesta Danorum*, V.135. Invaluable for tracking down such themes in the sagas is Boberg, *Motif-Index of Early Icelandic Literature*.

[137] Perhaps also to be included is the night-time battle with those 'water-monsters' (*nicoras*) that Beowulf, in his opening address to Hrothgar, reports himself as having slain (lines 419–24a), although there may be some overlap between this tale and the later account of Beowulf's encounter with Breca.

[138] See, for example, Anderson, 'Beowulf's Retreat from Frisia'; Earl, 'Beowulf's Rowing-Match'; Frank, ' "Mere" and "Sund": Two Sea-Changes in *Beowulf*'; Greenfield, 'A Touch of the Monstrous'; Griffith, '*Beowulf* 1495: *hwil dæges* = *momentum temporis*?'; Jorgensen, 'Beowulf's Swimming Contest with Breca'; Lawrence, 'The Breca Episode in *Beowulf*'; McNamara, 'Legends of Breca and Beowulf'; Puhvel, 'The Aquatic Contest'; Robinson, 'Elements of the Marvellous'; *idem*, 'Beowulf's Retreat from Frisia'; Wentersdorf, 'Beowulf's Adventure with Breca'; *idem*, 'Beowulf's Withdrawal from Frisia'.

[139] See below, pp. 230–2.

note that while there are a large number of analogues for Beowulf's supposed swimming-prowess to be found in the Norse *fornaldarsǫgur*, parallels for his alleged skill at rowing are harder to adduce.[140]

A particularly intriguing analogue for Beowulf's aquatic adventures is found in *Egils saga einhenda ok Ásmundar berserkjabana*, chapter 9;[141] the parallel is the more noteworthy since the saga in question also contains in an earlier chapter an analogue for part of the so-called 'two-troll' story-type, in which a hero descends into a grave-mound alone, battles with the resident undead warrior (*draugr*), decapitates him with a short sword (*sax*), and escapes with treasure.[142] The relevant passage reads as follows:

'Egill óx upp með hirð fǫður síns, þar til at hann var tólf vetra gamall. Hann var mikill fyrir sér ok óstýrilátr, kappsamr ok ódæll. Hann lagði lag sitt við drengi ok lagðist út á skóga at skjóta dýr ok fugla. Vatn mikit var í skóginum, ok váru þar í eyjar margar. Þar fóru þeir Egill á sund jafnan, því at þeir vǫndu sik mjǫk við íþróttir. Eitt sinn ræddi Egill um við þá, hverr lengst mundi geta lagist í vatnit, því at svá var langr vegrinn í þá ey, sem first var landi, at hana sá eigi, utan þeir gengi upp í há tré til. Nú leggjast þeir á vatnit, ok váru saman þrír tigir. Skyldi þar hverr eftir vera, sem hann treysti sér eigi lengra at fara. Leggjast þeir nú um vatnit, ok váru sum sundin breið mjǫk. Egill var fljótastr á sundinu, ok gat engi fylgt honum. Ok er þeir váru langt frá landi komnir, þá kom þoka svá myrk, at engi sá annan, ok gerði þá vind kaldan. Villtust þeir nú á sundinu, ok eigi vissi Egill, hvat af sínum mǫnnum varð. Hvarflaði hann nú um vatnit tvau dægr. Kom hann þá at landi ok var svá máttdreginn, at hann varð at skríða á land, ok reytti hann á sik mosa ok lá þar um nóttina.

['Egill grew up at his father's court, until he was twelve years old; he was self-willed and ungovernable, aggressive and unmanageable. He hooked up with a gang of lads and they used to go out in the woods to shoot animals and birds. There was a large lake in the woods, with many islands in it, and Egill and his gang often went swimming there, because they had trained themselves for all sorts of sports. One day Egill brought up the question among them of who could get the furthest into the lake, because it was such a long distance to the furthest island that it couldn't be seen unless they climbed a high tree. So they set off into the lake, thirty all told: each of them was to go only as far as he felt confident. So they set off into the lake, and some of the distances between the islands were very long. Egill was the swiftest swimmer, and no one could keep up with him. When they had come a long way from the shore, a mist came down so dark, that none of them could see the others, and the wind grew cold. Now they drifted in their swimming, and Egill did not know what had become of his companions. He wandered around in the lake for two days. Then he came to land, and was so exhausted, that he had to crawl ashore; he covered himself with moss and lay there overnight.]

---

140 See especially Jorgensen, 'Beowulf's Swimming Contest with Breca'.

141 *Egils saga einhenda ok Ásmundar berserkjabana* is ed. Guðni Jónsson, *Fornaldar sögur Norðurlanda*, III.323–65; and translated by Pálsson and Edwards, *Seven Viking Romances*, pp. 240–1.

142 Cf. Pálsson and Edwards, *Seven Viking Romances*, pp. 240–1.

This aquatic adventure has a number of close parallels to the encounter with Breca as seen from Beowulf's own point of view: a test of endurance rather than a challenge-match *per se*, in which the strongest individual becomes separated by bad weather, drifts alone for two days, and is finally washed ashore exhausted.[143] The number of Egill's fellow-swimmers is of interest too, since the thirty lads in Egill's gang equate both to the number of mail-shirts Beowulf recovers from Frisia, and to Beowulf's putative strength: we are told explicitly that he has the strength of thirty men in his grip (lines 379b–381a).[144]

The fact that both in his encounter with Breca and in his descent into the monster-mere Beowulf is wearing a mail-shirt that apparently prevents the various water-monsters from piercing his flesh is of some interest in this context too, since later on in *Egils saga einhenda* (chapter 15) reference is made to a shirt that no weapon could bite,[145] and which caused its wearer never to tire when swimming.[146] Several of the *fornaldarsǫgur* contain cases of shirts with similar aquatic and defensive properties. The most elaborate example of such a shirt is found in *Ǫrvar-Odds saga*, chapter 11,[147] where the eponymous hero is offered a magical shirt by a mysterious and beautiful woman he meets in a forest-clearing; she describes its properties in detail:[148]

> 'Þik skal aldri kala í henni, hvárki á sjó né á landi. Þik skal eigi sund mæða, ok eigi skal þér eldr granda, ok eigi skal þik hungr sækja, ok eigi skulu þik járn bíta, ok við ǫllum hlutum mun ek hana gera nema við einum.' – 'Hverr er sá inn eini?' sagði Oddr. – 'Þik munu járn bíta,' sagði hún, 'ef þú ert á flótta, þótt þú sért í skyrtunni.' – 'Annat vilda ek optar vinna í orrostum en flýja,' sagði Oddr, 'eða hvé nær skal hún ger?' – 'At ǫðru sumri,' sagði hún, 'jafnt í þat mund dags, sem nú er, ok er nú sól í suðri. Þá skulu vit hér finnast í þessu sama rjóðri.'

> ['You'll never get cold in it, either at sea or on land; you'll never get tired swimming, and fire won't harm you, and hunger won't afflict you, and iron won't bite on you, and it'll keep you from everything except one thing only.' 'And what's that?' said Oddr. 'Iron will bite you, if you're running away, even though you're wearing the shirt.' 'I'll have better things to do in battle than run away', said Oddr, 'how soon can it be made?' 'Next summer', she said, 'a year to the day, when the sun is in the south, as now. Then we shall meet here in the same clearing.']

---

[143] For a different view, cf. Puhvel, 'The Aquatic Contest in *Hálfdanar saga Brǫnufóstra*', p. 135; Puhvel is arguing against Jorgensen, 'Beowulf's Swimming Contest with Breca'.

[144] See further below, pp. 144–6.

[145] On this notion as a theme in the sagas see, for example, Beard, '*Á þá bitu engi járn*: a Brief Note on the Concept of Invulnerability in the Old Norse Sagas'.

[146] The shirt is made by the Russian princess Bekkhildr: *Bekkhildr hafði gert eina skyrtu, ok festi ekki vápn á, ok eigi mátti sá á sundi mæðast, er í henni var.*

[147] *Ǫrvar-Odds saga* is ed. Guðni Jónsson, *Fornaldar sögur Norðurlanda*, II.199–363; as with *Egils saga einhenda ok Ásmundar berserkjabana*, it is worth recording that *Ǫrvar-Odds saga* likewise contains further analogues to connect it to *Beowulf*.

[148] Cf. Pálsson and Edwards, *Seven Viking Romances*, pp. 240–1.

In fact, however, the majority of such shirts in the *fornaldarsǫgur* confer upon their wearer the advantages of that in *Egils saga*, namely invulnerability to weapons and tirelessness at swimming,[149] precisely those elements which are so important in the context of *Beowulf*. One can only suppose that as other *fornaldarsǫgur* are identified which appear to provide analogues to *Beowulf*, perhaps in areas other than swimming-prowess, invulnerability, and monster-slaying, a better understanding of the interrelationships between these texts will emerge. If the notion that *Beowulf* could have directly influenced Icelandic sagas still seems far-fetched to many, one notes that among the earliest settlers to Iceland was one Bjólfr, whose name appears to be cognate with that of Beowulf.[150] Moreover, if *Beowulf* had any currency in Anglo-Saxon England, as now seems not unlikely,[151] it remains possible that some aspects of the story could have travelled to Iceland with the early settlers, many of whom came from the British Isles or at least sojourned there in transit. As with so many aspects of the study of *Beowulf*, the success of scholars of the past in identifying parallels provides a keen incitement to future generations to do more.

Beowulf, however, is not the only surviving Old English poem to draw on aspects of the Germanic legendary past: *Deor*, *The Finnsburh Fragment*, *Waldere*, and *Widsith* certainly do, and *Wulf and Eadwacer* may.[152] Nor may *Beowulf* be the only surviving Old English poem to draw on aspects of Germanic myth, if the reference to the fact that 'all creation wept' at the death of Christ in the *Dream of the Rood* (*weop eall gesceaft*, line 55b) really does reflect the weeping of all creation required at the death of the god Baldr.[153] In the latter case, one notes that the apparent reference to a pagan god has been utterly sanctified by its context, just as in *Beowulf*, as we have seen, the apparent references to the death of Baldr or the Heimdallr's theft are likewise Christianised.[154] And if by giving his life in defence of his people when he defeats the dragon Beowulf may well reflect aspects of the monster-slaying pagan god Thor, it is important

---

149 A handy check-list of such garments in eleven separate (though doubtless related) *fornaldarsǫgur* is found in Andersson and Gade, *Morkinskinna*, p. 424, n. 10. Apart from *Egils saga einhenda* and *Ǫrvar-Odds saga*, the sagas in question are *Gǫngu-Hrólfs saga* (chapters 4, 30, and 32); *Hálfdanar saga Brǫnufóstra* (chapter 8); *Hervarar saga* (chapter 3); *Ragnars saga loðbrókar* (chapter 15), *Sǫgubrot af fornkonungum* (chapter 4), *Sǫrla saga sterka* (chapters 3, 6, and 18); *Vǫlsunga saga* (chapter 42); *Þáttr af Ragnars sonum* (chapter 3); *Þorsteins þáttr bœjarmagns* (chapters 3 and 5). See too Holtsmark, 'Olav den Hellige'.

150 Benediktsson, ed., *Landnámabók*, II.306/4–8; see too Einarsson, 'Bjólfr and Grendill'; *idem*, 'Beowulfian Place-Names'.

151 On the notion that some extant Old English poems echo *Beowulf* directly, see below, pp. 163–8. As evidence that some scribe or other appeared to recognise Beowulf's prime significance within the poem, one might note the extensive capitalisation of his name at the beginning of fitts XXI and XXII (see Table II above, pp. 94–5), as well as the apparent miscopying of Beow as Beowulf in lines 18a and 53b (see further above, pp. 103–4). Cf. Cassidy, 'Knowledge of *Beowulf* in Its Own Time'; Weinstock, 'Comment on "Knowledge of *Beowulf* in Its Own Time"'.

152 See, for example, Aertsen, '*Wulf and Eadwacer*: a Woman's *cri de coeur*'; Bouman, '*Leodum is minum*: Beaduhild's complaint'; D'Aronco, '*Wulf and Eadwacer*, analisi del testo'; Hough, '*Wulf and Eadwacer*: a Note on *ungelic*'; North, 'Metre and Meaning in *Wulf and Eadwacer*'.

153 See, for example, North, *Heathen Gods in Old English Literature*, pp. 287–303.

154 See above, pp. 114–19.

to realise that his self-sacrifice also reflects that of a figure from a quite different tradition, namely Christ.[155] It is therefore to that imported, written, Latin, Christian tradition that we now turn to seek other sources in the background to *Beowulf.*

---

[155] As Klaeber, ed., *Beowulf,* p. li, puts it: 'We might even feel inclined to recognize features of the Christian Savior in the destroyer of hellish fiends, the warrior brave and gentle, blameless in thought and deed, the king that dies for his people.' See further below, pp. 147–9.

5

Religion and Learning

The Christian background to 'Beowulf'

The older view that the surviving text of *Beowulf* represents a Christian re-working (or perhaps several re-workings) of an originally pagan text is no longer in vogue,[1] just as the efforts of *Beowulf*-scholars are no longer primarily directed towards the recovery of such a putative 'original' text.[2] In this respect, the developing study of *Beowulf* simply reflects that of other Old English poems, such as *The Wanderer*, long held to be an originally secular poem to which a Christian coda has been added,[3] or *Deor*, which if it contains unmistakable references to the pre-Christian legendary past, is often given a Christianised, even Boethian reading.[4] But there remain a number of issues of crucial importance to any understanding of the poem, namely the extent to which the *Beowulf*-poet may have been influenced by the literate Latinate culture that came into Anglo-Saxon England alongside Christianity itself, and the pervading effects of which on the Anglo-Saxon literary tradition have been increasingly recognised in recent years.[5] But this is not to say that Latin culture (any more than Christianity) was transmitted only through the medium of written texts: Christian-Latin tales, motifs, and ideas could as easily have been disseminated orally in much the same way as those of the secular heroic tradition, and it is often difficult to determine parallels of theme or even wording that

---

[1] See further above, pp. 6–7.

[2] Interesting (if very different) overviews of the way in which successive generations of Anglo-Saxon scholars have tended to focus on the background to Old English texts, rather than the texts themselves, are found in Frantzen, *Desire for Origins*; Frantzen and Venengoni, 'The Archaeology of Anglo-Saxon Studies'; Stanley, *Imagining the Past*.

[3] The comments of Anderson, *The Literature of the Anglo-Saxons*, pp. 159–60, can be taken as symptomatic of such an approach: 'The final lines of the poem, most likely a sop to Christianity from the hands of some pious scribe, succeed in being an anticlimax, for the heart of the poem is beating with triumphant pessimism'. For more recent criticism of *The Wanderer*, see Orchard, 'Re-reading *The Wanderer*'.

[4] See, for example, Bolton, 'Boethius, Alfred, and *Deor* Again'; many of the author's same preoccupations are evident in his later 'Boethius and a Topos in *Beowulf*'.

[5] The primary resources for assessing the extent of this influence on Anglo-Saxon literary culture are the two international research-projects *SASLC* and *Fontes Anglo-Saxonici* (on which, see the sites listed in section C of the Bibliography). Also crucial for assessing the manuscript evidence relating to this material is Gneuss, *Handlist*. See too Ogilvy, *Books Known to the English, 597–1066; idem*, 'Books Known to the English, A.D. 597–1066: Addenda et Corrigenda'.

are the result of direct borrowing or simply part of some wider pattern of influence.

As for *Beowulf*, there seems no getting rid of the poet's clear references to the biblical tales of Cain and Abel (lines 107–10 and 1261b–1265a) and the subsequent story of the Flood (lines 1260–1b and 1688b–1693) without doing irreparable damage to the transmitted text, and the debate has instead shifted to a consideration of the precise extent to which *Beowulf* has not simply been shaped by a Christian world-view,[6] but informed by the imported, literate, and Latinate learning that the Conversion brought to Anglo-Saxon England.[7] The difficulty of assessing how far *Beowulf* can be described as a truly 'Christian' poem has exercised many of the finest and most subtle of *Beowulf*-scholars: it might be noted that if Friedrich Klaeber can identify in Beowulf a type of Christ,[8] J. R. R. Tolkien, in the course of perhaps the most influential paper ever written on the poem, can still express doubts about the 'originality' of some of the Christian passages in the text.[9] Even in the introduction to one of the most recent editions of *Beowulf*, produced by two of the most distinguished *Beowulf*-scholars of their generation, the editors, Bruce Mitchell and Fred Robinson, feel obliged to offer 'Two Views of *Beowulf*', in which Mitchell downplays the Christian elements and Robinson emphasises them.[10]

But if *Beowulf* is reckoned free from the influence of the Christian-Latin tradition, then it is the only such text in the *Beowulf*-manuscript.[11] Indeed, in

---

6 Book-length studies of the putative influence of Christian themes on *Beowulf* include: Cherniss, *Ingeld and Christ*; Goldsmith, *The Mode and Meaning of 'Beowulf'*; Huppé, *The Hero in the Earthly City*; Klaeber, *The Christian Elements in 'Beowulf'*; Moe, 'The Christian Passages of "Beowulf"'; Parker, *'Beowulf' and Christianity*. Important and interesting articles on the topic include Blackburn, 'The Christian Coloring in the *Beowulf*'; Bloomfield, *'Beowulf* and Christian Allegory'; Britton, 'Unferth, Grendel and the Christian Meaning of *Beowulf*'; Cabaniss, *'Beowulf* and the Liturgy'; Campbell, 'The Death of Beowulf: Please Indicate Church Affiliation'; *idem*, 'Physical Signs of Spiritual Cleansing in Old English Poetry'; *idem*, 'The Decline and Fall of Hrothgar and His Danes'; Cassidy, 'A Symbolic Word-Group in *Beowulf*'; Donahue, *'Beowulf* and Christian Tradition'; *idem*, 'Beowulf, Ireland and the Natural Good'; Feldman, 'A Comparative Study of *feond, deofl, syn* and *hel* in *Beowulf*'; Garde, *'Sapientia, ubi sunt*, and the Heroic Ideal in *Beowulf*'; *idem*, 'Christian and Folkloric Tradition in *Beowulf*'; Frankis, 'The Thematic Significance of *enta geweorc*'; Goldsmith, 'The Christian Theme of *Beowulf*'; *idem*, 'The Christian Perspective in *Beowulf*'; Hamilton, 'The Religious Principle in *Beowulf*'; Hardy, 'The Christian Hero Beowulf and Unferð þyle'; Hill, 'The Christian Language and Theme of *Beowulf*'; Horgan, 'Religious Attitudes in Beowulf'; Irving, 'The Nature of Christianity in *Beowulf*'; *idem*, 'Christian and Pagan Elements'; McNamee, 'Beowulf, a Christian Hero'; McNamee, *'Beowulf* – An Allegory of Salvation?'; O'Brien O'Keeffe, 'Heroic Values and Christian Ethics'; Pigg, 'Cultural Markers in *Beowulf*'; Rollinson, 'The Influence of Christian Doctrine and Exegesis on Old English Poetry'; Smithson, 'The Old English Christian Epic'; Stevick, 'Christian Elements and the Genesis of *Beowulf*'; Whallon, 'The Christianity of *Beowulf*'; Whallon, Goldsmith, and Donahue, 'Allegorical, Typological, or Neither?'.

7 For useful overviews of the problems, see Niles, *'Beowulf': the Poem and the Tradition*, pp. 66–95; Irving, 'The Nature of Christianity in *Beowulf*'; *idem*, 'Christian and Pagan Elements'.

8 Klaeber, ed., *Beowulf*, p. li (quoted above, p. 129). Others of Klaeber's works, notably the four parts that make up 'Die christlichen Elemente im *Beowulf*', pursue the theme. There is a convenient translation of all four parts of 'Die christlichen Elemente' by Battles ('The Christian Elements in *Beowulf*'), and it is to the latter text that I shall primarily refer.

9 Tolkien, *'Beowulf*: the Monsters and the Critics', pp. 287–9.

10 Mitchell and Robinson, ed., *Beowulf*, pp. 36–8. It is interesting to note that in the course of brief analyses of broadly similar length, Mitchell uses the word 'Christian' three times (always citing the opinions of others), Robinson ten times.

11 See further above, pp. 22–5.

their range of unquestioned indebtedness to a variety of Latin works (secular, biblical, and hagiographical), the other texts in the manuscript provide a useful index to the sorts of material on which (at least some have argued) the *Beowulf*-poet may have drawn. It is important to stress, however, that (unlike all the other texts in the manuscript), no single Latin source has ever been certainly identified for *Beowulf* (nor is any likely to be), and only analogues have ever been seriously suggested;[12] and it seems quite possible that any Latinate elements in the poem may have been mediated through the vernacular. Therefore, any consideration of the putative influence of Christian or Latin texts on *Beowulf* needs also to consider apparent parallels between the poem and a variety of other, more explicitly Christian texts composed in Old English, most of which themselves are heavily endebted to biblical and patristic thought and diction.

Classical words and Christian contexts: Latin literary analogues for 'Beowulf'

It is a curious fact of literary history that the application of so-called 'oral-formulaic theory' to Old English has given new life to the moribund practice of drawing comparisons between Homeric epic and *Beowulf*,[13] although no one has yet been so bold as to take up cudgels again in arguing for direct influence from the Greek, or even for indirect influence mediated through texts such as the *Ilias Latina*.[14] Still more surprising, perhaps, given the vast amount of evidence for first-hand knowledge and study of Vergil in Anglo-Saxon England,[15] is the fact that the whole question of the influence of the *Aeneid* on the *Beowulf*-poet has become more or less a dead letter, ever since Tom Burns

---

12 For a useful discussion of the difference between sources and analogues, see Rauer, *Beowulf and the Dragon*, pp. 9–11. Here, I use the term 'analogue' to describe a parallel where intentional borrowing in one direction or the other cannot be demonstrated; the burden of evidence required of a 'source' is much higher: the would-be source-hunter must (rather like a detective) be able to demonstrate means, motive, and opportunity for borrowing to have taken place, rather than any more superficial (not to say circumstantial) evidence. See too Anderson, 'Sources and Analogues'.

13 On the 'oral-formulaic' debate, see above, pp. 85–91. Earlier attempts to align *Beowulf* with Homeric epic include Cook, 'Beowulfian and Odyssean Voyages'; *idem*, 'Greek Parallels to Certain Features of the *Beowulf*'; *idem*, 'Hellenic and Beowulfian Shields and Spears'; *idem*, 'The Beowulfian *maðelode*'; *idem*, '*Beowulf* 1039 and the Greek *archibasileus*'; Duff, 'Homer and *Beowulf*'; see too Brandl, 'Hercules und Beowulf'; Hagen, 'Classical Names and Stories in the *Beowulf*'. More recent attempts at such a comparison include Andersson, *Early Epic Scenery*; Foley, 'Feasts and Anti-Feasts in *Beowulf* and the *Odyssey*'; *idem*, *Traditional Oral Epic*; *idem*, *Homer's Traditional Art*; Lord, 'Beowulf and Odysseus'; Louden, 'A Narrative Technique in *Beowulf* and Homeric Epic'; Parks, 'Ring Structure and Narrative Embedding in Homer and *Beowulf*'; *idem*, *Verbal Dueling in Heroic Narrative*; *idem*, 'The Traditional Narrator in *Beowulf* and Homer'; Rose, 'Hrothgar, Nestor, and Religiosity as a Mode of Characterization in Heroic Poetry'; Whallon, 'Formulas for Heroes in the *Iliad* and in *Beowulf*'; *idem*, *Formula, Character, and Context*; see too *idem*, *Inconsistencies*. Even die-hard opponents of 'oral-formulaic' theory use Homer as a point of comparison: cf. Watts, *The Lyre and the Harp*.

14 Gneuss, *Handlist*, nos. 535 and 664, lists two manuscripts of the *Ilias Latina* written or owned in England up to 1100, but both date around the beginning of the twelfth century, and are too late for detailed consideration here.

15 See, for example, Orchard, *The Poetic Art of Aldhelm*, pp. 130–5 and the references there cited.

Haber presented the case most fully in English in 1931, building on (but certainly not improving) the pioneering work of Klaeber, which still stands in sore need of balanced reassessment.[16] Occasional voices timidly suggest the possible influence of other Classical poets,[17] but strong general objections have been raised;[18] and there the matter largely rests.

The main stumbling-block to widespread acceptance of Vergilian influence on *Beowulf* has been that none of the parallels suggested to date seems sufficiently specific. Klaeber pointed out long ago that an excellent parallel to Beowulf's comment that 'each of us shall experience an end of life in the world: let him who can gain glory before death' (*ure æghwylc sceal ende gebidan worolde lifes; wyrce se þe mote domes ær deaþe*, lines 1386–8a) is found in Jupiter's comment that 'to each there stands his own day; to all the time of life is short and irretrievable; but to extend one's fame with deeds, that is the task of valour' (*stat sua cuique dies, breve et irreperabile tempus / omnibus est vitae; sed famam extendere factis, hoc virtutis opus*, Aeneid X.467–9),[19] but such a sentiment seems simply a heroic commonplace. After a characteristically sensitive and thoughtful review of the evidence, Jack Niles finds the closest parallel between *Beowulf* and the *Aeneid* to lie in the shared use of the phrase 'they all fell silent', just before a key speech (*swigedon ealle*, line 1699b; *conticuere omnes*, Aeneid II.1).[20] While such a parallel is undoubtedly interesting, however, it might be pointed out that even if a parallel phrase in *Andreas* (*swigodon ealle*, line 762b) might be attributable to the direct influence on that poem of *Beowulf*,[21] the existence of a pair of parallel phrases in the Old Norse *Poetic Edda* (*þǫgþu allir*, found in *Brot af Sigurðarkviðu* 15.1 and *Sigurðarkvida in skamma* 50.1)[22] might suggest a wider currency for the phrase in Germanic verse. What is required is a connection still more specific.

A more promising line of enquiry might consider how Vergilian influence might have been mediated through later texts, and to compare the ways in which later authors and poets appropriated the pagan heroic material of the Classical past into undoubtedly Christian contexts. It has become increasingly clear in recent years the extent to which the authors of Christian-Latin epic, such as Juvencus, Caelius Sedulius, Prudentius, and Arator, formed the staple of the Anglo-Saxon school curriculum,[23] and of themselves provide a perfect model for the use of heroic verse for a Christian didactic purpose. Likewise, a Vergilian background for at least one curious text with a well-documented connection with *Beowulf* is assured. The *Liber monstrorum* ('Book of monsters') is an

---

16 Haber, *A Comparative Study of the 'Beowulf' and the 'Aeneid'*; Klaeber, 'Aeneis und Beowulf'. See too Brandl, '*Beowulf*-Epos und *Aeneis* in systematischer Vergleichung'; Renoir, 'The Terror of the Dark Waters'; Trnka, 'The *Beowulf* Poem and Virgil's *Aeneid*'.
17 Special mention should be made of Schrader, 'Beowulf's Obsequies and the Roman Epic'; *idem*, 'Sacred Groves, Marvellous Waters, and Grendel's Abode'. See too Cornelius, 'Palus inamabilis'.
18 Cf. Chadwick, *The Heroic Age*, pp. 73–6; Nist, '*Beowulf* and the Classical Epics'.
19 Klaeber, ed., *Beowulf*, p. 184.
20 Niles, *'Beowulf': the Poem and its Tradition*, pp. 74–8.
21 See further below, pp. 163–8.
22 Neckel, ed., *Edda*, pp. 200 and 215.
23 Cf. Lapidge, *Anglo-Latin Literature 600–899*, pp. 409–98; *idem*, *Anglo-Latin Literature 900–1066*, pp. 1–48; Orchard, *The Poetic Art of Aldhelm*, pp. 161–78.

extraordinary work, apparently composed by an Anglo-Saxon around the beginning of the eighth century, which meticulously catalogues more than 120 'monsters', divided into three books by type, namely whether they are humanoid, bestial, or serpentine.[24] Even this tripartite division might suggests a broad parallel with the monster-fights in *Beowulf*, and indeed the *Liber monstrorum* shares a number of curious details with the poem. In only its second chapter, the *Liber monstrorum* mentions Hygelac by name, albeit as a monster (I.2):

> Et fiunt monstra mirae magnitudinis, ut rex Higlacus, qui imperauit Getis et a Francis occisus est, quem equus a duodecimo aetatis anno portare non potuit. Cuius ossa in Rheni fluminis insula, ubi in Oceanum prorumpit, reseruata sunt, et de longinquo uenientibus pro miraculo ostenduntur.
>
> [And there are monsters of an amazing size, like King Hygelac, who ruled the Geats and was killed by the Franks, whom no horse could carry from the age of twelve. His bones are preserved on an island in the River Rhine, where it breaks into the Ocean, and they are shown as a wonder to travellers from afar.]

Apart from exaggerating Hygelac's size in a way familiar from a number of saga-narratives,[25] the author of the *Liber monstrorum* seems keen to align Hygelac with a whole race of giants, of whom he later notes (I.54):

> Gigantes enim ipsos tam enormis alebat magnitudo ut eis omnia maria pedum gressibus transmeabilia fuisse perhibeatur. Quorum ossa in litoribus et in terrarum latebris, ad indicium vastae quantitatis eorum, saepe conperta leguntur.
>
> [Indeed giants used to grow to such an enormous size that it is said that all the seas were passable to them on foot. And their bones are often found, according to books, on the shores and in the recesses of the world, as an indication of their vast size.]

That the bones of such creatures are found on the sea-shore seems an allusion to the narrative of their destruction in the Flood, an episode mentioned in the *Prologue* to the work.[26] Other heroes from the pagan past likewise turn up as monsters, notably the famed monster-slayer Hercules, who appears no fewer than seven times, in all three books (I.12; II.1, 6, and 14; III.1, 3, and 20). Recent work on the sources of the *Liber monstrorum* has shown it to be a highly sophisticated piece of work, based on a careful combination of three kinds of material, namely Christian prose sources, chiefly Isidore and Augustine; pagan prose sources, chiefly relating to the heroic exploits of Alexander the Great; and

---

[24] See, for example, Butturff, 'The Monsters and the Scholar'; Lapidge, '*Beowulf*, Aldhelm, the *Liber Monstrorum* and Wessex'; Lendinara, 'The *Liber monstrorum* and Anglo-Saxon Glossaries'; Orchard, *Pride and Prodigies*, pp. 86–115 and 254–320; idem, 'The Sources and Meaning of the *Liber monstrorum*'; Porsia, ed., *Liber Monstrorum*; Whitbread, 'The *Liber Monstrorum* and *Beowulf*'. All quotations and translations here are taken from the edition by Orchard, *Pride and Prodigies*, pp. 254–320.

[25] The classic example of a saga-hero of this type is Gǫngu-Hrólfr ('Walker-Hrólfr'), whom (as his name suggests) no horse could carry; cf. Jónsson, ed., *Fornaldar sögur Norðurlanda*, III.173.

[26] Cf. Orchard, *Pride and Prodigies*, pp. 254–7.

Vergil, including the commentary tradition.[27] The Christian author implicitly undermines and condemns the pagan and heroic material that he has apparently collected with such care, and presents the whole piece as a warning against the seductive power of pagan literature.[28]

Few of the individual chapters of the *Liber monstrorum* remain unsourced (that describing Hygelac being one of them), but among those few is an account of an extraordinarily venomous creature (II.23):

> Bestia autem illa inter omnes beluas dirissima fertur, in qua tantam ueneni copiam adfirmant ut eam sibi leones quamuis inualidioris feram corporis, timeant, et tantam uim eius uenenum habere arbitrantur, ut eo licet ferri acies intincta liquescat.

> [But that beast is said to be amongst the fiercest of all brutes, in which they assert that there is such a quantity of venom that lions fear it although it is an animal of weaker body, and they reckon that its poison has such strength, that the cutting-edge even of iron, dipped in it, melts.]

Such a creature seems to share this curious quality with Grendel, whose blood likewise causes the blade of the giant sword to melt, an image of which the *Beowulf*-poet gives two descriptions, first in his own voice (lines 1605b–1617), and then in Beowulf's (lines 1666b–1668a). The accounts of the melting of what the poet calls 'an ancient sword made by giants' (*ealdsweord eotenisc*, line 1558a)[29] and Beowulf calls 'an ancient and mighty sword' (*ealdsweord eacen*, line 1663a),[30] are strikingly similar; Beowulf's much briefer description has a number of unmistakable echoes of the earlier version by the poet, especially the simple statement that 'the decorated weapon burnt up', which is repeated almost verbatim (*forbarn brogdenmæl*, line1667a, cf. *forbarn brodenmæl*, line 1616a; *hildebil*, line 1666b, cf. *wigbil*, line 1607a; *blod . . . hatost heaþoswata*, line 1667b–1668a, cf. *heaþoswate . . . wæs þæt blod to þæs hat*, lines 1606a and 1616b). In fact, Vergil may have (inadvertently) suggested the image of the melting sword to both the author of the *Liber monstrorum* and to the *Beowulf*-poet (or indeed to one via the other):[31] long ago, Klaeber suggested that the fact that after Beowulf decapitates Grendel the giant sword 'entirely melted most like ice' (*hit eal gemealt ise gelicost*, line 1608) might relate to the famous scene in the *Aeneid* where the sword of Turnus, meeting the divine armour of

---

27 See especially Orchard, 'The Sources and Meaning of the *Liber monstrorum*'. It might be pointed out that among the Alexander-material employed by the author of the *Liber monstrorum* are the Latin texts that lie behind both the *Wonders of the East* and *The Letter of Alexander to Aristotle*.

28 Orchard, 'The Sources and Meaning of the *Liber monstrorum*', pp. 102–5.

29 The same term is used both of the sword that Weohstan takes from Eanmund (on which see Dane, 'Wiglaf's Sword'), which he is then given by Onela (line 2616a), and of the sword that Eofor uses to cleave through the 'helmet made by giants' worn by Ongentheow (line 2979b). See further, for example, Cronan, 'The Rescuing Sword'; Culbert, 'The Narrative function of Beowulf's Swords'; Dane, 'Wiglaf's Sword'; Kaske, 'Weohstan's Sword'; Köberl, 'The Magic Sword in *Beowulf*'; Nicholason, 'Hunlafing and the Point of the Sword'.

30 Here, as elsewhere in the poem (for example, lines 198a, 1621a, 2140a, 2280a, and 3051b), the term *eacen* has the sense 'increased (beyond normal measure)'. See Tolkien's remarks in Clark Hall, trans., *Beowulf*, pp. x–xi.

31 For an alternative (and rather unconvincing) suggestion that the image derives from Celtic sources, see Puhvel, 'The Melting of the Giant-Wrought Sword'.

Aeneas, 'shattered at the blow like brittle ice' (*glacies ceu futtilis ictu / dissiluit, Aeneid* XII.740–1).[32] Although as it stands the parallel might not seem very secure, one need only imagine a variant text reading *dissoluit* ('dissolves') to provide a much better match.[33] It must be said that extensive, cavalier, and 'creative' use of Vergil is something of a hallmark of the *Liber monstrorum*, whose author sometimes treats the text of the *Aeneid* with less than total respect.[34] At any rate, simply as an indication of the high level of literary sophistication in the interleaving of Christian, secular, and heroic themes by an Anglo-Saxon writing around the earliest supposed date of composition of *Beowulf*,[35] the *Liber monstrorum* probably deserves more attention from *Beowulf*-scholars than it has so far received.

Likewise, it may be instructive briefly to consider another Christian-Latin text, this time in verse and steeped in Vergilian influence, which shares with *Beowulf* a reassessment of Germanic heroic legend through Christian eyes. The probably ninth-century *Waltharius* has proved, like *Beowulf*, notoriously difficult to date with any precision, but it shares with the fragmentary Old English *Waldere* a concern to tell the story of the Germanic hero Walter of Aquitaine.[36] The author, to judge by learned and witty allusions to Vergil, Prudentius, and a range of other Latin poets, was a well-read individual who was very comfortable with the conventions of Latin heroic verse.[37] Yet some of the techniques the *Waltharius*-poet employs, namely formulaic repetition and the use of verbal echo,[38] onomastic puns on character's names,[39] and the subversive use of language,[40] have close parallels in *Beowulf*, and both poems seem steeped in the Germanic heroic ethos. The final scenes of the *Waltharius*, indeed, where Walther hides out in a mountainous cave with his treasure, and is besieged by thirteen warriors, of whom twelve fight and one refuses, read almost like a parody of Beowulf's dragon-fight (including the detail that one of Walther's

---

[32] Klaeber, 'Aeneis und Beowulf', p. 348

[33] Alas, no such variant is recorded by Mynors, ed., *P. Vergili Maronis Opera*, p. 416, nor anywhere else I have been able to find.

[34] Cf. Whitbread, 'The *Liber Monstrorum* and *Beowulf*', pp. 459–60.

[35] On the vexed question of the dating of *Beowulf*, see above, pp. 5–6.

[36] *Waltharius*, ed. Strecker; cf. Kratz, ed. and trans., *Waltharius and Ruodlieb*; Smyser and Magoun, *Survivals in Old Norwegian*, pp. 111–45. On the question of the dating of the *Waltharius*, see, for example, Dronke, '*Waltharius* and the *Vita Waltharii*'; Schaller, 'Ist der *Waltharius* früh-karolingisch?'. Neither of these scholars takes account of the close parallel between *Waltharius*, *Prologus*, line 15 (*det pater ex summis caelum terramque gubernans*) and Theodulf of Orléans, *Carmen* 71, line 91 (*det pater altithronus caelum terramque gubernans*) in their assessment of Carolingian literary connections with the text.

[37] See further, for example, Dronke, 'Functions of Classical Borrowing', and the *apparatus fontium* in Strecker's edition.

[38] With regard to internal echoes in the *Waltharius* itself, one might compare, for example, lines 241 and 551; 466 and 470; 625 and 1323; 752 and 938; 937 and 1060. Internal echoes in the *Waltharius* can be traced using Stiene, ed., *Konkordanz zum Waltharius-Epos*. On similar patterns in *Beowulf*, see above, pp. 85–91.

[39] Cf. Dumville, 'Ekiurid's *Celtica lingua*'; Morgan, 'Walther the Wood-Sprite'. On similar puns in *Beowulf*, see below, pp. 172–3.

[40] Cf. Parkes, 'Irony in *Waltharius*'. For similar use of *double entendre* and undercutting irony in *Beowulf*, see, for example, Shuman and Hutchings, 'The *Un*-Prefix: a Means of Germanic Irony in *Beowulf*'.

assailants actually describes him as a 'dragon').[41] This is not to suggest any direct connection, of course, simply to note that the *Beowulf*-poet was not the only Christian author to make use of Germanic legend in the service of Christian verse. Like the *Liber monstrorum*, then, the *Waltharius* seems to offer a potentially useful literary analogue to future generations of *Beowulf*-scholars.

But if the *Liber monstrorum* and the *Waltharius* demonstrate that in the early medieval period Christian poets and authors were well capable of making subtle literary use of their inherited pagan traditions, still closer connections can be established between *Beowulf* and a wide range of writings in both Latin and Old English, all of which ultimately lead back to the primary text of Christendom, namely the Bible, and it is to these texts that we now turn.

Doing it by the book: biblical references in 'Beowulf'

It is striking to note that both of the biblical narratives explicitly alluded to in *Beowulf* should be connected to Grendel and his kin; as Malcolm Godden has remarked: 'as Grendel is introduced by a reference to the Old Testament legend which describes the origin of monsters, so his end is announced by an allusion to the biblical myth of their destruction'.[42] The first of the poet's biblical allusions comes as part of a complicated sequence describing the fateful consequences of the building of Heorot (lines 86–114):[43]

> Ða se ellengæst   earfoðlice
> þrage geþolode,   se þe in þystrum bad,
> þæt he dogora gehwam   dream gehyrde
> hludne in healle;   þær wæs hearpan sweg,
> swutol sang scopes.   Sægde se þe cuþe   90
> frumsceaft fira   feorran reccan,
> cwæð þæt se ælmihtiga   eorðan worhte,
> wlitebeorhtne wang,   swa wæter bebugeð,
> gesette sigehreþig   sunnan ond monan
> leoman to leohte   landbuendum   95
> ond gefrætwade   foldan sceatas
> leomum ond leafum,   lif eac gesceop
> cynna gehwylcum   þara ðe cwice hwyrfaþ.
> Swa ða drihtguman   dreamum lifdon,
> eadiglice,   oð ðæt an ongan   100
> fyrene fremman   feond on helle;
> wæs se grimma gæst   Grendel haten,
> mære mearcstapa,   se þe moras heold,
> fen ond fæsten;   fifelcynnes eard
> wonsæli wer   weardode hwile,   105

---

41 *Waltharius*, line 790: *O versute dolis ac fraudis conscie serpens* (Strecker, ed., *Waltharius*, p. 56); cf. line 792 (*veluti coluber*).

42 Godden, 'Biblical Literature', p. 216.

43 In line 107a, the word *Caines* has been altered from *cames*; see further Pulsiano, ' "Cames cynne": Confusion or Craft?'.

siþðan him scyppend   forscrifen hæfde
in Caines cynne –   þone cwealm gewræc
ece Drihten,   þæs þe he Abel slog;
ne gefeah he þære fæhðe,   ac he hine feor forwræc,
Metod for þy mane   mancynne fram.   110
Þanon untydras   ealle onwocon,
eotenas ond ylfe   ond orcneas,
swylce gigantas,   þa wið Gode wunnon
lange þrage;   he him ðæs lean forgeald.

[Then the mighty spirit, who waited in the darkness, endured grievously
for a time that he heard each day joy, loud in the hall; there was the
sound of the harp, the clear voice of the poet. The one who could
recount from past ages the first-making of men spoke, said that the
Almighty created the earth, the fair bright plain which water encircles;
triumphing in might he set the sun and the moon as lamps to give light
to the dwellers on earth, and he adorned the earth's corners with
branches and leaves; he also fashioned life for each of the kinds that
move around alive. So those noble men lived in joys, happily, until one
began to perform wicked deeds, a fiend in hell; the grim spirit was
called Grendel, a well-known wanderer in the borderland wastes, he
who inhabited the moors, the fens and the fastnesses; the unhappy man
dwelt for a while in the land of the monster-race, after the Creator had
condemned him as one of the kin of Cain: the eternal Lord avenged that
killing, because Cain slew Abel; he did not rejoice in that feud, but the
Creator cast him far out for that crime, away from mankind. Thence
arose all the evil breed: giants and elves and evil monsters, also those
gigantic ones who strove against God for a long time; he repaid them for
that.]

That Grendel should have been roused to wrath by Hrothgar's poet singing a
song of Creation seems only fitting,[44] especially if, as has been suggested,[45]
lines 99–101 can be read both with what precedes (so alluding to Satan and the
Fall) and with what follows (a simple reference to Grendel);[46] certainly, similar
strategies appear to be used elsewhere in *Beowulf*.[47] Typically, the *Beowulf*-poet
is able to encompass here in just a few lines both the spawning of the kin of Cain
(*ealle onwocon*, line 111b) and their destruction by God (*he him ðæs lean
forgeald*, line 114b).[48]

Moreover, just as Cain and the Flood are invoked before Grendel's depreda-

44 Cf. Helder, 'The Song of Creation in *Beowulf* and the Interpretation of Heorot'; Manes, 'The Sub-
     stance of Earth in *Beowulf*'s Song of Creation'.
45 See Ball, '*Beowulf* 99–101'.
46 Cf. too Cronan, 'The Origin of Ancient Strife in *Beowulf*'.
47 For example, at the end of the so-called 'Finn-episode', on which see below, pp. 173–87. At the syn-
     tactical level there is evidence that constructions could face both ways (the so-called *apo kionou* con-
     struction): see Mitchell, '*apo koinou* in Old English Poetry?', a response to Stanley, ' "Ἀπὸ Κοινοῦ,"
     Chiefly in *Beowulf*'.
48 For more on the kin of Cain, see Orchard, *Pride and Prodigies*, pp. 58–85. Cf. here Osborn, 'The
     Great Feud: Scriptural History and Strife in *Beowulf*'.

tions begin, so too the vengeance of Grendel's mother is preceded by a parallel reference (lines 1258b–1267a):[49]

> Grendles modor,
> ides, aglæcwif, yrmþe gemunde,
> se þe wæteregesan wunian scolde,   1260
> cealde streamas, siþðan Cain wearð
> to ecgbanan angan breþer,
> fæderenmæge; he þa fag gewat,
> morþre gemearcod, mandream fleon,
> westen warode. Þanon woc fela   1265
> geosceaftgasta; wæs þæra Grendel sum,
> heorowearh hetelic.

[Grendel's mother, an awesome assailant in woman's form, called to mind her misery, she who had to inhabit the dread waters, the cold streams, since Cain became the sword-slayer to his only brother, his paternal kinsman: for that he went forth stained [or 'guilty'], marked by murder, fleeing the joys of men, dwelt in the wilderness. From there arose many fatal spirits; Grendel was one, a hateful and fierce outcast.]

Presumably, the *Beowulf*-poet is applying strict logic to the biblical tale: if the Flood was sent to destroy monstrous creatures, then the only ones who could survive were those who already inhabited watery depths.[50]

The final allusion to the biblical story of the Flood comes, fittingly enough, once Beowulf, who has despatched Grendel and his mother, brings back the hilt of the monstrous sword with which he had decapitated them both, and presents it to Hrothgar (lines 1687b–1693):

> hylt sceawode,
> ealde lafe, on ðæm wæs or writen
> fyrngewinnes, syðþan flod ofsloh,
> gifen geotende giganta cyn,   1690
> frecne geferdon; þæt wæs fremde þeod
> ecean Dryhtne; him þæs endelean
> þurh wæteres wylm Waldend sealde.

[He gazed on the hilt, the ancient heirloom, on which had previously been inscribed the origin of ancient struggle, when the flood, the streaming ocean, slew the race of Giants (they suffered terribly [or 'they dared boldly']); that was a race hostile to the eternal Lord; to them the Ruler gave recompense through the surging of the water.]

That this inscribed weapon of the monstrous races should survive the Flood can be paralleled in patristic sources: Cassian, for example, tells how Noah's wicked

---

[49] The manuscript reads *camp* at line 1261a; on the widespread emendation to *Cain* at line 1261a, see, for example, Pulsiano, ' "Cames cynne": Confusion or Craft?'

[50] On post-diluvial survival of giants and monsters, see, for example, Orchard, *Pride and Prodigies*, pp. 78–84.

son, Cham, a latter-day Cain,[51] inscribed on stone and metal his occult wisdom:[52]

> Quantum itaque traditiones ferunt, Cham filius Noe, qui superstitionibus istis et sacrilegis ac profanis erat artibus institutus, sciens nullum se posse super his memorialem librum in arcam prorsus inferre, in qua erat una cum patre iusto ac sanctis fratribus ingressurus, scelestas artes ac profana commenta diversorum metallorum laminis, quae scilicet aquarum conrumpi inundatione non passent, et durissimis lapidibus insculpsit. Quae peracto diluuio eadem quae celauerat curiositate perquirens sacrilegiorum ac perpetuae nequitiae seminarium transmisit in posteros.

> [Various traditions tell that Cham, the son of Noah, who was instructed in those superstitions and sacrileges and profane arts, knowing that he could not bring a book detailing these things into the Ark, in which he was about to go with his righteous father and holy brothers, inscribed these wicked arts and profane commentaries on sheets of various metals and on the hardest rocks, which would not be harmed by the surge of waters. When the Flood was over he sought them out with the same curiosity for sacrilegious things with which he had hidden them, and transmitted the seeds of perpetual wickedness to later generations.]

However much one may quibble about precisely what is depicted on the hilt that Hrothgar gazes upon,[53] the fact that the blade is said to have melted 'most like ice' in Grendel's hot blood, is surely meant to recall the Flood (lines 1607b–1611):

> Þæt wæs wundra sum,
> þæt hit eal gemealt   ise gelicost,
> ðonne forstes bend   fæder onlæteð,
> onwindeð wælrapas,   se geweald hafað   1610
> sæla ond mæla;   þæt is soð metod.

> [It was a wonder that it entirely melted, most like ice, when the Father releases the bonds of frost, unwinds the water-fetters, he who has control over times and seasons: that is the true Creator.]

The double invocation of God, with a change of verb-tense to signify his continuing power, inevitably calls to mind God's watery vengeance on the giants in the form of the Flood.[54]

But if the three scenes depicting Cain and the Flood are the only ones in *Beowulf* where biblical allusion is unquestionable, it might be noted that further Old Testament references may underlie other aspects of the activities of the kin of Cain. So, for example, given the commonplace biblical injunctions against

---

51 On the conflation of roles between Cham and Cain, see, for example, Hamilton, 'The Religious Principle in *Beowulf*', p. 320, n. 4; Donahue, 'Grendel and the *Clanna Cain*', p. 168. For an overview, see Orchard, *Pride and Prodigies*, pp. 69–70.

52 Petschenig, ed., *Iohannis Cassiani Conlationes*, *Conlatio* VIII.xxi.7–8, pp. 239/27–240/10; cf. Williams, *Cain and Beowulf*, p. 35.

53 See, for example, Köberl, 'The Magic Sword in *Beowulf*'; Schrader, 'The Language on the Giant's Sword Hilt in *Beowulf*'; Taylor, 'Grendel's Monstrous Arts'; Viswanathan, 'On the Melting of the Sword'; Whitman, 'Corrosive Blood in *Beowulf*'.

54 Cf. the use of the Flood-motif in the *Liber monstrorum* above, pp. 133–7.

drinking blood,[55] echoed in a range of Anglo-Saxon authors including Bede, Alfred, Ælfric, and Wulfstan,[56] a Christian Anglo-Saxon audience would have found the description of Grendel's eating-habits particularly loathsome (lines 739–45a):

> Ne þæt se aglæca   yldan þohte,
> ac he gefeng hraðe   forman siðe   740
> slæpende rinc,   slat unwearnum,
> bat banlocan,   blod edrum dranc,
> synsnædum swealh;   sona hæfde
> unlyfigendes   eal gefeormod,
> fet ond folma.   745

[Nor did the awesome assailant think to delay, but he quickly seized at the first opportunity a sleeping warrior, tore him greedily, bit the joints, drank the blood from the veins, swallowed in sinful gulps [or 'mighty gulps']; he had soon taken full care of the feet and hands of the unliving man.]

One might note that the reference to 'feet and hands' here may mask a further biblical reference: after all, even the dogs in the street who devour the corpse of the wicked Jezebel do not consume those extremities (II Reg. IX.35). Likewise, given the *Beowulf*-poet's explicit references to the Flood, it is important to point out both that after the Flood God prohibits the consumption of blood alongside flesh (Gen. IX.4) and that a range of commentators expressly connect such practices with those of the antediluvian giants; Bede is typical:[57]

Ferunt autem quod in hoc maxima fuerit preuaricatio gigantum, quia cum sanguine carnem comederent; ideoque Dominus, illis diluuio exstinctis, carne quidem uesci homines concesserit, sed ne id cum sanguine facerent prohibuerit.

[They say what has been in this matter the greatest collusion of the giants, that they consumed flesh with blood; and so the Lord, once he had obliterated them in the Flood, permitted men to eat flesh, but forbade that they eat it with blood.]

Similar traditions about the blood-drinking habits of antediluvian giants are found in the apocryphal Book of Enoch, a text certainly known in Anglo-Saxon England, and one which, as Kaske has argued, may lie behind a number of elements in *Beowulf* itself.[58] The possible use by the *Beowulf*-poet of apocryphal

---

55 See, for example, Lev. XVII.10–14 and XIX.26; Deut. XII.16 and 23, and XV.23.
56 See Robinson, 'Lexicography and Literary Criticism', pp. 102–3, who notes that these authors demonstrate 'an almost obsessive concern with the Old Testament injunction against the drinking of blood'.
57 Jones, ed., *Libri quatuor in principium Genesis*, p. 132, lines 2138–41; cf. Williams, *Cain and Beowulf*, pp. 14–15; Peltola, 'Grendel's Descent from Cain Reconsidered', p. 289.
58 Kaske, '*Beowulf* and the Book of Enoch', esp. pp. 421–3. See too Melinkoff, 'Cain's Monstrous Progeny in *Beowulf*: Part I, Noachic Tradition', p. 160; Dumville, 'Biblical Apocrypha and the Early Irish', pp. 330–1; Biggs, 'I Enoch', in Biggs, Hill, and Szarmach, ed., *Sources of Anglo-Saxon Literary Culture: a Trial Version*, pp. 25–7. A single manuscript-fragment of the Book of Enoch survives from Anglo-Saxon England: British Library, Royal 5. E. xiii, fols. 79v–80r, edited by James, *Apocry-*

traditions may attest to a fuller engagement with scripture than has sometimes been supposed: if the range of biblical reference in *Beowulf* may not be wide, it may be deep.

Biblical parallels and analogues

The very nature of the way in which the *Beowulf*-poet alludes to biblical traditions without apparently having recourse to quotation from the biblical text itself is of some interest when one considers the ways in which other Old Testament tales appear to have echoes in the poem. There are, for example, a significant number of interesting parallels which, it has been suggested, seem to connect the story of Beowulf and Grendel with the biblical narrative of David and Goliath.[59] The specific points of similarity might be schematised as in Table III, below. That there are no fewer than twelve such points of overlap is striking, to say the least; and the notion of the direct influence of the story of David and Goliath becomes still more attractive when it is noted that, according to Jerome's explanation (which had wide currency in Anglo-Saxon England), the Hebrew name David means 'strong in hand' (*manu fortis*).[60] Such parallels between *Beowulf* and David's battle against Goliath need not imply any direct connection, however: some biblical scholars regard the tale of David and Goliath itself as a 'folk epic' of wide currency,[61] and it is interesting to note that in at least one aspect the story of David and Goliath actually provides a closer parallel than *Beowulf* for a detail in the Icelandic *Grettis saga*, generally considered the best Norse analogue for the battles with Grendel and his mother.[62]

But if one need not imagine that *Beowulf* was composed pen in hand by an author carefully flicking through the biblical pages of I Samuel, the sheer number of parallels might suggest a general acquaintance with the story, perhaps heard rather than read. Certainly, it is instructive to turn to the story of David and Goliath as described in his homily on the Book of Kings by Ælfric, writing at a time roughly contemporary with that when the *Beowulf*-manuscript itself was written, many of the same essential narrative elements are found:[63]

> Þa forseah se ælmihtiga god þone Saul æt nextan
> and hine of his rice awearp be his agenum gewyrhtum

---

pha Anecdota, pp. 146–50. The manuscript is no. 459 in Gneuss, *Handlist*, where it is described as probably of ninth-century Breton origin, with a Worcester provenance; cf. Dumville, 'Biblical Apocrypha and the Early Irish', p. 331. For translations of the text, see Sparks, ed., *The Apocryphal Old Testament*.

59 The fullest analysis is by Horowitz, 'Beowulf, Samson, David, and Christ'.
60 See further Thiel, *Grundlagen und Gestalt der Hebräischkenntnisse des frühen Mittelalters*, p. 286.
61 See especially Jason, 'The Story of David and Goliath'.
62 On the links between *Beowulf* and *Grettis saga*, see Orchard, *Pride and Prodigies*, pp. 140–68; for an alternative view, see Fjalldal, *The Long Arm of Coincidence*. Whereas we do not learn what happens to the hilt of the monster-sword in *Beowulf* after it passes into the possession of Hrothgar (so prompting his so-called 'sermon', on which see below, pp. 155–62), David goes on to use Goliath's sword to perform heroic deeds, just as Grettir uses the short-sword (*sax*), Kársnautr, gained under similar circumstances, throughout his heroic career; see further Orchard, *Pride and Prodigies*, pp. 145–6.
63 Skeat, ed., *Ælfric's Lives of Saints*, I, pp. 384–5.

and geceas him to cynincge þone cenan Dauid
seðe butan wæpnum gewylde ða leon
and þæs beran ceaflas tobræc mid his handum
and ahredde þæt gelæhte scep of his scearpum toðum.
He ofwearp eac syððan þone swyþlican
ent Goliam þone gramlican þe Godes naman hyrwde
and mid gebeote clypode bysmor Godes folce
gearu to anwige mid ormettre wæpnunge.
Hwæt þa Dauid eode togeanes þam ente
and ofwearp mid his liþeran þone geleafleasan ent
bufon ðam eagan þæt he beah to eorðan.
Gelæhte þa of ðam ente his agen swurd
and his ormæte heafod mid þam of asloh
and hæfde ða gewunnen sige his leode.

[Then at last Almighty God rejected this Saul, and cast him out of his kingdom according to his own deeds, and chose for Himself as king the brave David, who without weapons had conquered the lion, and had torn apart the bear's jaws with his hands, and had delivered the captured sheep from its sharp teeth. He also overthrew afterwards the mighty giant, the cruel Goliath, who cursed God's name, and boastfully cried out against God's people, ready for single combat with huge weaponry. Listen! David went against that giant, and overthrew with his sling the faithless giant above the eye, so that he fell to the ground. Then he took from the giant his own sword, and struck off his huge head with it, and so gained victory for his people.]

While many of the bare bones of the same basic outline as found in both *Beowulf* and I Samuel are present here, several rather specific parallels are not: if the *Beowulf*-poet was working from a general paradigm of the biblical story of David and Goliath, then he clearly had access to one which was more detailed than Ælfric supplied.[64]

In this context, it seems worth pursuing other possible parallels with Old Testament heroes too.[65] One link with the story of the Old Testament strongman Samson has been detected in the episode in which Beowulf escapes alone by sea from the scene of Hygelac's death, apparently carrying thirty war-garments with him (lines 2359–69):[66]

---

64 One might note in passing the explicit reference to David killing the bear with his hands, since a different etymologising of David's name produces the sense 'bear-hand' (דוב יד); I am grateful to Samantha Zacher for pointing this out to me.

65 It is worth adding here that Bouman, 'Beowulf's Song of Sorrow', suggests that the grief of the old man described in *Beowulf*, lines 2444–62 has a parallel in the biblical story of David and Absalom in II Samuel.

66 For the connection, see Horowitz, 'Beowulf, Samson, David, and Christ'. The *Beowulf*-manuscript is damaged at this point, and a number of the words have to be completed or supplied (so, for example, *stag* in line 2362b has been filled out from manuscript . . . *g*, and *þorfton* in line 2363b from manuscript *þorf* . . .; the entire word *eorla* is lost at the corner of the page, and others conjecture *ana* ['alone'] instead). Also problematic is the vexed question as to whether Beowulf is swimming or rowing at this point, about which there has been much debate. See, for example, Anderson, 'Beowulf's Retreat from Frisia'; Frank, ' "Mere" and "Sund": Two Sea-Changes in *Beowulf*'; Greenfield, 'A Touch of the Monstrous in the Hero'; Puhvel, 'The Swim Prowess of Beowulf'; Robinson, 'Beowulf's Retreat from Frisia'; *idem*, 'Elements of the Marvellous'; Wentersdorf, 'Beowulf's Withdrawal from Frisia'; *idem*, 'Beowulf's Adventure with Breca'.

Table III: Parallels between Beowulf's fight with Grendel and David's with Goliath

#		
1.	King Hrothgar suffers the depredations of the giant Grendel (*Beowulf*, lines 115–93)	King Saul suffers the depredations of the giant Goliath (I Samuel XVII.3 and 23)
2.	King Hrothgar offers a rich reward for killing Grendel (*Beowulf*, lines 384–5 and 660b–661)	King Saul offers a rich reward for killing Goliath (I Samuel XVII.25)
3.	Beowulf appears from elsewhere, a promising youth (*Beowulf*, lines 247–51)	David appears from elsewhere, a promising youth (I Samuel XVI.12 and XVII.20)
4.	Early in his career, Beowulf had seemed of little worth (*Beowulf*, lines 2183b–2188a)	Early in his career, David had seemed of little worth (I Samuel XVI.11 and XVII.15)
5.	Beowulf's credentials as a suitable combatant are challenged (*Beowulf*, lines 506–28)	David's credentials as a suitable combatant are challenged (I Samuel XVII.28 and 33)
6.	Beowulf lists his previous experience tackling similarly frightening creatures (*Beowulf*, lines 530–606)	David lists his experience tackling similarly frightening creatures (I Samuel XVII.35–7)
7.	Beowulf is seen as heaven-sent, so his offer of help is accepted (*Beowulf*, lines 381b–384a)	David is seen as heaven-sent, so his offer of help is accepted (I Samuel XVII.37)
8.	Beowulf removes helmet, breastplate, and sword before the battle (*Beowulf*, lines 669–74)	David removes helmet, breastplate, and sword before the battle (I Samuel XVII.39)
9.	Beowulf boasts of victory, with God's help (*Beowulf*, lines 677–87)	David boasts of victory, with God's help (I Samuel XVII.46)
10.	Beowulf battles Grendel alone, and without a sword (*Beowulf*, lines 710–836)	David battles Goliath alone, and without a sword (I Samuel XVII.39, 42, and 50)
11.	Beowulf decapitates Grendel with Grendel's [mother's?] sword (*Beowulf*, lines 1584b–1590)	David decapitates Goliath with Goliath's own sword (I Samuel XVII.51)
12.	Beowulf returns with the sword and the head of Grendel (*Beowulf*, lines 1612–17)	David returns with the sword and the head of Goliath (I Samuel XVII.54)

> Þonan Biowulf com
> sylfes cræfte,   sundnytte dreah;   2360
> hæfde him on earme   eorla .XXX.
> hildegeatwa,   þa he to holme stag.
> Nealles Hetware   hremge þorfton
> feðewiges,   þe him foran ongean
> linde bæron;   lyt eft becwom   2365
> fram þam hildfrecan   hames niosan.
> Oferswam ða sioleða bigong   sunu Ecgðeowes,
> earm anhaga,   eft to leodum.

[Thence Beowulf came, by his own strength, undertook a sea-journey; he had in his arms the war-gear of thirty men, when he put to sea. Not at all did the Hetware need to exult about their pitched battle, those who bore their shields against him; few came back from that battle-warrior returning home. Then the son of Ecgtheow crossed the sea's expanse, a wretched lonely wanderer, back to his people.]

The figure 30 is elsewhere associated with both Beowulf and Grendel:[67] Grendel snatches thirty thanes from Heorot on his first visit (*þritig þegna*, line 123a; cf. *fyftyne men ond oðer swylc*, lines 1582b–1583a), and Beowulf has the strength of thirty men in his hand-grip (*.XXX.es manna mægencræft on his mundgripe*, lines 379b–380). That Samson, who had already killed a lion with his bare hands (Iud. XIV.6), should travel to Ashkelon, kill thirty of their men, and return home with their garments as spoils (Iud. XIV.19), seems indeed to provide a broad parallel for this episode, in much the same way that some have seen echoes of the finding of Moses as a waterbourne infant (whose burial-place no-one knows) in the story of Scyld Scefing, whose arrival and departure from Denmark are equally mysterious.[68] Moses, who is described in the bible as 'the gentlest man over all men' (Num. XII.3: *uir mitissimus super omnes homines*), and in the Old English poem *Exodus* as 'the mildest of men' the last time he is described at all (line 550a: *manna mildost*) has also been associated with Beowulf himself,[69] to whom similar qualities are attributed in the closing lines of the poem.[70]

These apparent parallels between Beowulf and such a variety of figures from the Old Testament as David, Samson, and Moses, the first two of whom in Christian exegetical texts were often identified as types of Christ,[71] surely encourages further speculation about other possible biblical analogues. Certainly, there seems a striking parallel to the fates of Grendel the persecutor

---

67 On numbers in general in *Beowulf*, see, for example, Berendsohn, *Zur Vorgeschichte des 'Beowulf'*, pp. 178–9; Whallon, *Formula, Character, and Context*, pp. 134–6.
68 See especially Owen-Crocker, *The Four Funerals in 'Beowulf'*, pp. 18–19.
69 See further above, p. 9.
70 One might also note that just as Beowulf is held to be 'of mankind the strongest in might on that day of this life' (*moncynnes mægenes strengest / on þæm dæge þysses lifes*, lines 196–7; cf. lines 789–90 and 806 [see further above, p. 55]), in the biblical account of the Flood Noah is held to be 'a righteous man, blameless among the people of his time' (*vir iustus atque perfectus fuit in generationibus suis* [Gen. VI.9]).
71 See, for example, Ælfric, *Catholic Homilies* I.xv.158–70 (Clemoes, ed., *Ælfric's Catholic Homilies*, p. 305); Blickling Homily III (Morris, ed., *Blickling Homilies*, p. 31).

of the Danes, beheaded and (literally) disarmed by Beowulf, and that of Nicanor, persecutor of the Jews, who meets a similar punishment at the hands of the hero Judas Maccabaeus.[72] In effect, the same biblical tale is told twice, in both longer and shorter forms. The briefer report gives the essentials (I Macc. VIII.47):[73]

> Et acceperunt spolia eorum et praedam et caput Nicanoris amputaverunt et dexteram eius quam extenderat superbe et adtulerunt et suspenderunt contra Hierusalem.

> [And they took the spoils of them for a booty, and they cut off Nicanor's head, and his right hand, which he had proudly stretched out, and they brought it, and they hung it up over Jerusalem.]

The longer account, however, adds several details of particular interest for a comparison with *Beowulf* (II Macc. XV.30–5):[74]

> Praecepit autem Iudas qui per omnia corpore et animo emori pro civibus paratus erat caput Nicanoris et manum cum umero abscisam Hierosolymam perferri, quo cum convenisset convocatis contribulibus et sacerdotibus ad altare arcersiit et eos qui in arce erant. Et ostenso capite Nicanoris et manu nefaria quam extendens contra domum sanctam omnipotentis Dei magnifice gloriatus est. Linguam etiam impii Nicanoris praecisam iussit particulatim avibus dari; manum autem dementis contra templum suspendi. Omnes igitur caeli Dominum benedixerunt dicentes benedictus qui locum suum incontaminatum conservavit. Suspendit autem Nicanoris caput in summa arce evidens ut esset et manifestum signum auxilii Dei.

> [And Judas, who was altogether ready in body and mind to die for his countrymen, commanded that Nicanor's head, and his hand with the shoulder be cut off, and carried to Jerusalem. And when he had come thither, having called together his countrymen, and the priests to the altar, he sent also for them that were in the castle. And shewing them the head of Nicanor, and the wicked hand which he had stretched out, with proud boasts, against the holy house of the Almighty God, he commanded also, that the tongue of the wicked Nicanor, should be cut out and given by pieces to birds, and the hand of the furious man to be hanged up over against the temple. Then all blessed the Lord of heaven, saying: Blessed be he that hath kept his own place undefiled. And he hung up Nicanor's head in the top of the castle, that it might be a clear and manifest sign of the help of God.]

The notion that Nicanor's tongue was also cut off, along with his head and hand, seems to align the story with the 'thought, word, and deed' triad that has been observed in *Beowulf*;[75] but more intriguing is the notion that both hand and arm of this 'furious man' (the connection with Grendel's well-documented rage is

---

72 I am grateful to Rob Getz for pointing out to me this parallel.
73 Here and throughout I use Fischer *et al.*, ed., *Biblia sacra iuxta vulgatam versionem* for the text of the Vulgate, and the Douai-Rheims translation (1582–1609), as revised by Richard Challoner (1749–50).
74 In view of the argument below, it should be pointed out that the reading *manifestum signum* is a variant; most texts (including the edition of the Vulgate by Fischer) prefer the reading *manifestum sit.*
75 See above, pp. 55 and 73. On the 'thought, word, and deed' triad, see Sims-Williams, 'Thought, Word, and Deed: an Irish Triad'.

instructive)[76] should be trophies for display, since the phrase 'manifest sign' (*manifestum signum*) calls to mind the description of how Beowulf made a similarly 'clear token' of Grendel's arm (lines 833b–836):[77]

> Þæt wæs tacen sweotol,
> syþðan hildedeor   hond alegde,
> earm ond eaxle   (þær wæs eal geador   835
> Grendles grape)   under geapne hrof.

[That was a clear token, once the battle-brave one placed the hand, arm, and shoulder (Grendel's grasp was all together) under the spacious roof.]

Another detail shared between this passage and the biblical account is the insistence that the trophy consists of the whole arm, from hand to shoulder; together, these two details might seem to support the notion of some connection between *Beowulf* and this heroic (indeed exemplary) biblical narrative.

By contrast with the poem's apparent links with the Old Testament, there are strikingly few direct connections to New Testament language and thought.[78] As Klaeber, perhaps the most persistent and persuasive of those who argue for substantial Christian influence on the text, rather wryly puts it: 'The overall character of the Christian elements [in *Beowulf*] is not particularly ecclesiastical or dogmatic.'[79] Most of the attempts to imply direct reference to New Testament events seem somewhat strained, to say the least. Certainly, given the general dearth of references to female characters in the poem, it is striking that Hrothgar should focus on Beowulf's (unnamed) mother in his praise of the hero after the latter has seen off Grendel (lines 942b–946a):

> 'Hwæt, þæt secgan mæg
> efne swa hwylc mægþa   swa ðone magan cende
> æfter gumcynnum,   gyf heo gyt lyfað,
> þæt hyre ealdmetod   este wære   945
> bearngebyrdo.'

['Lo, she may say, whichsoever of womankind bore that boy of human race, if she still lives, that the Old Creator was kind to her in her child-bearing.']

But to draw a parallel (as many do) with Luc. XI.27, in which an anonymous woman from the crowd praises Jesus by blessing the womb that bore him and the teats that gave him suck (*quaedam mulier de turba dixit illi beatus venter qui te portavit et ubera quae suxisti*), seems rather strained.[80] As C. L. Wrenn (who

---

76 See, for example, Orchard, *Pride and Prodigies*, p. 32; Henry, '*Furor heroicus*'; Pettitt, 'The Mark of the Beast and the Balance of Frenzy'.

77 On this passage, see further, for example, Bremmer, 'Grendel's Arm and the Law'; Miller, 'The Position of Grendel's Arm in Heorot'. The related phrase *sweotolan tacne*, again referring to Grendel's attacks, occurs in *Beowulf*, line 141b.

78 Cf. Cox, *Cruces of 'Beowulf'*, pp. 12–32.

79 Klaeber, *The Christian Elements*, p. 51.

80 Cf. Klaeber, ed., *Beowulf*, pp. 166–7.

nonetheless recognises that the lines in *Beowulf* 'may well be an echo' of the biblical verse) rather donnishly puts it: 'so natural and widespread a sentiment scarcely need have a definite "source" '.[81] The very language and context of the *Beowulf*-passage, however, surely speaks against imbuing it with specifically (and exclusively) Christian significance, for although the lines in question are certainly amply highlighted by word play (with puns on *mæg . . . mægþa . . . magan*, lines 942b–943; *cende . . . gumcynnum*, lines 943b–44a; *bearngebyrdo*, line 946a),[82] what is at issue is twofold: from Hrothgar's perspective, reference to Beowulf's mother leads naturally into his own intention to take Beowulf as an adopted son, which he does without pause (lines 946b–8a: *Nu ic, Beowulf, þec, / secg betsta, me for sunu wylle / freogan on ferhþe*); and from the poet's perspective, emphasis on Beowulf's mother (and his strictly human nature) paves the way for consideration of the fates and actions of three other mothers (Wealhtheow, Hildeburh, and Grendel's mother), whose contrastingly sad stories soon unfold.[83]

Likewise, the fact that Beowulf should be accompanied to his fight with the dragon by twelve retainers (of whom one is a thief),[84] has seemed to some a sign of his Christ-like qualities, especially given Beowulf's 'expression of gloomy forebodings' before the battle,[85] which has been taken as echoing Christ's agony in the Garden of Gethsemane (Matt. XXVI.36–46; Marc. XIV.32–42; cf. Luc. XXII.39–46).[86] Other elements seem to link the two narratives,[87] and it will be recalled that, just as Christ's Passion took place at the 'ninth hour' (*hora nona*, Matt. XXVII.46; Marc. XV.34), so too as Beowulf decapitates the dead Grendel, blood rises to the surface of the monster-mere and the Danes lose heart at the same hour (*non*, line 1600a).[88] Yet not everyone has been convinced. The number of companions who follow Beowulf to the dragon's lair is, after all, part of a descending sequence: Beowulf is one of fifteen when he heads to Denmark (line 207b),[89] and one of fourteen when he heads home (line 1641b), so perhaps it is not surprising that he should be one of thirteen in his last battle (line 2406b). As William Whallon, after a detailed analysis, puts it: 'the numerological arguments fail to show Christ behind *Beowulf*, and yet they were the chief reason for thinking that the poem said more than it seemed to'.[90] But if

---

81 Wrenn, ed., *Beowulf*, p. 133.

82 For other examples of wordplay in *Beowulf*, see above, pp. 73–6.

83 On the structural role of the women in *Beowulf*, see above, p. 84.

84 On the role of the thief in general, see Andersson, 'The Thief in *Beowulf*'.

85 For the passage in question, see below, pp. 228–9.

86 Klaeber, ed., *Beowulf*, p. 212; cf. Hoops, *Kommentar*, p. 276; Rauer, *Beowulf and the Dragon*, pp. 37 and 77–8.

87 The case is most forcefully put by Klaeber, ed., *Beowulf*, p. 217: 'the disloyalty of the ten cowardly followers of Beowulf, who flee for their lives, is not unlike the defection of the disciples of Christ, see [Marc. XIV.50 and Matt. XXVI.56]. (Also the injunction to the companions, [line] 2529 may recall [Marc. XIV.34 and Matt. XXVI.38].) Likewise, Wiglaf's heroic assistance is matched by the ἀριστεία of Peter ([Matt. XXVI.51 and Joh. XVIII.10])'. Cf. Klaeber, *The Christian Elements in 'Beowulf'*, p. 67.

88 On the use of this and other terminology apparently derived from the Christian-Latin tradition in *Beowulf*, see Whitelock, *The Audience of 'Beowulf'*, pp. 10–11.

89 The number matches that said to have been devoured by Grendel on his first visit (*fyftyne men*, line 1582b), although we are also told that he took away an equal number.

90 Whallon, *Formula, Character, and Context*, pp. 136–7.

the attempts to demonstrate that the life of Christ provided a model for the *Beowulf*-poet have not found universal acceptance,[91] they have at least sparked off a search for parallels among the lives of those who certainly did model themselves after Christ, namely the saints.

Saints alive: hagiographical analogues to 'Beowulf'

Given that there are so few narratives surviving from Anglo-Saxon England that focus on the life of a single figure and can match *Beowulf* in scale,[92] it is perhaps not surprising that critical attention has increasingly focused on those that can, namely Saints' Lives;[93] a number of parallels and analogues to episodes in *Beowulf* have been sought and identified among hagiographical material in a variety of languages,[94] most recently and fully by Christine Rauer, who offers a detailed comparison between the dragon-episode in *Beowulf* and around sixty parallel episodes in a range of hagiographical sources dating from the fourth century to the sixteenth.[95] One hagiographical passage in particular, from a ninth-century Life of Saint Samson of Dol (the so-called *Vita II S. Samsonis*),[96] has been identified by Rauer as showing the greatest number of parallels with the dragon-fight in *Beowulf*; the relevant passage deserves quotation in full:[97]

> Quadam uero die cum esset in monasterio Pentali, rem famosam audiuit de quodam serpente prioribus acriore. Tum ille, sicut mos ei erat, misericordia motus iter direxit ad montem in quo serpens habitabat, et de monte circa se respiciens uidit fumum igne mixtum de loco serpentis ascendere. Et dixit suis: 'Ecce locus serpentis.' Et illi contrementes dixerunt: 'Pater, non est consuetudo hominibus huc uenire. Et ille serpens nullum nocebit, eamus et dimittamus eum quia tu iam infirmaris.' Et ille respondens infit: 'Si ego infirmor, potens est Deus cuius anni nunquam deficient, et uirtus eius

---

91 In general, see Lee, 'Symbolism and Allegory'.

92 For a spirited attempt to connect *Beowulf* with one such secular narrative, see Chapman, '*Beowulf* and *Apollonius of Tyre*'.

93 An early attempt is that by Whitelock, *The Audience of 'Beowulf'*, pp. 80–2, to connect *Beowulf* to the mid-eighth-century *Vita S. Guthlaci* of Felix of Croyland; apart from the general similarity of a hero battling fen-monsters in a barrow, Whitelock indicates two verbal parallels: the devilish monsters are styled 'the seed of Cain' (*semen Cain* [Colgrave, ed., *Felix's Life of St Guthlac*, p. 106]), and the devil is called 'the ancient enemy of the human race' (*antiquus hostis prolis humanae* [Colgrave, ed., *Felix's Life of St Guthlac*, p. 94]; cf. the terms *ealdgewinna* and *feond mancynnes* [*mancynnes feond*] used of Grendel in *Beowulf*, lines 164b, 1276a, and 1776a).

94 Cameron, 'Saint Gildas and Scyld Scefing'; Chase, 'Saints' Lives, Royal Lives, and the Date of *Beowulf*'; idem, '*Beowulf*, Bede, and St. Oswine'; Herschend, '*Beowulf* and St. Sabas'; Goldsmith, *The Mode and Meaning of 'Beowulf'*, pp. 130–45; Lapidge, '*Beowulf*, Aldhelm, the *Liber Monstrorum* and Wessex', pp. 278–82; Meaney, 'Scyld Scefing', pp. 22–37; Sorrell, 'The Approach to the Dragon-Fight'.

95 Rauer, *Beowulf and the Dragon*, where she also analyses around fifty dragon-fights from Scandinavian sources, and concludes that: 'the hagiographical corpus would seem to lend itself more easily to a comparison with *Beowulf* than the corresponding Scandinavian material' (p. 136).

96 The complete Life was edited by Plaine, 'Vita antiqua Sancti Samsonis Dolensis episcopi'; see too Taylor, *The Life of St Samson of Dol*. For a full discussion of the background and significance of the Life, see Rauer, *Beowulf and the Dragon*, pp. 90–116.

97 Plaine, 'Vita antiqua Sancti Samsonis Dolensis episcopi', pp. 144–5; see too the text and translation by Rauer, *Beowulf and the Dragon*, pp. 158–9.

nobiscum est: Et uos constantes estote, et huc me expectate donec reuertar ad uos.' Tunc scutum fidei accipiens, gladium Spiritus sancti tenens, loricam spei induens, ad locum serpentis intrepide peruenit, et serpenti dixit: 'Nos necesse habemus hinc properare, et tu ne tardaueris foras uenire.' Tunc serpens audiens uocem eius, tremens cum magna reuerentia foras ueniebat. Sanctus Sanson extendens manum, stolam suam posuit circa collum eius, et iuxta se traxit ad uerticem montis, ubi fratres expectabant aduentum eius. Et ut uiderunt serpentem cum eo uenientem, timuerunt fugere uolentes. At ille ait: 'Nonne aliquando dixi uobis quod qui Deum timuerit, nullam aliam creaturam timere debet? Et uos timete Deum, et uiuet anima uestra, quoniam nihil deest timentibus eum.' Sanctus uero Sanson palam discipulis et aliis multis, ut uiderent euentum rei aduenientibus, serpenti dixit: 'In nomine Jesu Christi filii Dei altissimi praecipio tibi ut ad mare exeas, et exinde nunquam uiuas.' Et ille uoci obediens perrexit, et uidentibus illis, in mare extinctus est. Exinde collaudantes Deum ad monasterium reuersi sunt.

[One day, when [Saint Samson] was in the monastery of Pental, he heard a tale about a certain dragon fiercer than the previous ones. Then, impelled by compassion, as was his wont, he headed for the mountain that the dragon was inhabiting, and, looking around from the mountain, he saw smoke mixed with flame rising from the dragon's place; and he said to his men: 'There is the dragon's place'. In great fear they said: 'Father, it is not normal for men to come here. That dragon won't harm anyone; let's go and leave it alone, since you are already weak.' He answered: 'Though I am weak, God is strong, and His years never fail, and His power is with us. You stay here and wait for me until I come back to you.' Then, taking the shield of faith, holding the sword of the Holy Spirit, and wearing the breastplate of hope, he went fearlessly to the dragon's place and said to the dragon: 'We must leave this place soon, so you had better not waste time coming out.' Then, hearing his voice, the dragon came out, trembling with great reverence. Stretching out his hand, Saint Samson put his stole around its neck and dragged it beside him to the top of the mountain, where the brothers were expecting him to come. But when they saw the dragon coming with him, they became terrified, and wanted to run away. He said: 'Did I not tell you sometime that he who fears God, does not need to fear any other creature? Fear God, and your soul will live, for nothing fails those who fear Him.' In front of the disciples and many others, who came to see what would happen, Saint Samson said to the dragon: 'In the name of Jesus Christ, the Son of God most high, I order you to go into the sea, and live no more.' Obeying his voice, it went and in the sight of them all, was killed in the sea. Then, praising God, they returned to the monastery.]

The context of the episode, towards the end of the *Vita II S. Samsonis*, when Samson is an old man with a formidable reputation for getting rid of monsters, provides just one of a series of parallels with the dragon-fight in *Beowulf*;[98] moreover, a number of the features of this passage are repeated in other dragon-episodes both in the *Vita II S. Samsonis* and in its eighth-century foreunner, the imaginatively titled *Vita I S. Samsonis*,[99] and Rauer summarises

---

98 Cf. Pope, 'Beowulf's Old Age'.
99 On the relationship between the two works, see Rauer, *Beowulf and the Dragon*, pp. 92–3.

the narrative parallels between *Beowulf* and the whole sequence of dragon-episodes in these two early Lives of Saint Samson as follows:[100]

> the appearance of a dragon which represents the greatest threat in a sequence of dangerous monsters, the devastation of the land by the dragon, the secluded mountain by the sea from which smoke and fire can be seen to rise, the communal journey to the cave, led by a guide, the role played by the hero's companions (their attempt to dissuade the [hero] from approaching the dragon, their common procession to the dragon's cave, their terrified response, the particular loyalty of one companion, their function as witnesses to the [hero]'s encouraging speech and the subsequent [encounter], their waiting on the mountain and varying degrees of fear and disloyalty), the concomitant moral preoccupations, the old age of the hero, the dragon's sniffing, the summoning of the dragon from its cave and the sending of a messenger after the [encounter].

Such a list is certainly extremely impressive, and provides the most potent evidence to date for hagiographical influence on *Beowulf*. One clear difference between *Beowulf* and these texts, however, stands out: such encounters can scarcely be described as 'dragon-fights', since only rarely does any fighting occur; for dragon-slaying heroes, one must look elsewhere.[101]

Redeeming lost souls: patristic and homiletic influence on 'Beowulf'

Given the extent to which the written culture of the Anglo-Saxons demonstrably depended on a sweeping range of patristic authors, it is perhaps unsurprising that the influence of several of those authors (notably Gregory and Augustine, who were among the most influential) should have been sought in *Beowulf*.[102] Margaret Goldsmith's is perhaps the most sustained attempt to date to attribute a raft of motifs, themes, and phrases to the direct effect of Latin patristic and homiletic sources, but it is important to recognise that for a majority of Anglo-Saxons, such influence would have been mediated through the vernac-

---

100 *Ibid.*, pp. 112–13.
101 For example, to the Norse figures of Thor or Sigurðr, on whom see above, pp. 105–10 and 119–23. One might note in passing a curious resemblance to Beowulf's dragon-fight in Laȝamon's *Brut*, lines 3206–52; as McNelis, 'Laȝamon as Auctor', p. 254, n. 3, points out: 'Morpidus' monster-fight is oddly similar to that in *Beowulf*. In both fights, the king's anger is provoked by wholesale attack against the common people, particularly in lands near the sea, at which the king feels grief in his heart . . . Beowulf orders his retainers to await the result on a *beorge*; Morpidus orders his to wait in a *burȝe*. In both, the king seeks the monster out in his lair; he breaks his sword on the monster; he is killed by a bite rather than flame; he is criticised for exhibiting pointless courage in confronting such a monster single-handed; and the people are ambivalent in lamenting the king's loss while rejoicing in the monster's demise. These details do not correspond to [Laȝamon's main sources; these details are not found in] Geoffrey, in which the monster promptly swallows Morvid whole, or in Wace, where a brief fight is followed by a description of the dragon's slow death.'
102 Tom Hill has consistently argued for such patristic influence on a range of Old English poems; see, for example, 'Two Notes on Patristic Allusion in *Andreas*'; *idem*, '*Hwyrftum scriþað*: *Beowulf*, line 163'; *idem*, 'The Return of the Broken Butterfly'; *idem*, 'The Christian Language and Theme of *Beowulf*'. Cf. Greenfield, 'Old English Words and Patristic Exegesis'.

ular.[103] The apparent influence of vernacular homiletic sources is evident early on in *Beowulf*, when the *Beowulf*-poet chastises the Danes for sacrificing to heathen deities in an attempt to escape the depredations of Grendel (lines 175–88):[104]

> Hwilum hie geheton   æt hærgtrafum   175
> wigweorþunga,   wordum bædon
> þæt him gastbona   geoce gefremede
> wið þeodþreaum.   Swylc wæs þeaw hyra,
> hæþenra hyht;   helle gemundon
> in modsefan,   metod hie ne cuþon,   180
> dæda demend,   ne wiston hie drihten god,
> ne hie huru heofena helm   herian ne cuþon,
> wuldres waldend.   Wa bið þæm ðe sceal
> þurh sliðne nið   sawle bescufan
> in fyres fæþm,   frofre ne wenan,   185
> wihte gewendan;   wel bið þæm þe mot
> æfter deaðdæge   drihten secean
> ond to fæder fæþmum   freoðo wilnian.

[At times they vowed at heathen temples homage to idols, asked in words that the spirit-slayer grant them succour against their dire distress. Such was their custom, the hope of heathens: they recalled hell in their hearts. They did not know the Creator, the Judge of Deeds, nor did they recognise the Lord God, nor truly did they know how to praise the Protector of the Heavens, the Ruler of Glory. It shall be woe for the one who must through cruel emnity thrust his soul into the fire's embrace, not hope for comfort, or any change; it shall be well for the one who may seek the Lord after his death-day, and ask for protection in the father's embrace.]

The damning phrase 'hope of heathens' (*hæþenra hyht*, line 179a) says it all; in Christian eyes, heathens have no hope: 'to be a heathen is sin enough'.[105] But, as we have seen, the *Beowulf*-poet often seems to sanctify his heathen references,[106] and this, the most explicit reference to heathen practice in the entire poem, is no exception: the fervent variation on titles for God (there are five such in the three lines 180b–3a) is presumably intended to have an apotropaic effect.[107] The stark choice between Christianity and paganism is spelt out as that between 'the fire's embrace' (*fyres fæþm*, line 185a) and 'the father's embrace' (*fæder fæþmum*, line 188a); for some it shall be 'well' (*wel*, line 186b), for others 'woe' (*wa*, line 183b). Such parallel structures (and there are others, such as the pattern *ne cuþon . . . ne wiston . . . ne cuþon* in lines 180b–2b)[108] and other ornamental devices (such as the soundplay on *sliðne nið*, line 184a) clearly

---

103 Goldsmith, *The Mode and Meaning of 'Beowulf'*, *passim*.
104 The manuscript reads *hrærg trafum* at line 175b, presumably through dittography (on which see above, pp. 43–9).
105 Stanley, '*Hæthenra Hyht* in *Beowulf*', p. 150.
106 See above, pp. 118–19.
107 Cf. Payne, 'The Danes' Prayers to the "gastbona" in *Beowulf*'.
108 See further below, pp. 238–9.

mark this passage out as a set-piece, but the content of these lines has proved difficult for some to swallow; as Tolkien put it: 'unless my ear and judgment are wholly at fault, they have a ring and measure unlike their context, and indeed unlike that of the poem as a whole'.[109] Tolkien's 'ear and judgment' are justly celebrated, and it is perhaps no surprise that this brief passage contains two half-lines that Bliss was unable to make comply with his complicated metrical system.[110] That the two half-lines in question clearly have the same structure (*Wa bið þæm ðe sceal*, line 183b, and *wel bið þæm þe mot*, line 186b) which Hal Momma detects in no fewer than eighteen other cases in the extant Old English poetic corpus,[111] might suggest that the problem lies with Bliss's system, were it not also for the fact that the same structure is quite widely attested in Old English homiletic prose,[112] and may ultimately derive from the Beatitudes.[113] Once again, the *Beowulf*-poet seems to be sanctifying his pagan content through Christian language.

At the other end of the poem, a similarly homiletic tone has been detected in the report of the curse on the dragon's treasure, which Ted Irving has described as 'curious in that it describes a pagan curse in unmistakably Christian language'.[114] The passage is again one of the most controversial in the whole poem (since it has a direct bearing on whether or nor Beowulf himself is damned), and reads as follows (lines 3062b–75):[115]

> Wundur hwar þonne
> eorl ellenrof   ende gefere
> lifgesceafta,   þonne leng ne mæg
> mon mid his magum   meduseld buan.   3065
> Swa wæs Biowulfe,   þa he biorges weard
> sohte searoniðas;   seolfa ne cuðe
> þurh hwæt his worulde gedal   weorðan sceolde.
> Swa hit oð domes dæg   diope benemdon
> þeodnas mære,   þa ðæt þær dydon,   3070
> þæt se secg wære   synnum scildig,
> hergum geheaðerod,   hellbendum fæst,
> wommum gewitnad,   se ðone wong strude,
> næfne he goldhwæte   gearwor hæfde
> agendes est   ær gesceawod.   3075

109 Tolkien, '*Beowulf*: the Monsters and the Critics', p. 288.
110 Bliss, *The Metre of Beowulf*; cf. Vickman, *A Metrical Concordance to 'Beowulf'*, p. 46.
111 Momma, 'The "Gnomic Formula" '.
112 See, for example, Blickling Homily V, line 104 (Morris, ed., *The Blickling Homilies*, p. 61); Napier XXX.99 and 203; Napier XLIV.345.
113 For a more cautious assessment, see Momma, 'The "Gnomic Formula" ', pp. 424–5.
114 Irving, 'Christian and Pagan Elements', p. 178.
115 The word *magum* in line 3065a has to be supplied: the manuscript at present reads . . . *ū*; the manuscript likewise reads *strude* in line 3073b (on *a/u*-confusion, see above, pp. 42–6). The truly problematic line is 3074a, which in the manuscript reads *næs he*, but *s/f*-confusion is certainly attested elsewhere (see above, pp. 43–5) and a notional *–ne he* could appear as *he* through eyeskip (see above, pp. 45, 47, and 51). There are many discussions of this difficult passage; see, for example, Bliss, '*Beowulf* Lines 3074–3075'; Mitchell, *On Old English*, pp. 30–40; Stanley, '*Hæthenra Hyht* in *Beowulf*', pp. 143–7; Wetzel, '*Beowulf* 3074f. – ein *locus desperatus*?'.

[It is a wonder where a brave-hearted warrior will come to the end of his life's affairs, when he no longer may, a man among his kinsmen, dwell in the mead-hall. So it was for Beowulf, when he sought out the mound's guardian, cunning hostilities; he himself did not know how his parting from the world should come about. So the famous princes who put [the treasure] there gravely declared that until doomsday the man who plundered that place should be guilty of crimes, closed up in heathen temples, secure in the bonds of hell, punished with misfortunes, unless he had previously more readily perceived the gold-bestowing favour of the Lord.]

The passage moves from a general comment about the essential unknowability of death, to a specific comment about Beowulf's own ignorance concerning his own demise;[116] it then continues with an apparently explicit connection between Beowulf's own case and the curse on the one who plunders the dragon's hoard (*swa . . . swa*, lines 3066a and 3069a).[117] The curse itself, with its parallel syntactical structures (*synnum scildig, / hergum geheaðerod, hellbendum fæst, / wommum gewitnad*, lines 3071b–3073a) and evident references to 'doomsday', 'heathen temples', and 'hell-bonds' (*domes dæg*, line 3069a; *hergum*, line 3072a; *hellbendum*, line 3072b), is clearly a set-piece, and certainly seems to owe much to the Christian language of anathema and condemnation.[118] But it is important to note that the first time that the curse is mentioned (almost immediately before the quoted passage) there is an escape-clause provided (lines 3051–7):

> Þonne wæs þæt yrfe,   eacencræftig,
> iumonna gold   galdre bewunden,
> þæt ðam hringsele   hrinan ne moste
> gumena ænig,   nefne god sylfa,
> sigora soðcyning,   sealde þam ðe he wolde   3055
> he is manna gehyld   hord openian,
> efne swa hwylcum manna   swa him gemet ðuhte.

[Then that legacy, increased in power, the gold of ancient men, was enveloped in a spell, so that no man could be permitted to touch that ring-chamber, unless God himself, the true king of victories (he is man's protection) granted that he would open the hoard to whomsoever of men as seemed fitting to him.]

Elsewhere in the poem, the conjunction *nefne* ('unless', 'except that') is used, as here, to stress the difference between God's power and man's (*nefne him witig god*, line 1056a; *nemne . . . halig god*, lines 1052a and 1053b). Such parallels surely encourage the acceptance of the proposed emendation *næfne he* for manuscript *næs he* at line 3074a, with the important corollary that although the

---

116 One might compare the poet's repeated insistence on the ignorance of the Danes in the passage previously cited, at lines 180b–2b; see further below, pp. 238–9.

117 Cf. Doig, '*Beowulf* 3096b: Curse or Consequence?'.

118 Cf., for example, the same tone in Ælfric, *Catholic Homilies* II.v.131–3 (Godden, ed., *Ælfric's Catholic Homilies*, pp. 45–6): **Scyldig** he wæs to **hellicere** susle for his mandædum. ac he geandette his **synna** drihtne sylfum (emphasis added).

escape-clause *may* apply to *Beowulf*, it need not: the final decision is left in God's hands.[119] Indeed, the only person to whom God's protection in rifling the dragon's hoard has been apparently granted is the thief, of whom the poet rather curiously says 'so may an undoomed man easily endure hardship and exile, who maintains the Lord's favour' (*swa mæg unfæge eaðe gedigan / wean ond wræcsið, se ðe Wealdendes / hyldo gehealdeþ*, lines 2291–2293a).[120] If this quasi-gnomic statement is the poet's own equivalent of Beowulf's own motto, uttered many lines before, that 'fate often spares an undoomed man, if his courage endures' (*wyrd oft nereð / unfægne eorl, þonne his ellen deah*, lines 572b–573),[121] it is important to stress the difference between the two perspectives, one of which is explicitly Christian and the other not, just as the poet's insistence in the passage under scrutiny that Beowulf 'sought out . . . cunning hostilities' (*sohte searoniðas*, line 3067a) seems flatly to contradict Beowulf's own earlier proud boast that he 'did not seek out cunning hostilities' (*ne sohte searoniðas*, line 2738a). Nor is the poet the only one implicitly to undermine Beowulf's actions and assertions; in the passage immediately following the second expression of the curse, even Wiglaf seems to criticise his dead lord.[122]

Elsewhere in the poem, homiletic language seems mainly concentrated in just three passages, namely the two descriptions of the monster-mere (lines 1357–79 and 1408–17) and in Hrothgar's so-called 'sermon' (lines 1700–84).[123] It is interesting to note that two of these three passages should be put in the mouth of the pagan King Hrothgar, but here again the poet is at least demonstrating some consistency in the voices he gives his characters.[124] Hrothgar at any rate gives the first and longest of the descriptions of the monster-mere, speaking to Beowulf about the kin of Cain and their abode just before the latter heads off to confront Grendel's mother (lines 1357b–1379):[125]

> 'Hie dygel lond
> warigeað, wulfhleoþu, windige næssas,
> frecne fengelad, ðær fyrgenstream
> under næssa genipu niþer gewiteð, 1360
> flod under foldan. Nis þæt feor heonon
> milgemearces þæt se mere standeð;
> ofer þæm hongiað hrinde bearwas,
> wudu wyrtum fæst wæter oferhelmað.
> Þær mæg nihta gehwæm niðwundor seon, 1365
> fyr on flode. No þæs frod leofað
> gumena bearna, þæt þone grund wite.
> Ðeah þe hæðstapa hundum geswenced,
> heorot hornum trum, holtwudu sece,

---

119 See further below, pp. 238–62.
120 Note the soundplay in *Wealdendes / hyldo gehealdeþ*, lines 2292–3a, on which see above, pp. 61–9.
121 Cf. Liuzza, trans., *Beowulf: a New Verse Translation*, p. 123.
122 See below, pp. 261–3.
123 On the sermon itself, see, for example, Hansen, 'Hrothgar's "Sermon" in *Beowulf* as Parental Wisdom'; Ohba, 'Hrothgar's "Sermon" and Beowulf's Death'.
124 On which see further below, pp. 203–22.
125 For the emendation *helan* in line 1372a, see above, pp. 47–8.

feorran geflymed,   ær he feorh seleð,   1370
aldor on ofre,   ær he in wille
hafelan helan.   Nis þæt heoru stow.
Þonon yðgeblond   up astigeð
won to wolcnum,   þonne wind styreþ,
lað gewidru,   oðþæt lyft drysmaþ,   1375
roderas reotað.   Nu is se ræd gelang
eft æt þe anum.   Eard git ne const,
frecne stowe,   ðær þu findan miht
sinnigne secg;   sec gif þu dyrre.'

['They dwell in a secret land, wolf-slopes, windy headlands, dangerous
fen-tracts, where the mountain-stream goes down under the headlands'
mists, the flood under the ground. It is not far from here in the tally of
miles, where that mere stands, over which hang frosty groves, a wood
firm-rooted overshadows the water. There one can see each night a
dreadful wonder, fire on the flood. No one lives so wise of the sons of
men that knows the bottom. Even though the heath-stepper, driven by
the hounds, a hart, strong in its horns, may seek the wooded forest,
chased from afar, he will give up his life, his spirit on the brink, rather
than plunge in to save his head; that is no pleasant place. From there the
tumult of the waves rises up dark to the clouds, when the wind stirs up
hateful storms, until the sky turns grim, the heavens weep. Now once
again is a solution to be sought from you alone. You do not yet know the
dwelling-place, the dangerous spot where you can find the sinful creature. Seek if you dare.']

The geography of the place, which Stanley has rightly described as 'a
gallimauphry of devices',[126] is exceedingly hard to reconcile, and a number of
critics have remarked on the difficulty in particular of determining whether an
inshore lake or a sea-side location is intended.[127] The 'wulf-slopes' (*wulfhleoþu*,
line 1358a) would seem to accord well with the later descriptions of Grendel's
mother as a 'sea-wolf" (*brimwylf*, lines 1506a and 1599a), while both Grendel
and his mother are described by terms which would link them with the wolvish
wearh (Norse *vargr*, 'were-wolf"), namely *heorowearh* (line 1267a) and
grundwyrgen (line 1518b).[128] The image of the 'hart strong in horns' (*heorot
hornum trum*, line 1369a), which commences with two lines alliterating on *h*,
cannot help but conjure images of the imperilled Danish hall, Heorot, with its
wide gables (*horngeap*, line 82a; *hornreced*, line 704a). Up to this point, the
poet, speaking *in propria persona* has described Grendel as a 'fiend in hell'
(*feond on helle*, line 101b),[129] a 'captive of hell' (*helle hæfton*, line 788a), and a
'hellish spirit' (*helle gast*, line 1274a); he has described him as 'heathen'
(*hæþen*, lines 852b and 986a), 'enemy of mankind' (*feond mancynnes*, lines

---

126 Stanley, 'Old English Poetic Diction', p. 441.
127 See, for example, Butts, 'The Analogical Mere'; Lawrence, 'The Haunted Mere'; Mackie, 'The
     Demon's Home in Beowulf'; Schrader, 'Sacred Groves, Marvellous Waters'.
128 It is interesting to note that Beowulf appears to say of Unferth that he will experience *werhðo* in Hell
     for killing his brothers (lines 588b–99a), since it is precisely that fratricide which aligns him with
     the kin of Cain; on textual difficulties with this passage, however, see below, pp. 252–3.
129 Cf. Cosijn, *Notes on 'Beowulf'*, p. 3, speaking against those who would emend to *healle* ('hall').

164b and 1276a), and 'God's opponent' (*Godes andsaca*, lines 786b and 1682b), saying of Grendel, when held in Beowulf's grip, that 'he wished to flee into darkness, to seek the company of devils' (*wolde on heolstor fleon, / secan deofla gedræg*, lines 755b–756a).[130] Of Grendel's final descent into the mere, the poet simply says: 'joyless in the fen-refuge, he laid aside his life, his heathen soul: there hell received him' (*dreama leas / in fenfreoðo feorh alegde, / hæþene sawle; þær him hel onfeng*, lines 850b–852).[131] None of the characters in the poem have up to this point used comparable language, and afterwards only Hrothgar fleetingly seems unwittingly to apply a vernacular version of the Christian-Latin term 'old enemy' (*hostis antiquus*) to Grendel, whom he calls his 'ancient foe' (*ealdgewinna*, line 1776b);[132] and surely after twelve years of depredations Hrothgar has the right to do that. But the consistency of tone and perspective is perfect throughout.

Shortly following Hrothgar's chilling description, the poet gives his own potted version of the trip to the monster-mere (lines 1408–17):[133]

> Ofereode þa   æþelinga bearn
> steap stanhliðo,   stige nearwe,
> enge anpaðas,   uncuð gelad,   1410
> neowle næssas,   nicorhusa fela.
> He feara sum   beforan gengde
> wisra monna   wong sceawian,
> oþþæt he færinga   fyrgenbeamas
> ofer harne stan   hleonian funde,   1415
> wynleasne wudu;   wæter under stod
> dreorig ond gedrefed.

[Then the sons of princes passed over steep, rocky, slopes, thin courses, narrow single tracks, unknown paths, precipitous crags, many dwellings of water-monsters; [Beowulf] went on ahead with a few wise companions to view the place: until suddenly he perceived mountainous trees towering over the grey rock, a joyless wood; water stood below, grim and troubled.]

The two passages together produce an odd combination of images: of trees, and cliffs, and water; of hot and cold; and of curious creatures seething in the depths. Long ago, Richard Morris pointed out the close parallel to this description in that given by Saint Paul of Hell, according to Blickling Homily XVI:[134]

> Swa sanctus paulus wæs geseonde on norðanweardne þisne middangeard þær
> ealle wætero niðergewítað ⁊ he þær geseah ofer ðæm wætere sumne hárne

---

130 Cf. Malone, 'Grendel and His Abode', pp. 298–9; Maynard ' "Secan deofla gedræg" '. See too the later description of Grendel and his mother as 'devils' (*deofla*, line 1680a).

131 Tolkien, '*Beowulf*, the Monsters, and the Critics', pp. 278–80.

132 Whitelock, *The Audience of 'Beowulf'*, pp. 10–11; Malone, 'Grendel and His Abode', p. 298.

133 Cf. Cook, 'Old English Notes: *Beowulf* 1408ff'.

134 Morris, ed., *Blickling Homilies*, pp. vi–vii; the homily in question is in fact no. XVII in Morris's edition, but the fragment which Morris numbers XVI has been identified as a part of his Homily IV, causing a renumbering of Morris's Homilies XVII–XIX as XVI–XVIII. See further the facsimile by Willard, ed., *The Blickling Homilies*, pp. 38–40. For the text, cf. Collins, 'Blickling Homily XVI and the Dating of *Beowulf*', p. 62; for the translation, cf. Malone, 'Grendel and His Abode', pp. 304–5. See too Collins, 'Six Words in the Blickling Homilies', p. 141.

stán ⁊ wæron norð of ðæm stáne awexene swiðe hrimige bearwas ⁊ ðær wæron
þystrogenipo ⁊ under þæm stane wæs niccra eardung ⁊ wearga ⁊ he geseah
þæt on ðæm clife hangodan on ðæm ísgean bearwum manige swearte saula be
heora handum gebundne ⁊ þa fynd þara on nicra onlicnesse heora gripende
wæron swa swa grædig wulf ⁊ þæt wæter wæs sweart under þæm clife neoðan
⁊ betuh þæm clife on ðæm wætre wæron swylce twelf mila ⁊ ðonne ða twigo
forburston þonne gewitan þa saula niðer þa þe on ðæm twigum hangodan ⁊
him onfengon ða nicras.

[So Saint Paul was looking at the northern part of this world, where all the
waters go down, and he saw there above the water a certain grey rock, and
there had grown north of that rock very frosty woods, and there were dark
mists, and under that rock was a dwelling-place of water-monsters and
wolves; and he saw that on that cliff there hung in those icy woods many black
souls, tied by their hands, and their foes, in the guise of water-monsters, were
gripping them like greedy wolves, and the water was black underneath that
rock, and between that cliff and the water was a drop of twelve miles, and
when the branches broke, the souls who hung on those branches went down,
and the sea-monsters snatched them.]

Subsequent analyses have argued both vigorously and variously: for the direct
influence of *Beowulf* on Blickling Homily XVI;[135] for the reverse;[136] that both
authors were independently drawing on a vernacular version of the apocryphal
Visio S. Pauli;[137] or that both drew on shared homiletic motifs encountered
either through reading or listening.[138] The further parallels that apparently link
both these passages to sections of *The Letter of Alexander to Aristotle* need also
to be taken into account, however:[139] the introduction of a third putatively
connected text certainly complicates things. It is important to note, however,
that, as with motifs apparently borrowed from pagan myth,[140] in introducing
motifs of a description of hell ultimately endebted to the *Visio S. Pauli*, the
Beowulf-poet has naturalised them in their new setting; as Charlie Wright puts
it: 'while retaining the essential configuration, he divests particular elements of
their explicitly eschatological reference by literalising them: his "hell" is still in
the north, because that is where the Danes live; his frosty trees, bereft of the
souls that once were suspended from their branches, are left to "hang" over the
water below; and his water-monsters have been exorcised of their demons'.[141]

Much more explicitly homiletic is the 'sermon' on the dangers of pride that
Hrothgar issues to Beowulf immediately after the latter has emerged victorious
from the monster-mere (lines 1700–84).[142] Once again, however, such use of
Christian language is far from random, and seems intimately connected with the

---

135 So Morris, ed., *Blickling Homilies*, p. vii; Brown, '*Beowulf* and the *Blickling Homilies*', p. 909.
136 So Collins, 'Blickling Homily XVI and the Dating of *Beowulf*', pp. 67–8.
137 So Wright, *The Irish Tradition in Old English Literature*, pp. 116–36.
138 So (for different reasons) Clemoes, 'Style as Criterion', p. 181; Tristram, 'Stock Descriptions',
     p. 111.
139 See above, pp. 25–39; cf. Orchard, *Pride and Prodigies*, pp. 37–47.
140 On which see above, pp. 114–23.
141 Wright, *The Irish Tradition in Old English Literature*, p. 135.
142 For detailed analyses of the sermon, see, for example, Goldsmith, *Mode and Meaning*, pp. 183–209;
     Hansen, 'Hrothgar's "Sermon" in *Beowulf*'; Orchard, *Pride and Prodigies*, pp. 47–53.

fact that the speech is inspired by Hrothgar gazing on the hilt from the monster-mere, which is inscribed with the story of the biblical Flood.[143] Likewise, it is apparent that not all of the speech contains homiletic imagery: Klaeber describes it as 'conspicuous for the blending of heroic and theological motives',[144] and most of the Christian diction is restricted to just one (albeit the longest) section of the four into which the speech naturally falls.[145] Hrothgar briefly congratulates Beowulf (lines 1700–9a), before offering him a warning in the shape of the legendary Heremod (lines 1709b–1724a),[146] contemplation of whose fate leads Hrothgar into general musings on mankind's lot (lines 1724b–1768), after which he closes with a brief section on himself (lines 1769–84). It is the third of these sections that is of interest here (lines 1724b–1768):[147]

> 'Wundor is to secganne
> hu mihtig god   manna cynne   1725
> þurh sidne sefan   snyttru bryttað,
> eard ond eorlscipe;   he ah ealra geweald.
> Hwilum he on lufan   læteð hworfan
> monnes modgeþonc   mæran cynnes,
> seleð him on eþle   eorþan wynne   1730
> to healdanne   hleoburh wera,
> gedeð him swa gewealdene   worolde dælas,
> side rice,   þæt he his selfa ne mæg
> his unsnyttrum   ende geþencean.
> Wunað he on wiste;   no hine wiht dweleð   1735
> adl ne yldo,   ne him inwitsorh
> on sefan sweorceð,   ne gesacu ohwær
> ecghete eoweð,   ac him eal worold
> wendeð on willan;   he þæt wyrse ne con –
> oð þæt him on innan   oferhygda dæl   1740
> weaxeð ond wridað.   Þonne se weard swefeð,
> sawele hyrde;   bið se slæp to fæst,
> bisgum gebunden,   bona swiðe neah,
> se þe of flanbogan   fyrenum sceoteð.
> Þonne bið on hreþre   under helm drepen   1745
> biteran stræle   – him bebeorgan ne con –
> wom wundorbebodum   wergan gastes;
> þinceð him to lytel   þæt he lange heold,

---

143 Part of the relevant passage is cited above, pp. 110–11. The introduction to the speech (lines 1687–99) is the longest such in the whole poem (see Table IV below, pp. 206–7), and the connection between what Hrothgar says and what he sees (namely the hilt) is made apparent both by the fact that the poet uses rhyme to emphasise that 'Hrothgar spoke, gazed on the hilt' (*Hroðgar maðelode, hylt sceawode*, line 1687), and that almost the whole of the rest of the introduction is taken up with a description of what was inscribed on the hilt; at lines 1698b–99 we are reminded that 'Then the wise one spoke, the son of Healfdene, everyone was silent' (*Ða se wisa spræc / sunu Healfdenes swigedon ealle*).

144 Klaeber, ed. *Beowulf*, p. 190.

145 For arguments about the basic structure of the speech, see, for example, Cox, *Cruces*, p. 132; Klaeber, ed. *Beowulf*, p. 190; Hansen, 'Hrothgar's "Sermon" in *Beowulf*', p. 62.

146 On this section, see above, pp. 110–11.

147 The manuscript reads *fædde* at line 1750a, but the emendation adopted here is commonly accepted.

gytsað gromhydig,   nallas on gylp seleð
fætte beagas,   ond he þa forðgesceaft   1750
forgyteð ond forgymeð,   þæs þe him ær God sealde,
wuldres Waldend,   weorðmynda dæl.
Hit on endestæf   eft gelimpeð
þæt se lichoma   læne gedreoseð,
fæge gefealleð;   fehð oþer to,   1755
se þe unmurnlice   madmas dæleþ,
eorles ærgestreon,   egesan ne gymeð.
Bebeorh þe ðone bealonið,   Beowulf leofa,
secg betsta,   ond þe þæt selre geceos,
ece rædas;   oferhyda ne gym,   1760
mære cempa!   Nu is þines mægnes blæd
ane hwile;   eft sona bið
þæt þec adl oððe ecg   eafoþes getwæfeð,
oððe fyres feng,   oððe flodes wylm,
oððe gripe meces,   oððe gares fliht,   1765
oððe atol yldo;   oððe eagena bearhtm
forsiteð ond forsworceð;   semninga bið
þæt ðec, dryhtguma,   dead oferswyðeð.'

['It is wondrous to tell how mighty God, through his magnanimity deals
out to mankind wisdom, land, and rank; he has control of all things.
Sometimes he lets a well-born man's thoughts turn to pleasure, grants
him in his homeland to possess the joys of the earth, a sheltering stronghold of men, makes subject to him areas of the world, broad kingdoms,
so that he himself cannot in his folly perceive any end. He dwells in
prosperity; not at all do old age or sickness harm him, nor does grim
sorrow darken his spirit, nor does malice cause sword-hatred anywhere,
but the whole world moves at his whim; he knows nothing worse until a
portion of pride grows and flourishes; when the keeper sleeps, the
guardian of the soul; that sleep is too sound, fastened with worries, the
slayer very close, who shoots wickedly from his bow [or 'from a fiery
bow'?]. Then under his covering he is struck in the heart with a bitter
arrow, with the crooked commands of wonder of the accursed spirit: he
cannot defend himself; what he has long held seems to him too little,
angry at heart he grows niggardly, not at all honourably dispenses plated
rings, but he forgets and neglects the world to come, the portion of
glories that God, Ruler of Glory, had granted him. Finally it turns out
that the frail body droops and falls doomed, and another succeeds, who
doles out treasure recklessly, the ancient heirlooms of the warrior, does
not reckon of terror. Guard yourself against that dread horror, my dear
Beowulf, best of men, and choose for yourself the better part, eternal
rewards; care not for pride, famous warrior! Now the glory of your
might lasts for a time; but soon it will turn out that sickness or sword
will separate you from your strength, or the fire's embrace or the flood's
surge, or the bite of a blade, or the flight of a spear, or dreaded old age,
or the brightness of your eyes shall fail and grow dim; finally it shall be
that death, noble warrior, shall overpower you.']

It is striking that just as Hrothgar concluded his warning about Heremod with a
direct appeal to Beowulf, the list of dangers that face a man at the height of his

powers (lines 1735–9a) are echoed in a still longer list of the potential pitfalls facing Beowulf himself (lines 1762b–1769). The style of the whole 'sermon' at this point is highly homiletic: within the space of only twenty-three lines we find three examples of an alliterating pair of finite verbs (*weaxað ond wridað*, line 1741a; *forgyteð ond forgymeð*, line 1751a; *forsiteð ond forsworceð*, line 1767a) of a kind uncommon elsewhere in Beowulf, but frequently found in vernacular prose homilies, where very similar themes also occur.[148] So, for example, the motif of the arrows of the devil aimed at men's souls is explored in precisely the same context of overweening pride in Vercelli Homily IV:[149]

> Þonne hæfð þæt dioful geworht bogan ⁊ stræla. Se boga bið geworht of ofermettum, ⁊ þa stræla bioð swa manigra cynna swa swa mannes synna bioð . . . Ælce dæge hæbbað [we] twegen hyrdas: oðer cymð ufan of heofonum, þe us sceall gode bysene onstellan ⁊ us gode þeawas tæcan, ⁊ hæfð him on handa þa scyldas þe ic ær nemde ⁊ þæt sweord, ⁊ wyle us forstandan æt þam awyrgden diofle, þe of þære stylenan helle cymð mid his scearpum strælum us mid to scotianne.

> [Then the devil has made a bow and arrows. The bow is made of pride, and the arrows are of as many kinds as man's sins . . . Each day we have two guardians, and one comes from the heavens above, who is to establish a good example for us and teach us good virtues, and he has in his hand the shields which I mentioned earlier, and the sword, and he wants to defend us against the accursed devil, who comes from steely hell with his sharp arrows, with which to shoot us.]

The ultimate sources for such imagery are biblical, from both the Old and New Testaments. Most famous is that from Ephesians VI.13–17, which speaks of 'the flaming arrows of the evil one' (*tela nequissimi ignea*, Ephesians VI.13), but equally pertinent here is Psalm XC.4–6; both passages, alongside Prudentius's *Psychomachia*, which was widely read in Anglo-Saxon England,[150] popularised the use of the theme of spiritual warfare in Anglo-Saxon literature.[151] With specific regard to the passage from Ephesians, it may well be that the *Beowulf*-poet is here intentionally playing on the two senses of the term *fyren* (*fyrenum*, line 1744b), which means both 'crime' or 'sin' and 'fiery', in order to allude to the 'flaming arrows' of his ultimate source.[152] Likewise, this section of Hrothgar's sermon concludes with a familiar homiletic device: using a series of alliterative pairs linked by polysyndetic *oððe* (lines 1763–6); several examples might be cited which (as here) specifically focus on alternative ways to die.[153]

---

148 Clemoes, 'Style as a Criterion', pp. 180–1, lists only seven other examples of synonymous or near-synonymous pairings of finite verbs in the whole of the rest of *Beowulf*; cf. Klaeber, ed., *Beowulf*, p. 192.

149 Scragg, ed., *Vercelli Homilies*, pp. 102/308–10 and 104/337–42; cf. Atherton, 'The Figure of the Archer in *Beowulf* and the Anglo-Saxon Psalter'; Wright, *The Irish Tradition in Old English Literature*, pp. 260–1.

150 See further, for example, Orchard, *The Poetic Art of Aldhelm*, pp. 170–8.

151 In general, see Hermann, *Allegories of War*.

152 Cf. Robinson, 'A Sub-Sense of Old English *fyrn(-)*'.

153 A convenient set of examples is provide by Lapidge, 'The Archetype of *Beowulf*', pp. 38–9, to which might be added Bazire and Cross, ed., *Eleven Old English Rogationtide Homilies*, III.81–6 (pp. 50–1) and V.43–9 (p. 71).

Hrothgar concludes his sermon with an account of how his own past happiness and martial glory suffered a rebuff in the form of Grendel (lines 1769–81):[154]

'Swa ic Hringdena   hund missera
weold under wolcnum   ond hig wigge beleac   1770
manigum mægþa   geond þysne middangeard,
æscum ond ecgum,   þæt ic me ænigne
under swegles begong   gesacan ne tealde.
Hwæt, me þæs on eþle   edwenden cwom,
gyrn æfter gomene,   seoþðan Grendel wearð,   1775
ealdgewinna,   ingenga min;
ic þære socne   singales wæg
modceare micle.   Þæs sig metode þanc,
ecean dryhtne,   þæs ðe ic on aldre gebad
þæt ic on þone hafelan   heorodreorigne   1780
ofer ealdgewin   eagum starige.'

['So, under the skies, I ruled the Ring-Danes for fifty years, and protected them in battle against many nations throughout this world, with spears and swords, so that I did not reckon anyone an enemy to me under the expanse of the sky. Yet in my homeland a reversal occurred, grief after joy, once Grendel, the ancient adversary, became my invader; I continually bore that persecution, great sorrow of heart. Thanks be to the Creator, to the eternal Lord, that I should experience during my lifetime that I might stare with my eyes on that blood-stained head after the ancient struggle.']

Hrothgar's tragedy is that, after success abroad, he suffers reversal at home after a fifty-year reign; it is in this context that he uses an apparently Christian turn of phrase, describing Grendel as his 'ancient adversary' (*ealdgewinna*, line 1776a).[155] The cogency of Hrothgar's warning is underlined by the poet's repetition of precisely the same pattern in the cases of Grendel's mother, attacked at home after her successful raid of Heorot at the end of her fifty-year reign (lines 1497–8), and, later, Beowulf himself, who reigns for fifty years after his successes abroad, but is attacked at home by the dragon (lines 2208b–2211).[156] If Hrothgar is ostensibly here preaching to Beowulf on the dangers of pride, then the *Beowulf*-poet is implicitly preaching to us all.[157]

---

[154] The manuscript reads *ed wendan* at line 1774b.
[155] See above, p. 157.
[156] See above, p. 64.
[157] It is important to note that Hrothgar's sermon is not the only such in verse on the theme of pride to survive in Old English: *Vainglory* (ed. and trans. Shippey, *Poems of Wisdom and Learning in Old English*, pp. 54–7) provides a number of excellent parallels of thought and language to what Hrothgar says here.

Distant echoes of faraway voices: parallels with other Old English poems

The twin notions that the *Beowulf*-poet may have used existing Old English Christian verse as a source, or that *Beowulf* may have been sufficiently well known for other poets to echo it, were both swept aside in the wake of the oral-formulaic debate that dominated much of twentieth-century discussion of the poem:[158] the whole idea of direct borrowing between poems (and between poets) was subsumed in the supposition that Old English poets instead drew on a stock of shared diction, and that any perceived overlap between poems simply reflected the partial and incomplete nature of the extant corpus.[159] Such arguments ignored the fact that surviving Anglo-Latin poetry from the seventh century to the eleventh was demonstrably formulaic, and itself drew on the one hand on a stock of traditional formulas inherited from the Classical and Christian Latin poetic past, as well as on direct borrowings from other Anglo-Latin (and other) poets.[160] Moreover, modern computistical methods allow the quick and direct comparison of shared phrasing within the entire extant corpus of Old English at speeds unimagined by those late nineteenth-century scholars who laboriously compiled lists of *Parallelstellen* in order to demonstrate both the interdependence and comparative chronology of the whole range of Old English poems.[161] It seems likely that the identification and classification of formulaic language unique to individual texts and groups of texts will occupy scholars for a while to come, after which a serious and informed debate about the relationship between surviving Old English poems can be held.[162]

So, for example, striking parallels of diction have been identified between *Beowulf* and the Old English poem *Andreas*, preserved in the Vercelli Book, although scholars have long debated the significance of such overlapping diction:[163] in her 500-page doctoral dissertation, Carol Hughes Funk has meticulously charted the ebb and flow of academic opinion over the course of a century,[164] while the recent work of Anita Riedinger and Alison Powell strongly supports the notion of direct borrowing from *Beowulf* on the part of the *Andreas*-poet.[165] Powell's study in particular, by far the most thorough to date, is based on an assessment of around ninety parallels of diction and phrasing that are uniquely shared by *Beowulf* and *Andreas* in the extant corpus of Old

---

158 On which, see above, pp. 85–91.
159 For a quixotic counter-argument to the ongoing tide of debate, see, for example, Schaar, 'On a New Theory of Old English Poetic Diction'.
160 See, for example, Orchard, *The Poetic Art of Aldhelm*, esp. pp. 126–292.
161 On the widespread collection of *Parallelstellen*, see above, pp. 2 and 85.
162 I have in hand a project entitled 'An Anglo-Saxon Formulary', which seeks to collect examples of such parallel phrasing across the range of extant Anglo-Latin and Old English verse.
163 Significant stages in the debate include the contributions by Brooks, *Andreas and the Fates of the Apostles*; Cavill, '*Beowulf* and *Andreas*: Two Maxims'; Cook, 'The Old English *Andreas* and Bishop Acca of Hexham'; Klaeber, '*Beowulf* 769 und *Andreas* 1526ff'; Peters, 'The Relationship of the Old English *Andreas* to *Beowulf*'; Powell, 'Verbal Parallels in *Andreas*'; Schabram, '*Andreas* und *Beowulf*: Parallelstellen als Zeugnis für literarische Abhängigkeit'; Smithson, 'The Old English Christian'.
164 Funk, 'History of *Andreas* and *Beowulf*: Comparative Scholarship'.
165 Riedinger, 'The Formulaic Relationship between *Beowulf* and *Andreas*'; Powell, 'Verbal Parallels in *Andreas*'.

English. It may be that the traditional etymology of the name Andreas ('manly') first suggested to the *Andreas*-poet the martial tone that runs right through the poem,[166] and other broad parallels of theme and phrasing between *Andreas* and *Beowulf* have often been noted: the closing lines of *Andreas* depict the hero departing back home by sea in a manner which strongly recalls the funeral of Scyld Scefing, and there exist the oddly parallel (and equally odd) forms *ealuscerwen* (*Beowulf*, line 769a) and *meoduscerwen* (*Andreas*, line 1526b).[167]

Moreover, the sheer number of parallels (and their extensive nature) seems highly suggestive, and surely bespeaks more than two poets merely drawing on the same traditional stock. It is not simply that the *Andreas*-poet refers to the sea as a 'surging ocean' (*geofon geotende*, lines 393a and 1508a),[168] streets as 'stone-adorned' (*stræte stanfage*, line 1236a), an ancient construction as 'the old work of giants' (*enta ærgeweorc*, line 1235a), or a fine building as 'high and horn-gabled' (*heah ond horngeap*, line 668a) in the same way (unparalleled in the extant corpus) as the *Beowulf*-poet (cf. *gifen geotende*, line 1690a; *stræt wæs stanfah*, line 320a; *enta ærgeweorc*, line 1679a; *heah ond horngeap*, line 82a); but also in both poems people act 'as was their custom',[169] wealth is measured,[170] night falls,[171] ships are piled with treasure,[172] weapons melt,[173] ships float,[174] blood wells,[175] and the very expanse of the earth is assessed,[176] all

---

166 On the use of similarly meaningful names in *Beowulf*, see below, pp. 172–3.

167 See above, pp. 82–3.

168 One might note that in fact in both these cases (and again in 1585b, which is, interestingly enough, followed closely at 1590a by *geotende*, the third and last example of the verb *geotan* in *Andreas*) the manuscript actually reads *heofon* ('heaven'), which leave the lines in question without alliteration. Such confusion might suggest either that the term *geofon* was archaic (though it is copied correctly in *Andreas* at lines 498b, 852b, and 1624b [as *geofon*], and in the oblique case *geofone* in lines 1531a and 1615b; at line 489a the form *gifeðe* ['granted'] is found, presumably a mistake for *gifene*), or that the form *geotende*, which apart from the cited examples in *Andreas* and *Beowulf* only appears one other time in the extant poetic corpus (*Precepts*, line 41a: *geotende gielp*).

169 Compare *Andreas*, line 25 (*ðegon geond þa þeode swelc wæs þeaw hira*) and *Beowulf*, line 178 (*wið þeodþreaum swylc wæs þeaw hyra*).

170 Compare *Andreas*, line 303a (*landes ne locenra beaga*) and *Beowulf*, line 2995a (*landes ond locenra beaga*); the parallel is the more intriguing in that the genitive forms here seem grammatically out of place in their context in *Andreas*, but natural in that of *Beowulf*.

171 Compare *Andreas*, line 123 (*niwan stefne nihthelm toglad*) and *Beowulf*, line 1789 (*niowan stefne nihthelm geswearc*).

172 Compare *Andreas*, lines 360b–362a (*Æfre ic ne hyrde / þon cymlicor ceol gehladenne / heahgestreonum*) and *Beowulf*, lines 38 and 44a (*ne gehyrde ic cymlicor ceol gegyrwan . . . þeodgestreonum*).

173 Compare *Andreas*, lines 1145–6 (*Het wæpen wera wexe gelicost / on þam orlege eall formeltan*) and *Beowulf*, lines 1607b–1608 (*Þæt wæs wundra sum / þæt hit eal gemealt ise gelicost*).

174 Compare *Andreas*, line 497 (*færeð famigheals fugole gelicost*) and *Beowulf*, line 218 (*flota famiheals fugle gelicost*).

175 Compare *Andreas*, lines 1239b–1241a and 1275b–7a (*swate bestemed / banhus abrocen Blod yðum weoll / haton heolfre . . . swat yðum weoll / þurh bancofan blodlifrum swealg / hatan heolfre*) and *Beowulf*, lines 847–9, 1422–3a, and 2691–3 (*Ðær wæs on blode brim weallende / atol yðe geswing eal gemenged / haton heolfre, heorodreore weol . . . Flod blode weol (folc to sægon) / hatan heolfre . . . hat ond headogrim, heals ealne ymbefeng / biteran banum; he geblodegod wearð / sawuldriore swat yðum weoll*).

176 Compare *Andreas*, lines 332–4 (*Farað nu geond ealle eorðan sceatas / emne swa wide swa wæter bebugeð, / oððe stedewangas stræte gelicgaþ*) and *Beowulf*, lines 92b–93 and 1224–5 (*cwæð þæt se ælmihtiga eorðan worhte / wliteobeorhtne wang, swa wæter bebugeð . . . ealne wideferhþ weras ehtigað, / efne swa side swa sæ bebugeð*).

in ways which link these two poems perhaps more closely than any others in the extant corpus.

A still further chain of resonances links *Beowulf* not only to *Andreas*, but to the poem that immediately follows it in the Vercelli Book, namely *The Fates of the Apostles*, composed by Cynewulf.[177] So much is clear simply from the opening lines of all three poems, presented here in sequence, with parallels highlighted in italics:

Beowulf, lines 1–3:

> Hwæt! *We* Gardena *in* gear*dagum*,
> þeodcyninga, *þrym gefrunon*,
> hu ða æþelingas *ellen* fremedon.

> [Listen! We have heard of the power of the mighty kings of the spear-Danes in days long gone, how those noblemen did deeds of courage.]

Fates of the Apostles, lines 1–15:

> Hwæt! Ic þysne sang siðgeomor fand
> on seocum sefan, samnode wide
> *hu þa æðelingas ellen* cyðdon,
> torhte ond *tireadige. Twelfe* wæron,
> dædum domfæste, *dryhtne* gecorene, 5
> leofe on life. Lof wide sprang,
> miht ond mærðo, ofer middangeard,
> *þeodnes þegna, þrym* unlytel.
> Halgan heape *hlyt* wisode
> þær hie *dryhtnes* æ deman sceoldon, 10
> reccan fore rincum. Sume on Romebyrig,
> *frame, fyrdhwate*, feorh ofgefon
> þurg Nerones nearwe searwe,
> Petrus ond Paulus. Is se apostolhad
> wide geweorðod ofer werþeoda! 15

> [Listen! Sad at departing, I, sick at heart, put together this poem, collected far and wide how those noblemen, famed and honour-blessed, revealed deeds of courage. Twelve there were, glory-fast in deeds, chosen by the Lord, beloved in life. The praise spread wide, the might and esteem, across the world, of the prince's thegns, no little power. Their lot directed the holy band, to where they had to glorify the Lord's law, tell it before men. Some in Rome, bold, battle-brave, gave up their lives through Nero's narrow plotting: Peter and Paul. That apostolic state is widely honoured among men.]

Andreas, lines 1–11a:

> Hwæt! *We* gefrunan *on* fyrn*dagum*
> *twelfe* under tunglum *tireadige* hæleð,
> *þeodnes þegnas*. No hira *þrym* alæg
> camprædenne þonne cumbol hneotan,

---

177 Both poems are conveniently edited by Brooks, *'Andreas' and 'The Fates of the Apostles'*.

syððan hie gedældon, swa him *dryhten* sylf,   5
heofona heahcyning, *hlyt* getæhte.
Þæt wæron mære men ofer eorðan,
frome folctogan ond *fyrdhwate*,
rofe rincas, þonne rond ond hand
on herefelda helm ealgodon,   10
on meotudwange.

[Listen! We have heard of twelve honour-blessed heroes under the stars in days gone by, prince's thegns. Their power did not fail in fighting, when banners clashed, after they departed as the Lord himself, the high king of the heavens directed their lot. They were men famed across the earth, bold war-leaders and battle-brave, daring warriors, when shield and hand defended the helmet on the battle-field, on the plain of fate.]

The tissue of overlapping phrasing between the three poems is surely striking, and the incongruity of such martial and heroic diction in a hagiographical context strongly suggests that it is Cynewulf and the *Andreas*-poet who are borrowing here.[178] Earlier scholars often noted considerable parallels of diction and image between *Beowulf* the signed poems of Cynewulf (*Elene, Juliana, Christ II*, and *Fates of the Apostles*),[179] and the notion that Cynewulf is deliberately echoing and adapting *Beowulf* in the opening lines of *Fates of the Apostles* seems supported by the similarity of phrasing of the half-line *Lof wide sprang* (line 6b: 'fame spread widely') to a parenthetic half-line of like meaning at the beginning of *Beowulf: blæd wide sprang* (line 19b: 'renown spread widely').[180]

Apart from Cynewulf and the *Andreas*-poet, the most impressive parallels of diction have been noted between *Beowulf* and several of the biblical poems of the Junius manuscript.[181] Perhaps the most striking overlap is in the description of the path towards Grendel's mere taken by the Danish and Geatish warriors in *Beowulf* and that of the path towards the the Red Sea taken by the Israelites in *Exodus*: both are 'narrow solitary paths, an unknown way' (*enge anpaðas, uncuð gelad* [*Beowulf*, line 1410 and *Exodus*, line 58]). Nor is this the only overlap: Clare Lynch, in the course of the most detailed survey to date, notes no fewer than twenty-seven parallels within the half-lines of both poems that are

---

[178] See Orchard, 'Both Style and Substance: the Case for Cynewulf', pp. [20–1], where it is suggested that the *Andreas*-poet is borrowing from both Cynewulf and *Beowulf*. Powell, 'Verbal Parallels in *Andreas*', Appendix C points out some 180 parallels between *Andreas* and the signed poems of Cynewulf that are unique in the extant corpus. In short, the *Andreas*-poet seems to be borrowing from and consciously echoing earlier Old English poets much in the manner of the formulaic methods of composition of generations of Anglo-Saxons who chose to compose their verse in Latin; see further, for example, Orchard, *The Poetic Art of Aldhelm*, pp. 126–292; *idem*, 'After Aldhelm: the Teaching and Transmission of the Anglo-Latin Hexameter'.

[179] See in particular Cook, 'Cynewulf's Part in Our *Beowulf*'; Sarrazin, '*Beowulf* und Kynewulf'; *idem*, *Beowulf-Studien*; Schaar, *Critical Studies in the Cynewulf Group*, pp. 239–50.

[180] One might note further that in this line, Cynewulf indulges in characteristic sound-play or paronomasia (*leofe . . . life . . . lof*, on which see Orchard, 'Both Style and Substance: the Case for Cynewulf'), while in his, the *Beowulf*-poet may be punning on the name Beow (a name certainly associated with vegetation, as is the noun *blæd* ['growth', 'vigour']: see above, pp. 103–4). The only two further examples of parallel phrases in the extant poetic corpus are again from *Beowulf* (line 1588b: *Hra wide sprong*) and Cynewulf (*Juliana*, line 584b: *Lead wide sprong*).

[181] See, for example, Klaeber, ed., *Beowulf*, pp. cx–cxiii, who gives a conservative overview.

unique in the extant corpus, as well as eleven shared compounds.[182] While earlier scholars have argued both that *Beowulf* is borrowing from *Exodus* and vice versa (Klaeber, indeed, held both positions at different times),[183] Lynch argues powerfully for the priority of *Beowulf*.[184] More difficult to gauge at present are the apparent overlaps between *Beowulf* and *Genesis A*, which have been noted for a long time, with Klaeber asserting that the *Beowulf*-poet drew on the biblical epic.[185] Among the more striking parallels are the description of God's wrath against the people of the cities of the plains, who had offended against him 'for a long time: he paid them their reward for that' (*lange þrage: him þæs lean forgeald*, line 2546), since almost the same words in *Beowulf* are used to describe God's retribution against the giants (*lange þrage: he him ðæs lean forgeald*, line 114). Likewise, it is notable that the famous words used twice in *Beowulf* to describe its hero as one 'who was of mankind the strongest in might on that day of this life' (*se wæs moncynnes mægenes strengest / on þæm dæge þysses lifes*, lines 196–7; cf. *se þe manna wæs mægene strengest / on þæm dæge þysses lifes*, lines 789–90)[186] should appear to echo closely what the poet of *Genesis A* has to say about Nimrod, the giant hunter, of whom it is said 'that of mankind he had the most might and strength in those days' (*þæt he moncynnes mæste hæfde on þam mældagum mægen and strengo*, lines 1631–2).[187] Similarly, Wealhtheow's words to Hrothgar, encouraging him to leave his kingdom to his own sons when he 'has to [go] forth to see the decree of fate' (lines 1179b–1180a: *þonne ðu forð scyle / metodsceaft seon*)[188] have a parallel in the description of the death of Abraham's father in *Genesis A*, who 'went forth, wise in years, to see the decree of fate' (lines 1742b–1743: *þa he forð gewat / misserum frod metodsceaft seon*). Less convincing, perhaps, are those parallels in *Beowulf* to the account of the battle of the four kings against five kings in *Genesis A*, where we learn in quick succession that the defeated kings of Sodom and Gomorrah were 'bereft of their loved ones at the crowding of shields' (line 1998: *æt þæm lindcrodan leofum bedrorene*; cf. *Beowulf*, line 1073: *beloren leofum æt þæm lindplegan*) and that the king of Elam 'had war-success . . . controlled the place of slaughter' (lines 2003b and 2005a: *hæfde wigsigor . . . weold wælstowe*; cf. *Beowulf*, line 1554a: *geweold wigsigor*), since the apparent echoes in *Beowulf* are so widely scattered, and refer to the plight of Hildeburh in the Finn-episode and the victory of Beowulf himself over Grendel's mother. Evidently, more work needs to be done further to identify

---

182 Lynch, 'Enigmatic Diction in the Old English *Exodus*', pp. 171–256, 262–4, and 272.

183 See, for example, Brodeur, 'A Study of Diction and Style'; Klaeber, 'Concerning the Relation between *Exodus* and *Beowulf*'; idem, 'Noch einmal *Exodus* 56–58 und *Beowulf* 1408–10'.

184 Lynch, 'Enigmatic Diction in the Old English *Exodus*', pp. 171–256.

185 Klaeber, 'Die Ältere Genesis und der Beowulf'.

186 See above, p. 55.

187 On Nimrod (described in Genesis X.9 as 'mightie in the earth, and he was a valiaunt hunter before our Lord' [*potens in terra, et erat robustus uenator coram Domino*]), see further Orchard, *Pride and Prodigies*, pp. 77–8. According to Thiel, *Grundlagen und Gestalt der Hebräischkenntnisse des fruhen Mittelalters*, p. 367, the Hebrew name Nimrod (also spelt Nemrod, Nemroth, and Nembroth) had a range of (generally inauspicious) meanings, according to a variety of patristic sources, including 'bitterness' (*amaritudo*), 'temptation falling' (*tentatio descendens*), 'apostate' (*apostata*), and 'tyrant, exile, or transgressor' (*tyrannus uel profugus aut transgressor*).

188 See further below, pp. 219–22.

unique parallels across the whole range of extant Old English verse, the better to assess the strength of the connections suggested here.

Nevertheless, it is clear from the study of both the Christian and secular traditions that underlie *Beowulf* that the poet was drawing together a great range and variety of materials in producing his work. The skill and sophistication with which the *Beowulf*-poet brought together these disparate traditions has already been apparent, and as in the subsequent chapters we turn to consider other aspects of his art, such as characterisation, combination of speech and action, and shifting points of view, the extent to which *Beowulf* differs both in kind and in quality not only from any putative sources or models, but also from all other extant Old English verse will, it is hoped, become clear. *Beowulf* may not be the only Old English poem to survive, but in its combination of artistry and humanity, it is surely the best.

6

Heroes and Villains

Speaking parts and spear-carriers: the cast of 'Beowulf'

The sheer number of different characters mentioned in *Beowulf* is a major source of potential bewilderment for modern readers:[1] over seventy are named in the course of the poem, but almost half of these appear only once.[2] To be sure, some of these fleeting figures are well-attested outside *Beowulf*, such as the biblical Abel (line 108b),[3] the legendary smith, Weland (line 455a), or the ill-reputed Goth, Eormenric (line 1201a),[4] but many of the others pass by in a blur, named only in relation to other, more central, characters: all we ever learn of Yrmenlaf (line 1324a), for example, is that he is Æschere's younger brother.[5] In fact, only a dozen characters are named more than five times in the course of the poem, as follows (in descending order of frequency): Beowulf, Hrothgar, Grendel, Hygelac, Healfdene, Ecgtheow, Hrethel, Ongentheow, Weohstan, Finn, Wiglaf, and Wealhtheow.[6] Yet even this list is misleading, since (as with many of those who appear less frequently in the poem) several of these figures are named mainly because of their relationship to other (generally more significant) char-

---

[1] For an early attempt at clarification, see Björkman, *Studien über die Eigennamen im Beowulf.*

[2] Named more than once are Æschere, Beow, Beowulf, Breca, Cain, Ecglaf, Ecgtheow, Eofor, Finn, Fitela, Grendel, Hæreth, Hæthcyn, Healfdene, Heardred, Hemming, Hengest, Heorogar, Herebeald, Heremod, Hildeburh, Hnæf, Hrethel, Hrethric, Hrothgar, Hrothulf, Hygd, Hygelac, Offa, Ohthere, Onela, Ongentheow, Scyld, Sigemund, Unferth, Wealhtheow, Weohstan, Wiglaf, Wulf, and Wulfgar; named once are Abel, Ælfhere, Beanstan, Dæghrefn, Eadgils, Eanmund, Ecgwela, Eomer, Eormenric, Folcwalda, Freawaru, Froda, Garmund, Guthlaf, Halga, Hama, Heatholaf, Heoroweard, Hereric, Hoc, Hondscio, Hrothmund, Hunlafing, Ingeld, Oslaf, Swerting, Thryth, Wæls, Weland, Withergyld, Wonred, and Yrmenlaf.

[3] In Anglo-Saxon contexts, Abel generally appears (as in *Beowulf*) alongside his brother and slayer, Cain; see further, for example, Emerson, 'Legends of Cain'; Mellinkoff, 'Cain's Monstrous Progeny' (Parts I and II); Williams, *Cain and Beowulf.* See further above, pp. 63–4 and 137–40.

[4] See, for example, Lang, 'Sigurd and Weland'; Nedoma, 'The Legend of Wayland'; Brady, *The Legends of Ermanaric.* On all of these characters, see further above, pp. 105–10 and 114–16.

[5] Shippey, *Beowulf*, p. 24, describes Yrmenlaf as 'the poem's most redundant character'. Other characters named only in respect of other, more important figures are as follows (the names of the characters they identify are given in brackets): Hæreth (Hygd): lines 1929a and 1981b; Ælfhere (Wiglaf): line 2604a; Beanstan (Breca): line 524a; Folcwalda (Finn): line 1089b; Froda (Ingeld): line 2025b; Garmund (Eomor): line 1962a; Hemming (Offa): line 1944b, (Eomor): line 1961b; Hereric (Heardred): line 2206b; Hoc (Hildeburh): line 1076b; Swerting (Hygelac): line 1203a; Wæls (Sigemund): line 897a.

[6] For general background on these and othere figures, see, for example, the useful book by Gillespie, *A Catalogue of Persons Named in German Heroic Literature (700–1600).*

acters: only the names of Beowulf, Hrothgar, Grendel, and Hygelac occur as independent characters with any real frequency at all.

So, for example, Healfdene is named in his own right only once, on his first appearance in the text (at line 57a);[7] subsequently, his name is primarily used to identify his sons, particularly Hrothgar (fourteen times),[8] although once he is named as the father of Heorogar (line 469a), and also in relation to his sword (line 1020b).[9] An identical situation obtains with regard to Ecgtheow, Beowulf's father: the first two times he appears (lines 263b and 373b), it is in his own right, with his special significance signalled by alliteration; elsewhere, he is named fourteen times, always as part of a stock phrase identifying his son.[10] Likewise, Weohstan is mainly named in relation to his son, Wiglaf,[11] and even King Hrethel's name is invoked only three times in his own right (lines 374b, 2430b, and 2474b): otherwise he is named only to identify his son, Hygelac (lines 1485a, 1847b, 2358a, and 2992a), his mailcoat (*Hrædlan laf*, line 454b), and his sword (*Hreðles lafe*, line 2191b). Ecglaf is named five times in *Beowulf*, but only to identify his son, Unferth (lines 499b, 590b, 980b, 1465b, and 1808b); Ohthere's name is a similar cipher, invoked to identify his sons (lines 2380b, 2394b, and 2612b), his father (line 2928b), and his mother (line 2932b). In a striking reversal of the usual pattern, the Swedish king, Ongentheow, is named first in relation to his killer, Hygelac (line 1968a),[12] then his sons, Onela and Ohthere (lines 2387b and 2475a), before finally emerging in his last five appearances as an independent character with a role of his own (lines 2486a, 2924a, 2951a, 2961a, and 2986a). The attention paid to patronymics in the poem is indeed striking,[13] and only underlines the sinister implications of the fact that (for example) we are never told the name of Heremod's father,[14] while we learn that Grendel's father is not known at all (*no hie fæder cunnon*, line

---

7 It seems significant that of its seventeen appearances in the text, the name of Healfdene carries the main alliteration only here and in one other place (line 1064a).

8 At lines 189b, 268a, 344b, 645a, 1009b, 1040b, 1064a, 1474b, 1652b, 1699a, 1867a, 2011b, 2143b, and 2147a.

9 For the controversy surrounding the phrase *brand Healfdenes* ('sword of Healfdene') in line 1020b, which some would emend to *bearn Healfdenes* ('son of Healfdene'), see, for example, Kuhn, 'The Sword of Healfdene'; *idem*, 'Further Thoughts'; Mitchell, '*Beowulf*, line 1020b: *brand* or *bearn*?'; Watanabe, 'Final Words on *Beowulf* 1020b: *brand Healfdenes*'. One is tempted to suggest scribal eye-skip from a now-lost *bearn Healfdenes*, describing who gives Beowulf the gift (namely Hrothgar), to *brand Healfdenes*, describing what is given; certainly, two references to Healfdene (both identifying Hrothgar) occur in close proximity at lines 2143b (*maga Healfdenes*) and 2147a (*sunu Healfdenes*), and as it stands the passage from lines 1009b to 1064a contains no fewer than four references to Healfdene.

10 At lines 529b, 631b, 957b, 1383b, 1473b, 1651b, 1817b, 1999b, 2177b, 2425b, 1550b, 2367b, 2398b, and 2587b.

11 Weohstan appears in his own right at line 2613b; at lines 2602b, 2752b, 2862b, 2907b, 3076b, and 3120b he appears in phrases used to identify Wiglaf, his son.

12 We are to learn nearly a thousand lines later, in lines 2961–4a, that it was in fact one of Hygelac's men, namely Eofor, who actually slew Ongentheow, but the warrior's deed is credited here (as often) to his lord.

13 In this context, and in addition to the fathers already named, one need only think of Hæthcyn Hrethling (line 2925a), Hygelac Hrethling (line 1923a), Scyld Scefing (line 4a), Sigemund Wælsing (line 877a), and Wulf Wonreding (line 2965a).

14 On Heremod, see above, pp. 110–14.

1355b).[15] Family relationships are everything in this close-knit text,[16] which shows a keen interest both in blood-lines and (especially) in kings.[17]

Tribal names, particularly those derived from personal names, play a similarly important role in the poem: Beowulf himself is four times simply called 'the Geat' (lines 640a, 1301b, 1785a, and 1792b), and if in the first part of the poem Hrothgar is twice designated 'the aged Scylding' (*gamela Scylding*, lines 1792a and 2105b), it is surely significant that in the second part of the poem Ongentheow is likewise twice described in parallel terms as 'the aged Scylfing' (*gomela Scylfing*, lines 2487b and 2968a).[18] So too the Danes (*Dene*) are called by a multitude of allusive names, mainly for reasons of metre and alliteration:[19] not just 'bright-Danes', 'spear-Danes', and 'ring-Danes' (*Beorht-Dene*, *Gar-Dene*, and *Hring-Dene*), but also 'East Danes', 'West Danes', 'North Danes', and 'South Danes' (*East-Dene*, *West-Dene*, *Norð-Dene*, and *Suð-Dene*). Likewise, their designation as Scyldings is varied: they are associated with 'bounty', 'battle', 'victory', and 'greatness' (*Ar-Scyldingas*, *Here-Scyldingas*, *Sige-Scyldingas*, *Þeod-Scyldingas*).[20] Both the Geats (*Geatas*) and the Swedes (*Sweon*) are more simply described after the same pattern as the Danes, namely by elaborations on the basic tribal name (*Geatmæcgas*, *Guð-Geatas*, *Sæ-Geatas*, *Weder-Geatas*, *Wederas*; *Sweoðeod*), by reference to an eponymous founding king (*Hreþlingas*; *Scylfingas*), and by elaborations on the founder's eponym (*Hreðmenn*; *Guð-Scylfingas*). Of the three most important national or tribal groupings, however, it is important to stress that Beowulf's own, the Geats, remain much the most shadowy, with debate continuing as to their precise geographical location and prevailing attitudes towards them in the earlier medieval period.[21] But apart from the three main nations, we are presented in the poem with more than a dozen other family- or tribal-groupings (*Brondingas*, *Brosingas*, *Eotan*, *Finnas*, *Francan*, *Fresan*, *Gifðas*, *Heaðo-Beardnan*, *Heaþo-Ræmas*, *Helmingas*, *Hetware*, *Hugas*, *Wægmundingas*, *Wendlas*, and

---

15 As Irving, *A Reading of 'Beowulf'*, p. 16, notes: 'Since, in all epic poetry, a patronymic is at least as necessary to a hero as a sword, Grendel's title to heroic identity is wholly obscured.'

16 Considerable help in disentangling the complex and interconnected relationships between the main royal houses is offered by the genealogies on pp. xiv–xv above.

17 For a sensitive reading of the concept of kingship in *Beowulf*, see Clemoes, *Thought and Interaction*, pp. 3–67. See too Bloomfield, 'Benevolent Authoritarianism in Klaeber's *Beowulf*'; Carruthers, 'Kingship and Heroism in *Beowulf*'; Leyerle, 'Beowulf the Hero and the King'; Swanton, *Crisis and Development in Germanic Society, 700–800*; Wanner, 'Warriors, Wyrms, and Wyrd'; Waugh, 'Literacy, Royal Power, and King-Poet Relations in Old English and Old Norse Compositions'; Whitman, 'The Kingly Nature of Beowulf'.

18 It is possible that near the beginning of the poem Onela is similarly described as the 'battle-Scylfing' (*Heaðo-Scylfing*, line 63a), but the passage in question may well be corrupt. Tribal names also seem to lie behind the designations *Frescyning* (line 2503b) and *Merewioing* (line 2921a), both of which apparently refer to leaders of nations north and south, hostile to the Geats.

19 See above, pp. 69–72.

20 For *þeod-* as a compounding-element denoting 'greatness', compare within the poem *þeodcyning*, *þeodgestreon*, *þeodsceaða*, and *þeodþrea*. It might also be noted that the Danes are twice described as 'friends of Ing' (*Ingwine*, lines 1044a and 1319a), while the term 'half-Danes' (*Healf-Dene*, line 1069a) seems restricted to the family of Hoc, Hnæf, and Hildeburh.

21 See, for example, Farrell, '*Beowulf*, Swedes, and Geats'; *idem*, 'Beowulf and the Northern Heroic Age'; Greenfield, 'Geatish History: Poetic Art and Epic Quality in *Beowulf*'; Hardy; 'Some Thoughts on the Geats'; Leake, *The Geats of 'Beowulf'*; Lehmann, 'Ecgþeow the Wægmunding'; Storms, 'How did the *Dene* and the *Geatas* get into *Beowulf*?'.

Wylfingas); as with the personal names, the impression is given of a rich and textured background against which the main action of the story takes place.[22]

By contrast with its many and various personal and tribal names, *Beowulf* seems curiously unspecific with regard to place:[23] apart from Heorot, which is named no fewer than nineteen times, and always takes part in the main alliteration,[24] only eight other locations are named, none more than twice.[25] Like Heorot itself, the name of which transparently means 'hart',[26] a number of the place-names have a fictive quality and (again, like Heorot) allude to the natural world: the dead bodies of Beowulf and the dragon are laid out side by side at 'Eagles' bluff' (*Earnanæs*, line 3031b), Beowulf is buried on 'Whale's bluff' (*Hronesnæss*, lines 2805b and 3136b), and Ongentheow kills Hæthcyn at a place in Sweden variously called 'Ravens' wood' or 'Raven's holt' (*Hrefnawudu* or *Hrefnesholt*, lines 2925b and 2935a). In this context, one might well be tempted to emend the otherwise meaningless Geatish place-name *Hreosnaburh* (line 2477b), a site attacked by Ongentheow's sons, to read *Hrefnaburh* ('Ravens' stronghold'):[27] all the other place-names in the poem are national or regional.

Likewise, many of the personal names in the poem have a fictive quality, or at least one that seems particularly suited to their role. Several Old English poems make play with characters' names,[28] and *Beowulf* seems no exception.[29] Even leaving aside Unferth and Beowulf as two characters the meanings of whose names have been the source of long and sometimes bitter dispute,[30] it is hard to escape the conclusion that the *Beowulf*-poet has deliberately named (for example) an unavenged warrior 'recompense' (*Withergyld*), a headstrong queen 'power' (*Thryth*), a sensible queen 'reflection' (*Hygd*), and the two characters who so savagely slay Ongentheow 'boar' (*Eofor*) and 'wolf' (*Wulf*). That a character named 'glove' (*Hondscio*) should end up in Grendel's *glof* is in keeping

---

22 See too in this context such studies as Dederich, *Historische und Geographische Studien zum angelsächsischen Beowulfliede*; Leake, *The Geats of 'Beowulf'*.

23 For a recent account of a personal journey attempting to revisit the geography of *Beowulf*, see Overing and Osborn, *Landscape of Desire*.

24 Heorot is named in lines 78b, 166b, 403a, 432b, 475a, 497a, 593a, 766b, 991b, 1017b, 1176b, 1267b, 1279a, 1302a, 1330a, 1588a, 1671b, 1990a, and 2099a.

25 The places in question are *Earnanæs* (line 3031b), *Freslond* or *Frysland* (lines 1126b and 2357b), *Hrefnawudu* or *Hrefnesholt* (lines 2925b and 2935a), *Hreosnaburh* (line 2477b), *Hronesnæss* (lines 2805b and 3136b), *Scedeland* or *Scedenig* 19b and 1686b, *Swiorice* (lines 2383b and 2495a), and *Wedermearc* (line 298b). Obviously, I take the places given here with different names to be identical; unlike Klaeber, ed., *Beowulf*, p. 435, I do not consider *Freswæl* (line 1070a) a place-name, but a title, not unlike *Frescyning* (line 2503b).

26 Comparisons are often made with the *heorot hornum trum* ('hart strong in horns', line 1369a), pursued by hounds in a celebrated image; see, for example, Faraci, 'La caccia al cervo nel *Beowulf*'; Higley, '*Aldor on ofre*'; Tripp, 'The Exemplary Role of Hrothgar and Heorot'. For the image itself, see above, pp. 47–8.

27 On *s/f* scribal confusion in *Beowulf*, see above, pp. 43–5; for the variation *eo/e*, one might note, for example, the spellings *Heorogar* (line 61a) and *Heregar* (line 467b).

28 See in general Frank, 'Some Uses of Paronomasia in Old English Scriptural Verse'; Robinson, 'The Significance of Names in Old English Literature'; *idem*, 'Personal Names in Medieval Narrative and the Name of Unferth in *Beowulf*'.

29 Cf. Harris, 'Hands, Helms, and Heroes: the Role of Proper Names in *Beowulf*'; Weise, 'The Meaning of the Name "Hygd"'.

30 On the suggested meanings of Unferth's name, see below, p. 247; on Beowulf's, see above, p. 121.

with the same sensitivity (or lack of it),[31] and if the *Beowulf*-poet did not invent the names *Scyld* ('shield') and *Sigemund* ('victory-hand'), he certainly makes capital of their transparent meaning.[32] Other characters who have been argued to possess meaningful names include *Breca* ('breaker', 'wave'), *Heremod* ('battle-mind'), *Hygelac* ('thought-play'), and *Wealhtheow* ('foreign servant').[33] Against such a background, it seems hardly surprising to find the last of the Wægmundings called 'war-remnant' (*Wiglaf*):[34] he is but the last of a number of such 'remnants' in a poem that celebrates as it laments the end of a heroic age.[35]

The sheer number and variety of characters depicted by the *Beowulf*-poet, when compared with his comparative disinterest in the specifics of place, signals his overarching concern for individuals and their individual perspectives. So much is evident not merely from the main narrative, but from the lovingly detailed depiction of episodes which do not obviously advance the main plot. In describing the monster-fights with Grendel and his mother, the *Beowulf*-poet shows himself much interested in showing a range of perspectives, allowing the audience to see things even through monstrous eyes; likewise, his focus in many of the digressive episodes is on the minor characters, even on the victims,[36] a perspective that has sometimes been held to lend *Beowulf* its curiously melancholy, even elegiac feel.[37] In many ways, the *Beowulf*-poet reveals himself to be less concerned with the actions of his characters than with their reactions to what is being done both to them and around them.[38] Nowhere is this concern more evident than in the first two main monster-fights, and in the longest and most complex of the digressive episodes in the poem: the so-called Finn-episode.

Action and reaction: 'The Finnsburh fragment' and the Finn-episode

Much scholarly ink has been spilt on attempting to explain the relationship of *The Finnsburh fragment* to the Finn-episode in *Beowulf*,[39] and of both texts to a

---

31 See further above, pp. 122–3.
32 See further above, pp. 103–5.
33 On Wealhtheow in particular, see below, pp. 219–21.
34 Cf. Eliason, 'Beowulf, Wiglaf, and the Wægmundings'.
35 Also to be included on this list are Ecglaf, Guthlaf, Heatholaf, Hunlafing, Oslaf, and Yrmenlaf.
36 Cf. Richardson, 'Point of View and Identification in *Beowulf*'.
37 So Tolkien, '*Beowulf*: the Monsters and the Critics', p. 275.
38 Cf. Clemoes, 'Action in *Beowulf* and our Perception of It'.
39 The bibliography on the topic is vast; see in particular Albano, 'The Role of Women'; Aurner, *Interpretations of the Finnsburg Documents*; Ayres, 'The Tragedy of Hengest'; Brodeur, 'Design and Motive in the Finn Episode'; *idem*, 'The Climax of the Finn Episode'; Camargo, 'The Finn Episode'; Fry, '*Finnsburh*: a New Interpretation'; *idem*, ed., *Finnsburh: Fragment and Episode*; Girvan, 'Finnsburuh'; Gray, 'The Finn Episode in *Beowulf*'; Green, 'The Opening of the Episode of Finn in *Beowulf*'; Jorgensen, 'Hengest as an Indo-European Twin Hero'; Klaeber, 'Observations of the Finn Episode'; Lawrence, '*Beowulf* and the Tragedy of Finnsburg'; *idem*, '*Beowulf* and the Epic Tradition'; Malone, 'Hildeburg and Hengest'; *idem*, 'The Finn Episode in *Beowulf*'; Moore, 'The Relevance of the Finnsburh Episode'; North, 'Tribal Loyalties in the *Finnsburh Fragment* and Episode'; Östman and Wårvik, '*The Fight at Finnsburh*: Pragmatic Aspects of a Narrative Fragment'; Reino, 'The "Half-Danes" of Finnsburg and Heorot Hall'; Rosier, 'The *unhlitm* of Finn and Hengest'; Stanley, ' "Hengestes heap" '; Tolkien, *Finn and Hengest*; Turville-Petre, 'Hengest and Horsa'; Vickrey, 'On

catalogue-passage in *Widsith* which mentions how one 'Finn Folcwalding' ruled the Frisians, and Hnæf ruled the Hocings ([*weold* . . .] *Fin Folcwalding Fresna cynne* . . . *Hnæf Hocingum*, lines 27 and 29a),[40] and while the main structure of the general story seems agreed, there is great disagreement on the details. The conflict itself can be considered in two stages, beginning with an attack on the Danish prince, Hnæf, and his men while they are staying at Finn's stronghold, perhaps in connection with a visit to Hildeburh, Hnæf's sister and Finn's queen; it is this first attack which is the focus of the *Fragment*. The episode, by contrast, deals with the aftermath of that battle, and describes Hildeburh's grief at the outcome, the stalemate that exists between Finn and the survivors of Hnæf's warrior-band. Hnæf himself is dead, and his funeral, shared with at least one of Hildeburh's sons,[41] is described in detail. In the episode, the focus then shifts to Hengest, who has in some sense inherited Hnæf's mantle among the remnants of his warrior-band (*wealaf*, lines 1084a and 1098a);[42] although he has sworn oaths to Finn and passes an uneasy winter alongside Finn's men, nonetheless he seems clearly implicated in the revenge that follows, when Finn is killed and Hildeburh snatched back to her people.[43]

The text of the *Fragment* itself is deeply problematical, and numerous emendations have been suggested to the version printed by George Hickes in 1705, which apparently derives from a now-lost single manuscript-leaf described as originating from a manuscript of 'semi-Saxon' homilies in Lambeth Palace Library.[44] The *Fragment* clearly concerns an earlier stage of the narrative to that covered in the Finnsburh-episode in *Beowulf*, and again underlines the extent to which *Beowulf* as a whole tends to focus less on action than on reaction. The *Fragment* evidently describes the initial night-time conflict between the Danish leader Hnæf and his men, apparently attacked in their hall by troops loyal to

the *eorð*-Compounds in the Old English Finn-Stories'; *idem*, 'The Narrative Structure of Hengest's Revenge in *Beowulf*'; *idem*, '*Un[h]litme* "voluntarily" in *Beowulf* Line 1097'; Vries, 'Die Beiden Hengeste'; Ward, 'Hengest'; Williams, *The Finn Episode in Beowulf*.

40 Compare the appearances of Finn (lines 1068a, 1081a, 1096b, 1128b, 1146b, 1152b, and 1156a), Hnæf (lines 1069b and 1114b), Hoc (line 1076b), and Folcwalda (line 1089b) in *Beowulf* itself. See further above, pp. 115 and 128.

41 For the argument that more than one of Hildeburh's sons is involved, see below, pp. 181–2.

42 Cf. above, pp. 70 and 110.

43 Cf. Kahrl, 'Feuds in *Beowulf*'.

44 Hickes, *Thesaurus*, p. 192. The term 'semi-Saxon' refers to what might now be termed 'classical' Old English; Hickes used the term 'Dano-Saxon' to refer to the late and Scandinavian-influenced stage of the language immediately prior to the Norman Conquest. The widely held assumption that Hickes was the discoverer and transcriber of the *Fragment* is almost certainly wrong: as a fugitive charged with treason in the years 1691–9, he had neither the time nor the palaeographical expertise to be leafing through the manuscripts at Lambeth Palace. His close colleague and co-researcher Humfrey Wanley certainly had the palaeographical talent and acquaintance with medieval manuscripts to unearth and transcribe the *Fragment*, and in his extant letters records both his activities in Lambeth Palace Library in search of oddities, as well as his particular interest in paste-down and binding-fragments of precisely the right size to contain the *Fragment*. I am grateful to Dan Barrett for drawing all this material to my attention, and for suggesting Wanley as the likely discoverer of the text; much fuller documentation is to be found in his unpublished article '*The Finnsburh fragment* Reconsidered'. The notion that the *Fragment* is a forgery seems to me unlikely in the extreme: Hickes (and Wanley, for that matter) lacked the necessary motive and the close acquaintance with Old English heroic poetry required for such a task; no one would describe the Old English poetry composed in recent times by such scholars as J. R. R. Tolkien (who certainly had the necessary close acquaintance with Old English heroic poetry) as comparable in tone or style to the extant *Fragment*.

Finn. Finn himself is not named in the *Fragment*, although the action takes place at his stronghold (*Finnsburuh* is named in line 35a; the form **Finnesburuh* would, however, seem more likely).[45] The poem itself, although naturally incomplete, nonetheless has a vitality and an immediacy that is both powerful and attractive, no more so than in the speech usually attributed to Hnæf at the beginning of the *Fragment*,[46] as he apparently responds to a speech that evidently supplied an example of the so-called 'watchman-device' found elsewhere in heroic literature;[47] the watchman has attributed the glint of moonlight on the weaponry of the approaching troops to a variety of possible causes, which Hnæf proceeds to dismiss (lines 3–12):

> 'Ne ðis ne dagað eastan, ne her draca ne fleogeð,
> ne her ðisse healle hornas ne byrnað.
> Ac her forþ berað, fugelas singað,   5
> gylleð græghama, guðwudu hlynneð,
> scyld scefte oncwyð. Nu scyneð þes mona
> waðol under wolcnum. Nu arisað weadæda
> ðe ðisne folces nið fremman willað.
> Ac onwacnigeað nu, wigend mine,   10
> habbað eowre linda, hicgeaþ on ellen,
> winnað on orde, wesað onmode!'

> ['This is no dawning from the east, nor is a dragon flying here, nor are the gables of this hall burning. But here they are bearing forth (?), birds sing, the grey-coated [wolf] calls out, the war-wood resounds, shield speaks to shaft. Now this moon shines, wandering under the clouds, now woe-deeds arise, which will cause this people's enmity. But wake up now, my warriors, take up your linden-shields, think on courage, strive in the vanguard, be resolute.']

The use of such an evidently literary device is quite in keeping with the tone of the *Fragment* as a whole, which employs a number of standard devices, themes, and images well-attested in the extant Old English poetic corpus. So, for example, the *Fragment*, although brief, also bears witness to the so-called 'beasts of battle' theme (lines 5b–6a and 34b–35a), the notion that warriors must repay their mead to their lord (lines 39–40),[48] and the device (well-known from *Beowulf*) whereby the poet claims never to have heard a more impressive thing before (lines 37–40).[49]

The vigour and movement of this scene is finely conveyed by the bristling

---

45 One might compare the form *Finnesthorpe* in a Peterborough charter (Robertson, ed., *Anglo-Saxon Charters*, no. 40).

46 The speaker is simply identified as a 'battle-young king' (*heaþogeong cyning*, line 2b), although even this reading depends on Grundtvig's emendation of the phrase *hearogeong cyning* of Hickes' text; but several editors have considered that Hickes' *næfre* (line 1b) conceals a version of Hnæf's name, which only appears in the transmitted text at line 40a.

47 Sims-Williams, ' "Is it Fog or Smoke or Warriors Fighting?" '.

48 See further Rowland, 'OE *ealuscerwen/ meoduscerwen* and the Concept of "Paying for Mead" '.

49 For the 'I have not heard' theme (*Ne gefrægn ic* and variants), see, for example, *Exodus*, line 285b, *Beowulf*, lines 575b, 581b–582, and 1027a; see further Parks, ' "I Heard" Formulas in Old English Poetry'.

verbs: no fewer than sixteen verbs ending in *-að* or *-eð* (or equivalent) are packed into only ten lines. Moreover these verb-forms are carefully clustered, moving the focus from might be seen (*dagað . . . fleogeð . . . byrnað* [lines 3–4]) to what might be heard (*singað . . . gylleð . . . hlynneð . . . oncwyð* [lines 5–7]), and from an external consideration of the implications of those observations (*scyneð . . . arisað . . . fremman willað* [lines 7–9]) to a stirring series of commands to get ready for the fray (*onwacnigeað . . . habbað . . . hicgeaþ . . . winnað . . . wesað* [lines 10–12]); indeed, even the last four injunctions show careful patterning, alternating between exhortations to physical action and mental preparation.[50] The immediacy of all this action is underscored in this passage by overlapping repeated use of the terms 'here' (*her . . . her . . . her* [lines 3–5]), 'this' (*ðis . . . ðisse . . . þes . . . ðisne* [lines 3–9]), and 'now' (*Nu . . . Nu . . . nu* [lines 7–10]).

Similar concern with form and structure is apparent elsewhere in the *Fragment*, despite its incomplete state: the references in lines 3–7a to the sounds and sights of the approaching battle are recapitulated briefly after the initial exchange, when reference is made to the sound of slaughter and the clamour in the hall (*wælslihta gehlyn*, line 28b; *buruhðele dynede*, line 30b), as well as to the 'beasts of battle' motif and the contrast between the dark night and the light glinting off weapons that opens the *Fragment* (lines 34b–36):

> Hræfen wandrode,
> sweart and sealobrun.   Swurdleoma stod,   35
> swylce eal Finnsburuh   fyrenu wære.

[The raven wheeled, dark and dusky; there stood a sword-gleam as though all Finnsburh were aflame.]

Such parallels within the *Fragment* effectively provide a framing envelope-pattern that accounts for three-quarters of the extant text, and together demonstrate the skill of the poet. Likewise, no fewer than fifteen of the surviving forty-eight lines of the *Fragment* are in direct speech; it seems further likely that a speech follows shortly after the *Fragment* breaks off.[51] But these are not the lengthy, contemplative speeches that characterise so much of *Beowulf*: the only two complete speeches in the *Fragment* are only ten and four lines long respectively.[52] Again, pace and action seem to have been the chief concerns of the poet who produced the *Fragment*. Although we have no way of knowing how much of the text has been lost, what survives seems to indicate that in purely literary terms the loss has been great.

---

[50] Such clustering might well suggest that the otherwise opaque form *forþ berað* (line 5), which apparently does not fit into this ordered sequence, conceals a reference to further noise.

[51] The parallelism of lines 22–3 and 46–8 might suggest that speech is intended at some point after line 48. In the first case, a warrior (either Garulf or Guðere: the text is not clear) has asked (*frægn*) who is holding the door (*hwa þa duru heolde*), and is answered by Sigeferþ; in the second case, just after mention has been made of those who held the door (*ac hig ða duru heoldon*, line 42b), a wounded warrior is asked (*frægn*) by a leader (either Hnæf or Finn: the text is not clear) two questions, the first of which concerns how the warriors are bearing their wounds, and the second of which is incomplete. Presumably some answer in direct speech follows.

[52] Cf. Andersson, 'The Speeches in the *Waldere*-Fragments'.

By contrast with the forty-eight action-packed lines of the *Fragment*, the almost one hundred lines of the Finn-episode in *Beowulf* seem curiously detached and reflective.[53] Quite apart from the fact that the episode first focuses quite literally on the aftermath of the conflict described in the *Fragment*, describing in grisly detail the full horror of Hnæf's funeral-pyre (lines 1107–24) and the inner turmoil of Hengest (lines 1127b–1145), there is little in the way of genuine action in the episode except for a deliberately brief and telescoped account of the vengeance wrought for Hnæf, namely the killing of Finn and the return of his queen, Hildeburh, Hnæf's sister, back to her people, the Danes. This action-packed climax to the episode is recounted in five breathless half-lines, in which, significantly, all the verbs are expressed in the passive (lines 1151b–1153):[54]

> Ða wæs heal hroden
> feonda feorum,   swilce Fin slægen,
> cyning on corþre,   ond seo cwen numen.

> [Then was the hall adorned with the bodies of enemies, likewise Finn slain, a king among his retinue, and the queen taken.]

The use of passive forms here is surely telling: Finn and his queen have simply become pawns in a wider scheme, folk to whom things happen beyond their control. Likewise, the bulk of the episode as a whole focuses on two protagonists, namely Hildeburh and Hengest, and specifically on their reactions to the action in which they have become involved. Hildeburh in particular is at the heart of the episode, being named at the beginning (line 1071), towards the middle (line 1114), and appearing twice, now stripped even of her name, at the end (lines 1153b and 1158a).[55] The *Beowulf*-poet is at particular pains to highlight her impotence and passivity, as well as her innocence: she is portrayed

---

53 The precise extent of the Finn-episode in *Beowulf* is a matter of hot debate; Klaeber's relatively cautious estimate is that the episode extends from lines 1069–1159 (*Beowulf*, p. 170), but such an account requires the episode to begin in mid-sentence; similar difficulties exist with regard to estimating where the episode breaks off, as we shall see.

54 I preserve here the manuscript-reading *hroden* at 1151b, although it apparently violates a "rule" of Old English poetry that the fourth stressed syllable in a line does not participate in the main alliteration; most editors read *roden* ('reddened'). Yet the precise alliterative status of *h-* in *Beowulf* is uncertain, as has been pointed out by (amongst others) Taylor and Davis, 'Some Alliterative Misfits', pp. 615–20. Moreover, elsewhere in *Beowulf* (notably at 574b) the fourth stressed syllable *does* apparently participate in the main alliteration (the full line there reads *Hwæþere me gesælde þæt ic mid sweorde ofsloh*), although here too editors tend to emend the apparent anomaly away. The notion that Finn's hall is 'decorated' (rather than simply being 'reddened') with the bodies of enemies helps to connect it with Heorot, which at this point in the narrative is adorned with Grendel's torn-off arm (lines 833b–836 and 927–8). In what is surely a punning allusion to the grim decoration, the poet explicitly says that before the celebration-feast Heorot was 'decorated with arms' (*folmum gefrætwod*, line 992a). For other puns in the poem as a whole, see above, pp. 73–8.

55 It is intriguing to note that the author of the eleventh-century *Encomium Emmae Reginae* employs precisely the same structural device, deliberately highlighting Emma, Cnut's queen, at the beginning, middle, and end of his work. As the author explicitly states (*Encomium Emmae Reginae*, ed. Campbell, p. 6, lines 4–5): *Quod ita esse ipse fatebere, meque ab eius laudibus nusquam accipies deuiare, si prima mediis, atque si extima sagaci more conferas primis* ['But you will admit that this is the case, and allow that I nowhere deviate from her praises, if you wisely compare the beginning with the middle, and the end with the beginning']. See further Orchard, 'The Literary Background to the *Encomium Emmae Reginae*', p. 163.

purely as a victim. So, at the beginning of the episode, the poet concentrates on her hapless, helpless fall from grace (lines 1071–80a):[56]

> Ne huru Hildeburh   herian þorfte
> Eotena treowe;   unsynnum wearð
> beloren leofum   æt þam lindplegan,
> bearnum ond broðrum;   hie on gebyrd hruron,
> gare wunde.   Þæt wæs geomuru ides.   1075
> Nalles holinga   Hoces dohtor
> meotodsceaft bemearn,   syþðan morgen com,
> ða heo under swegle   geseon meahte
> morþorbealo maga,   þær heo ær mæste heold
> worolde wynne.   1080

[Truly Hildeburh had no reason to praise the good faith of the Jutes; guiltlessly she was deprived of her loved ones at that linden-play, sons and brothers;[57] they fell as fated, wounded by the spear: that was a sorrowful lady. Not at all without cause did the daughter of Hoc bemoan the outcome of events, once morning came, when she could see under the sky the murderous killing of kinsmen, where she had previously held the greatest joy in the world.]

The notion that the tragedy of the situation at Finnsburh derives from misplaced (or broken) 'good faith' (*treowe*, line 1072a) is one that again runs like a thread through the story, and seems a point of focus for the *Beowulf*-poet, who returns to the theme immediately after the Finn-episode, as we shall see. More important here is the utter exoneration of Hildeburh from responsibility: she suffers a terrible reversal of fortune (lines 1078–80a) 'guiltlessly' (*unsynnum*, line 1072b); and our sympathies are entirely with this 'sorrowful lady' (*geomoru ides*, line 1075b). The poet clearly echoes the last phrase in his next brief description of Hildeburh, as 'the lady grieved, sang sorrowful songs' (*ides gnornode, geomrode giddum*, lines 1117b–1118a) at the family funeral pyre. But it is the final reference to Hildeburh which really demonstrates the extent of her fall from grace: having lost a brother and at least one son, she now loses her husband in the revenge-killing of Finn, and is unceremoniously abducted (*seo cwen numen*, line 1153b). Worse, the poet's description of her restoration to Denmark makes it clear that, deprived even of her name, Hildeburh has become a mere chattel, simply listed alongside the other plunder (lines 1154–9a):

> Sceotend Scyldinga   to scypon feredon
> eal ingesteald   eorðcyninges,   1155
> swylce hie æt Finnes ham   findan meahton
> sigla, searogimma.   Hie on sælade

---

56 In fact the manuscript reads *he* ('he') at line 1079b, defended by some editors as a reference to Finn; the preceding *heo* ('she') in line 1078a surely strengthens the case for emendation. Likewise, most editors emend manuscript *hild plegan* ('war-play') to *lindplegan* at line 1073b (fol. 153r19) for reasons of alliteration; the scribal substitution of synonyms is apparently relatively frequent in *Beowulf* (see above, pp. 51 and 87–8), and in any case the element *hild-* (or *hilde-*) is found twice more on the same folio (at 153r11 and 17), making dittography a possibility.

57 On the plural forms, see below, pp. 181–2.

drihtlice wif   to Denum feredon,
læddon to leodum.

[The warriors of the Scyldings carried off to the ships all the possessions
of the great king that they could find at Finn's home, jewels and precious
gems. They carried off the noble woman on a sea-voyage to the Danes,
led her to her people.]

The deliberate parallelism of the phrasing here (*to scypon feredon . . . to Denum
feredon*, lines 1154 and 1158) surely only underlines Hildeburh's reduction in
status to a mere trophy, one to be carted home with the rest of the spoils.

What is striking about each of the references to Hildeburh is the
Beowulf-poet's deep sympathy for her plight; likewise, it is notable that in introducing the episode, the poet is careful to focus attention on the primary victims
of the first encounter, namely Hnæf and the sons of Finn. Indeed, this focus on
the victims considerably undermines and undercuts the ostensible joy of the
celebration-feast in Heorot, at which the Finn-episode apparently forms part of
the entertainment (lines 1063–70):[58]

Þær wæs sang ond sweg   samod ætgædere
fore Healfdenes   hildewisan,
gomenwudu greted,   gid oft wrecen,   1065
ðonne healgamen   Hroþgares scop
æfter medobence   mænan scolde
be Finnes eaferum,   ða hie se fær begeat,
hæleð Healfdena,   Hnæf Scyldinga,
in Freswæle   feallan scolde.   1070

[There was singing and clamouring all together, in the presence of
Healfdene's battle-leader, the joy-wood plucked, a tale often told, when
Hrothgar's poet had to mention hall-entertainment, all along the
mead-bench, about the sons of Finn, when a sudden attack overtook
them, the hero of the Half-Danes, Hnæf of the Scyldings, had to fall in
the Frisian slaughter.]

All commentators have felt these lines to form a jarring transition; but it is
particularly intriguing to note the *Beowulf*-poet's deliberate blurring of events in
Hrothgar's hall and events within the episode itself, telescoping the two
together: the description of Hrothgar himself as 'Healfdene's battle-leader'
(*Healfdenes hildewisan*, line 1064) seems echoed in the designation of Hnæf as
'the hero of the Half-Danes' (*hæleð Healfdena*, line 1069a); similarly juxtaposed is the parallel syntax describing how on the one hand Hrothgar's poet 'had
to mention' the tale (*mænan scolde*, line 1067b), and on the other Hnæf 'had to
fall' (*feallan scolde*, line 1070b); but perhaps most striking is how the description of the deaths of Hnæf and Finn's sons, killed together in hall-conflict, is
described as 'hall-entertainment' (*healgamen*, line 1066a): we are shortly to
hear the same dreadful slaughter described as 'linden-play' (*lindplegan*, line

---

[58] Along with several editors, I insert the word *be* in line 1068a, since it could easily have dropped out
through eye-skip after *scolde* in line 1067b; without it, the syntax of the passage is decidedly curious.

1073b).[59] In very much the same way, the end of the episode is signalled by some transitional lines which might plausibly refer either to celebrations marking the homecoming of Hildeburh, or to the end of the song sung in Heorot describing the Frisian slaughter, or to both (lines 1159b–62a):

> Leoð wæs asungen,
> gleomannes gyd.   Gamen eft astah,
> beorhtode bencsweg;   byrelas sealdon
> win of wunderfatum.

[Song was sung, a glee-man's lay; joy rose up again, bench-noise brightened; servants proffered wine from wondrous vessels.]

One might note in passing that the alliterating elements *gomen* and *gid* that signal the beginning of the episode (line 1065) are echoed in reverse (*gyd* and *gamen*) at the end, so forming a kind of chiastic envelope-pattern around the episode as a whole. That the scene has truly shifted back to Heorot is only made clear by a reference to Wealhtheow bustling in to serve a drink to her lord, husband, and king, Hrothgar (lines 1162b–8a):

> Þa cwom Wealhþeo forð
> gan under gyldnum beage,   þær þa godan twegen
> sæton suhtergefæderan;   þa gyt wæs hiera sib ætgædere,
> æghwylc oðrum trywe.   Swylce þær Unferþ þyle
> æt fotum sæt frean Scyldinga;   gehwylc hiora his ferhþe treowde,
> þæt he hæfde mod micel,   þeah þe he his magum nære
> arfæst æt ecga gelacum.

[Then Wealhtheow came forth, striding under a golden diadem, where the goodly pair, sat together, uncle and nephew; at that time their kinship was still intact, each true to the other. Likewise Unferð the *þyle* sat there at the foot of the lord of the Scyldings; each of them trusted his spirit, that he had great courage, even though he was not merciful to his kinsmen at the play of swords.]

That the poet marks these lines out by a change in metre suggests that they are meant to be taken together. But there is surely something disquieting (to say the least) about the picture of Wealhtheow's stately entrance coming so hard on the picture of the hapless and helpless Hildeburh's return to her home; after all, she too was once a stately queen, serving great men their liquor in a foreign hall. But it is not simply Wealhtheow's juxtaposition with Hildeburh that undercuts her; her very name (which appears to mean 'foreign servant' or somesuch) seems clearly not her own, even if it accords well with her function pouring drinks alongside the other 'servants' (*byrelas*, line 1161b) mentioned only the line before.[60] And since (as the episode shows) events proved that Hildeburh had little cause to praise the 'faith' of the Jutes (*Eotena treowe*, line 1072a), it is certainly disconcerting to see the same element of 'faith' raised here in consecutive (and parallel) lines with respect to Hrothgar and his nephew Hrothulf on the

---

[59] On the emendation *lindplegan* (for manuscript *hild plegan*) see n. 56 above.

[60] On the use of meaningful names in *Beowulf*, see above, pp. 172–3.

one hand (*æghwylc . . . trywe*, line 1165a), and Unferth (*gehwylc . . . treowde*, line 1166b) on the other; there is reason to suppose that subsequent events in Danish history proved such faith misplaced.[61] It is surely no coincidence that when Wealhtheow eventually speaks, first to Hrothgar (lines 1169–87), then to Beowulf (lines 1216–31), in both cases making what history was to prove a fruitless attempt to secure the succession for her sons, neither of those addressed actually answers.[62] Wealhtheow, like Hildeburh, is a passive onlooker in a much wider and more vicious game; and it is to such victims that the *Beowulf*-poet persistently draws our attention.

Within the episode itself, similar sympathy for the victims of heroic violence is witnessed in the gruesome account of Hnæf's funeral pyre (lines 1107–24):[63]

Ad wæs geæfned   ond icge gold
ahæfen of horde.   Here-Scyldinga
betst beadorinca   wæs on bæl gearu.
Æt þæm ade wæs   eþgesyne   1110
swatfah syrce,   swyn ealgylden,
eofer irenheard,   æþeling manig
wundum awyrded;   sume on wæle crungon.
Het ða Hildeburh   æt Hnæfes ade
hire selfre suna   sweoloðe befæstan,   1115
banfatu bærnan   ond on bæl don
earme on eaxle.   Ides gnornode,
geomrode giddum.   Guðrec astah,
wand to wolcnum   wælfyra mæst,
hlynode for hlawe;   hafelan multon,   1120
bengeato burston,   ðonne blod ætspranc,
laðbite lices.   Lig ealle forswealg,
gæsta gifrost,   þara ðe þær guð fornam
bega folces;   wæs hira blæd scacen.

[The pyre was prepared, and splendid (?) gold taken up from the hoard; the best of the battle-warriors of the warlike Scyldings was made ready on the funeral-pile. At that pyre was easily seen the blood-stained corselet, the all-golden swine, the iron-hard boar, many a noble killed by wounds; fine men had fallen in the slaughter. Then Hildeburh ordered

---

61   See further below, pp. 245–6.
62   On the careful choreography of speeches in the poem as a whole, see below, pp. 203–8.
63   Here I adopt the emendations *ad* ('pyre') for manuscript *að* ('oath') at line 1107a, *suna* ('sons') for manuscript *sunu* ('son') at line 1115a, and *guðrec* ('battle-smoke') for manuscript *guðrinc* ('battle-warrior') at line 1118b. In the first case, *ð* for *d* (and vice versa) is a relatively common scribal error in the text (see above, pp. 42–6), and the confusion is likely due to the fact that an 'oath' (*að*) has been mentioned in the immediately preceding lines 1095–1106. For the second case, see below, p. 182; on scribal confusion of *u* for *a*, see above, pp. 42–6. In the third case, mention of 'battle-smoke' (*guðrec*) seems more likely in context than to suggest that the phrase 'the battle-warrior mounted the pyre' (*guðrinc astah*) somehow stands alone, arresting as such a half-line might be: it is notable that in the description of Beowulf's own cremation, the poet comments that 'heaven swallowed the smoke' (*heofon rece swealg*, line 3155b) immediately after describing the grief of the chief female mourner (as here). On scribal transmission of *i* for *e* (and failure to expand a nasal suspension), see above, pp. 45–6; it is noteworthy that the manuscript reads 'here ric' for *hererinc* just over fifty lines later, at line 1176a. For a defence of the manuscript-readings, see (for example), Klaeber, ed., *Beowulf*, pp. 173–4; Wrenn, ed., *Beowulf*, pp. 140–1.

her own sons to be entrusted to the fire at Hnæf's pyre, their bone-vessels burn and be placed on the funeral-pile, wretched, side by side. The lady grieved and sang sorrowful songs. The battle-smoke went up, curled to the clouds, the greatest of slaughter-fires roared before the grave-mound; heads melted, wound-gashes burst; as blood spurted out, the cruel biting of the body. Flame, the greediest of spirits, swallowed all of those that battle took off of both peoples; their flowering had passed away.]

The incremental repetition *Ad . . . Æt þæm ade . . . æt Hnæfes ade* (lines 1107a, 1110a, and 1114b) focuses attention increasingly on the fact that this is no un-important funeral, but the cremation of some mighty men; the first two clauses are expressed in the passive, but it is Hildeburh herself who must actively entrust her brother and 'her own sons' (*hire selfre suna*, line 1115a) to the pyre.[64] Scholarly uncertainty over the number of Hildeburh's sons stems primarily from a desire to retain the apparently singular manuscript-form *sunu* ('son') in line 1115a; yet scribal confusion of *u* for *a* (and vice versa) is certain elsewhere in the *Beowulf*-manuscript,[65] and indeed many of those who retain the singular form here nonetheless emend the precisely parallel form in line 2013a, where Beowulf describes how he was placed by Hrothgar in a position of honour alongside the Danish king's own sons (the manuscript clearly reads *wið his sylfes sunu*).[66] But acceptance that Hildeburh loses more than one son only accords with the two previous assertions that the tale is to be one concerning Finn's sons (*Finnes eaferum*, line 1068a), and that Hildeburh was deprived of 'sons and brothers' (*bearnum ond broðrum*, line 1074a).[67] Moreover, a plural reading here makes it possible to construe 1117a as it stands, without emending manuscript *earme* ('wretched') to *eame* ('uncle');[68] the phrase is then grimly appropriate: it is as fitting for an 'arm' (*earm*) to be associated with a shoulder as it is for living warriors to fight shoulder-to-shoulder.[69] But these 'wretched' (*earme*) warriors are laid side-by-side, beyond any call to arms (of any kind).[70] Equally bitter is the poet's focus on the bloody corselet and boar-image, the latter presumably a protective image on the crest of a helmet:[71] neither has offered its promised protection to the dead warriors they once covered. The cremation itself is depicted as a kind of martial conflict, with 'war-smoke'

---

64 Cf. Feeny, 'The Funeral Pyre Theme in *Beowulf*'.

65 See above, pp. 42–6.

66 Thorpe, ed., *The Anglo-Saxon Poems of Beowulf, The Scop or Gleeman's Tale, and The Fight at Finnesburg* is alone in reading line 1115a (his line 2234) as plural, but line 2013a (his line 4030) as singular.

67 Editors often explain these plural forms away by various means: Klaeber, ed., *Beowulf*, p. 171, suggests that the former phrase means 'Finn's men', and the latter is '[g]eneric plural'. It is true that Hildeburh herself only loses one brother, but of course her sons are brothers too.

68 The emendation is Holthausen's, and is accepted by Sedgefield and Klaeber, amongst others; for an alternative explanation of the manuscript-reading (taking the form as a weak feminine adjective referring to Hildeburh), see Lester, '*Earme on eaxle* (*Beowulf* 1117a)'.

69 As witness the use of such terms as *eaxlgesteallā* ('close comrade', lines 1326a and 1714a); and note that Wiglaf sits down by the shoulder of the dying Beowulf (*frean eaxlum neah*, line 2853).

70 Stjerna, *Essays on Questions Connected with the Old English Poem of 'Beowulf'*, pp. 172–6, cites a number of examples of shoulder-to-shoulder burial from pagan Scandinavia.

71 On the boar-image as a (pagan) form of protection, see below, pp. 193 and 226.

(*guðrec*, line 1118b), 'the greatest of slaughter-fires' (*wælfyra mæst*, line 1119b), and a horrifyingly graphic description of freshly inflicted wounds (lines 1120b–1122a).[72] Finally, the depiction of the funeral-pyre is implicitly linked to the rest of the episode: the phrase 'those that battle took off there' (*þara ðe þær guð fornam*, line 1123b) harks back to a similar description of the fateful fray itself (*Wig ealle fornam*, line 1080b), while the final comment that 'their flowering had passed away' (*wæs hira blæd scacen*, line 1124b) looks ahead to the end of winter, and the beginning of Hengest's revenge (*Ða wæs winter scacen*, line 1136b).

Hengest too cuts rather a sorry figure in the context of the episode. He is named early on, in a brief passage which sets up his opposition to Finn (lines 1080b–1085a):

> Wig ealle fornam   1080
> Finnes þegnas   nemne feaum anum,
> þæt he ne mehte   on þæm meðelstede
> wig Hengeste   wiht gefeohtan,
> ne þa wealafe   wige forþringan
> þeodnes ðegne.   1085

[Battle took off all Finn's thegns except only a few, so that he could not in that meeting-place bring in any way the battle to finish against Hengest, nor dislodge by battle those survivors of woe from the chieftain's thegn.]

This passage is an excellent example of the compact style of the *Beowulf*-poet, who teases out the grim complexities of the situation through careful sound-play. The threefold repetition of the same term for 'battle' (*Wig . . . wig . . . wige*, lines 1080b, 1083a, and 1084b) not only identifies the main cause of the miserable dilemma, but is part of an orchestrated repetition of the same limited number of sounds, chiefly *f*, *w*, and *þ* that links individual lines. Finn and Hengest are likewise linked by alliteration in consecutive lines (*he . . . Hengeste*, lines 1082–3), as well as by parallel syntax: the reference to 'Finn's thegns' (*Finnes þegnas*, line 1081a) is closely followed by one to Hengest as 'the chieftain's (presumably Hnæf's) thegn' (*þeodnes ðegne*, line 1085a), in a way which only underscores the pain and problem on both sides, and the extent to which Finn and Hengest have become locked together in a deadly association.

Both sides make a truce, negotiated between Finn and Hengest, who is most likely a Jute in Hnæf's service.[73] The Finn-episode, like that of Sigemund and Heremod,[74] appears to play a double function according to the audience's perspective. From the point of view of most of the characters within the poem, the immediate rationale for the inclusion of the story of the deaths of Finn and Hnæf, would appear to be that of bolstering Danish pride and celebrating Beowulf's victory: in this case too the Danes recover from a humiliating setback

---

72 Compare the gruesome details supplied by Owen-Crocker, *Four Funerals*, pp. 51–5.
73 For a range of views on Hengest's tribal affiliations, see, for example, the summary tables provided by Aurner, *Hengest*, pp. 78–88.
74 On which, see above, pp. 105–14.

in a hall (the death of their leader, Hnæf, as opposed to Grendel's continued predations) through the killing of the perpetrator (Finn, as opposed to Grendel) through the agency of a foreign warrior (Hengest, as opposed to Beowulf). Tom Shippey has argued that at least two of the audience, namely Wealhtheow and Beowulf, see in the story a possible warning about the forthcoming wedding of Hrothgar's daughter Freawaru to Ingeld,[75] an episode with which, as Ted Irving has indicated, the story has a number of close parallels.[76] As we have seen, the *Beowulf*-poet himself offers yet another perspective to the audience of his own poem, focusing not on the characters of Finn and Hnæf, as might be expected, but on those of Hildeburh and Hengest.

The climax to the part of the episode which focuses on Hengest is told as follows (lines 1125–41):[77]

Gewiton him ða wigend   wica neosian,   1125
freondum befeallen,   Frysland geseon,
hamas ond heaburh.   Hengest ða gyt
wælfagne winter   wunode mid Finne
eal unhlitme,   eard gemunde,
þeah þe he ne meahte   on mere drifan   1130
hringedstefnan;   holm storme weol,
won wið winde,   winter yþe beleac
isgebinde,   oþðæt oþer com
gear in geardas,   swa nu gyt deð,
þa ðe syngales   sele bewitiað,   1135
wuldortorhtan weder.   Ða wæs winter scacen,
fæger foldan bearm.   Fundode wrecca,
gist of geardum;   he to gyrnwræce
swiðor þohte   þonne to sælade,
gif he torngemot   þurhteon mihte   1140
þæt he Eotena bearn   inne gemunde.

[Then the warriors, deprived of friends, went off to their dwellings, to visit Frisia, the homes and chief stronghold. Hengest still stayed with Finn a slaughter-stained winter, with ill-fated courage; he kept his homeland in mind, though he could not drive his ring-prowed ship on the sea: the ocean seethed with storms, buffeted against the wind; winter locked the waves, icebound, until another year came into the homefields, just as it still does, the seasons regularly keeping order, gloriously bright weather. The winter had passed, the lap of the earth was fair; the exile was anxious, the guest to get away; he thought more about vengeance than about a sea-voyage, if he could bring about a hostile encounter so that he might bring to mind the children of the Jutes in the land.]

---

[75] Shippey, *Old English Verse*, pp. 31–2; *idem, Beowulf*, pp. 32–3; Whitelock, *Audience*, pp. 34–8.
[76] Irving, *Reading 'Beowulf'*, pp. 169–78.
[77] In line 1130a, the word *ne* is missing in the manuscript, although it is easy to see why it could have dropped out as one of a sequence of words beginning in a similar way (*gemunde þeah þe he meahte*); the end of line 1128b and the beginning of line 1129a have evidently been run together in the manuscript, which reads *finnel unhlitme*.

The appalling weather acts as a perfect metaphor for Hengest's brooding thoughts,[78] and a solution comes in the spring when three (presumably Danish) warriors act: first the son of Hunlaf presents Hengest a sword which may well have been used to kill Jutes on Finn's side,[79] since 'its edges were well-known among the Jutes' (*þæs wæron mid Eotenum ecge cuðe*, line 1145), then Guthlaf and Oslaf utter reproach for their shameful situation (*sorge mændon, ætwiton weana dæl*, lines 1149b–50a).[80] In so doing, they appear explicitly to break the terms of the original treaty between Finn and Hengest, the details of which are given as follows (lines 1095–1106):[81]

> Đa hie getruwedon   on twa healfa   1095
> fæste frioðuwære.   Fin Hengeste
> elne unhlitme   aðum benemde
> þæt he þa wealafe   weotena dome
> arum heolde,   þæt ðær ænig mon
> wordum ne worcum   wære ne bræce,   1100
> ne þurh inwitsearo   æfre gemænden
> ðeah hie hira beaggyfan   banan folgedon
> ðeodenlease,   þa him swa geþearfod wæs;
> gyf þonne Frysna hwylc   frecnan spræce
> ðæs morþorhetes   myndgiend wære,   1105
> þonne hit sweordes ecg   syððan scolde . . .

[Then they made a pledge on two sides, a secure peace-treaty. Finn swore oaths to Hengest with ill-fated courage that he would treat the survivors honourably in the judgment of wise men, so that no man there should break the pact with words or deeds, nor ever mention it in vicious spite, even though they followed the slayer of their ring-giver, lordless, since they were so forced to do. If any of the Frisians, through dangerous talk should ever call to mind that murderous hatred, the sword's edge should later . . .]

The three Danes who bring matters to a head may well be related, if the reference in Arngrímr Jónsson's Latin abstract of the now-lost *Skjǫldunga saga* to three Scylding brothers called Gunnleifus (Old English Guthlaf), Oddleifus (Old

---

[78] The connection of the weather and the conflict is made explicit in the verbal echo between the description of the funeral pyre of young men (*wæs hira blæd scacen*, line 1124b) and the end of winter (*Đa wæs winter scacen*, line 1136b), especially since the word *blæd* carries the sense both of 'glory' and of 'vegetation'.

[79] This is to assume that Hunlafing (line 1143a) is not a sword (with a name formed like those of Nægling [line 2680b] and Hrunting [lines 1490b, 1659b, and 1807b]), but the unnamed son of a dead Dane, Hunlaf. For a range of alternative suggestions, see, for example, Klaeber, ed., *Beowulf*, pp. 175–6.

[80] Cf. Nicholson, 'Hunlafing and the Point of the Sword'.

[81] The manuscript reads *frecen* at 1104b, but the emendation is a common one; more problematic is the apparently unfinished syntax of line 1106b, so causing some editors to emend manuscript *syððan*, usually to an infinitive in *-an* (Klaeber invents a verb *sedan* ['declare', 'settle'], formed on the model of the noun *soð* ['truth': cf. *deman/dom*]. The unfinished syntax seems, however, not inappropriate in its implied threat, and, following Mitchell and Robinson, ed., *Beowulf*, I retain it here. For the phrase *elne unhlitme* of line 1097a (the manuscript reads *unflitme*), see, for example, Tolkien, *Finn and Hengest*, p. 120, n. 63; Vickrey, '*Un[h]litme* "voluntarily" in *Beowulf* Line 1097'. There seems a deliberate echo in the phrase *eal unhlitme* in line 1129a.

English Oslaf), and Hunleifus (Old English Hunlaf) is to be credited:[82] Hunlafing would then be a nephew of the other two; his father's name also appears (in the form 'Hunlapus') alongside other names from legend, including Rudolphus (Old English Hrothulf), in British Library, Cotton Vespasian D. IV.[83] The reference to a treaty existing 'on two sides' (*on twa healfa*, line 1095b), rather than 'on both sides', makes the pact very much a personal deal between Finn and Hengest, and the possible repetition of the charged phrase 'with ill-fated courage' (*elne unhlitme*, lines 1097a and 1129a) makes clear the extent of the risks each is taking.[84] To be sure, it is not the Frisians who 'mention' the shame of Hengest's party (*gemænden*, line 1101b), but Guðlaf and Oslaf (*mændon*, line 1149b); nor is it the Frisians who 'call to mind' (*myndgiend*, 1105b) the grim events, but Hengest himself (*gemunde*, lines 1129b and 1141b). Nonetheless, a 'sword's edge' certainly settles things.[85]

If both sides in the Finn-episode seem culpable, in that both sides seem to break a real or implied trust in their respective attacks, then it is equally true that innocents on both sides suffer. By placing the episode in the context of the rejoicing in Heorot after the defeat of Grendel, the poet offers a grim warning of disasters to come, for he closes his account of the feasting and celebrations at Heorot on a darker note, stressing the fact that for all their confidence, the future for the feasting Danes is far from certain (lines 1232b–1237a):

> Þær wæs symbla cyst;
> druncon win weras.   Wyrd ne cuþon,
> geosceaft grimne,   swa hit agangen wearð
> eorla manegum,   syþðan æfen cwom   1235
> ond him Hroþgar gewat   to hofe sinum,
> rice to ræste.

> [There was the best of feasts: men drank wine; they did not know fate, the grim destiny, as it came to pass, once evening came, and Hrothgar went to his home, the powerful one to bed.]

These words contain a grim echo of those that heralded Grendel's first attack: then too, the Danes went to bed after feasting in ignorance of what fate had in store (*sorge ne cuðon, wonsceaft wera*, lines 119b–20a).[86] Likewise, when we are told that after their celebratory feasting the Danes 'sank to sleep' (*Sigon þa to slæpe*, line 1251), we cannot fail to be reminded that the scene that greets Grendel on his first arrival at Heorot is similarly curiously calm: there, the warrior-band slumbers after their celebration-feast (*swefan æfter symble*, line

---

82 Benediktsson, ed., *Arngrimi Jonae Opera*, IX.336.
83 See Chambers, *Widsith*, p. 254.
84 For the textual problems associated with this phrase, see above, pp. 173 and 184.
85 Bearing in mind the aural background to *Beowulf* (on which see further above, pp. 61–9), one is tempted to assume a pun: one might easily mistake the phrase *sweordes ecg* ('sword's edge') for *sweorde secg* ('a man with a sword'), especially since in *Beowulf* swords and men are often identified, and in the *dénouement* to the episode both a specific man and a specific sword are highlighted. However the phrase is construed, the deep sense of implied threat remains.
86 See below, pp. 238–9.

119a).[87] In that case, the apparently peaceful image soon acquires grim over-tones as Grendel snatches up thirty warriors to take home and eat. A later passage, ironically discussing the ultimate fate of all men in the wake of Grendel's own demise, repeats the same image in substantially the same words (lines 1002b–1008a):[88]

> No þæt yðe byð
> to befleonne,   fremme se þe wille,
> ac gesecan sceal   sawlberendra,
> nyde genydde,   niþða bearna,   1005
> grundbuendra   gearwe stowe,
> þær his lichoma   legerbedde fæst
> swefeþ æfter symle.

[That is not an easy thing to escape, let him do it who will, but, forced by necessity, each of the children of men, earth-dwellers possessing a soul, must seek the place prepared, where, secure in the bed of death, he will sleep after the feast.]

This poignant image of mortality, stressed through repetition (*sawlberendra . . . niþða bearna / grundbuendra*, lines 1004 and 1005b–1006a) and punning (*nyde genydde*, line 1005a), portrays life as a feast that is followed by the certain sleep of death. As the Danes soon find out, falling asleep after their celebration-feast, Hildeburh and Wealhtheow are not the only grieving and anxious mothers: Grendel has a mother too, who is about to make her presence felt.[89]

Sons and mothers: fighting the kin of Cain

The central role of Grendel's mother is implicit in her role as the second of Beowulf's three main monstrous foes;[90] yet it might be argued that her struc-tural significance is greater still:[91] by focusing on a figure apparently 'wronged' by Beowulf, the poet again shows his characteristic sympathy for the victims, and allows his audience a fresh perspective on the mighty deeds they witness. The introduction of Grendel's mother comes hard on the description of the unsuspecting Danes and Geats asleep in Heorot (lines 1255b–1278):[92]

---

87 On the wider implications of this phrase in *Beowulf*, see below, pp. 239 and 254.
88 The manuscript reads *ge sacan* at line 1004a.
89 See above, pp. 84 and 148.
90 For Grendel's mother in general, see, for example, Alfano, 'The Issue of Feminine Monstrosity'; Bonjour, 'Grendel's Dam and the Composition of *Beowulf*'; Chance, 'The Structural Unity in *Beowulf*: the Problem of Grendel's Mother'; Huisman, 'The Three Tellings of Beowulf's Fight with Grendel's Mother'; Kiernan, 'Grendel's Heroic Mother'; Menzer, '*Aglæcwif* (*Beowulf* 1259a)'; Rob-inson, 'Did Grendel's Mother Sit on Beowulf?'; Stanley, 'Did Beowulf Commit *feaxfeng* against Grendel's Mother?'; Taylor, '*Beowulf* 1259a: the Inherent Nobility of Grendel's Mother'.
91 See in particular Chance, 'Structural Unity'. On the wider structure of poem, see above, pp. 91–7.
92 The manuscript reads *camp* at line 1261a and *þeod* at line 1278b. On the widespread emendation to *Cain* at line 1261a, see, for example, Pulsiano, ' "Cames cynne": Confusion or Craft?'; likewise, most editors emend *þeod* at line 1278b to *deod* or *deoð*, assuming *d/ð* confusion (on which, see above, pp. 42–6). For a (rather unconvincing) defence of the manuscript-reading, see Brown, '*Beowulf* 1278b: *sunu þeod wrecan*'.

                        Þæt gesyne wearþ,   1255
widcuþ werum,   þætte wrecend þa gyt
lifde æfter laþum,   lange þrage,
æfter guðceare   Grendles modor,
ides, aglæcwif,   yrmþe gemunde,
se þe wæteregesan   wunian scolde,   1260
cealde streamas,   siþðan Cain wearð
to ecgbanan   angan breþer,
fæderenmæge;   he þa fag gewat,
morþre gemearcod,   mandream fleon,
westen warode.   Þanon woc fela   1265
geosceaftgasta;   wæs þæra Grendel sum,
heorowearh hetelic,   se æt Heorote fand
wæccendne wer   wiges bidan.
Þær him aglæca   ætgræpe wearð;
hwæþre he gemunde   mægenes strenge,   1270
gimfæste gife   ðe him god sealde,
ond him to anwaldan   are gelyfde,
frofre ond fultum;   ðy he þone feond ofercwom,
gehnægde helle gast.   Þa he hean gewat,
dreame bedæled,   deaþwic seon,   1275
mancynnes feond,   ond his modor þa gyt,
gifre ond galgmod,   gegan wolde
sorhfulne sið,   sunu deoð wrecan.

[That became clear, widely-known to men, that an avenger still lived after the hateful one, a long time after the war-strife. Grendel's mother, an awesome assailant in woman's form, called to mind her misery, she who had to inhabit the dread waters, the cold streams, since Cain became the sword-slayer to his only brother, his paternal kinsman: for that he went forth stained [or 'guilty'], marked by murder, fleeing the joys of men, dwelt in the wilderness. From there arose many fatal spirits; Grendel was one, a hateful and fierce outcast, who found at Heorot a watchful man, waiting for battle. There the awesome assailant took hold of him, but he called to mind his mighty strength, the ample gift that God had given him, and trusted in the favour of the all-powerful, his comfort and support; thereby he laid low the hellish spirit. Then he went forth humiliated, deprived of joy, to seek a deadly abode, the enemy of mankind; and his mother still, ravenous and grimly determined, wanted to go on a sorrowful trip, to avenge her son's death.]

It is not, of course, literally true that Grendel's mother outlived her son 'for a long time' (*lange þrage*, line 1257b): even now, her days are numbered.[93] But it is striking that in the earlier passage in the poem introducing Grendel and describing Cain and his descendants (lines 102–14), precisely the same phrase is used to describe the feud of the Titans against God (line 114a); nor is that the only verbal parallel between the passages (compare *Þanon . . . onwocon*, line 111; *Þanon woc*, line 1265b). Within this passage, the poet uses both rhyme and verbal echo to connect the fates of both Cain and Grendel: Cain 'went forth

---

93 Cf. Klaeber, ed., *Beowulf*, p. 180.

stained [or 'guilty'], marked by murder, fleeing the joys of men, dwelt in the wilderness' (*he þa fag gewat / morþre gemearcod, mandream fleon, / westen warode*, lines 1263b–1265a); Grendel 'went forth humiliated, deprived of joy, to seek a deadly abode, the enemy of mankind' (*þa he hean gewat, dreame bedæled, deaþwic seon, mancynnes feond*, lines 1274b–1276a).[94] Even the word *gemearcod* ('marked', line 1264a) used of Cain, calls to mind the description of Grendel as a *mearcstapa* ('march-stepper', line 103a; cf. line 1348a).[95]

Despite being identified as female three times in quick succession as soon as she is introduced (*modor, ides, aglæcwif*, lines 1258b–1259a), the first time a pronoun is used of Grendel's mother it is grammatically masculine (line 1260a; cf. lines 1392b, 1394b; 1497b); Taylor's suggestion that Beowulf's own focus on Grendel largely leads to the confusion seems rather strained:[96] although two of these references occur in a speech by Beowulf, the other two are used by the poet. Moreover, although it is true both that on a handful of other occasions the poet follows a grammatically feminine antecedent with a masculine pronoun (*seo hand . . . se þe*, lines 1343b–1344a; *yldo . . . se þe*, lines 1886b–1887b; *sio hond . . . se ðe*, lines 2684b–2685a), and that while the *se þe* construction occurs in *Beowulf* around fifty times, a parallel *seo þe* is found only once (line 1445a), the poet's ambivalent depiction of Grendel's mother seems confirmed by the implicitly masculine designation of her as a *felasinnigne secg* (line 1379a; cf. *mihtig manscaða*, line 1339a; *gryrelicne grundhyrde*, line 2136). The confusion is compounded further when Grendel's mother is seen in action, and an explicit contrast is drawn between Grendel's approach to Heorot and that of his mother (lines 1279–95).[97]

Grendel's own nocturnal approach to Heorot is a masterful piece of suspenseful description (lines 702b–727):[98]

---

94 Similarly, the description of Grendel as 'deprived of joy' (*dreame bedæled*, line 1275a) echoes that given earlier, when he is described as 'deprived of joys' (*dreamum bedæled*, line 721a).

95 The alliterative collocation *mearc-/ mor-* is consistently applied in such contexts to Grendel and his kind (*mearcstapa . . . moras*, line 103; *morþre gemearcod*, line 1264a; *mearcstapan . . . moras*, line 1348; cf. *myrcan mor*, line 1405a). See further Sharma, 'Movement and Space as Metaphor in Old English Poetry', pp. 207–39.

96 Taylor, 'Beowulf's Second Grendel Fight'.

97 On the monsters in general, see, for example, Alfano, 'The Issue of Feminine Monstrosity'; Bonjour, 'Monsters Crouching and Critics Rampant'; Borsje, *From Chaos to Enemy*; Brynteston, '*Beowulf*, Monsters, and Manuscripts'; Butturff, 'The Monsters and the Scholar'; Carlsson, 'The Monsters of *Beowulf*'; Chadwick, 'The Monsters and Beowulf'; Chaney, 'Grendel and the *Gifstol*'; Cohen, 'The Use of Monsters and the Middle Ages'; Crépin, 'Beowulf: monstre ou modèle?'; Desmond, '*Beowulf*: the Monsters and the Tradition'; Dragland, 'Monster-Man in *Beowulf*'; Green-field, 'A Touch of the Monstrous in the Hero'; Huffines, 'OE *aglæce*: Magic and Moral Decline of Monsters and Men'; Kim, 'Monstrous and Bloody Signs'; Lapidge, '*Beowulf*, Aldhelm, the *Liber Monstrorum* and Wessex'; Lionarons, '*Beowulf*: Myth and Monsters'; Loganbill, 'Time and Monsters in *Beowulf*'; Mellinkoff, 'Cain's Monstrous Progeny in *Beowulf*: Part I'; idem, 'Cain's Monstrous Progeny in *Beowulf*: Part II'; Nicholls, 'Bede "Awe-Inspiring" not "Monstrous"'; Orchard, 'Tolkien, the Monsters, and the Critics'; idem, *Pride and Prodigies*; idem, 'The Sources and Meaning of the *Liber monstrorum*'; Parks, 'Prey Tell: How Heroes Perceive Monsters in *Beowulf*'; Tolkien, '*Beowulf*: the Monsters and the Critics'; Watanabe, 'Monsters Creep?'; Whitbread, 'The *Liber Monstrorum* and *Beowulf*'; Wiersma, 'A Linguistic Analysis of Words Referring to Monsters in *Beowulf*'. See too Gillam, 'The Use of the Term *æglæca* in *Beowulf* at Lines 813 and 2592'; Kuhn, 'Old English *aglæca* – Middle Irish *ochlach*'; Mizuno, 'Beowulf as a Terrible Stranger'.

98 The manuscript reads *syn scapa* ('sinful destroyer') at line 707a, but the emendation has been generally accepted. This passage has been discussed many times; see particularly Brodeur, *The Art of*

Com on wanre niht
scriðan sceadugenga.   Sceotend swæfon,
þa þæt hornreced   healdan scoldon,
ealle buton anum.   Þæt wæs yldum cuþ   705
þæt hie ne moste,   þa metod nolde,
se scynscaþa   under sceadu bregdan; –
ac he wæccende   wraþum on andan
bad bolgenmod   beadwa geþinges.
Ða com of more   under misthleoþum   710
Grendel gongan,   godes yrre bær;
mynte se manscaða   manna cynnes
sumne besyrwan   in sele þam hean.
Wod under wolcnum   to þæs þe he winreced,
goldsele gumena,   gearwost wisse,   715
fættum fahne.   Ne wæs þæt forma sið
þæt he Hroþgares   ham gesohte;
næfre he on aldordagum   ær ne siþðan
heardran hæle,   healðegnas fand!
Com þa to recede   rinc siðian,   720
dreamum bedæled.   Duru sona onarn,
fyrbendum fæst,   syþðan he hire folmum æthran;
onbræd þa bealohydig,   ða he gebolgen wæs,
recedes muþan.   Raþe æfter þon
on fagne flor   feond treddode,   725
eode yrremod;   him of eagum stod
ligge gelicost   leoht unfæger.

[Then there came in the dark night the shadow-walker stalking. The warriors slept, who ought to hold that gabled hall, all except one. It was known to men that the fiendish [or 'sinful'] destroyer could not drag them under shadows against the Creator's will; but he, vigilant, in malice against the foe, awaited with swollen heart the joining of battle. Then there came from the moor, under misty slopes, Grendel approaching: he bore God's anger; the wicked destroyer intended to ensnare one of mankind in that high hall. He walked under clouds until he could most clearly perceive the wine-building, the gold-hall of men, adorned with plate. That was not the first time that he had sought out Hrothgar's home; but never before nor afterwards in the days of his life did he come upon thegns in a hall with a harsher fate! Then there came travelling to that building the man deprived of joys. The door promptly sprang apart, secure with forged bands, when he touched it with his hands. The one intent on evil, since he was swollen with rage, tore open the building's mouth. Swiftly after that, the fiend stepped onto the decorated floor, advanced angry in spirit; from his eyes there stood, most like a flame, an unlovely light.]

'Beowulf', pp. 88–94; Greenfield, 'Grendel's Approach to Heorot', pp. 275–84; Irving, *A Reading of 'Beowulf'*, pp. 101–3; Lapidge, *'Beowulf* and the Psychology of Terror', pp. 383–4; O'Keeffe, *'Beowulf,* Lines 702b–836', pp. 487–8; Renoir, 'Point of View and Design for Terror', pp. 154–67; Storms, 'Grendel the Terrible', pp. 427–36; Tripp, 'A New Look at Grendel's Attack: *Beowulf* 804a–815a'.

The celebrated threefold repetition of *com* (lines 702b, 710a, and 720a), inexorably focusing in on the hall as Grendel emerges from the shadows, however, is not unique to *Beowulf*: elsewhere in the same manuscript a similar technique is used to describe the advancing army of the Jews in *Judith* (*stopon . . . stopon . . . stopon*, lines 200b, 212b, and 227a). Grendel approaches Heorot in much the same manner as the night itself had come upon the feasting warriors (lines 649–51a):

> oðþe nipende   niht ofer ealle,
> scaduhelma gesceapu   scriðan cwoman,
> wan under wolcnum.

> [Until the darkening night over all, the shape-concealing shadows came stalking, dark under the clouds.]

Unlike night itself, however, Grendel is depicted as a sentient being with plans of his own.[99] Three times in the course of the fight itself we are told of Grendel's intentions in identical terms (*mynte*, lines 712a, 731a, and 762a), and his eventual conflict with Beowulf is depicted as essentially a clash of wills (lines 750–61):[100]

> Sona þæt onfunde   fyrena hyrde   750
> þæt he ne mette   middangeardes,
> eorþan sceata,   on elran men
> mundgripe maran.   He on mode wearð
> forht on ferhðe;   no þy ær fram meahte.
> Hyge wæs him hinfus,   wolde on heolster fleon,   755
> secan deofla gedræg;   ne wæs his drohtoð þær
> swylce he on ealderdagum   ær gemette.
> Gemunde þa se modega,   mæg Higelaces,
> æfenspræce,   uplang astod
> ond him fæste wiðfeng;   fingras burston.   760
> Eoten wæs utweard;   eorl furþur stop.

> [The master of wicked deeds immediately perceived that he had not met in the world, on the face of the earth a greater hand-grip on any other

---

99   On Grendel in general, see Andrew, 'Grendel in Hell'; Baird, 'Grendel the Exile'; Bandy, 'Cain, Grendel, and the Giants of *Beowulf*'; Carens, 'Handscóh and Grendel: the Motif of the Hand in *Beowulf*'; Chambers, 'Beowulf's Fight with Grendel, and Its Scandinavian Parallels'; Chaney, 'Grendel and the *Gifstol*'; Chapman, 'Alas, Poor Grendel'; Crawford, 'Grendel's Descent from Cain'; Donahue, 'Grendel and the *Clanna Cain*'; Emerson, 'Grendel's Motive in Attacking Heorot'; Fajardo-Acosta, 'Intemperance, Fratricide, and the Elusiveness of Grendel'; Feldman, 'Grendel and Cain's Descendants'; Florey, 'Grendel, Evil, "Allegory", and Dramatic Development in *Beowulf*'; Greenfield, 'Grendel's Approach to Heorot: Syntax and Poetry'; Hanning, 'Sharing, Dividing, Depriving'; Harris, 'The Deaths of Grettir and Grendel'; Herben, 'Beowulf, Hrothgar, and Grendel'; Johansen, 'Grendel the Brave?'; Jorgensen, 'Grendel, Grettir, and Two Skaldic Stanzas'; Malmberg, 'Grendel and the Devil'; Malone, 'Grendel and Grep'; Ono, 'Grendel's Not Greeting the *gifstol* Reconsidered'; Peltola, 'Grendel's Descent from Cain Reconsidered'; Pepperdene, 'Grendel's Geis'; Puhvel, 'A Scottish Analogue to the Grendel Story'; Robinson, 'Why is Grendel's Not Greeting the Gifstol a Wræc Micel?'; Rosier, 'What Grendel Found: *heardran hæle*'; Skeat, 'On the Signification of the Monster Grendel in the Poem of *Beowulf*'; Storms, 'Grendel the Terrible'; Taylor, 'Grendel's Monstrous Arts'; Tripp, 'A New Look at Grendel's Attack'; Zachrisson, 'Grendel in *Beowulf*'.

100 For the reading *modega* for manuscript *goda*, see Bliss, *Metre of 'Beowulf'*, pp. 16–17, and Kendall, *Metrical Grammar*, p. 78. Likewise, the manuscript reads *sceatta* at line 752a (through dittography?).

man; in his heart he was frightened in spirit, none the sooner could he get away. His mind was eager to escape: he wanted to flee into the darkness, to seek the company of devils; his plight there was not such as he had met before in the days of his life. The courageous kinsman of Hygelac called to mind what was said that evening; he stood upright, and grasped him firmly; fingers burst: the giant was for heading off, the warrior came on.]

This description, in many ways the climax of the fight itself, is carefully constructed both to draw a stark contrast between the thoughts and actions of the two combatants, and to echo earlier parts of the poem. Grendel's thoughts and feelings are dealt with in a dense passage fairly stuffed with the vocabulary of mind and soul (*onfunde . . . on mode . . . on ferhðe . . . Hyge*, lines 750a, 753b, 754a and 755a), marked off in an envelope-pattern (*mette . . . gemette*, lines 751a and 757b); Beowulf's initial thoughts are linked to those of Grendel in this passage through rhyme (*onfunde . . . Gemunde*, lines 750a and 758a), but after remembering the speeches of the evening he is all action, a factor underlined with adverbial force (**uplang** *astod . . .* **fæste** *wiðfeng . . .* **furþur** *stop*, lines 759a, 760a, and 761b, emphasis added). Grendel's immediate perception that he had never in his life felt such a hand-grip confirms the earlier reports that Hrothgar says he has received concerning Beowulf's powers (lines 377–81a), and also reflects the earlier foreboding words of the poet himself about Grendel's ill-fated trip (lines 718–19):[101]

næfre he on aldordagum   ær ne siþðan
heardran hæle,   healðegnas fand!

[Never before nor afterwards in the days of his life did he come upon thegns in a hall with a harsher fate!]

Given Grendel's central role as a man-eating monster, it seems extraordinary that the *Beowulf*-poet should choose to depict him as a character with a point of view, one that is capable of evoking sympathy, at precisely this key moment in the battle, when the predator becomes prey.

Sympathy might be more naturally forthcoming for Grendel's mother, roused by grim circumstance to avenge her son. Her own approach to Heorot is rather less dramatic than her son's (lines 1279–95):[102]

Com þa to Heorote,   ðær Hringdene
geond þæt sæld swæfun.   Þa ðær sona wearð   1280
edhwyrft eorlum,   siþðan inne fealh
Grendles modor.   Wæs se gryre læssa
efne swa micle   swa bið mægþa cræft,
wiggryre wifes,   be wæpnedmen,
þonne heoru bunden,   hamere geþruen,   1285
sweord swate fah   swin ofer helme

---

101 For the translation, see Rosier, 'What Grendel Found'.
102 The manuscript reads *geþuren* at line 1285b, but several editors (including Mitchell and Robinson, ed., *Beowulf*, p. 91) assume metathesis, on which see further above, pp. 43–5.

ecgum dyhtig   andweard sċireð.
þa wæs on healle   heardecg togen
sweord ofer setlum,   sidrand manig
hafen handa fæst;   helm ne gemunde,   1290
byrnan side,   þa hine se broga angeat.
Heo wæs on ofste,   wolde ut þanon,
feore beorgan,   þa heo onfunden wæs.
Hraðe heo æþelinga   anne hæfde
fæste befangen,   þa heo to fenne gang.   1295

[Then she came to Heorot, where the Ring-Danes slept around the chamber; there was immediately a reverse for the warriors when Grendel's mother entered in. The terror was less, even as much as the power of females, the war-terror of women in contrast to armed men, when the ornamented blade, forged by the hammer, the sword stained with blood, strong in edge, cuts through the boar-image over the helmet. There was in the hall many a hard-edged sword drawn from above the benches, many a broad shield held fast in the hand; no one thought of their helmet, their broad mailcoat, when horror seized them. She was in haste, wanted out from there, to save her life, once she was discovered; quickly she seized one of the nobles, had him firmly grasped when she went to the fen.]

The speed of the description of this hit-and-run raid contrasts sharply with the leisurely account of Grendel's own foray into Heorot: Grendel's mother comes and goes in the space of seventeen lines; her son took more than 120 (lines 702b–823a). The difference in scale, aptly characterised here as the difference in 'terror' caused by the male and female creatures, is just that: the account of the attack by Grendel's mother contains many echoes of that of her son, of which it is in effect a perfect miniature. Grendel's own approach to Heorot is heralded by a threefold repetition of *com* (lines 702b, 710a, and 720a); that of his mother by a single occurrence of the same term (line 1279a). Grendel finds warriors sleeping (lines 728–30a); so does his mother (lines 1279b–1280a). When the alarm is raised about Grendel's raid, the warriors awaken, arm themselves, and prepare to fight (lines 794b–805a); Grendel's mother meets a similar reception (lines 1288–91). In the face of opposition, Grendel's instinct is to flee (lines 755–764a), as is that of his mother (lines 1292–3). Other verbal echoes heighten the parallel. So, for example, the repetition within this passage of the term 'terror' itself (*gryre*, line 1282b; *wiggryre*, line 1284a) echoes previous usages that are almost all specific to Grendel's own activities (*gryre*, lines 384a and 478a; *gryra*, line 591b; *gryreleoð*, line 786a; *færgryrum*, line 174a).[103]

Grendel's mother makes off with Æschere, Hrothgar's beloved thegn, snatched from his bed (*on ræste abreat, / blædfæstne beorn*, line 1298b–1299a; cf. *anne hæfde / fæste befangen, þa heo to fenne gang*, lines 1294b–1295) in a

---

103 Two other earlier usages seem to reflect the notion that Grendel's 'terror' can only be combated by other 'terror' (*gryrum*, line 483b; *gryregeatwum*, line 324a); a similar usage follows with respect to Grendel's mother (*gryresiðas*, line 1462a). Later references all relate to the dragon (*gryrebroga*, line 2227; *gryregieste*, line 2560a; *gryrefahne*, line 2576b; *gryrefah*, line 3041a), except for two, one of which refers to one of the creatures from the monster mere (*gryrelicne*, line 1441a), and another (albeit grammatically masculine) to Grendel's mother herself (*gryrelicne*, line 2136a).

further scaling down of her son's activities; in an earlier raid Grendel had snatched thirty men from their beds (*on ræste genam / þritig þegna*, lines 122b–123a). The poet's subsequent observation that in this raid Grendel has left the remains of fifteen of these unfortunates in Heorot, and carried off the fifteen others for later consumption (lines 1580–4a) is particularly intriguing in the light of Anderson's suggestion that the blood-spattered 'well-known hand' (*cuþe folme*, line 1303a) seized by Grendel's mother is not that of her son (as is usually thought), but that of Æschere, so promoting the feud by grim retaliation.[104] The poet's observation that 'grief was renewed' (*cearo wæs geniwod*, line 1303b) is echoed by Hrothgar's own immediate reaction that 'sorrow is renewed' (*sorh is geniwod*, line 1322b), and in any case the poet continues with a ringing condemnation of the nature of the vendetta (lines 1304b–1306a):[105]

> Ne wæs þæt gewrixle til,
> þæt hie on ba healfa   bicgan scoldon   1305
> freonda feorum.

[That was not a good exchange, that they on both sides had to pay with the lives of their friends.]

In fact, since the Geats and Danes later find Æschere's head by the monster-mere (line 1421b),[106] it is clear that Grendel's mother carried of more of her prey than just the arm, but the poet's use of the term *cuþe folme* here is but the first of a string of terms in close proximity based on words for 'arm' (*earm*), 'hand' (*hand*), or 'shoulder' (*eaxl*): Beowulf's troop are described as a *handscale* (line 1317a), Æschere as an *eaxlgestealla* (line 1325a), whose *hand* (1343b) now lies dead, Grendel's mother as a *handbana* (line 1330b); even Grendel, in a play on the two meanings of the word *earm* ('arm' and 'wretched') is described as *earmsceapen* (line 1351b).[107]

This last term occurs in the middle of Hrothgar's chilling description of the monster-mere (lines 1345–57a):

> 'Ic þæt londbuend,   leode mine,   1345
> selerædende,   secgan hyrde
> þæt hie gesawon   swylce twegen
> micle mearcstapan   moras healdan,
> ellorgæstas.   Ðæra oðer wæs,
> þæs þe hie gewislicost   gewitan meahton,   1350
> idese onlicnæs;   oðer earmsceapen
> on weres wæstmum   wræclastas træd,
> næfne he wæs mara   þonne ænig man oðer;
> þone on geardagum   Grendel nemdon
> foldbuende.   No hie fæder cunnon,   1355

---

104 Anderson, 'The *cuþe folme* in *Beowulf*'.
105 It may be worth noting that in the only other similar occurrence of the phrase in *Beowulf*, it is the 'lives of enemies' (*feonda feorum*, line 1152a) rather than of friends, which is stressed.
106 For the relevant scene, see above, pp. 82–3.
107 See further Rosier, 'The Uses of Association' and above, p. 182.

hwæþer him ænig wæs   ær acenned
dyrnra gasta.'

['I have heard the locals, my people, hall-counsellors, tell that they saw
two such mighty wanderers in the wastes inhabit the moors, alien spirits,
of whom one was, so far as they could most easily tell, the semblance of
a woman. The other wretched one whom, in past days, dwellers in the
land named Grendel, trod exile-paths in human form, except that he was
greater than any other man. They did not know of any father, whether
any such had been begotten of secret spirits.']

The reference to 'hall-counsellors' (*selerædende*, line 1346a) is potentially
loaded, since at the beginning of the poem (line 51b) it is their lack of knowledge of the ultimate destination of Scyld Scefing that is stressed.[108] A further
echo again aligns Grendel with his slayer: Hrothgar says of Grendel that 'he was
greater than any other man' (*he wæs mara þonne ænig man oðer*, line 1353),
whilst the Danish coastwarden had said of Beowulf that he had 'never seen a
greater warrior in the world' (*næfre ic maran geseah eorla ofer eorþan*, lines
247b–248a). The alignment of Grendel and his kin with 'secret spirits' (*dyrnra
gasta*, line 1357a) is surely revealing: Grendel's crime was precisely to make his
secret presence felt (*undyrne*, line 127b; *undyrne cuð*, lines 150b and 410b).[109]

There follows Hrothgar's celebrated description of the monster-mere,[110]
Beowulf's clumsy attempt to comfort the aged Dane,[111] and an account of the
arming of the hero.[112] Just before Beowulf plunges into the mere, he utters
another of his formal boasts: he will gain glory with Hrunting, or die in the
attempt (*ic mid Hruntinge / dom gewyrce oþðe mec dead nimeð*, lines
1490b–1491). Once again, however, the mask of Beowulf's perfection slips:
neither of the possibilities he outlines actually occurs.[113] Just before these
words, Beowulf had explicitly acknowledged the strength of his new relationship with Hrothgar, who had earlier made Beowulf, in effect, his son (lines
946b–949a); Beowulf's response here is equally unambiguous, an acceptance of
his new position (lines 1477–9):

'gif ic æt þearfe   þinre scolde
aldre linnan,   þæt ðu me a wære
forðgewitenum   on fæder stæle.'

['[Remember] if for your sake I had to lose my life, that you have always
been in a father's place to the one who is dead.']

Having addressed his speech to Hrothgar, Beowulf plunges into the mere, diving
down for an indeterminate time.[114] In a surely conscious echo of Grendel's own

---

108 See further below, pp. 238–9.
109 See below, p. 212.
110 On which, see above, pp. 155–8.
111 See below, pp. 215–16.
112 See above, pp. 80–2.
113 For a comparison with similarly thwarted expectations in Beowulf's other boasts before his main
     monster-fights, see below, pp. 215 and 233.
114 See, for example, Griffith, '*Beowulf* 1495: *hwil dæges = momentum temporis*?'.

thoughts in the earlier battle (*Sona þæt onfunde*, line 750a), we are told that when Beowulf could see the bottom, Grendel's mother 'immediately perceived it' (*Sona þæt onfunde*, line 1497a); likewise we learn that Grendel's mother, like Hrothgar before Grendel's first attack, like Beowulf himself before that of the dragon, had governed her domain for fifty years. Just as in Beowulf's earlier battle with Grendel, so too in the case of Grendel's mother we are told much of the perceptions of the individual participants. So, at the start of their conflict, Grendel's mother 'perceived' and 'beheld' (*onfunde . . . beheold*, lines 1497a and 1498a) her foe, whilst Beowulf 'noticed', 'saw', 'noticed', and 'perceived' his amazing surroundings (*ongeat . . . geseah . . . ongeat . . . onfand*, lines 1512b, 1516b, 1518a, and 1522b). Moreover, just as Beowulf's men had ineffectually attempted to pierce Grendel's impervious skin with their weapons (lines 794b–805a), so too do the minor inhabitants attempt to pierce Beowulf's impervious mailcoat (lines 1501–17):[115]

> Grap þa togeanes,   guðrinc gefeng
> atolan clommum.   No þy ær in gescod
> halan lice;   hring utan ymbbearh,
> þæt heo þone fyrdhom   ðurhfon ne mihte,
> locene leoðosyrcan   laþan fingrum.   1505
> Bær þa seo brimwylf,   þa heo to botme com,
> hringa þengel   to hofe sinum,
> swa he ne mihte,   no he þæs modig wæs,
> wæpna gewealdan,   ac hine wundra þæs fela
> swencte on sunde,   sædeor monig   1510
> hildetuxum   heresyrcan bræc,
> ehton aglæcan.   Ða se eorl ongeat
> þæt he in niðsele   nathwylcum wæs,
> þær him nænig wæter   wihte ne sceþede,
> ne him for hrofsele   hrinan ne mehte   1515
> færgripe flodes;   fyrleoht geseah,
> blacne leoman,   beorhte scinan.

[Then she made a grasp towards him, seized the warrior with her dread claws; yet she did not injure his unharmed body; the rings protected him without, so that she could not penetrate the battle-coat, the linked mail-shirt, with hostile fingers. When she came to the bottom the sea-wolf carried the prince of rings to her home, so that he could not, however brave he was, wield weapons, but a host of strange creatures oppressed him in the swell, many a sea-beast struck his war-shirt with their battle-tusks, pursued the awesome assailant (or 'awesome assailants pursued [him]'). Then the warrior perceived that he was in some kind of hostile hall, where no water could cause him any harm, nor could the sudden grip of the flood touch him; he saw fire-light, a gleaming beam, shining brightly.]

---

[115] The manuscript reads *brim wyl* at 1506a, *þæm* at line 1508b, and *swecte* at line 1510a; *in* does not appear in the manuscript at 1513a. All of the proposed emendations are straightforward and generally accepted by most editors.

The parallel between Grendel's attack on Heorot, and Beowulf's attack on the 'hall' (*niðsele*, line 1513a; *hrofsele*, line 1515a) of Grendel's mother, complete with the homely touch of fire-light, surely makes it most likely that he (rather than the sea-beasts) is the *aglæca* referred to in line 1512.[116] At this point, Beowulf attempts to bring Hrunting into play, striking Grendel's mother on the head, but the previously trusty weapon is simply not up to the task (lines 1522b–1528):

> Ða se gist onfand
> þæt se beadoleoma   bitan nolde,
> aldre sceþðan,   ac seo ecg geswac
> ðeodne æt þearfe;   ðolode ær fela   1525
> hondgemota,   helm oft gescær,
> fæges fyrdhrægl;   ða wæs forma sið
> deorum madme,   þæt his dom alæg.

> [Then the guest discovered that the battle-beam would not bite, harm the life, but the edge failed the prince in his need; previously it had endured many hand-to-hand encounters, often sliced a helmet, the battle-corselet of the doomed; that was the first time for the precious treasure, that its glory faltered.]

That Beowulf is described as a 'guest' (*gist*, line 1422b; cf. *selegyst*, line 1545a) in this hall, just like Grendel had been in Heorot, only underlines the parallel, whilst the fact that Beowulf is unable to penetrate the skin of Grendel's mother and 'harm life' (*aldre scepðan*, line 1524a) only echoes the impervious nature both of Grendel in Heorot, and of Beowulf's own mailcoat, which he dons explicitly so that nothing can penetrate and 'harm life' (*aldre gescepðan*, line 1447b). Moreover, the words used to describe Hrunting's failure are very close to those which had been used to extol the weapon earlier (lines 1460b–1464):

> næfre hit æt hilde ne swac   1460
> manna ængum   þara þe hit mid mundum bewand,
> se ðe gryresiðas   gegan dorste,
> folcstede fara;   næs þæt forma sið
> þæt hit ellenweorc   æfnan scolde.

> [It had never failed in battle any man who grasped it in his hand, who entered on dangerous deeds, the meeting-place of foes; that was not the first time that it had to perform a courageous deed.]

As Beowulf resorts first to hand-to-hand combat, then to the use of 'an ancient giant sword' (*ealdsweord eotenisc*, line 1558a), the actual mechanics of the combat are almost as oblique as in his battle against Grendel. First he grasps Grendel's mother by the hair (or perhaps shoulder),[117] and makes her fall towards the floor (*þæt heo on flet gebeah*, line 1540); next, couched in the same syntactic format, he trips (*þæt he on fylle wearð*, line 1544b). What happens

---

116 On the use of the term, see above, pp. 90 and 189.
117 Cf. Bammesberger, 'Further Thoughts on *Beowulf*, line 1537a: *Gefeng þa be [f]eaxe*'; Stanley, 'Did Beowulf Commit *feaxfeng* against Grendel's Mother?'.

next is unclear: it has usually been understood that Grendel's mother sits astride her foe, brandishing her knife (*Ofsæt þa þone selegyst ond hyre seax geteah*, line 1545), so spawning a whole series of comments on the supposed psycho-sexual imagery of the scene,[118] but Fred Robinson has recently suggested that the correct sense of *ofsittan* is no more than 'set upon' (rather than 'sit upon').[119] Nonetheless, from this apparently desperate situation, Beowulf evidently recovers, helped, the poet tells us, by his mail-shirt and by God (in that order, lines 1547b–1556).

Beowulf's salvation comes in the shape of a monstrous sword (lines 1557–69):[120]

> Geseah ða on searwum   sigeeadig bil,
> ealdsweord eotenisc,   ecgum þyhtig,
> wigena weorðmynd;   þæt wæs wæpna cyst,
> buton hit wæs mare   ðonne ænig mon oðer   1560
> to beadulace   ætberan meahte,
> god ond geatolic,   giganta geweorc.
> He gefeng þa fetelhilt,   freca Scyldinga
> hreoh ond heorogrim   hringmæl gebrægd,
> aldres orwena,   yrringa sloh,   1565
> þæt hire wið halse   heard grapode,
> banhringas bræc.   Bil eal ðurhwod
> fægne flæschoman;   heo on flet gecrong.
> Sweord wæs swatig,   secg weorce gefeh.

[He saw among the accoutrements a victory-blessed weapon, an ancient sword made by giants, strong in edge, a glory for warriors; it was the best of weapons, except that it was greater than any other man might carry to the play of battle, fine and splendid, the work of titans. The warrior of the Scyldings, fierce and deadly grim, drew the ring-patterned sword, without hope of his life, struck angrily, so that it caught her hard on the neck, broke the rings of bone. The sword passed right through the doomed body; she fell to the floor. The sword was bloody; the man rejoiced in his deed.]

This climactic scene is rich with meaning and allusion. The sword on the wall, one of many armaments, reminds us that the hall of Grendel's mother, like Heorot, is decked with weapons. The fact that 'it was greater than any other man might carry to the play of battle' (*hit wæs mare ðonne ænig mon oðer to beadulace ætberan meahte*, lines 1560–1) might suggest that it was Grendel's own weapon, since 'he was greater than any other man' (*he wæs mara þonne ænig mon oðer*, line 1353), except that we are told that he did not use a sword; at all events, it is a fit weapon for Beowulf too, of whom the Danish coastwarden had said in strikingly parallel terms that he had 'never seen a greater warrior in

---

118 See, for example, Chance, 'The Structural Unity in *Beowulf*', pp. 253–5.
119 Robinson, 'Did Grendel's Mother Sit on Beowulf?'; cf. Risden, 'Heroic Humor in *Beowulf*', p. 77, who argues that nonetheless 'the punning suggestion of "sat on" remains'.
120 The word *wæs* does not appear in the manuscript at line 1559b, having presumably been omitted through eye-skip to *wæpna*, but it is easily supplied on the basis of parallel formulas in line 1232b.

the world' (*næfre ic maran geseah eorla ofer eorþan*, lines 247b–248a). Certainly, if the sword is 'fine and splendid' (*god ond geatolic*, line 1562), then Beowulf himself is 'fierce and battle-grim' (*hreoh ond heorogrim*, line 1564a). Such a weapon would clearly have been beyond Unferð, although it is stressed that this sword, like Hrunting, is 'ring-patterned' (*hringmæl*, lines 1521b and 1564b). Unlike the rather leisurely account of the fight with Grendel, however, once Beowulf swings the sword, the movement is rapid, as we alternate swiftly between Beowulf's actions and those of the sword (*gefeng* . . . *gebrægd* . . . *sloh* . . . *grapode* . . . *bræc* . . . *ðurhwod*, lines 1563a–1566b) and then between the sword and Grendel's mother, and the sword and Beowulf (*Bil* . . . *heo* . . . *Sweord* . . . *secg*, lines 1567b–1569).

Immediately following the decapitation of Grendel's mother, the poet introduces a chiastic description of light flooding the hall (*Lixte se leoma, leoht inne stod*, line 1570), just as light shines after several of the monster-slayings. In the same spirit of anger that has characterised this and others of his undertakings (*gebolgen*, line 1539b; *yrringa*, line 1565b; *yrre*, line 1575a, *reþe*, line 1585a),[121] Beowulf turns to the recumbent form of Grendel, as the poet reminds us of Grendel's terrible crimes (lines 1584b–1590):

> He him þæs lean forgeald,
> reþe cempa, to ðæs þe he on ræste geseah　　　　　　1585
> guðwerigne Grendel licgan
> aldorleasne, swa him ær gescod
> hild æt Heorote. Hra wide sprong,
> syþðan he æfter deaðe drepe þrowade,
> heorosweng heardne, ond hine þa heafde becearf.　1590

> [He gave him his reward for that, the fierce champion, when he saw on the bed Grendel lying, battle-weary, lifeless, just as battle had damaged him at Heorot. The body burst open once he suffered a blow after death, a hard sword-stroke, as he cut off his head.]

The words used to describe Beowulf's revenge exactly echo those used of God's own conflict against the race of monsters (*he him ðæs lean forgeald*, line 114b).[122] Moreover, just as both Grendel and his mother had burst gloating into Heorot to attack sleeping warriors in their beds (*on ræste*, lines 122b, 747a, and 1298b), so now he is attacked in his bed; the poet's description of Grendel as 'battle-weary' (*guðwerigne*, line 1586a) momentarily sustains the illusion that he is merely asleep, a connection between sleep and death that occurs numerous times in the text.[123]

The immediate result of the beheading of Grendel is to cause consternation amongst those waiting above (lines 1591–1605a):[124]

---

121 On this repeated motif of anger, cf. Henry, '*Furor heroicus*'.
122 See further above, p. 167.
123 Cf. Beowulf's description of Grendel as *fylwerigne* (line 962b).
124 The manuscript reads *abreoten* at line 1599b and *secan* at line 1602b, but the emendations adopted here are commonplace; for the *c*/*t*-confusion implied in line 1602b, for example, see above, pp. 42 and 45.

> Sona þæt gesawon　snottre ceorlas,
> þa ðe mid Hroðgare　on holm wliton,
> þæt wæs yðgeblond　eal gemenged,
> brim blode fah.　Blondenfeaxe,
> gomele ymb godne,　ongeador spræcon　　　　　　　　1595
> þæt hig þæs æðelinges　eft ne wendon
> þæt he sigehreðig　secean come
> mærne þeoden;　þa ðæs monige gewearð
> þæt hine seo brimwylf　abroten hæfde.
> Ða com non dæges.　Næs ofgeafon　　　　　　　　　　1600
> hwate Scyldingas;　gewat him ham þonon
> goldwine gumena.　Gistas setan
> modes seoce　ond on mere staredon,
> wiston ond ne wendon　þæt hie heora winedrihten
> selfne gesawon.　　　　　　　　　　　　　　　　　　　1605

[Immediately the wise men, who gazed with Hrothgar into the water, saw that the surging waves were all disturbed, the swell stained with blood. The grey-haired old men spoke together about the good man, that they did not expect the prince, that he should come exulting in victory to seek the famous prince; many reckoned that the sea-wolf had destroyed him. Then came the ninth hour of the day, the bold Scyldings left the headland; the gold-friend of men went home from there. The strangers sat down, sick at heart, and stared into the mere; they wished but did not expect to see their lord and friend himself.]

The passage is delimited by an envelope pattern (*gesawon . . . gesawon*, lines 1591a–1605a), and concludes with a series of lines and half-lines which end in unstressed syllables in *-n*: (*ofgeafon . . . þonon . . . setan . . . staredon . . . wendon . . . winedrihten . . . gesawon*, lines 1600–5). Other verbal effects include paronomasia (*geblond . . . blondenfeaxe*, lines 1593a and 1594b) and the pointed use of formulaic epithets in inappropriate circumstances: elsewhere in the poem there are 'wise men' (*snottre ceorlas*, lines 202b and 416b; cf. *snotor ceorl*, line 908b), but nowhere else do they assess the situation so unwisely; likewise, elsewhere the Danes are called 'bold' (*hwate Scyldingas*, lines 2052b and 3005b),[125] when they are perhaps acting more heroically than their summary withdrawal here might suggest. The description of the waters of the mere mingled with blood (*yðgeblond eal gemenged, brim blode fah*, lines 1593–4a) is, in effect, an echo of the earlier sight of the mere suffused with Grendel's blood, when Beowulf and the Danes had first gone to view it before the advent of Grendel's mother (*on blode brim weallende, atol yða geswing eal gemenged, haton heolfre, heorodreore weol*, lines 847–9).[126]

Having offered us a glimpse of what is happening on the surface, the poet turns back to the hall beneath the mere (lines 1605b–17):[127]

125　On this repeated line, see pp. 90, 242, and 255.
126　Cf. Klaeber, 'A Few *Beowulf* Notes', pp. 15–16.
127　For further discussion of the motif of the melting sword, see, for example, above, p. 140.

> Þa þæt sweord ongan   1605
> æfter heaþoswate   hildegicelum,
> wigbil wanian.   Þæt wæs wundra sum,
> þæt hit eal gemealt   ise gelicost,
> ðonne forstes bend   fæder onlæteð,
> onwindeð wælrapas,   se geweald hafað   1610
> sæla ond mæla;   þæt is soð metod.
> Ne nom he in þæm wicum,   Wedergeata leod,
> maðmæhta ma,   þeh he þær monige geseah,
> buton þone hafelan   ond þa hilt somod
> since fage.   Sweord ær gemealt,   1615
> forbarn brodenmæl;   wæs þæt blod to þæs hat,
> ættren ellorgæst   se þær inne swealt.

[Then that sword, because of the combat-blood, the war-blade began to waste away in battle-icicles. It was a wonder, that it entirely melted, most like ice, when the Father releases the bonds of frost, unwinds the water-fetters, he who has control over times and seasons: that is the true Creator. The warrior of the Weather-Geats did not take from that dwelling any other precious objects, even though he saw many there, except for the head and the hilt as well, adorned with treasure. The sword had melted away, the patterned blade burned up; the blood was so hot, the venomous alien spirit, who had died inside.]

Once again, the passage is delimited by both an envelope pattern (*gemealt . . . gemealt*, lines 1608a–1615b) and end-rhyme (*gemealt . . . swealt*, lines 1615b and 1617b); other aural effects decorate the text (*wæl-/ sæl-/ mæl-*, lines 1610–11). Similarly careful patterned repetition marks out Beowulf's subsequent activities: as he dives up through the waters they are as cleansed as they had previously been disturbed (*wæron yðgebland eal gefælsod*, line 1620; cf. *þæt wæs yðgeblond eal gemenged*, line 1593), whilst the movements of Beowulf and his men towards Heorot are every bit as carefully choreographed as those of Grendel had been (*com . . . eodon . . . ferdon . . . comon . . . com*, lines 1623a, 1626a, 1632a, 1640b, and 1644a).[128]

In this way, the *Beowulf*-poet brings the episodes of Grendel and his mother to a close, ending, as it had begun, with an approach to Heorot from across the fens. Likewise, the second of the two main sequences of action that characterise the first part of the poem comes to a conclusion, leaving the characters themselves to consider the significance of the deeds that have been done. And just as the fight against Grendel arose out of boasting words, and was followed by the celebration and contemplation of the Finnsburh-episode,[129] so too the fight with Grendel's mother arose out of words and is followed by a lengthy period of speech and contemplation.[130] If the heroic deeds in *Beowulf* are presented for the ultimate consideration of the *Beowulf*-poet's own audience, including

---

128 Cf. above, pp. 78–9.
129 On which, see above, pp. 173–87.
130 On which, see above, pp. 158–62.

ourselves, the immediate reactions of the characters in the poem, voiced in speech, play a vital role in providing an extra perspective on all of the mighty deeds we witness. It is therefore to a close analysis of the many speeches in *Beowulf* that we now turn.

7

Words and Deeds

All talk and no action: the speeches in 'Beowulf'

For a poem in which action is often held to play a major role, there is an inordinate amount of talk in *Beowulf*; over 1200 lines (some 38%) of the poem are taken up with around forty separate speeches.[1] The speeches are largely confined to the major named characters;[2] Beowulf, Hrothgar, and Wiglaf together utter more than three-quarters of the lines spoken in the text. But it is also important to realise that not all of the major named characters speak (Grendel is an obvious exception, but Hygelac's own speaking-role is minimal), and indeed significant speeches are also accorded to unnamed characters, notably the coastwarden (lines 316–19, 286b–300, and 237–57), the so-called 'Last Survivor' (lines 2247–66), and, most chillingly, the anonymous messenger who foretells the doom of the Geats (lines 2900–3027). It is perhaps no surprise that Beowulf himself is by some way the most wordy character in the poem, breaking into speech on nineteen different occasions in addresses varying in length from a mere four lines (lines 316–19 and 2813–16) to an effusive 152 (lines 2000–151). The latter speech, the longest in the poem, in which Beowulf recounts his deeds in Denmark and makes a judicious prediction of the trouble in store for Ingeld and his bride,[3] follows, by contrast, the brief welcoming utterance of Hygelac that constitutes his only speech in the entire poem.[4] Hygelac's speech, for its very singularity, deserves special attention (lines 1983b–1998):[5]

> Higelac ongan
> sinne geseldan   in sele þam hean
> fægre fricgcean   hyne fyrwet bræc,   1985

---

[1] See Table IV below, pp. 206–7; for similar tables, see, for example, McConchie, 'The Use of the Verb *maþelian* in *Beowulf*', pp. 66–7; Parker, *'Beowulf' and Christianity*, pp. 187–8 (which, however, contains a number of factual errors). Significant studies of the speeches in *Beowulf* are to be found in, for example, Baker, 'Beowulf as Orator'; Bjork, 'Speech as Gift'; Levine, 'Direct Discourse in *Beowulf*: its Meaning and Function'; Shaw, 'The Speeches in *Beowulf*'; Shippey, 'Principles of Conversation'; Silber, 'Rhetoric as Prowess'. See too Andersson, 'The Speeches in the *Waldhere*-Fragments'.
[2] On which see above, pp. 169–73.
[3] See further below, pp. 242–4.
[4] On Hygelac's pivotal role in the poem as a whole, see, for example, Fast, 'Hygelac: a Centripetal Force in *Beowulf*'; Malone, 'Hygelac'; McNamara, 'Beowulf and Hygelac'.
[5] The manuscript reads *wið cuðne* at line 1991a, either through dittography or *ð/d*-confusion. See above, pp. 42–6.

hwylce Sægeata   siðas wæron:
'Hu lomp eow on lade,   leofa Biowulf,
þa ðu færinga   feorr gehogodest
sæcce secean   ofer sealt wæter,
hilde to Hiorote?   Ac ðu Hroðgare   1990
widcuðne wean   wihte gebettest,
mærum ðeodne?   Ic ðæs modceare
sorhwylmum seað,   siðe ne truwode
leofes mannes;   ic ðe lange bæd
þæt ðu þone wælgæst   wihte ne grette,   1995
lete Suðdene   sylfe geweorðan
guðe wið Grendel.   Gode ic þanc secge
þæs ðe ic ðe gesundne   geseon moste.'

[Hygelac began decorously to question his companion in that high hall;
he felt curious as to how the voyaging of the Sea-Geats had been: 'How
did it go for you on your trip, dear Beowulf, after you suddenly decided
to seek out a distant conflict over the salt-water, battle at Heorot? Did
you in any way remedy the well-known woe Hrothgar, that famous
prince? I seethed with surgings of sorrow for this heart-affliction, in no
way had confidence in the journey of a dear man. For a long time I
asked you in no way to meet this murderous spirit [or 'stranger'], but to
let the South-Danes themselves pick a fight with Grendel. I thank god
that I can see you safe.]

Effectively, the burden of Hygelac's speech is delived in the very first clipped
half-line: 'How did it go for you on your trip? (*Hu lomp eow on lade?*, line
1987a); all the rest is gloss. Quite apart from the fact that Hygelac here appears
to challenge both the poet and Beowulf himself (lines 202–4 and lines 415–18)
in asserting that he attempted to dissuade Beowulf from his trip,[6] there is an
important implication in Hygelac's claim on the one hand to have asked
Beowulf not to go 'for a long time' (*lange*, line 1994b) and his insistence that
Beowulf left 'suddenly' (*færinga*, line 1988a); indeed the description offered
here of a rash adventure overseas would seem better to fit the poet's assessment
of Hygelac's own final enterprise.[7] Likewise, even this brief speech, which
echoes in its introduction the initial questioning Beowulf faces in Denmark from
the coastwarden (compare *hine fyrwyt bræc*, line 232b, with *hyne fyrwet bræc*,
line 1985b; *meþelwordum frægn*, line 236b, with *fægre fricgcean*, line 1985a)
and Wulfgar (compare *frægn*, line 332b, with *fægre fricgcean*, line 1985a), is
carefully crafted. There seems, for example, deliberate patterning in the
pronouns: after a cursory enquiry about both Beowulf and his men (*eow*, line
1987a, is plural), the questioning focuses on Beowulf himself (*ðu . . . ðu*), and in
his self-commentary on the questions left hanging in the air, Hygelac makes it
clear that this is very much a personal matter between Beowulf and himself (*Ic
. . . ic ðe . . . ðu . . . ic . . . ic ðe*, lines 1992b–1998a). The speech ends, like many

---

6   One notes that on both occasions the poet stresses that it was 'wise men' (*snotere ceorlas*, lines 202b
     and 416b) who encouraged Beowulf to go to Denmark; is the poet here implying (as elsewhere) that
     wisdom is not necessarily a defining characteristic of Hygelac?
7   See above, pp. 98–9.

in the poem,[8] with a series of words sharing alliteration both across and within lines (*Suðdene sylfe . . . secge . . . gesundne geseon*, lines 1996–8). Such careful arrangement of words suggests that, for the *Beowulf*-poet, the speeches were an important part of his story, and that their disposition within the text itself casts light on the poet's intentions.

Table IV below provides an overview of all the speech-acts in *Beowulf*, analysed according to a number of different features such as audience, length, and setting. A number of clear patterns emerge. Most notable is the dramatic difference between Part I of the poem, describing Beowulf's youthful exploits in Denmark (lines 1–2199), and Part II, describing his battle in old age in Geatland against the dragon (lines 2200–3182).[9] Of the thirty speeches in Part I of the poem, all but five (nos. 4, 17, 20, 21, and 24) are part of decorously patterned exchanges in which two speakers talk in turn, and, uniquely in the special circumstances of Beowulf's approach to Heorot, the first speaker is granted a final word.[10] Only one of the thirty speeches is interrupted (no. 30), when Beowulf breaks off from his report to Hygelac to have gifts brought in. In Part II, by contrast, not a single one of the nine speeches is answered, and no fewer than three (nos. 32, 36, and 39) are interrupted. No more striking indication of the difference in tone between Parts I and II of the poem could be given,[11] and such a contrast throws into sharp relief the few instances where speeches in Part I go unanswered. Two of these cases (nos. 17 and 24) comprise the formal boasts made by Beowulf before his battles with Grendel and Grendel's mother respectively, to which no reply would surely be appropriate;[12] extended periods of action (with no speeches at all) follow both. A third instance of unanswered speech in Part I is the brief farewell offered by the coastwarden after he has escorted Beowulf and his men to Heorot, and is returning to his post (no. 4, lines 316–19); again, the casual nature of the speech (the joint shortest in the entire poem) scarcely warrants a reply.[13] In sharp contrast to these three examples of unanswered speech in Part I, it is surely significant that the only two speeches of Wealhtheow (nos. 20 and 21) in the poem, both articulating her concern for her sons' futures, and addressed to Hrothgar and Beowulf, should both meet with a resounding silence.[14]

In the face of such evidence of the artful disposition of speeches in the poem, one might well investigate the relationship between words and deeds in *Beowulf* by considering the patterning of the speeches themselves, concentrating on the carefully choreographed and decorous series of exchanges that take place between Beowulf's arrival in Denmark and his welcome by Hrothgar in Heorot,

---

8   On the artful use of alliteration in the poem, see above, pp. 61–9.
9   See further, for example, Klaeber, ed., *Beowulf*, p. lvi; Rauer, *Beowulf and the Dragon*, pp. 36–7.
10 See further below, pp. 208–18.
11 See further above, pp. 227–37.
12 On the function of the formal boast, see, for example, Conquergood, 'Boasting in Anglo-Saxon England: Performance and the Heroic Ethos'; Einarsson, 'Old English *Beot* and Old Icelandic *Heitstrenging*'; Nolan and Bloomfield, '*Beotword, gilpcwidas*, and the *gilphlædan* Scop of *Beowulf*'.
13 Only Beowulf's own last words (lines 2813–16) are as brief. Frank, 'Skaldic Verse and the Date of *Beowulf*', p. 132, argues that the opening words of the coastwarden's speech (which constitute a met-rically unusual half-line) provide 'a kind of pagan Norse colouring'.
14 See further below, pp. 219–22.

Table IV: Speech-acts in *Beowulf*

PART 1 (lines 1–2199)

No.	Lines	Speaker	Addressee	Extent	Setting	Episode	Introductory Verb
1	237–57	coastguard	Geats	21	Danish coast	Beowulf's arrival in Denmark	*meþelwordum frægn*
2	260–85	Beowulf	coastguard	26	Danish coast	Beowulf's arrival in Denmark	*andswarode . . . wordhord onleac*
3	287b–300	coastguard	Geats	13.5	Danish coast	Beowulf's arrival in Denmark	*maþelode*
4	316–19	coastguard	Geats	4	outside Heorot	Beowulf's arrival in Denmark	*word . . . cwæþ*
5	333–9	Wulfgar	Geats	7	outside Heorot	Beowulf's arrival at Heorot	*frægn*
6	342b–347	Beowulf	Wulfgar	5.5	outside Heorot	Beowulf's arrival at Heorot	*andswarode . . . word . . . spræc*
7	350b–355	Wulfgar	Beowulf	5.5	outside Heorot	Beowulf's arrival at Heorot	*maþelode*
8	361–70	Wulfgar	Hrothgar	10.5	inside Heorot	Beowulf announced at Heorot	*maþelode*
9	372–389a	Hrothgar	Wulfgar	17.5	inside Heorot	Beowulf announced at Heorot	*maþelode*
10	391–8	Wulfgar	Geats	8	outside Heorot	Beowulf announced at Heorot	*word . . . abead*
11	407–55	Beowulf	Hrothgar	49	inside Heorot	Beowulf welcomed at Heorot	*maþelode*
12	457–90	Hrothgar	Beowulf	34	inside Heorot	Beowulf welcomed at Heorot	*maþelode*
13	506–28	Unferth	Beowulf	23	inside Heorot	welcoming banquet at Heorot	*maþelode*
14	530–606	Beowulf	Unferth	77	inside Heorot	welcoming banquet at Heorot	*maþelode*
15	632–8	Beowulf	Danes	7	inside Heorot	welcoming banquet at Heorot	*maþelode*
16	655–61	Hrothgar	Beowulf	7	inside Heorot	welcoming banquet at Heorot	*gegrette . . . word acwæþ*
17	677–87	Beowulf	The company	11	inside Heorot	Beowulf's boast	*gespræc . . . gylpworda sum*
18	928–56	Hrothgar	Beowulf	29	outside Heorot	examining Grendel's torn-off arm	*maþelode*
19	958–79	Beowulf	Hrothgar	22	outside Heorot	examining Grendel's torn-off arm	*maþelode*
20	1169–87	Wealhtheow	Hrothgar	19	inside Heorot	celebration after Grendel's death	*spræc*
21	1216–31	Wealhtheow	Beowulf	16	inside Heorot	celebration after Grendel's death	*maþelode . . . spræc*

No.	Lines	Speaker	Addressee	Extent	Setting	Episode	Introductory Verb
22	1322–82	Hrothgar	Beowulf	61	inside Heorot	aftermath of visit by Grendel's mother	maþelode
23	1384–96	Beowulf	Hrothgar	13	inside Heorot	aftermath of visit by Grendel's mother	maþelode
24	1474–91	Beowulf	Hrothgar	18	at the mere's edge	Beowulf's boast	maþelode
25	1652–76	Beowulf	Hrothgar	25	inside Heorot	Beowulf and the monster-treasure	maþelode
26	1700–84	Hrothgar	Beowulf	85	inside Heorot	Beowulf and the monster-treasure	maþelode
27	1818–39	Beowulf	Hrothgar	22	inside Heorot	Beowulf's farewell	maþelode
28	1841–65	Hrothgar	Beowulf	25	inside Heorot	Beowulf's farewell	maþelode
29	1987–98	Hygelac	Beowulf	12	inside Hygelac's hall	Beowulf's return	ongan . . . fricgean
30	2000–151	Beowulf	Hygelac	152	inside Hygelac's hall	Beowulf's return	maþelode
[30]	2047–56	old warrior	young warrior	10	inside Ingeld's hall	old warrior's goading speech	word acwyð]
30	2155–52	Beowulf	Hygelac	8	inside Hygelac's hall	Beowulf's return	gyd . . . wræc

PART II (lines 2200–3182)

No.	Lines	Speaker	Addressee	Extent	Setting	Episode	Introductory Verb
31	2247–66	Last survivor	the earth	20	inside the barrow	lay of the last survivor	fea worda cwæþ
32	2426–509	Beowulf	Beowulf's men	84	outside the barrow	Beowulf's boast	maþelode
32	2511t–2515	Beowulf	Beowulf's men	4.5	outside the barrow	Beowulf's boast	maþelode
32	2518t–2537	Beowulf	Beowulf's men	18.5	outside the barrow	Beowulf's boast	gegrette
33	2633–60	Wiglaf	Beowulf's men	28	outside the barrow	Wiglaf joins the fray	maþelode
34	2663–8	Wiglaf	Beowulf	6	outside the barrow	Wiglaf joins the fray	fea worda cwæþ
35	2729–51	Beowulf	Wiglaf	23	outside the barrow	Beowulf's last words	maþelode
36	2794–808	Beowulf	Wiglaf?	15	outside the barrow	Beowulf's last words	*spræc
36	2813–16	Beowulf	Wiglaf	4	outside the barrow	Beowulf's last words	het
37	2864–91	Wiglaf	Beowulf's men	28	outside the barrow	Wiglaf's reproach	maþelode
38	2900–3027	messenger	Geatish people	128	inside Geats' stronghold	messenger's prophecy	sægde
39	3077–109	Wiglaf	Geatish people	33	outside the barrow	funeral preparations	maþelode

together with the equally well-managed pair of speeches that signal Beowulf's departure from Heorot, before focusing attention on a string of instances where speech fails (notably in the series of unanswered speeches that characterises Wealhtheow's utterances) or (as in the case of the dragon-fight) action intervenes.

Talking it up: Beowulf's arrival in and departure from Denmark

Almost as soon as he disembarks, Beowulf and his men encounter the Danish coastwarden, who gives the first of the many speeches in the poem. Although Beowulf reaches Denmark in line 229, he does not actually address Hrothgar, the Danish king, until almost 200 lines later (line 407).[15] In the interim, there are no fewer than ten separate speeches, carefully choreographed in an elaborate pattern which establishes the Danish court as a sophisticated and mannered milieu, where particular customs prevail. Beowulf establishes himself as fully in command of the appropriate usages, and indeed begins to demonstrate the considerable verbal dexterity that characterises his utterances in the poem.

Apart from the initial exchange with the coastwarden, all the speeches (with the exception of that of the wordy Hrothgar) in this sequence are relatively short. There is much careful repetition, particularly in the initial exchanges that both the coastwarden and Wulfgar have with the Geats. In each case, the Dane in question asks who the newcomers are (*Hwæt syndon ge searohæbbendra*, line 237; *hwanon eowre cyme syndon*, line 257b; *Hwanon ferigeað ge fætte scyldas*, line 333), states his own role (*Ic hwile wæs endesæta*, lines 240b–241a; *Ic eom Hroðgares ar ond ombiht*, lines 335b–336a), and expresses admiration for the travellers (*No her cuðlicor cuman ongunnon lindhæbbende*, lines 244–5a; *Ne geseah ic elþeodige þus manige men modiglicran*, lines 336b–7); in each case, Beowulf answers on behalf of the Geats in substantially the same terms, identifying them as Hygelac's retainers (*We synt gumcynnes Geata leode ond Higelaces heorðgeneatas*, lines 260–1; *We synt Higelaces beodgeneatas*, lines 342b–343a), specifying his own role (*wæs min fæder . . . Ecgþeow haten*, lines 262–3; *Beowulf is min nama*, line 343b), and outlining the nature of their errand to Hrothgar (*We . . . sunu Healfdenes secean cwomon . . . Habbað we to þæm mæran micel ærende*, lines 267–70; *Wille ic asecgan sunu Healfdenes, mæran þeodne, min ærende*, lines 344–5). Even the introductions to these three-part exchanges with the coastwarden and Wulfgar demonstrate clear echoes (*meþelwordum frægn . . . andswarode . . . wordhord onleac . . . maþelode* in lines 236b, 258b, 259b, and 286a is matched by *frægn . . . andswarode . . . word æfter spræc . . . maþelode* in lines 332b, 341b, 342b, and 348a).[16] Such repetition in the exchanges the Geats have with both the coastwarden and Wulfgar only highlights the poet's careful patterning; in some respects, then, Beowulf's own approach to Heorot is every bit as stylised as that of Grendel.[17]

---

15 Cf. Eliason, 'The Arrival at Heorot'.

16 On the particular overtones of *maþelode* in these lines, see, for example, McConchie, 'The Use of the Verb *maþelian* in *Beowulf*'.

17 On which see further above, pp. 78–9 and 189–9.

But in spite of their structural similarity, there are differences between the speeches the coastwarden and Wulfgar make to Beowulf and his men. In particular, the coastwarden, whose opening speech is altogether fuller and more complex than that of Wulfgar,[18] underlines the extraordinary nature of the Geats' arrival much more than Wulfgar, focusing swiftly on Beowulf himself (lines 247b–251a):[19]

> 'Næfre ic maran geseah
> eorla ofer eorþan   ðonne is eower sum,
> secg on searwum;   nis þæt seldguma,
> wæpnum geweorðad,   næfne him his wlite leoge,   250
> ænlic ansyn.'

['Never have I seen a mightier noble on earth, a warrior in armour, than is one of you; he is no hall-retainer made worthy with weapons: unless his appearance belies him, his peerless face.']

One might note that the coastwarden pitches his compliment in artful terms, through the use of interlinear alliteration (*geseah . . . sum secg . . . searwum . . . seldguma*, lines 247b and 248–9); by contrast, none of the negative terms carry the alliteration at all (*Næfre . . . nis . . . næfne*, lines 247b, 249b and 250b).[20] In his reply, Beowulf appears to claim that he has the only possible solution to the problems caused by Grendel's depredations (lines 277b–285):[21]

> 'Ic þæs Hroðgar mæg
> þurh rumne sefan   ræd gelæran,
> hu he frod ond god   feond oferswyðeþ,
> gyf him edwendan   æfre scolde   280
> bealuwa bisigu,   bot eft cuman,
> ond þa cearwylmas   colran wurðaþ;
> oððe a syþðan   earfoðþrage,
> þreanyd þolað,   þenden þær wunað
> on heahstede   husa selest.'   285

['I can offer Hrothgar advice from a magnanimous heart, how he, wise and good, can overcome the fiend, if a reverse of the tormenting afflictions should ever come, a remedy again, and those surgings of care grow cool, or else he will ever afterwards endure a time of hardship, while the best of houses remains there in the high place.']

The coastwarden replies with a gnomic utterance, again artfully decorated with interlinear alliteration,[22] that seems ambiguously phrased (lines 287b–289):[23]

---

18 Bjork, 'Speech as Gift'.
19 I accept the emendation of manuscript *næfre* to *næfne* at line 250b; the appearence of the word *næfre* at line 247b may well have confused the scribe, and in any case *n/r* confusion is well-attested elsewhere. See above, pp. 43–6, and cf. Hubert, 'The Case for Emendation of *Beowulf* 250b'; Robinson, 'Two Non Cruces in *Beowulf*', pp. 157–60.
20 Cf. Hill, 'Beowulf as Seldguma: *Beowulf*, lines 247–51'.
21 See further Baker, 'Beowulf as Orator', pp. 10–11; cf. Irving, *A Reading of 'Beowulf'*, pp. 54–5.
22 See further Orchard, 'Artful Alliteration', p. 435.
23 Cf. Greenfield, 'Of Words and Deeds: the Coastguard's Maxim Once More'; Kaske, 'The Coastwarden's Maxim in *Beowulf*'; Pepperdene, 'Beowulf and the Coast-Guard'.

'Æghwæþres sceal
scearp scyldwiga   gescad witan,
worda ond worca,   se þe wel þenceð.'

['A sharp schield-warrior, who thinks well, must know the difference
between (or 'have an understanding of') each, words and deeds.']

Either he is responding to Beowulf's suggestion that he alone can offer (presumably verbal) advice to Hrothgar by stating that it is deeds rather than words that count, or the coastwarden is affirming Beowulf's verbal dexterity as a fitting match to his (at this time supposed) martial valour. The latter possibility seems supported by the generally encouraging (not to say fawning) attitude towards Beowulf that the coastwarden exhibits throughout. Wulfgar too is unremittingly optimistic about the motives of Beowulf and his men (lines 338–9):

'Wen ic þæt ge for wlenco,   nalles for wræcsiðum,
ac for higeþrymmum   Hroðgar sohton.'

['I reckon that from pride, not from the journeys of exile, but from greatness of heart, you sought out Hrothgar.']

Hrothgar himself is similarly positive, twice attributing Beowulf's arrival to 'kindness' (*for arstafum*, lines 382a and 458a). Important here is the use of the phrase 'from pride' (*for wlenco*, line 338a), since the same phrase will occur twice more in the poem, with subtle changes of meaning. Here, it can hardly be anything other than a positive statement, varied as it is by the phrase 'from greatness of heart' (*for higeþrymmum*, line 339a), but within less then two hundred lines Unferth will use precisely the same words (*for wlence*, line 508b) to characterise pejoratively Beowulf's contest with Breca;[24] in the latter case, the term is varied with the phrase *for dolgilpe* ('for a foolish boast', line 509a).[25] The fact that two characters within the poem can apparently use the same phrase with opposite meaning, depending on how it is varied, makes it surely significant that the poet himself will later use the same phrase, without any variation at all, to describe Hygelac's final fateful trip (*for wlenco*, line 1206a).[26] Beowulf's voyage to Denmark has evidently been undertaken from loftier motives that Hygelac's raid on Frisia.

As if to emphasise this fact, Beowulf's response to Wulfgar is fittingly decorous and extremely well-measured (lines 342b–347):

'We synt Higelaces
beodgeneatas;   Beowulf is min nama.
Wille ic asecgan   sunu Healfdenes,
mærum þeodne,   min ærende,   345

---

[24] On which see further below, pp. 247–9.
[25] The element *dol-* ('foolish', 'mad', 'rash') here seems clearly pejorative: cf. the description of Grendel as a *dolsceaða* ('mad ravager', line 479a). Greater difficulties of interpretation come in line 2646a, where Wiglaf apparently describes Beowulf's 'deeds of glory' (*mærða*, line 2645b) as 'foolish deeds' or 'rash deeds' (*dollicra dæda*). For conflicting opinions, see Frisby, ' "Daring" and "Foolish" Renderings: On the Meaning of *dollic* in *Beowulf*'; Robinson, 'A Further Word on *dollicra* in *Beowulf* 2646'. On the passage in question, see below, pp. 261–2.
[26] See further below, pp. 249 and 261–2.

aldre þinum,   gif he us geunnan wile
þæt we hine swa godne   gretan moton.'

['We are Hygelac's hearth-companions: Beowulf is my name. I will tell
the son of Healfdene, the famous prince, my errand to your leader, if he
will grant us that we may greet him, good as he is.']

Once again, Beowulf identifies himself primarily through Hygelac, but here (for
the first time in the poem), also identifies himself by name. By contrast, he does
not name Hrothgar directly, but rather by a series of decorous circumlocutions
(*sunu Healfdenes / mærum þeodne . . . aldre þinum . . . hine swa godne*, lines
344b–345a, 346a and 347a) Beowulf shows that he recognises that his own
mission is a delicate one. Wulfgar's response is of exactly the same length
(five-and-a-half lines), and repeats several of the same elements back to
Beowulf, but instead begins by stressing Hrothgar's majesty (lines 350b–355):

'Ic þæs wine Deniga,   350
frean Scildinga,   frinan wille,
beaga bryttan,   swa þu bena eart,
þeoden mærne,   ymb þinne sið,
ond þe þa ondsware   ædre gecyðan
ðe me se goda   agifan þenceð.'   355

['I will ask the friend of the Danes about that, the Lord of the Scyldings,
giver of rings, since you are a petitioner, the famous prince about your
trip, and will swiftly report to you the answer which that good man
thinks to give.']

The repetition (with reversal) of some of the words from Beowulf's own speech
(*þeoden mærne*, line 353a; cf. *mærum þeodne*, line 345a; *se goda*, line 355a; cf.
swa godne, 347a), seems clearly deliberate, especially when one realises that the
phrases come at precisely the same relative points in each speech. Apart from
underlining Hrothgar's status, however, Wulfgar's speech is intended to highlight Beowulf's own role: 'since you are a petitioner' (*swa þu bena eart*, line
352b).

Wulfgar uses the same phrase when he addresses Hrothgar about the Geats:
'they are petitioners' (*hy benan synt*, line 364b). But he also in effect vouches for
the visiting Geats, naming Beowulf as the leader (but not mentioning Hygelac at
all), asking Hrothgar not to refuse them an audience, and saying of the visitors
that 'they seem worthy in their war-gear' (*hy on wiggetawum wyrðe þinceað*,
line 368). Hrothgar's response is one of immediate recognition of Beowulf's
name, his family-ties, and his prowess (lines 372–89a). The key thing, from
Hrothgar's point of view, is that Beowulf 'sought out a loyal friend' (*sohte
holdne wine*, line 376b); therefore, any supposed offer of help will come from
one repaying an old kindness. After more courtly manoeuvring, during which
Hrothgar tells Wulfgar to tell the Geats that they are 'welcome' (*wilcuman*, line
388b), he does so (*wilcuman*, line 394b), also telling them to leave their
weapons outside, Beowulf finally faces the king of Denmark.

Beowulf's opening speech to Hrothgar is highly crafted, and shows both the
poet and his hero in a fine light. The poet describes Beowulf standing arrayed in

the splendid mailcoat of a skilful smith (*on him byrne scan, searonet seowed smiþes orþancum*, lines 405b–406), but it is not until the end of Beowulf's own speech that we learn that it is the 'best of battle-dresses', and that the smith in question is none other than the legendary Weland (*beaduscruda betst . . . hrægla selest . . . Welandes geweorc*, lines 453–5a).[27] Beowulf does not merely bandy words, however, he gets right down to basics from the beginning (lines 407–10):

> 'Wæs þu, Hroðgar, hal!   Ic eom Higelaces
> mæg ond magoðegn;   hæbbe ic mærða fela
> ongunnen on geogoþe.   Me wearð Grendles þing
> on minre eþeltyrf   undyrne cuð.'   410

['Greetings, Hrothgar! I am Hygelac's kinsman and retainer; I have accomplished many bold deeds in my youth: the matter of Grendel was made plainly known to me in my home country.']

Even such a bland, even blunt, opening carries a number of resonances. As with his first speech to the coastwarden, and his first speech with Wulfgar, here for the third time Beowulf begins a speech by identifying himself primarily through his lord, Hygelac; since at the end of this speech Beowulf again nominates his lord to receive his mailshirt should he perish, the entire address can be said to be based on the so-called envelope-pattern that is so common throughout the poem.[28] Beowulf's gentle allusion to Hrothgar's difficulties as 'the matter of Grendel' (*Grendles þing*, line 409b) is likewise loaded; later in the same speech Beowulf undertakes to raise the matter formally with his foe (lines 425b–426a). Even the fact that Grendel's deeds have been made 'plainly known' to Beowulf (*wearð . . . undyrne cuð*, lines 409b–410) simply echoes the poet's own earlier assertion that tales of Grendel's wrongdoing had been made 'plainly known' to men through sorrowful songs (*wearð . . . undyrne cuð*, lines 149b–150). Beowulf goes on to establish his credentials in more detail: he has in the past, to avenge aggression against the Geats (line 423a), 'laid low the kin of giants, and in the waves slain sea-monsters by night' (*yðde eotena cyn ond on yðum slog niceras nihtes*, lines 421–2a). As a result, 'wise men' (*snotere ceorlas*, line 416b) encouraged him to offer help to the Danes. Beowulf's account squares with the poet's own earlier description of how 'wise men in no way discouraged him from that trip . . . they urged on the brave man' (*Ðone siðfæt him snotere ceorlas lythwon logon . . . hwetton higerofne*, lines 202–4), and sits uncomfortably with the later assertion of Hygelac that he tried to persuade Beowulf not to go, but to leave the Danes to their own devices (lines 1994b–1997a).[29] In any case, Beowulf, given his proven ability against 'the kin of giants' and 'sea-monsters', claims the right to fight the scourge of Heorot (lines 424b–426a):[30]

---

27 On Weland, see above, pp. 98, 115, and 169.
28 On the use of the envelope-pattern in general, see above, pp. 78–85.
29 See above, pp. 203–4.
30 Stanley, 'Two Old English Poetic Phrases Insufficiently Understood for Literary Criticism'.

'ond nu wið Grendel sceal,
wið þam aglæcan,   ana gehegan   425
ðing wið þyrse.'

['and now against Grendel, against that awesome assailant, against the
ogre, I ought alone to raise matters.']

Beowulf's threefold description of his foe is surely telling, as his insistence that
he will do the deed alone, as he later repeats (*ana*, line 431a).[31] Such self-
absorption is elsewhere typical of Beowulf's discourse and general attitude: here
he employs no fewer than twenty-eight first-person references in forty-nine
lines. In vowing to match Grendel and forsake the use of weapons, Beowulf
acknowledges the murderous (not to say all-consuming) nature of his opponent,
and exhibits a grim sense of humour about his own potential fate (lines
445b–451):

'Na þu minne þearft   445
hafalan hydan,   ac he me habban wile
dreore fahne,   gif mec dead nimeð.
Byreð blodig wæl,   byrgean þenceð,
eteð angenga   unmurnlice,
mearcað morhopu;   no ðu ymb mines ne þearft   450
lices feorme   leng sorgian.'

['You will not need to cover my head, but he will have me covered with
blood, if death takes me. He will bear off the bloody corpse, think to
savour it, the solitary wanderer will eat it without remorse, mark the
wetland-slopes; you will not need to grieve for long about how to take
care of my body.']

The whole passage is crafted after the familiar form of the envelope-pattern (*Na
þu . . . þearft*, line 445b; *no ðu . . . þearft*, line 450b), is divided into two by
echoic wordplay (*byr-/ byr-*, line 448; compare earlier in the speech *yð-/ yð-*, line
421), and hinges on a number of instances of paronomasia: *byrgean* means both
'to taste' and 'to bury';[32] *feorm* means both 'sustenance' and 'disposal (of a
corpse)';[33] *unmurnlice* means both 'without mourning' and 'ruthlessly'; the
verb *mearcað* (alliterating with both *unmurnlice* and especially *morhopu*) may
likewise carry some resonance of the fact that both Grendel and his mother are
'march-dwellers' (*mearcstapa*, line 103a; *mearcstapan*, line 1348a).[34] Thus,
Beowulf amply lives up to the Norse eddic injunction for a warrior to be glad
and cheerful right up until he dies.[35]

Hrothgar's response is likewise well in keeping with his character: he reas-

---

31 See below, pp. 261–2.
32 The same pun is found in *The Dream of the Rood*, line 101.
33 One might compare the usage in line 744b (*gefeormod*).
34 On the significance of the pun *mær-/ mearc-/ mor-*, which occurs elsewhere in the poem, see Sharma,
    'Movement and Space as Metaphor in Old English Poetry', pp. 207–39.
35 Cf. *Hávamál* 15/4–6: *Glaðr ok reifr / skyli gumna hverr / unz sinn biðr bana* (Neckel, ed., *Edda*, p.
    19).

serts his belief that Beowulf has come from the best motives,[36] gently reminds Beowulf that he settled his father's feud with money, and then spends some sixteen lines bemoaning his own problems with Grendel (lines 473–88); a final two lines rather abruptly seem simply to invite Beowulf to sit and enjoy the feast.[37] In fact, the feast in question is dominated by Beowulf's word-batttle with Unferth,[38] which, however, again needs to be seen as part of the carefully choreographed sequence of speeches preceding Beowulf's first fight. The notion that Unferth's verbal attack on Beowulf serves a formal purpose seems underlined by the delighted response of the Danes, who seem neither perturbed at the apparently harsh treatment meted out to their guest, nor offended at his unfavourable comparison of his own might and that of the Danes. Hrothgar in particular is depicted as delighted by Beowulf's unanswerable put-down of Unferth's attack (lines 607–12a):[39]

> Þa wæs on salum   sinces brytta,
> gamolfeax ond guðrof;   geoce gelyfde
> brego Beorhtdena,   gehyrde on Beowulfe
> folces hyrde   fæstrædne geþoht.   610
> Ðær wæs hæleþa hleahtor,   hlyn swynsode,
> word wæron wynsume.

> [Then the distributor of treasure filled with pleasure, grey-haired and battle-bold; the ruler of the Bright-Danes counted on help, the people's shepherd heard from Beowulf a firm resolution. There was the laughter of warriors, delight resounded, words were joyful.]

The noises of glee are echoed in the range of sound-effects in this short passage, which contains plentiful assonance (*gehyrde . . . hyrde*, lines 609b–610a; *hlyn swynsode . . . wynsume*, lines 611–12a), and which introduces the first appearance of Wealhtheow, Hrothgar's stately queen, decked in gold (*goldhroden*, line 614a).[40] After she has served the assembled company, Beowulf vows again to do or die (lines 632–41), and Wealhtheow, decked in gold (*goldhroden*, line 640b), goes to sit by her lord, who eventually leaves the hall to Beowulf, promising great rewards if he is successful.

Beowulf's final vow before the company all retire is revealing, since it demonstrates that he is not quite perfect: he vows to fight without a sword, although he asserts that he could readily slay Grendel with one (lines 679–80); such an assertion is wholly unfounded, as several of Beowulf's own retainers,

---

[36] Despite the difficulties with interpreting the manuscript-reading *fere fyhtum* at line 457a, whatever reading is adopted, the sense, varied by 'and out of kindness' (*ond for arstafum*, line 458a) is surely positive.

[37] The chief difficulty lies with line 489b (*ond onsæl meoto*), since the precise form and function of the word *meoto* in the line seems unclear. Mitchell and Robinson, ed., *Beowulf*, p. 64, propose translating lines 489–90 as follows: 'Sit now to the feast, and unbind [your] thought, the glory of victory to men, as your mind moves you'. As they put it: 'The meaning "thought" assigned here to the nonce-word *meoto* is conjectural'.

[38] On which see below, pp. 247–55.

[39] For the comparison, see below, pp. 254–5.

[40] The beginning of the description of Wealhtheow continues the assonance (*cynna gemyndig*, line 613b).

attempting to intervene in the fray, soon discover (lines 798–805a).[41] Nor is this the only time that one of Beowulf's assertions will prove untrue: before he fights Grendel's mother he says that 'I shall gain glory with Hrunting or death will take me off!' (*ic me mid Hruntinge / dom gewyrce oþðe mec deað nimeð*, lines 1490b–1491), and (in an obviously parallel construction) before he fights the dragon he says that 'I shall gain the gold by valour or battle, the perilous harm to life, will take off your lord!' (*Ic mid elne sceall / gold gegangen oðde guð nimeð / feorhbealu frecne frean eowerne*, lines 2535b–2537). In neither case does his confident prediction quite come true: against Grendel's mother, Hrunting fails him, but he still gains the victory, whereas against the dragon, he gets the gold and death gets him.

All of Beowulf's speeches, however, are marked by an authority and assurance that set him apart from the other figures in the poem. Part of this effect stems from his frequent use of gnomic or proverbial statements, which lend his utterances a sense of conviction, if not truth.[42] So, he concludes his first speech to Hrothgar with a simple gnomic statement: 'Fate always goes as it must!' (*Gæð a wyrd swa hio scel*, line 455b). The same kind of fatalistic confidence underlies his gnomic assertion in his speech to Unferth that 'fate often spares an undoomed man, if his courage endures' (*wyrd oft nereð / unfægne eorl, þonne his ellen deah*, lines 572b–573).[43] Even when attempting to comfort Hrothgar for the loss of his favourite thegn, Æschere, at the vengeful hands of Grendel's mother, Beowulf lapses into gnomic expression (lines 1384–9):

> 'Ne sorga, snotor guma; selre bið æghwæm
> þæt he his freond wrece, þonne he fela murne. 1385
> Ure æghwylc sceal ende gebidan
> worolde lifes; wyrce se þe mote
> domes ær deaþe; þæt bið drihtguman
> unlifgendum æfter selest.'

> ['Grieve not, wise man: it is better for everyone that he avenge his friend than mourn overmuch. Each of us has to endure an end to life in the world, let him who can gain glory before death: that is the best legacy for a dead noble.']

Beowulf's words of comfort are essentially restricted to the first two words of this speech (*Ne sorga*, line 1384a); what follows is a developing chain of three gnomic sentiments, couched in an envelope pattern (*selre . . . selest*), which turn the focus away from Hrothgar and his grief entirely, and pave the way for Beowulf's own action. Sandwiched between those twin pillars of heroic desire,

---

41 See above, p. 35.

42 In general, see, Burlin, 'Gnomic Indirection in *Beowulf*'; Cavill, '*Beowulf* and *Andreas*: Two Maxims'; *idem*, *Maxims in Old English Poetry*; Deskis, '*Beowulf*' and the Medieval Proverb Tradition; Jellinek and Kraus, 'Die Widersprüche im *Beowulf*'; Karkov and Farrell, 'The Gnomic Passages of *Beowulf*'.

43 On the concept of *wyrd* as it is applied in the poem in general, see, for example, Davis, '*Beowulf*' and the Demise of Germanic Legend in England, pp. 135–57; Major, 'A Christian *wyrd*: Syncretism in *Beowulf*'; North, ' "Wyrd" and "weorð" in *Beowulf*'; Phillpotts, 'Wyrd and Providence in Anglo-Saxon Thought'; Tietjen, 'God, Fate, and the Hero of *Beowulf*'.

namely vengeance and glory,[44] is a brief acceptance of the mortal lot that will be precisely echoed when the time for Beowulf's own death (and that of the dragon) draws near (lines 2341b–2344, with emphasis added; cf. 1386–7):[45]

> Sceolde liþendaga
> æþeling ærgod   *ende gebidan,*
> *worulde lifes,*   ond se wyrm somod,
> þeah ðe hordwelan   heolde lange.

[The prince, good of old, had to endure the end of his transitory days, of life's joy, and the dragon too, even though he had held the treasure long.]

No clearer indication could be given of the extent to which Beowulf himself, for all his attachment to gnomic sentiments, is himself ultimately powerless in the face of implacable fate.

The careful patterning of the first seventeen speeches in *Beowulf* seems clearly designed to point up Heorot as a courtly, cultured, mannered place.[46] Likewise, careful patterning is exhibited in the speeches exchanged by Beowulf and Hrothgar during the rest of his stay. After his defeat of Grendel, the two meet outside Heorot to marvel at Grendel's torn-off claw: Hrothgar speaks (lines 928–56) and Beowulf responds (lines 958–79); similarly, after the nocturnal visit of Grendel's mother, the pair meet again to commiserate, this time inside Heorot:[47] again, Hrothgar speaks (lines 1322–82) and Beowulf responds (lines 1384–96).[48] Beowulf's boast at the monster-mere (lines 1474–91) echoes that made in Heorot before the fight with Grendel (lines 677–87), just as the lengthy exchange when Beowulf hands over the hilt of the monstrous sword and Hrothgar ponders on it (lines 1652–76 and 1700–84) parallels their conversation gazing on Grendel's claw. Beowulf and Hrothgar speak just once more, when they have to part forever. The *Beowulf*-poet's careful disposition of the speeches is apparent.

Beowulf's final speech to Hrothgar (lines 1818–39) is likewise both generous

---

44 The secondary literature on precisely what constitutes 'heroism' in *Beowulf* is vast; see, for example, Carruthers, 'Kingship and Heroism in *Beowulf*'; Clark, 'The Hero and the Theme'; Fajardo-Acosta, *The Condemnation of Heroism in the Tragedy of Beowulf*; Farrell, 'Beowulf and the Northern Heroic Age'; Garde, '*Sapientia, ubi sunt*, and the Heroic Ideal in *Beowulf*'; Garmonsway, 'Anglo-Saxon Heroic Attitudes'; Greenfield, 'A Touch of the Monstrous in the Hero, or Beowulf Re-Marvellized'; idem, 'Beowulf and the Judgment of the Righteous'; Hanning, '*Beowulf* as Heroic History'; Hieatt, 'Beowulf's Last Words vs. Bothvar Bjarki's'; Huppé, 'The Concept of the Hero in the Early Middle Ages'; idem, *The Hero in the Earthly City*; Irving, 'Heroic Role-Models: Beowulf and Others'; Kaske, '*Sapientia et fortitudo* as the Controlling Theme in *Beowulf*'; Kindrick, 'Germanic *Sapientia* and the Heroic Ethos of *Beowulf*'; Leyerle, 'Beowulf the Hero and the King'; McNamee, 'Beowulf, a Christian Hero'; Morey, 'Beowulf's Androgynous Heroism'; O'Brien O'Keeffe, 'Heroic Values and Christian Ethics'; Puhvel, 'The Concept of Heroism in the Anglo-Saxon Epic'; Risden, 'Heroic Humor in *Beowulf*'; Smithers, 'Destiny and the Heroic Warrior in *Beowulf*'.

45 The manuscript is defective at line 2341b; for the reading *liþendaga*, see Mitchell and Robinson, ed., *Beowulf*, p. 131.

46 Cf. Stanley, 'Courtliness and Courtesy in *Beowulf* and Elsewhere in English Medieval Literature'.

47 It is striking how many of the speeches in Part I of the poem (lines 1–2199) take place inside (eighteen out of thirty), and how few in Part II (two out of nine); such a difference is symptomatic of the great differences in tone between the two parts of the poem.

48 It is worth noting that these are the only exchanges in the poem between the two when Hrothgar speaks first. See Table IV above, pp. 206–7.

and judicious: he mentions his own willingness to sail back to Denmark to give Hrothgar help in the future, should he need it, and suggests that Hrethric, Hrothgar's son, will find a warm welcome amongst the Geats, should he pay a visit. It seems odd that Beowulf should single out just one of Hrothgar's sons in this way, and it may be that there is some connection between Hrethric and the shadowy figure called Røricus, who, Saxo Grammaticus declares, was killed by Rolvo (Old English Hrothulf).[49] Beowulf may unwittingly be drawing the attention of the audience to the forthcoming usurpation of the Danish throne by Hrothulf. Certainly it is striking that, in a more explicit case later in the poem when the Swedish king, Onela, quarrels with his brother's two sons, they do flee to the land of the Geats, albeit with grim consequences. Moreover, the faith that Beowulf puts in the support of Hygelac for helping the Danes in future seems misplaced in the light of Hygelac's own later statement that, in the case of Grendel's depredations, he had wanted Beowulf simply to let the Danes deal with their own problems (lines 1994b–1997a):

> 'Ic ðe lange bæd
> þæt ðu þone wælgæst wihte ne grette, 1995
> lete Suðdene sylfe geweorðan
> guðe wið Grendel.'

['For a long time I asked you not to confront in any way that murderous spirit, to let the South-Danes themselves wage war against Grendel.']

In the light of what subsequently transpires on one of Hygelac's own foreign adventures, not to mention the disasters that face almost all the characters bar Beowulf who venture abroad, the gnomic statement with which Beowulf concludes his final speech to Hrothgar seems somewhat loaded (lines 1838b–1839):

> 'feorcyþðe beoð
> selran gesohte þæm þe him selfa deah.'

['distant lands are better sought by one who is himself of worth.']

Hrothgar's own final words (lines 1841–65) again reveal his preoccupation with death and dying: he focuses on the possible end of Hygelac with an abbreviated litany of catastrophes ('spear . . . sickness . . . sword': *gar . . . adl . . . iren*, lines 1846b and 1848a) which nonetheless echoes the grim warnings to Beowulf that he had uttered the night before (lines 1761b–1768):[50]

> Nu is þines mægnes blæd
> ane hwile. Eft sona bið
> þæt þec adl oððe ecg eafoþes getwæfeð,
> oððe fyres feng, oððe flodes wylm,
> oððe gripe meces, oððe gares fliht, 1765
> oððe atol yldo; oððe eagena bearhtm

---

[49] Cf. Chambers, *Beowulf: an Introduction*, pp. 26–7.
[50] For more on this passage, see above, pp. 160–1.

forsiteð ond forsworceð;   semninga bið
þæt ðec, dryhtguma,   dead oferswyðeð.

[Now the glory of your might lasts for a brief while; but suddenly it will happen that sickness or the sword will split you from your power, or the clutch of fire, or the surge of water, or a blade's grip, or a spear's flight, or dread old age, or the brightness of your eyes will fail and grow dim; at last it will happen that death will overcome you, brave warrior.]

Hrothgar's melancholy thoughts are heightened further by the fact of Beowulf's own imminent departure, and the aged king's esteem for the departing warrior could not be clearer; not only does he openly declare him a paragon in thought, word, and deed (*Þu eart mægenes strang ond on mode frod, wis wordcwida*, lines 1844–5a),[51] but he is greatly affected by Beowulf's departure, in a touchingly depicted scene (lines 1870–80a):[52]

Gecyste þa   cyning æþelum god,   1870
þeoden Scyldinga,   ðegn betstan
ond be healse genam;   hruron him tearas,
blondenfeaxum.   Him wæs bega wen,
ealdum infrodum,   oþres swiðor,
þæt hie seoððan no   geseon moston,   1875
modige on meþle.   Wæs him se man to þon leof
þæt he þone breostwylm   forberan ne mehte,
ac him on hreþre   hygebendum fæst
æfter deorum men   dyrne langað
beorn wið blode.   1880

[Then the king noble in descent, the ruler of the Scyldings, kissed the best of warriors, and embraced his neck; tears fell from the grey-haired man. Old, experienced, he thought of two outcomes, one more likely, that they would never see each other again, bold men in council. The man was too dear to him than that he could hold back his surging emotions, but in his heart, secure in thought, a hidden longing for the beloved man burned in his blood.]

This moving image brings to a close Beowulf's adventures in Denmark, and the sad and brooding tone established here looks ahead to the dominant mood that hangs over most of the second part of the poem. Before, during, and after the dragon-fight that forms the climax to events in Geatland, however, there is an unmistakable sense that the decorous patterning of speeches and actions that is the hallmark of activity in and around Heorot breaks down completely. Indeed, such is the care with which the *Beowulf*-poet has set up expectations of a patterned sequence of ordered speech that the sensitive reader cannot but feel disturbed when that expected arrangement fails. When, as is the case with the only female speeches in the poem, the sequence of speech and response is broken not once, but twice, a strong sense of foreboding seems only natural.

---

51 See Sims-Williams, 'Thought, Word, and Deed: an Irish Triad', and below, p. 255.
52 The manuscript reads *he seoðða . . . geseon* at line 1875a.

The sound of silence: Wealhtheow's unanswered speeches

As a character, Wealhtheow has excited a fair share of critical attention.[53] Her name, which apparently means 'foreign slave',[54] seems at odds with her queenly status, although in fact no character in the poem addresses her by name at all; it seems likely that she is meant to be interpreted as a non-Dane married off to Hrothgar for political reasons.[55] But if she is undermined by her very name and apparently precarious position, Wealhtheow herself seems to feel every inch a queen. In her very first speech in *Beowulf*, Wealhtheow is evidently at pains to address Hrothgar's intention, explicitly expressed in his preceding speech, that he will take Beowulf for a son (lines 946b–949a):

> 'Nu ic, Beowulf, þec,
> secg betsta,   me for sunu wylle
> freogan on ferhþe;   heald forð tela
> niwe sibbe.'

> ['Now I, Beowulf, best of men, will love you like a son in my heart; henceforth keep well this new kinship.']

In the more than two hundred lines intervening before Wealhtheow's majestic appearance in the hall, we have heard Beowulf's reply (lines 958–79), in which he makes no reference at all to his newly-won status, and have been given a detailed description of the celebration-banquet in Heorot, with its lavish gift-giving and recital of the story of Finn.[56]

Wealhtheow's subsequent speech to her lord deserves quotation in full (lines 1169–87):[57]

> 'Onfoh þissum fulle,   freodrihten min,
> sinces brytta.   Þu on sælum wes,   1170
> goldwine gumena,   ond to Geatum spræc
> mildum wordum,   swa sceal man don.
> Beo wið Geatas glæd,   geofena gemyndig,
> nean ond feorran   þe þu nu hafast.
> Me man sægde   þæt þu ðe for sunu wolde   1175
> hererinc habban.   Heorot is gefælsod,
> beahsele beorhta;   bruc þenden þu mote
> manigra medo,   ond þinum magum læf
> folc ond rice,   þonne ðu forð scyle
> metodsceaft seon.   Ic minne can   1180
> glædne Hroþulf,   þæt he þa geogoðe wile

---

53 See, for example, Bammesberger, 'The Conclusion of Wealhtheow's Speech (*Beowulf* 1231)'; Bloomfield, 'Diminished by Kindness: Frederick Klaeber's Rewriting of Wealhtheow'; Crépin, 'Wealhtheow's Offering of the Cup to Beowulf'; Damico, *Beowulf's Wealhtheow and the Valkyrie Tradition*; Gordon, '*Wealhþeow* and Related Names'; Hill, ' "Wealhtheow" as a Foreign Slave'; Robinson, 'Is Wealhtheow a Prince's Daughter?'; Stratyner, 'Wealhtheow's Threat: *Beowulf*: 1228–1231'.
54 On meaningful names elsewhere in the poem, see above, pp. 172–3.
55 See further above, pp. 83–4.
56 On which see above, pp. 173–87.
57 The manuscript omits *þe* in line 1174b (through haplography?), and reads *here ric* in line 1176a; see further above, p. 181.

arum healdan,   gyf þu ær þonne he,
wine Scildinga,   worold oflætest;
wene ic þæt he mid gode   gyldan wille
uncran eaferan,   gif he þæt eal gemon,   1185
hwæt wit to willan   ond to worðmyndum
umborwesendum ær   arna gefremedon.'

['Take this cup, my beloved lord, giver of treasure; be in high spirits,
gold-friend of men, and speak to the Geats with generous words, as one
ought to do. Be gracious to the Geats, mindful of the gifts far and near,
which you now possess. I've been told that you wished to have the
warrior as a son. Heorot is cleansed, bright ring-hall; enjoy while you
may the esteem of many, and leave the people and kingdom to your
kinsmen, when you have to pass on, experience fate's decree. I know my
gracious Hrothulf, that he will treat the youth kindly, if you, friend of
the Scyldings, should leave the world before him; I expect that he will
deal well with our sons, if he remembers all the kindnesses that the two
of us did him to please and honour him when he was young.']

From the opening word of her speech, Wealhtheow establishes herself as one
who speaks primarily in the imperative mood; she issues no fewer than four such
imperatives in the first six lines (*Onfoh . . . wes . . . spræc . . . Beo*, lines
1169–70, 1171b and 1173a), before coming to the point: 'I've been told that you
wished to have the warrior as a son' (*Me man sægde þæt þu ðe for sunu wolde /
hererinc habban*, lines 1175–6a). Two more imperatives follow (*bruc . . . læf*,
lines 1177b and 1178b). The weakness of her position is made crystal-clear in
the second part of the speech, which is basically composed of two conditional
sentences (*Ic . . . can . . . gyf; wene ic . . . gif*, lines 1180b–1181 and 1184–5), the
outcome of both of which an audience with any sense of dynastic Scylding
history would know: [58] Hrothulf did indeed outlive his uncle, and was less than
kind to his cousins.[58]

Wealhtheow knows none of this, of course: maternal concern alone shines
through this rather crude attempt to meddle in high politics, and immediately
after this speech, Wealhtheow heads straight for her sons (lines 1188–91):

Hwearf þa bi bence   þær hyre byre wæron,
Hreðric ond Hroðmund,   ond hæleþa bearn,
giogoð ætgædere;   þær se goda sæt,   1190
Beowulf Geata,   be þæm gebroðrum twæm.

[Then she turned along the bench, where her boys were, Hrethric and
Hrothmund, with warriors' sons, the youth together; there the good man
sat, Beowulf of the Geats, beside the two brothers.]

Beowulf's position is of course indicative of his new status, and it comes as no
surprise that Wealhtheow should, like her husband, seek to reward him for his
deeds against Grendel by offering him a number of gifts, including a splendid

---

[58] See below, pp. 246–7.

neck-ring (lines 1197–1214).[59] Wealhtheow's second speech is addressed to
Beowulf, just after she has presented the ring (lines 1216–31):[60]

'Bruc ðisses beages, Beowulf leofa,
hyse, mid hæle, ond þisses hrægles neot,
þeodgestreona, ond geþeoh tela,
cen þec mid cræfte ond þyssum cnyhtum wes
lara liðe; ic þe þæs lean geman. 1220
Hafast þu gefered þæt ðe feor ond neah
ealne wideferhþ weras ehtigað,
efne swa side swa sæ bebugeð,
windgeard, weallas. Wes þenden þu lifige,
æþeling, eadig. Ic þe an tela 1225
sincgestreona. Beo þu suna minum
dædum gedefe, dreamhealdende.
Her is æghwylc eorl oþrum getrywe,
modes milde, mandrihtne hold;
þegnas syndon geþwære, þeod ealgearo 1230
druncne dryhtguman doð swa ic bidde.'

['Enjoy this ring, dear Beowulf, with good fortune, young man, and
make use of this accoutrement, mighty treasures, and prosper well,
make yourself known through power, and be kind in advice to these
boys: I'll bear in mind a reward for you for that. You have brought it
about that far and near men will praise you always, as far as the sea, the
wind-enclosure, surrounds the cliffs. Be, as long as you live, a happy
prince. I grant you a multitude of precious treasures. Be to my sons kind
in deeds, joyful. Here is each warrior true to the other, mild of spirit,
loyal to their lord. The thegns are united, a people fully prepared, the
retainers have drunk [loyally]: they do as I bid.']

Once again, her speech is notable for the large number of imperatives employed:
I count at least seven (*Bruc . . . neot . . . geþeoh . . . cen . . . wes . . . Wes . . . Beo*,
lines 1216–19, 1224b and 1226b).[61] As with her previous speech to Hrothgar,
she expresses confidence in those around her, but again, she seems somewhat
undermined by circumstances: her comment that 'Here is each warrior true to
the other' (*Her is æghwylc eorl oþrum getrywe*, line 1228) echoes eerily a
comment made only a short time before by the poet when scanning over
Hrothulf and Hrothgar sitting together that 'at that time their kinship was still
intact, each true to the other' (*þa gyt wæs hiera sib ætgædere, æghwylc oðrum
trywe*, lines 1164b–5a). But that comment seemed to forecast the end of
peaceful co-existence.[62] Once again, Wealhtheow is not answered: she just heads
off to the bench (*Eode þa to setle*, line 1232a). The fact that neither Beowulf nor
Hrothgar sees fit to respond to Wealhtheow's speeches in any way is surely

---

59 On the significance of this neck-ring, see above, pp. 114–16.
60 The manuscript reads *þeo ge streona* at line 1218a and *hol* at line 1229b.
61 I say 'at least', since it has been argued by Bammesberger, 'The Conclusion of Wealhtheow's Speech
(*Beowulf* 1231)', that *doð* (line 1231b) should also be construed as an imperative. In that case,
Wealhtheow is effectively commanding Beowulf and Hrothgar to 'do as I say'.
62 See below, pp. 246–7.

striking in the context of the decorous speech-patterning that characterises the whole of the first part of the poem. If in a sense a woman's words are her only weapons,[63] then it must be concluded that none of Wealhtheow's words have hit home.

Words, gifts, and the gift of words: Beowulf's return home

But if the decorous and courtly nature of the Danish court is to some extent delimited and defined by the careful patterning of the speeches, it is interesting to note that in the telling of Beowulf's triumphant return to Geatland, speeches appear to play a quite different role. The mechanics of Beowulf's homecoming are crisply told: a sword is given to the Danish coastwarden (lines 1900–3a); the voyage is undertaken and briefly described (lines 1903b–1913), in a manner which matches in miniature the previous description of Beowulf's voyage to Denmark; even the distance from the coast to Hygelac's court is said to be short (lines 1920–4).[64] There follows, as commonly in *Beowulf*, what seems at first outright and unalloyed praise for the court of the Geats, which, however, gives way to more ominous words (lines 1925–31a):[65]

> Bold wæs betlic,   bregorof cyning,   1925
> heah in healle,   Hygd swiðe geong,
> wis, welþungen,   þeah ðe wintra lyt
> under burhlocan   gebiden hæbbe,
> Hæreþes dohtor;   næs hio hnah swa þeah,
> ne to gneað gifa   Geata leodum,   1930
> maþmgestreona.

[The building was magnificent, the king mighty, exalted in the hall, Hygd very young, wise and accomplished, even though she had lived few winters in the enclosed stronghold, the daughter of Hæreth; she was not niggardly, nor too sparing of gifts, precious treasures, to the people of the Geats.]

Once the hall, king, and queen of the Geats have been lavishly praised, the poet introduces a series of negatives concerning Hygd that seem paradoxically ungenerous: why not simply say that Hygd gave many gifts?[66] Unfortunately, the three half-lines that follow are obscure (lines 1931b–1932); the manuscript clearly reads *mod þryðo wæg fremu folces cwen firen ondrysne*, and indeed there is no controversy about the meaning of the last five words: a 'lofty queen of the people' (*fremu folces cwen*) is the subject, and 'dreadful wickedness' (*firen ondrysne*) is the object. Successive critics and editors, however, have been unsure whether a new character, called variously Modthrytho or Thryth, has

---

63 Cf. Strauss, 'Women's Words as Weapons'.
64 Cf. Irving, 'Beowulf Comes Home: Close Reading in Epic Context'.
65 The manuscript reads *hea healle* in line 1926a, but the sense seems incomplete.
66 On Hygd in general, see, for example, Kaske, ' "Hygelac" and "Hygd" '; Malone, 'Hygd'; Pope, '*Beowulf* 3150–3151: Queen Hygd and the Word "Geomeowle" '; Weise, 'The Meaning of the Name "Hygd" '.

been abruptly introduced, and it is she who is the 'lofty queen' who has 'commited' (*wæg*) the 'dreadful wickedness', or whether Hygd herself is being chastised for exercising earlier 'arrogance' (if that is the meaning of the otherwise unattested compound *modþrýðo*). The difficulty with the latter interpretation is how to square the poet's subsequent statement that the 'dreadful wickedness' perpetrated by this queenly figure consisted of the imperious slaughter of men who dared stare openly at her, a flaw cured by Offa in a standard rehearsal of the 'taming of the shrew' motif,[67] who caused her to become a model queen by marrying her on her father's advice; it is hard to believe that Hygd could have married Offa at some unspecified point in the past after a career of destruction, then later married Hygelac, and yet still be described as 'very young' (*swiðe geong*, line 1926b).[68] A third possibility seems plausible, which removes both the abruptness of a sudden change of subject at line 1931b, introducing a new character, and the otherwise cramped chronology of Hygd's early life, namely that the model behaviour of Hygd (whose name means something like 'thought') has resulted from the fact that she has 'weighed up' or 'pondered' (if *wæg* can bear this abstract sense) the 'mood' or 'pride' of Thryth (whose name means something like 'strength').[69]

At all events, it is striking that the poet has chosen to interject this episode into the narrative of Beowulf's homecoming: although the physical distance between the shore and Hygelac's hall is not far (as we are repeatedly told: *næs him feor þanon*, line 1921b; *sæwealle neah*, line 1924b), some fifty lines intervene between Beowulf's ship landing (line 1913) and him leaving the shore (line 1963). Hygelac is reintroduced, in terms which suggest a flattering comparison with the recently lauded Offa; just as Offa's martial prowess and generosity have been praised (*Offa wæs geofum ond guðum garcene man wide geweorðod*, lines 1957b–1959a), so too the same qualities are discerned in the young Hygelac, identified initially only as the 'slayer of Ongentheow' (*eorla hleo bonan Ongenþeoes . . . geongne guðcyning godne . . . hringas dælan*, lines 1967b–1970a). It may be more than an oversight that the poet fails to mention that Hygelac shares the third of Offa's virtues, namely that he 'governed his native land with wisdom' (*wisdome heold, eðel sinne*, lines 1959b–1960a); certainly wisdom is not the hallmark of Hygelac's known words and deeds.[70]

The most noticeable feature of Beowulf's own account of his battles with Grendel and his mother (lines 2069b–2143) is the extent to which it offers additional details to those already presented:[71] for example, here we learn for the first time the name of the Geat killed by Grendel – Hondscio (line 2076a) – and the fact that in his predations Grendel carried a 'glove' made of 'the skins of dragons' (*Glof*, line 2086b; *dracan fellum*, line 2088b).[72] Aside from these details, which are seemingly linked (the common noun *hondscio* would seem to

---

[67] Cf. Garmonsway *et al.*, *Beowulf and its Analogues*, pp. 222–37.

[68] See above, pp. 83–4.

[69] On meaningful personal names in the poem, see above, pp. 172–3.

[70] On Hygelac's wider role in the poem, see above, pp. 98–9, 134–5, and 210.

[71] Cf. Schwetman, 'Beowulf's Return'; Waugh, 'Competitive Narrators in the Homecoming Scene of *Beowulf*'.

[72] See above, pp. 121–3.

mean 'glove'), however, we are – most importantly – presented with Beowulf's own perspective. As Rosemary Huisman has pointed out, this is in fact the third account of the fight with Grendel in the poem: Beowulf has already made a brief report to Hrothgar (lines 958–79), although in that instance there is no mention of the motivation for his battle, nor of the reward.[73] Both of these aspects were, of course, more properly Hrothgar's own concern, and Beowulf also adds a touching description of the old king, worn down by his difficulties (lines 2105–14):

> 'Þær wæs gidd ond gleo: gomela Scilding,   2105
> felafricgende,   feorran rehte;
> hwilum hildedeor   hearpan wynne,
> gomenwudu grette,   hwilum gyd awræc
> soð ond sarlic,   hwilum syllic spell
> rehte æfter rihte   rumheort cyning.   2110
> Hwilum eft ongan,   eldo gebunden,
> gomel guðwiga   gioguðe cwiðan,
> hildestrengo;   hreðer inne weoll,
> þonne he wintrum frod   worn gemunde.'

> ['There was singing and joyful noise; the aged Scylding, having learned many things, recounted tales from long ago; sometimes the battle-brave one struck the delightful wood, the harp's joy, sometimes told a tale, true and mournful; sometimes the great-hearted king properly narrated a strange story; sometimes again, fettered by age, the old warrior began to mourn his youth, his battle-strength; his heart surged inside when, old in winters, he recalled many things.']

The careful patterning of this passage, with its fourfold repetition of 'sometimes' (*hwilum*),[74] offers a fresh perspective on Hrothgar, which again contrasts with that of Beowulf himself, who, for all his skill with words, seems prone to melancholy outburst only at the very end of his life.[75] In other respects, however, this passage echoes in miniature a pattern we have seen many times in *Beowulf*. Once again, we find joy giving way to sorrow in this passage (*gleo . . . wynne . . . gomenwudu . . . sarlic . . . cwiðan*, lines 2105–12).[76]

Throughout his speech to Hygelac, Beowulf presents the fight with Grendel very much as a matter of revenge for the murdered Hondscio, and as a personal struggle to prevent being placed in Grendel's 'glove' and so going the way of all human flesh hitherto. In what some modern readers may feel is an ironic observation in a speech of over 150 lines, Beowulf proclaims that the details of the fight are 'too long to tell', but goes on to assure his lord that the deed redounds to the glory of all the Geats (lines 2093–6a):[77]

---

[73] Huisman, 'The Three Tellings of Beowulf's Fight with Grendel's Mother'.
[74] On this incremental pattern, see above, pp. 78–85.
[75] See further below, pp. 227–37.
[76] On the frequency of this pattern in the poem as a whole, see above, pp. 63–4 and 77–8.
[77] Most emend *hondlean* to *ondlean* (for *andlean*, 'recompense'); *hondlean* seems wholly appropriate, as at line 1541b (again, *handlean forgeald*, here used of Beowulf's encounter with Grendel's mother); see too lines 2929b and 2972b.

'To lang ys to reccenne   hu ic ðam leodsceaðan
yfla gehwylces   hondlean forgeald;
þær ic, þeoden min,   þine leode   2095
weorðode weorcum.'

['It is too long to tell how I gave that people-destroyer hand-recompense
for every evil, where I, my lord, glorified your people by my deeds.']

Beowulf places his own might at the disposal of his lord (*þeoden min*, line
2095a), whose people (*þine leode*, line 2095b) are thereby honoured;[78] the
extent to which Beowulf diminishes his own role and exalts that of Hygelac is
implicit in the very structure of line 2095: words referring to Hygelac alliterate
(*þeoden* and, especially, *þine*), whilst words referring to Beowulf himself (*ic* and
min) do not. The same imperative seems to lie behind Beowulf's assertion that
he set off to slay Grendel's mother (presented as another tit-for-tat killing, after
her slaughter of Æschere) after being begged in Hygelac's name (literally 'on
your life': *ðine life*, line 2131b) to act; there is nothing comparable in Hrothgar's
own speech (lines 1321–82) to support it.

Hrothgar does, however, promise Beowulf a reward in the form of treasure, as
he had done in the case of his killing of Grendel (*swa ic ær dyde*, line 1381b),
and it is striking the number of times to which Beowulf returns to the subject of
treasure in his speech to Hygelac, when in Denmark he has seemed wholly
unconcerned with material gain. So, Beowulf tells Hygelac that Hrothgar 'paid
[him] well in decorated gold and many treasures' (*fættan golde fela leanode,
manegum maðmum*, lines 2102–3a) for killing Grendel, 'promised [him] a
reward' for undertaking his expedition against Grendel's mother (*he me mede
gehet*, line 2134b), and later fulfilled his promise (in an echo of the bounty he
received after slaying Grendel), when 'he gave [him] in return a multitude of
treasures' (*eft gesealde maðma menigeo*, lines 2142b–2143a). Likewise, the
whole closing section of Beowulf's speech to Hygelac, which begins in praise of
Hrothgar, again focuses on the treasure that Beowulf has brought (lines
2144–51):[79]

'Swa se ðeodkyning   þeawum lyfde.
Nealles ic ðam leanum   forloren hæfde,   2145
mægnes mede,   ac he me maðmas geaf,
sunu Healfdenes,   on minne sylfes dom;
ða ic ðe, beorncyning,   bringan wylle,
estum geywan.   Gen is eall æt ðe
lissa gelong;   ic lyt hafo   2150
heafodmaga   nefne, Hygelac, ðec.'

['So that mighty king lived in good customs, nor did I lack rewards, the
recompense for my strength, but he, the son of Healfdene, gave me treasures at my own choice; I shall bring them to you, brave king, bestow

---

[78] An implicit contrast between the suffering Danes and the (now) honoured Geats seems indicated by
the repetition of the element *leod-* in lines 2093b and 2095b.
[79] The word *maðmas* in line 2146b has been supplied; the manuscript is defective at this point; likewise,
minne has to be completed in line 2147b.

them in good will. I am still wholly dependent on you for my joys; I
have few chief kinsmen except you, Hygelac.']

So this long speech, which begins with Hygelac (*dryhten Higelac*, line 2000b),
ends too with mention of his name (*Hygelac, ðec*).

There follows a highly ritualised exchange of gifts, depicted in great detail
(lines 2152–99), and carefully marked off by chiastic repetition of introductory
phrases (*Het ða in beran . . . Hyrde ic . . . Hyrde ic . . . Het ða . . . in fetian*, lines
2152a, 2163a, 2172a, and 2190).[80] It is no surprise that the gifts which Beowulf
presents to Hygelac match closely what he was himself given by Hrothgar for
killing Grendel, although again we are given some supplementary detail here.
The four chief gifts bestowed by Hrothgar have earlier been carefully described
(lines 1020–34), where they are said to consist of 'Healfdene's sword' (*brand
Healfdenes*, line 1020b), a 'golden standard' (*segen gyldenne*, line 1021), and 'a
helmet and mailcoat' (*helm ond byrnan*, line 1022b); it is surely the same set of
weaponry that Beowulf passes on to Hygelac, described as 'a boar-headed standard, a helmet towering in battle, a grey mail-coat, a splendid war-sword' (*eofor
heafod segn, heaðosteapne helm, hare byrnan, guðsweord geatolic*, lines
2152b–2154a). We learn that the golden standard has a boar at its head, and, in
further elaboration (lines 2155–62), that the mailcoat is that of Hrothgar's elder
brother, Heorogar, who had refused to present it to his own son, Heoroweard.

As a further reward to Beowulf for killing Grendel, Hrothgar had given him
'eight horses' (*eahta mearas*, line 1035b) one of which was wearing Hrothgar's
own war-saddle (lines 1037b–1042), whilst Wealhtheow, not to be outdone, had
presented him with a number of baubles, including 'the greatest of neck-rings
(*healsbeaga mæst*, line 1195b).[81] In his own gift-giving on his return to the land
of the Geats, Beowulf gives Hygelac, in addition to the four golden treasures
already described, 'four horses' (*feower mearas*, line 2163b), and he gives a
further three (*þrio wicg somod*, line 2174b) to Hygd, Hygelac's queen, in addition to 'the neck-ring that Wealhtheow had given him' (*ðone healsbeah . . . ðone
þe him Wealhðeo geaf*, lines 2172a–2173b); one assumes that, having given
away seven of the eight horses with which he had been presented, Beowulf kept
the one wearing Hrothgar's war-saddle. What is striking in comparing these
scenes of gift-giving in Denmark and the land of the Geats, separated by over a
thousand lines, is the sheer extent of overlap: not only do the gifts Beowulf
hands over correspond closely with what he received for killing Grendel (presumably he also retains the twelve further gifts he was given for dealing with
Grendel's mother, mentioned in passing by the poet in lines 1866–9), but there
are numerous verbal echoes, not simply of the repeated 'structuring' phrases
(*Het ða in beran . . . Het ða eorla hleo in fetian*, lines 2152a and 2190: cf. *Heht
ða eorla hleo . . . on flet teon, in under eoderas*; *Hyrde ic . . . Hyrde ic*, lines
2163a and 2172a: cf. *gefrægn ic*, line 1027a), but also other specific diction (*he
him est geteah meara ond maðma*, lines 2165b–2166a: cf. *onweald geteah wicga
ond wæpna . . . mearum ond madmum*, lines 1044b–1045a and 1048a). Like-

---

[80] Cf. Van Meter, 'The Ritualized Presentation of Weapons and the Ideology of Nobility in *Beowulf*.
[81] For more on the significance of this ring, see below, pp. 114–16.

wise, it is striking that, just as there is a change of metre to predominantly long lines to mark out the arrival into the hall of Wealhtheow before she bestows on Beowulf the neck-ring (lines 1162b–1168), so too there is a similar change of metre when the neck-ring is reintroduced (lines 2171–2).[82] In short, the return to Geatland marks a further change in tempo of the speech-patterning, and prepares the audience for the quite different part that speeches play in Part II of the poem. At Hrothgar's court, the patterned trading of words provides the staple currency of courtly life, while at Hygelac's court it is the giving of gifts and reporting of deeds that seems paramount. As we shall see, a still different pattern prevails at the court of King Beowulf, where precious words are spent, but never exchanged.

Famous last words: dramatic monologues and the dragon-episode

If the total lack of response to Wealhtheow in Heorot seems disturbing precisely because of the careful choreography of the other speeches in Part I of the poem, and if exchanging words is made secondary to the exchange of gifts on Beowulf's return home, then pouring out words into unresponsive emptiness is simply the norm in Part II of *Beowulf*. It has often been noted that the whole of the dragon-episode has a different feel from the events depicted in Denmark, and that the dragon-fight itself is of a different stamp.[83] The bleakness of tone is set right from the start, with a speech from an anonymous 'last survivor' of a noble race (*æþelan cynnes*, line 2234b), mourning in a monologue the loss of his people (lines 2247–66):[84]

> 'Heald þu nu, hruse,   nu hæleð ne mostan,
> eorla æhte.   Hwæt, hyt ær on ðe
> gode begeaton.   Guðdeað fornam,
> feorhbealo frecne,   fyra gehwylcne   2250
> leoda minra,   þara ðe þis lif ofgeaf,
> gesawon seledream.   Nah hwa sweord wege
> oððe feormie   fæted wæge,

82 See further above, p. 67.
83 Several studies focus on the dragon-episode in *Beowulf*, including Amodio, 'Affective Criticism, Oral Poetics, and Beowulf's Fight with the Dragon'; Anderson, 'Treasure Trove in *Beowulf*'; Bonjour, 'Monsters Crouching and Critics Rampant'; Boyle, 'Historical Dragon-Slayers'; Braeger, 'Connotations of *(earm)sceapen*'; Brown, 'The Firedrake in *Beowulf*'; Davidson, 'The Hill of the Dragon'; Evans, 'Semiotics and Traditional Lore'; Garde, 'Christian and Folkloric Tradition in *Beowulf*'; Grinsell, 'Barrow Treasure in Fact, Tradition and Legislation'; Griffiths, *Meet the Dragon*; Keller, 'The Dragon in *Beowulf* Reconsidered'; Knipp, '*Beowulf* 2210b–2323'; Lawrence, 'The Dragon and his Lair in *Beowulf*'; Lionarons, *The Medieval Dragon*; Mitchell, ' "Until the Dragon Comes . . ." '; Rauer, *Beowulf and the Dragon*; Scherb, 'Setting and Cultural Memory in Part II of *Beowulf*'; Schichler, 'Heorot and Dragon-Slaying in *Beowulf*'; Shilton, 'The Nature of Beowulf's Dragon'; Sisam, 'Beowulf's Fight with the Dragon'; Sorrell, 'The Approach to the Dragon-Fight'; Talbot, 'Sigemund the Dragon-Slayer'; Taylor, 'The Dragon's Treasure in *Beowulf*'; Thornbury, '*eald enta geweorc* and the Relics of Empire'; Tripp, *More about the Fight with the Dragon*; Wild, 'Drachen im Beowulf und andere Drachen'.
84 The manuscript reads *mæstan* at 2247b, *fyrena* at 2250b, *þana ðe þis ofgeaf* at 2251b, and *seoc* at 2254b; *feormie* has been supplied in line 2253a: the manuscript reads *f.* . . .

dryncfæt deore;   duguð ellor scoc.
Sceal se hearda helm   hyrsted golde   2255
fætum befeallen;   feormynd swefað,
þa ðe beadogriman   bywan sceoldon,
geswylce seo herepad,   sio æt hilde gebad
ofer borda gebræc   bite irena,
brosnað æfter beorne.   Ne mæg byrnan hring   2260
æfter wigfruman   wide feran,
hæleðum be healfe.   Næs hearpan wyn,
gomen gleobeames,   ne god hafoc
geond sæl swingeð,   ne se swifta mearh
burhstede beateð.   Bealocwealm hafað   2265
fela feorhcynna   forð onsended.'

['Hold now, earth, what now warriors cannot, the possessions of men.
Indeed, good men obtained it once from you; battle-death, dread mortal
harm, has carried off every man of my people who have given up this
life: they have seen the last of the joy of the hall. There is no one to carry
the sword, or bear forth the plated cup, the precious drinking vessel; the
trusty troop has gone elsewhere. The hard helmet, gold-adorned, must
be bereft of its plated decorations; the burnishers sleep, who ought to
polish the battle-masks; and also the mail-coat, which in battle endured
the cut of iron above the clash of shields, decays after the warrior; the
mail-shirt's ring cannot journey widely behind the war-leader, by the
warriors' side. There is no joy from the harp, no delight from the
musical instrument, nor does the fine hawk fly through the hall, nor the
swift steed stamp the courtyard. Terrible death has sent forth many of
the living race.']

The artful nature of this set-piece speech is clear from the sheer number of
effects used: rhyme (*herepad . . . gebad*, line 2258), continued alliteration
(*gebad . . . borda gebræc bite . . . brosnað . . . beorne . . . byrnan*, lines
2258b–2260), paronomasia (*wege . . . wæge*, lines 2252b and 2253b), and
anaphora (*Næs . . . ne . . . ne*, lines 2262b–2264), all contained within an envelope pattern (*Guðdeað . . . feorhbealo . . . Bealocwealm . . . feorhcynna*, lines
2249b–2266a). Whether or not one accepts Gale Owen-Crocker's argument that
what is described here is, in effect, a funeral,[85] there is no mistaking the melancholy tone: the last survivor speaks to no one, is heard by no one, and answer
came there none.[86]

Within little more than a hundred and fifty lines, and some three hundred
years later,[87] we are back at the same scene, witnessing Beowulf's final speech
before facing the dragon. Beowulf's previous boasts before battle were both
relatively brief: eleven lines before fighting Grendel (lines 677–87) and eighteen before facing Grendel's mother (lines 1474–91). Now, prior to his last battle,
a very different Beowulf utters a very different speech of no fewer than 107

---

85 Owen-Crocker, *The Four Funerals in 'Beowulf' and the Structure of the Poem*, pp. 61–84.
86 Cf. Thormann, 'The Poetics of Absence: "The Lament of the Sole Survivor" in *Beowulf*'.
87 We are told that the dragon (who took possession of the treasure left by the last survivor) guarded the
    mound for *þreo hund wintra* (line 2278b).

lines, with two interruptions.[88] Those who wish to see in Beowulf a type of Christ find much significance in his final journey to meet the dragon, as Beowulf proceeds, one of twelve men (*twelfa sum*, line 2401a), with the thief thirteenth, tagging along unwillingly to guide the way (lines 2406–13a).[89] Certainly, Beowulf experiences a moment of personal reflection before his trial which resembles Christ's anguish at Gethsemane (lines 2417–24):[90]

> Gesæt ða on næsse   niðheard cyning,
> þenden hælo abead   heorðgeneatum,
> goldwine Geata.   Him wæs geomor sefa,
> wæfre ond wælfus,   wyrd ungemete neah,   2420
> se ðone gomelan   gretan sceolde,
> secean sawle hord,   sundur gedælan
> lif wið lice,   no þon lange wæs
> feorh æþelinges   flæsce bewunden.

[Then the attack-hardened king, the gold-friend of the Geats, sat on the headland, bid good luck to his hearth-companions. His heart was sad, restless and ready for death, the fate immeasureably close that had to overtake the aged one, seek out the soul's hoard, divide asunder the life from the body; not for long after that was the prince's life enclosed in flesh.]

Noteworthy here is the use of the phrase 'seek out the soul's hoard' (*secean sawle hord*, line 2422a), since earlier in the poem the parallel phrase 'seek out the soul' (*sawle secan*, line 801a) has been used of those intending (without result) to kill Grendel; the use of the term 'hoard' in this context, as Beowulf sets out to kill the dragon and plunder its hoard, seems distinctly loaded.[91] It may also be the case that in employing the phrase 'divide asunder the life from the body' (*sundur gedælan lif wið lice*, lines 2422b–2423a), the poet may be recalling the parallel expression, used of Grendel's frustrated murderous design, that he 'intended that he should divide . . . the life from the body of every single one of them' (*mynte þæt he gedælde . . . anra gehwylces lif wið lice*, lines 731a–733a). In Beowulf's case, fate and the dragon finally accomplish what Grendel could not.

At all events, the upshot of Beowulf's melancholy reverie is a lengthy speech of over one hundred lines (lines 2426–537, with brief interruptions at lines 2510–11a and 2516–18a), in which he reviews his past life. The speech begins with an assertion about his past conflicts which matches closely what the poet himself has twice recently said (lines 2426–7):[92]

> 'Fela ic on giogoðe   guðræsa genæs,
> orleghwila;   ic þæt eall gemon.'

---

88 See Table IV above, pp. 206–7.

89 See above, pp. 147–9.

90 See above, p. 148.

91 According to Klaeber, 'The Christian Elements', p. 40; cf. *Phoenix*, line 220: *lif bið on siðe fæges feorhhord*; *Guthlac B*, line 1141: *dead . . . sohte sawelhus*.

92 Compare lines 2349b–2351a (*forðon he ær fela nearo neðende niða gedigde, hildehlemma*) and 2397–9a (*Swa he niða gehwane genesen hæfde sliðra geslyhta, sunu Ecgðiowes, ellenweorca*).

['In my youth I survived many battle-onslaughts, times of war: I remember it all.']

Beowulf begins by reviewing his own life, but soon focuses instead on the calamities that befell old King Hrethel of the Geats, who saw one son kill another and could do nothing about it.[93] Beowulf follows up his musings on the sufferings of Hrethel by highlighting the case of how, after Hrethel died, another aged king, this time Ongentheow the Swede, died attempting to exact vengeance for an attack upon him by the Geats, led by Hæthcyn and Hygelac.[94] Ironically, Hæthcyn the fratricide is himself avenged by his other brother, Hygelac, in a passage which offers the first of several glimpses in the poem of the complex feuding that characterises the wars between the Swedes and the Geats (lines 2472–89). Although Hygelac is given the credit for the slaying of Ongentheow, the actual deed was performed by a hitherto unknown warrior, Eofor, in a vividly described killing, the savagery of which well suits a man whose name means 'boar' (lines 2484–9):[95]

> 'Þa ic on morgne gefrægn   mæg oðerne
> billes ecgum   on bonan stælan,   2485
> þær Ongenþeow   Eofores niosað –
> guðhelm toglad,   gomela Scylfing
> hreas heoroblac;   hond gemunde
> fæhðo genoge,   feorhsweng ne ofteah.'

['Then I heard that in the morning one kinsman took vengeance from the other's slayer with the edge of a sword, when Ongentheow encounters Eofor; the war-helmet split, the aged Scylfing fell, pale from battle: the hand remembered many hostile deeds, it did not hold back from the deadly blow.']

The violence of the aged king's death is dealt with in some detail; the notion that Eofor's hand 'did not hold back from the deadly blow' echoes what the poet has already said, nearly a thousand lines earlier, about Beowulf's own first blow against Grendel's mother (*hond sweng ne ofteah*, line 1520b). Beowulf follows his account of Ongentheow's death with a detailed discussion of his relationship with Hygelac (lines 2490–509):[96]

> 'Ic him þa maðmas,   þe he me sealde,   2490
> geald æt guðe,   swa me gifeðe wæs,
> leohtan sweorde;   he me lond forgeaf,
> eard, eðelwyn.   Næs him ænig þearf
> þæt he to Gifðum   oððe to Gardenum
> oððe in Swiorice   secean þurfe   2495
> wyrsan wigfrecan,   weorðe gecyþan.
> Symle ic him on feðan   beforan wolde,

---

93 See above, pp. 116–19.
94 See further above, pp. 170–2.
95 At line 2488a the manuscript simply reads *hreas blac*, but the metre is clearly defective.
96 The manuscript reads *fres cyning* at line 2503b and *incempan* at line 2505a; both emendations are widely accepted.

ana on orde,   ond swa to aldre sceall
sæcce fremman,   þenden þis sweord þolað,
þæt mec ær ond sið   oft gelæste,   2500
syððan ic for dugeðum   Dæghrefne wearð
to handbonan,   Huga cempan;
nalles he ða frætwe   Frescyninge,
breostweorðunge,   bringan moste,
ac in campe gecrong   cumbles hyrde,   2505
æþeling on elne;   ne wæs ecg bona,
ac him hildegrap   heortan wylmas,
banhus gebræc.   Nu sceall billes ecg,
hond ond heard sweord,   ymb hord wigan.'

['I repaid him in battle for those treasures which he gave me, as was
granted me with my bright sword; he presented me with land, a
dwelling, the joys of a home. There was no necessity for him, that he
need seek from the Gifthas, or the Spear-Danes, or in Sweden for a
worse warrior, obtain at a price. I always wanted to be before him
among the foot-soldiers, alone in the forefront, and so I shall throughout
my life do battle, while this sword lasts, which has often, in the early
days and lately, sustained me since the time when before the hosts I
became the hand-slayer of Dæghrefn, the champion of the Hugas. Not at
all was he permitted to bring back the accoutrements, breast-adornments, to the Frisian king, but he fell on the battle-field, the standard-bearer, the prince in valour; no sword was his slayer, but a
battle-grip shattered the surgings of his heart, his bone-house. Now
must a weapon's edge, hand and hard sword contend for the hoard.']

The opening of this section of Beowulf's speech focuses attention on the mutual
give and take which is the hallmark of heroic commerce, stressed by no fewer
that four terms for giving in three lines (*sealde geald . . . gifeðe . . . forgeaf*, lines
2490b–2492) of which the first two, the subjects of which are Hygelac and
Beowulf respectively, are highlighted by both contiguity and rhyme across a
line-break.[97] Although Beowulf mentions first of all that he received 'treasures'
(*maðmas*, line 2490a) from Hygelac, he quickly goes on to assert through repetition that what he really gained was a home (*lond . . . eard, eðelwyn*, lines
2492b–2493a). There is a striking emphasis here on Beowulf's sword (lines
2492a, 2499b, 2505b, 2508b and 2509a), as well as on his own raw
hand-strength (lines 2502a, 2507a and 2509a), an emphasis (and a construction)
which echoes closely his earlier comments about dealing with the creatures who
assailed him in his contest with Breca (lines 553b–558):

'Me to grunde teah
fah feondscaða,   fæste hæfde
grim on grape;   hwæþre me gyfeþe wearð   555
þæt ic aglæcan   orde geræhte,
hildebille;   heaþoræs fornam
mihtig meredeor   þurh mine hand.'

97 See above, pp. 61–9.

> ['A guilty aggressive ravager dragged me to the bottom, grim in its grip, and yet it was granted to me that I should pierce with my point the awesome assailant, with my war-sword; the rush of battle took off the mighty sea-creature through my hand.']

Here again, Beowulf's victory is seen as a combination of swordsmanship and sheer strength, much as was his triumph against Grendel's mother. The fact that just before he faces the dragon Beowulf should mention his defeat of Dæghrefn, apparently without the aid of a sword, would again seem to echo his triumphant earlier contest with Grendel.[98]

In breaking up Beowulf's speech before facing the dragon (lines 2510–11a and 2516–18a), the poet effectively twice stresses that this is the 'last time' he shall make such a speech (*niehstan siðe*, line 2511a; *hindeman siðe*, line 2517b); but these interjections by the poet also serve to highlight the wider structure of the speech as a whole. At its beginning, Beowulf had emphasised the depth of his experience (*Fela ic on gioguðe guðræsa genæs, orleghwila; ic þæt eall gemon*, lines 2426–7), and so too after the first of the poet's interruptions does he return to that theme (lines 2511b–2515):[99]

> 'Ic geneðde fela
> guða on geogoðe;   gyt ic wylle,
> frod folces weard,   fæhðe secan,
> mærðum fremman,   gif mec se mansceaða
> of eorðsele   ut geseceð.'   2515

> ['I endured many battles in my youth; as an experienced guardian of my people I still want to seek hostile encounters, perform gloriously, if that wicked ravager comes to me out of the earth-hall.']

Here, however, Beowulf turns quickly from the past to the future, and expresses a firm resolve, commencing immediately after the second of the poet's interruptions, and going on to the end of the speech (lines 2518b–2537):[100]

> 'Nolde ic sweord beran,
> wæpen to wyrme,   gif ic wiste hu
> wið ðam aglæcean   elles meahte   2520
> gylpe wiðgripan,   swa ic gio wið Grendle dyde.
> Ac ic ðær heaðufyres   hates wene,
> oreðes ond attres;   forðon ic me on haf
> bord ond byrnan.   Nelle ic beorges weard
> oferfleon fotes trem,   ac unc furður sceal   2525
> weorðan æt wealle,   swa unc wyrd geteoð,
> metod manna gehwæs.   Ic eom on mode from
> þæt ic wið þone guðflogan   gylp ofersitte.

---

98 See above, p. 121.

99 Following Mitchell and Robinson, ed., *Beowulf*, p. 137, I take *mærðum* in line 2514a as an adverbial dative; other editors simply emend to *mærðu* ('glorious deeds').

100 The manuscript reads *reðes & hattres* at line 2523a; *furður* is missing in line 2525b; and *wat* appears for *þæt* in line 2534a. On the phrase *oreðes ond attres*, see Cook, 'Aldhelm and the Source of *Beowulf* 2523'.

Gebide ge on beorge   byrnum werede,
secgas on searwum,   hwæðer sel mæge   2530
æfter wælræse   wunde gedygan
uncer twega.   Nis þæt eower sið
ne gemet mannes,   nefne min anes,
þæt he wið aglæcean   eofoðo dæle,
eorlscype efne.   Ic mid elne sceall   2535
gold gegangan,   oððe guð nimeð,
feorhbealu frecne,   frean eowerne.'

['I would not carry my sword, my weapon to the serpent, if I knew how
else I could according to my undertaking grapple with the awesome
assailant, as I previously did with Grendel; but I expect hot and destruc-
tive flame there, blast and venom; therefore I carry a shield and
mailcoat. I shall not flee away from the mountain's guardian the space of
a foot, but it must turn out for the pair of us further forward at the wall,
as fate decrees for the pair of us, the destiny of every man. I am firm in
heart that I should forbear from any further undertaking against the
flying enemy. Wait by the barrow, protected by mailcoats, men in arms,
to see which of the pair of us can better survive wounds after the deadly
onslaught. This is not an exploit for you, nor fitting for any man except
me alone, to match strength against a hostile assailant, perform deeds of
valour. I shall gain the gold with courage, or battle, the dread destroyer
of life, will take off your lord.']

For a speech expressing positive resolve, there are a striking number of negative
expressions here (*Nolde . . . Nelle . . . Nis*, lines 2518b, 2524b, and 2532b).
Moreover, the impression of Beowulf's otherness is underlined by the deliberate
way he distinguishes himself (and the dragon) from the rest: in a portion of the
speech remarkable for its first-person singular references (lines 2518b, 2519b,
2521b, 2522a, 2523b (twice), 2524b, 2527b, 2528a, 2533b, and 2535b),[101]
Beowulf aligns himself with the dragon through the use of the dual form three
times (lines 2525b and 2526b), and uses second-person plural forms to indicate
his men (lines 2532b and 2537b). Beowulf's closing vow to gain the treasure or
die in the attempt is typical of the (equally unfulfilled) vows made by him
earlier in the poem:[102] characteristically, he manages to do both.

The poet's own comment on Beowulf's actions stresses again the protective
measures that he has undertaken (lines 2538–41):

Aras ða bi ronde   rof oretta,
heard under helme,   hiorosercean bær
under stancleofu,   strengo getruwode   2540
anes mannes.   Ne bið swylc earges sið.

[Then the bold warrior arose by his shield, hard under his helmet, he
bore his battle-shirt under the stone cliffs, put his faith in the strength of
a single man: such is not the coward's way.]

---

101   On Beowulf's use of the first-person elsewhere in the poem, see above, p. 213.
102   See above, pp. 195 and 215.

By successively focusing on Beowulf's defensive arrangements (shield, helmet, and corselet) the poet effectively foreshadows the fact that Beowulf is to face the fiercest attack of his life.[103] The poet's remark that for Beowulf to put his faith in his own sole strength is not the mark of the coward would hardly seem appropriate were his opponent simply another man: we have already been told (twice) that Beowulf was the strongest man alive (lines 196–7 and 789–90). In his battles against superhuman creatures, however, Beowulf's (rightly placed) faith in his own might has already been expressed in very similar terms (and with similarly gnomic authorial endorsement); when Unferth's sword fails him against Grendel's mother, Beowulf is (quite literally) thrown back on his own resources (lines 1529–36):

> Eft wæs anræd, nalas elnes læt,
> mærða gemyndig mæg Hylaces.   1530
> Wearp ða wundenmæl wrættum gebunden
> yrre oretta, þæt hit on eorðan læg,
> stið ond stylecg; strenge getruwode,
> mundgripe mægenes. Swa sceal man don,
> þonne he æt guðe gegan þenceð   1535
> longsumne lof, na ymb his lif cearað.

> [Once again he was resolute, in no way slack in courage, mindful of great deeds, Hygelac's kinsman. He cast away the patterned weapon, inlaid with ornaments, the angry warrior, so that it lay on the ground, hard and steel-edged; he put his faith in his strength, his hand-grip of might. So ought a man to do when he thinks to gain lasting fame in battle: he will not care about his life.]

As he advances towards the dragon, however, Beowulf is not the only one of the protagonists to have put his faith in his defensive protection and martial ability; the poet has already noted ominously that a similar (and ultimately similarly misplaced) confidence is shared by the dragon itself (lines 2321–3):

> Hæfde landwara lige befangen,
> bæle ond bronde, beorges getruwode,
> wiges ond wealles; him seo wen geleah.

> [It had encircled the nation's people in flame, with fire and burning: it trusted in its barrow, its fighting-power and fortification; that hope deceived it.]

Once more, Beowulf and his final foe are linked, before they have even encountered one another. As Beowulf advances, the ominous collocation of surging fire that marked out the dwelling of Grendel and his mother is repeated at the scene of the dragon's lair (lines 2542–9):[104]

> Geseah ða be wealle se ðe worna fela,
> gumcystum god, guða gedigde,

---

103 Cf. above, pp. 65–6.
104 The manuscript reads *stodan* at line 2545a, presumably because of a missing nasal suspension.

hildehlemma,   þonne hnitan feðan,
stondan stanbogan,   stream ut þonan   2545
brecan of beorge.   Wæs þære burnan wælm
heaðofyrum hat;   ne meahte horde neah
unbyrnende   ænige hwile
deop gedygan   for dracan lege.

[He who, fine in his manly virtues, had endured a great number of
battles, war-clamours, when the foot-troops clashed, saw by the wall a
stone arch stand, and a stream break out from the mountain-side there.
The bubbling of that stream was hot with deadly fires; he could not
without burning endure the depths near the hoard for any length of time,
because of the dragon's flame.]

Wordplay underlines the extent to which the fiery surges of the dragon's flame
resemble streams of mountain water (*burnan* . . . *unbyrnende*, lines 2546b and
2548a), and, just as with the monster-mere, the combination of fire and water
may well suggest the familiar imagery of Doomsday.[105] Certainly, just as
Grendel is roused by the sound of a human voice, so too is the dragon enraged
by Beowulf's battle-cry (lines 2550–6a); once again references to Beowulf's
shield are common in the passage that describes the first encounter between
Beowulf and the dragon (lines 2559–75a):[106]

Biorn under beorge   bordrand onswaf
wið ðam gryregieste,   Geata dryhten;   2560
ða wæs hringbogan   heorte gefysed
sæcce to seceanne.   Sweord ær gebræd
god guðcyning,   gomele lafe,
ecgum ungleaw;   æghwæðrum wæs
bealohycgendra   broga fram oðrum.   2565
Stiðmod gestod   wið steapne rond
winia bealdor,   ða se wyrm gebeah
snude tosomne;   he on searwum bad.
Gewat ða byrnende   gebogen scriðan,
to gescipe scyndan.   Scyld wel gebearg   2570
life ond lice   læssan hwile
mærum þeodne   þonne his myne sohte,
ðær he þy fyrste,   forman dogore
wealdan moste   swa him wyrd ne gescraf
hreð æt hilde.   2575

[The warrior, lord of the Geats, swung the rim of his shield under the
barrow against that dreadful stranger; then was the heart of the coiled
creature aroused to seek out battle. The good war-king had drawn the
ancient heirloom, dull of edge; for each of those ones intent on destruction, there was horror of the other. The lord of the dear people stood
resolute by his towering shield as the dragon swiftly coiled together; he
waited in his armour. Then it came, burning and coiled, gliding swiftly

---

105 Cf. Orchard, *Pride and Prodigies*, pp. 42–4.
106 For the sense 'dull of edge' for *ecgum ungleaw* at line 2564a, see Mitchell and Robinson, ed.,
    Beowulf, p. 138; see too Kiernan, *'Beowulf' and the 'Beowulf'-Manuscript*, pp. 206–8.

to its fate. The shield protected life and limb less well than his purpose
required when on that occasion for the first time he had to battle when
fate had not decreed him the triumph in the fray.]

The whole passage builds on the same restricted series of sounds (*b*, *s*, and *sc*
[pronounced 'sh']), brilliantly brought together in the chilling description of the
rushing serpent (lines 2569–70). There is a sense that, for Beowulf, time is
running out: not only does his shield not protect him for as long as he intends
(lines 2570b–2572), but so too his sword 'bit less strongly than the mighty king
required, driven to dire straits' (*bat unswiðor þonne his ðiodcyning þearfe
hæfde, þysigum gebæded*, lines 2578b–2580a). Their mutual horror again
provides a link between Beowulf and the dragon (lines 2564b–2565), and the
poet represents this first phase of their encounter as essentially a battle between
equals: after Beowulf strikes his first (ineffective) sword-blow, the dragon retali-
ates in kind (lines 2580b–2583a):

> Þa wæs beorges weard   2580
> æfter heaðuswenge   on hreoum mode,
> wearp wælfyre;   wide sprungon
> hildeleoman.

[Then the mound's guardian following the aggressive blow became
enraged in his heart, cast out murderous fire, battle-flames sprang
widely.]

The poet's choice of the term 'battle-flames' (*hildeleoman*, line 2583a) here is
exquisite; elsewhere it and related terms are common kennings for 'sword' (as at
line 1143b).[107] By sandwiching the word between two (rhyming) references to
the failure of Beowulf's own sword (*sio ecg gewac . . . guðbill geswac*, lines
2577b and 2584b), and by using the term in its literal rather than metaphorical
sense, the poet makes of the dragon an almost human protagonist: just as
warriors wield their swords like flames, so too does the dragon wield its flames
like swords. At all events, we are clearly given to understand that Beowulf is
beaten back in the first attack, and has already failed to live up to his stated aim
that he 'will not flee away from the mountain's guardian the space of a foot'
(*Nelle ic beorges weard oferfeon fotes trem*, lines 2524b–2525a);[108] already this
small defeat is offered as a foretaste of the death that is to come (lines
2586b–2591a):[109]

> Ne wæs þæt eðe sið,
> þæt se mæra   maga Ecgðeowes
> grundwong þone   ofgyfan wolde;

---

[107] See further above, pp. 69–70.

[108] It is worth noting that the poet explicitly links the first attack of the dragon with Beowulf's earlier
expressed intention through the use of the term 'mountain's guardian' (*beorges weard*, line 2580b),
which has hitherto only been used by Beowulf to express his determination not to retreat (*beorges
weard*, line 2524b).

[109] The word *ofer* has been supplied in line 2589a, in line with most editions; the manuscript simply
reads *sceolde willan*.

sceolde ofer willan   wic eardian
elles hwergen,   swa sceal æghwylc mon   2590
alætan lændagas.

[It was no easy trip for the famous kinsman of Ecgtheow to want to give
up that piece of ground; he had against his will to inhabit a
dwelling-place elsewhere: so must every man abandon his transitory
days.]

Once again, Beowulf and his dragon are inextricably linked, as they are both
described as 'awesome assailants' (*aglæcean*, line 2592a) squaring up for a
second attack.[110] Beowulf's men all flee away to the woods (lines 2596–9a),
except one who, we infer, is related to Beowulf (lines 2599b–2601):

Hiora in anum weoll
sefa wið sorgum;   sibb æfre ne mæg   2600
wiht onwendan   þam ðe wel þenceð.

[In one of them his spirit surged with sorrows; nothing can ever deflect
the call of kinship for one who thinks properly.]

With such a gnomic sentiment fitt XXXV ends, and Wiglaf, a new and critical
voice, is (somewhat portentously) introduced.[111] His speeches, which form part
of the focus of the next chapter,[112] will be characterised by a clear-sightedness
and perspective hitherto denied the other characters in *Beowulf*. Wiglaf
comments freely on both Beowulf and his people in an openly analytical
fashion, and as such can be said to speak not only for the poet, but for us.

---

110 On the use of the term, see above, pp. 90 and 189.
111 On the sonorous introduction granted Wiglaf, see above, pp. 73–4.
112 See below, pp. 261–3.

8

Beowulf: Beyond Criticism?

'Beowulf' and the limits of human knowledge

According to Brigid Brophy, writing in 1967, first on the list (albeit for reasons of chronology) of dispensable texts in the canon of English literature was *Beowulf*.[1] What as early as 1705 Humfrey Wanley had called 'an outstanding example of Anglo-Saxon poetry' (*Poeseos Anglo-Saxonicae egregium exemplum*)[2] is unkindly described: 'Boring and unattractive as a story, pointlessly bloodthirsty but – we are always told – fundamentally christian, *Beowulf* is a fine example of primitive non-art. Admiring comment on its poetry is about as relevant as praise for the architecture of Stonehenge.'[3] Philip Larkin was equally scathing, if more pithy, writing to Kingsley Amis in 1942, after the latter had just joined the army: 'Life is a fanged monster, sonny, that lies in wait for you . . . Sometimes I think of *Beowulf* and *The Wanderer*. Oh boo hoo. You lucky man to be in the army away from it all.'[4]

But if some modern readers have failed to be impressed by *Beowulf*, it is equally clear that the poet himself is far from universally positive about the characters he has created, producing a perhaps surprising number of apparently critical or at least questionable comments, both by and of a whole range of individuals. Special pleading and even skilful emendation may do no real service to the poet and his piece. Certainly the poet often seems to circumscribe and undercut his creations, putting into sharp focus the limits of their shared mortality and the boundaries of all human knowledge. The closing words of the first (unnumbered) fitt stress as much, saying of the final destination of the departing Scyld Scefing (lines 50b–52):[5]

> Men ne cunnon   50
> secgan to soðe,   seleræ dende,
> hæleð under heofenum,   hwa þæm hlæste onfeng.

> [Men cannot say for sure, hall-counsellors, warriors under the heavens, who received that load.]

---

[1] Brophy, *Fifty Works*, pp. 1–2.
[2] Wanley, *Librorum Veterum Septentrionalium . . . Catalogus*, p. 219.
[3] Brophy, *Fifty Works*, p. 1.
[4] Larkin, *Selected Letters*, p. 39.
[5] The manuscript reads *sele rædenne* at line 51b, but the emendation is of a common type; see above, pp. 42 and 45.

This is but the first occasion on which the knowledge of the Danes (and, in this case, the wider audience also) is depicted as being sadly delimited in precisely parallel terms. Just as no one knows Scyld's ultimate fate, so too no one knows where creatures like Grendel venture in their wanderings (*men ne cunnon*, line 162b), nor whether Grendel has a father (*no hie fæder cunnon*, line 1355b). More seriously, the Danes go to sleep insensible of the sorrow of their sad mortal fate at Grendel's hands (*sorge ne cuðon, wonsceaft wera*, lines 119b–120a), and in their resultant panic fall into devilish ways, since they are ignorant of (the true) God (lines 180b–188):[6]

> Metod hie ne cuþon,   180
> dæda Demend,   ne wiston hie Drihten God,
> ne hie huru heofena Helm   herian ne cuþon,
> wuldres Waldend.   Wa bið þæm ðe sceal
> þurh sliðne nið   sawle bescufan
> in fyres fæþm,   frofre ne wenan,   185
> wihte gewendan;   wel bið þæm þe mot
> æfter deaðdæge   drihten secean
> ond to fæder fæþmum   freoðo wilnian.

[They did not know the Creator, the Judge of Deeds, nor did they recognise the Lord God, nor truly did they know how to praise the Protector of the Heavens, the Ruler of Glory. It shall be woe for the one who must through cruel emnity thrust his soul into the fire's embrace, not hope for comfort, or any change; it shall be well for the one who may seek the Lord after his death-day, and ask for protection in the father's embrace.]

Nor do the Danes ever learn. In what is evidently a deliberate echo of the earlier passage, we are later told how, even after the defeat of Grendel, the Danes are still in the dark (as it were), ignorant of the incipient arrival of his avenging mother (*wyrd ne cuþon, geasceaft grimme*, line 1233). On both occasions the Danes feast in empty celebration, before going to a sleep from which some will never arise.[7]

The utter helplessness and impotence of the Danes in the face of Grendel's predations are stressed twice in practically identical terms before Beowulf himself is introduced; we are told that (lines 133b–134a and 191b–192a):

> wæs þæt gewin to strang,
> lað ond longsum
>
> . . .
>
> wæs þæt gewin to swyð,
> laþ ond longsum.

[That struggle was too strong, hateful and longlasting . . . that struggle was too great, hateful and longlasting.]

---

6   These are famously among the lines that caused Tolkien such difficulty; see his 'The Monsters and the Critics', pp. 294–5, and see further above, pp. 152–3.

7   For the poet's use of sleep as a metaphor in this and similar contexts, see, for example, Kavros, '*Swefan æfter symble*: the Feast-Sleep Theme in *Beowulf*'; McFadden, 'Sleeping after the Feast'.

But if Grendel is beyond the power and comprehension of the Danes, the lines which introduce the (as yet unnamed) hero Beowulf provide an opportunity for the poet to make clear how much his hero outstrips other men (lines 194–8a):

> Þæt fram ham gefrægn Higelaces þegn,
> god mid Geatum, Grendles dæda; 195
> se wæs moncynnes mægenes strengest
> on þæm dæge þysses lifes,
> æþele ond eacen.

[Hygelac's thegn, a good man among the Geats, learned about Grendel's deeds from home; he was of men the strongest in might on that day of this life, noble and vast.]

Beginning with a near-rhyme (*gefrægn . . . þegn*, line 194),[8] these lines emphasise both Beowulf's nobility and his pre-eminence; the use of the term 'vast' (*eacen*, line 198a) is particularly interesting in this context, since elsewhere in the poem the term is used only of the giant sword from the monster mere (lines 1663a [*ealdsweord eacen*] and 2140a [*eacnum ecgum*]), the monster mere itself (*eacne eardas*, line 1621a), the dragon (*eacencræftig*, line 2280a), and the dragon's cursed treasure (*eacencræftig*, line 3051b). Still more striking, however, is the way in which the poet effectively circumscribes Beowulf's power both in time and sphere of influence through alliteration of elements which do not normally carry either stress or alliteration: he was the strongest on *that* day of *this* life.[9] The poet repeats the phrase twice more in the battle between Beowulf and Grendel, using it once of each protagonist (*se þe manna wæs mægene strengest on þæm dæge þysses lifes*, lines 789–90 [Beowulf]; *on ðæm dæge þysses lifes*, line 806 [Grendel]).[10]

Storm-clouds over Denmark: Ingeld, Hrothulf, and Unferth

But if the Danes are condemned for their impotent reliance on the tabernacles of idols,[11] Beowulf himself is measured circumspectly *sub specie aeternitatis*.[12] A similar technique is used to undercut Hrothgar at the height of his success, after having built Heorot and, in accordance with approved practice, liberally distributed treasure. Having praised the Danish king the poet characteristically glances ahead, towards the tragic end of Hrothgar's beloved hall (lines 80–5):[13]

---

8 On rhyme in *Beowulf*, see above, pp. 61–9; a similar use of end-rhyme between half-lines is found in line 2258 (*herepad . . . gebad*).

9 On the poet's use of the phrase, see in particular Frank, 'The *Beowulf* Poet's Sense of History', p. 54.

10 On the use of the variant phrase *mægene strengest* in line 789b, see above, p. 55.

11 See especially Stanley, '*Hæthenra Hyht* in *Beowulf*', esp. pp. 141–51.

12 A similar technique is used to emphasise a contrast between this world and the next by the poets of *The Wanderer* on the one hand (line 58: *Forþon ic geþence ne mæg geond þas woruld* [my emphasis]) and *Deor* on the other (line 31: *Mæg þonne geþencan þæt geond þas woruld* [my emphasis]); indeed, the closely parallel phrasing of these last two lines (both in the Exeter Book) may perhaps indicate some kind of connection. See further Orchard, 'Re-reading *The Wanderer*', pp. 18–19.

13 In fact, the manuscript reads *secg hete* at line 84a, almost always emended to *se ecghete* through an assumption of haplography (on which see above, pp. 43–6). Elsewhere in the poem, however, the poet

He beot ne aleh,   beagas dælde,   80
sinc æt symle.   Sele hlifade,
heah ond horngeap,   heaðowylma bad,
laðan liges;   ne wæs hit lenge þa gen
þæt se ecghete   aþumsweorum,
æfter wælniðe   wæcnan scolde.   85

[He did not break his vow: he distributed rings, treasure at the banquet.
The hall towered, high and wide-gabled, it awaited the hostile surges of
the hateful flame; the time was not yet at hand that the sword-hatred
between father-in-law and son-in-law should awaken after deadly
hatred.]

Even when the paint is barely dry on this 'best of houses' (*husa selest*, lines 146,
285, 658, and 935; *foremærost . . . receda*, lines 309–10a; *reced selesta*, line
412), we are told how it will perish as a result of feuding between in-laws,
namely Hrothgar and his future son-in-law Ingeld;[14] the term chosen to depict
the feuding parties (*aþumsweorum*, line 84) has a particularly ironic ring
following close on the assertion that Hrothgar himself 'did not break his vow'
(*beot ne aleh*, line 80).[15] If we flash forward to Beowulf's own prophetic
account of this feud, we find strikingly parallel terms used (lines 2063–9a):[16]

'Þonne bioð abrocene   on ba healfe
aðsweorð eorla;   syððan Ingelde
weallað wælniðas,   ond him wiflufan   2065
æfter cearwælmum   colran weorðað.
Þy ic Heaðobeardna   hyldo ne telge,
dryhtsibbe dæl   Denum unfæcne,
freondscipe fæstne.'

['Then is broken on both sides the oath-swearing of men; afterwards for
Ingeld deadly hatred wells up, and love of his wife grows cold after the
surgings of care. For that reason I do not reckon the loyalty of the
Heathobards, their portion of the marriage-peace, without danger for the
Danes, their friendship firm.']

Here, as elsewhere, alliteration is used in an artful manner,[17] linking key
concepts in the final two lines of the tale proper (2065–6), before Beowulf's
concluding analysis: continued alliteration (*weallað wælniðas . . . wiflufan . . .*

---

seems to engage in wordplay on the homograph *secg* (meaning both 'man' and 'sword'), as well as on
the soundplay between *secg* (meaning 'man') and *ecg* (meaning 'sword'); see further above, pp. 76
and 185–6. Likewise, the manuscript actually reads *aþum swerian* at line 84b; Klaeber's suggestion,
that 'a scribe blundered, having in mind *að* ['oath'] and *swerian* ['to swear]' (*Beowulf*, p. 130), is the
more intriguing given the putative connection with *aðsweorð* ('oath-swearing', line 2064a) noted
below. One is tempted to suggest a deliberate pun on the part of the poet.

14 Cf. Eliason, 'The Burning of Heorot'.
15 For useful commentary on this passage, see too Shippey, *Beowulf*, pp. 29–30.
16 The manuscript clearly reads *að sweorð* at 2064a, but given the common confusion of *d* for *ð* (and
vice versa: see further above, pp. 42–6), several editors emend to *aðsweord*; in any case, an oath that
is broken is clearly what is intended.
17 On the *Beowulf*-poet's artful use of alliteration, see further above, pp. 61–9.

cearwælmum . . . weorðað), cross-alliteration (*cearwælmum colran weorðað*), and paronomasia (*weall-* / *wæl-* / *wælm-*) all play their part, and Ingeld's shifting emotions, from 'love of his wife' to 'deadly hatred', are encapsulated in a single line. Still more significantly, the poet puts into Beowulf's mouth the otherwise unattested noun *aðsweorð* ('oath-swearing', line 2064a) to signify the bonds that link Ingeld to Hrothgar, and which rupture into 'deadly hatred' (*wælniðas*, line 2065a), in a clear echo of the poet's own predictions of the fate of Heorot almost 2,000 lines earlier. Then, the poet had predicted a later stage of the ongoing feud, when Ingeld will attack Hrothgar in his hall and set Heorot ablaze; the use of the unusual term *aþumsweorum* ('father-in-law and son-in-law', line 84b), later echoed in *aðsweorð* ('oath-swearing', line 2064a), and of the poetic compound *wælniðe* ('deadly hatred', line 85a), which does not occur in the poem again until line 2065a (*wælniðas*), points to a deliberate connection.

Certainly, Beowulf extrapolates from his brief acquaintance with Freawaru and his patchy knowledge of her forthcoming wedding-arrangements a vivid and depressing picture of problems ahead. We have already seen from his earlier dealings with Unferth that Beowulf is no slouch at speechifying,[18] and in this section of his report he pulls out all the stops (lines 2032–56):[19]

> 'Mæg þæs þonne ofþyncan   ðeodne Heaðobeardna
> ond þegna gehwam   þara leoda,
> þonne he mid fæmnan   on flett gæð
> dryhtbearn Dena,   duguða biwenede.   2035
> On him gladiað   gomelra lafe,
> heard ond hringmæl   Heaðabeardna gestreon
> þenden hie ðam wæpnum   wealdan moston,
> oððæt hie forlæddan   to ðam lindplegan
> swæse gesiðas   ond hyra sylfra feorh.   2040
> Þonne cwið æt beore   se ðe beah gesyhð,
> eald æscwiga,   se ðe eall geman,
> garcwealm gumena   him bið grim sefa,
> onginneð geomormod   geongum cempan
> þurh hreðra gehygd   higes cunnian,   2045
> wigbealu weccean,   ond þæt word acwyþ
> "Meaht ðu, min wine,   mece gecnawan
> þone þin fæder   to gefeohte bær
> under heregriman   hindeman siðe,
> dyre iren,   þær hyne Dene slogon,   2050
> weoldon wælstowe,   syððan Wiðergyld læg,
> æfter hæleþa hryre,   hwate Scyldungas?
> Nu her þara banena   byre nathwylces
> frætwum hremig   on flet gæð,
> morðres gylpeð,   ond þone maðþum byreð,   2055
> þone þe ðu mid rihte   rædan sceoldest."'

---

18 For a detailed analysis of Beowulf's contest of words with Unferth, see below, pp. 247–55.
19 The manuscript reads *ðeoden* at line 2032b and *heaðabearna* at 2037b, but the emendations accepted here are commonplace. Cf. Smithers, 'Four Cruces in *Beowulf*', pp. 427–30.

['That may cause resentment to the ruler of the Heathobards, and to each of the warriors of those peoples when he, the wedding-attendant of the Danes, steps onto the floor with the woman, when they are nobly entertained. On him there gleam ancient heirlooms, hard and ring-patterned, the treasures of the Heathobards while they were able to wield their weapons, until they led to destruction in that shield-play their beloved companions and their own lives. Then there will speak at the beer-drinking one who sees a precious object, an aged spear-warrior, who has recalled it all, the spear-slaying of men – his spirit is grim – sad at heart he begins through the thoughts of his mind to test the courage of a young fighter, to stir up war-malice; and speaks the following words: "My friend, can you recognise the sword that your father bore to the fray beneath his battle-mask the last time, the fine blade, when the Danes struck him down, controlled the battlefield once Withergyld lay dead, after the fall of heroes, those brave Danes? Now here the son of one of those killers, exulting in his trappings, steps onto the floor, boasts of the killing and carries the treasure which you by right should control." ']

There are signs of considerable artistry here. The passage begins with repeated alliteration on *þ* (lines 2032–3) which lays stress on '*those* peoples' (*þara leoda*, line 2033b), and the tension is built up through the use of an envelope pattern which delays the commencement of the speech of the 'aged spear-warrior' (*cwið . . . acwyð*, lines 2041a and 2046b) and thereby focuses attention on the psychological and emotional turmoil of the protagonists (*geman . . . sefa . . . geomormod . . . hreðra gehygd higes cunnian*); the fact that it is a 'spear-warrior' (*æscwiga*, line 2042a) who recalls 'spear-slaying' (*garcwealm*, line 2043a) echoes Beowulf's earlier apprehension about the 'killing-spear' (*bongar*, line 2031a). The speech of this 'aged spear-warrior' is linked back to Beowulf's own description through verbal repetition (*on flett gæð*, line 2034b; *on flet gæð*, line 2054b). Even the fact that the unnamed 'aged spear-warrior', in inciting the unnamed 'young fighter' should apparently allude to the death of the otherwise unknown Withergyld only underlines the rhetorical force of Beowulf's words: although the name is attested elsewhere (notably as Withergield in *Widsith*, line 124a), it seems as likely that it is a nonce-formation, signifying 'repayment' or 'recompense'.[20] Moreover, the power of the poetry blurs the complexity of viewpoints being simultaneously presented: we hear what the 'young fighter' hears, and are perhaps only dimly aware that these are the projected words of a supposed 'aged spear-warrior' as imagined by Beowulf in a speech to his lord that is his placed in his mouth by the poet. The audience is three-fold: the 'young fighter', Hygelac, and ourselves, each of whom is addressed by their own authority: the 'aged spear-warrior', Beowulf, and the poet. The passage as a whole demonstrates perfectly this poet's use of a triple perspective: just as Hrothgar cannot foresee the outcome of his daughter's betrothal, although Beowulf, with the growing wisdom proper to a hero who will one day assume the throne, can; so too Beowulf cannot know the end of the feud, although the

---

[20] On meaningful personal names elsewhere in *Beowulf*, see above, pp. 172–3.

poet (and his audience) can.[21] A similar use of perspective is implicit in the other passages discussed above: the Danes who sacrifice to false gods through 'the hope of heathens' (*hæþenra hyht*, line 179a) are perceived by the Christian poet to be in fatal error; and Beowulf is acknowledged to be the mightiest of men, but only from a strictly historical and secular perspective: final judgment is suspended. There are levels of ignorance implicit in the poem, and the poet himself claims no ultimate knowledge.

It has been suggested that precisely this technique of juxtaposing different points of view, of combining explicit praise with implicit censure can be seen in the lengthy passage describing the gifts given to Beowulf after he defeats Grendel (lines 1011–29):[22]

Ne gefrægen ic þa mægþe maran weorode	
ymb hyra sincgyfan sel gebæran.	
Bugon þa to bence blædagande,	
fylle gefægon; fægere geþægon	
medoful manig magas þara	1015
swiðhicgende on sele þam hean,	
Hroðgar ond Hroþulf. Heorot innan wæs	
freondum afylled; nalles facenstafas	
þeodscyldingas þenden fremedon.	
Forgeaf þa Beowulfe brand Healfdenes	1020
segen gyldenne sigores to leane;	
hroden hildecumbor, helm ond byrnan,	
mære maðþumsweord manige gesawon	
beforan beorn beran. Beowulf geþah	
ful on flette; no he þære feohgyfte	1025
for sceotendum scamigan ðorfte.	
Ne gefrægn ic freondlicor feower madmas	

---

21 Similar levels of perspective have been seen in the Finn-episode (above, pp. 173–87), with which, indeed, the Ingeld-episode is often directly compared; see, for example, Anderson, 'Formulaic Typescene Survival: Finn, Ingeld, and the *Nibelungenlied*'; Hart, 'Tectonic Design, Formulaic Craft, and Literary Execution'. Other noteworthy discussions of the Ingeld-episode include Hoops, 'Time and Place in the Ingeld Episode of *Beowulf*'; Malone, 'Ingeld'; *idem*, 'Freawaru'; *idem*, 'The Tale of Ingeld'; Steadman, 'The Ingeld-Episode in *Beowulf*: History or Prophecy?'. Most discussions of Ingeld include reference to Alcuin's famous question (derived from Jerome), berating monks for listening to secular heroic tales: 'What has Ingeld to do with Christ?' (*Quid Hinieldus cum Christo?*). On the historical background to Alcuin's outburst, see now Bullough, 'What has Ingeld to do with Lindisfarne?'.

22 The manuscript reads *hilte cumbor* at line 1022a and *scotenum* at line 1026a; the latter is apparently a scribal error of a common kind (see above, pp. 42–6), while the former is interesting in as much as the scribe has apparently mistaken the common element *hild(e)-* (on which see above, pp. 69–72) for a form of *hilt* ('hilt'; cf, lines 1574a, 1614b, 1668b, 1677a, 1687b, and 2987a), presumably because of the double mention of a sword (lines 1020b and 1023a). The syntax of line 1020, with Hrothgar apparently the unexpressed subject and the same sword apparently mentioned twice, has caused consternation to many, who would emend *brand* in 1020b to *bearn* ('son'). It may be that there has been eye-skip from a now-lost half-line *bearn Healfdenes* (describing who gave the sword) to *brand Halfdenes* (describing whose sword was given). See further Kuhn, 'The Sword of Healfdene'; *idem*, 'Further Thoughts on *brand Healfdenes*'; Mitchell, '*Beowulf*, line 1020b: *brand* or *bearn*?'; Watanabe, 'Final Words on *Beowulf* 1020b: *brand Healfdenes*'. It has been argued that similar eye-skip occurs elsewhere in the manuscript (see above, pp. 45–7), and the resulting identification of men and swords has been identified as another *leitmotif* of the poem (see above, pp. 76, 185–6, and 240–1).

golde gegyrede   gummanna fela
in ealobence   oðrum gesellan.

[I never heard of people in a greater company behave better in the presence of their treasure-giver. They went to the bench, exulting in glory,
rejoiced in the feast; courteously received many a mead-cup, their resolute kinsmen in that high hall, Hrothgar and Hrothulf. Heorot was filled
with friends; no wicked acts did the mighty Scyldings perform at that
time. Then [Hrothgar] gave Beowulf Healfdene's sword, and a golden
standard, a decorated battle-banner, as a reward for victory, also a
helmet and corslet; many saw the famous precious sword brought
before the warrior. Beowulf received the cup in the hall; he did not need
to be ashamed on account of that costly gift in the presence of
fighting-men. I never heard in a friendlier fashion of four treasures
decked with gold given to another on an ale-bench of many men.]

Sandwiched between the poet's assurance of the excellence of all that he is reporting (*Ne gefrægen . . . maran*, line 1011; *Ne gefrægn ic freondlicor*, line
1027a) is what has been interpreted as a darker vision: that of Hrothgar and
Hrothulf, uncle and nephew, apparent representatives of the old and young
factions in the hall (cf. *duguþe ond geogoþe*, lines 160b, 621a, and 1674a).
Amid the scenes of merriment, beautifully conveyed with rhyme (*gefægon . . .
gepægon*), assonance (*gefægon fægere gepægon*), and wordplay (*fylle . . .
medoful*) appearing together in three consecutive half-lines (lines 1014–15a),
other perspectives are offered.

From a number of other sources we know that Hrothulf, who of all the characters in *Beowulf* has been called 'the blankest',[23] was a major figure in Scandinavian legend,[24] much better known than Hrothgar whom (according to Norse
sources) he succeeded to the Danish crown, subsequently sending into exile
Hrothgar's sons, Hrethric and Hrothgar. In particular, Saxo Grammaticus tells
us that a certain Rolvo (Old English Hrothulf), son of Helgo (Old English
Halga), son of Haldanus (Old English Healfdene) killed Røricus (Old English
Hrethric), before he himself was killed by another of the Danish royal line of the
Scyldings, Hiarwarthus (Old English Heoroweard, son of Heorogar, son of
Healfdene).[25] But in *Beowulf* all these events are in the future, and Hrothulf's
precise role is unclear.[26] It has therefore been suggested that the poet is using
the word *þenden* ('at that time', line 1019b) in a loaded way, looking forward to
the end of the very friendship the poet is apparently celebrating.[27] As with the
earlier remark introducing Beowulf as the strongest on *that* day of *this* life, it is

23 Shippey, *Beowulf*, p. 32.
24 See above, pp. 219–21 and 244–7.
25 For the relevant chapters, see Olrik and Raeder, ed., *Saxonis Gesta Danorum*, II.vi–viii (pp. 48–63);
    cf. Davidson and Fisher, *Saxo Grammaticus*, I.51–64. See too the on-line text of the *Gesta Danorum*
    (details in section C of the Bibliography). For the family relationships of the Scyldings, see the Gene-
    alogy on p. xiv.
26 For a range of attempts to explain the role and function of Hrothulf in *Beowulf*, see, for example,
    Bremmer, 'The Importance of Kinship'; Kluge, 'Der Beowulf und die Hrolfs saga kraka'; McDavid,
    'Hroþulf, Hengest, and Beowulf'; Morgan, 'The Treachery of Hrothulf'.
27 Klaeber (*Beowulf*, p. 169) considers the comment 'unquestionably an allusion to Hro[th]ulf's treach-
    ery in later times', but Sisam, *The Structure of 'Beowulf'*, pp. 34–43, disagrees.

notable that the key word *þenden* ('at that time', line 1019b) is both stressed and carries alliteration, in a way which is unusual, to say the least.[28]

An equally ambiguous later scene in *Beowulf* also depicts Hrothgar and Hrothulf together, as Wealhtheow bustles about the hall immediately after the so-called Finn-episode,[29] itself of course a story of kin-slaying and betrayal in which the Danes are centrally involved (lines 1162b–68a):[30]

> Þa cwom Wealhþeo forð
> gan under gyldnum beage, þær þa godan twegen
> sæton suhtergefæderan; þa gyt wæs hiera sib ætgædere,
> æghwylc oðrum trywe. Swylce þær Unferþ þyle   1165
> æt fotum sæt frean Scyldinga; gehwylc hiora his ferhþe treowde,
> þæt he hæfde mod micel, þeah þe he his magum nære
> arfæst æt ecga gelacum.

> [Then Wealhtheow came forth, striding under a golden diadem, where the goodly pair, sat together, uncle and nephew; at that time their kinship was still intact, each true to the other. Likewise Unferth the *þyle* sat there at the foot of the lord of the Scyldings; each of them trusted his spirit, that he had great courage, even though he was not merciful to his kinsmen at the play of swords.]

These lines stand out from the surrounding material by reason of their metre, a factor which suggests that they need to be read as a unit.[31] The appearance of Wealhtheow follows hard upon the end of the Finn-episode, in which attention has been focused on the political impotence of Hildeburh, once a proud queen.[32] The very awkwardness of the juxtaposition ought to serve as a warning not to take the scene too readily at face value; the mention of Unferth, here acknowledged to be the kin-slayer that Beowulf had earlier reckoned him to be, is equally disturbing: the internal verbal echoes (*æghwylc . . . trywe*, line 1165a; *gehwylc . . . treowde*, line 1166b) only underline the fragility of the situation, and the extent to which 'faith' is not a commodity to be taken for granted among these people, or at least not taken for granted for too long. One might note that the two characters of Hrothgar and Hrothulf are found linked together in surviving Old English outside *Beowulf* also, in *Widsith*, lines 45–9:[33]

> Hroþwulf ond Hroðgar heoldon lengest   45
> sibbe ætsomne suhtorfædenan
> siþþan hy forwræcon Wicinga cynn
> ond Ingeldes ord forbigdan
> forheowan æt Heorote Heaðobeardna þrym

---

28 The word *þenden* occurs fourteen times in *Beowulf* (lines 30a, 57b, 284b, 1019b, 1177b, 1224b, 1859a, 2038a, 2418a, 2499b, 2649b, 2985a, 3027a, and 3100a), but only carries the alliteration here and (perhaps) in line 284b, in a parallel passage.

29 For a detailed discussion of the Finn-episode (including these very lines), see above, pp. 173–86.

30 The manuscript clearly reads *hun ferþ* at 1165b, its customary spelling of his name.

31 On the use of such metrical clues in *Beowulf*, see above, pp. 66–9.

32 On the juxtaposition, see above, pp. 219–22.

33 See further Chambers, *Widsith*, pp. 81–4; Malone, *Widsith*, p. 176.

[Hroþwulf [= Hrothulf] and Hrothgar kept peace together longest, uncle and nephew, after they had driven off the race of Wicingas and humiliated Ingeld's vanguard, cut down the might of the Heathobards at Heorot.]

One notes here the same *dvandva*-compound, *suhtorfœderan* (line 46b) that we find elsewhere in extant Old English only in the parallel passage from *Beowulf* (*suhtergefœderan*, line 1164a).[34]

It is against this background of the implicit undermining of positive images and the constant reminders that what we see is only a partial picture that the explicit verbal attack on Beowulf by Unferth is perhaps best to be viewed. Like Hrothulf, with whom he is seen in the unsettling tableau just discussed, Unferth appears an ambiguous figure who continues to fascinate generations of critics, for whom even the spelling of his name, let alone its meaning, is a point of contention.[35] We are told that Beowulf's father was well-known at Hrothgar's court, and perhaps even swore an oath of allegiance (if that is the force of what Hrothgar says in line 470b: *he me aþas swor*); Hrothgar himself claims to have known Beowulf as a boy (*Ic hine cuðe cnihtwesende*, line 372), the utter disingenuousness of the opening question posed by Unferth seems therefore particularly striking (lines 506–10a):[36]

'Eart þu se Beowulf,   se þe wið Brecan wunne,
on sidne sæ   ymb sund flite,
ðær git for wlence   wada cunnedon
ond for dolgilpe   on deop wæter
aldrum neþdon?'   510

['Are you that Beowulf who contended with Breca on the wide sea, competed in the surge, where the two of you out of pride made trial of the waters, and for a foolish boast risked your lives in deep water?']

Such an opening salvo cannot be interpreted as anything other than extremely aggressive, even ignoring the direct statement from the poet that in speaking Unferth 'unbound a battle-rune' (*onband beadurune*, line 501a). Unferth's precise position within the court has been much debated; some would reduce the

---

34 On the possibility of a direct connection between *Beowulf* and *Widsith*, see above, pp. 115–16.
35 There are a large number of discussions of Unferth's role in *Beowulf*, of which the following may be said to be symptomatic: Baird, 'Unferth the þyle'; Bjork, 'Unferth in the Hermeneutic Circle'; Bloomfield, '*Beowulf* and Christian Allegory'; Britton, 'Unferth, Grendel and the Christian Meaning of *Beowulf*'; Clover, 'The Germanic Context of the Unferþ Episode'; Enright, 'The Warband Context of the Unferth Episode'; Fulk, 'Unferth and his Name'; Gingher, 'The Unferth Perplex'; Hardy, 'The Christian Hero Beowulf and Unferð þyle'; Hollowell, 'Unferð the þyle in *Beowulf*'; Hughes, 'Beowulf, Unferth and Hrunting: an Interpretation'; Kabell, 'Unferð und die dänischen Biersitten'; Nagy, 'A Reassessment of Unferð's Fratricide in *Beowulf*'; Ogilvy, 'Unferth: Foil to Beowulf?'; Pope, '*Beowulf* 505, "gehedde", and the Pretensions of Unferth'; Roberts, 'Old English UN–Very and Unferþ'; Robinson, 'Personal Names in Medieval Narrative and the Name of Unferth in *Beowulf*'; Rosenberg, 'The Necessity of Unferth'; Rosier, 'Design for Treachery: the Unferth Intrigue'; Silber, 'Unferth: Another Look at the Emendation'; *idem*, 'Rhetoric as Prowess in the Unferð Episode'; Vaughan, 'A Reconsideration of "Unferð" '.
36 On Breca in general, see Lawrence, 'The Breca Episode in *Beowulf*'; McNamara, 'Legends of Breca and Beowulf'; Nelles, 'Beowulf's *sorhfullne sið* with Breca'; Wentersdorf, 'Beowulf's Adventure with Breca'.

status of his stated role as *þyle* (1165b and 1456b), sitting at Hrothgar's feet (*æt fotum sæt frean Scyldinga*, line 500 and 1166a) to no more than that of a kind of court-jester, but alongside the appearance of the word glossing Latin *scurra* ('buffoon') we find *gelæred þyle* glossing Latin *doctus orator* ('learned speaker').[37] As a character with a specific, even celebrated, lineage (Ecglaf, his father, is named four times in lines 499b, 590b, 1465b, and 1808a), who is the owner of a splendid sword (Hrunting is likewise named four times in lines 1457b, 1490b, 1659b, and 1807b), he appears to have played a significant (if perhaps not very honourable) role in the Danish succession. The lines immediately preceding his verbal assault on Beowulf describe not a coward or a scoundrel, but a man with a sense of his own status and a keen eye to personal glory (lines 501b–5):[38]

> wæs him Beowulfes sið,
> modges merefaran,   micel æfþunca,
> forþon þe he ne uþe   þæt ænig oðer man
> æfre mærða þon ma   middangeardes
> gehedde under heofenum   þonne he sylfa.   505

[To him the voyage of Beowulf, the bold seafarer, was a great irritant, since he would not allow that any other man in the world should ever pay more heed to glorious deeds under heaven than he did himself.]

At all events, Unferth's speech is a cunning, even witty, attack of a supposed piece of folly by both Beowulf and Breca (lines 510b–528):[39]

>   'Ne inc ænig mon,   510
> ne leof ne lað,   belean mihte
> sorhfullne sið,   þa git on sund reon.
> Þær git eagorstream   earmum þehton,
> mæton merestræta,   mundum brugdon,
> glidon ofer garsecg;   geofon yþum weol,   515
> wintrys wylmum.   Git on wæteres æht
> seofon niht swuncon;   he þe æt sunde oferflat,
> hæfde mare mægen.   Þa hine on morgentid
> on Heaþoræmas   holm up ætbær;
> ðonon he gesohte   swæsne .ᛟ.   520
> leof his leodum,   lond Brondinga,
> freoðoburh fægere,   þær he folc ahte,
> burh ond beagas.   Beot eal wið þe
> sunu Beanstanes   soðe gelæste.
> Ðonne wene ic to þe   wyrsan geþingea,   525
> ðeah þu heaðoræsa   gehwær dohte,
> grimre guðe,   gif þu Grendles dearst
> nihtlongne fyrst   nean bidan.'

---

37 Cf. the remarks of Bjork, 'Unferth in the Hermeneutic Circle'.

38 For the interpretation of *gehedde* (line 505a) I follow Pope, '*Beowulf* 505, "gehedde", and the Pretensions of Unferth'.

39 The manuscript reads *wylm* at 516a (through haplography?). On the use of the rune .ᛟ. for *eþel* in line 520b, see above, p. 40.

['Nor could any man, friend or foe, dissuade the two of you from your painful trip, when you two thrashed about in the surge, where the pair of you encompassed with your arms the flowing streams, measured out the briny paths, swept them with your hands, glided over the ocean. The deep seethed with waves, winter's swell; you two toiled for seven nights in the water's domain; he surpassed you in the surge, had greater might; then in the morning the sea swept him up on the land of the Heathoremes. From there he made for his dear homeland, dear to his people, the land of the Brondings, the fair stronghold. The son of Beanstan truly fulfilled his whole vow to you. So I expect a worse outcome from you, however much you have prospered everywhere in conflicts, grim battle, if you dare to wait close at hand for Grendel through the night.']

The verbal display is impressive, a piece of careful patterning: the fourfold description of Beowulf and Breca at sea is a splendid thumbnail sketch, with its steady repetition of preterite verbs and different patterns evident in the b-lines (*earmum þehton . . . mundum brugdon*) and the a-lines (*mæton merestræta . . . glidon ofer garsecg*). The ambiguity of all these terms, which might well apply to either rowing or swimming, is surely calculated; as Roberta Frank has indicated, Unferth seems deliberately to have used the equally ambiguous term *sund* no fewer than three times in the twenty-three lines of his speech (507a, 512b, and 517b), playing on the prosaic meaning 'swimming' of a term that in verse means 'sea', and so lending a fantastic quality to a marine contest that lasts a whole week.[40] Unferth's claim is that Beowulf failed to live up to his promise, and that the whole contest was undertaken 'for pride and a foolish boast' (*for wlence . . . ond for dolgilpe*, lines 508a and 509a), again terms which appear here to contain negative connotations.[41]

But if Unferth's speech is a cunning composition, it is more than matched by that of Beowulf.[42] Nowhere, however, does Beowulf deny the basic charge of youthful folly; indeed, he concedes it twice at the very start, as he effectively throws Unferth's words back in his face (lines 530–43):

'Hwæt! þu worn fela,   wine min Unferð,   530
beore druncen   ymb Brecan spræce,
sægdest from his siðe.   Soð ic talige,
þæt ic merestrengo   maran ahte,
earfeþo on yþum,   ðonne ænig oþer man.
Wit þæt gecwædon   cnihtwesende   535
ond gebeotedon   (wæron begen þa git
on geogoðfeore)   þæt wit on garsecg ut
aldrum neðdon,   ond þæt geæfndon swa.

40 Frank, ' "Mere" and "Sund": Two Sea-Changes in *Beowulf*'.
41 The phrase *for wlence* (in the form *for wlenco*) occurs in the poem on two further occasions: at 338a (where it is used by the coastguard in an apparently positive sense to describe Beowulf's own reasons for coming to Denmark), and at 1206a (where it is used in an apparently negative sense to refer to Hygelac's ill-fated final trip). On *dol-* compounds elsewhere in the poem, see below, pp. 261–2.
42 On Beowulf as a skilful speaker, see Baker, 'Beowulf the Orator'; Barringer, 'Adding Insult to the Inquiry'; Silber, 'Rhetoric as Prowess in the Unferð Episode'. Also see above, pp. 208–18.

Hæfdon swurd nacod,   þa wit on sund reon,
heard on handa;   wit unc wið hronfixas   540
werian þohton.   No he wiht fram me
flodyþum feor   fleotan meahte,
hraþor on holme;   no ic fram him wolde.'

['Listen! You have said a great deal, Unferth my friend, about Breca, spoken of his experience. I reckon it true that I had greater sea-strength, hardships on the waves, than any other man. We two spoke when we were lads, and made vows – we were at that time both young – that we would risk our lives out on the ocean; and we brought it about. We held drawn swords, hard in our hands when we two thrashed about in the surge – we thought to protect ourselves against whales – not a bit could he float far from me on the sea-waves, quicker in the water, nor did I want to leave him.']

Beowulf, however, does not simply repeat phrases from Unferth's own speech (*aldrum neþdon*, line 510a: *aldrum neðdon*, line 538a; *þa git on sund reon*, line 512b: *þa wit on sund reon*, line 539b), much in the same way as in *The Battle of Maldon*, Byrhtnoth casts back the words of the Viking messenger in his teeth;[43] he also seems to echo elements of Hrothgar's immediately preceding speech.[44] Just as Hrothgar began by courteously addressing Beowulf as his friend (*wine min Beowulf*, line 457b; cf. line 1704b), so too, in the only other occurrence of the phrase, Beowulf extends the courtesy to the distinctly discourteous Unferth (*wine min Unferð*, line 530b). Hrothgar had lamented the fact that while many of his retainers had sworn formal vows by the drinking of beer to defeat Grendel (*gebeotedon beore druncne*, line 480), none had accomplished their vow; Beowulf calmly points out that while Unferth has undoubtedly drunk some beer (*beore druncen*, line 531a), the vows that Beowulf and Breca swore (*gebeotedon*, line 536a) were fully accomplished.[45] Beowulf underlines the partial nature of Unferth's account by stating that he has only told what occurred from Breca's point of view (*ymb Brecan . . . from his siðe*, lines 531b–532a): a seven-day struggle that saw Breca, whose role as a prince of the Brondings is supported in *Widsith* (line 25a: *Breoca [weold] Brondingum*),[46] cast up on the shores of the Heathoreamas.

Beowulf, by contrast, vouches only for the five nights that he and Breca were together,[47] before the tides separated them (lines 544–8):

---

[43] So, for example, one might compare the messenger's *garræs mid gafole forgyldon* (line 32) with Byrhtnoth's *to gafole garras syllan* (line 46; note the reversal of word-order, and the phrase *gofol syllan* in line 61b); the messenger's *we willaþ mid þam sceattum us to scype gangan* (line 40) with Byrhtnoth's *þæt ge mid urum sceattum to scype gangon* (line 56); the messenger's *we swa hearde* (line 33a) with Byrhtnoth's *ge swa softe* (line 59a). See further Robinson, 'Some Aspects of the *Maldon*-Poet's Artistry'; Orchard, 'The *Hisperica famina* as Literature', p. 8.

[44] Again, a good parallel is to be found in *The Battle of Maldon*: compare the narrator's *se on beot abead brimliþendra* (line 27) with Byrhtnoth's *Brimmana boda abeod eft ongean* (line 49).

[45] The words need not imply, as they are usually taken, that Unferth was drunk; on the use of the term 'drunk' here, see in general Gould, 'Euphemistic Renderings of the Word *druncen* in *Beowulf*'; Magennis, 'The *Beowulf* Poet and his *druncne dryhtguman*'.

[46] See further Malone, *Widsith*, pp. 133–4.

[47] Some scholars have made heavy weather of the disparity between the two accounts, but there is no need to assume that the poet has slipped up here: Beowulf only comments on the time that he and Breca were together, and leaves Unferth to account for the rest. For an interesting analogue to the

'Đa wit ætsomne   on sæ wæron
fif nihta fyrst,   oþþæt unc flod todraf,   545
wado weallende,   wedera cealdost,
nipende niht,   ond norþanwind
heaðogrim ondhwearf;   hreo wæron yþa.'

['Then we two were on the sea together for the space of five nights, until the flood separated us, surging waves, coldest of weathers, darkening night, and the north wind battle-fierce drove us apart: the waves were rough.']

We can all applaud the undoubtedly heroic exploits of Breca, who clearly fulfils the terms of the vow that, according to Beowulf, they had both made: assuredly he 'risked his life out on the ocean'. But in Beowulf's description, there is no mention of a direct contest, merely a shared exploit in which, however hard Breca tried to shake off Beowulf, it was left to the might of a wintry storm that Unferth passes over in two half-lines (lines 515b–516a), and Beowulf elaborates in six (lines 546–8) to separate the pair. The great bulk of the rest of Beowulf's speech (and nearly half of the speech as a whole) is taken up not with any supposed contest with Breca but with Beowulf's own monster-slaying exploits after he and Breca had been separated. The whole of this section of the narrative appears to be an elaboration of Beowulf's earlier claim to Hrothgar that he had slain 'sea-monsters by night' (*niceras nihtes*, line 422a; cf. *niceras . . . on niht*, line 575), and, in effect, Beowulf tells the same tale twice (lines 549–58 and 559–79a).[48] The first of these accounts concludes by saying that, although harassed by these sea-beasts and protected by his mailshirt, nonetheless he was able to wield his sword to good effect (lines 555b–8):

'hwæþre me gyfeþe wearð   555
þæt ic aglæcan   orde geræhte,
hildebille;   heaþoræs fornam
mihtig meredeor   þurh mine hand.'

['Yet it was granted to me that I pierced the awesome assailants with my war-blade; a battle-rush snatched off the mighty sea-beasts through my hand.']

In the second account, which concludes in a very similar fashion (*hwæþere me gesælde þæt ic mid sweorde ofsloh niceras nigene*, lines 574–5a), Beowulf again echoes his earlier speech to Hrothgar by demonstrating his black humour, this time punning not on his own demise (as in lines 445–51),[49] but on that of the sea-monsters, whom he portrays as (quite literally) served ill by one they had hoped to have for dinner (lines 559–69a):[50]

Breca-episode from *Egils saga einhenda ok Ásmundar berserkjabana*, chapter 9, in which the hero gets separated in a swimming-match and wanders alone for two days, see above, pp. 126–7.

[48] For a similar technique of telling the same tale in multiple versions (Unferth's own account represents yet another perspective), see Huisman, 'The Three Tellings of Beowulf's Fight with Grendel's Mother'.

[49] On which, see above, p. 213.

[50] For the puns, see, for example, Rosier, 'The Uses of Association: Hands and Feasts in *Beowulf*'; Foley, 'Feasts and Anti-Feasts'.

'Swa mec gelome   laðgeteonan
þreatedon þearle.   Ic him þenode   560
deoran sweorde,   swa hit gedefe wæs.
Næs hie ðære fylle   gefean hæfdon,
manfordædlan,   þæt hie me þegon,
symbel ymbsæton   sægrunde neah;
ac on mergenne   mecum wunde   565
be yðlafe   uppe lægon,
sweordum aswefede,   þæt syðþan na
ymb brontne ford   brimliðende
lade ne letton.'

['So, often, the hateful persecutors closely oppressed me; I served them
with my splendid sword, as was fitting. In no way did those wicked creatures have joy of their feast, that they might consume me as they sat at
their feast near the sea-floor; but in the morning, wounded by my blade
they lay up along the sea-shore, put to sleep by my sword, so that never
afterwards did they hinder seafarers in their travels.']

Beowulf tops off this section of his reply with a typically gritty gnomic saying:
'fate often spares an undoomed man, if his courage suffices' (*Wyrd oft nereð /
unfægne eorl, þonne his ellen deah*, lines 572b–573). He continues his version
of the story with a clear echo of what he had said before (compare lines 574–5a
with 555b–556 above), before turning to criticise Unferth directly (lines
574–89):[51]

'Hwæþere me gesælde   þæt ic mid sweorde ofsloh
niceras nigene.   No ic on niht gefrægn   575
under heofones hwealf   heardran feohtan,
ne on egstreamum   earmran mannon;
hwaþere ic fara feng   feore gedigde,
siþes werig.   Ða mec sæ oþbær,
flod æfter faroðe   on Finna land,   580
wadu weallendu.   No ic wiht fram þe
swylcra searoniða   secgan hyrde,
billa brogan.   Breca næfre git
æt heaðolace,   ne gehwæþer incer,
swa deorlice   dæd gefremede   585
fagum sweordum.   No ic þæs soþæs gylpe,
þeah ðu þinum broðrum   to banan wurde,
heafodmægum;   þæs þu in healle scealt
werhðo dreogan,   þeah þin wit duge.'

['Yet it was granted me that I slew with my sword nine water-monsters. I
have not heard of a harder fight under the vault of heaven, nor a man

---

51 There are a number of textual problems here: the manuscript reads *hwaþere* in line 578a (on *a/æ*-
confusion, see above, pp. 42 and 45–6); *wudu* in line 581 (on *a/u*-confusion, see above, pp. 42–6); *no
ic þæs gylpe* in line 586b (*soþæs* has been supplied, following Bammesberger, 'The Emendation of
Beowulf, l. 586', and assuming eye-skip through homoeoteleuton [on which see above, pp. 45–7]); . . .
e sceall in line 588b (*healle* has been partly supplied from Thorkelin A and B, which both read *helle*;
on the change from *helle* to *healle*, see n. 54 below); *þeah þin . . . uge* in line 589b (the letters *wit d-*
have been supplied from Thorkelin A).

more wretched in the mighty streams; yet I escaped with my life the clutches of my foes, weary of my journey. Then the sea bore me up, the flood from the current in the land of the Finns, the surging waves. I have not heard tell a jot about such dire straits in your case, terror of swords. Breca never yet in battle-play, nor either of you pair, did so brave a deed with patterned swords. I don't brag of the truth, even though you turned out to be the slayer of your brothers, your chief kinsmen; for that you shall suffer condemnation in the hall, even though your wit may suffice.']

This section of Beowulf's speech is clearly structured through repetition (*No ic . . . No ic . . . No ic*, lines 575b, 581b, and 586b), as Beowulf turns the spotlight from his own heroism to Unferth's shame. The textual difficulties of the passage make the precise import of Beowulf's words difficult to assess, although evidently he is reacting to Unferth's criticisms with a few home-truths of his own. Given the commonplace nature of accusations of fratricide in such flytings or formal exchanges of abuse, generally exchanged before battle,[52] however, we cannot be sure that Unferth really is (at least at this point) a killer of his kin,[53] notwithstanding the poet's own later assertions that Unferth was a trusted figure in the Danish court 'even though he was not merciful to his kinsmen at the play of swords' (*þeah he his magum nære / arfæst æt ecga gelacum*, lines 1167b–8a). Likewise, despite the witness of both Thorkelin A and B that the manuscript read *helle* ('hell') rather than *healle* ('hall') at line 588b, it seems perhaps safer to assume that a christianising scribe rather than Beowulf himself has condemned Unferth to be damned in hell.[54]

At all events, and although this section of his speech might seem the peak of

---

52 See in particular Clover, 'The Germanic Context of the Unferþ Episode'; Harris, 'The *Senna*: From Description to Literary Theory'; Parks, 'Flyting and Fighting: Pathways in the Realization of the Epic Contest'; *idem*, *Vernal Duelling in Heroic Narrative*.

53 See now Nagy, 'A Reassessment of Unferð's Fratricide in *Beowulf*'.

54 For this reading, see Robinson, 'Elements of the Marvellous', pp. 129–30. For similar signs of a putative 'christianising scribe' see line 1983a, where the *ð* of the original reading *hæðnū* ('heathens') has been erased by the scribe, who is presumably as puzzled as modern scholars by an apparently random reference to Geats as 'heathens' in his exemplar; most modern editions emend to *hæleðum* ('warriors'). A similar case may be found in line 1816a, where the manuscript clearly reads *helle*, and most editors emend to *hæle* ('man', 'hero'). Likewise, the manuscript clearly reads *fyrena* ('sins') at line 2250b, generally emended to *fyra* ('fires'). More problematic cases where a scribe may have introduced a christianising reading are *drihten wereda* ('lord of hosts') at line 2186a and *for metode* ('for god') at line 169a. In the first instance, the phrases *wereda drihten* and *drihten wereda* apply to god in a large number of extant Old English poems (*Genesis*, lines 255b, 352b, 386b, 1362a, 1411b, and 2382b; *Exodus*, lines 8b and 92a; *Daniel*, line 220b; *Christ and Satan*, lines 197b and 580b; *Andreas*, lines 173a, 435a, 727b, 1206b, and 1663b; *Soul and Body I*, line 14b; *Homiletic Fragment I*, lines 7b and 10b; *Elene*, line 896b; *Christ I*, line 428b; *Guthlac A*, line 134b; *Descent into Hell*, lines 120b, 126b, and 133b; *Judith*, line 342a; *Metres of Boethius* 20, line 86b; *Paris Psalter* 79.16, line 4, 83.3, line 1, 88.5, line 1, and 103.29, line 1b; *Psalm 50*, lines 30a, 36a, 94b, and 121a; *Psalm Fragment* 50.13, line 3b; *Instructions to Christians*, line 193b; *Gloria 2*, line 1), and most editors emend to *drihten Wedera* ('lord of the Geats'); in the second instance, it has been argued that what is intended is the past tense of a notional verb *formetian* (on the model of *forhicgan*), meaning 'despise': see further Bammesberger, 'Five *Beowulf* Notes', pp. 243–8, and on the general problem Chaney, 'Grendel and the *Gifstol*: a Legal View of Monsters'; Kaske, 'The *Gifstol* Crux in *Beowulf*'; Ono, 'Grendel's Not Greeting the *gifstol* Reconsidered'; Robinson, 'Why is Grendel's Not Greeting the Gifstol a Wræc Micel?'. For an apparent example of a christianising scribe elsewhere in Old English, see *Christ II*, line 485a, where the manuscript reads clearly *heofonum* ('heavens'), but editors generally emend to *hæþnum* ('heathens').

his response, it is interesting to observe that Beowulf continues his reply to
Unferth in a way which subtly seems to undermine not merely Unferth, but all
the Danes (lines 590–603a):[55]

> 'Secge ic þe to soðe,   sunu Ecglafes,   590
> þæt næfre Grendel swa fela   gryra gefremede,
> atol æglæca,   ealdre þinum,
> hynðo on Heorote,   gif þin hige wære,
> sefa swa searogrim,   swa þu self talast.
> Ac he hafað onfunden   þæt he þa fæhðe ne þearf,   595
> atole ecgþræce   eower leode
> swiðe onsittan,   Sigescyldinga;
> nymeð nydbade,   nænegum arað
> leode Deniga,   ac he lust wigeð,
> swefeð ond snedeþ,   secce ne weneþ   600
> to Gardenum.   Ac ic him Geata sceal
> eafoð ond ellen   ungeara nu,
> guþe gebeodan.'

['I tell you for a truth, son of Ecglaf, that Grendel would never have
carried out such terrors, that dread assailant, against your lord, humilia-
tion in Heorot, if your spirit, your heart was as cunningly fierce, as you
yourself reckon. But he has found out that he does not need greatly to
fear the enmity and dread sword-clash of your people, the
Victory-Scyldings; he extracts a needful contribution, he honours none
of the people of the Danes, but he exercises his will, he kills and preys,
and expects no fighting from the Spear-Danes. But I shall show him
very soon the power and courage and conflict of the Geats.']

Beowulf begins by asserting 'truth', just as he did at the opening of his reply
(*Soð ic talige*, line 532b),[56] but moves quickly away from a personal attack on
Unferth to more general comments on his people: the change from 'your
[singular] lord' (*ealdre þinum*, line 592b) to 'your [plural] people' (*eower leode*,
line 596b) is masterful, and the repeated references to the Danes (*Sigescyldinga
. . . Deniga . . . Gardenum*, lines 597b, 599a, and 601a) emphasise the switch.
That the Danes at this point are described as 'Victory-Scyldings' (*Sigescyldinga*,
line 597b) and 'Spear-Danes' (*Gardenum*, line 601a) at this least martial and

---

55 In fact, the manuscript reads *gre del* at line 591a, but the emendation is a simple one, and (almost)
universally accepted. Likewise, the manuscript reads *sendeþ* ('sends') at line 600a, a reading which
some (like Klaeber, ed., *Beowulf*, pp. 151–2) retain on the grounds of a supposed parallel with the
Vergilian *mittere Orco* ('to send to the underworld') or *mittere umbris* ('to send to the shades'). See
too Liberman, 'Germanic *Sendan* "To Make a Sacrifice"'. It seems, however, easier to assume scribal
metathesis (on which see above, pp. 43–5) for *snedeþ* or *snædeþ* (on e for æ see above, pp. 42 and
45–6), and to posit a verb *snædan* meaning 'to eat', 'swallow' (cf. line 743a: *synsnædum swealh*
['(Grendel) swallowed in huges bites']). Such a reading has the advantage of providing with *swefeþ*
(lit. 'put to sleep') an association between feasting and sleeping that is a *leitmotif* of the poem as a
whole: see, for example, Kavros, '*Swefan æfter symble*: the Feast-Sleep Theme in *Beowulf*';
Magennis, '*Beowulf*, 1008a: *swefeþ æfter symle*'; McFadden, 'Sleeping after the Feast: Deathbeds,
Marriage Beds, and the Power-Structure of Heorot'.
56 Truth would again be stressed in line 586b, if we accept the suggestion of Bammesberger, 'The
Emendation of *Beowulf*, l. 586', that manuscript *þæs* conceals an original *þæs soþæs*.

heroic point in their national life is striking, to say the least;[57] the emphasis that follows on the valour of the Geats (*Geata . . . eafoð ond ellen . . . guþe*, lines 601b–3a) creates a surely deliberate point of contrast.

Clearly, such an outstanding rhetorical display is important in the context of establishing Beowulf's credentials to fight Grendel: unlike Unferth, whose words and deeds do not tally, Beowulf can transform his words into courage and his courage into deeds; little wonder that when Beowulf takes his leave of Hrothgar over twelve hundred lines later, the grateful old king declares the young hero a paragon in thought, word, and deed (*Þu eart mægenes strang ond on mode frod, wis wordcwida*, lines 1844–5a).[58] Against this unqualified praise, however, it is important to note that the poet's final judgment on Beowulf in the part of the poem based on Beowulf's Danish exploits is perhaps somewhat curiously phrased (lines 2166b–2171 and 2177–89):[59]

> Swa sceal mæg don,
> nealles inwitnet   oðrum bregdon
> dyrnum cræfte,   dead renian
> hondgesteallan.   Hygelace wæs,
> niða heardum,   nefa swyðe hold,   2170
> ond gehwæðer oðrum   hroþra gemyndig.
>
> . . .
>
> Swa bealdode   bearn Ecgðeowes,
> guma guðum cuð,   godum dædum,
> dreah æfter dome,   nealles druncne slog
> heorðgeneatas;   næs him hreoh sefa,   2180
> ac he mancynnes   mæste cræfte
> ginfæstan gife,   þe him god sealde,
> heold hildedeor.   Hean wæs lange,
> swa hyne Geata bearn   godne ne tealdon,
> ne hyne on medobence   micles wyrðne   2185
> drihten Wedera   gedon wolde;
> swyðe wendon   þæt he sleac wære,
> æðeling unfrom.   Edwenden cwom
> tireadigum menn   torna gehwylces.

[So must a kinsman do, in no way weave a malice-net for another, with concealed cunning prepare death for a close companion. To Hygelac, a man brave in conflicts, his nephew was very loyal, and each mindful of benefits for the other . . . So did Ecgtheow's son show himself brave, a man known for battles, good deeds; he acted for glory, in no way did he slay drunk hearth-companions: his heart was not savage, but the

---

57 Compare the poet's description of the Danes who leave the monster-mere once they assume that Beowulf has been killed by Grendel's mother as 'brave' (*Næs ofgeafon / hwate Scyldingas*, lines 1601b–1602a).

58 On this figure, see Sims-Williams, 'Thought, Word, and Deed: an Irish Triad'. See too above, pp. 55, 73, 146, and 218.

59 The manuscript reads *wereda* at line 2186a, presumably as a result of scribal confusion with the common (Christian) formula *wereda drihten* ('lord of hosts'), which occurs numerous times in Old English poetry (see above, n. 54). On the notion that Beowulf was a 'slack' youth, cf. Bonjour, 'Young Beowulf's Inglorious Period'; Eliason, 'Beowulf's Inglorious Youth'; Tripp, 'Did Beowulf Have an "Inglorious Youth"?'.

battle-warrior with very great strength kept the liberal gift that God had granted him. For a long time he was of low esteem, so that the children of the Geats did not reckon him good, nor was the lord of the Weders willing to honour him much on the mead-bench; they greatly thought that he was slack, a feeble prince. A reversal of every affliction came for the glorious man.]

Both these passages, it might be noted, are rich in alliterative effect: the first concludes with three consecutive lines alliterating on 'h' (lines 2169–71), whilst the second ends with consecutive examples of cross-alliteration (lines 2186–7) and with paronomasia (*wendon . . . Edwenden*, lines 2187–8). Praise of Beowulf is somewhat undermined by the implied criticism of others: the fact that he never plotted to kill a close companion or slew his drunken hearth-companions might be thought scarcely to constitute a ringing endorsement of his moral probity, although it should be stressed that both crimes might be attributed to the Danes Unferth, Heremod, and (perhaps) Hrothulf.[60] If Hrothgar clearly considers Beowulf a paragon amongst men, the poet implicitly reminds us both at the beginning and at the end of his adventures in Denmark that the men against whom he is measured are not themselves beyond reproach.

Enter the dragon: Wiglaf struggles to defend the hero

But if the first part of *Beowulf*, dealing with his youthful exploits in Denmark, contains a disturbingly high number of implicit and explicit criticisms of the characters depicted, the second part of poem, dealing with the dragon-fight, is still darker in tone. After fifty years on the throne, Beowulf, like Hrothgar, has an unwelcome visitor.[61] Like Hrothgar gazing on the hilt from the monster-mere, the thief's lord (perhaps Beowulf himself) is depicted gazing in uncomprehending inaction at the dragon's stolen cup.[62] But in the very moment that the thief's lord is frozen in silent contemplation of the stolen cup,[63] the dragon itself is all action (lines 2287–311):[64]

> Þa se wyrm onwoc,   wroht wæs geniwad;
> stonc ða æfter stane,   stearcheort onfand
> feondes fotlast;   he to forð gestop
> dyrnan cræfte   dracan heafde neah.   2290
> Swa mæg unfæge   eaðe gedigan
> wean ond wræcsið,   se ðe waldendes
> hyldo gehealdeþ.   Hordweard sohte

60 See further above, pp. 240–55.
61 On the significance of the fifty-year period, see above, pp. 64, 162, and 196.
62 See further above, pp. 50, 100, and 113.
63 On parallel tableaux elsewhere in the poem, see above, p. 216.
64 The manuscript reads *hlæwū* at line 2296b, *hilde* at line 2298b, *fela ða* at line 2305a, and *læg* at 2307b. For the emendation of *hilde* to *wiges* at line 2298b (effectively, a substitution of one synonym which will not alliterate for another which will), see above, pp. 51 and 178. On the *f/s*-confusion that appears to account for the reading at line 2305a, see above, pp. 42 and 44–5; a missing nasal-suspension (on which see above, p. 181) will account for the manuscript-reading at 2307b.

georne æfter grunde,   wolde guman findan,
þone þe him on sweofote   sare geteode,   2295
hat ond hreohmod   hlæw oft ymbehwearf
ealne utanweardne,   ne ðær ænig mon
on þære westenne;   hwæðre wiges gefeh,
beaduwe weorces,   hwilum on beorh æthwearf,
sincfæt sohte.   He þæt sona onfand   2300
ðæt hæfde gumena sum   goldes gefandod,
heahgestreona.   Hordweard onbad
earfoðlice   oððæt æfen cwom;
wæs ða gebolgen   beorges hyrde
wolde se laða   lige forgyldan   2305
drincfæt dyre.   Þa wæs dæg sceacen
wyrme on willan;   no on wealle læng,
bidan wolde,   ac mid bæle for,
fyre gefysed.   Wæs se fruma egeslic
leodum on lande,   swa hyt lungre wearð   2310
on hyra sincgifan   sare geendod.

[Then the dragon awoke, wrath was renewed, it snuffled along the stone, fierce-hearted found the track of the foe; he had stepped forward with cunning craft close by the dragon's head. So may an undoomed man easily survive misery and exile, when he keeps the favour of the Ruler. The guardian of the hoard searched eagerly along the ground; it wished to find the man who had grievously treated him in his sleep. Hot and fierce in heart it often stalked around the mound, all around the outside: there was no one there in the wilderness, yet it exulted in war, deeds of battle. Sometimes it stalked back into the barrow, sought out the precious vessel; it immediately discovered that a man had tampered with the gold, the rich treasures. The guardian of the hoard waited with difficulty until the evening came; then the keeper of the barrow was enraged, the hateful foe wished to pay back with flame for the precious drinking-vessel. Then the day was done, as the dragon wished; no longer would it wait by the wall, but it went with flame, ready with fire. The beginning was terrible for the people in the land, as it swiftly was brought to a dreadful end on their treasure-giver.]

The dragon's frantic movement is suggested by the insistent repetition of both words (mainly verbs) and sounds within this brief twenty-five line passage (*onfand . . . onfand*, lines 2288b and 2300b; *Hordweard . . . Hordweard*, lines 2293b and 2302b; *sohte . . . sohte*, lines 2293b and 2300a; *ymbehwearf . . . æthwearf*, lines 2296b and 2299; *onfand . . . gefandod*, lines 2300b and 2301b).[65] The poet's perspective is introduced twice. On the first occasion the poet ascribes the lucky escape of the thief with the dragon's cup to God: it seems unclear why such a character should be regarded as 'undoomed' (*unfæge*, line 2291),[66] nor why (with emphasising assonance) he should 'keep the favour of the Ruler' (*waldendes hyldo gehealdeþ*, lines 2292b–2293a), unless perhaps the

65 On the use of such 'echo-words', see, for example, Beaty, 'The Echo-Word in *Beowulf*'; Rosier, 'Generative Composition in *Beowulf*'. See too above, p. 78.
66 One might note that elsewhere in the poem the only other time that the word 'undoomed' is used is in

poet means to imply that the thief's own lord (who, we later learn, may be Beowulf himself) was wrong to condemn the man in the first place. The second of the poet's interventions is still more ominous, effectively predicting the death of Beowulf (lines 2309b–2311) almost nine hundred lines before the end of the poem.

Nor is this the last of the many grim predictions that occur before Beowulf even steps up to face his final foe; the poet concludes at least three other passages in the next hundred lines or so with similarly portentous words (lines 2341b–2344, 2399b–2400, and 2423b–2424). Furthermore, just as the poet depicts Beowulf gazing statically at the dragon's cup while the dragon is in a frenzy of impatient action, so too, when the dragon's dreadful vengeance comes about, Beowulf himself is pictured first in a paralysis of anguish (lines 2312–36):[67]

> Đa se gæst ongan gledum spiwan,
> beorht hofu bærnan; bryneleoma stod
> eldum on andan. No ðær aht cwices
> lað lyftfloga læfan wolde.   2315
> Wæs þæs wyrmes wig wide gesyne,
> nearofages nið nean ond feorran,
> hu se guðsceaða Geata leode
> hatode ond hynde; hord eft gesceat,
> dryhtsele dyrnne, ær dæges hwile.   2320
> Hæfde landwara lige befangen,
> bæle ond bronde, beorges getruwode,
> wiges ond wealles; him seo wen geleah.
> Þa wæs Biowulfe broga gecyðed
> snude to soðe, þæt his sylfes ham,   2325
> bolda selest, brynewylmum mealt,
> gifstol Geata. Þæt ðam godan wæs
> hreow on hreðre, hygesorga mæst;
> wende se wisa þæt he wealdende
> ofer ealde riht, ecean dryhtne,   2330
> bitre gebulge. Breost innan weoll
> þeostrum geþoncum, swa him geþywe ne wæs.
> Hæfde ligdraca leoda fæsten,
> ealond utan, eorðweard ðone
> gledum forgrunden; him ðæs guðkyning,   2335
> Wedera þioden, wræce leornode.

[Then the stranger began to spew flames, to burn the bright dwellings; the fire-glow remained in malice for men: the hateful flying-creature would not leave anything alive. The dragon's fighting-power was widely visible, the wickedness of the difficult and hostile one both near and far, how that warlike ravager hated and humiliated the people of the Geats; it hastened back to the hoard, the secret noble hall before day. It had encir-

---

Beowulf's gnomic observation (discussed above, p. 252) that 'fate often spares an undoomed man, if his courage suffices' (*Wyrd oft nereð / unfægne eorl, þonne his ellen deah*, lines 572b–573).

[67] The manuscript reads *him* at line 2325b.

cled the nation's people in flame, with fire and burning: it trusted in its barrow, its fighting-power and fortification; that hope deceived it. Then the terror was made known to Beowulf, swiftly and truly, that his own home, best of buildings had melted in surges of flames, the gift-throne of the Geats. For that good man there was sorrow in his heart, the greatest of griefs, the wise one reckoned that he had severely offended the Ruler, the eternal Lord, contrary to ancient law; his breast welled up inside with dark thoughts, as was not customary for him. The fire-dragon had destroyed with flame that people's stronghold, the fortress and coastal land beyond; for that the warlike king, the prince of the Weder-Geats, planned vengeance.]

Beowulf's initial maudlin inactivity is cleverly contained within an envelope pattern of the dragon's action (*Hæfde . . . lige befangen . . . Hæfde . . . gledum forgrunden*, lines 2321 and 2333a–2335a), and seems to stem from a sense that he has somehow acted wrongly in God's eyes. The dragon too is compromised, since its hope in its own protection is immediately said by the poet to be misplaced (*him seo wen geleah*, line 2323b),[68] more chillingly, we infer from the passage that follows, Beowulf's hope for his own protection in the form of a specially made iron shield (lines 2337–41a) is likewise misplaced, as both Beowulf and his foe are equally doomed (lines 2341b–2344):

> Sceolde lændaga
> æþeling ærgod ende gebidan,
> worulde lifes, ond se wyrm somod,
> þeah ðe hordwelan heolde lange.

[The prince, good of old, had to endure the end of his transitory days, of life in the world, and the dragon too; even though he had held the treasure-hoard for long.]

The link between Beowulf and his foe is enforced by the ambiguity of the final clause: both king and dragon have 'held the treasure-hoard for long'. Equally striking is the fact that the poet here echoes Beowulf's own earlier words to Hrothgar after the death of Æschere that (lines 1386–9):

> 'Ure æghwylc sceal ende gebidan
> worolde lifes; wyrce se þe mote
> domes ær deaþe; þæt bið drihtguman
> unlifgendum æfter selest.'

['Each of us must endure an end to life in the world; let him who can win fame before death: that is the best thing afterwards for the noble warrior once he is gone.']

Such a link back to Beowulf's glorious past in the light of his impending death is typical of this poet's approach, strengthened by the fact that the only previous times in the poem when the word 'good of old' (*ærgod*, line 2342a) has been

---

68 On the significance of this phrase, see, for example, Ringler, '*Him seo wen geleah*: the Design for Irony in Grendel's Last Visit to Heorot'.

applied to humans (as opposed to weapons)[69] it was used of Hrothgar, brooding over Grendel's first attack in precisely the same way as Beowulf over that of the dragon (line 130a), and of Æschere, in the very speech by Hrothgar that prompts Beowulf's observations on the mutability of human life (line 1329a).[70]

The poet immediately backs up his statement that Beowulf was 'good of old' by offering a resumé of his career to date; the dispatch of Grendel and his mother are dealt with in three lines (lines 2351b–2354a), and instead the poet focuses on his exploits in Frisia when Hygelac was killed (lines 2354b–2366), on his initial refusal of the Geatish crown (lines 2367–76), on his finally becoming king after Heardred was killed by Onela (lines 2377–90), and on his role in helping Eadgils to kill Onela (lines 2391–6). The poet had prefaced this litany of heroic endeavour by stating that Beowulf had confidence in his chances against the dragon 'because previously risking danger he had endured many attacks, battle-tumults' (*forðon he ær fela/ nearo neðende niða gedigde,/ hildehlemma*, lines 2349b–2351a); he concludes his account of Beowulf's *curriculum uitae* in precisely the same way (lines 2397–400):

> Swa he niða gehwane   genesen hæfde,
> sliðra geslyhta,   sunu Ecgðiowes,
> ellenweorca,   oð ðone anne dæg
> þe he wið þam wyrme   gewegan sceolde.   2400

> [So the son of Ecgtheow had survived each of the attacks, cruel slaughters, mighty deeds, until that one day when he had to contend with the dragon.]

Beowulf's gloriously successful past, the poet makes clear, is no guarantee of his future.

Before outlining the reasons for Beowulf's faith in his own abilities against the dragon, the poet again apparently undercuts his hero by implying of Beowulf's decision (based on his self-belief) not to attack the dragon mob-handed that it was the result of over-confidence; the verb used (*oferhogode*, line 2345) cannot but recall the twin use of the related noun in Hrothgar's so-called 'sermon' (*oferhygda* and *oferhyda*, lines 1740b and 1760b),[71] in which Hrothgar explicitly warns Beowulf of the dangers of pride. The implication seems clear: Beowulf goes to face the dragon doomed.

Moreover, he seems to sense his doom: not only does the poet depict Beowulf's heart seething with uncustomarily dark thoughts (*breost innan weoll / þeostrum geþoncum, swa him geþywe ne wæs*, lines 2331b–2332).[72] He goes on to make an extraordinary speech in which he muses on the fate of the Geatish King Hrethel and compares his suffering over the killing of one son by another with that of an old man who loses his son to the gallows;[73] whatever the precise parallels invoked, it is clear enough that Beowulf is here brooding on the impo-

---

[69] On the poet's common connection of men and swords, see above, pp. 76, 185–6, 240–1, and 263.
[70] For the speech, see above, p. 89.
[71] See further above, pp. 155–62.
[72] On these dark thoughts, see above, pp. 149 and 229.
[73] On this episode, see further above, pp. 116–18.

tent grief and frustrated desire for requital of two old men in a manner which surely suggests something of his own anguish in the case of the dragon. Moreover, Beowulf continues to ponder the sufferings of Hrethel by ruminating further on how, after Hrethel's death, the aged Swedish King Ongentheow also died attempting to avenge an attack upon him by the Geats Hæthcyn and Hygelac. Ironically, the fratricide Hæthcyn is himself avenged by his surviving brother, Hygelac, in a passage which introduces the complex series of descriptions of the long-standing wars between the Swedes and the Geats (lines 2472–89).[74] The struggles and sufferings of the secular heroic world are painted by the poet in far from glowing terms; and Beowulf, who as a young man in Denmark was all action, is now seen in a welter of reflection and reaction.

But in the absence of a dynamic and positive Beowulf in the second part of the poem, the heroic mantle falls on Wiglaf. It has often been noted that just as the epithets used of Hrothgar in Part I are used of Beowulf in Part II, so too Wiglaf inherits the descriptions used of the young Beowulf.[75] But (it is important to note) he speaks with a quite different voice. Like Beowulf, Wiglaf speaks no fewer than five times in Part II, but the whole tone of his addresses is distinct.[76] Unlike the carefully choreographed speeches of Part I, including, for example, the entire series of courteous exchanges between Beowulf and the coastguard, Beowulf and Wulfgar, Wulfgar and Hrothgar, and Hrothgar and Beowulf before Unferth ever opens his mouth,[77] all such niceties break down in Part II, which includes a series of twelve unanswered addresses by Beowulf, Wiglaf, the so-called 'last survivor', and the Geatish messenger.[78] The very first of Wiglaf's speeches is typical (lines 2633–50a):

> 'Ic ðæt mæl geman, þær we medu þegun,
> þonne we geheton   ussum hlaforde
> in biorsele,   ðe us ðas beagas geaf,   2635
> þæt we him ða guðgetawa   gyldan woldon
> gif him þyslicu   þearf gelumpe,
> helmas ond heard sweord.   Ðe he usic on herge geceas
> to ðyssum siðfate   sylfes willum,
> onmunde usic mærða,   ond me þas maðmas geaf,   2640
> þe he usic garwigend   gode tealde,
> hwate helmberend,   þeah ðe hlaford us
> þis ellenweorc   ana aðohte
> to gefremmanne,   folces hyrde,
> forðam he manna mæst   mærða gefremede,   2645
> dæda dollicra.   Nu is se dæg cumen

---

74 Simple summaries of this complicated sequence of action and counter-action are hard to come by: useful overviews are offered by Liuzza, trans., *Beowulf*, pp. 157–8; Mitchell and Robinson, ed., *Beowulf*, pp. 181–2. For a rather fuller (but still excellent) summary and analysis, see Lawrence, '*Beowulf*' and Epic Tradition, pp. 77–106. See too North, 'Saxo and the Swedish Wars in *Beowulf*'.

75 For example, by Whallon, *Formula, Character, and Context*, pp. 105–6.

76 For the patterning of these speeches, see Table IV above, pp. 206–7.

77 See further above, pp. 208–18.

78 For the role of the messenger in particular, see, for example, Carnicelli, 'The Function of the Messenger in *Beowulf*'.

> þæt ure mandryhten   mægenes behofað,
> godra guðrinca;   wutun gongan to,
> helpan hildfruman,   þenden hyt sy,
> gledegesa grim.'

['I remember the time when we drank mead, and promised in the mead-hall our lord who gave us these rings that we would repay him for the war-trappings, helmets and hard swords, if a need like this should arise. That is why he chose us of his own will for the war-band on this expedition, because he reckoned us worthy of these glories, and gave me these treasures, since he counted us good spear-warriors, bold helmet-wearers, even though our lord intended to undertake this courageous task alone, the people's keeper, since he had accomplished most glories of men, audacious (or 'foolish') deeds. Now the day has come that our liege lord needs the strength of good warriors. Let us go to him, help our battle-leader, while this lasts, the grim fire-terror.']

The speech is almost wholly focused on Beowulf, although it does contain a number of dialect-forms of the first-person plural pronoun and pronominal adjective (*usic, ussum*).[79] Wiglaf reasserts Beowulf's uniqueness (*ana*), in a striking echo of Beowulf's first speech to Hrothgar, when he states twice in the space of six lines that he alone can bring the Danes relief (*ana*, line 425b; *ana*, line 431a).[80] Equally striking is the way in which Wiglaf effectively echoes Unferth's assertion that Beowulf is impervious to sensible advice. But perhaps the most intriguing part of this speech is that in which Wiglaf characterises Beowulf's deeds of derring-do as *dæda dollicra*. Robinson argues that here (uniquely in Old English), the term *dollic* is being used ironically, and carries a different sense to the implied usages elsewhere in the poem (*dolgilp, dolsceaþa*): 'audacious' 'bold'.[81] Such special pleading would be more convincing were this the only occasion on which Wiglaf appears to criticise his dead lord, but the opening words of Wiglaf's penultimate speech seem still more unequivocal (lines 3077–84a):[82]

> 'Oft sceall eorl monig   anes willan
> wræc adreogan,   swa us geworden is.
> Ne meahton we gelæran   leofne þeoden,
> rices hyrde,   ræd ænigne,   3080
> þæt he ne grette   goldweard þone,
> lete hyne licgean   þær he longe wæs,
> wicum wunian   oð woruldende;
> heold on heahgesceap.   Hord ys gesceawod,
> grimme gegongen;   wæs þæt gifeðe to swið   3085
> þe ðone þeodcyning   þyder ontyhte.'

---

79 Such dialect-forms perhaps lend Wiglaf's speech a distinctive flavour, although their use in the poem is not restricted to him: the *usic* form, for example, is used by Hrothgar at line 458b.

80 See further above, p. 213.

81 Robinson, 'A Further Word on *dollicra* in *Beowulf* 2646'; Robinson is responding to a suggestion by Frisby, ' "Daring" and "Foolish" Renderings: On the Meaning of *dollic* in *Beowulf*'.

82 The manuscript reads *adreogeð* at line 3078a; *þeodcyning* has been supplied in line 3086a; there is no gap in the manuscript.

['Often must many a man suffer grief through the will of one (or 'for the sake of one', as has happened to us. We could not suggest to our dear lord, the kingdom's protector any plan, so that he would not meet that gold-guardian, let him lie where he had been long, stay in his dwelling until the world's end; he held to a high destiny. The hoard is revealed, grimly gained; the fate was too powerful, that brought the nation's king there.']

There must be an element of criticism here, where the many suffer because of one extraordinary man (*anes*, line 3077b),[83] and where in a sense Wiglaf takes on the voice of the poet, marvelling at a heroism that he cannot quite condone. Just as Heremod's selfish acts appear to have plunged the Danes into the lord-less danger they faced before the mysterious arrival of Scyld Scefing at the beginning of the poem,[84] so Beowulf's own deeds condemn the Geats to a predictably grim future at the poem's end.[85] Unlike in the case of Heremod, however, the poet seems very careful not to condemn Beowulf in similarly explicit terms.[86]

We can still argue (as I suppose we are supposed to) over the significance of the cursed treasure,[87] or precisely what it means to be *lofgeornost* ('most eager for praise').[88] In considering the great deeds of the pagan past, this poet does not put them entirely beyond criticism, nor yet does he seek to suggest that they are unworthy of sincere celebration. This poet seems all too aware of human limita-tions, and judiciously suspends judgment. We might do worse than follow his example, however quixotic such a course of action may seem. Indeed, in his overwhelming and deep-felt involvement with and sympathy for the heroic past, the *Beowulf*-poet seems to have more than a touch of Don Quixote about him, of whom Cervantes says:[89]

In short, he so buried himself in his books that he spent the nights reading from twilight till daybreak, and the days reading from dawn till dark; and so from little sleep and much reading, his brain dried up and he lost his wits. He filled his mind with all that he had read in them, with enchantments, quarrels, battles, challenges, wounds, wooings, loves, torments, and other impossible nonsense; and so deeply did he steep his imagination in the belief that all the fanciful stuff he read was true, that to his mind no history in the world was more authentic.

In attempting to make sense of deeds way back then (*in geardagum*) in a foreign land (*Gar-Dena*), and in celebrating a hero who was the greatest at that time (*þam dægum*) and in this life (*þisses lifes*), the *Beowulf*-poet carefully

---

83 Attempts to explain the term *anes* as referring here to the dragon or the thief (see, for example, Mitchell and Robinson, ed., *Beowulf*, p. 157) seem all the more unconvincing given the poet's consis-tent characterisation of Beowulf (and indeed Beowulf's own characterisation of himself) as 'unique' (*ana*), on which see further above, p. 213.
84 See above, pp. 110–13.
85 Cf. Malone, 'Beowulf the Headstrong'.
86 See above, pp. 255–6.
87 See above, pp. 153–5. See too Helder, 'Beowulf and the Plundered Hoard'.
88 See above, pp. 180–1.
89 Cohen, trans., *Don Quixote*, p. 32.

views his subject through a number of distancing lenses, and yet still produces a
work which casts light on his own world and which (even through the further
lenses of time and translation) can still do the same for us today. Is *Beowulf*,
then, in any sense beyond criticism? Like so many of the questions that the
poem poses, it may be that the answer is that there is no final answer: it depends
on the audience-perspective.[90] One is left in sheer admiration of this deeply
layered and textured work, the resonances of which remain long after it is read
or heard read: it is not so much that *Beowulf* is beyond criticism, but rather that
any all-embracing solution to the poem's mysteries remains, for the moment at
least, clearly beyond its critics.[91]

[90] Cf. Niles, 'Introduction: *Beowulf*, Truth and Meaning'.
[91] For a range of brief attempts to give an overview of the poem, see, for example, Clark, *Beowulf*;
Kaske, '*Beowulf*'; Robinson, '*Beowulf*'; Smithers, 'The Making of *Beowulf*'; Stanley, '*Beowulf*'.

9

Afterword: Looking Forward

A hundred years from now, a reader of *Beowulf*, should such an exotic creature still exist, will have access to a vast array of material unimaginable today. And much of that access will be instant. Even now, at the turn of the twentieth century, a well-equipped (which is to say well-funded) scholar can easily travel the world carrying not only the entire surviving corpus of Old English, but also vast bibliographies, together with books and articles complete and in progress, large numbers of downloaded dissertations, and a range of high quality manu-script-facsimiles, all collected together on a laptop computer that can be plugged into the internet to gain relatively speedy access not merely to friends and colleagues for questioning, commiseration, and companionship, but to a splendid array of library-catalogues, bibliographies, and other multimedia resources. In the future (and the not-so-distant future, if we are to believe the cyber-prophets who have virtually predicted it already), almost every would-be reader of *Beowulf* will have access to much more information than anyone today, in a much more compact form, and all at the click of a button, or (since doubt-less buttons will seem quite quaint by then) at least in the wink of an eye.

All of the great collaborative projects now in progress, such as *Fontes Anglo-Saxonici, SASLC: Sources of Anglo-Saxon Literary Culture*, and the *Dic-tionary of Old English*, will be long finished, available instantly, and likely undergoing long-term revision (if the funding is available, naturally); others now planned or in embryonic form, such as a complete database of formulaic phrasing in Old English and Anglo-Latin, or a comprehensive searchable bibli-ography of Anglo-Saxon studies, will simply be taken for granted. Every new edition will as a matter of course preserve the editorial emendations of the past, alongside a range of translations, recordings, facsimiles, notes, and commen-taries. Electronic facsimiles of every item in Helmut Gneuss's doubtless still standard *Handlist* will have been published (if that is then the right term) in time for the centenary celebrations, each one prefaced by a learned discussion that assigns date and provenance not so much on palaeographical, codicological, or art-historical grounds, as on a chemical analysis of the ink and a microscopic DNA-analysis of the poor creatures first flayed in its production.

More Old English will be known, recovered from binding-strips and frag-ments in much later books put to repair, alongside a handful of larger serendipi-tous discoveries in obscure and unlikely places. More too will have turned up in the likeliest of places, lost or unrecognised in libraries inaccessible for long periods or seldom visited for one reason or another. Much closer study of the activities of the earliest Anglo-Saxon scholars of the sixteenth, seventeenth, and eighteenth centuries will reveal in their early annotations and transcriptions of manuscripts now lost still more Old English unknown today; and amidst much rejoicing the original manuscript of the *Finnsburh fragment* will (let us hope) be recovered, still in the back of the book where Wanley placed it for safe-keeping after copying it all those years before.

More too will be known about the Old English we do have. The large amount that even now languishes in the critical apparatuses of all or most editions, or sits unprinted in manuscript, unregarded by most (and certainly no part of the collected corpus as it now stands), will by then have been welcomed back into the fold. We will know more about the different varieties and registers of Old English, and in particular about the idiolects expressed by individual authors, scribes, texts, manuscripts, and even schools. A broad consensus will (perhaps) have been reached on the scansion of *Beowulf* (though not on the fact or nature of any likely musical accompaniment), but (as now) individual scholars will still quibble about the propriety of individual conjectural emendations, which will be measured against a complete and detailed database of scribal corrections and suggested emendations of every extant Old English text.

A spurt of much-needed parallel editorial activity in that vast area of unprinted medieval texts not only in Latin but in a range of vernaculars (especially Irish and Old Norse-Icelandic) will shed great light on the intellectual and cultural background of *Beowulf*. The possible influence on *Beowulf* of Christian-Latin school-text authors, the debt to whom of Old English poets such as Cynewulf will have long since been demonstrated, will become a topic of close study. Analogues to *Beowulf* will be much more widely sought, as a direct consequence of wider familiarity with the text by students whose first language is not necessarily English. The precise nature of the relationships between *Beowulf* and an ever-growing range of other Old English texts both in prose and verse will continue to be investigated, even though the relative chronology of Old English poems and their supposed interdependence will have been established long before.

In short, we can be sure both that more will be known and that there will be more to know about *Beowulf* in the century ahead: the intensive academic study of *Beowulf* will be a distinct possibility (if not a choice) for a far broader spectrum of prospective readers from a greater variety of backgrounds than ever before. This highly necessary (and highly desirable) democratisation of information will doubtless have a profound impact on the way *Beowulf* is read, taught, and studied. Old English studies in general, and *Beowulf*-studies in particular, have always benefited from the concentrated activities of a handful of mavericks; and if the future of single-site geographically localised universities looks uncertain, prospects have never been brighter for the solitary scholar. The real engagements will take place, as now, not only with other readers past and present, present and absent, but primarily with the poem itself.

But looking back is a salutary lesson to those who would look ahead: few would have predicted at the end of the nineteenth century, when the overwhelming proportion of serious scholarship on *Beowulf* was being conducted by

Germans in German, that by the end of the twentieth century the bulk of research would be being carried out in English in North America; global politics are of course what will ultimately decide what gets studied where, but the globalisation of *Beowulf*-studies has had a profoundly positive effect that looks set to continue. With a leap of faith we can perhaps permit ourselves to allow that as long as English remains the dominant language of international electronic communication, then someone somewhere will care where all that English came from. Moreover, if *Beowulf* looks to be increasingly marginalised on university curricula, a century from now we may expect it still to be studied in some other context: surely Seamus Heaney and J. R. R. Tolkien have and will continue to serve the poem well. Certainly, then, *Beowulf* has a future, whatever that future may bring.

For anyone, of any age, it is a strange and strangely awesome thing to stand between worlds, straining to gaze both forward and back. However much faith one has in the future, there is a deep comfort in the things that comforted those we knew and loved before. But there, between worlds, is precisely where the *Beowulf*-poet himself stands, honouring and admiring a past he has outgrown, but pinning all his hopes on what he fervently believes is to come. It is right that as readers of *Beowulf* we should honour those who have read the text before, however much we can no longer have faith in their convictions. Our views too will soon enough seem quaint and myopic, and perhaps in a century's time the students of our students' students will crack a wry smile at the assumptions and follies of those of us writing on *Beowulf* today, and do what, after all, we did: read (some of) what was thought and said about *Beowulf* before, and try to say something different and from a different point of view.

A hundred years from now, for all the new data and analyses and hypotheses about *Beowulf* that will doubtless arise, at the heart of it all will still remain the poem itself, still read so many centuries after it was first composed, a poem the meaning of which will even then continue to excite debate and admiration because, like all great works, *Beowulf* still retains enormous power, across the centuries, to move. And if a hundred years from now someone not yet born can perhaps, even 'in a place far from libraries', still take pleasure reading *Beowulf*, then surely it seems a future worth looking forward to after all.

Appendix I: The Foliation of *Beowulf*

Note: The transcriptions here follow those of Kiernan, ed., *Electronic Beowulf*, although the lineation is that of more traditional editions.

'Old' foliation	1884 foliation	line	Transcription	MS lines	verse lines
129r	132r	1a	HWÆT WE GARDE	19	21.5
129v	132v	21b	. . .)me þæt hine onylde eft ge wunigen wi(. . .	20	25
130r	133r	46b	sende þagyt hie him asetton segen g(. . .	20	22.5
130v	133v	69a	. . .]ærn micel mengewyrcean þone yldo	20	23
132r	134r	92a	cwæ(ð) þæt se ælmihtiga eorðan w(o. . .	20	21
132v	134v	113a	. . .](. . .) þa wið gode wunnon lange þrag(. . .	20	21.5
133r	135r	134b	. . .)yrst acym(. . .) ane niht ef(. . .	20	25
133v	135v	159b	. . .h)tende wæs deorc deaþ sc(. . .	20	22.5
134r	136r	182a	. . .) huru heofena helm herian (. . .	20	21.5
134v	136v	203b	. . .) he him leof wære hwetton hige (. . .	20	25.5
135r	137r	229a	. . .) of wealle geseah weard scildinga seþe (. . .	20	23.5
135v	137v	252b	. . .n)an leas scea weras onland den(. . .	20	21
136r	138r	273b	secgan hydon þætmid scyldingum scea(. . .	20	25.5
136v	138v	297a	. . .as) leofne mannan wudu wunden hals	20	22
137r	139r	319a	. . .)ra(ð) werod wearde healdan.	20	20
137v	139v	339a	. . .)m mum hroð gar sohton. himþa elle(. . .	20	21.5
138r	140r	360b	to[h]i(s) wine drihtne her syndon ge(. . .	20	19
138v	140v	379b	. . .)es manna mægen cræft onhis (mund)	20	22

139r	141r	401b	. . . ea)rda be bead. snyredon ætsomn(. . .	20	21.5
139v	141v	423a	. . .)[. . .]ra nið wean ahsodon for grand g(r . . .	20	21.5
140r	142r	444b	oft dyde mægen hreð manna na (. . .	20	20
140v	142v	464b	. . .)dinga ðaic furþum weold folce de	20	21.5
141r	143r	486a	benc þelu blode bestymed heall heor(. . .	20	18
141v	143v	504a	mærða þon ma middan geardes ge	20	19.5
142r	144r	523b	beot ealwið þe sunu beanstanes so[. . .	20	20.5
142v	144v	544a	. . .)om ne onsæ wæron fifnihta fyrst	20	20.5
143r	145r	565b	wunde beyðlafe uppe lægon swe(. . .	20	23
143v	145v	588b	. . .)e scealt werhðo dreogan þeah þin	20	20.5
144r	146r	609a	brego beorht dena gehyrde on (. . .	20	20.5
144v	146v	629b	. . .)ealhþeon ⁊ þagyddode guþe gefysed	20	24.5
145r	147r	654a	geweald ⁊ þæt word acwæð. Næfre ic ænegum	20	22
145v	147v	676a	geata ærhe on bed stige no ic me[:]an	20	20.5
146r	148r	697b	wedera leodum frofor ⁊ fult(. . .	20	21
146v	148v	718b	. . .)siþðan heardran hæle heal ðegnas	20	21.5
147A(131)r	149r	740a	feng hraðe forman siðe slæpendn(. . .	20	22.5
147A(131)v	149v	762b	. . .](. . .) he meahte swa. widre gewindan ⁊	20	20
147r	150r	782b	up astag. niwe geneahhe norð denum st(. . .	20	22
147v	150v	804b	. . .o)rsworen hæfde ecga gehwylcre scolde	20	22.5
148r	151r	827a	niðe niht weorce gefeh ellen mær (þ . . .	20	21.5
148v	151v	849b	. . .)ro dreore weol deað fæge deog. siððan	20	23
149r	152r	872b	styrian ⁊ on sped wrecan spel ge ra de	20	23
149v	152v	895b	sæ bat ge hleod bær on bearm scipes beo	20	23
150r	153r	918b	eode scealc monig swið hicgende tosele	20	20.5
150v	153v	939a	scuc cum ⁊ scinnum nu scealc hafað þurh	20	24.5
151r	154r	963b	heardan clam mum on wæl bedde wriþan	20	23
151v	154v	986b	hilde rinces egl unheoru æghwylc ge cwæð	20	22.5

'Old' foliation	1884 foliation	line	Transcription	MS lines	verse lines
152r	155r	1009a	gang healf denes sunu wolde self cyni(n . . .	20	23
152v	155v	1032a	. . .)ffrecne ne meahton scur heard sceþ	20	21
153r	156r	1053a	fe lafe ꝼ þone ænne heht golde forgy(. . .	20	22
153v	156v	1075a	. . .)unde þætwæs geomuru ides nalles holinga	20	22.5
154r	157r	1097b	be nemde. þæt he þa wealafe weotena	20	21.5
154v	157v	1119a	. . .o) wolcnum wæl fyra mæst hlynode	20	20
155r	158r	1139a	þohte þonne to sælade gifhe tor(n. . .	20	20
155v	158v	1159a	. . .)eodum leoð wæs asungen gleoman	20	16.5
156r	159r	1175b	(þ)u(ð)e for sunu wolde here ric hab(b. . .	20	19.5
156v	159v	1195a	. . .)s heals beaga mæst þara þe ic on fol(. . .	20	22.5
157r	160r	1217b	. . .)isses hrægles neot þeo ge streona (. . .	20	24
157v	160v	1241b	. . .g) set ton him toheafdon hilde randas	20	23
158r	161r	1264b	. . .a)n (. . .)ream fleon westen warode þ(. . .	20	23
158v	161v	1287a	. . .) andweard scireð. þawæs on hea(. . .	20	20
159r	162r	1307b	. . .)de syðþan he aldor begnunly(. . .	20	21
159v	162v	1328b	. . .) colde eorl wesan ærgod swylc æsc(. . .	20	24
160r	163r	1352b	træd næfne he wæs mara þonne ænig m(a . . .	20	24.5
160v	163v	1377a	. . .)e anum eard git ne const frecne stowe	20	21.5
161r	164r	1398b	. . .ræc) þa wæs hroðgare hors ge(. . .	20	24.5
161v	164v	1423a	. . .) heolfre horn stundum song fu(. . .	20	25.5
162r	165r	1448b	. . .)afelan werede seþe meregrundas men(. . .	20	22.5
162v	165v	1471a	. . .)rðum ne wæs þæm oðrum swa syð þan	20	20.5
163r	166r	1491b	opðe mec deað nimeð. æfter þæ(. . .	22	25
163v	166v	1516b	. . .h)t ge seah blacne leoman beorht(. . .	22	25.5
164r	167r	1542a	man grapum ꝼ him to geanes feng ofer wear[þ]	22	25.5

164v	1565b	...)loh þæt hire wið halse heard grapode ban	22	26
165r	1591b	ceorlas þaðe mid hroð gare on holm (...	22	25
165v	1616b	..æ)s hat æt tren ellor gæst se þær	22	23.5
166r	1640a	semninga tosele comon frome fyrd	22	22.5
‾66v	1662b	..)ngian eald sweord eacen oftost wisode	22	23
‾67r	1685b	sæm tweonum ðara þe on scedenigge (s ...	22	23.5
‾67v	1709a	..)eðum to helpe ne wearð here mod	22	23
168r	1732a	ge deð him swa ge weal dene worolde (...	22	20
168v	1752a	..)dend weorð mynda dæl. hit on ende	22	25
169r	1777a	Ic þære socne singales wæg mod cear(...	22	25.5
169v	1802b	..)om beorht scacan scaþan onet ton	22	23.5
170r	1826a	fricge ofer floda begang þæt þec ymb	22	24
170v	1850a	..)æ geatas selran næbban toge ceosen	22	24
171r	1874a	frodum oþres swiðor þæt he seoðða ...	20	19
171v	1893a	...) grette achim to geanes rad	20	21
172r	1914a	holme hyð weard geara seþe ær lange	20	22.5
172v	1936b	(w)eotode tealde hand gewriþene hraþe	20	21
173r	1957b	wæs geo fum ⁊ guðum gar cene man wid(...) (...	20	21
173v	1978b	..)lyððan man dryhten þurh hleoðor	20	21.5
174r	2000a	þæt is un dyrne dryhten hige[...	20	19
174v	2019a	..) ær hie to setle geong. hwilum fo(...	21	22.5
175r	2041b	gesyhð eald æsc wiga seðe eall g(...	21	20.5
175v	2062a	..)de con him land geare þon(...) bio(ð)	21	23
176r	2085a	grapode geareo folm glof (...	21	20.5
176v	2105b	..) fela fricgen de feorran reh(...	20	22
177r	2127b	(h)ioþætlic æt bær feondes fæð[m] ...	20	19
177v	2146b	..) geaf sunu healfdenes on	20	20
178r	2166b	mæg dón. nealles inwit net oðr(...	20	19.5

'Old' foliation	1884 foliation	line	Transcription	MS lines	verse lines
178v	181v	2186a	. . .]hten wereda gedon wolde swyðe	20	21
179r	182r	2207a	beowulfe br[æ]de rice onhand ge[. . .	21	22
179v	182v	2229a	[. . . roga][s] [hwæþre] [fyren] sceapen	21	23.5
180r	183r	2252b	nah hwa sweord wege oððe f[:g] . . .	21	22.5
180v	183v	2275a	. . . nan hege secan sceall [hearm]	21	21.5
181r	184r	2296b	hl(. . .)wum oftymbe hwearf ealn[. . .	21	19
181v	184v	2315b	. . .). wæs þæs wyrmes wig wide gesy(. . .	21	24
182r	185r	2339b	wisse hegearwe þæt him holt wudu he . . .	21	22
182v	185v	2361b	xxx. hilde geat wa þahe to holm(. . .	21	22.5
183r	186r	2384a	(þ)eoden him þæt to mearce wearð he (þ . . .	21	21
183v	186v	2405a	. . .) ma(. . .)þum fæt mære þurh ðæs me(. . .	21	23
184r	187r	2428a	icwæs syfan wintre þa mec sin(. . .	21	23
184v	187v	2451a	. . .)ran ellor sið oðres negymeð	21	21
185r	188r	2472a	. . .) synn ʒ sacu sweona ʒ geata of(. . .	21	24
185v	188v	2496a	. . .s)an wig frecan weorðe gecypa(. . .	21	23.5
186r	189r	2519b	gificwiste hu wiððam aglæcean elle(s)	21	23
186v	189v	2542b	. . .)e worna fela gum cystum gód guða ge	21	23
187r	190r	2565b	. . .)ga fram oðrum stið mod gestod (w . . .	21	25
187v	190v	2590b	. . .) æg hwylc mon. alætan læn dag(. . .	21	21.5
188r	191r	2612a	. . .u)na ohtere þam æt sæcce wearð w(r . . .	21	21
188v	191v	2633a	. . .) geman þær we medu þegun þon(. . .	21	22.5
189A(197)r	192r	2655b	(f)eorh. ealgian wedra ðeod nes icwat gear(e)	21	26.5
189A(197)v	192v	2682a	gomol ʒ græg mæl him þæt gifeðe ne wæs (. . .	21	23
189r	193r	2705a	helm wyrm on middan feond gefyldan	21	26
189v	193v	2731a	weard æfter wurde lice gelenge ic ðas leo(. . .	21	26

Appendix II: Repeated Formulas in *Beowulf*

The following Appendix seeks to chart the majority of repeated formulas in *Beowulf*; it does not claim to be exhaustive,[1] but is rather intended to point up the most significant parallels of phrasing, in so far as they might throw light on the poem's structure or the poet's compositional technique (or both). I present the lines without punctuation and with minimal capitalisation, highlighting in italics overlapping phrasing, and have indicated suggested emendations with an asterisk (*), in as much as they are derived from formulaic phrasing and have been conjectured by earlier editors; however, the recording of such conjectural emendations here should not necessarily be taken as a sign of an acceptance on my part of their validity.[2] I have only indicated a handful of other conjectural emendations in the lines cited, in so far as they have a bearing on the formulaic character of the lines in question. In all cases of emendation, I have supplied the manuscript-reading in square brackets following the line. This Appendix may be used in conjuction with Appendix III below to identify formulaic phrasing in specific lines.

1	hwæt we Gardena	in *geardagum*
1354	þone on *geardagum*	Grendel nemdon
2233	swa hy on *geardagum*	gumena nathwylc

2	*þeodcyninga*	*þrym gefrunon*
2694	ða ic æt þearfe *gefrægn**	*þeodcyninges*	[NOT IN MS]

5	*monegum mægþum*	*meodosetla ofteah*
75	*manigre mægþe*	*geond þisne middangeard*
1771	*manigum mægþa*	*geond þysne middangeard*

6	egsode eorlas	*syððan ærest wearð*
1947	inwitniða	*syððan ærest wearð*

8	weox *under wolcnum*	weorðmyndum þah
651	wan *under wolcnum*	werod eall aras
714	wod *under wolcnum*	to þæs þe he winreced

---

[1] Those in search of a much fuller (and sometimes rather speculative) register should consult Creed, 'Studies in the Techniques of Composition'. Many of the formulas and formulaic systems listed here can be augmented with recourse to Bessinger and Smith, *A Concordance to the Anglo-Saxon Poetic Records*; idem, *A Concordance to Beowulf*; Cook, *A Concordance to Beowulf* [details of which are in section B of the Bibliography].

[2] See further the discussion above, pp. 42–56.

| 1631 | wæter *under wolcnum*   wældreore fag |
| 1770 | weold *under wolcnum*   ond hig wigge beleac |

| 9 | oðþæt him æghwylc   þara *ymbsittendra* |
| 2734 | *ymbesittendra*   ænig ðara |

11	gomban gyldan *þæt wæs god cyning*
863	glædne Hroðgar ac *þæt wæs god cyning*
2390	geatum wealdan *þæt wæs god cyning*

16	*lange hwile* him þæs liffrea
2159	leod Scyldunga *lange hwile*
2780	*longe hwile* ligegesan wæg

17	*wuldres wealdend* woroldare forgeaf
183	*wuldres waldend* wa bið þæm ðe sceal
1752	*wuldres waldend* weorðmynda dæl

29	*swæse gesiþas* swa he *selfa* bæd
1934	*swæsra gesiða* nefne sinfrea
2040	*swæse gesiðas* ond hyra *sylfra* feorh
2518	*swæse gesiðas* nolde ic sweord beran

30	þenden wordum weold *wine Scyldinga*	
148	*wine Scyldinga** weana gehwelcne	[MS *scyldenda*]
170	þæt wæs wræc micel *wine Scyldinga*	
1183	*wine Scildinga* worold oflætest	
1418	*winum Scyldinga* weorce on mode	
2026	hafað þæs geworden *wine Scyldinga*	
2101	me þone wælræs *wine Scildunga*	

32	þær æt hyðe stod *hringedstefna*
1131	*hringedstefnan* holm storme weol
1897	hladen herewædum *hringedstefna*

| 34 | aledon þa   *leofne þeoden* |
| 3079 | ne meahton we gelæran   *leofne þeoden* |

	aledon þa leofne þeoden
	beaga bryttan on bearm scipes
34–6	*mærne be mæste* þær wæs madma fela
	alegdon ða tomiddes mærne þeoden
3141–2	hæleð hiofende hlaford *leofne*

35	*beaga bryttan on bearm scipes*
352	*beaga bryttan* swa þu bena eart
896	bær *on bearm scipes* beorhte frætwa

1487   *beaga bryttan*   breac þonne moste

40   *billum ond byrnum*   him on bearme læg
2621   *bill ond byrnan*   oððæt his byre mihte

41   *madma mænigo*   þa him mid scoldon
2143   *maðma menigeo*   maga Healfdenes

44   *þeodgestreonum*   þon þa dydon
1218   *þeodgestreona**   ond geþeoh tela   [MS *þeo ge streona*]

45   þe hine æt frumsceafte   *forð onsendon*
2266   fela feorhcynna   *forð onsended*

46   ænne ofer yðe   *umborwesende*
1187   *umborwesendum* ær   arna gefremedon

47   þa gyt hie him asetton   *segen gyldenne**   [MS *g . . . denne*]
1021   *segen gyldenne*   sigores to leane

48   heah *ofer* heafod   *leton* holm beran
3132   wyrm *ofer* weallclif   *leton* weg niman

49   geafon on garsecg   *him wæs geomor sefa*
2419   goldwine geata   *him wæs geomor sefa*
2632   sægde gesiðum   *him wæs sefa geomor*

50   murnende mod   *men ne cunnon*
162   mistige moras   *men ne cunnon*

51   *secgan to soðe*   *seleræedende**   [MS *sele ræedenne*]
1346   *seleræedende*   *secgan* hyrde

52   hæleð *under heofenum*   hwa þæm hlæste onfeng
505   gehedde *under heofenum*   þonne he sylfa

54   leof leodcyning   *longe þrage*
114   *lange þrage*   he him ðæs lean forgeald
1257   lifde æfter laþum   *lange þrage*

58   *gamol ond guð*reouw   glæde Scyldingas
608   *gamol*feax *ond guð*rof   geoce gelyfde

65   *wiges weorðmynd*   þæt him his winemagas
1559   *wigena weorðmynd*   þæt wæs wæpna cyst

72   geongum ond ealdum   swylc *him god sealde*

1271	*gimfæste gife ðe him god sealde*
1751	forgyteð ond forgymeð *þæs þe him ær god sealde*
2182	*ginfæstan gife þe him god sealde*

86	ða se ellengæst *earfoðlice*
1636	*earfoðlice* heora æghwæþrum
1657	*earfoðlice* ætrihte wæs
2303	*earfoðlice* oððæt æfen cwom
2822	*earfoðlice* þæt he on eorðan geseah
2934	oððæt hi oðeodon *earfoðlice*

89	hludne in healle *þær wæs hearpan sweg*
2458	hæleð in hoðman nis *þær hearpan sweg*
3023	hæfen on handa nalles *hearpan sweg*

99	*swa* ða drihtguman dreamum *lifdon*
2144	*swa* se ðeodkyning þeawum *lyfde*

100	eadiglice *oððæt an ongan*
2210	eald eþelweard *oððæt an ongan*

103	mære *mearcstapa* se þe *moras heold*
1348	micle *mearcstapan* *moras healdan*

108	*ece drihten* þæs þe he Abel slog
1692	*ecean dryhtne* him þæs endelean
1779	*ecean dryhtne* þæs ðe ic on aldre gebad
2330	ofer ealde riht *ecean dryhtne*

114	lange þrage *he him ðæs lean forgeald*	
1541	heo *him* eft hraþe *andlean* forgeald*	[MS *handlean*]
1584	laðlicu lac *he him þæs lean forgeald*	
2094	yfla gehwylces *ondlean forgeald*	

118	fand þa ðær inne æþelinga *gedriht*	
357	eald ond anhar mid his eorla *gedriht*	
431	þæt ic mote ana ond* minra eorla *gedryht*	[NOT IN MS]
633	sæbat gesæt mid minra secga *gedriht*	
662	ða him Hroþgar gewat mid his hæleþa *gedryht*	
1672	sorhleas swefan mid þinra secga *gedryht*	

119	*swefan æfter symble* sorge nu cuðon
1008	*swefeþ æfter symle* þa wæs sæl ond mæl

121	*grim ond grædig* gearo sona wæs
1499	*grim ond grædig* þæt þær gumena sum

123   þritig þegna   *þanon eft gewat*
853   *þanon eft gewiton*   ealdgesiðas

124   huðe *hremig*   to ham faran
1882   since *hremig*   sægenga bad
2054   frætwum *hremig*   on flet gæð

125   mid þære wælfylle   *wica neosan*
1125   gewiton him ða wigend   *wica neosian*

129   micel morgensweg   *mære þeoden*
201   *mærne þeoden*   þa him wæs manna þearf
345   *mærum þeodne*   min ærende
353   *þeoden mærne*   ymb þinne sið
797   *mæres þeodnes*   ðær hie meahton swa
1046   swa manlice   *mære þeoden*
1598   *mærne þeoden*   þa ðæs monige gewearð
1715   *mære þeoden*   mondreamum from
1992   *mærum ðeodne*   ic ðæs modceare
2384   *mærne þeoden*   him þæt to mearce wearð
2572   *mærum þeodne*   þonne his myne sohte
2721   *þeoden mærne*   þegn ungemete till
2788   he ða mid þam maðmum   *mærne þioden*
3141   alegdon ða tomiddes   *mærne þeoden*

130   *æþeling ærgod*   unbliðe sæt
1329   *æþeling* ærgod*   swylc Æschere wæs   [NOT IN MS]
2342   *æþeling ærgod*   ende gebidan

133   *wergan gastes*   wæs þæt gewin to strang
1747   wom wundorbebodum   *wergan gastes*

       wergan gastes   *wæs þæt gewin to* strang
133–4 *lað ond longsum*   næs hit lengra fyrst
       wean onwendan   *wæs þæt gewin to* swyð
191–2 *laþ ond longsum*   þe on ða leode becom

137   *fæhðe ond fyrene*   wæs to fæst on þam
153   *fyrene ond fæhðe*   fela missera
879   *fæhðe ond fyrena*   buton fitela mid hine
2480   *fæhðe ond fyrene*   swa hyt gefræge wæs

141   gesægd soðlice   *sweotolan tacne*
833   torn unlytel   þæt wæs *tacen sweotol*

146   *husa selest*   wæs seo hwil micel

285	on heahstede *husa selest*
658	hafa nu ond geheald *husa selest*
935	*husa selest* heorodreorig stod

| 148 | wine Scyldinga *weana gehwelcne* |
| 1396 | *weana gehwylces* swa ic þe wene to |

150	*ylda bearnum undyrne cuð*
410	on minre eþeltyrf *undyrne cuð*
605	ofer *ylda bearn* oþres dogores

| 153 | fyrene ond fæhðe *fela missera* |
| 2620 | he frætwe geheold *fela missera* |

| 156 | feorhbealo feorran *fea þingian* |
| 470 | siððan þa fæhðe *feo þingode* |

159	ac* se* *æglæca* ehtende wæs	[GAP AT EDGE OF MS]
592	*atol æglæca* ealdre þinum
732	*atol aglæca* anra gehwylces
816	*atol æglæca* him on eaxle wearð

160	deorc deaþscua *duguþe ond geogoþe*
621	*duguþe ond geogoþe* dæl æghwylcne
1674	*duguðe ond iogoþe* þæt þu him ondrædan ne þearft

| 164 | swa fela fyrena *feond mancynnes* |
| 1276 | *mancynnes feond* ond his modor þa gyt |

| 165 | *atol* angengea *oft gefremede* |
| 2478 | *eatolne* inwitscear *oft gefremedon** | [MS *ge gefremedon*] |

| 168 | no he þone gifstol *gretan moste* |
| 347 | þæt we hine swa godne *gretan moton* |

| 174 | wið færgryrum *to gefremmanne* |
| 2644 | *to gefremmanne* folces hyrde |

| 177 | þæt him gastbona *geoce gefremede* |
| 2674 | geongum garwigan *geoce gefremman* |

| 178 | wið þeodþreaum swylc *wæs þeaw hyra* |
| 1246 | þrecwudu þrymlic *wæs þeaw hyra* |

| 182 | ne hie *huru* heofena helm *herian* ne cuþon |
| 1071 | ne *huru* Hildeburh *herian* þorfte |

| 187 | *æfter deaðdæge* | drihten secean |
| 885 | *æfter deaðdæge* | dom unlytel |

189	swa ða mælceare	*maga Healfdenes*
1474	geþenc nu *se mæra*	*maga Healfdenes*
1867	*mago Healfdenes*	*maþmas* xii
2011	sona me *se mæra*	*mago Healfdenes*
2143	*maðma* menigeo	*maga Healfdenes*

194	þæt fram ham gefrægn	*Higelaces þegn*
1574	*heard* be hiltum	*Higelaces ðegn*
2977	let se *hearda*	*Higelaces þegn*

	se wæs moncynnes	*mægenes strengest*
196–7	on þæm dæge	*þysses lifes*
	se þe manna wæs	*mægene strengest*
789–90	on þæm dæge	*þysses lifes*

197	*on þæm dæge*	*þysses lifes*
790	*on þæm dæge*	*þysses lifes*
806	*on ðæm dæge*	*þysses lifes*

| 200 | ofer swanrade | *secean wolde* |
| 645 | sunu healfdenes | *secean wolde* |

	ofer swanrade	*secean* wolde
200–1	*mærne þeoden*	þa him wæs manna þearf
	þæt he sigehreðig	*secean* come
1597–8	*mærne þeoden*	þa ðæs monige gewearð

| 201 | mærne þeoden | þa him wæs *manna þearf* |
| 1835 | mægenes fultum | þær ðe bið *manna þearf* |

202	ðone siðfæt him	*snotere ceorlas*
416	þa selestan	*snotere ceorlas*
1591	sona þæt gesawon	*snottre ceorlas*

| 203 | lythwon logon | þeah he *him leof wære* |
| 2467 | laðum dædum | þeah him *leof* ne waes |

205	hæfde se goda	*Geata leoda*
260	we synt gumcynnes	*Geata leode*
362	ofer geofenes begang	*Geata leode*
443	in þæm *guð*sele	*Geotena leode*
1213	æfter *guð*sceare	*Geata leode*
1856	*Geata leodum*	ond Gardenum
1930	ne to gneað gifa	*Geata leodum*

2318	hu se gu*ð*sceaða *Geata leode*
2927	*Geata leode* Gu*ð*scilfingas
3137	him ða gegiredan *Geata leode*
3178	swa begnornodon *Geata leode*

207	*findan mihte* xvna sum
1156	swylce hie æt finnes ham *findan meahton*
1378	frecne stowe ðær þu *findan miht*
2373	no ðy ær feasceafte *findan meahton*
2870	ower feor oððe neah *findan meahte*
3162	foresnotre men *findan mihton*

214	*on bearm* nacan *beorhte frætwe*
896	bær *on bearm* scipes *beorhte frætwa*

	on bearm nacan *beorhte* frætwe
214–15	gu*ð*searo geato*lic* guman ut scufon
	beran ofer bolcan *beorhte* randas
231–2	fyrd*searu* fus*licu* hine fyrwyt bræc
896	*bær on bearm* scipes *beorhte frætwa*

217	gewat þa ofer wægholm winde *gefysed*
630	ond þa gyddode guþe *gefysed*
2309	fyre *gefysed* wæs se fruma egeslic
2561	ða wæs hringbogan heorte *gefysed*

218	*flota famiheals* fugle *gelicost*
727	ligge *gelicost* leoht unfæger
985	stiðra nægla gehwylc style *gelicost*
1608	þæt hit eal gemealt ise *gelicost*
1909	*fleat famigheals* forð ofer yðe

219	oðþæt ymb antid o*þres dogores*
605	ofer ylda bearn o*þres dogores*

225	*Wedera leode* on wang stigon
697	wigspeda gewiofu *Wedera leodum*
1894	cwæð þæt wilcuman *Wedera leodum*
2900	nu is wilgeofa *Wedra leoda*
3156	geworhton þa *Wedra leode*

227	gu*ð*gew*æ*do *gode þancedon*
625	grette geata leod *gode þancode*
1397	ahleop ða se gomela *gode þancode*
1626	eodon him þa togeanes *gode þancodon*
2617	his gædelinges *guðgewædu*
2623	geaf him ða mid geatum *guðgewæda*

2730	*guðgewædu* *þær* me gifeðe swa
2851	*guðgewædu* *þær* se gomela læg
2871	þæt he genunga *geðgewædu*

| 230 | se þe holmclifu   *healdan scolde* |
| 704 | þa þæt hornreced   *healdan scoldon* |

232	*fyrdsearu fuslicu* *hine fyrwyt bræc*
1985	fægre fricgcean *hyne fyrwet bræc*
2618	*fyrdsearo fuslic* no ymbe ða fæhðe spræc
2784	frætwum gefyrðred *hyne fyrwet bræc*

| 238 | *byrnum werede*   þe þus brontne ceol |
| 2529 | gebide ge on beorge   *byrnum werede* |

| 242 | þe *on land Dena*   laðra nænig |
| 253 | leassceaweras   *on land Dena* |

| 245 | *lindhæbbende*   ne ge leafnesword |
| 1402 | *lindhæbbendra*   lastas wæron |

246	guðfremmendra *gearwe ne wisson*
715	goldsele *gumena* *gearwost wisse*
878	þara þe *gumena* bearn *gearwe ne wiston*

249	*secg on searwum* nis *þæt* seldguma
2530	*secgas on searwum* hwæðer sel mæge
2700	*secg on searwum* þæt ðæt sweord gedeaf

| 250 | *wæpnum geweorðad*   næfne him his wlite leoge |
| 331 | *wæpnum gewurþad*   þa ðær wlonc hæleð |

| 252 | frumcyn witan   ær ge *fyr heonan* |
| 1361 | under foldan   nis þæt *feor heonon* |

| 256 | anfealdne geþoht   *ofost is* selest |
| 3007 | eorlscipe efnde   nu* *is ofost* betost | [MS *me*] |

| 258 | *him* se yldesta   *ondswarode* |
| 340 | *him* þa ellenrof   *andswarode* |

261	ond Higelaces *heorðgeneatas*
1580	þonne he Hroðgares *heorðgeneatas*
2180	*heorðgeneatas* næs him hreoh sefa
2418	þenden hælo abead *heorðgeneatum*
3179	hlafordes hryre *heorðgeneatas*

263	æþele ordfruma *Ecgþeow haten*
373	wæs his ealdfæder *Ecgþeo haten*

266	witena welhwylc *wide geond eorþan*
3099	wigend weorðfullost *wide geond eorðan*

268	*sunu Healfdenes secean cwomon*
344	wille ic asecgan *sunu Healfdenes*
645	*sunu Healfdenes secean* wolde
1009	þæt to healle gang *Healfdenes sunu*
1040	ðonne sweorda gelac *sunu Healfdenes*
1597	þæt he sigehreðig *secean come*
1652	hwæt we þe þas sælac *sunu Healfdenes*
1699	*sunu Healfdenes* swigedon ealle
2147	*sunu Healfdenes* on minne sylfes dom

271	*Deniga frean* ne sceal þær dyrne sum
359	*Deniga frean* cuþe he duguðe þeaw
1680	æfter deofla hryre *Denigea frean*

273	swa we *soþlice secgan hyrdon*
582	swylcra searoniða *secgan hyrde*
875	þæt he fram sigemundes *secgan hyrde*
1346	selerædende *secgan hyrde*
2899	ac he *soðlice sægde* ofer ealle

275	deogol dædhata *deorcum nihtum*
2211	*deorcum nihtum* draca ricsian

282	ond þa *cearwylmas colran wurðaþ*
2066	æfter *cearwælmum colran weorðað*

289	*worda ond worca se þe wel þenceð*
1100	*wordum* ne *worcum* wære ne bræce
1833	*wordum* ond worcum* þæt ic þe *wel* herige [MS *weordum*]
2601	wiht onwendan *þam ðe wel þenceð*

291	*frean Scyldinga* gewitaþ forð beran
351	*frean Scildinga* frinan wille
500	þe æt fotum sæt *frean Scyldinga*

292	wæpen ond gewædu *ic eow wisige*
3103	wundur under wealle *ic eow wisige*

296	*arum healdan* oþðæt eft byreð
1099	*arum heolde* þæt ðær ænig mon
1182	*arum healdan* gyf þu ær þonne he

297	ofer lagustreamas	*leofne mannan*	
1915	se þe ær lange tid	*leofra manna*	
1943	æfter ligetorne	*leofne mannan*	
1994	*leofes mannes*	ic ðe lange bæd	
2080	*leofes mannes*	*lic* eall forswealg	
2127	*leofne mannan*	hio þæt *lic* ætbær	
2897	*leofes monnes*	lyt swigode	
3108	*leofne mannan*	þær he longe sceal	

	seomode on *sale**	*sidfæþmed scip*	[MS *onsole*]
302–3	on *ancre fæst*	eoforlic scionon	
	sælde to sande	*sidfæþme scip*	
1917–18	*oncer*bendum* *fæst*	þy læs hym yþa ðrym	[MS *oncear bendum*]

308	geatolic ond goldfah	*ongyton mihton*
1496	*ær he þone grundwong*	*ongytan mehte*
1911	*þæt hie* geata clifu	*ongitan meahton*
2770	*þæt he þone grundwong*	*ongitan meahte*

309	þæt wæs foremærost	*foldbuendum*
1355	*foldbuende*	no hie fæder cunnon

311	*lixte se leoma*	ofer landa fela
1570	*lixte se leoma*	leoht inne stod

315	wicg gewende	*word æfter* cwæð
341	wlanc wedera leod	*word æfter* spræc

321	gumum ætgædere	guð*byrne scan*
405	beowulf maðelode	on him *byrne scan*

322	*heard hondlocen*	hringiren scir
551	*heard hondlocen*	helpe gefremede

327	*bugon þa to bence*	byrnan hringdon
1013	*bugon þa to bence*	blædagande

329	sæmanna searo	*samod ætgædere*
387	seon *sibbegedriht*	*samod ætgædere*
729	swefan *sibbegedriht*	*samod ætgædere*
1063	þær wæs sang ond sweg	*samod ætgædere*

332	*oretmecgas*	æfter æþelum frægn
363	þone yldestan	*oretmecgas*
481	ofer ealowæge	*oretmecgas*

| 336 | ar ond ombiht | *ne seah ic* elþeodige |
| 2014 | weorod wæs on wynne | *ne seah ic* widan feorh |

338	*wen ic þæt ge for wlenco*	nalles for wræcsiðum
442	*wen ic þæt* he wille	gif he wealdan mot
508	ðær git *for wlence*	wada cunnedon
1206	syþðan he *for wlenco*	wean ahsode

342	*heard under helme*	we synt higelaces
404	*heard under helme*	þæt he on heoðe gestod
2539	*heard under helme*	hiorosercean bær

| 343 | *beodgeneatas* | beowulf is min nama |
| 1713 | breat bolgenmod | *beodgeneatas* |

| 348 | *Wulfgar maþelode* | þæt wæs Wendla leod |
| 360 | *Wulfgar maðelode* | to his winedrihtne |

| 361 | her syndon geferede | *feorran cumene* |
| 1819 | *feorran cumene* | þæt we fundiaþ |

| 366 | *wordum wrixlan* | no ðu him wearne geteoh |
| 874 | *wordum wrixlan* | welhwylc gecwæð |

371	*Hroðgar maþelode*	*helm Scyldinga*
456	*Hroðgar maþelode*	*helm Scyldinga*
1321	*Hroðgar maþelode*	*helm Scyldinga*

| 372 | ic hine cuðe | *cnihtwesende* |
| 535 | wit þæt gecwædon | *cnihtwesende* |

| 375 | *angan dohtor* | is his eafora nu |
| 2997 | ond ða Iofore forgeaf | *angan dohtor* |

| 381 | heaþorof hæbbe | hine *halig god* |
| 1553 | herenet hearde | ond *halig god* |

| 382 | *for arstafum* | *us* onsende |
| 458 | ond *for arstafum* | *usic* sohtest |

383	*to westdenum*	þæs ic wen hæbbe
1578	ðara þe he geworhte	*to westdenum*
3000	wælnið weia	*ðæs ðc ic wen* hafo*	[NOT IN MS]

| 384 | wið *Grendles gryre* | ic þæm godan sceal |
| 478 | on *Grendles gryre* | god eaþe mæg |

386	beo ðu *on ofeste* hat in gan
2747	bio nu on ofoste þæt ic ærwelan

389	*Deniga leodum*
599	*leode Deniga* ac he lust wigeð
696	*Denigea leode* ac him dryhten forgeaf
1323	*Denigea leodum* dead is Æschere
1712	ond to deaðcwalum *Deniga leodum*
2125	deaðwerigne *Denia leode*

394	*heardhicgende* hider wilcuman
799	*heardhicgende* hildemecgas

396	*under heregriman* Hroðgar geseon
2049	*under heregriman* hindeman siðe
2605	*under heregriman* hat þrowian

400	*þryðlic þegna heap* sume þær bidon
1627	*ðryðlic þegna heap* þeodnes gefegon

415	þa me þæt gelærdon *leode mine*
1336	forþan he to lange *leode mine*
1345	ic þæt londbuend *leode mine*
2797	þæs ðe ic moste *minum leodum*
2804	se scel to gemyndum *minum leodum*

416	*þa selestan* snotere ceorlas	
1406	*þone selestan* sawolleasne	
1685	*ðæm selestan* be sæm tweonum	
1956	*þone* selestan* bi sæm tweonum	[MS *þæs*]
2382	*þone selestan* sæcyninga	

	þa selestan *snotere ceorlas*
416–17	þeoden *Hroðgar* þæt ic þe sohte
	sona þæt gesawon *snottre ceorlas*
1591–2	þa ðe mid *Hroðgare* on holm wliton

423	wræc wedera nið *wean ahsodon*
1206	syþðan he for wlenco *wean ahsode*

427	*brego beorhtdena* biddan wille
482	þæt hie in beorsele *bidan woldon*
609	*brego beorhtdena* gehyrde on Beowulfe
1494	*bidan wolde* brimwylm onfeng
2308	*bidan wolde* ac mid bæle for

428	*eodor Scyldinga* anre bene

663   *eodur Scyldinga*   ut of healle

429   þæt ðu me ne forwyrne   *wigendra hleo*
899   ofer werþeode   *wigendra hleo*
1972   þæt ðær on worðig   *wigendra hleo*
2337   heht him þa gewyrcean   *wigendra hleo*

430   *freowine folca*   nu ic þus feorran com
2357   *freawine folca*   freslondum on
2429   *freawine folca*   æt minum fædergenam

437   þæt ic sweord bere   oþðe *sidne scyld*
325   setton sæmeþe   *side scyldas*

441   dryhtnes *dome*   se *þe hine deað nimeð*
452   onsend Higelace   *gif mec hild nime*
447   dreore fahne   *gif mec deað nimeð*
1436   sundes þe sænra   *ðe hyne* swylt *fornam*
1481   hondgesellum   *gif mec hild nime*
1491   *dom* gewyrce   *oþðe mec deað nimeð*
2536   gold gegangan   *oððe guð nimeð*

442   wen ic þæt he wille   gif he *wealdan mot*
2038   þenden hie ðam wæpnum   *wealdan moston*
2574   *wealdan moste*   swa him wyrd ne gescraf
2827   wyrm wohbogen   *wealdan ne moste*
2984   þæt hie wælstowe   *wealdan moston*

443   *in þæm guðsele*   Geotena leode
2139   *in ðam guðsele*   Grendeles modor   [MS *sele*]

446   *hafalan hydan*   ac he me habban wile
1372   *hafelan hydan*   nis þæt heoru stow   [NOT IN MS]

457   for gewyrhtum þu   *wine min Beowulf*
1704   geond widwegas   *wine min Beowulf*

460   *wearþ* he Heaþolafe   *to handbonan*
1330   *wearð* him on Heorote   *to handbanan*
2502   *to handbonan*   Huga cempan

463   *þanon he gesohte*   Suðdena folc
520   *ðonon he gesohte*   swæsne .ᛋ.

464   ofer yða gewealc   *Arscyldinga*
1710   eaforum Ecgwelan   *Arscyldingum*

465	ða ic furþum weold *folce Deniga**	[MS *deninga*]
1582	*folces Denigea* fyftyne men	

467	burh hæleþa *ða wæs Heregar dead*
2372	ealdan cuðe *ða wæs Hygelac dead*

468	min yldra mæg *unlifigende*
744	*unlyfigendes* eal gefeormod
1389	*unlifgendum* æfter selest
2908	eorl ofer oðrum *unlifigendum*

470	siððan þa fæhðe *feo* þingode
1380	ic þe þa fæhðe *feo* leanige

474	*gumena ængum* hwæt me Grendel hafað
2416	to gegangenne *gumena ænigum*
3054	*gumena ænig* nefne god sylfa

475	*hynðo on Heorote* mid his heteþancum
593	*hynðo on Heorote* gif þin hige wære

477	wigheap gewanod hie *wyrd forsweop*	
2814	Wægmundinga ealle *wyrd forsweop**	[MS *for speof*]

478	on Grendles gryre god *eaþe mæg*
2764	searwum gesæled sinc *eaðe mæg*

480	ful oft gebeotedon *beore druncne*
531	*beore druncen* ymb Brecan spræce
1467	wine *druncen* þa he þæs wæpnes onlah

488	deorre duguðe þe þa *deað fornam*
695	in þæm winsele *wældeað fornam*
2119	siðode sorhfull sunu *deað fornam*
2236	deore maðmas ealle hie *deað fornam*
2249	gode begeaton *guðdeað fornam*

492	*on beorsele* benc gerymed
1094	*on beorsele* byldan wolde
2635	in *biorsele* ðe us ðas beagas geaf

494	þryðum dealle þegn *nytte beheold*
667	seleweard aseted sundor*nytte beheold*
3118	scoc ofer scildweall sceft *nytte heold*

500	þe æt fotum sæt *frean Scyldinga*
1166	*æt fotum sæt frean Scyldinga* gehwylc hiora his ferhþe treowde

504	æfre *mærða* þon ma *middangeardes*	
751	þæt he ne mette *middangeardes*	
2996	mon on *middangearde* syððan hie ða *mærða* geslogon	

510	*aldrum neþdon* ne inc ænig mon	
538	*aldrum neddon* ond þæt geæfndon swa	

512	*sorhfullne sið þa git on sund reon*	
539	hæfdon swurd nacod *þa wit on sund reon*	
1278	*sorhfulne sið sunu dead*** wrecan	[MS *þeod*]
1429	*sorhfulne sið* on seglrade	
2119	*siðode sorhfull sunu dead* fornam	

529	*Beowulf maþelode bearn Ecgþeowes*	
631	*Beowulf maþelode bearn Ecgþeowes*	
957	*Beowulf maþelode bearn Ecþeowes*	
1383	*Beowulf maþelode bearn Ecgþeowes*	
1473	*Beowulf maðelode bearn Ecgþeowes*	
1651	*Beowulf maþelode bearn Ecgþeowes*	
1817	*Beowulf maþelode bearn Ecgþeowes*	
1999	*Biowulf maðelode bearn Ecgðioes*	
2425	*Biowulf maþelade bearn Ecgðeowes*	

530	hwæt þu *worn fela* wine min Unferð	
1783	wiggeweorþad unc sceal *worn fela*	

541	werian þohton *no he wiht fram me*	
581	wadu weallendu *no ic wiht fram þe*	

546	*wado weallende* wedera cealdost	
581	*wadu*** weallendu* no ic wiht fram þe	[MS *wudu*]

547	*nipende niht* ond norþanwind	
649	oðþe *nipende niht* ofer ealle	

551	heard hondlocen *helpe gefremede*	
1552	nemne him heaðobyrne *helpe gefremede*	

553	*golde gegyrwed* me to grunde teah	
1028	*golde gegyrede* gummanna fela	
2192	*golde gegyrede* næs mid Geatum ða	

555	grim on grape *hwæþre me* gyfeþe wearð	
574	*hwæþere me* gesælde þæt ic mid sweorde ofsloh	

557	*hildebille* heaþoræs fornam	
1520	*hildebille* hond sweng ne ofteah	

559   swa mec gelome   *laðgeteonan*
974   no þy leng leofað   *laðgeteona*

561   *deoran sweorde   swa hit gedefe wæs*
1670   deaðcwealm denigea   *swa hit gedefe wæs*
3048   discas lagon   ond *dyre swyrd*
3174   duguðum demdon   *swa hit gedefe* bið**   [MS ḡd . . .]

562   næs hie ðære fylle   *gefean hæfdon*
2740   feorhbennum seoc   *gefean habban*

565   ac *on mergenne   mecum* wunde
2939   cwæð he *on mergenne   meces* ecgum

571   *þæt ic* sænæssas   *geseon mihte*
648   siððan *hie* sunnan leoht   *geseon meahton*
961   *þæt* ðu hine selfne   *geseon moste*
1078   ða heo under swegle   *geseon meahte*
1628   *þæs þe hi* hyne gesundne   *geseon moston*
1875   *þæt hie** seoððan no   *geseon moston*   [MS *he seoðð* . . .]
1911   *þæt hie* Geata clifu   ongitan *meahton*
1998   *þæs ðe ic* ðe gesundne   *geseon moste*

576   *under heofones hwealf*   heardran feohtan
2015   *under heofones hwealf*   healsittendra

578   *hwaþere ic* fara feng   feore *gedigde*
661   gif þu þæt ellenweorc   *aldre gedigest*
1655   *ic þæt* unsofte   *ealdre gedigde*

579   *siþes werig   ða mec sæ oþbær*
1794   sona him seleþegn   *siðes wergum*

585   swa deorlice   *dæd gefremede*
940   þurh drihtnes miht   *dæd gefremede*
954   *dædum gefremed   þæt þin dom* lyfað

587   þeah ðu þinum broðrum   *to banan wurde*
2203   under bordhreoðan   *to bonan wurdon*

590   secge ic þe to soðe   *sunu Ecglafes*
980   ða wæs swigra secg   *sunu Eclafes*
1808   *sunu Ecglafes*   heht his sweord niman

597   swiðe onsittan   *Sigescyldinga*
2004   *Sigescyldingum*   sorge gefremede

599	*leode* Deniga ac *he lust* wigeð
618	*leodum* leofne *he* on *lust* geþeah
1653	*leod* Scyldinga *lustum* brohton
602	*eafoð ond ellen* ungeara nu
902	*eafoð ond ellen* he mid eotenum wear
2349	*eafoð ond ellen* forðon he ær fela
607	þa *wæs on salum* *sinces brytta*
1170	*sinces brytta* þu *on sælum wes*
1922	to gesecanne *sinces bryttan*
2071	*sinces brytta* to hwan syððan wearð
610	*folces hyrde* fæstrædne geþoht
1832	*folces hyrde* þæt he mec *fremman* wile
1849	*folces hyrde* ond þu þin *feorh* hafast
2644	to *gefremmanne* *folces hyrde*
2981	*folces hyrde* wæs in *feorh* dropen
612	word wæron wynsume eode *Wealhþeow forð*
1162	win of wunderfatum þa cwom *Wealhþeo forð*
613	cwen Hroðgares cynna *gemyndig*
868	guma gilphlæden gidda *gemyndig*
1173	beo wið Geatas glæd geofena *gemyndig*
1530	mærða *gemyndig* mæg Hylaces
2082	bona blodigtoð bealewa *gemyndig*
2171	ond gehwæðer oðrum hroþra *gemyndig*
2689	frecne fyrdraca fæhða *gemyndig*
626	wisfæst wordum þæs ðe hire se *willa gelamp*
824	æfter þam wælræse *willa gelumpen*
635	willan geworhte oþðe *on wæl crunge*
1113	wundum awyrded sume *on wæle crungon*
644	sigefolca sweg *oþþæt semninga*
1640	*oþðæt semninga* to sele comon
646	*æfenræste* wiste þæm ahlæcan
1252	*æfenræste* swa him ful oft gelamp
651	wan under wolcnum *werod eall aras*
1790	ofer dryhtgumum duguð *eal aras*
3030	wyrda ne worda *weorod eall aras*
652	*gegrette* þa guma* oþerne [MS *grette*]

2516   *gegrette ða   gumena* gehwylcne

653   Hroðgar Beowulf   ond him *hæl abead*
2418   þenden *hælo abead*   heorðgeneatum

654   winærnes geweald   *ond þæt word acwæð*
2046   wigbealu weccean   *ond þæt word acwyþ*

659   *gemyne mærþo   mægen*ellen cyð
1530   *mærða gemyndig*   mæg Hylaces
2678   *mærða* gemunde   mægen*strengo sloh   [MS *m* . . .]

660   waca wið wraþum   *ne bið þe wilna gad*
        niwe sibbe   *ne bið þe* nænigra *gad*
949–50 worulde *wilna*   þe ic geweald hæbbe

662   ða *him Hroþgar gewat*   mid his hæleþa gedryht
1236   ond *him Hroþgar gewat*   to hofe sinum

        helm of hafelan   sealde his hyrsted *sweord*
672–3   *irena cyst*   ombihtþegne
        geseted ond gesæd   hwam þæt *sweord* geworht
1696–7 *irena cyst*   ærest wære

673   *irena cyst*   ombihtþegne
802   ænig ofer eorþan   *irenna cyst*
1232   þa to setle   þær *wæs* symbla *cyst*
1559   wigena weorðmynd   þæt *wæs** wæpna *cyst*   [NOT IN MS]
1697   *irena cyst*   ærest wære

674   ond gehealdan het   *hildegeatwe*
2362   *hildegeatwa*   þa he to holme beag

676   *Beowulf Geata*   ær he on bed stige
1191   *Beowulf Geata*   be þæm gebroðrum twæm

678   *guþgeweorca*   þonne Grendel hine
981   on gylpspræce   *guðgeweorca*
1825   *guðgeweorca*   ic beo gearo sona

685   wig ofer wæpen   ond siþðan *witig god*
1056   nefne him *witig god*   wyrd forstode

687   mærðo deme   *swa him gemet þince*
3057   efne swa hwylcum manna   *swa him gemet ðuhte*

698   *frofor ond fultum*   þæt hie *feond* heora

1273	*frofre ond fultum* ðy he þone *feond* ofercwom
701	þæt *mihtig god* *manna cynnes*
712	mynte se manscaða *manna cynnes*
735	þæt he ma moste *manna cynnes*
810	modes myrðe *manna cynne*
914	mæg Higelaces *manna cynne*
1716	ðeah þe hine *mihtig god* *mægenes wynnum*
1725	hu *mihtig god* *manna cynne*
706	þæt *hie ne* moste *þa metod nolde*
967	ic *hine ne mihte* *þa metod nolde*
713	sumne besyrwan *in sele þam hean*
919	*swiðhicgende* to *sele þam hean*
1016	*swiðhicgende* on *sele þam hean*
1984	sinne geseldan *in sele þam hean*
716	fættum fahne *ne wæs þæt forma sið*
1463	folcstede fara *næs þæt forma sið*
1527	fæges fyrdhrægl *ða wæs forma sið*
2625	frod on forðweg *þa wæs forma sið*
721	*dreamum bedæled* duru sona onarn
1275	*dreame bedæled* deaþwic seon
723	onbræd þa bealohydig *ða he* gebolgen* wæs*
	[MS *he ge* VERY FADED]
1539	*brægd þa* beadwe heard *þa he gebolgen wæs*
2220	bufolc beorna *þæt he gebolgen* wæs* [MS *gebolge . . .*]
2550	let ða of breostum *ða he gebolgen wæs*
732	atol aglæca *anra gehwylces*
784	atelic egesa *anra gehwylcum*
733	*lif wið lice* þa him alumpen wæs
2423	*lif wið lice* no þon lange wæs
2571	*life* ond *lice* læssan hwile
2743	*lif* of *lice* nu ðu lungre geong
737	*mæg Higelaces* hu se manscaða
758	gemunde þa se goda *mæg Higelaces*
813	ac hine se modega *mæg Hygelaces*
914	*mæg Higelaces* manna cynne
740	ac he gefeng hraðe *forman siðe*
2286	fira fyrngeweorc *forman siðe*

750	*sona þæt onfunde* fyrena hyrde	
809	ða *þæt onfunde* se þe fela æror	
1497	*sona þæt onfunde* se ðe floda begong	
2226	secg synbysig *sona þæt* onfunde**	[MS *mwatide*]

762	mynte se *mæra* *þær** he meahte swa	[MS ILLEGIBLE AT EDGE]
797	*mæres* þeodnes *ðær hie meahton swa*	

763	widre gewindan ond *on weg þanon*
844	hu he werigmod *on weg þanon*

767	dryhtsele dynede *Denum eallum wearð*
823	dogera dægrim *Denum eallum wearð*
913	.Ⴟ. Scyldinga he þær *eallum wearð*
1417	dreorig ond gedrefed *Denum eallum wæs*

776	medubenc monig *mine gefræge*
837	ða wæs on morgen *mine gefræge*
1955	ealles moncynnes *mine gefræge*
2685	se ðe meca gehwane *mine gefræge*
2837	mægenagendra *mine gefræge*

782	swulge on swaþule sweg *up astag*
1373	þonon yðgeblond *up astigeð*

786	gryreleoð galan *godes ondsacan*
1682	gromheort guma *godes ondsaca*

791	nolde *eorla hleo* *ænige þinga*
1035	*heht ða eorla hleo* eahta mearas
1866	ða git him *eorla hleo* inne gesealde
1967	elne geeodon to ðæs ðe *eorla hleo*
2142	ac me *eorla hleo* eft gesealde
2190	*het ða eorla hleo* in gefetian
2374	æt ðam æðelinge *ænige ðinga*
2905	on ðam aglæcean *ænige þinga*

795	eorl Beowulfes *ealde lafe*
1488	ond þu Unferð læt *ealde lafe*
1688	*ealde lafe* on ðæm wæs or writen

796	wolde freadrihtnes *feorh ealgian*
2655	fane gefyllan *feorh ealgian*
2668	*feorh ealgian* ic ðe fullæstu

	wolde freadrihtnes *feorh ealgian*
796–7	*mæres þeodnes* *ðær hie meahton swa*

	fane gefyllan *feorh ealgian*
2655–6	wedra ðeodnes ic wat geare

801	*sawle secan* þone synscaðan
2820	*sawol secean* soðfæstra dom

808	*on feonda geweald* feor siðian
903	*on feonda geweald* forð forlacen

814	hæfde be honda wæs *gehwæþer oðrum*
2171	ond *gehwæðer oðrum* hroþra gemyndig

824	*æfter þam wælræse* willa gelumpen
2531	*æfter wælræse* wunde gedygan

827	genered wið niðe niht*weorce gefeh*
1569	sweord wæs swatig secg *weorce gefeh*

828	*ellenmærþum* hæfde Eastdenum
1471	*ellenmærðum* ne wæs þæm oðrum swa

831	*inwid*sorge *þe hie ær drugon*
1858	*inwit*niþas *þe hie ær drugon*

835	*earm ond eaxle* þær wæs eal geador
972	*earm ond eaxle* no þær ænige swa þeah

839	ferdon folctogan *feorran ond nean*
1174	*nean ond feorran* þu nu hafast
2317	nearofages nið *nean ond feorran*

840	*geond widwegas* *wundor sceawian*
1704	*geond widwegas* wine min Beowulf
3032	wollenteare *wundur sceawian*

848	atol *yða* geswing *eal gemenged*
1593	þæt wæs *yð*geblond *eal gemenged*

849	*haton heolfre* heorodreore weol
1423	*hatan heolfre* horn stundum song

858	þætte suð ne norð *be sæm tweonum*	
1297	on gesiðes had *be sæm tweonum*	
1685	ðæm selestan *be sæm tweonum*	
1956	þone* selestan *bi sæm tweonum*	[MS þæs]

þætte suð ne norð   *be sæm tweonum*

858–9   ofer *eormen*grund   oþer nænig
         þone selestan   *bi sæm tweonum*
1956–7   *eormen*cynnes   forðam Offa wæs

860   *under swegles begong*   selra nære
1773   *under swegles begong*   gesacan ne tealde

865   on *geflit* faran   *fealwe* mearas
916   hwilum *flitende   fealwe* stræte

867   *cystum cuðe*   hwilum cyninges þegn
923   *cystum gecyþed*   ond his cwen mid him

870   *worn gemunde*   word oþer fand
2114   þonne he wintrum frod   *worn gemunde*

872   *sið Beowulfes*   snyttrum styrian
1971   *sið Beowulfes*   snude gecyðed

874   wordum wrixlan   wel*hwylc gecwæð*
987   eglu unheoru   æg*hwylc gecwæð*

876   *ellendædum*   uncuþes fela
900   *ellendædum*   he þæs ær onðah

887   hordes hyrde   he *under harne stan*
1415   ofer *harne stan*   hleonian funde
2553   heaðotorht hlynnan   *under harne stan*
2744   hord sceawian   *under harne stan*

888   *æþelinges bearn*   ana geneðde
1408   ofereode þa   *æþelinga bearn*
2597   *æðelinga bearn*   ymbe gestodon
3170   *æþelinga bearn*   ealra twelfe

892   dryhtlic iren   draca *morðre swealt*
2782   middelnihtum   oðþæt he *morðre swealt*

893   hæfde aglæca   *elne gegongen*
1967   *elne geeodon*   to ðæs ðe eorla hleo
2676   *elne geeode*   þa his agen wæs
2917   *elne geeodon*   mid ofermægene

894   þæt he beahhordes   *brucan moste*
2241   *brucan moste*   beorh eallgearo
3100   þenden he burhwelan   *brucan moste*

| 895 | *selfes dome* | sæbat gehleod |
| 2776 | *sylfes dome* | segn eac genom |

907	swylce oft bemearn	*ærran mælum*
2237	*ærran mælum*	ond se an ða gen
3035	*ærran mælum*	þa wæs endedæg

| 910 | þæt þæt *ðeodnes bearn* | geþeon scolde |
| 1837 | geþingeð *þeodnes bearn* | he mæg þær fela |

| 920 | searo*wundor seon* | swylce self cyning |
| 1365 | þær mæg nihta gehwæm | nið*wundor seon* |

| 933 | weana ne wende | to *widan feore* |
| 2014 | werod wæs on wynne | ne seah ic *widan feorh* |

934	bote gebidan	þonne *blode fah*
1594	brim *blode fah*	blondenfeaxe
2974	þæt he *blode fah*	bugan sceolde

	bearngebyrdo	nu ic *Beowulf* þec
946–7	*secg betsta*	me for sunu wylle
	bebeorh þe ðone bealonið	*Beowulf* leofa
1758–9	*secg betsta*	ond þe þæt selre geceos

| 950 | worolde wilna | þe ic *geweald hæbbe* |
| 1610 | onwindeð wælrapas | se *geweald hafað* |

956	gode forgylde	*swa he nu gyt dyde*
1058	*gumena* cynnes	*swa he nu git deð*
1134	gear in geardas	*swa nu gyt deð*
1824	*gumena* dryhten	*ðonne ic gyt dyde*
2859	*gumena* gehwylcum	*swa he nu gen deð*

961	þæt ðu *hine selfne*	*geseon moste*
1605	*selfne gesawon*	þa þæt sweord ongan
1628	þæs þe hi *hyne gesundne*	*geseon moston*
1875	þæt hie seoððan no	*geseon moston*
1998	þæs ðe ic ðe *gesundne*	*geseon moste*

| 963 | ic hine hrædlice | *heardan clammum* |
| 1335 | þurh hæstne had | *heardum clammum* |

969	*feorhgeniðlan*	wæs to foremihtig
1540	*feorhgeniðlan*	þæt heo on flet gebeah
2933	ond ða folgode	*feorhgeniðlan*

971   to lifwraþe   *last weardian*
2164   lungre gelice   *last weardode*

974   no þy *leng leofað   laðgeteona*
2008   se ðe *lengest leofað   laðan* cynnes

982   *siþðan æþelingas*   eorles cræfte
2888   idel hweorfan   *syððan æðelingas*

986   hæþenes handsporu   *hilderinces*   [MS *hild . . . derinces*]
1495   *hilderince*   ða wæs hwil dæges
1576   *hilderince*   ac he hraþe wolde

989   *iren ærgod*   þæt ðæs ahlæcan
2586   *iren ærgod*   ne wæs þæt eðe sið

1002   *aldres orwena*   no þæt yðe byð
1565   *aldres orwena*   yrringa sloh

1012   ymb *hyra sincgyfan*   sel gebæran
2311   on *hyra sincgifan*   sare geendod

1014   *fylle gefægon*   fægere geþægon
1333   *fylle gefægnod*   heo þa fæhðe wræc   [MS *ge frægnod*]

1022   hroden hildecumbor   *helm ond byrnan*
1629   ða wæs of þæm hroran   *helm ond byrne*
2868   healsittendum   *helm ond byrnan*

1038   sadol searwum fah   *since gewurþad*
1450   secan sundgebland   *since geweorðad*

1045   wicga ond wæpna   *het hine wel brucan*
2812   beah ond byrnan   *het hyne brucan well*

             swa manlice   *mære þeoden*
1046–7   hordweard *hæleþa*   heaþoræsas geald
             alegdon ða tomiddes   *mærne þeoden*
3141–2   *hæleð* hiofende   hlaford leofne

1047   *hordweard hæleþa*   heaþoræsas geald
1852   *hordweard hæleþa*   gyf þu healdan wylt

1048   *mearum ond madmum*   swa hy næfre man lyhð
1898   *mearum ond maðmum*   mæst hlifade
2166   *meara ond maðma*   swa sceal mæg don

1050	ða gyt æghwylcum *eorla drihten*
2338	eallirenne *eorla dryhten*

	on þære medubence maþðum gesealde	
1052–3	*yrfelafe* ond þone ænne heht	
	on meodubence maþme* þy weorþra*	[MS *maþma; weorþre*]
1902–3	*yrfelafe* gewat him on naca	

1061	*leofes ond laþes* se þe longe her
2910	*leofes ond laðes* nu ys leodum wen

1065	*gomenwudu greted* *gid* oft *wrecen*
2108	*gomenwudu grette* hwilum *gyd awræc*
2446	giong on galgan þonne he *gyd wrece*
3172	word*gyd wrecan* ond ymb wer sprecan

1068	be Finnes eaferum *ða hie se fær begeat*
2230	*þa* hyne* se fær begeat* [MS DAMAGED AND ILLEGIBLE]

1077	meotodsceaft bemearn *syþðan morgen com*
1784	maþma gemænra *siþðan morgen* bið
2103	manegum maðmum *syððan mergen com*
2124	noðer hy hine ne moston *syððan mergen cwom*

1079	*morþorbealo maga* þær heo ær mæste he
2742	*morðorbealo maga* þonne min sceaceð

1088	wið *eotena bearn* agan moston
1141	þæt he *eotena bearn* inne gemunde

1092	efne swa swiðe *sincgestreonum*
1226	*sincgestreona* beo þu suna minum

1093	*fættan goldes* swa he fresena cyn
2102	*fættan golde* fela leanode
2246	*fættan goldes* fea worda cwæð

1097	elne *unhlitme** aðum benemde [MS *unflitme*]
1129	eal *unhlitme* eard gemunde

1110	æt þæm ade wæs *eþgesyne*
1244	ofer æþelinge *yþgesene*

1111	*swatfah* syrce *swyn* ealgyldcn
1286	sweord *swate fah* *swin* ofer helme

1119	wand *to wolcnum* wælfyra mæst
1374	won *to wolcnum* þonne wind styreþ
3143	ongunnon þa on beorge bælfyra mæst

| 1122 | laðbite *lices*   lig *ealle forswealg* |
| 2080 | leofes mannes   *lic eall forswealg* |

| 1143 | þonne him Hunlafing   *hildeleoman* |
| 2583 | *hildeleoman*   hreðsigora ne gealp |

| 1147 | sweordbealo sliðen   æt *his selfes ham* |
| 2325 | snude to soðe   þæt *his sylfes ham**   [MS *him*] |

| 1152 | feonda *feorum*   swilce Fin slægen |
| 1306 | freonda *feorum*   þa wæs frod cyning |

| 1165 | *æghwylc oðrum trywe*   swylce þær Unferþ þyle |
| 1228 | her is *æghwylc*   eorl *oþrum getrywe* |

1171	*goldwine gumena* ond to Geatum spræc
1476	*goldwine gumena* hwæt wit geo spræcon
1602	*goldwine gumena* gistas setan

1172	mildum wordum *swa sceal man don*
1534	mundgripe mægenes *swa sceal man don*
2166	meara ond maðma *swa sceal mæg don*

| 1184 | wene ic þæt he mid gode   *gyldan wille* |
| 2636 | þæt we him ða guðgetawa   *gyldan woldon* |

1185	uncran eaferan gif he þæt *eal gemon*
1701	fremeð on folce feor *eal gemon*
2427	orleghwila ic þæt *eall gemon*

| 1193 | wordum bewægned   ond *wunden gold* |
| 3134 | þa wæs *wunden gold*   on wæn hladen |

| 1203 | nefa Swertinges   *nyhstan siðe* |
| 2511 | *niehstan siðe*   ic geneðde fela |

| 1211 | *breostgewædu*   ond se beah somod |
| 2162 | *breostgewædu*   bruc ealles well |

1212	*wyrsan wigfrecan* *wæl reafedon*
2496	*wyrsan wigfrecan* weorðe gecyþan
3027	þenden he wið wulf *wæl reafode*

1216	bruc ðisses beages *Beowulf leofa*	
1758	bebeorh þe ðone bealonið *Beowulf leofa*	
1854	licað leng swa wel *leofa Beowulf*	
1987	hu lomp eow on lade *leofa Biowulf*	
2663	*leofa Biowulf* læst eall tela	
1221	*hafast þu gefered* *þæt* ðe feor ond neah	
1855	*hafast þu gefered* *þæt* þam folcum sceal	
1232	*eode þa to setle* þær wæs *symbla* cyst	
1782	*ga* nu *to setle* *symbel*wynne dreoh	
1235	eorla manegum *syþðan æfen cwom*	
2303	earfoðlice oððæt *æfen cwom*	
1236	ond him Hroþgar gewat *to hofe sinum*	
1507	hringa þengel *to hofe sinum*	
1241	*fus ond fæge* fletræste gebeag	
3025	*fus ofer fægum* fela reordian	
1245	*heaþosteapa helm* *hringed byrne*	
2153	*headosteapne helm* hare *byrnan*	
2615	brunfagne *helm* *hringde byrnan*	
1258	æfter *guðceare* *Grendles modor*	
1282	*Grendles modor* wæs se gryre læssa	
1538	Guðgeata leod *Grendles modor*	
2118	gearo gyrnwræce *Grendeles modor*	
2139	in ðam *guð*sele* *Grendeles modor*	[MS *sele*]
1277	gifre ond galgmod *gegan* wolde	
1462	se ðe gryresiðas *gegan* dorste	
1535	þonne he æt guðe *gegan* þenceð	
2630	syððan hie togædre *gegan* hæfdon	
1281	edhwyrft eorlum siþðan *inne fealh*	
2225	ærnes þearfa ond ðær *inne fealh**	[MS *weall*]
1287	*ecgum þyhtig** andweard scireð	[MS *dyhtig*]
1558	ealdsweord eotenisc *ecgum þyhtig*	
1303	cuþe folme cearu *wæs geniwod*	
1322	ne frin þu æfter sælum sorh *is geniwod*	
2287	þa se wyrm onwoc wroht *wæs geniwad*	
1306	freonda feorum *þa wæs frod cyning*	

2209   fiftig wintra   *wæs ða frod cyning*

1307   *har hilderinc   on hreon mode*
2581   æfter heaðuswenge   *on hreoum mode*
3136   *har hilderinc   to Hronesnæsse*

1311   *sigoreadig secg   samod ærdæge*
2352   *sigoreadig secg   sele fælsode*
2942   sarigmodum   *somod ærdæge*

1313   *self mid gesiðum   þær se snotera bad*
1924   *selfa mid gesiðum   sæwealle neah*

1327   *hafelan weredon   þonne hniton feþan*
1448   ac se hwita helm   *hafelan werede*
2544   hildehlemma   *þonne hnitan feðan*

1326   *eaxlgestealla   ðonne we on orlege*
1714   *eaxlgesteallan   oþþæt he ana hwearf*

1338   *ealdres scyldig   ond nu oþer cwom*
2061   *ealdres scyldig   him se oðer þonan*

1341   *þæs þe þincean mæg   þegne monegum*
1419   to geþolianne   *ðegne monegum*

1343   hreþerbealo hearde   *nu seo hand ligeð*
2745   wiglaf leofa   *nu se wyrm ligeð*

1353   næfne *he wæs mara   þonne ænig man oðer*
1560   buton *hit wæs mare   ðonne ænig mon oðer*

1360   under næssa *genipu   niþer gewiteð*
2808   ofer floda *genipu   feorran drifað*

1381   *ealdgestreonum   swa ic ær dyde*
1458   þæt wæs an foran   *ealdgestreona*
1891   eftsið eorla   *swa he ær dyde*

         ure æghwylc sceal   *ende gebidan*
1386–7 *worolde lifes   wyrce se þe mote*
         æþeling ærgod   *ende gebidan*
2342–3 *worulde lifes   ond se wyrm somod*

1403   æfter waldswaþum   *wide gesyne*
2316   wæs þæs wyrmes wig   *wide gesyne*
2947   wælræs weora   *wide gesyne*

3158   wægliðendum *wide gesyne*

1404   gang *ofer grundas*   þær heo gegnum for
2073   glad *ofer grundas*   gæst yrre cwom

1421   on *þam holmclife*   *hafelan* metton
1635   from *þæm holmclife*   *hafelan* bæron

1426   sellice sædracan   *sund cunnian*
1444   sid ond searofah   *sund cunnian*

1434   *yðgewinnes*   þæt him on aldre stod
2412   *yðgewinne*   se wæs innan full

1439   *niða genæged*   ond on næs togen
2206   *niða genægdan*   nefan hererices

1440   wundor*lic* wægbora   *weras* sceawedon
1650   wliteseon wræt*lic*   *weras* on sawon

1442   eorlgewædum   *nalles for* ealdre *mearn*
1537   gefeng þa be eaxle   *nalas for* fæhðe *mearn*

1446   þæt *him hildegrap*   hreþre ne mihte
2507   ac *him hildegrap*   heortan wylmas

1447   eorres inwitfeng   *aldre gesceþðan*
1524   *aldre sceþðan*   ac seo ecg geswac

1459   *ecg wæs iren*   atertanum fah
2778   *ecg wæs iren*   ealdhlafordes

1461   manna ængum   þara þe hit mid *mundum bewand*
3022   monig morgenceald   *mundum bewunden*

1469   under yða gewin   *aldre geneþan*
2133   eorlscipe efnde   *ealdre geneðde*

1474   geþenc nu *se mæra*   *maga Healfdenes*
2011   sona me *se mæra*   *mago Healfdenes*
2587   þæt *se mæra*   *maga Ecgðeowes*

1475   *snottra fengel*   nu ic eom siðes fus
2156   *snotra fengel*   sume worde het

1478   *aldre linnan*   þæt ðu me a wære
2443   æðeling unwrecen   *ealdres linnan*

1482   swylce þu *ða madmas   þe þu me sealdest*
2490   ic him *þa maðmas   þe he me sealde*

1484   mæg þonne on þæm golde ongitan   *Geata dryhten*
1831   *Geata dryhten   þeah ðe he geong sy*
2402   *dryhten Geata*   dracan sceawian
2483   *Geata dryhtne   guð* onsæge
2560   wið ðam *gryregieste   Geata dryhten*
2576   *Geata dryhten   gryre*fahne sloh
2901   *dryhten Geata*   deaðbedde fæst
2991   geald þone *guðræs   Geata dryhten*

        mæg þonne on þæm golde ongitan   *Geata dryhten*
1484–5   geseon sunu *Hrædles*   þonne he on þæt sinc starað
        geald þone guðræs   *Geata dryhten*
2991–2   *Hreðles* eafora   þa he to ham becom

1490   heardecg habban   ic me *mid Hruntinge*
1659   ne meahte ic æt hilde   *mid Hruntinge*

1492   æfter þæm *wordum   Wedergeata leod*
1612   ne nom he in þæm wicum   *Wedergeata leod*
2551   *Wedergeata leod   word* ut faran

1496   ær he *þone grundwong*   ongytan mehte
2588   *grundwong þone   of*gyfan wolde

1498   heorogifre beheold   *hund missera*
1769   swa ic Hringdena   *hund missera*

1505   *locene leoðosyrcan*   laþan fingrum
1890   *locene leoðosyrcan*   landweard onfand

1507   *hringa fengel**   to hofe sinum   [MS *þengel*]
2345   oferhogode ða   *hringa fengel*

1515   ne him for hrof*sele   hrinan ne* mehte
3053   þæt ðam hring*sele   hrinan ne* moste

1528   *deorum madme*   þæt his dom alæg
2236   *deore maðmas*   ealle hie deað fornam
3131   *dyre maðmas*   dracan ec scufun

1533   stið ond stylecg   *strenge getruwode*
2540   under stancleofu   *strengo getruwode*

1544   *feþecempa*   þæt he on fylle wearð

2853	*feðecempa* frean eaxlum neah

1550	hæfde ða forsiðod *sunu Ecgþeowes*
2367	oferswam ða sioleða bigong *sunu Ecgðeowes*
2398	sliðra geslyhta *sunu Ecgðiowes*

1554	geweold wigsigor *witig drihten*
1841	þe þa wordcwydas *wigtig drihten*

1558	*ealdsweord eotenisc* ecgum þyhtig
2616	*ealdsweord etonisc* þæt him Onela forgeaf
2979	*ealdsweord eotonisc* entiscne helm

1587	*aldorleasne* swa him ær gescod
3003	*ealdorleasne* þone ðe ær geheold

1590	heorosweng heardne *ond hine þa heafde becearf*
2138	holm heolfre weoll *ond ic heafde becearf*

1593	þæt *wæs yðgeblond* *eal* gemenged
1620	*wæron yðgebland* *eal* gefælsod

1594	brim blode fah *blondenfeaxe*
	wolde *blondenfeax* beddes neosan
1873	*blondenfeaxum* him wæs bega wen
2962	*blondenfexa* on bid wrecen

1599	þæt hine seo brimwylf *abroten* hæfde*	[MS *abreoten*]
2707	ond hi hyne þa begen *abroten hæfdon*	

1601	*hwate Scyldingas* gewat him ham þonon
2052	*æfter hæleþa hryre hwate Scyldungas*
3005	*æfter hæleða hryre hwate Scildingas*

1616	*forbarn brodenmæl* wæs *þæt blod* to þæs hat
1667	*forbarn brogdenmæl* swa *þæt blod* gesprang

1637	*felamodigra* feower scoldon
1888	cwom þa to flode *felamodigra*

1639	to *þæm goldsele Grendles heafod*
1648	*Grendles heafod* þær guman druncon
2083	of *ðam goldsele* gongan wolde

1641	*frome fyrdhwate* feowertyne
2476	*frome fyrdhwate* freode ne woldon

1646	*hæle hildedeor Hroðgar gretan*
1816	*hæle hildedeor Hroðgar grette*
2010	to ðam hringsele *Hroðgar gretan*
3111	*hæle hildedior* hæleða monegum

1673	*ond þegna gehwylc þinra leoda*
1708	eal langtwidig *leodum þinum*
2033	*ond þegna* gehwam þara *leoda*
2095	þær ic þeoden min *þine leode*

| 1675 | þeoden Scyldinga   *on þa healfe* |
| 2063 | þonne bioð abrocene   *on ba healfe* |

1679	*enta ærgeweorc* hit on æht gehwearf
2717	gesæt on sesse seah *on enta geweorc*
2774	eald *enta geweorc* anne mannan

| 1684 | on geweald gehwearf   *woroldcyninga* |
| 3180 | cwædon þæt he wære   *wyruldcyninga**   [MS *wyruldcyning*] |

	on geweald gehwearf worold*cyninga*
	ðæm selestan be sæm tweonum
1684–6	*ðara þe* on Scedenigge sceattas dælde
	þone selestan sæcyninga
2382–3	þara ðe in swiorice sinc brytnade

1692	*ecean dryhtne* him þæs endelean
1779	*ecean dryhtne* þæs ðe ic on aldre gebad
2330	ofer ealde riht *ecean dryhtne*
2796	*ecum dryhtne* þe ic her on starie

| 1700 | *þæt la mæg secgan   se þe soð* ond riht |
| 2864 | *þæt la mæg secgan   se ðe* wyle *soð* specan |

| 1702 | *eald .Ⴟ.weard*   þæt ðes eorl wære |
| 2210 | *eald eþelweard*   oððæt an ongan |

1709	*hæleðum to helpe* ne wearð Heremod swa
1830	*hæleþa to helpe* ic on Higelac wat
1961	*hæleðum to helpe* Hemminges mæg

| 1716 | þe hine mihtig god   *mægenes wynnum* |
| 1887 | *mægenes wynnum*   se þe oft manegum scod |

1719	breosthord blodreow nallas *beagas geaf*
2635	in biorsele ðe us ðas *beagas geaf*
3009	ond þone gebringan þe us *beagas geaf*

1724	awræc *wintrum frod* wundor is to secganne
2114	þonne he *wintrum frod* worn gemunde
2277	waráð *wintrum frod* ne byð him wihte ðy sel

| 1730 | seleð him on eþle   *eorþan wynne* |
| 2727 | *eorðan wynne**   ða wæs eall sceacen   [MS *wyn . . .*] |

| 1733 | *side rice*   þæt he his selfa ne mæg |
| 2199 | *side rice*   þam ðær selra wæs |

1736	*adl* ne yldo ne him inwitsorh
1763	þæt þec *adl oððe* ecg eafoþes getwæfeð
1848	*adl oþðe* iren ealdor ðinne

| 1781 | ofer ealdgewin   *eagum starige* |
| 1935 | þæt hire an dæges   *eagum starede* |

| 1784 | *maþma gemænra*   siþðan morgen bið |
| 1860 | *maþmas gemæne*   manig oþerne |

| 1788 | *fletsittendum*   fægere gereorded |
| 2022 | þa ic Freaware   *fletsittende* |

| 1789 | *niowan stefne*   nihthelm geswearc |
| 2594 | *niwan stefne*   nearo ðrowode |

1792	*gamela Scylding* geat unigmetes wel
2105	þær wæs gidd ond gleo *gomela Scilding*
2487	guðhelm toglad *gomela Scylfing*
2968	*gomela Scilfing* ac forgeald hraðe

| 1798 | *heaþoliðende*   habban scoldon |
| 2955 | *heaðoliðendum*   hord forstandan |

1810	cwæð he þone guðwine *godne tealde*
2641	þe he usic garwigend *gode tealde*
2184	swa hyne Geata bearn *godne* ne *tealdon*

1812	*meces ecge* þæt wæs modig secg
2614	*meces ecgum* ond his magum ætbær
2939	cwæð he on mergenne *meces ecgum*

1847	hild heorugrimme *hreþles eaferan*
2358	*hreðles eafora* hiorodryncum swealt
2992	*hreðles eafora* þa he to ham becom

| 1858 | *inwitniþas*   þe hie ær drugon |

| 1947 | *inwitniða*   syððan ærest wearð |

| 1874 | ealdum infrodum   *oþres swiðor* |
| 2198 | eard eðelriht   *oðrum swiðor* |

| 1889 | hægstealdra heap   *hringnet bæron* |
| 2754 | hyran heaðosiocum   *hringnet beran* |

| 1899 | ofer Hroðgares   *hordgestreonum* |
| 3092 | *hordgestreona*   hider utætbær |

| 1929 | *Hæreþes dohtor*   næs hio hnah swa þeah |
| 1981 | geond þæt healreced   *Hæreðes dohtor* |

| 1944 | huru þæt onhohsnode   *Hemminges* mæg* | [MS *hem ninges*] |
| 1961 | hæleðum to helpe   *Hemminges* mæg* | [MS *hem inges*] |

1948	gyfen goldhroden *geongum cempan*
2044	onginneð geomormod *geongum cempan*
2626	*geongan cempan* þæt he guðe ræs

| 1953 | *lifgesceafta*   lifigende breac |
| 3064 | *lifgesceafta*   þonne leng ne mæg |

| 1963 | *gewat him ða se* hearda   *mid his* hondscole |
| 2949 | *gewat him ða se* goda   *mid his* gædelingum |

| 2003 | wearð on ðam wange   þær he *worna fela* |
| 2542 | geseah ða be wealle   se ðe *worna fela* |

| 2006 | swa begylpan ne þearf   *Grendeles maga* |
| 2353 | ond æt guðe forgrap   *Grendeles mægum* |

| 2008 | se ðe lengest leofað   *laðan cynnes* |
| 2354 | *laðan cynnes*   no þæt læsest wæs |

| 2015 | under heofones hwealf   *healsittendra* |
| 2868 | *healsittendum*   helm ond byrnan |

| 2027 | *rices hyrde*   ond þæt ræd talað |
| 3080 | *rices hyrde*   ræd ænigne |

| 2030 | æfter leodhryre   *lytle hwile* |
| 2097 | *lytle hwile*   lifwynna breac |

| 2034 | þonne he mid fæmnan   *on flett gæð* |
| 2054 | frætwum hremig   *on flet gæð* |

2036	on him gladiað	*gomelra lafe*	
2563	god guðcyning	*gomele lafe*	
2049	under heregriman	*hindeman siðe*	
2517	hwate helmberend	*hindeman siðe*	
2073	glad ofer grundas	*gæst yrre cwom*	
2669	æfter ðam wordum	*wyrm yrre cwom*	
2076	þær wæs Hondscio	*hild* onsæge*	[MS *hilde*]
2483	Geata dryhtne	*guð onsæge*	
2090	dior dædfruma	*gedon wolde*	
2186	drihten Wedera	*gedon wolde*	
2107	hwilum hildedeor	*hearpan wynne*	
2262	hæleðum be healfe	*næs hearpan wyn*	
2113	hildestrengo	*hreðer inne weoll*	
2331	bitre gebulge	*breost innan weoll*	
2593	hyne hordweard	*hreðer æðme weoll*	
2133	*eorlscipe efnde*	ealdre geneðde	
2535	*eorlscype efne*	ic mid elne sceall	
2622	*eorlscipe efnan*	swa his ærfæder	
3007	*eorlscipe efnde*	nu is ofost betost	
2134	*mærðo fremede*	he me mede gehet	
2514	*mærðu fremman*	gif mec se mansceaða	
2135	ic ða ðæs wælmes	þe is *wide cuð*	
2923	wihte ne wene	ac wæs *wide cuð*	
2141	feorh oðferede	*næs ic fæge þa gyt*	
2975	feoll on foldan	*næs he fæge þa git*	
2146	mægnes mede	ac he *me maðmas* geaf*	
		[WORD LOST AT EDGE OF MS]	
2640	onmunde usic mærða	ond *me þas maðmas geaf*	
2865	þæt se mondryhten	se eow ða *maðmas geaf*	
2147	sunu Healfdenes	on minne *sylfes dom*	
2776	*sylfes dome*	segn eac genom	
2156	*snotra fengel*	sume worde het	
1475	*snottra fengel*	nu ic eom siðes fus	

| 2159 | *leod* Scyldunga | lange hwile |
| 2603 | leoflic lindwiga | *leod* Scylfinga |

| 2160 | no ðy ær *suna sinum* | *syllan wolde* |
| 2729 | nu ic *suna minum* | *syllan wolde* |

| 2162 | breostgewædu | *bruc* ealles *well* |
| 2812 | beah ond byrnan | het hyne *brucan well* |

| 2168 | *dyrnum cræfte* | deað renian |
| 2290 | *dyrnan cræfte* | dracan heafde neah |

| 2169 | *hondgesteallan* | Hygelace wæs |
| 2596 | nealles him on heape | *handgesteallan** | [MS *heand gesteallan*] |

| 2200 | eft þæt geiode | *ufaran dogrum* |
| 2392 | *uferan dogrum* | eadgilse wearð |

2201	*hildehlæmmum*	*syððan* hygelac læg
2351	*hildehlemma*	*syððan* he hroðgares
2544	*hildehlemma*	þonne hnitan feðan

| 2209 | *fiftig wintra* | *wæs* ða frod *cyning* |
| 2733 | *fiftig wintra* | *næs* se folc*cyning* |

| 2222 | *sylfes willum* | se ðe him sare gesceod |
| 2639 | to ðyssum siðfate | *sylfes willum* |

| 2246 | fættan goldes | *fea worda cwæð* |
| 2662 | frean on fultum | *fea worda cwæð* |

| 2250 | *feorhbealo frecne* | fyra gehwylcne |
| 2537 | *feorhbealu frecne* | frean eowerne |

| 2253 | oððe feormie | *fæted wæge* |
| 2282 | *fæted wæge* | frioðowære bæd |

| 2254 | *dryncfæt deore* | duguð ellor sceoc |
| 2306 | *drincfæt dyre* | þa wæs dæg sceacen |

| 2256 | fætum befeallen | feormynd *swefað* |
| 2457 | reote berofene | ridend *swefað* |

| 2274 | *fyre befangen* | hyne foldbuend |
| 2595 | *fyre befongen* | se ðe ær folce weold |

| 2277 | waráð wintrum frod | *ne byð him wihte ðy sel* |

2687   wæpen wundrum heard   *næs him wihte ðe sel*

2279   heold *on hrusan   hordærna* sum
2831   hreas *on hrusan   hordærne* neah

2280   *eacencræftig*   oðð æt hyne an abealch
3051   þonne wæs þæt yrfe   *eacencræftig*

2300   sincfæt sohte   *he þæt sona onfand*
2713   swelan ond swellan   *he þæt sona onfand*

2306   drincfæt dyre   *þa wæs* dæg *sceacen*
2727   eorðan wynne   *ða wæs* eall *sceacen*

2316   wæs *þæs wyrmes wig*   wide gesyne
2348   ne him *þæs wyrmes wig*   for wiht dyde

2335   *gledum forgrunden*   him ðæs *guðkyning*
2677   *gledum forgrunden*   þa gen *guðcyning*

gledum forgrunden   him ðæs *guðkyning*
2335–6   *Wedera þioden*   wræce leornode
godum gegongen   þæt se *guðcyning*
3036–7   *Wedra þeoden*   wundordeaðe swealt

2336   *Wedera þioden*   wræce leornode
2656   *Wedra ðeodnes*   ic wat geare
2786   in ðam wongstede   *Wedra þeoden*
3037   *Wedra þeoden*   wundordeaðe swealt

2339   wigbord wrætlic   *wisse he gearwe*
2725   wunde wælbleate   *wisse he gearwe*

nearo neðende   *niða gedigde*
2350–1   *hildehlemma*   syððan he Hroðgares
gumcystum god   guða *gedigde*
2543–4   *hildehlemma*   þonne hnitan feðan

2366   fram þam hildfrecan   *hames niosan*
2388   *hames niosan*   syððan heardred læg

2369   þær him hygd gebead   *hord ond rice*
3004   wið hettendum   *hord ond rice*

2380   *ofer sæ* sohtan   *suna Ohteres*
2394   *ofer sæ* side   *sunu Ohteres*
2612   *suna Ohteres**   þam æt sæcce wearð   [MS *ohtere*]

| 2419 | *goldwine geata*   him wæs geomor sefa |
| 2584 | *goldwine geata*   guðbill geswac |

| 2420 | wæfre ond wælfus   wyrd *ungemete neah* |
| 2728 | dogorgerimes   deað *ungemete neah* |

| 2427 | *orleghwila*   ic þæt eall gemon |
| 2911 | *orleghwile*   syððan underne |

| 2445 | *to gebidanne*   þæt his byre ride |
| 2452 | *to gebidanne*   burgum in innan |

| 2462 | wongas ond wicstede   swa *wedra helm* |
| 2705 | forwrat *wedra helm*   wyrm on middan |

| 2472 | þa wæs synn ond sacu   *Sweona ond Geata* |
| 2946 | wæs sio swatswaðu   *Sweona* ond Geata*   [MS *swona*] |

| 2485 | *billes ecgum*   on bonan stælan |
| 2508 | banhus gebræc   nu sceall *billes ecg* |

| 2516 | gegrette ða   *gumena gehwylcne* |
| 2859 | *gumena gehwylcum*   swa he nu gen deð |

| 2517 | *hwate helmberend*   hindeman siðe |
| 2642 | *hwate helmberend*   þeah ðe hlaford us |

| 2524 | bord ond byrnan   nelle ic *beorges weard* |
| 2580 | bysigum gebæded   þa wæs *beorges weard* |

| 2591 | alætan *læn*dagas   *næs ða long to ðon* |
| 2845 | *læn*an lifes   *næs ða lang to ðon* |

| 2602 | *Wiglaf* wæs haten   *Weoxstanes sunu* |
| 2862 | *Wiglaf* maðelode   *Weohstanes sunu* |

| 2607 | wicstede weligne   *Wægmundinga* |
| 2814 | *Wægmundinga*   ealle wyrd forsweop |

| 2624 | *æghwæs unrim*   þa he of ealdre gewat |
| 3135 | *æghwæs unrim*   æþeling boren |

| 2647 | *þæt* ure *mandryhten*   mægenes behofað |
| 2865 | *þæt* se *mondryhten*   se eow ða maðmas geaf |

| 2670 | atol inwitgæst   *oðre siðe* |
| 3101 | uton nu efstan   *oðre siðe**   [NOT IN MS] |

| 2674 | *geongum garwigan* geoce gefremman | |
| 2811 | *geongum garwigan* goldfahne helm | |

| 2683 | þæt him *irenna ecge* mihton | |
| 2828 | ac hine *irenna ecga* fornamon | |

| 2738 | ne *sohte searoniðas* ne me swor fela | |
| 3067 | *sohte searoniðas* seolfa ne cuðe | |

| 2740 | feorh*bennum seoc* gefean habban | |
| 2904 | sex*bennum seoc* sweorde ne meahte | |

2631	*Wiglaf maðelode* wordrihta fela	
2752	ða ic snude gefrægn *sunu Wihstanes*	
2862	*Wiglaf maðelode Weohstanes sunu*	
3076	*Wiglaf maðelode Wihstanes sunu*	
3120	huru se snotra *sunu Wihstanes*	

2759	*wundur on wealle* ond þæs wyrmes denn	
3060	wræte* *under wealle* weard ær ofsloh	[MS *wræce*]
3103	*wundur under wealle* ic eow wisige	

| 2772 | onsyn ænig ac hyne *ecg fornam* | |
| 2828 | ac hine irenna *ecga fornamon* | |

| 2782 | *middelnihtum* oðþæt he morðre swealt | |
| 2833 | *middelnihtum* maðmæhta wlonc | |

| 2793 | *gomel on giohðe** gold sceawode | [MS *giogoðe*] |
| 3095 | *gomol on gehðo* ond eowic gretan het | |

| 2799 | nu ic on *maðma hord* mine bebohte | |
| 3011 | mid þam modigan ac þær is *maðma hord* | |

| 2805 | heah hlifian on *Hronesnæsse* | |
| 3136 | har hilderinc to *Hronesnæsse* | |

| 2907 | ofer Biowulfe *byre Wihstanes* | |
| 3110 | het ða gebeodan *byre Wihstanes* | |

	þæt se byrnwiga *bugan sceolde*	
2918–19	*feoll on* feðan nalles frætwe geaf	
	þæt he blode fah *bugan sceolde*	
2974–5	*feoll on* foldan næs he fæge þa git	

| 2929 | *eald* ond egesfull *ondslyht** ageaf | [MS *hond slyht*] |
| 2972 | *ealdum* ceorle *ondslyht** giofan | [MS *hond slyht*] |

| 2931 | gomela iomeowlan | *golde berofene* | |
| 3018 | ac sceal geomormod | *golde bereafod* | |

| 2957 | eald *under eorðweall* | þa wæs æht boden | |
| 3090 | inn *under eorðweall* | ic on ofoste gefeng | |

| 2970 | syððan *ðeodcyning þyder on*cirde | | |
| 3086 | þe ðone *þeodcyning* þyder on*tyhte | | [NOT IN MS] |

| 3002 | syððan hie gefricgeað | *frean userne* | |
| 3107 | ond þonne geferian | *frean userne* | |

| 3014 | beagas gebohte | þa *sceall* brond *fretan* | |
| 3114 | godum togenes | nu *sceal* gled *fretan* | |

| 3024 | *wigend weccean* | ac se wonna hrefn | |
| 3144 | *wigend weccan* | wudurec astah | |

| 3082 | lete hyne licgean | *þær he longe* wæs | |
| 3108 | leofne mannan | *þær he longe* sceal | |

Appendix III: A Concordance of Repeated Formulas in *Beowulf*

The following concordance is based on Appendix II above, to which readers should refer for full texts of the lines in question.

1	see lines 1354 and 2233
2	see line 2694
5	see lines 75 and 1771
6	see line 1947
8	see lines 651, 714, 1631, and 1770
9	see line 2734
11	see lines 863 and 2390
16	see lines 2159 and 2780
17	see lines 183 and 1752
29	see lines 1934, 2040, and 2518
30	see lines 148, 170, 1183, 1418, 2026, and 2101
32	see lines 1131 and 1897
34	see line 3079
34–6	see lines 3141–2
35	see lines 352, 896, and 1487
40	see line 2621
41	see line 2143
44	see line 1218
45	see line 2266
46	see line 1187
47	see line 1021
48	see line 3132
49	see lines 2419 and 2632
50	see line 162
51	see line 1346
52	see line 505
54	see lines 114 and 1257
58	see line 608
65	see line 1559
72	see lines 1271, 1751, and 2182
75	see lines 5 and 1771
86	see lines 1636, 1657, 2303, 2822, and 2934
89	see lines 2458 and 3023
99	see line 2144
100	see line 2210
103	see line 1348
108	see lines 1692, 1779, 2330, and 2796
114	see lines 54, 1257, 1541, 1584, and 2094
118	see lines 357, 431, 633, 662, and 1672
119	see line 1008
121	see line 1499
123	see line 853
124	see lines 1882 and 2054
125	see line 1125
129	see lines 201, 345, 353, 797, 1046, 1598, 1715, 1992, 2384, 2572, 2721, 2788, and 3141
130	see lines 1329 and 2342
133	see lines 191 and 1747
133–4	see line 191–2
137	see lines 153, 879, and 2480
141	see line 833
146	see lines 285, 658, and 935
148	see lines 30, 170, 1183, 1396, 1418, 2026, and 2101
150	see lines 410 and 605
153	see lines 137, 879, 2480, and 2620
156	see line 470
159	see lines 592, 732, and 816
160	see lines 621 and 1674
162	see line 50
164	see line 1276
165	see line 2478
168	see line 347
170	see lines 30, 148, 1183, 1418, 2026, and 2101
174	see line 2644
177	see line 2674
178	see line 1246
182	see line 1071
183	see lines 17 and 1752
187	see line 885
189	see lines 1474, 1867, 2011, and 2143
191–2	see lines 133–4
194	see lines 1574 and 2977
196–7	see lines 789–90
197	see lines 790 and 806
200	see line 645
200–1	see lines 1597–8
201	see lines 129, 345, 353, 797, 1046, 1598, 1715, 1835, 1992, 2384, 2572, 2721, 2788, and 3141
202	see lines 416 and 1591
203	see line 2467
205	see lines 260, 362, 443, 1213, 1856, 1930, 2318, 2927, 3137, and 3178
207	see lines 1156, 1378, 2373, 2870, and 3162
214	see line 896
217	see lines 630, 2309, and 2561

478	see lines 384 and 2764
480	see lines 531 and 1467
481	see lines 332 and 363
482	see lines 427, 609, 1494, and 2308
488	see lines 695, 2119, 2236, and 2249
492	see lines 1094 and 2635
494	see lines 667 and 3118
500	see lines 291, 351, and 1166
504	see lines 751 and 2996
505	see line 52
508	see lines 338 and 1206
510	see line 538
512	see lines 539, 1278, 1429, and 2119
520	see line 463
529	see lines 631, 957, 1383, 1473, 1651, 1817, 1999, and 2425
530	see line 1783
531	see lines 480 and 1467
535	see line 372
538	see line 510
539	see line 512
541	see line 581
546	see line 581
547	see line 649
551	see line 322 and 1552
553	see lines 1028 and 2192
555	see line 574
557	see line 1520
559	see line 974
561	see lines 1670, 3048, and 3174
562	see line 2740
565	see line 2939
571	see lines 648, 961, 1078, 1628, 1875, 1911, and 1998
574	see line 555
576	see line 2015
578	see lines 661 and 1655
579	see line 1794
581	see lines 541 and 546
582	see lines 273, 875, and 1346
585	see lines 940 and 954
587	see line 2203
590	see lines 980 and 1808
592	see lines 159, 732, and 816
593	see line 475
597	see line 2004
599	see lines 389, 618, 696, 1323, 1653, 1712, and 2125
602	see lines 902 and 2349
605	see lines 150 and 219
607	see lines 1170, 1922, and 2071
608	see line 58
609	see lines 427, 482, 1494, and 2308
610	see lines 1832, 1849, 2644, and 2981
612	see line 1162
613	see lines 868, 1173, 1530, 2082, 2171, and 2689
618	see lines 599 and 1653
621	see lines 160 and 1674
625	see lines 227, 1397, and 1626
626	see line 824
630	see lines 217, 2309, and 2561
631	see lines 529, 957, 1383, 1473, 1651, 1817, 1999, and 2425
633	see lines 118, 357, 431, 662, and 1672
635	see line 1113
644	see line 1640
645	see lines 200, 268, 344, 1009, 1040, 1597, 1652, 1699, and 2147
646	see line 1252
648	see lines 571, 961, 1078, 1628, 1875, 1911, and 1998
649	see line 547
651	see lines 8, 714, 1631, 1770, 1790, and 3030
652	see line 2516
653	see line 2418
654	see line 2046
658	see lines 146, 285, and 935
659	see lines 1530 and 2678
660	see lines 949–50
661	see lines 578 and 1655
662	see lines 118, 357, 431, 633, 1236, and 1672
663	see line 428
667	see lines 494 and 3118
672–3	see lines 1696–7
673	see lines 802, 1232, 1559, and 1697
674	see line 2362
676	see line 1191
678	see lines 981 and 1825
685	see line 1056
687	see line 3057
695	see lines 488, 2119, 2236, and 2249
696	see lines 389, 599, 1323, 1712, and 2125
697	see lines 225, 1894, 2900, and 3156
698	see line 1273
701	see lines 712, 735, 810, 914, 1716, and 1725
704	see line 230
706	see line 967
712	see lines 701, 735, 810, 914, and 1725
713	see lines 919, 1016, and 1984
714	see lines 8, 651, 1631, and 1770
715	see lines 246 and 878
716	see lines 1463, 1527, and 2625
721	see line 1275
723	see lines 1539, 2220, and 2550
727	see lines 218, 985, and 1608
729	see lines 329, 387, and 1063
732	see lines 159, 592, 784, and 816
733	see lines 2423, 2571, and 2743
735	see lines 701, 712, 810, 914, and 1725
737	see lines 758, 813, and 914
740	see line 2286
744	see lines 468, 1389, and 2908
750	see lines 809, 1497, and 2226
751	see line 504
758	see lines 737, 813, and 914
762	see line 797
763	see line 844
767	see lines 823, 913, and 1417
776	see lines 837, 1955, 2685, and 2837

782   see line 1373
784   see line 732
786   see line 1682
789–90 see lines 196–7
790   see lines 197 and 806
791   see lines 1035, 1866, 1967, 2142, 2190, 2374, and 2905
795   see lines 1488 and 1688
796   see lines 2655 and 2668
796–7 see lines 2655–6
797   see lines 129, 201, 345, 353, 762, 1046, 1598, 1715, 1992, 2384, 2572, 2721, 2788, and 3141
799   see line 394
801   see line 2820
802   see lines 673, 1232, 1559, and 1697
806   see lines 197 and 790
808   see line 903
809   see lines 750, 1497, and 2226
810   see lines 701, 712, 735, 914, and 1725
813   see lines 737, 758, and 914
814   see line 2171
816   see lines 159, 592, and 732
823   see lines 767, 913, and 1417
824   see lines 626 and 2531
827   see line 1569
828   see line 1471
831   see line 1858
833   see line 141
835   see line 972
837   see lines 776, 1955, 2685, and 2837
839   see lines 1174 and 2317
840   see lines 1704 and 3032
844   see line 763
848   see line 1593
849   see line 1423
853   see line 123
858   see lines 1297, 1685, and 1956
860   see line 1773
863   see lines 11 and 2390
865   see line 916
867   see line 923
868   see lines 613, 1173, 1530, 2082, 2171, and 2689
870   see line 2114
872   see line 1971
874   see lines 366 and 987
875   see lines 273, 582, and 1346
876   see line 900
878   see lines 246 and 715
879   see lines 137, 153, and 2480
885   see line 187
887   see lines 1415, 2553, and 2744
888   see lines 1408, 2597, and 3170
892   see line 2782
893   see lines 1967, 2676, and 2917
894   see lines 2241 and 3100
895   see line 2776
896   see lines 35 and 214
899   see lines 429, 1972, and 2337
900   see line 876
902   see lines 602 and 2349
903   see line 808

907   see lines 2237 and 3035
910   see line 1837
913   see lines 767, 823, and 1417
914   see lines 701, 712, 735, 737, 758, 810, 813, and 1725
916   see line 865
919   see lines 713, 1016, and 1984
920   see line 1365
923   see line 867
933   see line 2014
934   see lines 1594 and 2974
935   see lines 146, 285, and 658
940   see lines 585 and 954
946–7 see lines 1758–9
947   see line 1759
949–50 see line 660
950   see line 1610
954   see lines 585 and 940
956   see lines 1058, 1134, 1824, and 2859
957   see lines 529, 631, 1383, 1473, 1651, 1817, 1999, and 2425
961   see lines 571, 648, 1078, 1605, 1628, 1875, 1911, and 1998
963   see line 1335
967   see line 706
969   see lines 1540 and 2933
971   see line 2164
972   see line 835
974   see lines 559 and 2008
980   see lines 590 and 1808
981   see lines 678 and 1825
982   see line 2888
985   see lines 218, 727, and 1608
986   see lines 1495 and 1576
987   see line 874
989   see line 2586
1002   see line 1565
1008   see line 119
1009   see lines 268, 344, 645, 1040, 1652, 1699, and 2147
1012   see line 2311
1013   see line 327
1014   see line 1333
1016   see lines 713, 919, and 1984
1021   see line 47
1022   see lines 1629 and 2868
1028   see lines 553 and 2192
1035   see lines 791, 1866, 1967, 2142, and 2190
1038   see line 1450
1040   see lines 268, 344, 645, 1009, 1652, 1699, and 2147
1045   see line 2812
1046   see lines 129, 201, 345, 353, 797, 1598, 1715, 1992, 2384, 2572, 2721, 2788, and 3141
1046–7 see lines 3141–2
1047   see line 1852
1048   see lines 1898 and 2166
1050   see line 2338
1052–3 see lines 1902–3
1056   see line 685
1058   see lines 956, 1134, 1824, and 2859

1061	see line 2910	1244	see line 1110
1063	see lines 329, 387, and 729	1245	see lines 2153 and 2615
1065	see lines 2108, 2446, and 3172	1246	see line 178
1068	see line 2230	1252	see line 646
1071	see line 182	1257	see lines 54 and 114
1077	see lines 1784, 2103, and 2124	1258	see lines 1282, 1538, 2118, and 2139
1078	see lines 571, 648, 961, 1628, 1875, 1911, and 1998	1271	see lines 72, 1751, and 2182
1079	see line 2742	1273	see line 698
1088	see line 1141	1275	see line 721
1092	see line 1226	1276	see line 164
1093	see lines 2102 and 2246	1277	see lines 1462, 1535, and 2630
1094	see lines 492 and 2635	1278	see lines 512, 1429, and 2119
1097	see line 1129	1281	see line 2225
1099	see lines 296 and 1182	1282	see lines 1258, 1538, 2118, and 2139
1100	see lines 289 and 1833	1286	see line 1111
1110	see line 1244	1287	see line 1558
1111	see line 1286	1297	see lines 858, 1685, and 1956
1113	see line 635	1303	see lines 1322 and 2287
1119	see lines 1374 and 3143	1306	see lines 1152 and 2209
1122	see line 2080	1307	see lines 2581 and 3136
1125	see line 125	1311	see lines 2352 and 2942
1129	see line 1097	1313	see line 1924
1131	see lines 32 and 1897	1321	see lines 371 and 456
1134	see lines 956, 1058, 1824, and 2859	1322	see lines 1303 and 2287
1141	see line 1088	1323	see lines 389, 599, 696, 1712, and 2125
1143	see line 2583	1326	see line 1714
1147	see line 2325	1327	see lines 1448 and 2544
1152	see line 1306	1329	see lines 130 and 2342
1156	see lines 207, 1378, 2373, 2870, and 3162	1330	see lines 460 and 2502
1162	see line 612	1333	see line 1014
1165	see line 1228	1335	see line 963
1166	see line 500	1336	see lines 415, 1345, 2797, and 2804
1170	see lines 607, 1922, and 2071	1338	see line 2061
1171	see lines 1476 and 1602	1341	see line 1419
1172	see lines 1534 and 2166	1343	see line 2745
1173	see lines 613, 868, 1530, 2082, 2171, and 2689	1345	see lines 415, 1336, 2797, and 2804
1174	see lines 839 and 2317	1346	see lines 51, 273, 582, and 875
1182	see lines 296 and 1099	1348	see line 103
1183	see lines 30, 148, 170, 1418, 2026, and 2101	1353	see line 1560
1184	see line 2636	1354	see lines 1 and 2233
1185	see lines 1701 and 2427	1355	see line 309
1187	see line 46	1360	see line 2808
1191	see line 676	1361	see line 252
1193	see line 3134	1365	see line 920
1203	see line 2511	1372	see line 446
1206	see lines 338, 423, and 508	1373	see line 782
1211	see line 2162	1374	see line 1119
1212	see lines 2496 and 3027	1378	see lines 207, 1156, 2373, 2870, and 3162
1213	see lines 205, 260, 362, 443, 1856, 1930, 2318, 2927, 3137, and 3178	1380	see line 470
1216	see lines 1758, 1854, 1987, and 2663	1381	see lines 1458 and 1891
1218	see line 44	1383	see lines 529, 631, 957, 1473, 1651, 1817, 1999, and 2425
1221	see line 1855	1386–7	see lines 2342–3
1226	see line 1092	1389	see lines 468, 744, and 2908
1228	see line 1165	1396	see line 148
1232	see lines 1559 and 1782	1397	see lines 227, 625, and 1626
1235	see line 2303	1402	see line 245
1236	see lines 662 and 1507	1403	see lines 2316, 2947, and 3158
1241	see line 3025	1404	see line 2073
		1406	see lines 416, 1685, 1956, and 2382
		1408	see lines 888, 2597, and 3170
		1415	see lines 887, 2553, and 2744

1417   see lines 767, 823, and 913
1418   see lines 30, 148, 170, 1183, 2026, and 2101
1419   see line 1341
1421   see line 1635
1423   see line 849
1426   see line 1444
1429   see lines 512, 1278, and 2119
1434   see line 2412
1436   see lines 441, 452, 447, 1481, 1491, and 2536
1439   see line 2206
1440   see line 1650
1442   see line 1537
1444   see line 1426
1446   see line 2507
1447   see line 1524
1448   see line 1327
1450   see line 1038
1458   see line 1381
1459   see line 2778
1461   see line 3022
1462   see lines 1277, 1535, and 2630
1463   see lines 716, 1527, and 2625
1467   see lines 480 and 531
1469   see line 2133
1471   see line 828
1473   see lines 529, 631, 957, 1383, 1651, 1817, 1999, and 2425
1474   see lines 189, 1867, 2011, 2143, and 2587
1475   see line 2156
1476   see lines 1171 and 1602
1478   see line 2443
1481   see lines 441, 452, 447, 1436, 1491, and 2536
1482   see line 2490
1484   see lines 1831, 2402, 2483, 2560, 2576, 2901, and 2991
1484–5   see lines 2991–2
1487   see lines 35 and 896
1488   see lines 795 and 1688
1490   see line 1659
1491   see lines 441, 452, 447, 1436, 1481, and 2536
1492   see lines 1612 and 2551
1494   see lines 427, 482, 609, and 2308
1495   see lines 986 and 1576
1496   see lines 308, 1911, 2588, and 2770
1497   see lines 750, 809, 1826, and 2226
1498   see line 1769
1499   see line 121
1505   see line 1890
1507   see lines 1236 and 2345
1515   see line 3053
1520   see line 557
1524   see line 1447
1527   see lines 716, 1463, and 2625
1528   see lines 2236 and 3131
1530   see lines 613, 659, 868, 1173, 2082, 2171, 2678, and 2689
1533   see line 2540
1534   see lines 1172 and 2166

1535   see lines 1277, 1462, and 2630
1537   see line 1442
1538   see lines 1258, 1282, 2118, and 2139
1539   see lines 723, 2220, and 2550
1540   see lines 969 and 2933
1541   see lines 114, 1584, and 2094
1544   see line 2853
1550   see lines 2367 and 2398
1552   see line 551
1553   see line 381
1554   see line 1841
1558   see lines 1287, 2616 and 2979
1559   see lines 65, 673, 802, 1232, and 1697
1560   see line 1353
1565   see line 1002
1569   see line 827
1570   see line 311
1574   see lines 194 and 2977
1576   see lines 986 and 1495
1578   see line 383
1580   see lines 261, 2180, 2418, and 3179
1582   see line 465
1584   see lines 114, 1541, and 2094
1587   see line 3003
1590   see line 2138
1591   see lines 202 and 416
1591–2   see lines 416–17
1593   see lines 848 and 1620
1594   see lines 934, 1791, 1873, 2962, and 2974
1597   see lines 268, 344, 645, 1009, 1040, 1652, 1699, and 2147
1597–8   see lines 200–1
1598   see lines 129, 201, 345, 353, 797, 1046, 1715, 1992, 2384, 2572, 2721, 2788, and 3141
1599   see line 2707
1601   see lines 2052 and 3005
1602   see lines 1171 and 1476
1605   see line 961
1608   see lines 218, 727, and 985
1610   see line 950
1612   see lines 1492 and 2551
1616   see line 1667
1620   see line 1593
1626   see lines 227, 625, and 1397
1627   see line 400
1628   see lines 571, 648, 961, 1078, 1605, 1875, 1911, and 1998
1629   see lines 1022 and 2868
1631   see lines 8, 651, 714, and 1770
1635   see line 1421
1636   see lines 86, 1657, 2303, 2822, and 2934
1637   see line 1888
1639   see lines 1648 and 2083
1640   see line 644
1641   see line 2476
1646   see lines 1816, 2010, and 3111
1648   see line 1639
1650   see line 1440
1651   see lines 529, 631, 957, 1383, 1473, 1817, 1999, and 2425

1652	see lines 268, 344, 645, 1009, 1040, 1699, and 2147
1653	see lines 599 and 618
1655	see lines 578 and 661
1657	see lines 86, 1636, 2303, 2822, and 2934
1659	see line 1490
1667	see line 1616
1670	see lines 561 and 3174
1672	see lines 118, 357, 431, 633, and 662
1673	see lines 1708, 2033, and 2095
1674	see lines 160 and 621
1675	see line 2063
1679	see lines 2717 and 2774
1680	see lines 271 and 359
1682	see line 786
1684	see line 3180
1684–6	see lines 2382–3
1685	see lines 416, 858, 1297, 1406, 1956, and 2382
1688	see lines 795 and 1488
1692	see lines 108, 1779, 2330, and 2796
1696–7	see lines 672–3
1697	see lines 673, 802, 1232, and 1559
1699	see lines 268, 344, 645, 1009, 1040, 1652, and 2147
1700	see line 2864
1701	see lines 1185 and 2427
1702	see line 2210
1704	see lines 457 and 840
1708	see lines 1673, 2033, and 2095
1709	see lines 1830 and 1961
1710	see line 464
1712	see lines 389, 599, 696, 1323, and 2125
1713	see line 343
1714	see line 1326
1715	see lines 129, 201, 345, 353, 797, 1046, 1598, 1992, 2384, 2572, 2721, 2788, and 3141
1716	see lines 701 and 1725
1719	see lines 2635 and 3009
1724	see lines 2114 and 2277
1725	see lines 701, 712, 735, 810, 914, and 1716
1730	see line 2727
1733	see line 2199
1736	see lines 1763 and 1848
1747	see line 133
1751	see lines 72, 1271, and 2182
1752	see lines 17 and 183
1758	see lines 1216, 1854, 1987, and 2663
1758–9	see lines 946–7
1759	see line 947
1763	see lines 1736 and 1848
1769	see line 1498
1770	see lines 8, 651, 714, and 1631
1771	see lines 5 and 75
1773	see line 860
1779	see lines 108, 1692, 2330, and 2796
1781	see line 1935
1782	see line 1232
1783	see line 530
1784	see lines 1077, 1860, 2103, and 2124
1788	see line 2022

1789	see line 2594
1790	see lines 651 and 3030
1791	see lines 1594, 1873, and 2962
1792	see lines 2105, 2487, and 2968
1794	see line 579
1798	see line 2955
1808	see lines 590 and 980
1810	see lines 2641 and 2184
1812	see lines 2614 and 2939
1816	see lines 1646, 2010, and 3111
1817	see lines 529, 631, 957, 1383, 1473, 1651, 1999, and 2425
1819	see line 361
1824	see lines 956, 1058, 1134, and 2859
1825	see lines 678 and 981
1826	see line 1497
1830	see lines 1709 and 1961
1831	see lines 1484, 2402, 2483, 2560, 2576, 2901, and 2991
1832	see lines 610, 1849, 2644, and 2981
1833	see lines 289 and 1100
1835	see line 201
1837	see line 910
1841	see line 1554
1847	see lines 2358 and 2992
1848	see lines 1736 and 1763
1849	see lines 610, 1832, 2644, and 2981
1852	see line 1047
1854	see lines 1216, 1758, 1987, and 2663
1855	see line 1221
1856	see lines 205, 260, 362, 443, 1213, 1930, 2318, 2927, 3137, and 3178
1858	see lines 831 and 1947
1860	see line 1784
1866	see lines 791, 1035, 1967, 2142, and 2190
1867	see lines 189, 1474, 2011, and 2143
1873	see lines 1594, 1791, and 2962
1874	see line 2198
1875	see lines 571, 648, 961, 1078, 1628, 1911, and 1998
1882	see lines 124 and 2054
1887	see line 1716
1888	see line 1637
1889	see line 2754
1890	see line 1505
1891	see line 1381
1894	see lines 225, 697, 2900, and 3156
1897	see lines 32 and 1131
1898	see lines 1048 and 2166
1899	see line 3092
1902–3	see lines 1052–3
1909	see line 218
1911	see lines 308, 571, 648, 961, 1078, 1496, 1628, 1875, 1998, and 2770
1915	see lines 297, 1943, 1994, 2080, 2127, 2897, and 3108
1917–18	see lines 302–3
1922	see lines 607, 1170, and 2071
1924	see line 1313
1929	see line 1981
1930	see lines 205, 260, 362, 443, 1213, 1856, 2318, 2927, 3137, and 3178

2211	see line 275	2372	see line 467
2220	see lines 723, 1539, and 2550	2373	see lines 207, 1156, 1378, 2870, and
2222	see line 2639		3162
2225	see line 1281	2374	see lines 791 and 2905
2226	see lines 750, 809, and 1497	2380	see lines 2394 and 2612
2230	see line 1068	2382	see lines 416, 1406, 1685, and 1956
2233	see lines 1 and 1354	2382–3	see lines 1684–6
2236	see lines 488, 695, 1528, 2119, 2249, and	2384	see lines 129, 201, 345, 353, 797, 1046,
	3131		1598, 1715, 1992, 2572, 2721, 2788,
2237	see lines 907 and 3035		and 3141
2241	see lines 894 and 3100	2388	see line 2366
2246	see lines 1093, 2102, and 2662	2390	see lines 11 and 863
2249	see lines 488, 695, 2119, and 2236	2392	see line 2200
2250	see line 2537	2394	see lines 2380 and 2612
2253	see line 2282	2398	see lines 1550 and 2367
2254	see line 2306	2402	see lines 1484, 1831, 2483, 2560, 2576,
2256	see line 2457		2901, and 2991
2262	see line 2107	2412	see line 1434
2266	see line 45	2416	see lines 474 and 3054
2274	see line 2595	2418	see lines 261, 653, 1580, 2180, and
2277	see lines 1724, 2114, and 2687		3179
2279	see line 2831	2419	see lines 49, 2584, and 2632
2280	see line 3051	2420	see line 2728
2282	see line 2253	2423	see lines 733, 2571, and 2743
2286	see line 740	2425	see lines 529, 631, 957, 1383, 1473,
2287	see lines 1303 and 1322		1651, 1817, and 1999
2290	see line 2168	2427	see lines 1185, 1701, and 2911
2300	see line 2713	2429	see lines 430 and 2357
2303	see lines 86, 1636, 1235, 1657, 2822, and	2443	see line 1478
	2934	2445	see line 2452
2306	see lines 2254 and 2727	2446	see lines 1065, 2108, and 3172
2308	see lines 427, 482, 609, and 1494	2452	see line 2445
2309	see lines 217, 630, and 2561	2457	see line 2256
2311	see line 1012	2458	see lines 89 and 3023
2316	see lines 1403, 2348, 2947, and 3158	2462	see line 2705
2317	see lines 839 and 1174	2467	see line 203
2318	see lines 205, 260, 362, 443, 1213, 1856,	2472	see line 2946
	1930, 2927, 3137, and 3178	2476	see line 1641
2325	see line 1147	2478	see line 165
2330	see lines 108, 1692, 1779, and 2796	2480	see lines 137, 153, and 879
2331	see line 2113	2483	see lines 1484, 1831, 2076, 2402, 2560,
2335	see line 2677		2576, 2901, and 2991
2335–6	see lines 3036–7	2485	see line 2508
2336	see lines 2656, 2786, and 3037	2487	see lines 1792, 2105, and 2968
2337	see lines 429, 899, and 1972	2490	see line 1482
2338	see line 1050	2496	see line 1212
2339	see line 2725	2502	see lines 460 and 1330
2342	see lines 130 and 1329, and 1386	2507	see line 1446
2342–3	see lines 1386–7	2508	see line 2485
2345	see line 1507	2511	see line 1203
2348	see line 2316	2514	see line 2134
2349	see lines 602 and 902	2516	see lines 652 and 2859
2350–1	see lines 2543–4	2517	see lines 2049 and 2642
2351	see lines 2201 and 2544	2518	see lines 29, 1934, and 2040
2352	see line 1311	2524	see line 2580
2353	see line 2006	2529	see line 238
2354	see line 2008	2530	see lines 249 and 2700
2357	see lines 430 and 2429	2531	see line 824
2358	see lines 1847 and 2992	2535	see lines 2133, 2622, and 3007
2362	see line 674	2536	see lines 441, 452, 447, 1436, 1481, and
2366	see line 2388		1491
2367	see lines 1550 and 2398	2537	see line 2250
2369	see line 3004	2539	see lines 342 and 404

2540	see line 1533
2542	see line 2003
2543	see line 2350
2544	see lines 1327, 2201, and 2351
2550	see lines 723, 1539, and 2220
2551	see lines 1492 and 1612
2553	see lines 887, 1415, and 2744
2560	see lines 1484, 1831, 2402, 2483, 2576, 2901, and 2991
2561	see lines 217, 630, and 2309
2563	see line 2036
2571	see lines 733, 2423, and 2743
2572	see lines 129, 201, 345, 353, 797, 1046, 1598, 1715, 1992, 2384, 2721, 2788, and 3141
2574	see lines 442, 2038, 2827, and 2984
2576	see lines 1484, 1831, 2402, 2483, 2560, 2901, and 2991
2580	see line 2524
2581	see line 1307
2583	see line 1143
2584	see line 2419
2586	see line 989
2587	see lines 1474 and 2011
2588	see line 1496
2591	see line 2845
2593	see line 2113
2594	see line 1789
2595	see line 2274
2596	see line 2169
2597	see lines 888, 1408, and 3170
2601	see line 289
2602	see line 2862
2603	see line 2159
2605	see lines 396 and 2049
2607	see line 2814
2612	see lines 2380 and 2394
2614	see lines 1812 and 2939
2615	see lines 1245 and 2153
2616	see lines 1558 and 2979
2617	see lines 227, 2623, 2730, 2851, and 2871
2618	see line 232
2620	see line 153
2621	see line 40
2622	see lines 2133, 2535, and 3007
2623	see lines 227, 2617, 2730, 2851, and 2871
2624	see line 3135
2625	see lines 716, 1463, and 1527
2626	see lines 1948 and 2044
2630	see lines 1277, 1462, and 1535
2631	see lines 2752, 2862, 3076, and 3120
2632	see lines 49 and 2419
2635	see lines 492, 1094, 1719, and 3009
2636	see line 1184
2639	see line 2222
2640	see lines 2146 and 2865
2641	see lines 1810 and 2184
2642	see line 2517
2644	see lines 174, 610, 1832, 1849, and 2981
2647	see line 2865
2655	see lines 796 and 2668

2656	see lines 2336, 2786, and 3037
2662	see line 2246
2663	see lines 1216, 1758, 1854, and 1987
2668	see lines 796 and 2655
2669	see line 2073
2670	see line 3101
2674	see lines 177 and 2811
2676	see lines 893, 1967, and 2917
2677	see line 2335
2678	see lines 659 and 1530
2683	see line 2828
2685	see lines 776, 837, 1955, and 2837
2687	see line 2277
2689	see lines 613, 868, 1173, 1530, 2082, and 2171
2694	see line 2
2700	see lines 249 and 2530
2705	see line 2462
2707	see line 1599
2713	see line 2300
2717	see lines 1679 and 2774
2721	see lines 129, 201, 345, 353, 797, 1046, 1598, 1715, 1992, 2384, 2572, 2788, and 3141
2725	see line 2339
2727	see lines 1730 and 2306
2728	see line 2420
2729	see line 2160
2730	see lines 227, 2617, 2623, 2851, and 2871
2733	see line 2209
2734	see line 9
2738	see line 3067
2740	see lines 562 and 2904
2742	see line 1079
2743	see lines 733, 2423, and 2571
2744	see lines 887, 1415, and 2553
2745	see line 1343
2747	see line 386
2752	see lines 2631, 2862, 3076, and 3120
2754	see line 1889
2759	see lines 3060 and 3103
2764	see line 478
2770	see lines 308, 1496, and 1911
2772	see line 2828
2774	see lines 1679 and 2717
2776	see lines 895 and 2147
2778	see line 1459
2780	see lines 16 and 2159
2782	see lines 892 and 2833
2784	see lines 232 and 1985
2786	see lines 2336, 2656, and 3037
2788	see lines 129, 201, 345, 353, 797, 1046, 1598, 1715, 1992, 2384, 2572, 2721, and 3141
2793	see line 3095
2796	see lines 108, 1692, 1779, and 2330
2797	see lines 415, 1336, 1345, and 2804
2799	see line 3011
2804	see lines 415, 1336, 1345, and 2797
2805	see line 3136
2808	see line 1360
2811	see line 2674

2812   see lines 1045 and 2162
2814   see lines 477 and 2607
2820   see line 801
2822   see lines 86, 1636, 1657, 2303, and 2934
2827   see lines 442, 2038, 2574, and 2984
2828   see lines 2683 and 2772
2831   see line 2279
2833   see line 2782
2837   see lines 776, 837, 1955, and 2685
2845   see line 2591
2851   see lines 227, 2617, 2623, 2730, and
       2871
2853   see line 1544
2859   see lines 956, 1058, 1134, 1824, and
       2516
2862   see lines 2602, 2631, 2752, 3076, and
       3120
2864   see line 1700
2865   see lines 2146, 2640, and 2647
2868   see lines 1022, 1629, and 2015
2870   see lines 207, 1156, 1378, 2373, and
       3162
2871   see lines 227, 2617, 2623, 2730, and
       2851
2888   see line 982
2897   see lines 297, 1915, 1943, 1994, 2080,
       2127, and 3108
2899   see line 273
2900   see lines 225, 697, 1894, and 3156
2901   see lines 1484, 1831, 2402, 2483, 2560,
       2576, and 2991
2904   see line 2740
2905   see lines 791 and 2374
2907   see line 3110
2908   see lines 468, 744, and 1389
2910   see line 1061
2911   see line 2427
2917   see lines 893, 1967, and 2676
2918–19 see lines 2974–5
2923   see line 2135
2927   see lines 205, 260, 362, 443, 1213, 1856,
       1930, 2318, 3137, and 3178
2929   see line 2972
2931   see line 3018
2933   see lines 969 and 1540
2934   see lines 86, 1636, 1657, 2303, and 2822
2939   see lines 565, 1812, and 2614
2942   see line 1311
2946   see line 2472
2947   see lines 1403, 2316, and 3158
2949   see line 1963
2955   see line 1798
2957   see line 3090
2962   see lines 1594, 1791, and 1873
2968   see lines 1792, 2105, and 2487
2970   see line 3086
2972   see line 2929
2974   see lines 934, 1594, and 2918
2974–5 see lines 2918–19
2975   see line 2141
2977   see lines 194 and 1574
2979   see lines 1558 and 2616
2981   see lines 610, 1832, 1849, and 2644

2984   see lines 442, 2038, 2574, and 2827
2991   see lines 1484, 1831, 2402, 2483, 2560,
       2576, and 2901
2992   see lines 1847 and 2358
2996   see linc 504
2997   see line 375
3000   see line 383
3002   see line 3107
3003   see line 1587
3004   see line 2369
3005   see lines 1601 and 2052
3007   see lines 256, 2133, 2535, and 2622
3009   see lines 1719 and 2635
3011   see line 2799
3014   see line 3114
3018   see line 2931
3022   see line 1461
3023   see lines 89 and 2458
3024   see line 3144
3025   see line 1241
3027   see line 1212
3030   see lines 651 and 1790
3032   see line 840
3035   see lines 907 and 2237
3036–7 see lines 2335–6
3037   see lines 2336, 2656, and 2786
3048   see line 561
3051   see line 2280
3053   see line 1515
3054   see lines 474 and 2416
3057   see line 687
3060   see lines 2759 and 3103
3064   see line 1953
3067   see line 2738
3076   see lines 2631, 2752, 2862, and 3120
3079   see line 34
3080   see line 2027
3082   see line 3108
3086   see line 2970
3090   see line 2957
3092   see line 1899
3095   see line 2793
3099   see line 266
3100   see lines 894 and 2241
3101   see line 2670
3103   see lines 292, 2759 and 3060
3107   see line 3002
3108   see lines 297, 1915, 1943, 1994, 2080,
       2127, 2897, and 3082
3110   see line 2907
3111   see lines 1646 and 1816
3114   see line 3014
3118   see lines 494 and 667
3120   see lines 2631, 2752, 2862, and 3076
3131   see lines 1528 and 2236
3132   see line 48
3134   see line 1193
3135   see line 2624
3136   see lines 1307 and 2805
3137   see lines 205, 260, 362, 443, 1213,
       1856, 1930, 2318, 2927, and 3178

3141   see lines 129, 201, 345, 353, 797, 1046,
        1598, 1715, 1992, 2384, 2572, 2721, and
        2788
3141–2 see lines 34–6 and 1046–7
3143   see line 1119
3144   see line 3024
3156   see lines 225, 697, 1894, and 2900
3158   see lines 1403, 2316, and 2947
3162   see lines 207, 1156, 1378, 2373, and
        2870

3170   see lines 888, 1408, and 2597
3172   see lines 1065, 2108, and 2446
3174   see lines 561 and 1670
3178   see lines 205, 260, 362, 443, 1213,
        1856, 1930, 2318, 2927, and 3137
3179   see lines 261, 1580, 2180, and 2418
3180   see line 1684

Bibliography

A: Bibliographies and encyclopaedias

Fry, Donald K., ed., *Beowulf and the Fight at Finnsburh: a Bibliography* (Charlottesville, VA, 1969)

Greenfield, Stanley B., and Fred C. Robinson, *A Bibliography of Publications on Old English Literature to the End of 1972* (Toronto, 1980)

Hasenfratz, Robert J., *'Beowulf' Scholarship: an Annotated Bibliography 1979–1990* (New York, 1993)

———, *'Beowulf* Bibliography 1979–1994' [*see section C*]

Lapidge, Michael, John Blair, Simon Keynes, and Donald Scragg, ed., *The Blackwell Encyclopaedia of Anglo-Saxon England* (Oxford, 1999)

Pulsiano, Phillip, ed., *An Annotated Bibliography of North American Doctoral Dissertations on Old English Language and Literature* (East Lansing, MI, 1988), esp. pp. 134–67

Pulsiano, Phillip, *et al.*, ed., *Medieval Scandinavia: an Encyclopedia* (New York, 1993)

Robinson, Fred C., *Old English Literature: a Select Bibliography*, Toronto Medieval Bibliographies 2 (Toronto, 1970)

Short, Douglas D., *'Beowulf' Scholarship: an Annotated Bibliography* (New York, 1980)

Szarmach, Paul E., M. Teresa Tavormina, and Joel T. Rosenthal, ed., *Medieval England: an Encyclopedia* (New York, 1998)

Tinker, Chauncey B., *The Translations of Beowulf: a Critical Bibliography*, updated by Marijane Osborn, with a new foreword by Fred C. Robinson (Hamden, CT, 1974)

Wolf, Kirsten, ed., *An Annotated Bibliography of North American Doctoral Dissertations on Old Norse-Icelandic* (Ithaca, NY, 1998)

Wülcker, Richard P., *Grundriss zur Geschichte der angelsächsischen Litteratur; mit einer Übersicht der angelsächsischen Sprachwissenschaft* (Leipzig, 1885)

B: Dictionaries and concordances

Bessinger, Jess B., *A Concordance to the Anglo-Saxon Poetic Records*, programmed by Philip H. Smith (Ithaca, NY, 1978)

———, *A Concordance to Beowulf*, programmed by Philip H. Smith (Ithaca, NY, 1969)

Bosworth, Joseph, and T. Northcote Toller, *An Anglo-Saxon Dictionary Based on the Manuscript Collections of Joseph Bosworth* (Oxford, 1881–98); *An Anglo-Saxon Dictionary: Supplement*, by T. Northcote Toller (Oxford, 1908–21); *Enlarged Addenda and Corrigenda to the Supplement by T. Northcote Toller to An Anglo-Saxon Dictionary Based on the Manuscript Collections of Joseph Bosworth*, by Alistair Campbell (Oxford, 1972)

Campbell, Alistair [*see* Bosworth–Toller]

Cook, Albert S., *A Concordance to Beowulf* (Halle, 1911)

Grein, Christian W. M., *Sprachschatz der angelsächsischen Dichter* (Cassel, 1861–4); rev. ed. J. Köhler, with the help of F. Holthausen (Heidelberg, 1912)

Hall, John R. Clark, *A Concise Anglo-Saxon Dictionary for the Use of Students* (London, 1894)

Healey, Antonette diPaolo, *et al.*, ed., *The Dictionary of Old English* (Toronto, 1986–)

Holthausen, Ferdinand, *Altenglisches etymologisches Wörterbuch* (Heidelberg, 1932–4)
Sweet, Henry, *The Student's Dictionary of Anglo-Saxon* (New York, 1897)
Toller, T. Northcote [*see* Bosworth–Toller]
Venezky, Richard L., and Antonette diPaolo Healey, ed., *A Microfiche Concordance to Old English* (Newark, DE, 1980)
Venezky, Richard L., and Sharon Butler, eds., *A Microfiche Concordance to Old English: The High Frequency Words* (Toronto and Newark, DE, 1985)

C: Electronic corpora, databases, and useful websites

'Alternative *Beowulf*' [by Syd Allen: www.jagular.com/beowulf/]
'ASPR Text of *Beowulf*' [www.georgetown.edu/labyrinth/library/oe/texts/a4.1.html]
'*Beowulf* Bibliography 1979–1994' [by Bob Hasenfratz: www.lib.uconn.edu/Medieval/beowulf.html]
'*Beowulf*: a Study Guide' [by Roy Liuzza: www.tulane.edu/~beowulf/]
'Dictionary of Old English' [www.doe.utoronto.ca/]
Dictionary of Old English Corpus in Electronic Form, ed. Antonette diPaolo Healey, Joan Holland, Ian McDougall, and Peter Mielke (Toronto, 2000)
'Electronic Scansions for Old Germanic Metre' [by Rick Russom: www.stg.brown.edu/webs/russom/]
'Fontes Anglo-Saxonici' [fontes.english.ox.ac.uk/data/]
'Graphotactics Page' [by Bob Stevick: faculty.washington.edu/stevickr/graphotactics/index.html]
'Icelandic texts' [www.snerpa.is/net/]
Íslendinga sögur: orðstöðulykill og texti (Reykjavík, 1996)
'Old English Corpus' [ets.umdl.umich.edu/o/oec/]
'Old English Pages' [by Cathy Ball: www.georgetown.edu/cball/oe/old_english.html]
'Old Norse Legendary Sagas' [www.humnet.ucla.edu/humnet/scandinavian/leghome.html]
'Old Norse texts' [www.forn-sed.org/n-text/; home.nvg.org/~gjerde/norn/]
'Oral Formulaic Theory and Research: an Introduction and Annotated Bibliography' [by John Miles Foley; updated through 1992: www.missouri.edu/~csottime/biblio.html]
'Patrologia Latina Database' [pld.chadwyck.com/]
PoetriaNova: a CD-ROM of Latin Medieval Poetry (650–1250 A.D.) (Florence, 2001)
'ProQuest Digital Dissertations' [wwwlib.umi.com/dissertations/gateway]
'SASLC, Sources of Anglo-Saxon Literary Culture' [www.wmich.edu/medieval/saslc/index.html]
'Saxo Grammaticus, Electronic Text of the *Gesta Danorum*' [www.kb.dk/elib/lit/dan/saxo/index.htm]

D: Editions and facsimiles of Beowulf

Alexander, Michael, ed., *Beowulf* (London, 1995)
Chickering, Howell D., Jr, ed., *Beowulf: a Dual-Language Edition* (Garden City, NY, 1977)
Crépin, André, ed., *'Beowulf': édition diplomatique et texte critique, traduction française, commentaire et vocabulaire*, Göppinger Arbeiten zur Germanistik 329, 2 vols. (Göppingen, 1991)
Dobbie, Elliott van Kirk, ed., *Beowulf and Judith*, ASPR 4 (New York, 1953)
Ettmüller, Ludwig, ed., *Carmen de Beovvlfi Gavtarvm regis rebvs praeclare gestis atqve interitv, qvale fverit ante qvam in manvs interpolatoris, monachi Vestsaxonici, inciderat* (Zürich, 1875)
Grundtvig, N. F. S., ed., *Beowulfes beorh eller Bjovulfs-drapen, det old-angelske helte digt, paa grund-sproget* (Copenhagen, 1861)

Heyne, Moritz, ed., *Beowulf* (Paderborn, 1863); 5th ed. rev. Adolf Socin (1888); 8th ed. rev. Levin L. Schücking (1908); 17th ed. rev. Else von Schaubert (1961)

Holthausen, Ferdinand, ed., *Beowulf nebst dem Finnsburg-Bruchstück*, 2 vols. (Heidelberg, 1905–6)

Jack, George, ed., *'Beowulf': a Student Edition* (Oxford, 1997)

Kemble, John M., ed., *The Anglo-Saxon Poems of Beowulf, The Travellers Song, and The Battle of Finnesburh*, 2nd ed. (London, 1835)

Kiernan, Kevin S., *et al.*, ed., *Electronic Beowulf*, 2 CDs (London, 2000)

Klaeber, Friedrich, ed., *Beowulf*, 3rd ed. (Boston, 1950)

Magoun, Francis P., ed., *Beowulf and Judith Done in a Normalized Orthography and Edited*, rev. ed. Jess B. Bessinger (Cambridge, MA, 1966)

Malone, Kemp, ed., *The Nowell Codex, British Museum Cotton Vitellius A. xv, Second MS*, EEMF 12 (Copenhagen, 1963)

——, ed., *The Thorkelin Transcripts of 'Beowulf'*, EEMF 1 (Copenhagen, 1951)

Mitchell, Bruce, and Fred C. Robinson, ed., *'Beowulf': an Edition with Relevant Shorter Texts* (Oxford, 1998)

Nickel, G., *et al.*, ed., *'Beowulf' und die kleineren Denkmäler der altenglischen Heldensage 'Waldere' und 'Finnsburg'*, 3 vols. (Heidelberg, 1976–82)

Sedgefield, Walter J., ed., *Beowulf Edited with Introduction, Bibliography, Notes, Glossary, and Appendices*, 3rd ed. (Manchester, 1935)

Thorkelin, Grímur Jónsson, ed., *De Danorum rebus gestis seculi III & IV: Poëma Danicum dialecto Anglo-Saxonica* (Copenhagen, 1815)

Thorpe, Benjamin, ed., *The Anglo-Saxon Poems of Beowulf, The Scop or Gleeman's Tale, and The Fight at Finnesburg* (London, 1855; rptd Woodbury, NY, 1962)

Trautmann, Moritz, ed., *Das Beowulflied: als Anhang das Finn-Bruchstück und die Waldhere-Bruchstücke*, Bonner Beiträge zur Anglistik 16 (Bonn, 1904)

Wrenn, C. L., ed., *Beowulf with the Finnesburg Fragment* (London, 1953)

Wyatt, Alfred J., ed., *Beowulf* (Cambridge, 1894)

——, *Beowulf edited with Textual Foot-Notes, Index of Proper Names, and Alphabetical Glossary*, rev. R. W. Chambers (Cambridge, 1914)

Zupitza, Julius, *Beowulf: Autotypes of the Unique Cotton MS. Vitellius A. XV in the British Museum, with a Transliteration*, EETS 77 (London, 1882); 2nd ed. rev. Norman Davis, EETS 245 (London, 1959)

E: Translations of Beowulf

Alexander, Michael, *Beowulf: a Verse Translation* (Harmondsworth, 1973)

Ayres, Harry Morgan, trans., *Beowulf: a Paraphrase* (Williamsport, PA, 1933)

Björnsson, Halldóra B., trans., *Bjólfskviða (Beowulf)*, ed. Pétur Knútsson Ridgewell (Reykjavík, 1983)

Bone, Gavin D., trans., *Beowulf: a New Verse Translation* (Oxford, 1945)

Bradley, S. A. J., trans., *Anglo-Saxon Poetry* (London, 1982)

Conybeare, John J., *Illustrations of Anglo-Saxon Poetry*, ed. William D. Conybeare (London, 1826)

Crossley-Holland, Kevin, trans., *Beowulf* (London, 1968)

Donaldson, E. Talbot, trans., *Beowulf* (New York, 1966)

Earle, John, trans., *The Deeds of Beowulf: an English Epic of the Eighth Century Done into Modern Prose* (Oxford, 1892)

Garmonsway, G. Norman, Jacqueline Simpson, and Hilda Ellis Davidson, *Beowulf and its Analogues* (London, 1971)

Gordon, Robert K., trans., *The Song of Beowulf* (London, 1923)

Greenfield, Stanley B., trans., *A Readable 'Beowulf': the Old English Epic Newly Translated* (Carbondale, IL, 1982)

Grundtvig, N. F. S., *Bjowulfs drape: Et gothisk helte-digt* (Copenhagen, 1820)

Gummere, Francis B., trans., *The Oldest English Epic: Beowulf, Finnsburg, Waldere, Deor, Widsith, and the German Hildebrand* (New York, 1909)

Hall, John R. Clark, trans., *'Beowulf' and the 'Fight at Finnsburg': a Translation into Modern English Prose* (London, 1901); rev. ed. C. L. Wrenn, with a preface by J. R. R. Tolkien (London, 1940)

Heaney, Seamus, trans., *Beowulf: a New Translation* (New York, 2000)

Hieatt, Constance B., trans., *Beowulf and Other Old English Poems* (New York, 1967)

Hudson, Marc, trans., *Beowulf: a Translation and Commentary* (Lewisburg, PA, 1990)

Kemble, John M., trans., *A Translation of the Anglo-Saxon Poem of Beowulf, with a Copious Glossary, Preface, and Philological Notes* (London, 1837)

Kennedy, Charles W., trans., *Beowulf: the Oldest English Epic* (Oxford, 1968)

Lehmann, Ruth P. M., trans., *'Beowulf': An Imitative Translation* (Austin, TX, 1988)

Leonard, William Ellery, trans., *Beowulf: a New Verse Translation for Fireside and Classroom* (New York, 1939)

Liuzza, Roy Michael, trans., *Beowulf: a New Verse Translation* (Toronto, 2000)

Morgan, Edwin, trans., *Beowulf: a Verse Translation into Modern English* (Aldington, 1952)

Morris, William, and Alfred J. Wyatt, trans., *The Tale of Beowulf, Sometime King of the Weder Geats* (Hammersmith, 1895)

Nye, Robert, trans., *Beowulf: a New Telling* (New York, 1968)

Osborn, Marijane, trans., *Beowulf: a Verse Translation with Treasures of the Ancient North* (Berkeley, CA, 1984)

Porter, John, trans., *Beowulf: Text and Translation* (Pinner, 1991)

Raffel, Burton, trans., *Beowulf* (New York, 1963)

Rebsamen, Frederick R., trans., *'Beowulf': a Verse Translation* (New York, 1991)

Swanton, Michael, ed. and trans., *Beowulf*, rev. ed. (Manchester, 1997)

Swearer, Randolph, Raymond Oliver, and Marijane Osborn, trans., *Beowulf: a Likeness*, with introduction by Fred C. Robinson (New Haven, CT, 1990)

Trask, Richard M., trans., *Beowulf and Judith: Two Heroes* (Lanham, MD, 1997)

F: Recordings of Beowulf

Ayres, Harry Morgan, *Selections from Chaucer/ On Reading Chaucer* (Urbana, IL, 1965) [includes selections from *Beowulf*]

Bessinger, Jess B., Jr, *Beowulf and Other Poetry (in Old English)* (New York, 1996) [includes *Beowulf*, lines 1–125, 195–225, 702–852, and 3137–82]

Brodeur, Arthur G., *Selections from Beowulf* (Berkeley, CA, 1955) [includes *Beowulf*, lines 1–52, 499–606, 702b–836, 1999–2013, 2069b–2104, 2115–51, 2200–20, 2231b–66, 2312–44, 2538–91a, 2792b–2820, and 3156–82; limited edition of 175 copies on red vinyl]

Coghill, Neville, and Norman Davis, *Beowulf* (New Rochelle, NY, 1969) [includes *Beowulf*, lines 1–25, 405–55, 710–70, 1251–1305, 2538–91, and 3137–82]

Creed, Robert P., *The O/Aural Tradition, Parts I and II. Part I: Beowulf and the Grendel Kind. Part II: Beowulf and the Dragon* (New York, 1978) [extracts]

Dunn, Charles W., *Early English Poetry* (Princeton, NJ, 1958) [includes *Beowulf*, lines 2724–927, 2999–3057, and 3076–182]

Eaton, Trevor, *'Beowulf', Read in Anglo-Saxon* (Wadhurst, 1997)

Glover, Julian, *Beowulf* (London, 1995)

Heaney, Seamus, *Beowulf: a New Translation* (Harmondsworth, 1999)

Irving, Edward B., Jr, *Favorite Passages from 'Beowulf'* (Provo, UT, 1997) [includes *Beowulf*, lines 1–52, 205–28, 405–55, 710–45a, 1537–69, 2032–66, 2236b–2270a, 2425–2471, 2694–723, 2860–891, 3007b–27, and 3156–82]

Kökeritz, Helge, *A Thousand Years of English Pronunciation* (Pleasantville, NY, 1956) [includes *Beowulf*, lines 205–28, 405–32, 2801–20, and 3156–82]

Malone, Kemp, *Beowulf* (New York, 1967)

Pope, John C., and Helge Kökeritz, *Beowulf-Chaucer* (Pleasantville, NY, 1956) [includes *Beowulf*, lines 1–11, 26–53, 205–24a, 736b–70, 1159b–74, 1345–72, 2247–66, and 3156–82]

G: Other works cited

Abraham, Lenore, 'The Decorum of *Beowulf*', *PQ* 72 (1993), 267–87

Aðalbjarnarson, Bjarni, ed., *Heimskringla*, ÍF 26–8, 3 vols. (Reykjavik, 1941–51)

Aertsen, Henk, '*Wulf and Eadwacer*: a Woman's *cri de coeur* – For Whom? For What?', in *Companion to Old English Poetry*, ed. Aertsen and Bremmer, pp. 119–44

Aertsen, Henk and Rolf H. Bremmer Jr, ed., *Companion to Old English Poetry* (Amsterdam, 1994)

Albano, Robert A., 'The Role of Women in Anglo-Saxon Culture: Hildeburh in *Beowulf* and a Curious Counterpart in the *Volsunga Saga*', *ELN* 32.1 (1994), 1–10

Alfano, Christine, 'The Issue of Feminine Monstrosity: a Reevaluation of Grendel's Mother', *Comitatus* 23 (1992), 1–16

Allen, M. J. B., and D. G. Calder, trans., *Sources and Analogues of Old English Poetry: the Major Latin Texts in Translation* (Cambridge, 1976)

Amodio, Mark C., 'Affective Criticism, Oral Poetics, and Beowulf's Fight with the Dragon', *OT* 10 (1995), 54–90

Amos, Ashley Crandell, 'An Eleventh-Century *Beowulf*?', *Review* 4 (1982), 335–42

———, *Linguistic Means of Determining the Dates of Old English Literary Texts*, Medieval Academy Books 90 (Cambridge, MA, 1990)

Anderson, Earl R., 'A Submerged Metaphor in the Scyld Episode', *YES* 2 (1972), 1–4

———, 'Treasure Trove in *Beowulf*: a Legal View of the Dragon's Hoard', *Mediaevalia* 3 (1977 [1978]), 141–64

———, 'Formulaic Typescene Survival: Finn, Ingeld, and the *Nibelungenlied*', *ES* 61 (1980), 293–301

———, 'Beowulf's Retreat from Frisia: Analogues from the Fifth and Eighth Centuries', *ELN* 19 (1981), 89–93

———, 'Grendel's *glof* (*Beowulf* 2085b–88), and Various Latin Analogues', *Mediaevalia* 8 (1982), 1–8

Anderson, George K., *The Literature of the Anglo-Saxons* (Oxford, 1949)

Anderson, J. J., 'The *cuþe folme* in *Beowulf*', *Neophilologica* 67 (1983), 126–30

Andersson, Theodore M., *Early Epic Scenery: Homer, Virgil, and the Medieval Legacy* (Ithaca, NY, 1976)

———, 'Tradition and Design in *Beowulf*', in *Old English Literature in Context*, ed. Niles, pp. 90–106 and 171–2

———, 'The Dating of *Beowulf*', *UTQ* 52 (1983), 288–301

———, 'The Thief in *Beowulf*', *Speculum* 59 (1984), 493–508

———, 'Heathen Sacrifice in *Beowulf* and Rimbert's *Life of Ansgar*', *MH* n.s. 13 (1985), 65–74

———, 'The Speeches in the *Waldere*-Fragments', in *De Gustibus*, ed. Foley, pp. 21–9

———, 'Sources and Analogues', in *Handbook*, ed. Bjork and Niles, pp. 125–48

Andersson, Theodore M., and Kari Ellen Gade, *Morkinskinna: the Earliest Icelandic Chronicle of the Norwegian Kings (1030–1157)*, Islandica 51 (Ithaca, NY, 2000)

Andrew, Malcolm, 'Grendel in Hell', *ES* 62 (1981), 401–10

Andrew, Samuel O., *Syntax and Style in Old English* (Cambridge, 1940)

———, *Postscript on 'Beowulf'*, 2nd ed. (New York, 1969)

Anlezark, Daniel Charles, 'The Old Testament Patriarchs in Anglo-Saxon England: Abraham and Noah' (unpublished DPhil thesis, University of Oxford, 1997)

Arent, A. Margaret, 'The Heroic Pattern: Old Germanic Helmets, *Beowulf*, and *Grettis saga*', in *Old Norse Literature and Mythology: a Symposium*, ed. Edgar C. Polomé (Austin, TX, 1969), pp. 130–99

Atherton, Mark, 'The Figure of the Archer in *Beowulf* and the Anglo-Saxon Psalter', *Neophilologus* 77 (1993), 653–7

Atwood, E. Bagby, and Archibald A. Hill, ed., *Studies in Language, Literature, and Culture of the Middle Ages and Later* (Austin, TX, 1969)

Aurner, Nellie S., *An Analysis of the Interpretations of the Finnsburg Documents*, University of Iowa Humanistic Studies 1.6 (1917), 1–36

———, *Hengest: a Study in Early English Heroic Legend*, University of Iowa Humanistic Studies 2.1 (1918), 1–121

Ayres, Harry M., 'The Tragedy of Hengest in *Beowulf*', *JEGP* 16 (1917), 282–95

Baird, Joseph L., 'Grendel the Exile', *NM* 67 (1966), 375–81

———, 'Unferth the Þyle', *MÆ* 39 (1970), 1–12

Baker, Peter S., 'Beowulf the Orator', *Journal of English Linguistics* 21 (1988), 3–23

———, ed., *'Beowulf': Basic Readings*, BRASE 1 (New York, 1995)

Baker, Peter S., and Nicholas Howe, ed., *Words and Works: Studies in Medieval English Language and Literature in Honour of Fred C. Robinson*, TOES 10 (Toronto, 1998)

Bald, Wolf-Dietrich, and Horst Weinstock, ed., *Medieval Studies Conference, Aachen, 1983*, Bamberger Beiträge zur englischen Sprachwissenschaft 15 (Frankfurt am Main, 1984)

Ball, C. J. E., '*Beowulf* 99–101', *NQ* 18 (1971), 163

Bammesberger, Alfred, 'Three Beowulf Notes', *ES* 61 (1980), 481–4

———, 'A Note on Beowulf 83b', *NM* 83 (1982), 24–5

———, 'Hidden Glosses in Old English Poetic Texts', *ASE* 13 (1984), 43–9

———, *Linguistic Notes on Old English Poetic Texts*, Anglistische Forschungen 189 (Heidelberg, 1986)

———, 'Die Lesart in *Beowulf* 1382a', *Anglia* 108 (1990), 314–26

———, 'The Conclusion of Wealhtheow's Speech (*Beowulf* 1231)', *NM* 91 (1990), 207–8

———, 'Five Beowulf Notes', in *Words, Texts and Manuscripts*, ed. Korhammer, pp. 239–55

———, 'A Note on Old English *gedræg/gedreag*', *NM* 94 (1993), 243–8

———, 'Zu *Beowulf* 386–394', *Anglia* 112 (1994), 107–14

———, 'A Textual Note on *Beowulf* 431–432', *ES* 76 (1995), 297–301

———, 'Beowulf's Descent into Grendel's Mere', *NM* 96 (1995), 225–7

———, 'Beowulf's Last Will', *ES* 77 (1996), 305–10

———, 'The Emendation of *Beowulf*, l. 586', *NM* 97 (1996), 379–82

———, 'The Half-Line *freond on frætewum* (*Beowulf* 962a)', *NM* 99 (1998), 237–9

———, 'The Half-Line *Grendeles mægum* (*Beowulf* 2353b)', *NQ* 45 (1998), 2–4

———, 'The Reading of *Beowulf*, l. 31b', *NM* 99 (1998), 125–9

———, 'In What Sense was Grendel an *angeng(e)a*?', *NQ* 46 (1999), 173–6

———, 'Old English *reote* in *Beowulf*, line 2457a', *NQ* 47 (2000), 158–9

———, 'The Superlative of OE *god* in *Beowulf*', *NM* 101 (2000), 519–21

———, 'What does *he* in lines 1392b and 1394b Refer to?', *NQ* 47 (2000), 403–5

———, 'Beowulf's Landing in Denmark', *ES* 81 (2001), 97–9

———, 'Further Thoughts on *Beowulf*, line 1537a: *Gefeng þa be [f]eaxe*', *NQ* 48 (2001), 3–4

———, 'The Syntactic Analysis of *Beowulf*, lines 4–5', *NM* 102 (2001), 131–3

Bandy, Stephen C., 'Cain, Grendel, and the Giants of *Beowulf*', *PLL* 9 (1973), 235–49

Barquist, Claudia Russell, 'Phonological Patterning in *Beowulf*', *Literary and Linguistic Computing* 2 (1987), 19–23

Barringer, Bob, 'Adding Insult to the Inquiry: a Study of Rhetorical Jousting in *Beowulf*', *In Geardagum* 19 (1998), 19–26

Bartlett, Adeline Courtney, *The Larger Rhetorical Patterns in Anglo-Saxon Poetry* (New York, 1935)

Baskervill, W. M., 'The Anglo-Saxon Version of the *Epistola Alexandri ad Aristotelem*', *Anglia* 4 (1881), 139–67

Batchelor, C. C., 'The Style of the *Beowulf*: a Study of the Composition of the Poem', *Speculum* 12 (1937), 330–42

Bately, Janet, 'Old English Prose before and during the Reign of Alfred', *ASE* 17 (1988), 93–138

———, 'Linguistic Evidence as a Guide to the Authorship of Old English Verse: a Reappraisal, with Special Reference to *Beowulf*', in *Learning and Literature*, ed. Lapidge and Gneuss, pp. 409–31

Battles, Paul, 'The Art of the Scop: Traditional Poetics in the Old English *Genesis A*' (unpublished PhD dissertation, University of Illinois at Urbana-Champaign, 1998)

———, '*Genesis A* and the Anglo-Saxon "Migration Myth"', *ASE* 29 (2000), 43–66

Baum, Paull F., 'The Meter of the *Beowulf*', *MP* 46 (1948–49), 73–91, 145–62

———, 'The *Beowulf* Poet', *PQ* 39 (1960), 389–99 [also in *Anthology*, ed. Nicholson, pp. 353–65]

Bazelmans, Jos, *By Weapons Made Worthy: Lords, Retainers, and their Relationship in 'Beowulf'* (Amsterdam, 1999)

Bazire, Joyce, and J. E. Cross, ed., *Eleven Rogationtide Homilies* (Toronto, 1982)

Beard, D. J., '*Á þá bitu engi járn*: a Brief Note on the Concept of Invulnerability in the Old Norse Sagas', in *Studies in English Language and Early Literature*, ed. Tilling, pp. 13–31

Beaty, John O., 'The Echo-Word in *Beowulf* with a Note on the *Finnsburg Fragment*', *PMLA* 49 (1934), 365–73

Belden, H. M., 'Onela the Scylfing and Ali the Bold', *MLN* 28 (1913), 149–53

Benediktsson, Jakob, ed., *Arngrimi Jonae Latine Conscripta*, Bibliotheca Arnamagnaeana IX–XII (Copenhagen, 1950–7)

———, 'Icelandic Traditions of the Scyldings', *SBVS* 15 (1957–61), 48–66

———, ed., *Landnámabók*, ÍF 1 (Reykjavik, 1968)

Bennett, Helen, 'Extra Alliteration as a Stylistic Device in *Beowulf*' (unpublished PhD dissertation, Brown University, 1980)

———, 'The Female Mourner at Beowulf's Funeral: Filling in the Blanks / Hearing the Spaces', *Exemplaria* 4 (1992), 35–50

Benson, Larry D., 'The Literary Character of Anglo-Saxon Formulaic Poetry', *PMLA* 81 (1966), 334–41 [also in Benson, *Contradictions*, pp. 1–14]

———, 'The Pagan Coloring of *Beowulf*', in *Old English Poetry: 15 Essays*, ed. Robert P. Creed (Providence, RI, 1967), pp. 193–213 [also in Benson, *Contradictions*, pp. 15–31; *'Beowulf': Basic Readings*, ed. Baker, pp. 35–50]

———, 'The Originality of *Beowulf*', in *The Interpretation of Narrative: Theory and Practice*, ed. Morton W. Bloomfield, Harvard English Studies 1 (Cambridge, MA, 1970), pp. 1–43 [also in Benson, *Contradictions*, pp. 32–69]

———, *Contradictions: from 'Beowulf' to Chaucer. Selected Studies of Larry D. Benson*, ed. Theodore M. Andersson and Stephen A. Barney (Aldershot, 1995)

Benson, Larry D., and Siegfried Wenzel, ed., *The Wisdom of Poetry: Essays in Early English Literature in Honor of Morton W. Bloomfield* (Kalamazoo, MI, 1982)

Berendsohn, Walter A., *Zur Vorgeschichte des 'Beowulf'* (Copenhagen, 1935)

Berkhout, Carl T., and Renée Medine, '*Beowulf* 770a: *reþe renweardas*', *NQ* 33 (1986), 433–4

Bessinger, Jess B., and Robert P. Creed, ed., *Franciplegius: Medieval and Linguistic Studies in Honor of Francis Peabody Magoun, Jr* (New York, 1965)

Bessinger, Jess B., Jr, and Stanley J. Kahrl, ed., *Essential Articles for the Study of Old English Poetry* (Hamden, CT, 1968)

Bessinger, Jess B., Jr, and Robert Y. Yeager, ed., *Approaches to Teaching Beowulf* (New York, 1984)

Biddle, Martin, 'Excavations at Winchester 1965 Fourth Interim Report', *Antiquaries Journal* 46 (1966), 308–32

Biggs, Frederick M., Thomas D. Hill, and Paul E. Szarmach, *Sources of Anglo-Saxon Literary Culture: a Trial Version*, MRTS 74 (Binghamton, NY, 1990)

Bjork, Robert E., 'Unferth in the Hermeneutic Circle: a Reappraisal of James L. Rosier's "Design for Treachery: the Unferth Intrigue" ', *PLL* 16 (1980), 133–41

———, 'Speech as Gift in *Beowulf*', *Speculum* 69 (1994), 993–1022

———, 'Grímur Jónsson Thorkelin's Preface to the First Edition of *Beowulf*, 1815', *SS* 68 (1996), 291–320

———, 'Digressions and Episodes', in *Handbook*, ed. Bjork and Niles, pp. 193–212

Bjork, Robert E., and John D. Niles, ed., *A 'Beowulf' Handbook* (Lincoln, NE, 1997)

Bjork, Robert E., and Ann Obermeier, 'Date, Provenance, Author, Audiences', in *Handbook*, ed. Bjork and Niles, pp. 13–34

Björkman, E., *Studien über die Eigennamen im Beowulf*, Studien zur englischen Philologie 58 (Halle, 1920)

Blackburn, F. A., 'The Christian Coloring in the *Beowulf*', *PMLA* 12 (1897), 205–25 [also in *Anthology*, ed. Nicholson, pp. 1–21]

Blake, Norman F., 'The Heremod Digressions in *Beowulf*', *JEGP* 61 (1962), 278–87

Bliss, Alan J., *The Metre of Beowulf* (Oxford, 1958)

———, *An Introduction to Old English Metre* (Oxford, 1962)

———, 'The Appreciation of Old English Metre', in *English and Medieval Studies*, ed. Davis and Wrenn, pp. 27–40

———, 'The Origin and Structure of the Old English Hypermetric Line', *NQ* n.s. 19 (1972), 242–8

———, '*Beowulf* Lines 3074–3075', in *J. R. R. Tolkien, Scholar and Storyteller*, ed. Mary Salu and Robert T. Farrell (Ithaca, NY, 1979), pp. 41–63

———, *The Scansion of 'Beowulf'*, ed. Peter J. Lucas, OEN Subsidia 22 (Kalamazoo, MI, 1995)

Blockley, Mary and Thomas Cable, 'Kuhn's Laws, Old English Poetry, and the New Philology', in *'Beowulf': Basic Readings*, ed. Baker, pp. 261–79

Blomfield, Joan, 'The Style and Structure of *Beowulf*', *RES* 14 (1938), 396–403 [also in *'Beowulf'-Poet*, ed. Fry, pp. 57–65]

Bloom, Harold, ed., *'Beowulf': Modern Critical Interpretations* (New York, 1987)

Bloomfield, Josephine, 'Diminished by Kindness: Frederick Klaeber's Rewriting of Wealhtheow', *JEGP* 93 (1994), 183–203

———, 'Benevolent Authoritarianism in Klaeber's *Beowulf*: an Editorial Translation of Kingship', *MLQ* 60 (1999), 129–59

Bloomfield, Morton W., ' "Interlace" as a Medieval Narrative Technique, with Special Reference to *Beowulf*', in *Magister Regis*, ed. Groos *et al.*, pp. 49–59

———, '*Beowulf* and Christian Allegory: an Interpretation of Unferth', *Traditio* 7 (1949–51), 410–15 [also in *'Beowulf'-Poet*, ed. Fry, pp. 68–75; *Anthology*, ed. Nicholson, pp. 155–64]

Boberg, Inger M., *Motif-Index of Early Icelandic Literature*, Bibliotheca Arnamagnæana 27 (Copenhagen, 1966)

Boer, Richard C., 'Zur Grettissaga', *ZdP* 30 (1898), 1–71

Boer, W. W., ed., *Epistola Alexandri ad Aristotelem*, Beiträge zur klassischen Philologie 50 (Meisenheim am Glan, 1973)

Bolton, Whitney F., 'Boethius, Alfred, and *Deor* Again', *MP* 69 (1972), 222–7

———, *Alcuin and 'Beowulf': an Eighth-Century View* (New Brunswick, NJ, 1978)

———, 'Boethius and a Topos in *Beowulf*', in *Saints, Scholars and Heroes*, ed. King and Stevens, I, 15–43

Bond, George, 'Links between *Beowulf* and Mercian History', *SP* 40 (1943), 481–93

Bonjour, Adrien, 'Grendel's Dam and the Composition of *Beowulf*', *ES* 30 (1949), 113–24 [also updated in his *Twelve 'Beowulf' Papers*, pp. 29–50]

———, *The Digressions in Beowulf*, MÆ Monographs 5 (Oxford, 1950)

———, 'The Problem of Dæghrefn', *JEGP* 51 (1952), 355–9 [also updated in his *Twelve 'Beowulf' Papers*, pp. 76–96]

———, 'Monsters Crouching and Critics Rampant, or the *Beowulf* Dragon Debated', *PMLA* 68 (1953), 304–12 [also updated in his *Twelve 'Beowulf' Papers*, pp. 135–49]

————, 'Young Beowulf's Inglorious Period', *Anglia* 70 (1952), 339–44 [also updated in his *Twelve 'Beowulf' Papers*, pp. 89–96]

————, '*Beowulf* and the Beasts of Battle', *PMLA* 72 (1957), 563–73

————, *Twelve 'Beowulf' papers* (Neuchâtel, 1962)

Borroff, Marie, 'Systematic Sound Symbolism in the Long Alliterative Line in *Beowulf* and *Sir Gawain*', in *English Historical Metrics*, ed. McCully and Anderson, pp. 120–33

Borsje, Jacqueline, *From Chaos to Enemy: Encounters with Monsters in Early Irish Texts; an Investigation related to the Process of Christianization and the Concept of Evil*, Instrumenta Patristica 29 (Turnhout, 1996)

Bouman, A. C., '*Beowulf*'s Song of Sorrow', in *Mélanges de Linguistique et de Philologie: Fernand Mossé in Memoriam* (Paris, 1959), pp. 41–3

————, '*Leodum is minum*: Beaduhild's complaint', in his *Patterns in Old English and Old Icelandic Literature* (Leiden, 1962), pp. 93–1

Bowden, Betsy, *Listeners' Guide to Medieval English: a Discography* (New York, 1988)

Boyle, J. A., 'Historical Dragon-Slayers', in *Animals in Folklore*, ed. J. R. Porter and W. M. S. Russell (Ipswich, 1978), pp. 23–32

Boyle, Leonard E., 'The Nowell Codex and the Dating of *Beowulf*', in *Dating of 'Beowulf'*, ed. Chase, pp. 23–32

Bracher, Frederick, 'Understatement in Old English Poetry', *PMLA* 52 (1937), 915–34 [also in *Essential Articles*, ed. Bessinger and Kahrl, pp. 228–54]

Bradley, Henry, 'The Numbered Sections in Old English Poetical MSS', *PBA* 7 (1915–16), 165–87

Brady, Caroline, *The Legends of Ermanaric* (Berkeley, CA, 1943)

————, 'The Synonyms for "Sea" in *Beowulf*', *Studies in Honor of Albert Morey Sturtevant*, Humanistic Studies 29 (Lawrance, KS, 1952), pp. 22–46

————, ' "Weapons" in *Beowulf*: an Analysis of the Nominal Compounds and an Evaluation of the Poet's Use of them', *ASE* 8 (1979), 79–141

————, ' "Warriors" in *Beowulf*: an Analysis of the Nominal Compounds and an Evaluation of the Poet's Use of them', *ASE* 11 (1983), 199–246

Braeger, Peter C., 'Connotations of *(earm)sceapen: Beowulf* ll. 2228–2229 and the Shape-Shifting Dragon', *Essays in Literature* (Western Illinois University) 13 (1986), 327–30

Brandl, Alois, 'Die angelsächsische Literatur', in *Grundriss der germanischen Philologie*, ed. Hermann Paul, 3 vols. (Strassburg, 2nd ed., 1901–9), II, pp. 941–1134

————, 'Hercules und Beowulf', *Sitzungsberichte der Preussischen Akademie der Wissenschaften*, Phil.-hist. Klasse 14 (1928), 161–7

————, '*Beowulf*-Epos und *Aeneis* in systematischer Vergleichung', *ASnSL* 171 (1937), 161–73

Braun, Adolf, *Lautlehre der angelsächsischen Version der 'Epistola Alexandri ad Aristotelem'* (Leipzig, 1911)

Bray, Dorothy Ann, *A List of Motifs in the Lives of the Early Irish Saints*, Folklore Fellows' Communications 252 (Helsinki, 1992)

Breeze, Andrew, '*Beowulf* 875–902 and the Sculptures at Sangüesa, Spain', *NQ* 38 (1991), 2–13

————, '*Beowulf* and *The Battle of Maldon*: *trem* "pace" and Welsh *tremyn* "journey" ', *NQ* 40 (1993), 9–10

————, '*Wered* "sweet drink" at *Beowulf* 496: Welsh *gwirod* "liquor, drink" ', *NQ* 40 (1993), 433–4

Bremmer, Rolf H., Jr, 'The Importance of Kinship: Uncle and Nephew in *Beowulf*', *ABäG* 15 (1980), 21–38

————, 'Grendel's Arm and the Law', in *Studies in English Language and Literature*, ed. Toswell and Tyler, pp. 121–32

Britton, G. C., 'Unferth, Grendel and the Christian Meaning of *Beowulf*', *NM* 72 (1971), 246–50

Brodeur, Arthur Gilchrist, 'Design and Motive in the Finn Episode', *UCPE* 14 (1943), 1–42

——, 'The Climax of the Finn Episode', *UCPE* 3 (1943), 285–361

——, 'The Structure and the Unity of *Beowulf*', *PMLA* 68 (1953), 1183–95

——, 'A Study of Diction and Style in Three Anglo-Saxon Narrative Poems', in *Nordica et Anglica: Studies in Honor of Stefán Einarsson*, ed. Allan H. Orrick (The Hague, 1968), pp. 97–114

——, '*Beowulf:* One Poem or Three?', in *Medieval Literature and Folklore Studies*, ed. Mandel and Rosenberg, pp. 3–26

——, *The Art of 'Beowulf'* (Berkeley, LA, 1971)

Brooke, Stopford A., *English Literature from the Beginning to the Norman Conquest* (London, 1898)

Brooks, Kenneth R., ed., *'Andreas' and 'The Fates of the Apostles'* (Oxford, 1961)

Brophy, Bridgid, Michael Levey, and Charles Osborne, *Fifty Works of English (and American) Literature We Could Do Without* (London, 1967)

Brown, Alan K., 'The Firedrake in *Beowulf*', *Neophilologus* 64 (1980), 439–60

Brown, Carleton, '*Beowulf* and the *Blickling Homilies* and Some Textual Notes', *PMLA* 53 (1938), 905–16

Brown, George Hardin, '*Beowulf* 1278b: *sunu þeod wrecan*', *MP* 72 (1974), 172–4

Brown, P. R., G. R. Crampton, and F. C. Robinson, ed., *Modes of Interpretation in Old English Literature: Essays in Honour of Stanley B. Greenfield* (Toronto, 1986)

Bryan, William F., '*Ærgod* in *Beowulf*, and other Old English Compounds of *ær*', *MP* 28 (1930–1), 157–61

Brynteston, William I., '*Beowulf*, Monsters, and Manuscripts: Classical Associations', *Res Publica Litterarum* 5.2 (1982), 41–57

Bullough, Donald A., 'What has Ingeld to do with Lindisfarne?', *ASE* 22 (1993), 93–125

Burlin, Robert B., 'Inner Weather and Interlace: a Note on the Semantic Value of Structure in *Beowulf*', in *Old English Studies*, ed. Burlin and Irving, pp. 81–9

——, 'Gnomic Indirection in *Beowulf*', in *Anglo-Saxon Poetry*, ed. Nicholson and Frese, pp. 41–9

Burlin, Robert B., and Edward B. Irving, Jr, ed., *Old English Studies in Honour of John C. Pope* (Toronto, 1974)

Burton, Richard, 'Woman in Old English Poetry', *Sewanee Review* 4 (1895), 1–14

Busse, Wilhelm, 'Assumptions in the Establishment of Old English Poetic Texts: P. J. Lucas's Edition of *Exodus*', *Arbeiten aus Anglistik und Amerikanistik* 6 (1981), 197–219

——, *Altenglische Literatur und ihre Geschichte: zur Kritik des gegenwärtigen Deutungssystems* (Düsseldorf, 1987)

Busse, W. G., and R. Holtei, 'Beowulf and the Tenth Century', *BJRL* 63.2 (1981), 285–329

Butts, Richard, 'The Analogical Mere: Landscape and Terror in *Beowulf*', *ES* 68 (1987), 113–21

Butturff, Douglas R., 'The Monsters and the Scholar: an Edition and Critical Study of the *Liber Monstrorum*' (unpublished PhD dissertation, University of Illinois, 1968)

Byock, Jesse L., *The Saga of King Hrolf Kraki* (London, 1998)

Cabaniss, Allen, '*Beowulf* and the Liturgy', *JEGP* 54 (1955, 1963), 195–201 [also in *Anthology*, pp. 223–32]

Cable, Thomas M., *The Meter and Melody of Beowulf*, Illinois Studies in Language and Literature 64 (Urbana, IL, 1974)

——, 'Metrical Style as Evidence for the Date of *Beowulf*', in *Dating of 'Beowulf'*, ed. Chase, pp. 77–82

Calder, Daniel G., ed., *Old English Poetry: Essays on Style* (Berkeley, CA, 1979)

——, 'The Study of Style in Old English Poetry: a Historical Introduction', in *Old English Poetry*, ed. Calder, pp. 1–65

Camargo, Martin, 'The Finn Episode and the Tragedy of Revenge in *Beowulf*', *SP* 78 (1981), 120–34

Cameron, Angus F., 'Saint Gildas and Scyld Scefing', *NM* 70 (1969), 240–6

Cameron, Angus [F.], and Roberta Frank, ed., *A Plan for the Dictionary of Old English*, TOES 2 (Toronto, 1973)

Cameron, Angus [F.], Ashley Crandell Amos, and Gregory Waite, with the assistance of Sharon Butler and Antonette DiPaolo Healey, 'A Reconsideration of the Language of *Beowulf*', in *Dating of 'Beowulf'*, ed. Chase, pp. 33–75

Cameron, Angus F., Ashley Crandell Amos, Antonette diPaolo Healey, *et al.*, ed., *A Dictionary of Old English* (Toronto, 1986–)

Campbell, A. P., 'The Death of Beowulf: Please Indicate Church Affiliation', *RUO* 44 (1974), 539–42

————, 'Physical Signs of Spiritual Cleansing in Old English Poetry', *RUO* 45 (1975), 382–91

————, 'The Decline and Fall of Hrothgar and His Danes', *RUO* 45 (1975), 417–29

Campbell, Alistair, 'The Old English Epic Style', in *English and Medieval Studies*, ed. Davis and Wrenn, pp. 13–26

————, ed., *Chronicon Æthelweardi* (London, 1962)

————, 'The Use in *Beowulf* of Earlier Heroic Verse', in *England Before the Conquest: Studies in Primary Sources presented to Dorothy Whitelock*, ed. Peter Clemoes and Kathleen Hughes (Cambridge, 1971), pp. 283–92

————, ed., *Encomium Emmae Reginae*, with a supplementary introduction by Simon Keynes, Camden Classic Reprints 4 (Cambridge, 1998)

Carens, Marilyn M., 'Handscóh and Grendel: the Motif of the Hand in *Beowulf*', in *Aeolian Harps: Essays in Literature in Honor of Maurice Browning Cramer*, ed. Donna G. Fricke and Douglas C. Fricke (Bowling Green, OH, 1976), pp. 39–55

Carlsson, Signe M., 'The Monsters of *Beowulf*: Creations of Literary Scholars', *JAF* 80 (1967), 357–64

Carney, James, *Studies in Irish Literature and History* (Dublin, 1955)

Carnicelli, Thomas A., 'The Function of the Messenger in *Beowulf*', *SP* 72 (1975), 246–57

Carr, C. T., *Nominal Compounds in Germanic* (London, 1939)

Carrigan, E., 'Structure and Thematic Development in *Beowulf*', *PRIA* 66C (1967), 1–51

Carruthers, Leo, 'Kingship and Heroism in *Beowulf*', in *Heroes and Heroines*, ed. Carruthers, pp. 19–29

————, ed., *Heroes and Heroines in Medieval English Literature: a Festschrift for Professor André Crépin* (Cambridge, 1994)

Carver, Martin, ed., *The Age of Sutton Hoo* (Woodbridge, 1992)

Cassidy, Frederic G., 'How Free Was the Anglo-Saxon Scop?', in *Franciplegius*, ed. Bessinger and Creed, pp. 75–85

————, 'A Symbolic Word-Group in *Beowulf*', in *Medieval Literature and Folklore Studies*, ed. Mandel and Rosenberg, pp. 27–35

————, 'Knowledge of *Beowulf* in Its Own Time', *Yearbook of Research in English and American Literature* 1 (1982), 1–12

Cavill, Paul, '*Beowulf* and *Andreas*: Two Maxims', *Neophilologus* 77 (1993), 479–87

————, *Maxims in Old English Poetry* (Cambridge, 1999)

Chadwick, Hector M., *The Cult of Othin* (Cambridge, 1899)

————, *The Heroic Age* (Cambridge, 1912)

Chadwick, Nora K., 'Norse Ghosts: a Study in the *draugr* and the *haugbúi*', *Folk-Lore* 57 (1946), 50–65 and 106–27

————, 'The Monsters and Beowulf', in *The Anglo-Saxons: Studies in Some Aspects of their History and Culture Presented to Bruce Dickins*, ed. Peter Clemoes (London, 1959), pp. 171–203

Chambers, R. W., *Widsith: a Study in Old English Heroic Legend* (Cambridge, 1912)

————, 'Beowulf's Fight with Grendel, and Its Scandinavian Parallels', *ES* 11 (1929), 81–100

————, *Beowulf: an Introduction to the Study of the Poem with a Discussion of the*

Stories of Offa and Finn, third ed., with a supplement by C. L. Wrenn (Cambridge, 1959)

Chance, Jane, *Woman as Hero in Old English Literature* (Syracuse, 1986)

——, 'The Structural Unity in *Beowulf*: the Problem of Grendel's Mother', in *New Readings on Women*, ed. Damico and Olsen, pp. 248–61

Chaney, William A., 'Grendel and the *Gifstol*: a Legal View of Monsters', *PMLA* 77 (1961), 513–20

Chapman, Coolidge Otis, '*Beowulf* and *Apollonius of Tyre*', *MLN* 46 (1931), 439–43

Chapman, Richard L., 'Alas, Poor Grendel', *CE* 17 (1956), 334–7

Chase, Colin, 'Opinions on the Date of *Beowulf*, 1815–1980', in *Dating of 'Beowulf'*, ed. Chase, pp. 3–8

——, 'Saints' Lives, Royal Lives, and the Date of *Beowulf*', in *Dating of 'Beowulf'*, ed. Chase, pp. 161–71

——, ed., *The Dating of 'Beowulf'*, TOES 6 (Toronto, 1981; reptd 1997)

——, '*Beowulf*, Bede, and St. Oswine: the Hero's Pride in Old English Hagiography', in *The Anglo-Saxons: Synthesis and Achievement*, ed. J. Douglas Woods and David A. E. Pelteret (Waterloo, 1985), pp. 37–48 (also in *'Beowulf': Basic Readings*, ed. Baker, pp. 181–93]

Cherniss, Michael D., *Ingeld and Christ: Heroic Concepts and Values in Old English Christian Poetry* (The Hague, 1972)

Chickering, Howell, 'Lyric Time in *Beowulf*', *JEGP* 91 (1992), 489–509

Christensen, T., 'Lejre beyond Legend–the Archaeological Evidence', *Journal of Danish Archaeology* 10 (1991), 163–85

Clark, Francelia Mason, *Theme in Oral Epic and in 'Beowulf'* (New York, 1995)

Clark, George, 'Beowulf's Armor', *ELH* 32 (1965), 409–41

——, '*Beowulf* and *Njálssaga*', in *Proceedings of the First International Saga Conference, University of Edinburgh, 1971*, ed. Peter Foote, Hermann Pálsson, and Desmond Slay. London, 1973), pp. 66–87

——, *Beowulf*, Twayne's English Authors Series 477 (Boston, MA, 1990)

——, '*Beowulf*: the Last Word', in *Old English and New*, ed. Hall *et al.*, pp. 15–30

——, 'The Hero and the Theme', in *Handbook*, ed. Bjork and Niles, pp. 271–90

Clausen, Julius, ed., *Illustreret Verdens-Litteraturhistorie* (Copenhagen, 1901)

Clement, Richard W., 'Codicological Consideration in the *Beowulf* Manuscript', in *Proceedings of the Illinois Medieval Association*, ed. Roberta Bux Bosse *et al.* (Macomb, IL, 1984), pp. 13–27

Clemoes, Peter, 'Action in *Beowulf* and our Perception of It', in *Old English Poetry*, ed. Calder, pp. 147–68

——, 'Style as a Criterion for Dating the Composition of *Beowulf*', *Dating of 'Beowulf'*, ed. Chase, pp. 173–85

——, *Interactions of Thought and Language in Old English Poetry*, CSASE 12 (Cambrige, 1995)

——, ed., *Ælfric's Catholic Homilies: the First Series*, EETS SS 17 (Oxford, 1997)

Clover, Carol J., 'The Germanic Context of the Unferþ Episode', *Speculum* 55 (1980), 444–68 [also in *'Beowulf': Basic Readings*, ed. Baker, pp. 127–54]

Clunies Ross, Margaret, 'Two of Þórr's Great Fights according to *Hymiskviða*', *LSE* n.s. 20 (1989), 7–27

Coffin, R. N., '*Beowulf* and its Relationship to Norse and Finno-Uguric Beliefs and Narratives' (unpublished PhD dissertation, Boston University, 1962)

Cohen, J. M., trans., *Don Quixote* (London, 1950)

Cohen, Jeffrey J., 'The Use of Monsters and the Middle Ages', *SELIM: Journal of the Spanish Society of Medieval English Language and Literature* 2 (1992), 47–69

Colgrave, Bertram, 'A Mexican Version of the "Bear's Son" Folk Tale', *JAF* 64 (1951), 109–13

——, ed., *Felix's Life of Saint Guthlac* (Cambridge, 1956)

Collins, Rowland L., 'Blickling Homily XVI and the Dating of *Beowulf*', in *Medieval Studies Conference*, ed. Bald and Weinstock, pp. 61–9

————, 'Six Words in the Blickling Homilies', in *Philological Essays*, ed. Rosier, pp. 137–41

Conner, Patrick W., 'The Section Numbers in the *Beowulf* Manuscript', *ANQ* 24 (1985), 33–8

Conquergood, Dwight, 'Boasting in Anglo-Saxon England: Performance and the Heroic Ethos', *Literature in Performance* 1 (1981), 24–35

Cook, Albert S., ed., *Judith: an Old English Epic Fragment* (Boston, MA 1888; rev. 1889)

————, 'An Irish Parallel to the Beowulf Story', *ASnSL* 103 (1899), 154–56

————, 'Old English Notes: *Beowulf* 1408ff', *MLN* 17 (1902), 418–19; 22 (1907), 146–47

————, 'The Old English *Andreas* and Bishop Acca of Hexham', *TCAAS* 26 (1922–24), 245–332

————, '*Beowulf* 1422', *MLN* 39 (1924), 77–82

————, 'Aldhelm and the Source of *Beowulf* 2523', *MLN* 40 (1925), 137–42

————, 'Cynewulf's Part in Our *Beowulf*', *TCAAS* 27 (1925), 385–406

————, 'Beowulfian and Odyssean Voyages', *TCAAS* 28 (1926), 1–20

————, 'Greek Parallels to Certain Features of the *Beowulf*', *PQ* 5 (1926), 226–34

————, 'Hellenic and Beowulfian Shields and Spears', *MLN* 41 (1926), 360–63

————, 'The Beowulfian *maðelode*', *JEGP* 25 (1926), 1–6

————, '*Beowulf* 1039 and the Greek *archibasileus*', *Speculum* 3 (1928), 75–81

Cornelius, Roberta D., 'Palus Inamabilis', *Speculum* 2 (1927), 321–5

Cosijn, P. J., *Notes on 'Beowulf'*, ed. and trans. Rolf H. Bremmer Jr, Jan van den Berg, and David F. Johnson, Leeds Texts and Monographs 12 (Leeds, 1991)

Cox, Betty S., *Cruces of 'Beowulf'*, Studies in English Literature 60 (The Hague, 1971)

Cramp, Rosemary J., '*Beowulf* and Archaeology', *Medieval Archaeology* 1 (1957), 57–77 [also in *'Beowulf'-Poet*, ed. Fry, pp. 114–40]

————, 'The Hall in *Beowulf* and in Archaeology', in *Heroic Poetry*, ed. Damico and Leyerle, pp. 331–46

Crawford, Samuel J., ed., *Exameron Anglice or The Old English Hexameron* (Hamburg, 1921; prtd Darmstadt, 1968)

————, 'Grendel's Descent from Cain', *MLR* 23 (1928), 207–8; 24 (1929), 63

Creed, Robert P., 'Studies in the Techniques of Composition of the "Beowulf" Poetry in British Museum MS. Cotton Vitellius A. xv' (unpublished PhD disertation, Harvard University, 1955)

————, 'The *Andswarode*-System in Old English Poetry', *Speculum* 32 (1957), 523–8

————, 'The Making of an Anglo-Saxon Poem', *ELH* 26 (1959), 445–54 [also in *'Beowulf'-Poet*, ed. Fry, pp. 141–53; *Essential Articles*, ed. Bessinger and Kahrl, pp. 363–73; *Old English Literature*, ed. Stevens and Mandel, pp. 52–72]

————, 'On the Possibility of Criticizing Old English Poetry', *TSLL* 3 (1961), 97–106

————, 'The Singer Looks at His Sources', *CL* 14 (1962), 44–52

————, ' " . . . Wel-hwelc Gecwaeþ . . . ": the Singer as Architect', *TSL* 11 (1966), 131–43

————, ed., *Old English Poetry: Fifteen Essays* (Providence, RI, 1967)

————, 'The *Beowulf*-Poet: Master of Sound-Patterning', in *Oral Traditional Literature*, ed. Foley, pp. 194–216

————, 'The Remaking of *Beowulf*', in *Oral Tradition in Literature*, ed. Foley, pp. 136–46

————, *Reconstructing the Rhythm of 'Beowulf'* (Columbia, MO, 1990)

————, 'Sutton Hoo and the Recording of *Beowulf*', in *Voyage to the Other World*, ed. Kendall and Wells, pp. 65–75

Crépin, André, 'Wealhtheow's Offering of the Cup to Beowulf: a Study in Literary Structure', in *Saints, Scholars and Heroes*, ed. King and Stevens, I, 45–58

————, 'Beowulf: monstre ou modèle?', *Études Anglaises* 51 (1998), 387–98

Cronan, Dennis, 'Alliterative Rank in Old English Poetry', *SN* 58 (1986), 145–58

————, '*Lofgeorn*: Generosity and Praise', *NM* 92 (1991), 187–94

————, 'The Rescuing Sword', *Neophilologus* 77 (1993), 467–78

————, 'The Origin of Ancient Strife in *Beowulf*', in *Germanic Studies*, ed. Goblirsch, Mayou, and Taylor, pp. 57–68

Crook, Eugene J., 'Pagan Gold in *Beowulf*', *ABR* 25 (1974), 218–34

Crowne, David K., 'The Hero on the Beach: an Example of Composition by Theme in Anglo-Saxon Poetry', *NM* 61 (1960), 362–72

Culbert, Taylor, 'The Narrative Function of Beowulf's Swords', *JEGP* 59 (1960), 13–20

Damico, Helen, '*Sörlaþáttr* and the Hama Episode in *Beowulf*', *SS* 5 (1983), 222–35

————, *Beowulf's Wealhtheow and the Valkyrie Tradition* (Madison, WI, 1984)

————, ed., *Medieval Scholarship: Biographical Studies on the Formation of a Discipline 2: Literature and Philology*, Garland Reference Library of the Humanities 2071 (New York, 1998)

Damico, Helen, and Alexandra Hennessey Olsen, ed., *New Readings on Women in Old English Literature* (Bloomington, IN, 1990)

Damico, Helen, and John Leyerle, ed., *Heroic Poetry in the Anglo-Saxon Period: Studies in Honor of Jess B. Bessinger*, Studies in Medieval Culture 32 (Kalamazoo, MI, 1993)

Damon, John, 'The Raven in *Beowulf* 1801: Bird of a Different Color', *Work in Progress* (Department of English, University of Arizona), 1.1 (1990), 60–70

Dane, Joseph A., 'The Notion of Ring Composition in Classical and Medieval Studies: a Comment on Critical Method and Illusion', *NM* 94 (1993), 61–7

————, 'Wiglaf's Sword', *SN* 65 (1993), 129–39

D'Aronco, Maria Amalia, '*Wulf and Eadwacer*, analisi del testo', *AIUON* 26, Filologia germanica (1983), 67–133

Davidson, Charles, 'Differences between the Scribes of Beowulf', *MLN* 5 (1890), 43–5 [see too the reply by C. F. McClumpha and Davidson's response in the same issue, pp. 123 and 189–90]

Davidson, Hilda R. Ellis, 'The Hill of the Dragon: Anglo-Saxon Burial Mounds in Literature and Archaeology', *Folk-Lore* 61 (1950), 169–85

Davidson, Hilda R. Ellis, and Peter Fisher, trans. and comm., *Saxo Grammaticus: the History of the Danes*, 2 vols. (Cambridge, 1979)

Davis, Craig R., 'Cultural Assimilation in the Anglo-Saxon Royal Genealogies', *ASE* 21 (1992), 23–39

————, *'Beowulf' and the Demise of Germanic Legend in England*, Albert Bates Lord Studies in Oral Tradition 17 (New York and London, 1996)

Davis, Norman, ' "Hippopotamus" in Old English', *RES* 4 (1953), 141–2

Davis, Norman, and C. L. Wrenn, ed., *English and Medieval Studies Presented to J.R.R. Tolkien on the Occasion of his Seventieth Birthday* (London, 1962)

Dean, Paul, '*Beowulf* and the Passing of Time', *ES* 75 (1994), 193–209 and 293–302

Dederich, Hermann, *Historische und Geographische Studien zum angelsächsischen Beowulfliede* (Cologne, 1877)

Deskis, Susan E., 'An Addendum to Beowulf's Last Words', *MÆ* 63 (1994), 301–5

————, *'Beowulf' and the Medieval Proverb Tradition*, MRTS 155 (Tempe, AZ, 1996)

Desmond, Marilynn, '*Beowulf*: the Monsters and the Tradition', *OT* 7 (1992), 258–83

Diamond, Robert E., 'Theme as Ornament in Anglo-Saxon Poetry', *PMLA* 76 (1961), 461–68 [also in *Essential Articles*, ed. Bessinger and Kahrl, pp. 374–92]

Diller, Hans-Jürgen, 'Contiguity and Similarity in the *Beowulf* Digressions', in *Medieval Studies Conference*, ed. Bald and Weinstock, pp. 71–83

Doane, A. N., 'Oral Texts, Intertexts, and Intratexts: Editing Old English', *Influence and Intertextuality in Literary History*, ed. Jay Clayton and Eric Rothstein (Madison, WI, 1991), pp. 75–113

Doane, A. N., and Carol Braun Pasternack, ed., *Vox Intexta: Orality and Textuality in the Middle Ages* (Madison, WI, 1991)

Doig, J. F., '*Beowulf* 3096b: Curse or Consequence?', *ELN* 19 (1981), 3–6

Donahue, Charles, 'Grendel and the *Clanna Cain*', *Journal of Celtic Studies* 1 (1950), 167–75

——, '*Beowulf* and Christian Tradition: a Reconsideration from a Celtic Stance', *Traditio* 21 (1965), 55–116

——, 'Beowulf, Ireland and the Natural Good', *Traditio* 7 (1949–51), 263–77

Dragland, S. L., 'Monster-Man in *Beowulf*', *Neophilologus* 61 (1977), 606–18

Dronke, Peter, 'Functions of Classical Borrowing in Medieval Latin Verse', in *Classical Influences on European Culture, A.D. 500–1500*, ed. R. R. Bolgar (Cambridge, 1969), pp. 159–64

——, '*Waltharius* and the *Vita Waltharii*', *BGdSL* 106 (1984), 390–402

Dronke, Ursula, '*Beowulf* and Ragnarök', *SBVS* 17 (1969), 302–25

Duff, J. Wight, 'Homer and *Beowulf*', *SBVS* 4 (1905–6), 382–406

Duggan, Hoyt N., 'Scribal Self-Correction and Editorial Theory', *NM* 91 (1990), 215–27

Dümmler, Ernst, ed., *Alcuini Epistolae*, MGH, Epistolae Aevi Karolini 4.2 (Berlin, 1895)

Dumville, David N., 'Biblical Apocrypha and the Early Irish: a Preliminary Investigation', *PRIA* 73C (1973), 299–338

——, '*Beowulf* and the Celtic World: the Uses of Evidence', *Traditio* 37 (1981), 109–60 [rptd in *Britons and Anglo-Saxons in the Early Middle Ages*]

——, 'Ekiurid's *Celtica lingua*: an Ethnological Difficulty in *Waltharius*', *Cambridge Medieval Celtic Studies* 6 (1983), 87–94

——, 'The West Saxon Genealogical Regnal List: Manuscripts and Texts', *Anglia* 104 (1986), 1–32

——, 'Beowulf Come Lately. Some Notes on the Palaeography of the Nowell Codex', *ASnSL* 225 (1988), 49–63 [rptd in *Britons and Anglo-Saxons in the Early Middle Ages*]

——, *Britons and Anglo-Saxons in the Early Middle Ages* (Aldershot, 1993)

——, 'The *Beowulf*-Manuscript and How Not to Date It', *MESN* 39 (1998), 21–27

Düwel, Klaus, 'On the Sigurd Representations in Great Britain and Scandinavia', in *Languages and Cultures: Studies in Honour of Edgar C. Polomé*, ed. M. A. Jazayery and W. Winter (Berlin, 1988), pp. 133–56

Earl, James W., 'Beowulf's Rowing-Match', *Neophilologus* 63 (1979), 285–90

Egilsson, Sveinbjörn, *Lexicon Poeticum Antiquae Linguae Septentrionalis*, 2nd ed. by Finnur Jónsson (Copenhagen, 1966)

Einarsson, Stefán, 'Old English *Beot* and Old Icelandic *Heitstrenging*', *PMLA* 49 (1934), 99–103 [also in *Essential Articles*, ed. Bessinger and Kahrl, pp. 99–123]

——, 'Bjólfur and Grendill in Iceland', *MLN* 71 (1956), 79–80

——, 'Beowulfian Place-Names in East Iceland', *MLN* 76 (1961), 385–92

Einenkel, Eugen, 'Das altenglische Cristoforus-fragment', *Anglia* 17 (1895), 11–22

Eliason, Norman E., 'The "Improvised Lay" in *Beowulf*', *PQ* 31 (1952), 171–9

——, 'The "Thryth-Offa" Digression in *Beowulf*', in *Franciplegius*, pp. 124–38 [also in *English Essays Literary and Linguistic*, ed. Robert G. Benson and Erika C. D. Lindemann (Grand Prairie, TX, 1975), pp. 83–98]

——, 'The Arrival at Heorot', in *Studies in Language, Literature, and Culture*, ed. Atwood and Hill, pp. 235–42

——, 'Beowulf, Wiglaf, and the Wægmundings', *ASE* 7 (1978), 95–105

——, 'Beowulf's Inglorious Youth', *SP* 76 (1979), 101–8

——, 'The Burning of Heorot', *Speculum* 55 (1980), 75–83

Eller, Allan Louis, 'Semantic Ambiguity as a Structural Element in *Beowulf*' (unpublished PhD dissertation, State University of New York at Binghamton, 1978)

Emerson, Oliver F., 'Legends of Cain, Especially in Old and Middle English', *PMLA* 21 (1906), 831–929

——, 'Grendel's Motive in Attacking Heorot', *MLR* 16 (1921), 113–9

Enright, Michael J, 'The Warband Context of the Unferth Episode', *Speculum* 73 (1998), 297–337

Ettmüller, Ludwig, *Engla and Seaxna Scôpas and Bôceras* (Quedlinburg, 1850)

Evans, D. R., 'The Sequence of Events in *Beowulf*, ll. 207–16', *MÆ* 32 (1963), 214–16

Evans, Jonathan D., 'Semiotics and Traditional Lore: the Medieval Dragon Tradition', *Journal of Folklore Research* 22 (1985), 85–112

Evans, Stephen S., *The Heroic Poetry of Dark-Age Britain: and Introduction to its Dating, Composition, and Use as a Historical Source* (Lanham, MD, 1997)

Fajardo-Acosta, Fidel, *The Condemnation of Heroism in the Tragedy of Beowulf: a Study in the Characterization of the Epic.* Studies in Epic and Romance Literature 2 (Lewiston, NY, 1989)

——, 'Intemperance, Fratricide, and the Elusiveness of Grendel', *ES* 73 (1992), 205–10

Fakundiny, Lydia, 'The Art of Old English Verse Composition', *RES* n.s. 21 (1970), 129–42 and 257–66

Faraci, Dora, 'La caccia al cervo nel *Beowulf*', *Romanobarbarica* 14 (1996–97 [1998]), 375–420

Farrell, Robert T., '*Beowulf*, Swedes, and Geats', *SBVS* 18 (1972), 225–86

——, 'Beowulf and the Northern Heroic Age', in *The Vikings*, ed. Robert T. Farrell (London, 1982), pp. 180–216

Fast, Lawrence E., 'Hygelac: a Centripetal Force in *Beowulf*', *AM* 12 (1972), 90–9

Faulkes, Anthony, ed., *Snorri Sturluson, Edda. Prologue and Gylfaginning* (Oxford: Clarendon, 1982)

——, trans., *Snorri Sturluson: Edda* (London, 1987)

Fee, Christopher, '*Beag & beaghroden*: Women, Treasure and the Language of Social Structure in *Beowulf*', *NM* 97 (1996), 285–94

Feeny, Sarah J., 'The Funeral Pyre Theme in *Beowulf*', in *De Gustibus*, ed. Foley, pp. 185–200

Feldman, Thalia Phillies, 'Grendel and Cain's Descendants', *Literary Onomastics Studies* 8 (1981), 71–87

——, 'A Comparative Study of *feond, deofl, syn* and *hel* in *Beowulf*', *NM* 88 (1987), 159–74

Fell, Christine, *Women in Anglo-Saxon England* (Oxford, 1984)

——, 'Paganism in *Beowulf*: a Semantic Fairy-Tale', in *Pagans and Christians: the Interplay between Christian Latin and Traditional Germanic Cultures in Early Medieval Europe*, ed. T. Hofstra *et al.*, Mediaevalia Groningana 16 (Groningen, 1995), pp. 9–34

Finch, R.G. ed., *Völsunga saga: the Saga of the Volsungs* (London, 1965)

Fischer, Bonifatius, *et al.*, ed., *Biblia sacra iuxta vulgatam versionem* (Stuttgart, 1969)

Fjalldal, Magnús, *The Long Arm of Coincidence: the Frustrated Connection between 'Beowulf' and 'Grettis saga'* (Toronto, 1998)

Fleming, Damian, '*Eþel-weard*: the First Scribe of the *Beowulf*-Manuscript', *NM* (forthcoming)

Florey, Kenneth, 'Grendel, Evil, "Allegory", and Dramatic Development in *Beowulf*', *Essays in Arts and Sciences* 17 (1988), 83–95

Förster, Max, *Die 'Beowulf'-Handschrift*, Berichte über die Verhandlungen der sächsischen Akademie der Wissenschaften zu Leipzig, phil.-hist. Klasse 71 (Leipzig, 1919)

Foley, Joanne De Lavan, 'Feasts and Anti-Feasts in *Beowulf* and the *Odyssey*', in *Oral Traditional Literature*, ed. Foley, pp. 235–61

Foley, John Miles, 'Formula and Theme in Old English Poetry', in *Oral Literature and the Formula*, ed. Benjamin A. Stolz and Richard S. Shannon (Ann Arbor, MI, 1976), pp. 207–32

——, ed., *Oral Traditional Literature: a Festschrift for Albert Bates Lord* (Columbus, OH, 1981)

——, ed., *Oral-Formulaic Theory and Research: an Introduction and Annotated Bibliography* (New York, 1985)

——, [for an update of *Bibliography* through 1992] [*see section C*]

——, ed., *Oral Tradition in Literature: Interpretation in Context* (Columbia, MO, 1986)

————, *The Theory of Oral Composition: History and Methodology* (Bloomington, IN, 1988)

————, *Traditional Oral Epic: 'The Odyssey', 'Beowulf', and the Serbo-Croatian Return Song* (Berkeley, CA, 1990)

————, *Immanent Art: From Structure to Meaning in Traditional Oral Epic* (Bloomington, IN, 1991)

————, ed., *De Gustibus: Essays for Alain Renoir* (New York, 1992)

————, *The Singer of Tales in Performance* (Bloomington, IN, 1995)

————, *Homer's Traditional Art* (University Park, PA, 1999)

Fox, Denton, and Hermann Pálsson, trans., *Grettir's Saga* (Toronto, 1974)

Frank, Roberta, 'Some Uses of Paronomasia in Old English Scriptural Verse', *Speculum* 47 (1972), 207–26

————, 'Skaldic Verse and the Date of *Beowulf*', in *Dating of 'Beowulf'*, ed. Chase, pp. 123–99 [also in *'Beowulf': Basic Readings*, ed. Baker, pp. 155–80]

————, 'The *Beowulf* Poet's Sense of History', in *The Wisdom of Poetry*, ed. Benson and Wenzel, pp. 53–65 [also in *'Beowulf'*, ed. Bloom, pp. 51–61]

————, 'Old Norse Memorial Eulogies and the Ending of *Beowulf*', *Acta* 6 (1982 [1979]), 1–19

————, ' "Mere" and "Sund": Two Sea-Changes in *Beowulf*', in *Modes of Interpretation*, ed. Brown *et al.*, pp. 153–72

————, 'Germanic Legend in Old English Literature', in *Cambridge Companion*, ed. Godden and Lapidge, pp. 88–106

————, '*Beowulf* and Sutton Hoo: the Odd Couple', in *Voyage to the Other World*, ed. Kendall and Wells, pp. 47–64

Frankis, Peter J., 'The Thematic Significance of *enta geweorc* and Related Imagery in *The Wanderer*', *ASE* 2 (1973), 253–70

Frantzen, Allen J., *Desire for Origins: New Language, Old English, and Teaching the Tradition* (New Brunswick, NJ, 1990)

————, 'Writing the Unreadable Beowulf: "writan" and "forwritan," the Pen and the Sword', *Exemplaria* 3 (1991), 327–57

————, ed., *Speaking Two Languages: Traditional Disciplines and Contemporary Theory in Medieval Studies* (Albany, NY, 1991)

Frantzen, Allen J., and Charles L. Venegoni, 'An Archaeology of Anglo-Saxon Studies', *Style* 20 (1986), 142–56

Frese, Dolores Warwick, 'The Scansion of *Beowulf* Critical Implications', in *Approaches to Beowulfian Scansion*, ed. Renoir and Hernández, pp. 37–46

Frisby, Deborah S., ' "Daring" and "Foolish" Renderings: On the Meaning of *dollic* in *Beowulf*', *ANQ* n.s. 4 (1991), 59–63

Fritzsche, Arthur, 'Das angelsächsische Gedicht *Andreas* und Cynewulf', *Anglia* 2 (1879), 441–96

Fry, Donald K., 'Old English Formulas and Systems', *ES* 48 (1967), 193–204

————, 'Old English Formulaic Themes and Type-Scenes', *Neophilologus* 52 (1968), 48–54

————, ed., *The 'Beowulf'-Poet: a Collection of Critical Essays* (Englewood Cliffs, NJ, 1968)

————, '*Finnsburh*: a New Interpretation', *Chaucer Review* 9 (1974), 1–14

————, ed., *Finnsburh: Fragment and Episode* (London, 1974)

————, 'Launching Ships in *Beowulf* 210–216 and *Brunanburh* 32b–36', *MP* 79 (1981), 61–6

Fulk, R. D., 'Dating *Beowulf* to the Viking Age', *PQ* 61 (1982), 341–59

————, 'Unferth and his Name', *MP* 85 (1987), 113–27

————, 'An Eddic Analogue to the Scyld Scefing Story', *RES* 40 (1989), 313–22

————, 'Contraction as a Criterion for Dating Old English Verse', *JEGP* 89 (1990), 1–16

————, ed., *Interpretations of Beowulf: a Critical Anthology* (Bloomington, IN, 1991)

————, *A History of Old English Meter* (Philadelphia, PA, 1992)

——, 'Inductive Methods in the Textual Criticism of Old English Verse', *MH* 23 (1996), 1–24

——, 'Textual Criticism', in *Handbook*, ed. Bjork and Niles, pp. 35–53

Funk, Carol Hughes, 'History of *Andreas* and *Beowulf*: Comparative Scholarship' (unpublished PhD dissertation, University of Denver, 1998)

Gang, T. M., 'Approaches to *Beowulf*', *RES* 33 (1952), 1–12

Garde, Judith [N.], '*Sapientia, ubi sunt*, and the Heroic Ideal in *Beowulf*', *SN* 66 (1994), 159–73

——, 'Christian and Folkloric Tradition in *Beowulf*: Death and the Dragon Episode', *Literature and Theology* (1997), 325–46

Gardner, John, *Grendel* (New York, 1971)

——, 'Fulgentius's *Expositio Vergiliana Continentia* and the Plan of *Beowulf*: Another Approach to the Poem's Style and Structure', *PLL* 6 (1970), 227–62

Gardner, Thomas J., *Semantic Patterns in Old English Substantival Compounds* (Hamburg, 1968)

——, 'The Application of the term "Kenning" ', *Neophilologus* 56 (1972), 464–8

——, 'How Free Was the *Beowulf* Poet?' *MP* 71 (1973), 111–27

——, 'Compositional Techniques of the Beowulf Poet', in *Anglo-Saxonica*, ed. Grinda and Wetzel, pp. 209–23

Garmonsway, G. N., 'Anglo-Saxon Heroic Attitudes', in *Franciplegius*, ed. Bessinger and Creed, pp. 139–46

Gatch, Milton, McC., 'Humfrey Wanley (1672–1726)', in *Medieval Scholarship*, ed. Damico, pp. 45–57

Georgianna, Linda, 'King Hrethel's Sorrow and the Limits of Heroic Action in *Beowulf*', *Speculum* 62 (1987), 829–50

Gering, Hugo, 'Der Béowulf und die isländische Grettissaga', *Anglia* (1880), 74–87

Gerritsen, Johan, 'British Library MS Cotton Vitellius A.xv – a Supplementary Description', *ES* 69 (1988), 293–302

——, 'Emending *Beowulf* 2253 – Some Matters of Principle. With a Supplement on 389–90, 1372 & 240', *Neophilologus* 73 (1989), 448–52

——, 'Have with You to Lexington! The *Beowulf* Manuscript and *Beowulf*', in *In Other Words: Transcultural Studies in Philology, Translation and Lexicology Presented to Hans Heinrich Meier*, ed. J. Lachlan Mackenzie and Richard Todd (Dordrecht, 1989), pp. 15–34

——, 'A Reply to Dr Kiernan's "Footnote" ', *ES* 72 (1991), 497–500

——, 'The Thorkelin Transcripts of *Beowulf*: a Codicological Description, with Notes on Their Genesis and History', *The Library*, 6th series 13 (1991), 1–22

——, '*Beowulf* Revisited', *ES* 79 (1998), 82–6

——, 'What Use are the Thorkelin Transcripts of *Beowulf*?', *ASE* 28 (1999), 23–42

Gillam, Doreen M. E., 'The Use of the Term *æglæca* in *Beowulf* at Lines 813 and 2592', *Studia Germanica Gandensia* 3 (1961), 145–69

Gillespie, G. T., *A Catalogue of Persons Named in German Heroic Literature (700–1600)* (Oxford, 1973)

Gingher, Robert S., 'The Unferth Perplex', *Thoth* 4 (1974), 19–28

Girvan, Ritchie, 'Finnsburuh', *PBA* 26 (1940), 327–60

——, *Beowulf and the Seventh Century*, with a chapter on Sutton Hoo by R. Bruce-Mitford (London, 1971)

Gneuss, H., *Handlist of Anglo-Saxon Manuscripts: a List of Manuscripts and Manuscript Fragments Written or Owned in England up to 1100* (Tempe, AZ, 2001)

Goblirsch, Kurt Gustav, Martha Berryman Mayou, and Marvin Taylor, ed., *Germanic Studies in Honor of Anatoly Liberman* (Odense, 1997)

Godden, Malcolm, ed., *Ælfric's Catholic Homilies: the Second Series*, EETS SS 5 (Oxford, 1997)

——, 'Literary Language', in *The Cambridge History of the English Language I: the Beginnings to 1066*, ed. Richard M. Hogg (Cambridge, 1992), pp. 490–535

—, 'Biblical Literature: the Old Testament', in *Cambridge Companion*, ed. Godden and Lapidge, pp. 206–26

Godden, Malcolm, and Michael Lapidge, ed., *The Cambridge Companion to Old English Literature* (Cambridge, 1991)

Goffart, Walter, '*Hetware* and *Hugas:* Datable Anachronisms in *Beowulf*', in *Dating of 'Beowulf'*, ed. Chase, pp. 83–100

Goldsmith, Margaret E., 'The Christian Theme of *Beowulf*', *MÆ* 29 (1960), 81–101

—, 'The Christian Perspective in *Beowulf*', *CL* 14 (1962), 71–90 [also in *Anthology*, ed. Nicholson, pp. 373–86; *Interpretations*, ed. Fulk, pp. 103–19]

—, *The Mode and Meaning of 'Beowulf'* (London, 1970)

Goossens, L., ed., *The Old English Glosses of MS. Brussels, Royal Library 1650* (Brussels, 1974)

Gordon, Eric V., '*Wealhþeow* and Related Names', *MÆ* 4 (1935), 169–75

Gough, Alfred Bradley, 'The Thrytho Saga, and Offa and Cynethryth of Mercia', in *The Constance Saga*, Palaestra 23 (Berlin, 1902), pp. 53–83

Gould, David, 'Euphemistic Renderings of the Word *druncen* in *Beowulf*', *NQ* 44 (1997), 443–50

Gray, John, 'The Finn Episode in *Beowulf*: Line 1085(b), *ac hig him geþingo budon*', in *Words and Wordsmiths: a Volume for H. L. Rogers*, ed. Geraldine Barnes *et al.* (Sydney, 1989), pp. 32–39

Green, Alexander, 'The Opening of the Episode of Finn in *Beowulf*', *PMLA* 31 (1916), 759–97

Green, Martin, 'Man, Time, and Apocalypse in *The Wanderer, The Seafarer*, and *Beowulf*', *JEGP* 74 (1975), 502–18

Greenfield, Stanley B., 'The Formulaic Expression of the Theme of "Exile" in Anglo-Saxon Poetry', *Speculum* 30 (1955), 200–6 [also in *Essential Articles*, ed. Bessinger and Kahrl, pp. 352–62; *Hero and Exile*, pp. 125–31]

—, ed., *Studies in Old English Literature in Honor of Arthur G. Brodeur* (Eugene, OR, 1963),

—, 'Geatish History: Poetic Art and Epic Quality in *Beowulf*', *Neophilologus* 47 (1963), 211–17 [also in *Hero and Exile*, pp. 19–26; *Interpretations*, ed. Fulk, pp. 120–6]

—, '*Beowulf* 207b–228: Narrative and Descriptive Art', *NQ* n.s. 13 (1966), 86–90 [also in *Hero and Exile*, pp. 27–32]

—, 'Grendel's Approach to Heorot: Syntax and Poetry', in *Old English Poetry*, ed. Creed, pp. 275–84

—, 'Old English Words and Patristic Exegesis – *hwyrftum scriþað*: a Caveat', *MP* 75 (1977), 44–8

—, 'A Touch of the Monstrous in the Hero, or Beowulf Re-Marvellized', *ES* 63 (1982), 294–300

—, 'Of Words and Deeds: the Coastguard's Maxim Once More', in *The Wisdom of Poetry*, ed. Benson and Wenzel, pp. 45–51

—, 'Beowulf and the Judgment of the Righteous', in *Learning and Literature*, ed. Lapidge and Gneuss, pp. 393–407

—, *Hero and Exile: the Art of Old English Poetry*, ed. George H. Brown (London, 1989)

Griffith, Mark S., 'Convention and Originality in the Old English "Beasts of Battle" Typescene', *ASE* 22 (1993), 179–99

—, '*Beowulf* 1495: *hwil dæges = momentum temporis?*', *NQ* 239 (1994), 144–6

—, 'Some Difficulties in *Beowulf*, lines 874–902: Sigemund Reconsidered', *ASE* 24 (1995), 11–41

—, ed., *Judith* (Exeter, 1997)

Griffiths, Bill, *Meet the Dragon: an Introduction to Beowulf's Adversary* (Loughborough, 1996)

Grinda, Klaus R., and Claus-Dieter Wetzel, ed., *Anglo-Saxonica: Beiträge zur Vor- und*

Frühgeschichte der englischen Sprache und zur altenglischen Literatur: Festschrift für Hans Schabram (Munich, 1993)

Grinsell, Lynne V., 'Barrow Treasure in Fact, Tradition and Legislation', *Folk-Lore* 78 (1967), 1–38

Groos, Arthur, *et al.*, ed., *Magister Regis: Studies in Honor of Robert Earl Kaske* (New York, 1986)

Gruber, Loren C., 'Motion, Perception, and *oþþæt* in *Beowulf*', *In Geardagum: Essays on Old English Language and Literature*, ed. Loren C. Gruber and Dean Loganbill (Denver, 1974), pp. 31–7

Guðnason, Bjarni, *Um Skjöldunga sögu* (Reykjavík, 1963)

Haarder, Andreas, *'Beowulf': the Appeal of a Poem* (Viborg, 1975)

Haber, Tom Burns, *A Comparative Study of the 'Beowulf' and the 'Aeneid'* (Princeton, NJ, 1931)

Hagen, Sivert N., 'Classical Names and Stories in the Beowulf', *MLN* 19 (1904), 65–74

Hall, J. R., 'Old English Literature', in *Scholarly Editing: an Introduction to Research*, ed. D. C. Greetham (New York, 1995), pp. 149–83

——, 'The First Two Editions of *Beowulf*, Thorkelin's (1815), and Kemble's (1833)', *The Editing of Old English*, ed. Scragg and Szarmach, pp. 239–50

Hall, Joan H., Nick Doane, and Dick Ringler, ed., *Old English and New: Studies in Language and Linguistics in Honor of Frederic G. Cassidy* (New York, 1992)

Hamilton, Marie Padgett, 'The Religious Principle in *Beowulf*', *PMLA* 61 (1946), 309–31

Handelman, Anita F., 'Wulfgar at the Door: *Beowulf*, ll. 389b–90a', *Neophilologus* 72 (1988), 475–7

Hanning, Robert W., 'Sharing, Dividing, Depriving: the Verbal Ironies of Grendel's Last Visit to Heorot', *TSLL* 15 (1973), 203–13

——, '*Beowulf* as Heroic History', *MH* 5 (1974), 77–102

Hansen, Elaine Tuttle, 'From *freolicu folccwen* to *geomuru ides:* Women in Old English Poetry Reconsidered', *Michigan Academician* 9 (1976), 109–17

——, 'Hrothgar's "Sermon" in *Beowulf* as Parental Wisdom', *ASE* 10 (1982), 53–67

Hardy, Adelaide, 'The Christian Hero Beowulf and Unferð þyle', *Neophilologus* 53 (1969), 55–69

——, 'Some Thoughts on the Geats', *Parergon* 9 (August 1974), 27–39

——, 'Historical Perspective and the *Beowulf*-Poet', *Neophilologus* 63 (1979), 430–49

Harris, A. Leslie, 'Hands, Helms, and Heroes: the Role of Proper Names in *Beowulf*', *NM* 83 (1982), 414–21

Harris, Joseph, 'The Masterbuilder Tale in Snorri's Edda and in Two Sagas', *ANF* 91 (1976), 66–101

——, 'The *Senna:* From Description to Literary Theory', *Michigan Germanic Studies* 5 (1979), 65–74

——, '*Beowulf* in Literary History', *PCP* 17 (1982), 16–23 [also in *Interpretations*, ed. Fulk, pp. 235–41]

——, '*Beowulf*'s Last Words', *Speculum* 67 (1992), 1–32

——, 'A Nativist Approach to *Beowulf*: the Case of Germanic Elegy', in *Companion to Old English Poetry*, ed. Aertsen and Bremmer, pp. 45–62

——, 'The Dossier on Byggvir, God and Hero: *Cur deus homo*', *Arv* 55 (1999), 7–23

Harris, Richard L., 'The Deaths of Grettir and Grendel: a New Parallel', *SI* 24 (1973), 25–53

Hart, Thomas Elwood, 'Tectonic Design, Formulaic Craft, and Literary Execution: the Episodes of Finn and Ingeld in *Beowulf*', *ABäG* 2 (1972), 1–61

——, 'Tectonic Methodology and an Application to *Beowulf*', in *Essays in the Numerical Criticism of Medieval Literature*, ed. Caroline D. Eckhardt (London and Lewisburg, PA, 1980), pp. 185–210

——, 'Calculated Casualties in *Beowulf*: Geometrical Scaffolding and Verbal Symbol', *SN* 3 (1981), 3–35

Haruta, Setsuko, 'The Women in *Beowulf*', *Poetica* (Tokyo), 23 (1986), 1–15

Hasenfratz, Robert J., 'A Decade's Worth of *Beowulf* Scholarship: Observations on Compiling a Bibliography', *OEN* 27.3 (1994), 35–40

Haymes, Edward R., trans., *The Saga of Thidrek of Bern* (New York, 1988)

Heinemann, Fredrik J., '*Ealuscerwen-Meoduscerwen*, the Cup of Death and *Baldrs Draumar*', *SN* 55 (1983), 3–10

Helder, Willem, 'Beowulf and the Plundered Hoard', *NM* 78 (1977), 317–25

———, 'The Song of Creation in *Beowulf* and the Interpretation of Heorot', *ESC* 13 (1987), 243–55

Helterman, Jeffrey, '*Beowulf*: the Archetype Enters History', *ELH* 35 (1968), 1–20

Henry, P. L., '*Furor heroicus*', in *Studies in English Language and Early Literature*, ed. Tilling, pp. 53–61

Herben, Stephen J., 'Beowulf, Hrothgar, and Grendel', *ASnSL* 173 (1938), 24–30

Hermann, John P., *Allegories of War: Language and Violence in Old English Poetry* (Ann Arbor, MI, 1989)

Herschend, Frands, 'Beowulf and St. Sabas: the Tension between the Individual and the Collective in Germanic Society around 500 A.D', *Tor: tidskrift för arkeologi* 24 (1992), 145–64

Hickes, George, *Linguarum Veterum Septentrionalium Thesaurus Grammatico-Criticus et Archaeologicus*, 2 vols. (Oxford, 1703–5; rptd Hildesheim, 1970)

Hieatt, Constance B., 'Envelope Patterns and the Structure of *Beowulf*', *ESC* 1 (1975), 249–65

———, 'Modþryðo and Heremod: Intertwined Threads in the *Beowulf* Poet's Web of Words', *JEGP* 83 (1984), 173–82

———, 'Beowulf's Last Words vs. Bothvar Bjarki's: How the Hero Faces His God', in *Heroic Poetry*, ed. Damico and Leyerle, pp. 403–24

Higley, Sarah Lynn, '*Aldor on ofre*, or The Reluctant Hart: a Study of Liminality in *Beowulf*', *NM* 87 (1986), 342–53

Hill, John M., 'Beowulf and the Danish Succession: Gift Giving as an Occasion for Complex Gesture', *MH* n.s. 11 (1982), 177–97

———, 'Hrothgar's Noble Rule: Love and the Great Legislator', in *Social Approaches to Viking Studies*, ed. Ross Samson (Glasgow, 1991), pp. 169–78

———, *The Cultural World in 'Beowulf'*, Anthropological Horizons 6 (Toronto, 1995)

———, 'Social Milieu', in *Handbook*, ed. Bjork and Niles, pp. 255–69

Hill, Thomas D., 'Two Notes on Patristic Allusion in *Andreas*', *Anglia* 84 (1966), 156–62

———, '*Hwyrftum scriþað*: *Beowulf*, line 163', *MS* 33 (1971), 379–81

———, 'The Return of the Broken Butterfly: *Beowulf* Line 163, Again', *Mediaevalia* 5 (1979), 271–81

———, 'The Confession of Beowulf and the Structure of *Vǫlsunga Saga*', in *The Vikings*, ed. Farrell, pp. 165–79

———, 'Scyld Scefing and the *stirps regia*: Pagan Myth and Christian Kingship in *Beowulf*', in *Magister Regis*, ed. Groos *et al.*, pp. 37–47

———, 'The Myth of the Ark-Born Son of Noah and the West Saxon Royal Genealogical Tables', *Harvard Theological Review* 80 (1987), 379–83

———, ' "Wealhtheow" as a Foreign Slave: Some Continental Analogues', *PQ* 69 (1990), 106–12

———, 'Beowulf as Seldguma: *Beowulf*, lines 247–51', *Neophilologus* 74 (1990), 637–9

———, 'The Christian Language and Theme of *Beowulf*', in *Companion to Old English Poetry*, ed. Aertsen and Bremmer, pp. 63–77

Hills, Catherine M., '*Beowulf* and Archaeology', in *Handbook*, ed. Bjork and Niles, pp. 291–310

Hintz, Howard W. 'The "Hama" Reference in *Beowulf* 1197–1201', *JEGP* 33 (1934), 98–102

Hodges, Kenneth, 'Beowulf's Shoulder Pin and *wið earm gesæt*', *ELN* 34.3 (1997), 4–10

Hollis, Stephanie, '*Beowulf* and the Succession', *Parergon* n.s. 1 (1983), 39–54

Hollowell, Ida M., 'Unferð the *þyle* in *Beowulf*', *SP* (1976), 239–65

Holtsmark, Anne, 'Olav den Hellige og "Seierskjorten" ', *MM* (1954), 104–8

Hoops, Johannes, *Beowulfstudien*, Anglistische Forschungen 74 (Heidelberg, 1931)

———, 'Time and Place in the Ingeld Episode of *Beowulf*', *JEGP* 39 (1940), 76–92

Hoover, David L., *A New Theory of Old English Meter*, American University Studies 4 (New York, 1985)

———, 'Evidence for the Primacy of Alliteration in Old English Metre', *ASE* 14 (1985), 75–96

Horgan, A. D., 'Religious Attitudes in *Beowulf*', in *Essays and Poems Presented to Lord David Cecil*, ed. W. W. Robson (London, 1970), pp. 9–17

Horowitz, Sylvia Huntley, 'Beowulf, Samson, David and Christ', *Studies in Medieval Culture* 12 (1978), 17–23

———, 'The Ravens in *Beowulf*', *JEGP* 80 (1981), 502–11

———, 'The Interrupted Battles in *Beowulf*', *NM* 85 (1984), 295–303

Houwen, L. A. J. R., and A. A. MacDonald, ed., *Loyal Letters: Studies on Mediaeval Alliterative Poetry & Prose*, Mediaevalia Groningana 15 (Groningen, 1994)

Howlett, David, 'Form and Genre in *Beowulf*', *SN* 46 (1974), 309–25

———, 'New Criteria for Editing *Beowulf*', in *The Editing of Old English*, ed. Scragg and Szarmach, pp. 69–84

———, *British Books in Biblical Style* (Dublin, 1997)

Hubert, Susan J, 'The Case for Emendation of *Beowulf* 250b', *In Geardagum* 19 (1998), 51–4

Huffines, Marion Lois, 'OE *aglæca*: Magic and Moral Decline of Monsters and Men', *Semasia* 1 (1974), 71–81

Hughes, Geoffrey, 'Beowulf, Unferth and Hrunting: an Interpretation', *ES* 58 (1977), 385–95

Huisman, Rosemary, 'The Three Tellings of Beowulf's Fight with Grendel's Mother', *LSE* n.s. 20 (1989), 217–48

Hulbert, James R., 'The Accuracy of the B-Scribe of *Beowulf*', *PMLA* 43 (1928), 1196–9

———, 'A Note on Compounds in *Beowulf*', *JEGP* 31 (1932), 504–8

Hume, Kathryn, 'The Function of the *hrefn blaca*: *Beowulf* 1801', *MP* 67 (1969), 60–3

———, 'The Theme and Structure of *Beowulf*', *SP* 72 (1975), 1–27

Huppé, Bernard F., *The Web of Words* (Albany, NY, 1970)

———, 'The Concept of the Hero in the Early Middle Ages', in *Concepts of the Hero in the Middle Ages and the Renaissance*, ed. Norman T. Burns and Christopher R. Reagan (Albany, NY, 1975), pp. 1–26

———, *The Hero in the Earthly City: a Reading of 'Beowulf'*, MRTS 33 (Binghamton, NY, 1984)

Hutcheson, B. R, *Old English Poetic Metre* (London, 1995)

Irving, Edward B., Jr, ed., *The Old English Exodus* (New Haven, CT, 1953)

———, *A Reading of 'Beowulf'* (New Haven, CT, 1968)

———, 'Beowulf Comes Home: Close Reading in Epic Context', in *Acts of Interpretation: the Text in its Contexts, 700–1600: Essays on Medieval and Renaissance Literature in Honour of E. Talbot Donaldson*, ed. Mary J. Carruthers and Elizabeth D. Kirk (Norman, OK, 1982), pp. 129–43

———, 'The Nature of Christianity in *Beowulf*', *ASE* 13 (1984), 7–21

———, *Rereading 'Beowulf'* (Philadelphia, PA, 1989)

———, 'Heroic Role-Models: Beowulf and Others', in *Heroic Poetry*, ed. Damico and Leyerle, pp. 347–72

———, 'Christian and Pagan Elements', in *Handbook*, ed. Bjork and Niles, pp. 175–92

Jackson, Kenneth, 'Incremental Repetition in the Early Welsh *Englyn*', *Speculum* 16 (1941), 304–21

Jacobs, Nicolas, 'Anglo-Danish Relations, Poetic Archaism, and the Date of *Beowulf*', *Poetica* (Tokyo) 8 (1978), 23–43

Jager, Eric, 'Speech and Chest in Old English Poetry: Orality or Pectorality?', *Speculum* 65 (1990), 845–59

James, Montague Rhodes, ed., *Apocrypha Anecdota: a Collection of Thirteen Apocryphal Books and Fragments*, Texts and Studies: Contributions to Biblical and Patristic Literature II.3 (Cambridge, 1893)

———, ed., *Marvels of the East, A Full Reproduction of the Three Known Copies* Roxburghe Club Publications 191 (Oxford, 1929)

Jason, Heda, 'The Story of David and Goliath: a Folk Epic?', *Biblica* 60 (1979), 36–70

Jellinek, M. H., and Carl Kraus, 'Die Widersprüche im *Beowulf*', *ZdA* 35 (1891), 265–81

Johansen, J. G., 'Grendel the Brave? *Beowulf*, Line 834', *ES* 63 (1982), 193–7

John, Eric, '*Beowulf* and the Margins of Literacy', *BJRL* 56 (1974), 388–422 [also in '*Beowulf*': *Basic Readings*, ed. Baker, pp. 51–77]

Jones, Charles W., ed., *Bedae Venerabilis Libri quatuor in Genesim*, CCSL 118A (Turnhout, 1967)

Jones, Gwyn, *Kings, Beasts, and Heroes* (London, 1972)

Jónsson, Finnur, ed., *Den norsk-islandske skjaldedigtning*, 4 vols (Copenhagen, 1912–15)

———, *Edda Snorra Sturlusonar* (Copenhagen, 1931)

Jónsson, Guðni, ed., *Grettis saga Ásmundarsonar*, ÍF 7 (Reykjavik, 1936), pp. 3–290

———, ed., *Fornaldar sögur Norðurlanda*, 4 vols. (Akureyri, 1954)

———, ed., *Þiðreks saga af Bern* (Reykjavík, 1954)

Jorgensen, Peter A., 'Grendel, Grettir, and Two Skaldic Stanzas', *SI* 24 (1973), 54–61

———, 'The Two-Troll Variant of the Bear's Son Folktale in *Hálfdanar saga Brönufóstra* and *Gríms saga loðinkinna*', *Arv* 31 (1975), 35–43

———, '*Beowulf*'s Swimming Contest with Breca: Old Norse Parallels', *Folk-Lore* 89 (1978), 52–9

———, 'Old English Hengest as an Indo-European Twin Hero', *Mankind Quarterly* 24 (1983), 105–15

———, 'The Gift of the Useless Weapon in *Beowulf* and the Icelandic Sagas', *ANF* 94 (1979), 82–90

———, 'Additional Icelandic Analogues to *Beowulf*', in *Sagnaskemmtun: Studies in Honour of Hermann Pálsson on his Sixty-Fifth Birthday*, ed. Rudolf Simek, Jónas Kristjánsson, and Hans Bekker-Nielsen (Vienna, 1986), pp. 201–8

Judd, Elizabeth, 'Women before the Conquest: a Study of Women in Anglo-Saxon England', *Papers in Women's Studies* 1 (1974), 127–49

Kabell, Aage, 'Unferð und die dänischen Biersitten', *Arkiv för Nordisk Filologi* 94 (1979), 31–41

Kahrl, Stanley J., 'Feuds in *Beowulf*: a Tragic Necessity?', *MP* 69 (1972), 189–98

Kail, Johannes, 'Über die Parallelstellen in der angelsächsischen Poesie', *Anglia* 12 (1889), 21–40

Karkov, Catherine, and Robert Farrell, 'The Gnomic Passages of *Beowulf*', *NM* 91 (1990), 295–310

Kaske, Robert E., '*Sapientia et fortitudo* as the Controlling Theme in *Beowulf*', *SP* 55 (1958), 423–57 [also in *Anthology*, ed. Nicholson, pp. 269–310]

———, 'The Sigemund-Heremod and Hama-Hygelac Passages', *PMLA* 74 (1959), 489–94

———, 'Weohstan's Sword', *MLN* 75 (1960), 465–8

———, ' "Hygelac" and "Hygd" ', in *Studies in Old English Literature*, ed. Greenfield, pp. 200–6

———, 'The *eotenas* in *Beowulf*', in *Old English Poetry*, ed. Creed, pp. 285–310

———, '*Beowulf*', in *Critical Approaches to Six Major English Works: Beowulf through Paradise Lost*, ed. Robert M. Lumiansky and Herschel Baker (Philadelphia, PA, 1968), pp. 3–40

———, '*Beowulf* and the Book of Enoch', *Speculum* 46 (1971), 421–31

———, 'The Coastwarden's Maxim in *Beowulf*: a Clarification', *NQ* 229 (1984), 16–18

———, 'The *Gifstol* Crux in *Beowulf*', *LSE*, n.s. 16 (1985), 142–51

Kavros, Harry E., 'Swefan æfter symble: the Feast-Sleep Theme in *Beowulf*', *Neophilologus* 65 (1981), 120–8

Keefer, Sarah Larratt, and Katherine O'Brien O'Keeffe, ed., *New Approaches to Editing Old English Verse* (Cambridge, 1998)

Keller, Thomas L., 'The Dragon in *Beowulf* Reconsidered', *Aevum* 55 (1981), 218–28

Kelly, Birte, 'The Formative Stages of *Beowulf* Textual Scholarship: Part I', *ASE* 11 (1982), 247–74

———, 'The Formative Stages of *Beowulf* Textual Scholarship: Part II', *ASE* 12 (1983), 239–75

Kendall, Calvin B., *The Metrical Grammar of 'Beowulf'*, CSASE 5 (Cambridge, 1991)

Kendall, Calvin B., and Peter S. Wells, ed., *Voyage to the Other World: the Legacy of Sutton Hoo*, Medieval Studies at Minnesota 5 (Minneapolis, MN, 1992)

Ker, N. R., *Catalogue of Manuscripts Containing Anglo-Saxon* (Oxford, 1957; rptd. 1990)

Kermode, Frank, 'The Geat of Geats', *New York Review*, July 20, 2000, 18–21

Kershaw, Nora, *Stories and Ballads of the Far Past* (Cambridge, 1921)

Kiernan, Kevin S., *'Beowulf' and the 'Beowulf'-Manuscript* (New Brunswick, NJ, 1981); rev. ed. with foreword by Katherine O'Brien O'Keeffe (Ann Arbor, MI, 1996)

———, 'Grendel's Heroic Mother', *In Geardagum* 6 (1984), 13–33

———, *The Thorkelin Transcripts of Beowulf*, Anglistica 25 (Copenhagen, 1986)

———, 'A Long Footnote for J. Gerritsen's "Supplementary" Description of BL Cotton MS Vitellius A.XV', *ES* 72 (1991), 489–96

———, 'The State of the *Beowulf* Manuscript 1882–1983', *ASE* 13 (1983), 23–42 [also in his *'Beowulf' and the 'Beowulf' Manuscript*, rev. ed., pp. 305–28]

———, 'Old Manuscripts / New Technologies', in *Anglo-Saxon Manuscripts*, ed. Richards, pp. 37–54

———, 'The Eleventh-Century Origin of *Beowulf* and the *Beowulf* Manuscript', in *Anglo-Saxon Manuscripts*, ed. Richards, pp. 277–99

———, 'The Legacy of Wiglaf: Saving a Wounded Beowulf', in *'Beowulf': Basic Readings*, ed. Baker, pp. 195–218

Kim, Susan Marie, 'Monstrous and Bloody Signs: the *Beowulf* Manuscript' (unpublished PhD dissertation, University of Chicago, 1996)

Kindrick, Robert L., 'Germanic *Sapientia* and the Heroic Ethos of *Beowulf*', *MH* n.s. 10 (1981), 1–17

King, Margot H., and Wesley M. Stevens, ed., *Saints, Scholars and Heroes: Studies in Medieval Culture in Honour of Charles W. Jones*, 2 vols. (Collegeville, MN, 1979)

King, Richard John, 'Traces of Sigmund the Wælsing in Popular Tradition', *Athenaeum* (1850), 636–7

Kistenmacher, Richard, *Die wörtlichen Wiederholungen im Bêowulf* (Berlin, 1898)

Klaeber, Friedrich, 'A Few *Beowulf* Notes', *MLN* 16 (1901), 14–18

———, 'Die Ältere Genesis und der Beowulf', *EStn* 42 (1910), 321–38

———, 'Aeneis und Beowulf', *ASnSL* 126 (1911), 40–8 and 339–59

———, 'Die christlichen Elemente im *Beowulf*', *Anglia* 35 (1911–12), 111–36; 249–70; 453–82; 36 (1912), 169–99

———, 'Observations of the Finn Episode', *JEGP* 14 (1915), 544–49

———, 'Concerning the Relation between *Exodus* and *Beowulf*', *MLN* 33 (1918), 218–24

———, '*Beowulf* 769 und *Andreas* 1526ff', *EStn* 73 (1938–39), 185–89

———, 'Noch einmal *Exodus* 56–58 und *Beowulf* 1408–10', *ASnSL* 187 (1950), 71–2

———, *The Christian Elements in 'Beowulf'*, trans. Paul Battles, OEN Subsidia 24 (Kalamazoo, MI, 1997 [1996])

Kluge, Friedrich, 'Der Beowulf und die Hrolfs saga kraka', *EStn* 22 (1896), 144–5

Knappe, Fritz, *Das angelsächsische Prosastück Die Wunder des Ostens. Überlieferung, Quellen, Sprache und Text nach beiden Handschriften* (Berlin, 1906)

Knipp, Christopher, '*Beowulf* 2210b–2323: Repetition in the Description of the Dragon's Hoard', *NM* 73 (1972), 775–85

Köberl, Johann, 'The Magic Sword in *Beowulf*', *Neophilologus* 71 (1987), 120–8
———, 'Referential Ambiguity as a Structuring Principle in *Beowulf*', *Neophilologus* 79 (1995), 481–95
Kölbing, Eugen, 'Zur Béowulf-handschrift', *Archiv* 56 (1876), 91–118
Korhammer, Michael, ed., *Words, Texts and Manuscripts: Studies in Anglo-Saxon Culture Presented to Helmut Gneuss on the Occasion of his Sixty-Fifth Birthday* (Cambridge, 1992)
Kratz, Dennis M., ed. and trans., *Waltharius and Ruodlieb* (New York, 1984)
———, *Mocking Epic: Waltharius, Alexandreis, and the Problem of Christian Heroism* (Madrid, 1980)
Krusch, B., and W. Levison, ed., *Gregorii Episcopi Turonensis Libri Historiarum X*, MGH, Scriptores Rerum Merovinigicarum 1 (Hanover, 2nd ed., 1951)
Kuhn, Sherman M., 'The Sword of Healfdene', *JEGP* 42 (1943), 82–95
———, '*Beowulf* and the Life of Beowulf: a Study in Epic Structure', in *Studies in Language, Literature, and Culture*, ed. Atwood and Hill, pp. 243–64
———, 'Further Thoughts on *brand Healfdenes*', *JEGP* 76 (1977), 231–7
———, 'Old English *aglæca* – Middle Irish *ochlach*', in *Linguistic Method: Essays in Honor of Herbert Penzl*, ed. I. Rauch and G. F. Carr, Janua linguarum series maior 79 (The Hague, 1979), pp. 213–30
Laborde, E. D., 'Grendel's Glove and his Immunity from Weapons', *MLR* 18 (1923), 202–4
Lang, J. T., 'Sigurd and Weland in Pre-Conquest Carving from Northern England', *Yorkshire Archaeological Journal* 48 (1976), 83–94
Lapidge, Michael, 'Aldhelm's Latin Poetry and Old English Verse', *CL* 31 (1979), 249–314
———, '*Beowulf*, Aldhelm, the *Liber Monstrorum* and Wessex', *SM*, 3rd series, 23 (1982), 151–92
———, 'Textual Criticism and the Literature of Anglo-Saxon England', *BJRL* 73 (1991), 17–45
———, 'The Edition, Emendation and Reconstruction of Anglo-Saxon Texts', in *The Politics of Editing Medieval Texts*, ed. Roberta Frank (New York, 1993), pp. 131–57
———, *Anglo-Latin Literature, 900–1066* (London, 1993)
———, '*Beowulf* and the Psychology of Terror', in *Heroic Poetry*, ed. Damico and Leyerle, pp. 373–402
———, *Anglo-Latin Literature, 600–899* (London, 1996)
———, 'The Archetype of *Beowulf*', *ASE* 29 (2000), 5–41
———, '*Beowulf* and Perception', *PBA* 111 (2001), 61–97
Lapidge, Michael, and Helmut Gneuss, ed., *Learning and Literature in Anglo-Saxon England: Studies Presented to Peter Clemoes on the Occasion of his Sixty-Fifth Birthday* (Cambridge, 1985)
Larkin, Phillip, *Selected Letters of Phillip Larkin 1940–1985*, ed. Anthony Thwaite (London, 1992)
Lawrence, William Witherle, 'The Haunted Mere in *Beowulf*', *PMLA* 27 (1912), 208–45
———, 'The Breca Episode in *Beowulf*', *Anniversary Papers by Colleagues and Pupils of George Lyman Kittredge* (Boston, MA, 1913), pp. 359–66
———, '*Beowulf* and the Tragedy of Finnsburg', *PMLA* 30 (1915), 372–432
———, 'The Dragon and his Lair in *Beowulf*', *PMLA* 33 (1918), 547–83
———, '*Beowulf* and the Epic Tradition* (Cambridge, MA, 1928)
———, '*Beowulf* and the *Saga of Samson the Fair*', in *Studies in English Philology*, ed. Malone and Ruud, pp. 172–81
———, *Beowulf and Epic Tradition* (Cambridge, MA, 1930)
———, 'Grendel's Lair', *JEGP* 38 (1939), 477–80
Leake, Jane Acomb, *The Geats of 'Beowulf': a Study in the Geographical Mythology of the Middle Ages* (Madison, WI, 1967)
Lee, Alvin A., 'Symbolism and Allegory', in *Handbook*, ed. Bjork and Niles, pp. 233–54
———, *Gold-Hall and Earth-Dragon: 'Beowulf' as Metaphor* (Toronto, 1998)

Lehmann, Ruth P. M., 'Ecgþeow the Wægmunding: Geat or Swede?', *ELN* 31.3 (1994), 1–5

Lehmann, Winfred P., 'On Posited Omissions in the *Beowulf*', in *Studies in Language, Literature, and Culture*, ed. Atwood and Hill, pp. 220–9

Lehmann, Winfred P., and Takemitsu Tabusa, *The Alliterations of the 'Beowulf'* (Austin, TX, 1958)

Lendinara, Patrizia, 'The *Liber monstrorum* and Anglo-Saxon Glossaries', in her *Anglo-Saxon Glosses and Glossaries* (Aldershot, 1999), pp. 113–38

Lerer, Seth, *Literacy and Power in Anglo-Saxon Literature* (Lincoln, NE, 1991)

———, 'Grendel's Glove', *ELH* 61 (1994), 721–51

———, '*Beowulf* and Contemporary Critical Theory', in *Handbook*, ed. Bjork and Niles, pp. 325–39

Lester, Graham A., '*Earme on eaxle* (*Beowulf* 1117a)', *SN* 58 (1986), 159–63

Levine, Robert, 'Direct Discourse in *Beowulf*: its Meaning and Function' (unpublished PhD dissertation, University of California, Berkeley, 1963)

Lewis, Richard A., '*Beowulf* 992A: Ironic Use of the Formulaic', *PQ* 54 (1975), 663–4

Leyerle, John, 'Beowulf the Hero and the King', *MÆ* 34 (1965), 89–102

———, 'The Interlace Structure of *Beowulf*', *UTQ* 37 (1967), 1–17 [also in *Interpretations*, ed. Fulk, pp. 146–67]

Liberman, Anatoly, 'Germanic *Sendan* "To Make a Sacrifice"', *JEGP* 77 (1978), 473–88

———, 'Beowulf-Grettir', in *German Dialects: Linguistic and Philological Investigations*, ed. Bela Brogyanyi and Thomas Krömmelbein, Amsterdam Studies in the Theory and History of Linguistic Science 38 (Amsterdam, 1986), pp. 353–91

———, 'The "Icy" Ship of Scyld Scefing: *Beowulf* 33', *Bright Is the Ring of Words: Festschrift für Horst Weinstock*, ed. Clausdirk Pollner, Helmut Rohlfing, and Frank-Rutger Hausmann (Bonn, 1996), pp. 183–94

Lionarons, Joyce Tally, '*Beowulf*: Myth and Monsters', *ES* 77 (1996), 1–14

———, *The Medieval Dragon: the Nature of the Beast in Germanic Literature* (Enfield Lock, 1998)

Liuzza, Roy Michael, 'On the Dating of *Beowulf*', in *'Beowulf': Basic Readings*, ed. Baker, pp. 281–302

Locherbie-Cameron, Margaret A. L., 'Structure, Mood and Meaning in *Beowulf*', *Poetica* (Tokyo), 10 (1978), 1–11

Loganbill, Dean, 'Time and Monsters in *Beowulf*', *In Geardagum* 3 (1979), 26–35

Lönnroth, Lars, 'The Noble Heathen: a Theme in the Sagas', *SS* 41 (1969), 1–29

Looze, Laurence N. de, 'Frame Narratives and Fictionalization: Beowulf as Narrator', *TSLL* 26 (1984), 145–56 [also in *Interpretations*, ed. Fulk, pp. 242–50]

Lord, Albert Bates, *The Singer of Tales* (Cambridge MA, 1960)

———, 'Beowulf and Odysseus', in *Franciplegius*, ed. Bessinger and Creed, pp. 86–91

———, *The Singer Resumes the Tale*, ed. Mary Louise Lord (Ithaca, NY, 1995)

Louden, Bruce, 'A Narrative Technique in *Beowulf* and Homeric Epic', *OT* 11 (1996), 346–62

Lowe, E. A., 'The Oldest Omission Signs in Latin Manuscripts: their Origins and Significance', in his *Palaeographical Papers 1907–1965*, ed. Ludwig Bieler, 2 vols. (Oxford, 1972), II, 349–80

Lowe, Kathryn A., 'Never say *Nefa* Again', *NM* (1993), 27–35

Lucas, Peter J., ed., *Exodus* (London, 1977)

———, 'The Place of *Judith* in the *Beowulf*-Manuscript', *RES* 41 (1990), 463–78

Luehrs, Phoebe M., 'A Summary of Sarrazin's "Studies in Beowulf"', *Western Reserve University Bulletin* 7 (1904), 146–65

Lynch, Clare, 'Enigmatic Diction in the Old English *Exodus*' (unpublished PhD dissertation, University of Cambridge, 2001)

Mackie, William S., 'The Demons' Home in *Beowulf*', *JEGP* 37 (1938), 455–61

Magennis, Hugh, '*Beowulf*, 1008a: *swefeþ æfter symle*', *NQ* 29 (1982), 391–2

———, 'The *Beowulf* Poet and his *druncne dryhtguman*', *NM* 86 (1985), 159–64

Magoun, Francis P., Jr, 'Recurring First Elements in Different Nominal Compounds in *Beowulf* and the *Elder Edda*', in *Studies in Philology*, ed. Malone and Ruud, pp. 73–8
——, 'The Oral-Formulaic Character of Anglo-Saxon Narrative Poetry', *Speculum* 28 (1953), 446–67 [also in *Anthology*, ed. Nicholson, pp. 189–221; *Essential Articles*, ed. Bessinger and Kahrl, 319–51; *'Beowulf'-Poet*, ed. Fry, pp. 83–113; *Interpretations*, ed. Fulk, pp. 45–65]
——, 'The Geography of Hygelac's Raid on the Lands of the West Frisians and the Hætt-ware, *circa* 530 A.D.', *ES* 34 (1953), 160–3
——, 'Béowulf and King Hygelác in the Netherlands: Lost Anglo-Saxon Verse-Stories about This Event', *ES* 35 (1954), 193–204
——, 'The Theme of the Beasts of Battle in Anglo-Saxon Poetry', *NM* 56 (1955), 81–90
——, ' "*Beowulf A*": a Folk-Variant', *Arv* 14 (1958), 95–101
——, '*Beowulf B*: a Folk-Poem on Beowulf's Death', in *Early English and Norse Studies Presented to Hugh Smith in Honour of His Sixtieth Birthday*, ed. Arthur Brown and Peter Foote (London, 1963), pp. 127–40
Major, C. Tidmarsh, 'A Christian *wyrd*: Syncretism in *Beowulf*', *ELN* 32.3 (1995), 1–10
Malmberg, Lars, 'Grendel and the Devil', *NM* 78 (1977), 241–3
Malone, Kemp, 'The Finn Episode in *Beowulf*', *JEGP* 25 (1926), 157–72
——, 'Ingeld', *MP* 27 (1930), 257–76
——, 'Hygelac', *ES* 21 (1939), 108–19
——, 'Freawaru', *ELH* 7 (1940), 39–44
——, 'Hygd', *MLN* 56 (1941), 356–8
——, 'Grendel and Grep', *PMLA* 57 (1942), 1–14
——, 'Hildeburg and Hengest', *ELH* 10 (1943), 257–84
——, 'Grendel and his Abode', in *Studia Philologica et Litteraria in Honorem L. Spitzer*, ed. A. G. Hatcher and K-L. Selig (Bern, 1958), pp. 297–308
——, 'The Tale of Ingeld', in his *Studies in Heroic Legend and in Current Speech*, ed. Stefán Einarsson and Norman E. Eliason (Copenhagen, 1959), pp. 1–62
——, 'Readings from Folios 94 to 131, Cotton Vitellius A xv', in *Studies in Medieval Literature in Honor of Professor Albert Croll Baugh*, ed. MacEdward Leach (Philadelphia, PA, 1961), pp. 255–71
——, ed., *Widsith*, Anglistica 13 (Copenhagen, rev. ed., 1962)
——, Review of Westphalen, *Beowulf 3150–55*, *Speculum* 44 (1969), 182–6
——, 'A Reading of *Beowulf* 3169–3182', in *Medieval Literature and Folklore Studies*, ed. Mandel and Rosenberg, pp. 35–8
——, 'Beowulf the Headstrong', *ASE* 1 (1972), 139–45
Malone, Kemp, and Martin B. Ruud, ed., *Studies in Philology: a Miscellany in Honor of Frederick Klaeber* (Minneapolis, MN, 1929)
Mandel, Jerome, and Bruce Rosenberg, ed., *Medieval Literature and Folklore Studies: Essays in Honor of Francis Lee Utley* (New Brunswick, NJ, 1970)
Manes, Christopher, 'The Substance of Earth in *Beowulf*'s Song of Creation', *ELN* 31.4 (1994), 1–5
Margeson, Sue, 'The Völsung Legend in Medieval Art', in *Medieval Iconography and Narrative: a Symposium*, ed. F. G. Andersen (Odense, 1980), pp. 183–211
Martin-Clarke, Daisy E., 'The Office of Thyle in *Beowulf*', *RES* 12 (1936), 61–6
Maynard, Stephen, ' "Secan deofla gedræg": a Note on *Beowulf* 756', *NM* 93 (1992), 87–91
Mazo, Jeffrey Alan, 'Compound Diction and Traditional Style in *Beowulf* and *Genesis A*', *OT* 6 (1991), 79–92
McClintock, Ellery, 'Translation and *Beowulf* in Translation' (unpublished PhD dissertation, Georgia State University, 2000)
McClumpha, C. F. [*see* Davidson, Charles]
McConchie, R. W., 'Grettir Ásmundarson's Fight with Kárr the Old: a Neglected *Beowulf* Analogue', *ES* 63 (1982), 481–86
——, 'The Use of the Verb *maþelian* in *Beowulf*', *NM* 99 (1998), 59–68

McCone, Kim, *Pagan Past and Christian Present in Early Irish Literature* (Maynooth, 1990)

McCully, C. B., and J. J. Anderson, ed. *English Historical Metrics* (Cambridge, 1996)

McDavid, Raven I., Jr, 'Hroþulf, Hengest, and Beowulf: Two Structural Parallels', in *Studies in Language, Literature, and Culture*, ed. Atwood and Hill, pp. 230–4

McFadden, Brian, 'Sleeping after the Feast: Deathbeds, Marriage Beds, and the Power-Structure of Heorot', *Neophilologus* 84 (2000), 629–46

McGuiness, Daniel, 'Beowulf's Byrnies', *ELN* 26.3 (1989), 1–3

McGurk, P. M. J., D. N. Dumville, and M. R. Godden, ed., *An Eleventh-Century Anglo-Saxon Illustrated Miscellany (British Library Cotton Tiberius B. V Part I)*, EEMF 21 (Copenhagen, 1983)

McNamara, John, 'Beowulf and Hygelac: Problems for Fiction in History', *Rice University Studies* 62.2 (1976), 55–63

——, 'Legends of Breca and Beowulf', *SF* 53 (1996), 153–69

McNamee, Maurice B., 'Beowulf, a Christian Hero', in *Honor and the Epic Hero: a Study of the Shifting Concept of Magnanimity in Philosophy and Epic Poetry* (New York, 1960), pp. 86–117

——, '*Beowulf* – An Allegory of Salvation?', *JEGP* 59 (1960), 190–207 [also in *Anthology*, ed. Nicholson, pp. 331–52; *Interpretations*, pp. 88–102]

McNelis, James I., III, 'Laȝamon as Auctor', in *The Text and Tradition of Laȝamon's 'Brut'*, ed. Françoise Le Saux (Cambridge, 1994), pp. 253–72

——, 'The Sword Mightier Than the Pen? Hrothgar's Hilt, Theory, and Philology', in *Studies in English Language and Literature*, ed. Toswell and Tyler, pp. 175–85

McTurk, Rory W., 'Variation in *Beowulf* and the Poetic *Edda*: a Chronological Experiment', in *Dating of 'Beowulf'*, ed. Chase, 141–60

——, *Studies in 'Ragnars saga loðbrókar' and its Major Scandinavian Analogues*, MÆ Monographs, n.s. 15 (Oxford, 1991)

Meaney, Audrey L., 'Scyld Scefing and the Dating of *Beowulf* – Again', *BJRL* 71 (1989), 7–40

Mellinkoff, Ruth, 'Cain's Monstrous Progeny in *Beowulf*: Part I, Noachic Tradition', *ASE* 8 (1979), 143–62

——, 'Cain's Monstrous Progeny in *Beowulf*: Part II, Post-Diluvian Survival', *ASE* 9 (1981), 183–97

Menzer, Melinda J., '*Aglæcwif* (*Beowulf* 1259a): Implications for -*wif* Compounds, Grendel's Mother, and Other *aglæcan*', *ELN* 34.1 (1996), 1–6

Meyer, Richard M., *Die altgermanische Poesie nach ihren formelhaften Elementen beschrieben* (Berlin, 1889)

Miller, T., 'The Position of Grendel's Arm in Heorot', *Anglia* 12 (1889), 396–400

Mitchell, Bruce, ' "Until the Dragon Comes . . ." Some Thoughts on *Beowulf*', *Neophilologus* 47 (1963), 126–38 [also in his *On Old English*, pp. 3–15]

——, 'Linguistic Facts and the Interpretation of Old English Poetry', *ASE* 4 (1975), 11–28 [also in his *On Old English*, pp. 152–71]

——, 'The Dangers of Disguise: Old English Texts in Modern Punctuation', *RES* 31 (1980), 385–413 [also in his *On Old English*, pp. 172–202]

——, *Old English Syntax*, 2 vols. (Oxford, 1985)

——, *On Old English* (Oxford, 1988)

——, '*Beowulf*, line 1020b: *brand* or *bearn*?', *Romanobarbarica* 10 (1988–9), 283–92

——, 'Literary Lapses: Six Notes on *Beowulf* and Its Critics', *RES* 43 (1992), 1–17

——, '*apo koinou* in Old English Poetry?', *NM* 100 (1999), 477–97

Mitchell, Bruce, and Susan Irvine, '*Beowulf*' *Repunctuated*, OEN Subsidia 29 (Kalamazoo, MI, 2000)

Mizuno, Tomaki, 'Beowulf as a Terrible Stranger', *Journal of Indo-European Studies* 17 (1989), 1–46

——, 'The Magical Necklace and the Fatal Corselet in *Beowulf*', *ES* 80 (1999), 377–97

Moe, Lawrence Dalton, 'The Christian Passages of "Beowulf"' (unpublished PhD dissertation, University of Minnesota,1991)

Moffat, Douglas, 'Anglo-Saxon Scribes and Old English Verse', *Speculum* 67 (1992), 805–27

Moisl, Hermann, 'Anglo-Saxon Royal Genealogies and Germanic Oral Tradition', *Journal of Medieval History* 7 (1981), 215–48

Momma, Haruko, 'The "Gnomic Formula" and Some Additions to Bliss's Old English Metrical Ststem', *NQ* 37 (1989), 423–6

Moore, Bruce, 'The Relevance of the Finnsburh Episode', *JEGP* 75 (1976), 317–29

——, 'The Thryth-Offa Digression in *Beowulf*', *Neophilologus* 64 (1980), 127–33

Moorman, Charles, 'The Essential Paganism of *Beowulf*', *MLQ* 28 (1967), 3–18

Morey, Robert, '*Beowulf*'s Androgynous Heroism', *JEGP* 95 (1996), 486–96

Morgan, G., 'The Treachery of Hrothulf', *ES* 53 (1972), 23–39

Morgan, Gareth, 'Walther the Wood-Sprite', *MÆ* 41 (1972), 16–19

Morris, R., ed., *The Blickling Homilies of the Tenth Century*, EETS OS 58, 63, 73 (London, 1874–80; rptd in one vol., 1967)

Müllenhoff, Karl, 'Der Mythus von Beovulf', *ZdA* 7 (1849), 419–41

——, 'Die innere Geschichte des *Beovulfs*', *ZdA* 14 (1869), 193–244

Müller-Zimmermann, Gunhild, 'Beowulf: zur Datierungs- und Interpretationsproblematik', *Medieval Insular Literature between the Oral and the Written II: Continuity of Transmission*, ed. Hildegard L. C. Tristram, ScriptOralia 97 (Tübingen, 1997), pp. 29–64

Murray, Alexander Callander, 'Beowulf, the Danish Invasions, and Royal Genealogy', in *Dating of 'Beowulf'*, ed. Chase, pp. 101–11

Mussett, Griselda Cann, and Paul Wilkinson, *'Beowulf' in Kent* (Faversham, 1998)

Mynors, R. A. B., ed., *P. Vergili Maronis Opera* (Oxford, 1969)

Mynors, R. A. B., R. M. Thomson, and M. Winterbottom, ed. and trans., *William of Malmesbury, Gesta Regum Anglorum*, 2 vols. (Oxford, 1998–9)

Nagler, Michael N., '*Beowulf* in the Context of Myth', in *Old English Literature in Context*, ed. Niles, pp. 143–56

Nagy, Joseph F., 'Beowulf and Fergus: Heroes of Their Tribes?', in *Connections between Old English and Medieval Celtic Literature*, ed. Patrick K. Ford and Karen G. Borst, OEC 2 (Lanham, MD, 1982), pp. 31–44

Nagy, Michael S., 'A Reassessment of Unferð's Fratricide in *Beowulf*', *PMAM* 3 (1996 [1995]), 15–30

Napier, Arthur S., ed., *Wulfstan: Sammlung der ihm zugeschriebenen Homilien nebst Untersuchungen über ihre Echtheit* (Berlin, 1883; rptd with an appendix by K. Ostheeren, Berlin, 1966)

——, ed., *Old English Glosses*, Anecdota Oxoniensia, Medieval and Modern Series 11 (Oxford, 1900; rptd Hildesheim, 1969)

Near, Michael R., 'Anticipating Alienation: *Beowulf* and the Intrusion of Literacy', *PMLA* 108 (1993), 320–32 [response by A. J. Frantzen and G. R. Overing, reply by Near, pp. 1177–79]

Neckel, Gustav, ed., *Die Lieder des Codex Regius nebst verwandten Denkmälern I: Text*, rev. Hans Kuhn, 5th ed. (Heidelberg, 1983)

Nedoma, Robert, 'The Legend of Wayland in *Deor*', *ZAA* 38 (1990), 129–45

Nelles, William, '*Beowulf*'s *sorhfullne sið* with Breca', *Neophilologus* 83 (1999), 299–312

Neville, Jennifer, *Representations of the Natural World in Old English Poetry*, CSASE 27 (Cambridge, 1999)

Newton, Sam, *The Origins of 'Beowulf' and the Pre-Viking Kingdom of East Anglia* (Cambridge, 1993)

Nicholls, Alex, 'Bede "Awe-Inspiring" not "Monstrous": Some Problems with Old English *aglæca*', *NQ* 38 (1991), 147–8

Nicholson, Lewis E., ed., *An Anthology of 'Beowulf' Criticism* (Notre Dame, IN, 1963)

————, 'The Literal Meaning and Symbolic Structure of *Beowulf*', *Classica et Mediaevalia* 25 (1964), 151–201

————, 'Hunlafing and the Point of the Sword', in *Anglo-Saxon Poetry*, ed. Nicholson and Frese, pp. 50–61

————, 'The Art of Interlace in *Beowulf*', *SN* 52 (1980), 237–49

————, '*Beowulf* and the Pagan Cult of the Stag', *SM* 3rd series 27 (1986), 637–69

Nicholson, Lewis E., and Dolores Warwick Frese, ed., *Anglo-Saxon Poetry: Essays in Appreciation for John C. McGalliard* (Notre Dame, IN, 1975)

Niles, John D., 'Ring-Composition and the Structure of *Beowulf*', *PMLA* 94 (1979), 924–35

————, ed., *Old English Literature in Context: Ten Essays* (Cambridge, 1980)

————, 'Compound Diction and the Style of *Beowulf*', *ES* 62 (1981), 489–503

————, 'Formula and Formulaic System in *Beowulf*', in *Oral Traditional Literature*, ed. Foley, pp. 394–415

————, *Beowulf: the Poem and its Tradition* (Cambridge, MA, 1983)

————, 'Toward an Anglo-Saxon Oral Poetics', in *De Gustibus*, ed. Foley, pp. 359–77

————, 'Pagan Survivals and Popular Belief', in *Cambridge Companion*, ed. Godden and Lapidge, pp. 126–41

————, 'Locating *Beowulf* in Literary History', *Exemplaria* 5 (1993), 79–109

————, 'Editing *Beowulf*: What Can Study of the Ballads Tell Us?', *OT* 9 (1994), 440–67

————, 'Introduction: *Beowulf*, Truth and Meaning', in *Handbook*, ed. Bjork and Niles, pp. 1–12

————, 'Myth and History', in *Handbook*, ed. Bjork and Niles, pp. 213–32

————, 'Understanding *Beowulf*: Oral Poetry Acts', *JAF* 106 (1993), 131–55

Nist, John A., *The Structure and Texture of Beowulf* (São Paulo, 1959)

————, '*Beowulf* and the Classical Epics', *CE* 24 (1963), 257–62

Nolan, Barbara, and Morton W. Bloomfield, '*Beotword, gilpcwidas*, and the *gilphlædan* Scop of *Beowulf*', *JEGP* 79 (1980), 499–516

North, Richard, 'Tribal Loyalties in the *Finnsburh Fragment* and Episode', *LSE* 21 (1990), 13–43

————, *Pagan Words and Christian Meanings*, Costerus n.s. 81 (Amsterdam, 1991)

————, 'Saxo and the Swedish Wars in *Beowulf*', in *Saxo Grammaticus tra storiografia e letteratura*, ed. Carlo Santini (Rome, 1992), pp. 175–88

————, 'Metre and Meaning in *Wulf and Eadwacer*: Signý Reconsidered', in *Loyal Letters*, ed. Houwen and MacDonald, pp. 29–54

————, ' "Wyrd" and "wearð" in *Beowulf*', *LSE* 25 (1994), 69–82

————, *Heathen Gods in Old English Literature*, CSASE 22 (Cambridge, 1997)

O'Keef[f]e, Katherine O'Bri[e]n, '*Beowulf*, Lines 702b–836: Transformations and the Limits of the Human', *TSLL* 23 (1981), 484–94

————, *Visible Song: Transitional Literacy in Old English Verse*, CSASE 4 (Cambridge, 1990)

————, 'Heroic Values and Christian Ethics', in *Cambridge Companion*, ed. Godden and Lapidge, pp. 107–25

————, 'Diction, Variation, and the Formula', in *Handbook*, ed. Bjork and Niles, pp. 85–104

————, ed., *The Anglo-Saxon Chronicle: a Collaborative Edition. MS C* (Cambridge, 2001)

Ogilvy, J. D. A., *Books Known to the English, 597–1066* (Cambridge, MA, 1967)

————, 'Books Known to the English, A.D. 597–1066: Addenda et Corrigenda', *Mediaevalia* 7 (1981), 281–325

————, 'Unferth: Foil to Beowulf?', *PMLA* 79 (1964), 370–5

Ogura, Michiko, 'An Ogre's Arm: Japanese Analogues of *Beowulf*', in *Words and Works*, ed. Baker and Howe, pp. 59–66

Ohba, Keizo, 'Hrothgar's "Sermon" and Beowulf's Death', *Annual Reports of Studies, Doshisha Women's College of Liberal Arts*, Kyoto 24 (1973), 1–19

Olrik, J., and H. Raeder, ed., *Saxonis Gesta Danorum*, 2 vols. (Copenhagen, 1931–7)

Olsen, Alexandra Hennessey, 'Women in *Beowulf*', in *Approaches to Teaching Beowulf*, ed. Bessinger and Yeager, pp. 150–6

———, 'Oral-Formulaic Research in Old English Studies: I', *OT* 1 (1986), 548–606

———, 'Oral-Formulaic Research in Old English Studies: II', *OT* 3 (1988), 138–90

———, 'Gender Roles', in *Handbook*, ed. Bjork and Niles, pp. 311–24

———, '*Beowulf*', in *Teaching Oral Traditions*, ed. John Miles Foley (New York, 1998), pp. 351–8

Olson, Oscar L., '*Beowulf* and *The Feast of Bricriu*', *MP* 11 (1913–14), 1–21

———, *The Relation of the Hrólfs saga kraka and the Bjarkarímur to Beowulf* (Chicago, 1916)

Ono, Shigeru, 'Grendel's Not Greeting the *gifstol* Reconsidered–with Special Reference to *motan with the Negative', *Poetica* (Tokyo), 41 (1994), 11–17

Opland, Jeff, 'A *Beowulf* Analogue in *Njálssaga*', *SS* 45 (1973), 54–8

———, '*Beowulf* on the Poet', *MS* 38 (1976), 442–67

———, *Anglo-Saxon Oral Poetry: a Study of the Traditions* (New Haven, CT, 1980)

Orchard, Andy, 'Crying Wolf: Oral Style and the *Sermones Lupi*', *ASE* 21 (1992), 239–64

———, 'After Aldhelm: the Teaching and Transmission of the Anglo-Latin Hexameter', *Journal of Medieval Latin* 2 (1992), 96–133

———, 'Tolkien, the Monsters, and the Critics: Back to *Beowulf*', in *Scholarship and Fantasy: Proceedings of the 'The Tolkien Phenomenon', Turku May 1992*, ed. Keith Battarbee, Anglicana Turkuensia 12 (1993), 73–84

———, *The Poetic Art of Aldhelm*, CSASE 8 (Cambridge, 1994)

———, 'Artful Alliteration in Anglo-Saxon Song and Story', *Anglia* 113 (1995), 429–63

———, *Pride and Prodigies: Studies in the Monsters of the 'Beowulf'-Manuscript* (Cambridge, 1995)

———, 'Oral Tradition', in *Reading Old English Texts*, ed. Katherine O'Brien O'Keeffe (Cambridge, 1997), pp. 101–23

———, 'The Sources and Meaning of the *Liber monstrorum*', in *I 'monstra' nell'inferno Dantesco: Tradizione e Simbologie*, Atti del XXXIII Convegno storico internazionale, Todi, 13–16 ottobre 1996, ed. E. Menestò (Spoleto, 1997), pp. 73–105

———, 'Unrecoverable Magic', *Times Literary Supplement*, 20 June 1997, p. 20 [review of Trevor Eaton's *Beowulf* recording]

———, *Cassell Dictionary of Norse Myth and Legend* (London, 1997)

———, 'Wish you were here: Alcuin's Courtly Verse and the Boys Back Home', in *Courts and Regions in Medieval Europe*, ed. Sarah Rees Jones, Richard Marks, and A. J. Minnis (York, 2000), pp. 21–43

———, 'The *Hisperica famina* as Literature', *Journal of Medieval Latin* 10 (2000), 1–45

———, 'The Literary Background to the *Encomium Emmae Reginae*', *Journal of Medieval Latin* 11 (2001), 157–84

———, 'Old Sources, New Resources: Finding the Right Formula for Boniface', *ASE* 30 (2001), 15–38

———, 'Re-Reading *The Wanderer*: the Value of Cross References', in *Via Crucis: Essays on Early Medieval Sources and Ideas in Memory of J. E. Cross*, ed. Thomas N. Hall (Morgantown, WV, 2002), pp. 1–26

———, 'Both Style and Substance: the Case for Cynewulf', in *Anglo-Saxon Styles*, ed. Catherine E. Karkov and George Hardin Brown (Binghamton, NY, 2003), pp. 271–305.

Orton, Peter, *The Transmission of Old English Poetry*, Westfield Publications in Medieval and Renaissance Studies 12 (London, 2000)

Osborn, Marijane, 'The Great Feud: Scriptural History and Strife in *Beowulf*', *PMLA* 93 (1978, 1995), 973–81 [also in '*Beowulf*': *Basic Readings*, ed. Baker, pp. 111–25]

——, 'Translations, Versions, Illustrations', in *Handbook*, ed. Bjork and Niles, pp. 341–72

——, 'Two-Way Evidence in *Beowulf* Concerning Viking-Age Ships', *ANQ* 13.2 (2000), 3–6

Östman, Jan-Ola, and Brita Wårvik, '*The Fight at Finnsburh*: Pragmatic Aspects of a Narrative Fragment', *NM* 99 (1998), 207–27

Overing, Gillian R., *Language, Sign, and Gender in Beowulf* (Carbondale, IL, 1990)

——, 'The Women of *Beowulf*: a Context for Interpretation', in *'Beowulf': Basic Readings*, ed. Baker, pp. 219–60

Overing, Gillian R., and Marijane Osborn, *Landscape of Desire: Partial Stories of the Medieval Scandinavian World* (Minneapolis, MN, 1994)

Owen-Crocker, Gale R., *The Four Funerals in 'Beowulf' and the Structure of the Poem* (Manchester, 2000)

Page, R. I., 'The Audience of *Beowulf* and the Vikings', in *Dating of 'Beowulf'*, ed. Chase, pp. 113–22

——, 'Back to the Manuscripts: Some Thoughts on Editing Old English Texts', in *Back to the Manuscripts: Papers from the Symposium 'The Integrated Approach to Manuscript Studies: a New Horizon', Tokyo, December 1992*, Centre for Medieval English Studies, Tokyo, Occasional Papers 1 (Tokyo, 1997), pp. 1–27

Pálsson, Hermann, and Paul Edwards, *Legendary Fiction in Medieval Iceland*, Studia Islandica 30 (Reykjavík, 1971)

——, trans., *Seven Viking Romances* (Harmondsworth, 1985)

Panzer, Friedrich, *Studien zur germanischen Sagengeschichte*, 2 vols. (Munich, 1910)

Parker, Mary A., *'Beowulf' and Christianity*, American University Studies, Series 4: English Language and Literature (New York, 1987)

Parkes, Ford B., 'Irony in the *Waltharius*', *MLN* 89 (1974), 459–65

Parks, Ward, 'Flyting and Fighting: Pathways in the Realization of the Epic Contest', *Neophilologus* 70 (1986), 292–306

——, ' "I Heard" Formulas in Old English Poetry', *ASE* 16 (1987), 45–66

——, 'Ring Structure and Narrative Embedding in Homer and *Beowulf*', *NM* 89 (1988), 237–51

——, *Verbal Dueling in Heroic Narrative: the Homeric and Old English Traditions* (Princeton, NJ, 1990)

——, 'The Traditional Narrator in *Beowulf* and Homer', in *De Gustibus*, ed. Foley, pp. 456–79

——, 'Prey Tell: How Heroes Perceive Monsters in *Beowulf*', *JEGP* 92 (1993), 1–16

Pàroli, Teresa, ed., *La funzione dell'eroe germanico: storicità, metafora, paradigma, Atti del Convegno internazionale di studio, Roma, 6-8 maggio 1993*, Philologia, 2 (Rome, 1995)

Parry, Adam, *The Making of Homeric Verse: the Collected Papers of Milman Parry* (Oxford, 1971)

Pasternack, Carol Braun, *The Textuality of Old English Poetry*, CSASE 13 (Cambridge, 1995)

Payne, F. Anne, 'The Danes' Prayers to the "gastbona" in *Beowulf*', *NM* 80 (1979), 308–14

Pearson, Michael Parker, Robert van de Noort, and Alex Woolf, 'Three Men and a Boat: Sutton Hoo and the East Saxon Kingdom', *ASE* 22 (1993), 27–50

Peltola, Niilo, 'Grendel's Descent from Cain Reconsidered', *NM* 73 (1972), 284–91

Pepperdene, Margaret W., 'Grendel's Geis', *Journal of the Royal Society of Antiquarians of Ireland* 85 (1955), 188–92

——, 'Beowulf and the Coast-Guard', *ES* 47 (1966), 409–19

Peters, F[rank] J. J., 'The Wrestling in *Grettis saga*', *PLL* 25 (1989), 235–41

——, 'The Wrestling in *Beowulf*', *ELN* 29.4 (1992), 10–12

Peters, Leonard J., 'The Relationship of the Old English *Andreas* to *Beowulf*', *PMLA* 66 (1951), 844–63

Petschenig, M., ed., *Iohannis Cassiani Conlationes*, CSEL 13.2 (Vienna, 1886)

Pettitt, Thomas, 'The Mark of the Beast and the Balance of Frenzy', *NM* 77 (1976), 526–35

Phillpotts, Bertha S., 'Wyrd and Providence in Anglo-Saxon Thought', *E&S* 13 (1928), 7–27 [also in *Interpretations*, ed. Fulk, pp. 1–13]

Pickles, John Drayton, 'Studies in the Prose Texts of the *Beowulf* Manuscript' (unpublished PhD dissertation, University of Cambridge, 1971)

Pigg, Daniel F., 'Cultural Markers in *Beowulf*: a Re-evaluation of the Relationship between Beowulf and Christ', *Neophilologus* 74 (1990), 601–7

Plaine, F., ed., 'Vita antiqua Sancti Samsonis Dolensis episcopi', *AB* 6 (1887), 77–150

Planta, Joseph, *A Catalogue of the Manuscripts in the Cottonian Library, Deposited in the British Museum* (London, 1802)

Ploss, Emile, *Siegfried-Sigurd, der Drachenkämpfer: Untersuchungen zur germanisch-deutschen Heldensage*, Beihefte der Bonner Jahrbücher 17 (Cologne, 1966)

Pope, John C., '*Beowulf* 3150–3151: Queen Hygd and the Word "Geomeowle"', *MLN* 70 (1955), 77–87

———, *The Rhythm of 'Beowulf': an Interpretation of the Normal and Hypermetric Verse-Forms in Old English Poetry* (New Haven, CT, 1942; rev. ed., 1966)

———, 'Beowulf's Old Age', in *Philological Essays*, ed. Rosier, pp. 55–81

———, 'On the Date of Composition of *Beowulf*', in *Dating of 'Beowulf'*, ed. Chase, pp. 187–96

———, '*Beowulf* 505, "gehedde", and the Pretensions of Unferth', in *Modes of Interpretation*, ed. Brown *et al.*, pp. 173–87

———, 'The Irregular Anacrusis in *Beowulf* 9 and 402: Two Hitherto Untried Remedies, with Help from Cynewulf', *Speculum* 63 (1988), 104–13

Porsia, Franco, ed., *Liber Monstrorum* (Bari, 1976)

Porru, Giulia Mazzuoli, '*Beowulf*, v. 33: *isig ond utfus*', in *Studi linguistici e filologici per Carlo Alberto Mastrelli* (Pisa, 1985), pp. 263–74

Poussa, Patricia, 'The Date of *Beowulf* Reconsidered: the Tenth Century', *NM* 82 (1981), 276–88

Powell, Alison M., 'Verbal Parallels in *Andreas* and its Relationship to *Beowulf* and Cynewulf' (unpublished PhD dissertation, University of Cambridge, 2002)

Prescott, Andrew, ' "Their Present Miserable State of Cremation": the Restoration of the Cotton Library', in *Sir Robert Cotton as Collector: Essays on an Early Stuart Courtier and his Legacy*, ed. C. J. Wright (London, 1997), pp. 391–454

Prokosch, E., 'Two Types of Scribal Error in the *Beowulf* MS', in *Studies in English Philology*, ed. Malone and Ruud, pp. 196–207

Puhvel, Martin, 'Beowulf and Celtic Under-Water Adventure', *Folk-Lore* 76 (1965), 254–61

———, 'Beowulf's Slaying of Daghræfn – a Connection with Irish Myth?', *Folk-Lore* 77 (1966), 282–5

———, 'The Swiming Prowess of Beowulf', *Folk-Lore* 82 (1971), 276–80

———, 'The Blithe-Hearted Morning Raven in *Beowulf*', *ELN* 10 (1973), 241–7

———, '*Beowulf* and Celtic Tradition* (Waterloo, 1979)

———, 'The Melting of the Giant-Wrought Sword', in his *'Beowulf' and Celtic Tradition*, pp. 39–44

———, 'A Scottish Analogue to the Grendel Story', *NM* 81 (1980), 395–8

———, 'The Ride around Beowulf's Barrow', *Folk-Lore* 94 (1983), 108–12

———, 'The Concept of Heroism in the Anglo-Saxon Epic', in *La funzione dell'eroe germanico*, ed. Pàroli, pp. 57–73

———, 'The Aquatic Contest in *Hálfdanar saga Brönufóstra* and Beowulf's Adventure with Breca. Any Connection?', *NM* 99 (1998), 131–8

Pulsiano, Phillip, ' "Cames cynne": Confusion or Craft?', *PPMRC* 7 (1985 [1982]), 33–8

Pulsiano, Phillip, and Joseph McGowan, '*Fyrd, here* and the Dating of *Beowulf*', *Studia Anglica Posnaniensia* 23 (1990), 3–13

Ramsey, Lee C., 'The Sea Voyages in *Beowulf*', *NM* 72 (1971), 51–9

Rauer, Christine, *Beowulf and the Dragon: Parallels and Analogues* (Cambridge, 2000)

Raw, Barbara C., 'Royal Power and Royal Symbols in *Beowulf*', in *The Age of Sutton Hoo*, ed. Carver, pp. 167–74

Reinhard, Mariann, *On the Semantic Relevance of the Alliterative Collocations in 'Beowulf'*, Schweizer Anglistische Arbeiten (Swiss Studies in English) 92 (Bern, 1976)

Reino, Joseph, 'The "Half-Danes" of Finnsburg and Heorot Hall', *Modern Language Studies* 2 (1972), 29–43

Renoir, Alain, 'Point of View and Design for Terror in *Beowulf*', *NM* 63 (1962), 154–67

———, 'The Terror of the Dark Waters: a Note on Virgilian and Beowulfian Techniques', in *The Learned and the Lewed: Studies in Chaucer and Medieval Literature*, ed. Larry D. Benson, Harvard English Studies 5 (Cambridge, MA, 1974), pp. 147–60

———, 'Old English Formulas and Themes as Tools for Contextual Interpretation', in *Modes of Interpretation*, ed. Brown et al., pp. 65–79

Renoir, Alain, and Ann Hernández, ed., *Approaches to Beowulfian Scansion*, OEC 1 (Berkeley, CA, 1982)

Richards, Mary P., 'A Reexamination of *Beowulf* ll. 3180–3182', *ELN* 10 (1973), 163–7

———, ed., *Anglo-Saxon Manuscripts: Basic Readings*, BRASE 2 (New York, 1994)

Richardson, Peter, 'Imperfective Aspect and Episode Structure in *Beowulf*', *JEGP* 93 (1994), 313–25

———, 'Point of View and Identification in *Beowulf*', *Neophilologus* 81 (1997), 289–98

Rickert, Edith, 'The Old English Offa Saga', *MP* 2 (1904–5), 29–76, 321–76

Riedinger, Anita R., 'The Old English Formula in Context', *Speculum* 60 (1985), 294–317

———, 'The Formulaic Relationship between *Beowulf* and *Andreas*', in *Heroic Poetry*, ed. Damico and Leyerle, pp. 283–312

Rigg, A. G., '*Beowulf* 1368–72: an Analogue', *NQ* 29 (1982), 101–2

———, *A History of Anglo-Latin Literature* (Cambridge, 1992)

Riley, Samuel M., '*Beowulf*, Lines 3180–82', *Explicator* 40 (1982), 2–3

Ringler, Richard N., '*Him seo wen geleah*: the Design for Irony in Grendel's Last Visit to Heorot', *Speculum* 41 (1966), 49–67

Risden, Edward L., *Beasts of Time: Apocalyptic 'Beowulf'*, Studies in the Humanities 8 (New York, 1994)

———, 'Heroic Humor in *Beowulf*', in *Humour in Anglo-Saxon Literature*, ed. Wilcox, pp. 71–8

Roberts, Jane, 'Old English UN–Very and Unferþ', *ES* 61 (1980), 289–92

Robertson, A. J., ed., *Anglo-Saxon Charters*, 2nd edition (Cambridge, 1956)

Robinson, Fred C., 'Variation: a Study in the Diction of *Beowulf*' (unpublished PhD dissertation, University of North Carolina at Chapel Hill, 1961)

———, 'Is Wealhtheow a Prince's Daughter?', *ES* 45 (1964), 36–9 [also in his *The Editing of Old English*, pp. 71–3]

———, 'Beowulf's Retreat from Frisia: Some Textual Problems in ll. 2361–2362', *SP* 62 (1965), 1–16 [also in his *The Editing of Old English*, pp. 56–68]

———, 'Two Non-Cruces in *Beowulf*', *TSL* 11 (1966), 151–60 [also in his *The Editing of Old English*, pp. 47–55]

———, 'The Significance of Names in Old English Literature', *Anglia* 86 (1968), 14–58

———, 'Lexicography and Literary Criticism: a Caveat', in *Philological Essays*, ed. Rosier, pp. 99–110 [also in his *Tomb of Beowulf*, pp. 140–52]

———, 'Personal Names in Medieval Narrative and the Name of Unferth in *Beowulf*', in *Essays in Honor of Richebourg Gaillard McWilliams*, ed. Howard Creed (Birmingham, AL, 1970), pp. 43–8

———, 'Some Aspects of the *Maldon*-Poet's Artistry', *JEGP* 75 (1976), 25–40

———, 'Two Aspects of Variation in Old English Poetry', in *Old English Poetry*, ed. Calder (Berkeley, CA, 1979), pp. 127–45 [also in his *Tomb of Beowulf*, pp. 71–86]

———, 'Old English Literature in its Most Immediate Context', in *Old English Liter-*

ature in Context, ed. Niles, pp. 11–29 [also in his *Editing of Old English*, pp. 3–24; *Old English Shorter Poems*, ed. O'Keeffe, pp. 3–29]

———, 'Elements of the Marvellous in the Characterization of Beowulf: a Reconsideration of the Textual Evidence', in *Old English Studies*, ed. Burlin and Irving, pp. 119–37 [also in his *Tomb of Beowulf*, pp. 20–35; *'Beowulf': Basic Readings*, ed. Baker, pp. 79–96]

———, *'Beowulf' and the Appositive Style* (Knoxville, TN, 1985)

———, 'Metathesis in the Dictionaries: a Problem for Lexicographers', in *Problems of Old English Lexicography: Studies in Memory of Angus Cameron*, ed. Alfred Bammesberger (Regensburg, 1985), pp. 245–65 [also in his *The Editing of Old English*, pp. 131–48

———, *'Beowulf'*, in *Cambridge Companion*, ed. Godden and Lapidge, pp. 142–59

———, 'Why is Grendel's Not Greeting the Gifstol a Wræc Micel?', in *Words, Texts and Manuscripts*, ed. Korhammer, pp. 257–62

———, 'A Further Word on *dollicra* in *Beowulf* 2646', *ANQ* n.s. 6 (1993), 11–13

———, 'Textual Notes on *Beowulf*', in *Anglo-Saxonica*, ed. Grinda and Wetzel, pp. 107–12 [also in his *The Editing of Old English*, pp. 89–95]

———, 'The Tomb of Beowulf', in *Tomb of Beowulf*, pp. 3–19

———, *The Tomb of Beowulf and Other Essays on Old English* (Oxford, 1993)

———, 'Did Grendel's Mother Sit on Beowulf?', in *From Anglo-Saxon to Early Middle English*, ed. Malcolm Godden, Douglas Gray, and Terry Hoad (Oxford, 1994), pp. 1–7

———, ed., *The Editing of Old English* (Oxford, 1994)

———, *'Beowulf* in the Twentieth Century', *PBA* 94 (1997), 45–62

———, 'Sigemund's *fæhðe ond fyrena*: *Beowulf* 879a', *To Explain the Present: Studies in the Changing English Language in Honour of Matti Rissanen*, ed. Terttu Nevalainen and Leena Kahlas-Tarkka, Mémoires de la Société Néophilologique de Helsinki 52 (Helsinki, 1997), pp. 200–8

———, 'The Language of Paganism in *Beowulf*: a Response to an Ill-Omened Essay', *Multilingua* 18 (1999), 173–83

———, 'A Sub-Sense of Old English *fyrn(-)*', *NM* 100 (1999), 471–5

Rogers, H. L., 'Beowulf's Three Great Fights', *RES* n.s. 6 (1955), 339–55 [also in *Anthology*, ed. Nicholson, pp. 233–56]

———, 'The Crypto-Psychological Character of the Oral Formula', *ES* 47 (1966), 89–102

———, *'Beowulf*, line 804', *NQ* 229 (1984), 289–92

Rollason, D. W., 'List of Saints' Resting-Places in Anglo-Saxon England', *ASE* 7 (1978), 61–93

Rollinson, Philip, 'The Influence of Christian Doctrine and Exegesis on Old English Poetry: an Estimate of the Current State of Scholarship', *ASE* 2 (1973), 271–84

Rose, Gregory F., 'A Look Back at Kevin S. Kiernan's *Beowulf and the Beowulf-Manuscript. The Kiernan Theory Revisited: Beowulf* at the Court of Cnut?', *Envoi* 6 (1997), 135–45

Rose, Nancy, 'Hrothgar, Nestor, and Religiosity as a Mode of Characterization in Heroic Poetry', *Journal of Popular Culture* 1 (1967), 158–65

Rosenberg, Bruce A., 'The Necessity of Unferth', *JFI* 6 (1969), 50–60

———, 'Folktale Morphology and the Stucture of *Beowulf*: a Counter-Proposal', *JFI* 11 (1975), 199–209

Rosier, James L., 'Design for Treachery: the Unferth Intrigue', *PMLA* 77 (1962), 1–7

———, 'The Uses of Association: Hands and Feasts in *Beowulf*', *PMLA* 78 (1963), 8–14

———, 'The *unhlitm* of Finn and Hengest', *RES* n.s. 17 (1966), 171–4

———, 'The Two Closings of *Beowulf*', *ES* 54 (1973), 1–6

———, ed., *Philological Essays: Studies in Old and Middle English Literature in Honour of Herbert Dean Meritt* (The Hague, 1970)

———, 'What Grendel Found: *heardran hæle*', *NM* 75 (1974), 40–9

——, 'Generative Composition in *Beowulf*', *ES* 58 (1977), 193–203

Rowland, Jenny, 'OE *ealuscerwen/ meoduscerwen* and the Concept of "Paying for Mead" ', *LSE* n.s. 21 (1990), 1–12

Rudanko, Martii Juhani, *Towards Classifying Verbs and Adjectives Governing the Genitive in 'Beowulf'*, University of Tampere Publications of the Department of English and German Series A, no. 6 (Tampere, 1983)

Ruggerini, Maria Elena, 'L'eroe germanico contro avversari mostruosi: tra testo e iconografia', in *La funzione dell'eroe germanico*, ed. Pàroli, pp. 201–57

Russom, Geoffrey R., *Old English Meter and Linguistic Theory* (Cambridge, 1987)

——, 'Purely Metrical Replacements for Kuhn's Laws', in *English Historical Metrics*, ed. McCully and Anderson, pp. 30–41

——, *'Beowulf' and Old Germanic Metre*, CSASE 23 (Cambridge, 1998)

Rypins, Stanley I., ed., *Three Old English Prose Texts in MS Cotton Vitellius A. xv*, EETS OS 161 (London, 1924, rptd. 1971)

Sandbach, Mary, 'Grettir in Thorisdal', *SBVS* 12 (1937–8), 93–106

Sarrazin, Gregor, '*Beowulf* und Kynewulf', *Anglia* 9 (1886), 515–50

——, *Beowulf-Studien: Ein Beitrag zur Geschichte altgermanischer Sage und Dichtung* (Berlin, 1888)

Savage, Anne, 'The Story's Voyage through the Text: Transformations of the Narrative in *Beowulf*', in *Shifts and Transpositions in Medieval Narrative: a Festschrift for Dr Elspeth Kennedy*, ed. Karen Pratt (Cambridge, 1994), pp. 121–38

Schaar, Claes, *Critical Studies in the Cynewulf Group*, Lund Studies in English 17 (Lund, 1949; repr. New York, 1967)

——, 'On a New Theory of Old English Poetic Diction', *Neophilologus* 40 (1956), 301–5

Schabram, Hans, '*Andreas* und *Beowulf*: Parallelstellen als Zeugnis für literarische Abhängigkeit', *Nachrichten der Giessener Hochschulgesellschaft* 34 (1965), 201–18

Schaefer, Ursula, *Vokalität: Altenglische Dichtung zwischen Mündlichkeit und Schriftlichkeit*, ScriptOralia 39 (Tübingen, 1992)

——, 'Rhetoric and Style', in *Handbook*, ed. Bjork and Niles, pp. 105–24

Schaller, Dieter, 'Ist der *Waltharius* frühkarolingisch?', *Mittellateinisches Jahrbuch* 18 (1983), 63–83

Scherb, Victor I, 'Setting and Cultural Memory in Part II of *Beowulf*', *ES* 79 (1998), 109–19

Schichler, Robert Lawrence, 'Heorot and Dragon-Slaying in *Beowulf*', *PPMRC* 11 (1986), 159–75

Schlauch, Margaret, *Romance in Iceland* (London, 1934)

Schneider, Karl, *Sophia Lectures on Beowulf*, ed. Shoichi Watanabe and Norio Tsuchiya (Tokyo, 1986)

Schrader, Richard J., 'Beowulf's Obsequies and the Roman Epic', *CL* 24 (1977), 237–59

——, 'Sacred Groves, Marvellous Waters, and Grendel's Abode', *Florilegium* 5 (1983), 76–84

——, 'The Deserted Chamber: an Unnoticed Topos in the "Father's Lament" of *Beowulf*', *Journal of the Rocky Mountain Medieval and Renaissance Association* 5 (1984), 1–5

——, 'Succession and Glory in *Beowulf*', *JEGP* 90 (1991), 491–504

——, 'The Language on the Giant's Sword Hilt in *Beowulf*', *NM* 94 (1993), 141–7

Schück, Henrik, *Studier i Beowulfsagen* (Uppsala, 1909)

Schwetman, John W., 'Beowulf's Return: the Hero's Account of His Adventures among the Danes', *Medieval Perspectives* 13 (1998), 136–48

Scowcroft, R. M., 'The Irish Analogues to *Beowulf*', *Speculum* 74 (1999), 22–64

Scragg, Donald G., 'The Nature of Old English Verse', in *Cambridge Companion*, ed. Godden and Lapidge, pp. 54–70

——, ed., *The Vercelli Homilies*, EETS OS 300 (London, 1992)

Scragg, Donald G., and Paul E. Szarmach, ed., *The Editing of Old English: Proceedings of the 1990 Manchester Conference* (Cambridge, 1995)

Scull, C. J., 'Before Sutton Hoo: Structures of Power and Society in Early East Anglia', in *The Age of Sutton Hoo*, ed. Carver, pp. 3–23

Senra Silva, Immaculada, 'The Rune "Eþel" and Scribal Writing Habits in the *Beowulf* MS', *NM* 99 (1998), 241–7

Sharma, Manish, 'Movement and Space as Metaphor in Old English Poetry' (unpublished PhD dissertation, University of Cambridge, 2002)

Shaw, Brian A., 'The Speeches in *Beowulf*: a Structural Study', *Chaucer Review* 13 (1978), 86–92

Shilton, Howard, 'The Nature of Beowulf's Dragon', *BJRL* 79.3 (1997), 67–77

Shippey, Thomas A., 'The Fairy-Tale Structure of *Beowulf*', *NQ* 214 (1969), 2–11

———, *Old English Verse* (London, 1972)

———, *Poems of Wisdom and Learning in Old English*, (Cambridge, 1976)

———, *Beowulf* (London, 1978)

———, 'Principles of Conversation in Beowulfian Speech', *Techniques of Description: Spoken and Written Discourse: a Festschrift for Malcolm Coulthard*, ed. John M. Sinclair, Michael Hoey, and Gwyneth Fox (London, 1993), pp. 109–26

———, 'Structure and Unity', in *Handbook*, ed. Bjork and Niles, pp. 149–74

Shippey, Thomas A., and Andreas Haarder, ed., *'Beowulf': the Critical Heritage* (London and New York, 1998)

Shuman, Baird, and H. Charles Hutchings, 'The *Un*-Prefix: a Means of Germanic Irony in *Beowulf*', *MP* 57 (1960), 217–22

Sievers, Eduard, 'Miscellen zur Angelsächsischen Grammatik', *BGdSL* 9 (1884), 197–300

———, *Altgermanische Metrik* (Halle, 1893)

Silber, Patricia, 'Unferth: Another Look at the Emendation', *Names* 28 (1980), 101–11

———, 'Rhetoric as Prowess in the Unferð Episode', *TSLL* 23 (1981), 471–83

Sims-Williams, Patrick, ' "Is it Fog or Smoke or Warriors Fighting?": Irish and Welsh Parallels to the *Finnsburg Fragment*', *Bulletin of the Board of Celtic Studies* 27 (1978), 505–14

———, 'Thought, Word, and Deed: an Irish Triad', *Ériu* 29 (1978), 78–111

Sisam, Kenneth, 'The *Beowulf* ms', *MLR* 11 (1916), 335–7 [rptd in his *Studies in the History of Old English Literature*, pp. 61–4]

———, 'Anglo-Saxon Royal Genealogies', *PBA* 39 (1953), 287–346

———, *Studies in the History of Old English Literature* (Oxford, 1953)

———, 'The Authority of Old English Poetical Manuscripts', in his *Studies in the History of Old English Literature*, pp. 29–44 [also in *Old English Literature*, ed. Stevens and Mandel, pp. 36–51]

———, 'The Compilation of the Beowulf Manuscript', in his *Studies in the History of Old English Literature*, pp. 65–96

———, 'Beowulf's Fight with the Dragon', *RES* n.s. 9 (1958), 129–40

———, *The Structure of 'Beowulf'* (Oxford, 1965)

Skeat, Walter William, ed., *Ælfric's Lives of Saints*, EETS o.s. 76, 82, 94, and 114 (London, 1881–1900; 4 vols. in 2, 1966)

———, 'On the Signification of the Monster Grendel in the Poem of *Beowulf*; with a Discussion of lines 2076–2100', *The Journal of Philology* 15 (1886), 120–31

Smith, C., 'Beowulf Gretti', *The New Englander* 4 (1881), 49–67

Smith, Roger, 'Ships and the Dating of *Beowulf*', *ANQ* 3 (1990), 99–103

Smith, Steven E., 'The Provenance of the *Beowulf*-Manuscript', *ANQ* 13.1 (2000), 3–7

Smithers, Geoffrey V., *The Making of 'Beowulf*: Inaugural Lecture of the Professor of English Language Delivered . . . on 18 May, 1961* (Durham, 1961)

———, 'Four Cruces in *Beowulf*', in *Studies in Language and Literature in Honor of Margaret Schlauch*, ed. Mieczysław Brahmer, Stanisław Helsztynski, and Julian Krzyżanowski (Warsaw, 1966), pp. 413–30

———, 'Destiny and the Heroic Warrior in *Beowulf*', in *Philological Essays*, ed. Rosier, pp. 65–81

Smithson, George A., 'The Old English Christian Epic: a Study in the Plot Technique of

Juliana, the *Elene*, the *Andreas*, and the *Christ*, in Comparison with the *Beowulf* and with the Latin Literature of the Middle Ages', *University of California Publications in Modern Philology* 1.4 (1910), 303–400

Smyser, H. M., 'Ibn Fadlan's Account of the Rus with Some Commentary and Some Allusions to *Beowulf*', in *Franciplegius*, ed. Bessinger and Creed, pp. 92–119

Smyser, H. M., and F. P. Magoun, Jr, *Survivals in Old Norwegian of Medieval English, French, and German Literature together with Latin Versions of the Heroic Legend of Walther of Aquitaine* (Baltimore, MD, 1941)

Sorrell, Paul, 'Oral Poetry and the World of *Beowulf*', *OT* 7 (1992), 28–65

——, 'The Approach to the Dragon-Fight in *Beowulf*, Aldhelm, and the "*traditions folkloriques*" of Jacques LeGoff', *Parergon*, n.s. 12 (1994), 57–87

Sparks, H. F. D., ed., *The Apocryphal Old Testament* (Oxford, 1984)

Spolsky, Ellen, 'Old English Kinship Terms and *Beowulf*', *NM* 78 (1977), 233–38

Standop, Ewald, 'Alliteration und Akzent: "schwere" und "leichte" Verse im *Beowulf*', in *Anglo-Saxonica*, ed. Grinda and Wetzel, pp. 167–79

Stanley, Eric G., 'Old English Poetic Diction and the Interpretation of *The Wanderer, The Seafarer*, and *The Penitent's Prayer*', *Anglia* 73 (1955), 413–66 [also in *Essential Articles*, ed. Nicholson, 458–514]

——, '*Hæthenra Hyht* in *Beowulf*', in *Studies in Old English Literature*, ed. Greenfield, pp. 136–51

——, '*Beowulf*', in *Continuations and Beginnings*, ed. E. G. Stanley (London, 1966), pp. 104–41 [also in '*Beowulf*': *Basic Readings*, pp. 3–34

——, *The Search for Anglo-Saxon Paganism* (Cambridge, 1975)

——, 'Did Beowulf Commit *feaxfeng* against Grendel's Mother?', *NQ* 23 (1976), 339–40

——, 'Two Old English Poetic Phrases Insufficiently Understood for Literary Criticism: *þing gehegan* and *seoneþ gehegan*', in *Old English Poetry*, ed. Calder, pp. 76–82

——, 'The Date of *Beowulf*: Some Doubts and No Conclusions', in *Dating of 'Beowulf'*, ed. Chase, pp. 197–211

——, 'Unideal Principles of Editing Old English Verse', *PBA* 70 (1984), 231–73

——, *A Collection of Papers with Emphasis on Old English Literature* (Toronto, 1987)

——, 'Rhymes in English Medieval Verse: from Old English to Middle English', in *Medieval English Studies Presented to George Kane*, ed. E. D. Kennedy, *et al.* (Woodbridge, 1988), pp. 19–54

——, ' "Hengestes heap", *Beowulf* 1091', in *Britain 400–600: Language and History*, ed. Alfred Bammesberger and Alfred Wollmann, Anglistische Forschungen 205 (Heidelberg, 1990), pp. 51–63

——, ' "Ἀπὸ Κοινοῦ," Chiefly in *Beowulf*', in *Anglo-Saxonica*, ed. Grinda and Wetzel, pp. 181–207

——, *In the Foreground: 'Beowulf'* (Cambridge, 1994)

——, 'Courtliness and Courtesy in *Beowulf* and Elsewhere in English Medieval Literature', in *Words and Works*, ed. Baker and Howe, pp. 67–103

——, *Imagining the Past: the Search for Anglo-Saxon Paganism and Anglo-Saxon Trial by Jury* (Cambridge, 2000)

Steadman, J. M., Jr, 'The Ingeld-Episode in *Beowulf*: History or Prophecy?', *MLN* 45 (1930), 522–5

Stedman, Douglas, 'Some Points of Resemblance between *Beowulf* and the Grettla (or *Grettis saga*)', *SBVS* 8 (1913–14), 6–28

Stefanovic, Svetislav, 'Zur Offa-Thryðo-Episode im *Beowulf*', *EStn* 69 (1934), 15–31

Stévanovitch, Colette, 'Envelope Patterns and the Unity of the Old English *Christ and Satan*', *ASnSL* 233 (1996), 260–7

——, 'Envelope Patterns in *Genesis A* and *B*', *Neophilologus* 80 (1996), 465–78

——, '*Beowulf*': *de la forme au sens* (Paris, 1998)

Stevens, Martin, 'The Structure of *Beowulf:* From Gold-Hoard to Word-Hoard', *MLQ* 39 (1978), 219–38

Stevens, Martin, and Jerome Mandel, ed., *Old English Literature: Twenty-two Analytical Essays* (Lincoln, NE, 1968)

Stevenson, J., ed. *Chronicon Monasterii de Abingdon*, 2 vols. (London, 1858)

Stevick, Robert D., 'The Oral-Formulaic Analysis of Old English Verse', *Speculum* 37 (1962), 382–9 [also in *Essential Articles*, ed. Bessinger and Kahrl, pp. 393–403; *Old English Literature*, ed. Stevens and Mandel, pp. 62–72]

——, 'Christian Elements and the Genesis of *Beowulf*', *MP* 61 (1963), 79–89

——, 'Representing the Form of *Beowulf*', in *Old English and New*, ed. Hall, Doane, and Ringler, pp. 3–14

Stiene, Heinz Erich, ed., *Konkordanz zum Waltharius-Epos* (Frankfurt, 1982)

Stitt, J. Michael, *'Beowulf' and the Bear's Son: Epic, Saga, and Fairytale in Northern Germanic Tradition*, Albert Bates Lord Studies in Oral Tradition 8 (New York, 1992)

Stjerna, Knut, *Essays on Questions Connected with the Old English Poem of 'Beowulf'*, trans. J. R. Clark Hall, Viking Club Extra Series 3 (Coventry, 1912)

Stockwell, Robert P., 'On Recent Theories of Metrics and Rhythm in *Beowulf*', in *English Historical Metrics*, ed. McCully and Anderson, pp. 73–94

Stockwell, Robert P. and Donka Minkova, 'Old English Metrics and the Phonology of Resolution', in *Germanic Studies*, ed. Goblirsch, Mayou, and Taylor, pp. 389–406

——, 'Prosody', in *Handbook*, ed. Bjork and Niles, pp. 55–83

Storms, Godfrid, 'The Significance of Hygelac's Raid', *NMS* 14 (1970), 3–26

——, 'Grendel the Terrible', *NM* 73 (1972), 427–36

——, 'How did the *Dene* and the *Geatas* get into *Beowulf?*', *ES* 80 (1999), 46–9

Stratyner, Leslie, 'Wealhtheow's Threat: *Beowulf:* 1228–1231', *In Geardagum* 14 (1993), 39–44

Strauss, Barrie Ruth, 'Women's Words as Weapons: Speech as Action in *The Wife's Lament*', *TSLL* 23 (1981), 268–85

Strecker, Karl, ed., *Waltharius*, MGH, Poetae Latini Medii Aevi VI.1 (Weimar, 1951), pp. 1–85

Stryker, W. G., ed., 'The Latin-Old English Glossary in MS. Cotton Cleopatra A. III' (unpublished PhD dissertation, Stanford University, 1951)

Stuhmiller, Jacqueline, 'On the Identity of the *eotenas*', *NM* 100 (1999), 7–14

Suchier, Hermann, 'Über die Sage von Offa und Þrytho', *BGdSL* 4 (1877), 500–21

Suzuki, Seiichi, 'Anacrusis in the Meter of *Beowulf*', *SP* 92 (1995), 141–63

——, *The Metrical Organization of 'Beowulf': Prototype and Isomorphism*, Trends in Linguistics, Studies and Monographs 95 (Berlin, 1996)

Swanton, Michael J., *Crisis and Development in Germanic Society, 700–800: Beowulf and the Burden of Kingship*, Göppinger Arbeiten zur Germanistik 333 (Göppingen, 1982)

Sweringen, Grace Fleming von, 'Women in the Germanic Hero-Sagas', *JEGP* 8 (1909), 501–12

Talbot, Annelise, 'Sigemund the Dragon-Slayer', *Folk-Lore* 94 (1983), 153–62

Taylor, A. R., 'Two Notes on Beowulf', *LSE* 7–8 (1952), 5–17

Taylor, Keith P, '*Beowulf* 1259a: the Inherent Nobility of Grendel's Mother', *ELN* 31.3 (1994), 13–25

Taylor, Paul Beekman, 'Heorot, Earth, and Asgard: Christian Poetry and Pagan Myth', *TSL* 11 (1966), 119–30 [reworked in 'Heorot, Earth, and Ásgarðr: Christian Poetry and Pagan Myth', in his *Sharing Story*, pp. 107–22]

——, 'The Epithetical Style in *Beowulf*', *NM* 91 (1990), 195–206

——, '*searoniðas*: Old Norse Magic and Old English Verse', *SP* 80 (1983), 109–25 [reworked in '*searoniðas*: Etymology, Magic, and Poetry', in his *Sharing Story*, pp. 33–52]

——, 'Grendel's Monstrous Arts', *In Geardagum* 6 (1984), 1–12 [reworked in 'Swords and Words: Grendel and the Norse *þursar*', in his *Sharing Story*, pp. 123–37]

——, 'Beowulf's Second Grendel Fight', *NM* 86 (1985), 62–9

————, 'The Language of Sacral Kingship in *Beowulf*', *SN* 66 (1994), 129–45 [reworked in 'Nordic Sacral Kingship in *Beowulf*', in his *Sharing Story*, pp. 53–77]

————, 'The Dragon's Treasure in *Beowulf*', *NM* 98 (1997), 229–40

————, *Sharing Story: Medieval Norse-English Literary Relationships* (New York, 1998)

————, 'Vestiges of Old Norse Charms in *Beowulf*', in his *Sharing Story*, pp. 79–90

Taylor, Paul Beekman, and R. Evan Davis, 'Some Alliterative Misfits in the *Beowulf* MS', *Neophilologus* 66 (1982), 614–21

Taylor, Paul Beekman, and Peter H. Salus, 'The Compilation of Cotton Vitellius A XV', *NM* 69 (1968), 199–204

Taylor, T., *The Life of St Samson of Dol* (London, 1925)

Thiel, Matthias, *Grundlagen und Gestalt der Hebräischkenntnisse des frühen Mittelalters* (Spoleto, 1973)

Thormann, Janet, 'The Poetics of Absence: "The Lament of the Sole Survivor" in *Beowulf*', *De Gustibus*, ed. Foley, pp. 542–50

Thornbury, E. V., '*eald enta geweorc* and the Relics of Empire: Revisiting the Dragon's Lair in *Beowulf*', *Quaestio* 1 (2000), 82–92

Thundy, Zacharias P., '*Beowulf*: Date and Authorship', *NM* 87 (1986), 102–16

Tietjen, Mary C. Wilson, 'God, Fate, and the Hero of *Beowulf*', *JEGP* 74 (1975), 159–71

Tilling, P. M., ed., *Studies in English Language and Early Literature in Honour of Paul Christophersen* (Coleraine, 1981)

————, 'William Morris's Translation of *Beowulf*: Studies in his Vocabulary', in *Studies in English Language and Early Literature*, ed. Tilling, pp. 163–75

Tolkien, J. R. R., '*Beowulf*: the Monsters and the Critics', *PBA* 22 (1936), 245–95; rptd Oxford, 1956 [also in '*Beowulf*', ed. Bloom, pp. 5–31; '*Beowulf*'-*Poet*, ed. Fry, pp. 8–56; *Interpretations*, ed. Fulk, pp. 14–44; *Anthology*, ed. Nicholson, pp. 51–103]

————, *Finn and Hengest: the Fragment and the Episode*, ed. Alan Bliss (London, 1982)

Tolley, Clive, '*Beowulf*'s Scyld Scefing Episode: Some Norse and Finnish Analogues', *Arv* 52 (1996), 7–48

Tonsfeldt, H. Ward, 'Ring Structure in *Beowulf*', *Neophilologus* 61 (1977), 443–52

Toswell, M. J., ed., *Prosody and Poetics in the Early Middle Ages: Essays in Honour of C. B. Hieatt* (Toronto, 1995)

Toswell, M. J., and E. M. Tyler, ed., *Studies in English Language and Literature. 'Doubt Wisely': Papers in Honour of E. G. Stanley* (London, 1996)

Tripp, Raymond P., Jr, 'A New Look at Grendel's Attack: *Beowulf* 804a–815a', *In Geardagum: Essays on Old English Language and Literature*, ed. Loren C. Gruber and Dean Loganbill (Denver, CO, 1974), pp. 8–11

————, 'The Exemplary Role of Hrothgar and Heorot', *PQ* 56 (1977), 123–9

————, *More about the Fight with the Dragon: 'Beowulf' 2208b–3182, Commentary, Edition, and Translation* (Lanham, MD, New York and London, 1983)

————, 'Did Beowulf Have an "Inglorious Youth"?', *SN* 61 (1989), 129–43

————, *Literary Essays on Language and Meaning in the Poem Called 'Beowulf': Beowulfiana Literaria* (Lewiston, NY, 1992)

————, 'Wulfgar at the Door? A Literary Solution to *Beowulf* "389–90" ', *ELN* 29.4 (1992), 1–9

————, 'Humor, Wordplay, and Semantic Resonance in *Beowulf*', in *Humour in Anglo-Saxon Literature*, ed. Wilcox, pp. 49–70

Tristram, Hildegard L. C., 'Stock Descriptions of Heaven and Hell in Old English Literature', *NM* 75 (1976), 102–13

————, 'Der insulare Alexander', in *Kontinuität und Transformation der Antike im Mittelalter*, ed. Willi Erzgräber (Sigmaringen, 1989), pp. 129–55

————, 'More Talk of Alexander', *Celtica* 21 (1990), 658–63

————, 'What's the Point of Dating "Beowulf"?', in *Medieval Insular Literature between the Oral and the Written II: Continuity of Transmission*, ed. Hildegard L. C. Tristram, ScriptOralia 97 (Tübingen, 1997), pp. 65–80

Trnka, Bohumil, 'The *Beowulf* Poem and Virgil's *Aeneid*', *Poetica* 12 (1981), 50–6

Turville-Petre, E. O. G., *Myth and Religion of the North: the Religion of Ancient Scandinavia* (New York, 1964)

Turville-Petre, Joan E., 'Hengest and Horsa', *SBVS* 14 (1953–7), 273–90

——, '*Beowulf* and *Grettis saga*: an Excursion', *SBVS* 19 (1977), 347–57

Van Meter, David C., 'The Ritualized Presentation of Weapons and the Ideology of Nobility in *Beowulf*', *JEGP* 95 (1996), 175–89

Vaughan, M. F., 'A Reconsideration of "Unferð" ', *NM* 77 (1976), 32–48

Vickman, Jeffrey, *A Metrical Concordance to 'Beowulf'*, with Preface by R. D. Fulk, OEN Subsidia 16 (Binghamton, NY, 1990)

Vickrey, John F., '*Egesan ne gymeð* and the Crime of Heremod', *MP* 71 (1974), 295–300

——, 'The Narrative Structure of Hengest's Revenge in *Beowulf*', *ASE* 6 (1977), 91–103

——, '*Un[h]litme* 'voluntarily' in *Beowulf* Line 1097', *JEGP* 87 (1988), 315–28

——, 'On the *eorð*-Compounds in the Old English Finn-Stories', *SN* 65 (1993), 19–27

Vigfusson, Gudbrand, 'Prolegomena', in his *Sturlunga saga*, 2 vols. (Oxford, 1878)

Vigfusson, Gudbrand, and F. York Powell, ed., *Corpus Poeticum Boreale: the Poetry of the Old Northern Tongue from the Earliest Times to the Thirteenth Century*, 2 vols. (Oxford, 1883)

Viswanathan, S., 'On the Melting of the Sword: *wæl-rapas* and the Engraving on the Sword-Hilt in *Beowulf*', *PQ* 58 (1979), 360–3

Vries, Jan de, 'Die Beiden Hengeste', *ZdP* 72 (1953), 125–43

Wachsler, Arthur A., 'Grettir's Fight with a Bear: another Neglected Analogue of *Beowulf* in the *Grettis Sag[a] Ásmundarsonar*', *ES* 66 (1985), 381–90

Wanley, Humphrey, *Librorum Veterum Septentrionalium, qui in Angliae Bibliothecis extant, nec non multorum Veterum Codicum Septentrionalium alibi extantium Catalogus Historico-Criticus, cum totius Thesauri Linguarum Septentrionalium sex Indicibus* (London, 1705) [vol. II of Hickes, *Linguarum Veterum Septentrionalium Thesaurus*]

Wanner, Kevin J., 'Warriors, Wyrms, and Wyrd: the Paradoxical Fate of the Germanic Hero/King in *Beowulf*', *Essays in Medieval Studies* 16 (1999), 1–15

Ward, Gordon, 'Hengest', *Archaeologia Cantiana* 61 (1949), 77–97

Watanabe, Hideki, 'Monsters Creep?: the Meaning of the Verb *scriðan* in *Beowulf*', *Studies in Language and Culture* (Osaka University), 14 (1988), 107–20

——, 'Final Words on *Beowulf* 1020b: *brand Healfdenes*', *NM* 101 (2000), 51–7

Watts, Ann Chalmers, *The Lyre and the Harp: a Comparative Reconsideration of Oral Tradition in Homer and Old English Epic Poetry* (New Haven, CT, 1969)

Waugh, Robin, 'Competitive Narrators in the Homecoming Scene of *Beowulf*', *Journal of Narrative Technique* 25 (1995), 202–22

——, 'Literacy, Royal Power, and King-Poet Relations in Old English and Old Norse Compositions', *CL* 49 (1997), 289–315

Webster, Leslie, 'Archaeology and *Beowulf*', in *Beowulf: an Edition*, ed., Mitchell and Robinson, pp. 183–94

Wehlau, Ruth, ' "Seeds of Sorrow": Landscapes of Despair in *The Wanderer*, *Beowulf*'s Story of Hrethel and *Sonatorrek*', *Parergon* 15.2 (1998), 1–17

Weinstock, Horst, 'Comment on "Knowledge of *Beowulf* in Its Own Time" by Professor Frederic G. Cassidy', *Yearbook of Research in English and American Literature* 1 (1982), 13–25

Weise, Judith, 'The Meaning of the Name "Hygd": Onomastic Contrast in *Beowulf*', *Names* 34 (1986), 1–10

Wells, David M., 'The Sections in Old English Poetry', *YES* 6 (1976), 1–4

Welsh, Andrew, '*Branwen*, *Beowulf*, and the Tragic Peaceweaver Tale', *Viator* 22 (1991), 1–13

Wentersdorf, Karl P., 'Beowulf's Withdrawal from Frisia: a Reconsideration', *SP* 68 (1971), 395–415

———, 'Beowulf's Adventure with Breca', *SP* 72 (1975), 140–66

———, '*Beowulf*: the Paganism of Hrothgar's Danes', *SP* 72 (1981), 91–119

Westphalen, Tilman, *Beowulf 3150–55: Textkritik und Editionsgeschichte*, 2 vols. (Munich, 1967)

Wetzel, Claus-Dieter, 'Die Datierung des *Beowulf*: Bemerkungen zur jüngsten Forschungsentwicklung', *Anglia* 103 (1985), 371–400

———, '*Beowulf* 3074f. – ein *locus desperatus*?', in *Anglo-Saxonica*, ed. Grinda and Wetzel, pp. 113–66

Whallon, William, 'The Diction of Beowulf', *PMLA* 76 (1961), 309–19

———, 'The Christianity of *Beowulf*', *MP* 60 (1962), 81–94

———, 'Formulas for Heroes in the *Iliad* and in *Beowulf*', *MP* 63 (1965), 95–104

———, *Formula, Character, and Context: Studies in Homeric, Old English, and Old Testament Poetry* (Washington, DC, 1969)

———, *Inconsistencies: Studies in the New Testament, the 'Inferno', 'Othello', and 'Beowulf'* (Cambridge, 1983)

Whallon, William, Margaret Goldsmith, and Charles Donahue, 'Allegorical, Typological, or Neither? Three Short papers on the Allegorical Approach to *Beowulf* and a Discussion', *ASE* 2 (1973), 285–302

Whitbread, L., '*Beowulf* and Archaeology: Two Further Footnotes', *NM* 69 (1968), 63–72

———, 'The *Liber Monstrorum* and *Beowulf*', *MS* 36 (1974), 434–71

Whitelock, Dorothy, '*Beowulf* 2444–71', *MÆ* 8 (1939), 198–204

———, 'Anglo-Saxon Poetry and the Historian', *TRHS* 4th series 31 (1949), 75–94

———, *The Audience of 'Beowulf'* (Oxford, 1951)

Whitesell, J.E., 'Intentional Ambiguities in *Beowulf*', *TSL* 11 (1966), 145–9

Whitman, F. H., 'The Meaning of "Formulaic" in Old English Verse Composition', *NM* 76 (1975), 529–37

———, 'Corrosive Blood in *Beowulf*', *Neophilologus* 61 (1977), 276

———, 'The Kingly Nature of Beowulf', *Neophilologus* 61 (1977), 277–86

Wieland, Gernot, '*Manna mildost*: Moses and Beowulf', *PCP* 23 (1988), 86–93

Wiersma, Stanley Martin, 'A Linguistic Analysis of Words Referring to Monsters in *Beowulf*' (unpublished PhD dissertation, University of Wisconsin, 1961)

Wilcox, Jonathan, ed., *Humour in Anglo-Saxon Literature* (Cambridge, 2000)

Wild, F., 'Drachen im Beowulf und andere Drachen', *Sitzungsberichte der österreichischen Akademie der Wissenschaften*, phil.-hist. Klasse 238 (1962), 3–62

Willard, Rudolf, ed., *The Blickling Homilies*, EEMF 10 (Copenhagen, 1960)

Williams, David, 'The Exile as Uncreator', *Mosaic* 8.3 (1975), 1–14

———, *Cain and Beowulf: a Study in Secular Allegory* (Toronto, 1982)

Williams, R. A., *The Finn Episode in Beowulf: an Essay in Interpretation* (Cambridge, 1924)

Wilson, David M., *Anglo-Saxon Paganism* (London, 1992)

Wilson, R. M., *The Lost Literature of Medieval England* (London, 1952)

Wrenn, C. L., 'Sutton Hoo and *Beowulf*', in *Mélanges de Linguistique et de Philologie: Fernand Mossé in Memoriam* (Paris, 1959), pp. 495–507

Wright, C. E., *The Cultivation of Saga in Anglo-Saxon England* (Edinburgh, 1939)

———, 'Humfrey Wanley: Saxonist and Library-Keeper', *PBA* 46 (1961), 99–129

Wright, Charles D., *The Irish Tradition in Old English Literature*, CSASE 6 (Cambridge, 1993)

———, 'Moses, *manna mildost* (*Exodus*, 550a)', *NQ* 31 (1994), 440–3

Wright, Louise E., '*Merewioingas* and the Dating of *Beowulf*: a Reconsideration', *NMS* 24 (1980), 1–6

Wülcker, Richard P., *Geschichte der englischen Literatur von den ältesten Zeiten bis zur Gegenwart* (Leipzig, 1896)

Wyld, Henry Cecil, 'Diction and Imagery in Anglo-Saxon Poetry', *E&S* 11 (1925), 49–91 [also in *Essential Articles*, ed. Bessinger and Kahrl, pp. 183–227]

Zacher, Samantha, 'Sin, Syntax, and Synonyms: Rhetorical Style and Structure in Vercelli Homily X', *JEGP* (forthcoming)

Zachrisson, R. E., 'Grendel in *Beowulf*', in *Festschrift Otto Jespersen* (Copenhagen, 1930), pp. 39–44

Zettersten, Arne, ed., *Waldere* (Copenhagen, 1979)

Index of Lines and Passages Cited and Discussed

A passage is defined here as containing three complete lines of verse, or at least six half-lines, while a citation is two-and-a-half lines, or five half-lines, or fewer. Passages and citations are arranged numerically by line, and then by length. Citations of half-lines and whole verses have in certain cases been combined for considerations of space; the intention has been throughout to provide as full an index as possible of the verses of *Beowulf* discussed or cited within this book without complicating the index unnecessarily.

Passages cited and discussed

Lines cited and discussed

Index of Scholars Cited

General Index

CPSIA information can be obtained at www.ICGtesting.com
Printed in the USA
BVOW012234240113

311535BV00002B/10/P